Using Assembly Language

2nd Edition

Allen L. Wyatt, Sr.

Revised for 2nd Edition
by Allen L. Wyatt, Sr. and Jim Kyle

PROGRAMMING
S E R I E S

que®
CORPORATION
LEADING COMPUTER KNOWLEDGE

Using Assembly Language

2nd Edition

This book was written for DOS version 4.0. The examples in this book should work with the following software through the versions shown:

LINK.EXE 4.06	QuickC 2.01
MASM.EXE 5.1	TurboC 2.0
LIB.EXE 3.14	QuickBASIC 4.5
TASM.EXE 2.0	QuickPascal 1.0
TCREF 1.01	Turbo Pascal 5.5
TLINK 2.0	dBase III+ 1.1
TLIB.EXE 2.0	dBase IV 1.0
OptLib.EXE 1.9	FoxBase+ 2.1
OptLink.EXE 1.0	Clipper Summer 87

DEDICATION ▼

Dedicated to my God,
who gives me talents to develop and the ability to work,
and to my wife, Debbie,
who gives me the freedom and latitude to do so.

Programming Books Director

Allen L. Wyatt, Sr.

Cover and Book Design

Dan Armstrong

Production

Bill Basham
Claudia Bell
Brad Chinn
Don Clemons
Sally Copenhaver
Tom Emrick
Dennis Hager
Bill Hurley
Jodi Jensen
David Kline
Larry Lynch
Lori A. Lyons
Jennifer Matthews
Cindy L. Phipps
Joe Ramon
Dennis Sheehan
Louise Shinault
Bruce Steed
Mary Beth Wakefield

Senior Editor

Gregory Croy

Editor

Andy Saff

Editorial Assistant

Ann K. Taylor

Illustrations

Susan Moore

Keyboarding

Mary Croy

Indexed by

Joelynn Gifford
Hilary Adams

Composed in Garamond and OCRB by Que Corporation

ABOUT THE AUTHOR ▼

Allen L. Wyatt, Sr.

Allen Wyatt has been working with small computers for more than a dozen years, and has worked in virtually all facets of programming. He has authored many books related to programming and programming languages. He is the president of Discovery Computing, Inc., a microcomputer consulting and services corporation based in Indiana. He is also Programming Books Director for the Macmillan Computer Books Division. Allen likes to spend his spare time (what little there is of it) with his wife and children doing the things that families do together.

CONTENT OVERVIEW

TABLE OF CONTENTS ▼

II   Assembly Language Tools

8   Choosing and Using Your Assembler 151

17 Processor Instruction Sets 631

TRADEMARK ACKNOWLEDGMENTS

Que Corporation has made every attempt to supply trademark information about company names, products, and services mentioned in this book. Trademarks indicated below were derived from various sources. Que Corporation cannot attest to the accuracy of this information.

Advanced Trace86 is a trademark of Morgan Computing Co., Inc.

AT Probe, PC Probe, Software Source Probe, and Mini Probe I, II, and III are trademarks of Atron Division of Northwest Instrument Systems.

AztecC is a registered trademark of Manx Software Systems, Inc.

Clipper is a trademark of Nantucket, Inc.

CodeSmith-86 is a trademark of Visual Age.

COMPAQ 386 is a registered trademark of COMPAQ Computer Corporation.

dBASE III, dBASE III+ and dBASE IV are registered trademarks of Ashton-Tate Company.

FoxBase+ is a trademark of Fox Software, Inc.

ICD286, PDT-AT, PDT-PC, and RBUG86 are trademarks of Answer Software Corp.

IBM is a registered trademark of International Business Machines Corporation. OS/2, PCjr, PC XT, and Personal System/2 are trademarks of International Business Machines Corporation.

Intel is a registered trademark of Intel Corporation. I²ICE is a trademark of Intel Corporation.

LATTICE C is a registered trademark of Lattice, Inc.

Microcosm is a trademark of Microcosm, Inc.

Microsoft, Microsoft QuickBASIC, Microsoft QuickC, Microsoft QuickPascal, MS-DOS, and XENIX are registered trademarks of Microsoft Corporation. CodeView is a trademark of Microsoft Corporation.

Motorola is a registered trademark of Motorola, Inc.

Periscope I, Periscope II, Periscope III, and Periscope II-X are trademarks of The Periscope Co., Inc.

Pfix86+ is a trademark of Phoenix Technologies Ltd.

ProKey is a trademark of Rosesoft, Inc.

SideKick, Turbo C and Turbo Pascal are registered trademarks of Borland International, Inc.

Introduction

Welcome to *Using Assembly Language*, 2nd Edition, a book written to help you learn how to use assembly language subroutines to increase the performance of your programs.

If you write programs in BASIC, Pascal, or C on the IBM family of microcomputers and you want to make the most of your programming, you'll find *Using Assembly Language*, 2nd Edition, a helpful learning aid and reference guide. Each carefully designed chapter is packed with detailed information about the use of assembly language subroutines in high-level language programs.

This book is written from a programmer's perspective. Precepts and examples are included to teach you the information you need to become proficient in the use of assembly language. Also included are detailed reference materials. Building on the framework developed in the first edition, *Using Assembly Language*, 2nd Edition, covers more languages, more assemblers, and more assembly language tools than any other assembly language book available.

To help you understand *why* programming works, and what happens when you program, I've emphasized the effects of assembly language instructions, commands, and functions—how they are used and what they produce. There will be no "black boxes" here—nothing mysterious or questionable left unexplained. By understanding assembly language, you will learn how to make better use of your particular IBM environment.

The computer field changes quickly, seeming to go from simple to complex overnight. *Using Assembly Language*, 2nd Edition, lays a firm foundation of the precepts and underlying concepts on which the field's complex ideas are built. I've tried to simplify many of the concepts that the assembly language programmer must understand so that your interest in and focus on these guiding precepts are not lost.

I've included many examples that you can try on your computer. Working through these examples on the computer (or even in your mind) should help you retain key ideas. I recommend that you use the computer. The programs in this book are available on disk. You can order a copy using the order form on the last page of the book.

Clearly, *Using Assembly Language*, 2nd Edition, is not intended as light, after-dinner reading. It is meant to provide a sound basis in the principles of developing assembly language subroutines, tapping the internal power of BIOS and DOS functions, and interfacing assembly language subroutines to high-level language programs. You can use many sections of the book as reference.

Why Use Assembly Language?

You may ask, "Why should I use assembly language?" There's no easy answer. The reasons for using assembly language vary, depending on the application in which you use it and the high-level language you use as the controlling program. A brief look at the development of high-level languages may help you better understand the value of assembly language.

Assembly language once was the only language available for microcomputers. But with the advent of such powerful high-level languages as BASIC, Pascal, and C, many programmers learned only these languages. Compared to assembly language, these languages were easy to learn and provided most of the functions ordinarily needed to program. Assembly language was often relegated to programmers in research labs (and padded cells).

Over time, as applications became increasingly complex, the limits of various high-level languages were tested and pushed about as far as they could go. Surely you have experienced the frustration of knowing that there must be a faster, slicker, more efficient way to do something than what you can do with the high-level language you're using. This frustration has led some programmers either to change languages (hoping to find one that addressed most, if not all, of their needs) or to accept the limitations of their current high-level language.

No language is perfect. High-level languages are no exception—they all have strong points and corresponding weak points. And that's where assembly language subroutines come in: you can use them to augment the capabilities of the high-level languages in which you program.

The benefits of programming well-defined tasks in assembly language fall into four general areas: *speed*, *versatility*, *flexibility*, and *compact code*.

Assembly language is *fast*. To paraphrase an old saying, "It don't get any faster." During the assembly process, assembly language mnemonics translate directly into machine language—the native language for computers. No language is faster than machine language; its execution speed is the fastest possible on any given computer. Because assembly language is the root of all high-level programming languages, assembly language runs faster than any of these languages.

High-level languages can be *interpretive*, *compiled*, or *pseudocode*. Interpretive and pseudocode (a cross between interpretive and compiled code) languages require some translation into machine language at the time of execution. It is true that, depending on the implementation of the language, some high-level languages, once compiled, require no such translation at run-time. But assembly language source code files, once assembled, never require translation; they have no overhead penalty of greater execution time.

Assembly language is *versatile*. Anything that can possibly be done with a computer can be done with assembly language. The only limiting factor is the capacity of the computer system you're using.

Many high-level languages are designed to execute on a wide variety of computers, each of which has different capabilities and peripherals. These languages are designed for the "lowest common denominator" so that they cover the capabilities and peripherals likely to be on virtually every machine on which they might run. Assembly language has no such artificial limitation. Because the capabilities of your specific machine are the only limiting factor, assembly language allows great versatility in program development.

Although specifically suited only to one particular type of CPU, assembly language is *flexible*. Assembly language gives you a multitude of ways to accomplish one task. Some languages have rigid coding restraints that restrict the number of approaches to coding a particular task. Assembly language has no coding restraints. If your coding style is undisciplined, this degree of freedom may present drawbacks; you can easily end up with "spaghetti code." But if you are a disciplined, structured person (or at least write disciplined, structured code), you'll find the flexibility of assembly language refreshing. Mastering the language can be both challenging and rewarding.

Assembly language produces *compact code*. Because assembly language routines are written for a specific purpose in a language that translates directly into machine language, these routines will include code that only you, the programmer, want included.

High-level languages, on the other hand, are written for a general audience and include extraneous code. For instance, many high-level languages include intrinsic graphics functions or file-handling functions that are used by only a few applications. Needed or not, this irrelevant coding is included in every application.

Because assembly language mnemonic instructions translate directly into one or, at most, several bytes of data, there is no overhead unless you specifically choose to include it in your executable file.

What You Should Know

In any book, assumptions are made about what the reader knows. Those assumptions may be stated up front or may become clear after you've read the book. Before you read this book, you need to know what the assumptions are.

First, it is assumed that you know at least one high-level language—BASIC, Pascal, or C—or one of the database languages such as dBASE. These are used throughout this book. (If you know more than one of these languages, you will benefit even more from *Using Assembly Language*, 2nd Edition.)

You should be familiar with ASCII, the native coding scheme used for character representation on the IBM PC family of microcomputers. Many assembly language subroutines in this book (and elsewhere) use and manipulate ASCII characters. You don't need to memorize the entire code, but you may want to keep an ASCII table within reach while you work through this book. Appendix A is an ASCII chart.

Because you're reading this book, I assume that at one time or another you have had experience programming and that you are familiar with the different numbering systems commonly used with microcomputers: binary (base 2), decimal (base 10), and hexadecimal (base 16). If you're familiar with octal (base 8), so much the better, but familiarity with octal is not necessary. If you have trouble working with any of these systems, writing assembly language code should quickly provide all the familiarity you could ever want. *Using Assembly Language*, 2nd Edition, doesn't delve into the differences between numbering systems or the reasons for using binary or hexadecimal systems.

Depending on your programming background, you may be familiar with many differing notations for numbering systems. Because of the inherent possibilities for confusion when you work with binary, decimal, and hexadecimal numbers, some sort of notation is needed to differentiate between the systems.

This book's approach to notation is simple and straightforward: a lowercase *b* is appended to *binary* numbers, and a lowercase *h* to *hexadecimal* numbers; decimal numbers have no appendage (see table I.1).

Table I.1. *Number representation.*

Binary	Decimal	Hexadecimal
00001110b	14	0Eh
01101011b	107	6Bh
10111011b	187	BBh
11010101b	213	D5h
0000000110110000b	432	01B0h
0000001001010101b	597	0255h
0000001101100111b	871	0367h
0000101111111111b	3071	0BFFh
0101111111111000b	24568	5FF8h

As you can see from this table, binary and hexadecimal numbers occupy an even number of digits. Every digit within a binary number represents a *bit*. Every two digits of a hexadecimal number represent a *byte*, or eight bits, and every four digits represent a *word*, or two bytes. As an assembly language programmer, you must learn to think in groupings—bits, bytes, and words.

Speaking of words—the other kind—you should be familiar with certain rudimentary terms. You'll find a glossary at the end of this book, but the following definitions should prove helpful at this point and throughout the book:

Assembler: The software program that translates (assembles) assembly language mnemonics into machine language for direct execution by the computer. Typical assemblers include MASM from Microsoft, Turbo Assembler from Borland International, and OptAsm from SLR Inc.

Assembly: A process of code conversion, done by an assembler, that translates assembly language source code into machine language.

Assembly Language: The English-style language (also called *source code*) that is understandable to humans. Assembly language is not directly executable by computers. The previously listed assemblers share a common assembly language subset, but each includes some unique language elements that are missing from the others. This book concentrates on the common subset.

Linker: A program that performs the linking process. Typical linkers include Link from Microsoft, Tlink from Borland, and OptLink from SLR Inc.

Linking: The process of resolving external references and address references in object code. The resulting machine language instructions are directly executable by a computer.

Machine Language: The series of binary digits executed by a microprocessor to accomplish individual tasks. People seldom (if ever) program in machine language. Instead, they program in assembly language and use an assembler to translate their instructions into machine language.

Object Code: A half-way step between source code and executable machine language. Object code, which is not directly executable by a computer, must go through a *linking* process that resolves external references and address references.

Source Code: The assembly-language instructions written by a programmer and then translated into object code by an assembler.

What Is Covered in This Book

Whenever I pick up a book, the first thing I want to know is whether the book will help me. Will it teach me what I need to know?

You can see from the table of contents that *Using Assembly Language*, 2nd Edition, covers many technical areas related to assembly language programming. For easy reference, the book is divided into four parts. The following is a quick outline of the contents of each chapter.

Part I, "Interfacing Assembler with Other Languages." Chapter 1, "An Overview of Assembly Language," introduces you to the basics of programming in assembly language. This chapter touches on the structure, main commands, and operations needed to use assembly language.

Chapter 2, "Interfacing Subroutines," covers general information about interfacing assembly language subroutines with high-level language programs.

Chapter 3, "Interfacing with BASIC," provides specific information and examples on using assembly language subroutines from both interpretive and compiled BASIC.

Chapter 4, "Interfacing with Pascal," gives you specific interfacing information for programs written in Pascal.

Chapter 5, "Interfacing with C," details how to interface assembly language subroutines with the popular C language.

Chapter 6, "Interfacing with dBASE and FoxBase," explains how to interface assembly language subroutines with the most widely used DBMS language.

Chapter 7, "Interfacing with Clipper," shows how to create user-defined functions" in assembly language for use with the Clipper database compiler.

Part II, "Assembly Language Tools." Chapter 8, "Choosing and Using Your Assembler," explains what the assembler does, describes the three most popular assembler programs, and shows how to use each of these assembler programs to translate assembly language instructions into machine code.

Chapter 9, "Choosing and Using Your Linker," compares the most popular linker programs and explains how to link assembled programs. LINK parameters and file types are included in this chapter.

Chapter 10, "Debugging Assembly Language Subroutines," shows how to use the DEBUG program that comes with DOS, or one of the three most popular "symbolic debuggers," to locate, isolate, and correct errors and problems in assembly language subroutines.

Chapter 11, "Developing Libraries," covers the creation, use, and management of object file libraries of assembly language subroutines.

Chapter 12, "Using Makefiles," explains why these tools are so popular and describes how to use them.

Part III, "Advanced Assembly Language Topics." Chapter 13, "Video Memory," provides extremely detailed information on how to manipulate (from assembly language) the memory areas that control the display of information on a computer monitor.

Chapter 14, "Accessing Hardware Ports," covers working at the hardware level from assembly language. Examples include accessing the keyboard and speaker controllers.

Part IV, "Reference." Chapter 15, "Accessing BIOS Services," details the different BIOS interrupts and services and the various tasks they perform. Corresponding information for the different DOS interrupts and services is included in Chapter 16, "Accessing DOS Services."

Chapter 17, "Processor Instruction Sets," provides detailed reference information for the Intel 8086/8088, 80286, 80386, 80486, 8087, 80287, and 80387.

Using Assembly Language, 2nd Edition, contains three useful appendixes. Appendix A presents the standard ASCII character codes. Appendix B lists the disk base table, a set of parameters that controls the operation of a disk drive. The BIOS keyboard codes and keyboard controller codes are included in Appendix C.

Finally, *Using Assembly Language*, 2nd Edition, contains a brief glossary, and index, and an order form for the program diskette.

What Is Not Covered in This Book

Using Assembly Language, 2nd Edition, is packed with information but cannot possibly cover all related subjects. This book has limits.

First, this book does not teach high-level languages. In fact, it does not purport to teach any language. Its purpose is to show how to make two languages—assembly language and either BASIC, Pascal, C, or your database language—work together for the benefit of both the program and programmer.

As you read and work through this book, you probably will learn something about each of these languages. You'll undoubtedly learn a great deal about assembly language, but please don't feel that you've learned it all. Learning how to do things well takes *years*—and by then the rules have all changed. And don't be surprised if someday you learn from another source a quicker, easier way to do a task than what you learn here. Part of the fun of living is that people keep developing new ideas and methods.

Programming style is a big deal for many authors. Style is fine and pro-motes logical thinking, but I believe that coding must meet only a few criteria:

- ❏ *Is the code intelligible?* Adequate remarks (perhaps for every line) and appropriate line formatting help.

- ❏ *Will others understand the code?* Because you may not be around to decipher any sloppy, obtuse, or idiosyncratic coding when changes to the code must be made in a month or a year, you must write for those who follow. In case you are around to make the changes, don't challenge yourself to remember months or years from now what you had in mind when you wrote some cryptic gobbledygook; keep it clear and simple.

- ❏ *Does it work?* In my opinion, this is the most important criterion of all.

This book does not adhere to any published or unpublished set of pro-gramming conventions or techniques. The goal for this book is to provide clear, concise, intelligent, working code to help you become more pro-ductive. You can organize and optimize your software by simply applying to assembly language programming the same logical structures and com-mon sense encouraged by high-level languages.

Graphics programming, because of its specialized nature, is beyond the scope of this book. Entire volumes can be written about true graphics and graphic manipulation. Indeed, graphics routines are well suited for being written in assembly language. For example, the sheer volume of data that must be processed to perform animation demands a level of speed avail-able only through assembly language.

Writers, programmers, and others often misuse the word *graphics*. Text screens are frequently referred to as "graphics" screens. This confusion arises because, on the IBM, certain ASCII codes correspond to special characters that are neither textual nor numeric, but clearly graphic. Although these characters permit you to enhance an otherwise bland text screen, the screen is not a true graphics screen. Text screens deal with data on a character level; graphics screens manipulate data on a pixel level.

Using Assembly Language, 2nd Edition, *does* cover the use of textual graphics and color. Library routines that allow all sorts of snazzy screen creations (using text characters) with assembly language drivers from high-level languages are discussed and developed.

Summary

I hope that you now have a sense of what this book is, as well as what it isn't. Because I've felt the need for this type of book, writing it has been important to me. Ideally, you also have felt that need. Items missing from the first edition have now been included in the second edition, and technology has yielded new information, which has been included. If you feel any information that belongs in this book is missing, I would like to know about it. Feel free to contact me either through the publisher or on CompuServe (72561,2207).

Now, if you're ready, let's begin the process. May yours be a fruitful journey.

Part I

Interfacing Assembler with Other Languages

1

An Overview of Assembly Language

Before examining how assembly language routines are used with (or from) high-level languages, let's look at assembly language. This is a *quick* introduction to assembly language, not an exhaustive discussion of assembly language programs. It is meant to touch on the structure, main commands, and operations of the language. You should gain a feel for the language and subsequently learn what you must know to use the language effectively from BASIC, Pascal, or C.

Conceptual Guide to Assembly Language

Assembly language is similar to many other computer languages. At their root, languages provide building blocks that the programmer can arrange to create programs. The building blocks in assembly language are smaller (and less singularly powerful) than those in high-level languages.

13

The building block concept should already be familiar to you. You program using commands, variables, and words that are almost like English to instruct the computer what to do. These words are translated into machine code, a series of numbers that the computer understands. But the work appears to be done with the building blocks, not with the numbers used by the computer.

As I've already stated, the building blocks in assembly language are smaller and less singularly powerful than those in high-level languages. Let's take a moment to examine this statement.

Programmers who use high-level languages need not concern themselves directly with many operations that occur "behind the scenes." For instance, you usually do not need to even think about *where* and *how* your data will reside in the computer's memory. These matters are arranged by either the compiler or the *run-time system* used by your language. A run-time system is a manager that oversees the program execution.

Another example of these "behind the scenes" operations is the use of what I will call *compound commands*. For instance, consider the BASIC statement

```
PRINT "This is a test"
```

Pascal uses this syntax to accomplish the same task:

```
writeln('This is a test');
```

C uses this syntax:

```
printf("This is a test\n");
```

All of these statements accomplish the same task. They print to the output device (usually the display monitor) a string of characters followed by a carriage return and line feed. Inherent in the PRINT, writeln(), and printf() commands, however, are several smaller commands that do other tasks related to displaying the information. These smaller commands locate the information to display, determine where to display it, decide how the information is displayed, and handle the carriage return and line feed at the end of the string.

With assembly language, little happens "behind the scenes." You must specify virtually everything related to the composition, storage, and execution of your program or subroutine. For example, if you want to perform the equivalent of printing a string in assembly language, the following lines accomplish the task:

```
          MOV       DX,OFFSET MSG
          MOV       AH,09h
          INT       21h
MSG       DB        'This is a test',13,10,'$'
```

Although many other elements (covered later in this book) must be added before this code can be executed, this example should clearly indicate how extremely specific you need to be when working in assembly language. This need for specificity, to perform even relatively simple tasks, requires that you use much more source code than you would with a high-level language.

Another point may not be quite as obvious in this example: data must be declared explicitly. If you are accustomed to working in Pascal or C, you will not have to change your habits much. BASIC programmers, however, must get used to explicitly declaring data elements. Later, this chapter discusses how data is defined and manipulated in assembly language.

Conceptually, assembly language is the same as any other computer language: it enables you to instruct the computer to perform specific tasks. Depending on your background, however, you may find the application of the concepts radically different.

The assembly language development process is similar to that for many high-level languages. There are several distinct phases:

- ❏ Source code generation or editing
- ❏ Assembly
- ❏ Linking
- ❏ Execution

If your high-level language uses a compiler and linker, this process will seem familiar. The second step (assembly) is analogous to the compilation step of high-level language development. The third step (linking) uses the same linker that you currently use. So the assembly language development process is no different from the steps most high-level language programmers currently perform.

The 25-Cent Tour of Memory

Because assembly language inherently involves working at a level that is much closer to the computer than other languages, you need to understand how your computer uses memory. (Memory and memory management are generally handled automatically and "behind the scenes" by other languages.)

The IBM PC, running under PC DOS or MS-DOS, has up to 640K of memory available (655,360 bytes of storage). However, the entire 640K is not available to the assembly language programmer. Certain areas are reserved for the Basic Input/Output System (BIOS) and DOS. Other areas are considered system areas that hold information enabling BIOS and DOS to function properly. Still other areas may have user-installed resident programs such as SideKick or ProKey. Figure 1.1 is typical memory map.

Fig. 1.1. *Sample memory map.*

| BIOS/DOS Interrupt Vector Tables |
| DOS Work/System Area |
| Device Drivers |
| COMMAND.COM (resident portion) |
| KBFIX2.COM (resident keyboard program) |
| MSPOOL2.COM (resident print spooler) |
| SMARTKEY.COM (resident program) |
| SK.COM (SideKick resident program) |
| Free memory |
| Video Buffers |
| ROM Area |

If it weren't for some of the memory management functions built into DOS, the average programmer would have to struggle with memory conflicts among programs. Later, this book will explain how to use DOS functions to request blocks of memory for your program.

Microprocessors use an address register to keep track of memory locations where operations should be occurring. The size of the address register usually dictates the maximum amount of memory a computer can use. Table 1.1 shows how much memory is addressable by various address register capacities.

Table 1.1. *Addressable memory by address register size.*

Address Register Bits	Addressable Memory (bytes)	Memory Size
8	256	
9	512	
10	1,024	1K
11	2,048	2K
12	4,096	4K
13	8,192	8K
14	16,384	16K
15	32,768	32K
16	65,536	64K
17	131,072	128K
18	262,144	256K
19	524,288	512K
20	1,048,576	1M
21	2,097,152	2M
22	4,194,304	4M
23	8,388,608	8M
24	16,777,216	16M
25	33,554,432	32M
26	67,108,864	64M
27	134,217,728	128M
28	268,435,456	256M
29	536,870,912	512M
30	1,073,741,824	1G
31	2,147,483,648	2G
32	4,294,967,296	4G

Each memory location requires its own unique address. Two memory locations cannot have the same address; if they did, operations affecting the locations would become jumbled. Imagine what would happen if your house and your neighbor's house had the same address. Without additional information, the mailman wouldn't know what mail went to which house.

The IBM processor uses an instruction pointer (IP) to keep track of the machine-language instructions that are currently being executed. This pointer is simply a 16-bit address register specialized for this purpose. From table 1.1, you can determine that 16 bits can hold unsigned integers in the range of 0 to 65,535.

The IBM (running under PC DOS or MS-DOS) can have up to 640K of memory. If the IP can hold only 65,536 values, how can each of 655,360 possible memory locations be addressed? Holding the 655,360 values necessary for 640K of memory would require an address register of at least 20 bits. The obvious solution would have been to use a larger register size. But Intel (the developers of the CPUs used in IBM microcomputers) used a more indirect and potentially confusing solution.

Intel used a *segment register* to control the general area of memory being pointed to, with the IP as an offset pointer into that segment. Each segment of memory can be up to 65,536 bytes (64K) in size. This scheme was a radical departure not only from the memory addressing schemes used in earlier microprocessors but also from those schemes used by other microprocessors such as the Motorola 68000 family. Suddenly, the program could directly address a maximum of only 64K of memory.

Through segment notation, each memory location can be addressed individually in the format

   SSSS:OOOO

where SSSS is the segment, and OOOO is the offset. Memory locations given in this format are always in hexadecimal notation. The segment portion of the address can range from 0 to FFFFh; and, depending on the segment, the offset portion also can range from 0 to FFFFh.

The absolute address of any memory location can be determined by multiplying the segment value by 10h, which is the same as 16 decimal, and then adding the offset value. Thus, the absolute location of 1871:321F is determined by 18710h plus 321Fh, or 1B92Fh. Based on this addressing notation, it would seem logical that the total addressable memory could range from 0000:0000 (0) to FFFF:FFFF (1,114,095)—slightly over 1 megabyte of memory. Remember, however, that the limit for PC DOS or MS-DOS is 640K; therefore, the calculated absolute memory address cannot exceed 655,360. (The "missing" 384K is actually used by the ROM-BIOS, video RAM, and other system components; it's not really missing at all, just unavailable to your programs.)

Clearly, memory segments can overlap, and one memory location can be addressed in many ways. Table 1.2 shows the notation of several memory addresses, all of which refer to the same absolute memory location.

Table 1.2. *Segment/offset pairs address absolute memory location 027920h.*

2792:0000	2515:27D0
2791:0010	2292:5000
2790:0020	1F93:7FF0
278F:0030	1D90:A020
2777:01B0	1AFF:C930
26D0:0C20	1A74:D1E0
2654:13E0	17A5:FED0

To create figure 1.2, addresses were attached to the memory map shown in figure 1.1. The address in your system may vary (sometimes greatly) depending on your memory configuration, DOS version, program use, and other factors.

When you program in assembly language, you need not be concerned about which actual memory address your program will physically reside in. The linking process, and subsequent DOS loaders, take care of positioning your program and getting it ready to execute. If you want more information about where the program will reside, several technical manuals deal with how programs are loaded and how they begin execution. If you find this topic interesting, you may want to note the differences between COM and EXE files as outlined in those manuals.

Although you don't need to worry about *program* addresses, you do need to know about segment and offset notation for addressing specific *data* in memory, such as system parameters or vector addresses. That specific topic is covered shortly.

The Stack

A special segment of memory, called the *stack*, is reserved for the temporary storage of data. To program effectively in assembly language, you must understand the stack. Even if you're already familiar with the concepts behind a stack, let's take just a moment to review them. Because later sections of this book present assembly language instructions and routines that rely on the stack, the basics must be covered now.

Fig. 1.2. Sample memory map with addresses.

00000h	BIOS/DOS Interrupt Vector Tables
00500h	DOS Work/System Area
04C00h	Device Drivers
05400h	COMMAND.COM (resident portion)
0E0A0h	KBFIX2.COM (resident keyboard program)
0E8E0h	MSPOOL2.COM (resident print spooler)
1E720h	SMARTKEY.COM (resident program)
26F70h	SK.COM (SideKick resident program)
37A80h	Free memory
A0000h	Video Buffers
C0000h	ROM Area

If you have never worked with one, a stack can be confusing at first. A stack is a last-in, first-out (LIFO) queue; it operates much like the spring-loaded plate servers in a cafeteria line. Each plate placed on the server makes the lower plates inaccessible. Conversely, removing a plate makes the one under it immediately available. Plates can only be removed in the reverse order of their placement on the server. The last plate added is always the first to be removed.

In the conceptual representation of the stack shown in figure 1.3, each box contains one word (16 bits) of data. The boxes can be removed in the reverse order of their placement on the stack. Only data at the top of the stack is accessible by conventional means. Data is shown as individual bytes, even though it can be deposited or extracted from the stack only one word (two bytes) at a time.

Fig. 1.3. *Conceptual representation of the stack.*

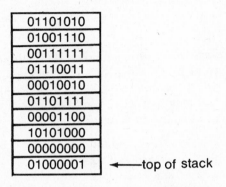

On the IBM PC, data is always stored on and removed from the stack one word (16 bits) at a time. Even if you need to store only one byte of data, you must deposit (and later remove) a full word.

Throughout this book, you will see references to the stack. Some specific assembly language commands cause information to be deposited in the stack; others cause the information to be removed. This depositing and removing frequently results from another action that you want to perform. As I discuss the assembly language mnemonic commands, I will touch on the specific operations that affect the stack.

The stack is integral to passing information from the high-level language to assembly language. Generally, information to be passed is pushed onto the stack, then removed as needed by the assembly language routine. This process is covered in detail when passing parameters to assembly language subroutines is discussed.

If you are a little confused about how the stack works and why it is important in assembly language programming, don't despair; such confusion is normal. As you work through the examples in this book, pay particular attention to how operations affect the stack. Doing so should clarify the concepts introduced here.

If you are quite confused about the stack, reread this section until you begin to grasp the concepts. Before you can understand the concepts behind assembly language programming, you must first understand the stack.

Segments and Classes

The IBM family of microcomputers uses processors that address memory by using segment addresses and offset addresses. When you program in assembly language, segment addresses are set either explicitly, by loading the segment registers, or implicitly, through assembler directives to the linker.

But there are segment addresses—and then there are segments. So far, I have talked about segment addresses and how they are used. This is the logical use of the word *segment* for the Intel 8086/8088/80286/80386 microprocessors. To program effectively in assembly language, you must understand these segments and their use.

Another definition of the word *segment*, however, is used in reference to the macro assembler and linker developed by Microsoft. Because many (if not most) other assemblers and linkers are based on standards established by Microsoft, you need to be familiar with this alternate (and potentially confusing) use of the word segment.

When you write assembly language source code, a segment is simply a group of instructions that all operate relative to the same segment address. It is difficult not to confuse such *program segments* with *memory segments*, but they are not directly related. A program segment is just a block of code delineated by explicit starting and ending points. To avoid confusion, some assemblers call these coding sections PSECTs (for program sections) rather than SEGMENTs.

At the beginning of any group of instructions (usually at the beginning of the code in the file), the assembler directive SEGMENT is used to signify the start of a segment. At the close of the group of instructions, the ENDS directive is used. The assembler and linker then use these directives to delineate the explicit start and end of groups of assembly language code.

The following example shows how the SEGMENT and ENDS directives might be used in an assembly language file:

```
TEXT            SEGMENT BYTE PUBLIC 'CODE'
assembly language coding goes in this area
TEXT            ENDS
```

Let's look at each part of this example. The word TEXT is the name of the segment (I've used TEXT arbitrarily). Notice also the corresponding appearance of the name TEXT with the ENDS directive.

The word BYTE directs the assembler to place this segment at the next available byte in the object file. In the example, BYTE is the *align type* of the segment. A segment can be aligned to a byte, word, paragraph, or page. BYTE starts the segment at the byte following the end of the preceding segment. WORD begins the segment at the next even address. PARAgraph begins the segment at the next hexadecimal address that ends in a 0. PAGE begins the segment at the next hexadecimal address that ends in 00. Table 1.3 summarizes these align types.

Table 1.3. *Align types possible with the Microsoft Assembler.*

Type	Description
BYTE	Segment is placed at the next available byte in the object file
WORD	Segment is placed at the next available even byte in the object file
PARAGRAPH	Segment is placed at the next available paragraph boundary in the object file. Address of the segment will end in a 0.
PAGE	Segment is placed at the next available page boundary in the object file. Address of the segment will end in a 0.

The word PUBLIC is a declaration of the segment's *combine type*. The combine type, which is optional, denotes how a segment will be combined with other segments that have the same name. Several different combine types are possible (see table 1.4). For most purposes that involve writing subroutines which will be incorporated into high-level language programs, the combine type will be PUBLIC.

The word 'CODE' is the segment's *class type*. This name, which must be enclosed in single quotation marks, signifies the groupings to be used when the different segments are linked. All segments of a given class type are loaded contiguously in memory before another class type is begun. In the directives example, the segment belongs to the 'CODE' class type. It will be grouped with other segments of the same class type.

Normally, you will use only one class type when you prepare assembly language subroutines for use from high-level languages. Sometimes this class type is specified by the high-level language you are using.

Table 1.4. *Combine types possible with the Microsoft Assembler and Linker.*

Type	Description
PUBLIC	Joins all segments with the same name into one segment when linked. All addresses and offsets in the resulting segment are relative to a single segment register.
STACK	Joins all segments with this combine type to form one segment when linked. All addresses and offsets in the resulting segment are relative to the stack segment register. The stack pointer (SP) register is initialized to the ending address of the segment. This combine type normally is used to define the stack area for a program. The linker requires that exactly one stack segment be defined for an EXE program.
COMMON	Same as PUBLIC, except that the segments are not joined to form a new, large segment. All COMMON segments with the same name begin at the same point; the resulting segment is equal in length to the longest individual segment.
MEMORY	Works exactly like the PUBLIC combine type.
AT	Used to prepare a template that will be used for accessing fixed location data. In the format AT XXXX (where XXXX is a memory address), AT signifies that addresses and offsets are to be calculated relative to the specified memory address.

Registers and Flags

The 8086/8088 and subsequent generations of microprocessors use *registers* to operate on data and to perform tasks. Registers are special storage areas built into the microprocessor. All registers are 16 bits (one word) wide, but some operations can be performed on only one byte (eight bits) of specific registers. Table 1.5 shows the 8086/8088 register set.

The four general-purpose registers (AX, BX, CX, and DX) can also be addressed by their component bytes. For instance, AH and AL are the individual bytes that make up the word register AX. The H and L indicate,

Table 1.5. *The 8086/8088 register set.*

Name	Category	Purpose
AX	General Purpose	Accumulator
BX	General Purpose	Base
CX	General Purpose	Counter
DX	General Purpose	Data
SI	Index	Source index
DI	Index	Destination index
SP	Stack	Stack pointer
BP	Stack	Base pointer
CS	Segment	Code segment
DS	Segment	Data segment
SS	Segment	Stack segment
ES	Segment	Extra segment
IP		Instruction pointer
FLAGS		Operation flags

respectively, either the high byte or low byte. Similarly, BH and BL form BX, CH and CL make up CX, and DH and DL form DX.

The stack, segment, and instruction pointer registers are discussed in the following section. Understanding the flag register will help you understand the 8086/8088 instruction set introduced in the next section of this chapter.

The flag register is the same size as the other registers (16 bits), but the 8086/8088 uses only nine bits to signify status flags (see Chapter 17 for differences in later processor versions). These flags, shown in table 1.6, are set or cleared based on the results of individual operations.

Notice from table 1.6 that only nine flags are represented in the flag register. Bits 1, 3, 5, and 12 through 15 of this register are not used. Each of the other bits can, of course, be set to either 0 or 1. A 0 indicates that the flag is clear; a 1 indicates that the flag is set.

Certain assembly language instructions are used to set or clear individual flags. These instructions, often referred to as *Flag* and *Processor Control* instructions, will be detailed shortly. Other instructions set or clear individual flags to indicate the result of a previous operation. For instance, the zero flag (ZF) is set if the result of an arithmetic operation is zero, and cleared if the result is not zero.

A group of instructions referred to as *Control Transfer* instructions is used to test the value of the flags and then, based on the result, to condi-

Table 1.6. *Use of the 8086/8088 flag register.*

Bit	Use
0	Carry flag (CF)
1	
2	Parity flag (PF)
3	
4	Auxiliary carry flag (AF)
5	
6	Zero flag (ZF)
7	Sign flag (SF)
8	Trap flag (TF)
9	Interrupt flag (IF)
10	Direction flag (DF)
11	Overflow flag (OF)
12	
13	
14	
15	

tionally transfer program control. To program effectively in assembly language, you must understand what the flags are and how they are used.

The Segment Registers

The processors used in the IBM family of microcomputers have four different segment registers for addressing: the code, data, extra, and stack segments.

The code segment register (CS) contains the segment used with the instruction pointer register (IP). Thus, CS:IP contains the segment and off-set of the next instruction to be executed by the processor.

The data segment register (DS) contains the segment used by general-purpose data operations. It is used also as the source segment for string operations.

The extra segment register (ES) is used as the target segment for string operations. It can be used also as a secondary segment register for general-purpose data operations.

The stack segment register (SS) is used as the reference segment for the stack and is used with the stack pointer (SP). Thus, SS:SP points to the top of the stack, the last place where information was stored in the stack segment.

When you write small routines for use from high-level languages, most segment registers are set to the same addresses. In many instances, the code and data segments can be set to the same values so that the data used by the subroutines is actually part of the coding. This simplifies subroutine development. Exceptions occur when you want to use a specialized data area, in which case the DS or ES registers would be changed. The most common such occurrence makes these registers point into the data areas used by the high-level language. Many sample programs in this book use this technique.

When you write subroutines, don't change the stack segment. The controlling program usually sets this register, so you don't need to change it within your routines. Changing the stack segment without knowing the full use of the stack or without restoring its value, can result in undesirable side effects (usually a "system crash").

The Assembly Language Instruction Set

The actual instructions used by the assembler and translated into machine language depend on the microprocessor being used in the computer. The IBM PC and PC XT and their clones use the Intel 8088; the IBM Personal Computer AT uses the Intel 80286; newer computers use the Intel 80386. The new generation of MS-DOS or OS/2 computers, including the IBM Personal System/2 line, all use one of these three microprocessors.

All of these microprocessor chips are *upward compatible*, which means that anything programmed for the 8086/8088 will run on the 80286 and 80386, and anything programmed for the 80286 will run on the 80386. However, these processors are not *downward compatible*, which means that software written for the 80386 will not necessarily run on the 80286, and that written for the 80286 may not run on the 8086/8088.

Each generation of microprocessor has added different instructions and operating modes to the basic set used in the 8086/8088. These improvements prevent the processors from being downward compatible. In addition, you might have a numeric coprocessor in your computer that will make it possible to add even more assembly language instructions. These chips are usually called the 8087, 80287, or 80387 numeric coprocessors.

Because of the diversity of possible assembly language instructions, and because of the installed base of computers using the 8086/8088 and the upward compatibility of 8086/8088 code, the discussions of specific assembly language instructions focus on the 8086 instruction set. All assembly language examples in this book are written to work on the 8086/8088; they will also work on computers that use the 80286 and 80386 microprocessors.

Approximately 116 different assembly language mnemonics for the 8086/8088 can translate to 180 different machine language codes, depending on their context usage. The assembler takes care of the actual translation into machine language.

While this may seem like a formidable number of assembly language instructions, it's not as bad as it sounds. Most of the time, only a handful of these instructions are used. Others are used less often but are still available as you need them. Other microcomputer chips include even more instructions and provide correspondingly greater power to the programmer.

Because of the sheer number of instructions, this chapter lists only those for the 8086/8088. They are listed also, with detailed instruction information, in Part IV, as are the corresponding instruction sets for the 80286, 80386, 8087, and 80287.

Table 1.7 lists the different classes of assembly language mnemonics for the 8086/8088. Notice that the instructions are divided into six different groups, depending on the type of operation performed. Also listed are the individual assembly language instructions that form each group.

Table 1.7. The 8086/8088 microprocessor instruction set.

Data Transfer Instructions

IN	Input from port
LAHF	Load AH register with flags
LDS	Load DS register
LEA	Load effective address
LES	Load ES register
MOV	Move
OUT	Output to port
POP	Remove data from stack
POPF	Remove flags from stack
PUSH	Place data on stack

PUSHF	Place flags on stack
SAHF	Store AH into flag register
XCHG	Exchange
XLAT	Translate

Arithmetic Instructions

AAA	ASCII adjust for addition
AAD	ASCII adjust for division
AAM	ASCII adjust for multiplication
AAS	ASCII adjust for subtraction
ADC	Add with carry
ADD	Add
CBW	Convert byte to word
CMP	Compare
CWD	Convert word to doubleword
DAA	Decimal adjust for addition
DAS	Decimal adjust for subtraction
DEC	Decrement by 1
DIV	Divide, unsigned
IDIV	Integer divide
IMUL	Integer multiply
INC	Increment by 1
MUL	Multiply
NEG	Negate
SBB	Subtract with carry
SUB	Subtract

Bit Manipulation Instructions

AND	Logical AND on bits
NOT	Logical NOT on bits
OR	Logical OR on bits
RCL	Rotate left through carry
RCR	Rotate right through carry
ROL	Rotate left
ROR	Rotate right
SAL	Arithmetic shift left
SAR	Arithmetic shift right
SHL	Shift left
SHR	Shift right
TEST	Test bits
XOR	Logical exclusive-or on bits

Table 1.7. continues

Table 1.7. *continued*

String Manipulation Instructions

CMPSB	Compare strings, byte for byte
CMPSW	Compare strings, word for word
LODSB	Load a byte from string into AL
LODSW	Load a word from string into AX
MOVSB	Move string, byte by byte
MOVSW	Move string, word by word
REP	Repeat
REPE	Repeat if equal
REPNE	Repeat if not equal
REPNZ	Repeat if not zero
REPZ	Repeat if zero
SCASB	Scan string for byte
SCASW	Scan string for word
STOSB	Store byte in AL at string
STOSW	Store word in AX at string

Control Transfer Instructions

CALL	Perform subroutine
INT	Software interrupt
INTO	Interrupt on overflow
IRET	Return from interrupt
JA	Jump if above
JAE	Jump if above or equal
JB	Jump if below
JBE	Jump if below or equal
JC	Jump on carry
JCXZ	Jump if CX$=$0
JE	Jump if equal
JG	Jump if greater
JGE	Jump if greater or equal
JL	Jump if less than
JLE	Jump if less than or equal
JMP	Jump
JNA	Jump if not above
JNAE	Jump if not above or equal
JNB	Jump if not below
JNBE	Jump if not below or equal
JNC	Jump on no carry
JNE	Jump if not equal
JNG	Jump if not greater than

JNGE	Jump if not greater than or equal
JNL	Jump if not less than
JNLE	Jump if not less than or equal
JNO	Jump on no overflow
JNP	Jump on no parity
JNS	Jump on not sign
JNZ	Jump on not zero
JO	Jump on overflow
JP	Jump on parity
JPE	Jump on parity even
JPO	Jump on parity odd
JS	Jump on sign
JZ	Jump on zero
LOOP	Loop
LOOPE	Loop while equal
LOOPNE	Loop while not equal
LOOPNZ	Loop while not zero
LOOPZ	Loop while zero
RET	Return from subroutine

Flag and Processor Control Instructions

CLC	Clear carry flag
CLD	Clear direction flag
CLI	Clear interrupt flag
CMC	Complement carry flag
ESC	Escape
HLT	Halt
LOCK	Lock bus
NOP	No operation
STC	Set carry flag
STD	Set direction flag
STI	Set interrupt flag
WAIT	Wait

Although table 1.7 lists quite a few assembly language mnemonics, don't be overly concerned. Some mnemonics, although they appear to be different in this table, translate to the same machine language value. For instance, JZ and JE test the same flags and make the same branching decisions based on the condition of those flags. They translate to the *same* machine code, but more than one mnemonic is provided so that you can write code that is easier to understand in the context of the task being done.

Although this chapter does not discuss each of these instructions in any depth, you need to understand what each instruction does and how the instructions affect the flags and registers. Each instruction is covered in Part IV.

Data Storage in Memory

Data is stored in the computer's memory as a series of bytes. In the discussion of addressing, I stated that the IBM PC, operating under PC DOS or MS-DOS, could normally address up to 640K of memory. Special hardware or software makes expanded memory above the 640K boundary accessible, but the use of such expanded memory is beyond the scope of this book. The normal 640K work area has 655,360 individual bytes, each of which can store a specific, individual value. Because each byte is made up of 8 bits, and each bit can have a value of 0 or 1, each byte can store a value in the range of 0 through 255.

As you program in assembly language and then assemble and link the programs you create, your instructions (if syntactically correct) will be translated into individual bytes of information that the microprocessor later uses to perform tasks. To the computer, no physical difference exists between *machine language program instruction bytes* and *data bytes*. To the programmer, a distinction is vital to ensure that data bytes do not overwrite coding bytes while the program is executing.

Several methods are available for setting aside data areas in an assembly language program. The usual method involves the use of data definition *directives* or *pseudo-ops*. Another related but distinctly different method of defining data is through the use of *equates*. Let's take a look at each of these methods, focusing on equates first.

Equates

Equates do not set aside memory area for data. Instead, the assembler uses equates as substitute values later in the program. For instance, the following set of equates can be used to define the IBM color set:

```
; ----------------------------------------------------------
BLACK          EQU          0
BLUE           EQU          1
GREEN          EQU          2
CYAN           EQU          3
```

```
RED           EQU       4
MAGENTA       EQU       5
BROWN         EQU       6
WHITE         EQU       7
GRAY          EQU       8
LT_BLUE       EQU       9
LT_GREEN      EQU       10
LT_CYAN       EQU       11
Lt_RED        EQU       12
LT_MAGENTA    EQU       13
YELLOW        EQU       14
BR_WHITE      EQU       15
; ------------------------------------------------------
```

Equates are helpful because remembering RED is much easier than remembering that four is equal to the color red. For example, although the following commands are functionally the same, the first one is considerably more understandable to humans:

```
MOV       AH,LT_BLUE
MOV       AH,9
```

Both commands result in the value nine being placed in the AH register. In the following section, other uses for the EQU directive will become apparent.

Data Definition Pseudo-ops

A pseudo-op is simply an assembly language mnemonic that the assembler interprets and uses. No corresponding machine language instruction is generated. Pseudo-ops vary, depending on the assembler being used. Many assemblers use the word *directive* for this category of mnemonics.

In assembly language programs, data is defined through the use of several different pseudo-ops that instruct the assembler to set aside specific amounts of memory for the program to use at a later time. Optionally, you can direct the memory to be filled with specific values. Table 1.8 shows the different data-definition pseudo-ops for assembly language programs.

Each of the data-definition pseudo-ops sets aside memory for subsequent use by your program. They can be further modified and made more powerful through the use of the DUP and OFFSET operators. Understanding how all these pseudo-ops function may be easier if you see how they are

Table 1.8. *Data-definition pseudo-ops and their meanings.*

DB	Define Byte (1 byte)
DW	Define Word (2 bytes)
DD	Define Doubleword (4 bytes)
DQ	Define Quadword (8 bytes)
DT	Define ten bytes (10 bytes)

used in a program. Look at the following selected data declarations in a program:

```
; --------------------------------------------------------------
ORIG_DRIVE       DB     00
ORIG_PATH        DB     64 DUP(0)
PRE_PATH         DB     '\'
PATH             DB     64 DUP(0)

ANY_FILE         DB     '*.*',0

DIR_TABLE        DB     256 DUP(19 DUP(0))

BREAK_INT_OFF    DW     00
BREAK_INT_SEG    DW     00
CMD_TABLE        EQU    THIS BYTE
                 DW     OFFSET ACTION_CMD
                 DW     OFFSET DOIT_CMD
                 DW     OFFSET DRIVE_CMD
                 DW     OFFSET PATH_CMD
                 DW     OFFSET EXIT_CMD

ACTION_CMD       DB     'SELECT',0
DOIT_CMD         DB     'DELETE',0
DRIVE_CMD        DB     'DRIVE',0
PATH_CMD         DB     'PATH',0
EXIT_CMD         DB     'EXIT',0
ONE-MOMENT       DB     'Examining diskette ... One moment please!',0

; --------------------------------------------------------------
```

These few lines set aside and define a data area 5,084 bytes long. Further, they provide a means by which data can later be referenced. Referring to each line by its name, I'll describe what the data-definition pseudo-ops accomplish in this example.

ORIG_DRIVE is defined as a variable one byte long, initially set to 0. Also, ORIG_PATH is set to an initial value of 0; but through use of the DUP function, ORIG_PATH is defined as 64 consecutive zeros. ORIG_PATH can only be referenced directly as a byte value. For instance, the command

```
MOV     AH,ORIG_PATH
```

would work because a byte value (the first of the 64 bytes of ORIG_PATH) is being loaded into a byte register. However, the line

```
MOV     AX,ORIG_PATH
```

would not work because the assembler will not allow 8 bits to be loaded directly into 16.

The following example shows how to override this declared reference to ORIG_PATH as byte values only:

```
MOV     AX,WORD PTR ORIG_PATH
```

The use of WORD PTR tells the assembler that even though the label ORIG_PATH is a reference to a byte value, you want to reference the word that begins at the address associated with ORIG_PATH.

PRE_PATH is similar to ORIG_DRIVE, except that here the byte is being set to 92, the ASCII value of the backslash character. ANY_FILE translates directly to the following four individual bytes:

```
42      46      42      00
 *       .       *
```

DIR_TABLE becomes an area of zeros 256 × 19, or 4,864 bytes long. You can use DUP multiple times in the same declaration to make it more readable.

BREAK_INT_OFF and BREAK_INT_SEG set aside one word each and initially set the contents of those memory locations to zero. Later, the contents of this named memory location can be loaded directly into a register by a line similar to the following:

```
MOV     AX,BREAK_INT_SEG
```

Through the use of EQU and THIS BYTE, CMD_TABLE is set up to reference the first byte of an area that will later be used as an offset table to other values. For this example, the five words beginning at CMD_TABLE are set equal to the offset addresses of other variables. In this way, the messages ACTION_CMD, DOIT_CMD, DRIVE_CMD, PATH_CMD, and EXIT_CMD can all be accessed by address, even though the length of each message is different.

Finally, ONE_MOMENT is a series of bytes that spells the message Examining diskette ... One moment please!, followed by a zero, or null byte.

Addressing

The 8086/8088 offers a multitude of ways to address data: register-to-register, immediate addressing, direct addressing, and several different types of indirect addressing. Because you will use each of these modes as you program, you need to understand them now.

Each addressing mode always has a source and a destination. The destination is always to the left of the comma; the source is always to the right. In addition, both direct and indirect addressing assume an implied addressing segment. Let's take a look at each type of addressing and any applicable segment addressing assumptions.

Register Addressing

Register addressing is the fastest mode of data addressing. These instructions take fewer physical bytes and are entirely executed in the CPU. If your data needs are small within certain subroutines, always perform manipulations within registers. Some examples of this type of addressing are

```
MOV    AX,BX
MOV    DX,CX
MOV    DI,SI
```

These instructions result in the contents of the register to the right of the comma being copied into the register to the left of the comma. Thus the contents of BX, CX, and SI are copied into AX, DX, and DI, respectively. Notice that the contents are *copied*, not simply *moved*. Therefore, after the first instruction is completed, AX and BX contain the same values.

Immediate Addressing

Immediate addressing causes a constant numeric value to be placed into a register or a memory location. Consider the following instructions:

```
RED       EQU       4
LOC_1     DB        00
LOC_2     DW        0000

          MOV       AX,5
          MOV       BL,RED
          MOV       LOC_1,RED
          MOV       LOC_2,5
```

In all instances, a constant value (right of the comma) is being placed at the specified destination (left of the comma). The specified destination is either a register or a memory location. Although several of these instructions use equates instead of specific numbers, the correct numbers will replace the equates when the coding is assembled. Thus, all occurrences of RED will be replaced by 4 to provide the constant numeric value required by immediate addressing.

Direct Addressing

While immediate addressing only places data at either a register or a memory location, direct addressing moves data from a memory location to a register, or from a register to a memory location, as the following instructions illustrate:

```
LOC_1     DB        00
LOC_2     DW        0000

          MOV       AL,LOC_1
          MOV       BX,LOC_2
          MOV       LOC_1,AH
          MOV       LOC_2,CX
```

As with the other addressing modes, the values contained in the memory location or register to the right of the comma are copied into the memory location or register to the left of the comma.

Indirect Addressing

Indirect addressing is the most difficult addressing mode to master but is also the most powerful. The three methods of indirect addressing are *register indirect, indexed* (or *based*), and *based and indexed with displacement*. Rather than considering each of these methods individually, this section will cover the general category of indirect addressing as a whole.

To illustrate the various indirect addressing methods, consider the following code fragments:

```
CMD_TABLE        EQU         THIS BYTE
                 DW          OFFSET ACTION_CMD
                 DW          OFFSET DOIT_CMD
                 DW          OFFSET DRIVE_CMD
                 DW          OFFSET PATH_CMD
                 DW          OFFSET EXIT_CMD

ACTION_CMD       DB          'SELECT',0
DOIT_CMD         DB          'DELETE',0
DRIVE_CMD        DB          'DRIVE',0
PATH_CMD         DB          'PATH',0
EXIT_CMD         DB          'EXIT',0
CMD_NUM          DW          0003

                 MOV         AX,CMD_NUM
                 MOV         BX,OFFSET CMD_TABLE
                 SHL         AX,1
                 ADD         BX,AX
                 MOV         SI,[BX]
```

Suppose that the variable CMD_NUM contains the value 3. The first instruction in this fragment uses direct addressing to copy the contents of CMD_NUM (3) into AX. Then immediate addressing is used to load BX with the offset address of CMD_TABLE. Remember that when this code is assembled, the directive OFFSET CMD_TABLE will be replaced with a literal number that represents the desired offset. Then the contents of AX are multiplied by 2 (which *always* happens when you shift the bits one position to the left), and this value is added to what is already in BX. At this point, BX contains a value 6 greater than the address of the start of CMD_TABLE, which is the address of the table entry for PATH_CMD.

The next statement is a specific example of indirect addressing. This statement results in SI being loaded with the contents of the location addressed by BX, which is the address for the string PATH_CMD. This indirect addressing usage always assumes that BX contains an address. The brackets (as used in this example) instruct the assembler to use the content of the memory location pointed to by the register within the brackets. Only the registers BX, BP, SI, or DI may be used within brackets.

Don't be misled by the preceding paragraph into believing that the brackets *always* indicate indirect addressing; the Microsoft assembler also lets them be used for other purposes and in some versions even requires their use under certain circumstances to obtain special forms of direct addressing! This is covered in much more detail in Chapter 8, when the differences between the most popular assemblers are examined.

Clearly, indirect addressing is inherently powerful. As used in the sample routine, a different address can be loaded into SI simply by changing the number in CMD_NUM. In this instance, because it contains an address used as a base, BX is referred to as the *base register*.

Variations on this basic indirect-addressing method provide even greater flexibility in addressing:

```
MOV        SI,[BX]
MOV        SI,[BP+2]
MOV        AX,[BX+SI+2]
```

The first instruction shows the indirect-addressing method already described. The second and third examples, however, show some variations. The second example uses the base register and a *displacement value*. The displacement value is added to the contents of the base register, producing a value that is assumed to be the address of the source value to be copied to the destination.

The third example uses the base register, an *index register*, and a displacement value that are all added together, resulting in a value that is again assumed to be the address of the source value from which the destination is loaded.

In all of these indirect-addressing methods, the specifications of the source and destination can be reversed, as with each of the other addressing schemes. Thus,

```
MOV        [BX],SI
MOV        [BP+2],SI
MOV        [BX+SI+2],AX
```

are all perfectly acceptable as destinations for data.

Segment Assumptions

When addressing data, the destination and source are always assumed to be in the data segment or relative to the DS register. The exception to this assumption is when the base pointer, BP, is used as the base register in indirect addressing; in this instance the stack segment, SS, is used.

The default segment can be overridden by explicit use of the desired segment, as follows:

```
MOV         CS:LOC_2,5
MOV         AL,CS:LOC_1
MOV         CS:LOC_2,CX
MOV         SI,ES:[BX]
MOV         DS:[BP+2],SI
MOV         ES:[BX+SI+2],AX
```

Notice that in the fifth line of these examples, DS must be stated explicitly as an override segment because the BP register is being used as the base register. Normally, SS would be assumed, but in this case DS is used.

Subroutines and Procedures

Subroutines are essential to programs of any magnitude. They enable a programmer to break a task down into smaller tasks, and continue breaking it down as necessary to complete a project. Using subroutines is much like outlining. You start with the main idea and break it down further and further until the entire topic is covered.

A subroutine is basically the same as a procedure or function. Although some technical distinction may exist between subroutines, procedures, and functions, this book assumes that they are essentially the same. All of these terms describe coding developed to perform a specialized task or set of tasks, and called (either singularly or repetitively) from a higher-level controlling program. Because assembly language uses the terms *procedure* and *proc* to identify such an entity, so have I.

In high-level languages, you can easily define procedures that other programs can call. BASIC uses the GOSUB command to invoke a subroutine and the RETURN command to signal its end. Pascal and C enable you to call a procedure or function by using a user-defined name. In Pascal, control is subsequently returned to the calling program by use of the end marker; and in C, the closing brace (or optional return statement) marks the end of the function.

Because assembly language requires much more interaction on the programmer's part to accomplish a given task, and because the amount of source code written to accomplish the task can be prodigious, using procedures becomes even more important than with other languages. Two types of procedures (NEAR and FAR) are used in assembly language. They are procedurally the same, differing only in how a CALL to and RETurn from each affects the stack and CS:IP registers.

NEAR procedures are contained within the same code segment as the program invoking the procedure. The declaration of a NEAR procedure is accomplished with the PROC NEAR directives. The following example shows a subroutine to load the AX register with the contents of the word that DS:SI points to, after which SI is incremented to point to the next word:

```
GET_WORD        PROC    NEAR
                MOV     AX,[SI]
                INC     SI
                INC     SI
                RET
GET_WORD        ENDP
```

This example is declared as a NEAR procedure because it will reside in the same segment as the routine from which it is called. The only change necessary to make this routine a FAR procedure would be to change NEAR to FAR.

The following line executes either a NEAR or FAR procedure:

```
CALL    GET_WORD
```

In the case of a NEAR procedure, this invocation results in the offset address of the instruction *following* the CALL being pushed on the stack, and the address of CS:GET_WORD being loaded into the IP (thus, execution begins at GET_WORD). When the subsequent RET is encountered, the value of the IP is retrieved from the stack, and execution continues from the point following the original CALL.

Because this is a NEAR routine, only offset addresses, one word long, are pushed on and subsequently popped from the stack.

A FAR procedure operates exactly the same way, except that two address words (the value of the code segment and the offset address) are pushed on and later popped from the stack. Also, both the CS and IP registers are set to point to the beginning of the subroutine.

The vast majority of procedures you use will be of the NEAR persuasion. FAR procedures are usually used for controlling programs, for extremely large programs, and for interrupt handler routines. However, when you write routines to use with certain high-level languages, these languages will require that your routines be defined as FAR procedures.

The Assembly Language Subroutine Skeleton

By this point, programmers who have done most of their work with high-level languages are usually shaking their heads in amazement and starting to visualize assembly language programmers in padded cells with small, barred windows.

Don't despair! All this information about memory usage, program organization, data storage, and procedures is necessary so that you can see the structure and power of assembly language. The following statement may help simplify everything discussed on the last several pages: Virtually all assembly language programs and subroutines can be written using a standard program skeleton. Through the use of a program skeleton, you can concentrate on task completion rather than administrative overhead.

A program skeleton is a template that gives a bare-bones (pardon the pun) outline of the program header, data declaration areas, and other "overhead" information. For example, most subroutines and COM files have data and code in the same memory segment. Thus, the following program skeleton can be entered, saved as a file, and used as a starting point for future assembly language programs or subroutines:

```
        page 60,132
;   ***************************************************************
;   *                                                             *
;   * Author:    [your name goes here]                            *
;   * Date:      [date program written]                           *
;   *                                                             *
;   * File:      [file name goes here]                            *
;   *                                                             *
;   * Descrpt:   [description of program or routine]              *
;   *                                                             *
;   * Format:    [syntax of calling statement]                    *
;   *                                                             *
;   ***************************************************************

; *** Public declaration of subroutines and data

            PUBLIC  [list entry points and data here]

; *** External data needed by these subroutines
```

```
                EXTRN    [data and its type goes here]

; *** External subroutines called by these subroutines

                EXTRN    [routine and its type goes here]

                NAME     [routine name goes here]
CODE            SEGMENT BYTE PUBLIC 'CODE'
                ASSUME  CS:CODE

; *** Declaration of equates

PARMD           EQU      12              ;These are sample equates.
PARMC           EQU      10              ;       The ones you use will
PARMB           EQU      08              ;       vary as your program
PARMA           EQU      06              ;       needs change.

; *** Declaration of data

DATA1           DW       0000            ;These are sample data
DATA2           DW       0000            ;       definitions. Yours
DATA3           DW       0000            ;       will vary.


; ---------------------------------------------------------------
; START OF MAIN CODING
; ---------------------------------------------------------------


XXXXXX          PROC     FAR

                                         ;Your program statements are
                                         ;       inserted at this point.


XXXXXX          ENDP
; ---------------------------------------------------------------
CODE            ENDS
                END
```

Notice the liberal use of comments. Getting into the habit of documenting your programs will help make your job much easier. In assembly language, comments are denoted by a semicolon. When the program is assembled, everything following a semicolon is disregarded until the end of the current line is reached. Thus, the comments you place in a source file do not make your program longer or slower; they only increase the size of the source file and make it more easily understood later.

In this program skeleton, information within brackets is to be supplied when the skeleton is developed into a real program. Also, the locations indicated by XXXXXX are to be replaced with the name of the routine or program. This is the name that will be used to call this routine from other programs; it is also the name that the linker uses when the program modules are put together.

How you use a program skeleton is up to you; your individual programming habits and needs necessarily differ from everyone else's. If you do not have a skeleton developed already, develop one, and store it in a file. Then you can copy the file and edit the skeleton each time you start a new program.

Summary

Assembly language is quick, compact, and powerful. Because the "building blocks" provided by the language are so small, quite a few more blocks are needed to create a large structure. Resulting programs, however, can yield benefits—such as speed and compact code—not possible with other languages. Other benefits are outlined in the introduction to this book.

This chapter is a quick overview of some features and basic tenets of the language. Detailed information on the use of individual instructions can be gleaned from studying the examples through the rest of this book or by referring to Part IV.

Interfacing Subroutines

When you interface assembly language subroutines with a high-level language, you must address the following:

❏ How the subroutine is invoked

❏ How parameters are passed

❏ How values are returned

This chapter does not attempt to address the specifics of all these points. The nitty-gritty details of each of these considerations are covered in Chapters 3 through 7. The way you invoke an assembly language subroutine, for example, largely depends on the high-level language from which that subroutine is called. The information in this chapter is more or less common to the process of interfacing assembly language subroutines, no matter which high-level language you may be using.

Let's look first at how parameters are passed to assembly language subroutines. Later in this chapter, you will see how values are returned to a high-level language.

Passing Parameters

Generally, you use the stack to pass parameters to subroutines. As you learned from Chapter 1, the stack is a general-purpose work area, and using it correctly is critical to successful program execution.

Not all languages pass parameters on the stack. The parameters can also be passed in the CPU registers or in some other memory area (usually called a *parameter block*). However, neither of these methods is widely used; you probably will only use them when working with DBMS languages. Chapters 6 and 7 discuss these methods in more detail.

Because each high-level language uses memory in different ways, a common area is needed for subroutine interfacing. The accepted standard for this area is the stack. If you push the parameters on the stack before you call a subroutine, the subroutine can access and modify the data. To prepare for the discussion of how parameters are accessed on the stack, let's look at how the data is placed on the stack and how parameters are formatted.

How Parameters Are Placed on the Stack

The specifics of how parameters are pushed on the stack depend on the type of data the parameter represents and on the high-level language you are using. However, individual parameters usually are passed either as data values or as pointers to the values.

Normally, if the parameter is a short numeric integer (16 bits or shorter), its data value is pushed on the stack. If the parameter is an alphanumeric string, a pointer to the string is passed. A parameter that is a large numeric integer or a floating-point number can be passed by either method.

Because parameter placement differs from language to language, later chapters cover the specifics for each language.

How Parameters Are Formatted

Individual parameter format may vary from language to language. For instance, if the data value of a floating-point number is being passed on the stack, the high-level language you are using determines the way in which the number is encoded.

Parameters must occupy at least one complete word (16 bits) on the stack although, depending on the high-level language, additional words can be used. If that one word is a pointer to the variable in the high-level language's data segment, the translation of the data at that memory location will differ from language to language. The number of bytes that each data element uses is particularly open to variation. Again, later chapters cover specifics for parameter format.

Accessing Parameters on the Stack

To access information passed through the stack, the routines in this book use the BP register (the base pointer, introduced in Chapter 1). This register is used as a secondary stack pointer, primarily for accessing data on the stack relative to a given location.

The specific way you use the BP register largely depends on the type of subroutine being called. Let's take a look at the contents of the stack when the assembly language subroutine is a NEAR procedure.

When the subroutine is invoked, each individual parameter is pushed on the stack, followed by the calling program's return address. In a NEAR procedure, this return address is the segment offset—technically, the incremented contents of the Instruction Pointer (IP) register. Thus, at the start of the assembly language subroutine to which three 16-bit parameters are being passed, the stack would look like that shown in figure 2.1.

Fig. 2.1. Stack at beginning of execution of a NEAR procedure.

| ???? |
| ???? |
| ???? |
| ???? |
| high byte of return address offset |
| low byte of return address offset |

◄── stack pointer (SP) is here

If the routine being called were a FAR procedure, the stack contents would look like those in figure 2.2.

Fig. 2.2. Stack at beginning of execution of a FAR *procedure.*

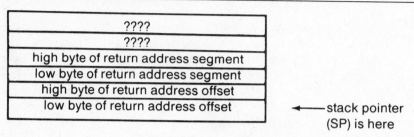

Notice that invoking a FAR procedure involves pushing one additional word of data. This word is the segment of the calling program, technically the contents of the Code Segment (CS) register.

Other than the number of bytes pushed for the return address, the information for both procedures is in the same format and in a predictable position on the stack. To access the information, you simply set the BP register and use offsets to retrieve values from the stack. The following code segment shows the proper way to do this in a NEAR procedure assuming that the parameters have been placed on the stack by a C compiler, and that each occupies 16 bits; the code segment would be slightly different for other languages:

```
PARM_A              EQU     4
PARM_B              EQU     6
PARM_C              EQU     8

TEST                PROC    NEAR
                    PUSH    BP
                    MOV     BP,SP

                    MOV     AX,[BP]+PARM_A
                    MOV     BX,[BP]+PARM_B
                    MOV     CX,[BP]+PARM_C

; REST OF PROGRAM GOES HERE

                    POP     BP
                    RET
TEST                ENDP
```

Notice that the three parameters are called PARM_A, PARM_B, and PARM_C in this subroutine. These symbols are equated with a specific offset value at the front of the program. When the subroutine executes, the first commands encountered set the base pointer so that it can be used with the offset values to access the parameters. Let's follow what happens in this coding segment step by step.

Remember that, on entry, the stack looks like the one shown in figure 2.1. At this point, the return address occupies the two bytes at stack offset 0, and the parameters begin with the byte at offset 2. However, to save the contents of the BP register, you must push the register on the stack. After you push BP on the stack, the value of BP occupies the two bytes at stack offset 0, followed by the two-byte return address, and the parameters then begin at an offset of 4.

The next instruction sets BP equal to the current Stack Pointer (SP), which means that BP contains the stack offset address of the old BP value. Because you know that the parameters begin at offset 4, you can access them through indirect addressing, using BP and an offset.

At the end of the subroutine, you must pop BP off the stack. Doing so leaves the stack clean and restores BP (BP must be restored because it is almost always used in the calling program).

Because a call to a FAR procedure results in an additional word on the stack, the only change necessary to the preceding coding segment is that of changing the equates (EQU) to

```
PARM_A          EQU     6
PARM_B          EQU     8
PARM_C          EQU     10
```

This change compensates for the additional word placed on the stack when the FAR procedure is called.

Most assembly language programmers use BP to access the contents of the stack; this method commonly is used to access parameters passed to assembly language subroutines.

Returning Values

Values usually are returned from an assembly language subroutine in one of the following ways:

❏ Through the stack

❏ Through a register

❏ Through memory

None of these methods is automatic; you must predetermine how you will return values. The high-level language with which you are interfacing is the major determinant for selecting which method to use. Some languages require that you use a certain method. Others, such as C, allow some programming flexibility.

Let's take a look at each of these methods.

Returning Values through the Stack

The stack can be used not only for passing parameters but also for returning values. For example, if the calling program pushes four unsigned integer numbers on the stack before calling an assembly language subroutine, the subroutine can use and even modify these four words of data. On return to the controlling program, the four values remain on the stack. The controlling program can retrieve and use these values, which may have been altered by the subroutine. This is a common method, in some languages, for passing information both to and from a subroutine.

Returning Values through a Register

In some languages, such as C, you can provide a return value in a register. Because the expected register varies from language to language and possibly from version to version, be sure to verify which registers to use for your particular language.

As an example of this method of returning values, assume that a calling program uses the following command line to invoke an assembly language subroutine:

```
x=whizbang();
```

Clearly, whatever the purpose of the whizbang subroutine, a return value is expected and will be assigned to the variable x. The value's expected format depends on the format of x. If we assume that x is a 16-bit integer, a value can be returned in a register, such as AX, and the high-level language then will assign the contents of AX to the variable x.

Returning Values through Memory

If your high-level language passes pointers to data instead of passing data values, you can modify high-level language variables directly.

When passing string variables to a subroutine, many high-level languages pass only a pointer to the string's memory location. Because the length of the string may vary, passing the entire string on the stack is unrealistic. However, using the pointer, you can access the string directly and even make changes to it, which are then available to the high-level language.

Although this method has powerful possibilities, it also has a drawback. For example, an assembly language subroutine cannot readily change the length of a string. Changing memory allocation is dangerous when that allocation is under the control of a high-level language. Many pointers and assumptions that affect the high-level language's use of the variable may be in play and, by changing the data length, you may overwrite other data or invalidate other pointers. Either of these possibilities is dangerous to successful program execution.

You can prevent most potential problems by making sure that you pass a string long enough for any reasonable amount of data you might need to return. For instance, dBASE permits strings to be up to 255 bytes long; therefore, passing a string of 255 blanks to your routine provides buffer space big enough to handle *any* string that the language permits. However, if you know that you will never need more than 64 bytes in the return value, then passing a 64-byte string in will be adequate.

Other Considerations

In addition to the observations already made about the stack and its use, I want to point out several other considerations. These are mainly tips for you to keep in mind when doing any programming that will manipulate the stack.

As you've learned, additional data is pushed on the stack when a procedure is invoked. One item of this data (which I call *overhead data*) that is common to all high-level languages is the return address for the calling program.

Inadvertently changing this overhead data can, and usually does, have disastrous effects. For example, if the return address is modified, program execution will not resume at the proper point in the calling program. If you are lucky, the entire system may "hang" and require rebooting; if you are unlucky, control could accidentally drop into the DOS routine that reformats your hard disk!

A more common error is failure to remove information that was pushed on the stack or failure to restore the stack pointer properly after using the stack for temporary storage. This leaves the stack "dirty." Figure 2.3 illustrates what may happen if you inadvertently leave an extra word of data on the stack.

Fig. 2.3. Corrupted stack; too much data left at end of procedure.

????
????
????
????
12
6F
0C
A8	◄——actual return address
00
41	◄——stack pointer (SP) is here

When a RET (return) instruction is executed, execution will resume at 0CA8:0041 instead of resuming at 126F:0CA8 (the proper return address). The return address will vary, depending on what is left on the stack. And the results of this error will vary, depending on the memory contents beginning at the erroneous return address. This address may be in the program or, as in figure 2.3, it may be somewhere outside the program area. To solve the problem of program execution that does not continue as you want it to, make sure that everything pushed on the stack is subsequently popped off. Then execute the return.

A similar error occurs if you pop too much data from the stack; execution continues at an unintended memory address.

These two errors bring up an interesting (and potentially devastating) possibility, which has already been mentioned. Many hard disk manufacturers include a set of low-level routines in ROM. These routines, which include low-level hard disk formatting and other preparation software, lie quietly in wait until you call them—either purposely or inadvertently. It is possible, although unlikely, that an erroneous return address on the stack could cause program execution to resume at a memory address located at the start of the formatting (or other dangerous) code for the hard disk. The results could be devastating. To guard against such a possibility, back up your hard disk at regular intervals, and make sure that your routines leave the proper return address undisturbed.

Data Manipulation Tips

When working with data passed to assembly language subroutines, you should follow several safety guidelines:

1. Never manipulate data values unless you need to.

2. Use intermediate working variables or registers during execution of assembly language subroutines.

3. *Always* remember to leave the stack as it was when the routine was called. The stack should be free of extraneous data.

4. Make sure not to pop too much data from the stack.

5. Determine your subroutine procedure ahead of time, and make allowance for it. Is it NEAR or FAR? The type of subroutine affects how data is accessed.

6. Take special care to preserve the calling program's return address unchanged.

Summary

Because different high-level languages use memory in different ways, a common method of passing information to assembly language subroutines is mandatory. The accepted method is to pass information on the stack, where that data can be accessed by the assembly language subroutines.

This chapter introduced and explained some general concepts, but did not cover language-specific information. In the following five chapters you will discover how to interface specific high-level languages with assembly language subroutines.

CHAPTER 3

Interfacing with BASIC

B ASIC (Beginner's All-purpose Symbolic Instruction Code) is perhaps the most popular of all computer languages. Its free-form structure, easy English-like vocabulary, and low cost make it the most widely distributed language in the world of microcomputers.

Although BASIC is popular, it has several shortcomings that have caused some people to disdain the language and other people to adopt apparently unorthodox methods of circumventing the problem areas.

BASIC's slowness is its most serious and noticeable problem. By nature, BASIC is an interpretive language; every line of source code is parsed to its machine language equivalent when the code is executed, which ultimately slows down BASIC programs. The best way to get around this problem is to use a BASIC compiler, which translates the BASIC source code into machine language for subsequent execution. Although using a compiler greatly increases speed, it also increases development time and destroys the interactive nature of the language. However, the frustration of this dilemma was somewhat alleviated after Microsoft's QuickBASIC and Borland's Turbo BASIC were introduced. In these environments, you get both the interactive advantages of interpretive BASIC and the increased power and speed of a compiled language.

To overcome the slowness of interpretive BASIC (and some compiled BASIC routines), many programmers have resorted to the technique of

55

reducing time-consuming procedures to their assembly language equivalent, and then combining them with the BASIC program. This technique, which is certainly not without perils, is the type of assembly language interfacing covered in this chapter.

Those who turned to compiled BASIC seemed to solve the speed problem—for a while. IBM's BASIC compiler (introduced in the early 1980s and made to work with DOS versions prior to 2.0) did not support such features as hierarchical directories and path names, but programmers could use assembly language subroutines to sidestep these deficiencies. Many programmers converted other routines to assembly language; execution time for those routines was noticeably faster. The newer Quick-BASIC and Turbo BASIC compilers removed many of the barriers to compiler use.

This chapter examines both interpretive and compiled BASIC. First, let's look at the process of interfacing with interpretive BASIC.

Interpretive BASIC

Shielded from the computer's day-to-day, machine-level intricacies, most interpretive BASIC programmers do not have to concern themselves with where code or data reside, or how peripherals are interfaced with the computer. The BASIC interpreter takes care of all these matters behind the scenes. However, a limited number of commands enable you to examine BASIC's internal workings more closely. These commands, which include VARPTR and DEF SEG, are not used frequently in the course of normal, BASIC-only programming.

You can use several methods to interface assembly language subroutines with BASIC. This chapter focuses on two methods: storing short routines in string variables, and storing long routines in a set position in memory. Each method is well-suited for different types of subroutines, based on their length.

Interfacing Short Subroutines

You can enter short subroutines directly into memory by placing them in the variable space used by BASIC strings. These subroutines must (by definition) be short because, under interpretive BASIC, strings cannot be longer than 255 characters.

To place an assembly language subroutine into a string, follow these steps:

1. Determine the length (in bytes) of the machine language subroutine.

2. Set aside a string variable that is equal in length to the number of bytes determined in step 1.

3. Move the subroutine, byte by byte, into the memory space occupied by the string variable.

After completing these steps, you can call the subroutine at any time by simply calling the address associated with the string variable.

To understand this method of interfacing an assembly language subroutine, let's look at a practical example; BASIC has CLS but no "clear to end of line" capability, so let's create a subroutine that provides it. First comes the actual assembly language coding:

```
        Page 60,132
;       **********************************************************
;       *                                                        *
;       * File:     CLREOL.ASM                                   *
;       * Date:     10/20/89                                     *
;       *                                                        *
;       * Descrpt: Subroutine designed to clear screen from current *
;       *          cursor position to end of line. Designed to be *
;       *          called from interpretive BASIC.               *
;       *                                                        *
;       * Format:   CALL D                                       *
;       *              D =  Address of subroutine                *
;       *                                                        *
;       **********************************************************

                PUBLIC  CLREOL

CODE            SEGMENT 'CODE'
                ASSUME  CS:CODE


;       ----------------------------------------------------------
CLREOL          PROC    FAR

                MOV     AH,OFh          ; get video mode data
                INT     10h             ; using BIOS function
                XCHG    AH,AL           ; set up COLS data
                XOR     AH,AH
```

```
          PUSH      AX                    ; and save it

          MOV       AH,03h                ; get current cursor pos
          INT       10h
          XOR       DH,DH                 ; ignore row
          POP       CX                    ; get width back
          SUB       CX,DX                 ; calc number left on line
          MOV       AX,0A20h              ; write char only, blank
          INT       10h

          RET
CLREOL    ENDP
;         ----------------------------------------------------------------


CODE      ENDS
          END
```

This simple little subroutine first checks how many character positions are on a line (since BASIC can have either 40 or 80 columns), then finds out which column the cursor is currently in, calculates how many characters will be needed to reach the end of the line, and finally writes that many blank spaces, starting at the current position, without moving the cursor. All of this magic is done by three calls to the video BIOS routine.

After completing the three steps outlined at the beginning of this section, you must then determine the number of bytes required by the preceding routine. To make this simpler you can use the following BASIC program, once you have assembled the assembler source program into an OBJ file:

```
 1' ****************************************************************
 2' *                                                            *
 3' * File:    OBJREAD.BAS                                       *
 4' * Date:    10/20/89                                          *
 5' *                                                            *
 6' * Descrpt: Creates overlay DATA lines for use with          *
 7' *          examples, from OBJ files created by MASM, TASM,   *
 8' *          or OPTASM. Just change filename "xxx" in line     *
 9' *          20, then RUN the program.                         *
10' *                                                            *
11' ****************************************************************
15 CLS
20 OPEN "xxx.obj" AS #1 LEN=1
30 FIELD #1, 1 AS A$
```

```
40 P% = 1
50 GET #1, P%
60 IF ASC(A$)= 160 THEN GOTO 110
70 P%=P%+1
80 GET #1, P%
90 P% = P%+2+ASC(A$)
100 GOTO 50
110 P%=P%+1
120 GET #1,P%
130 N% = ASC(A$)-4
140 PRINT "1000 DATA";N%;
150 L%=1001
160 P%=P%+5
170 WHILE N%>0
180 IF Z%=0 THEN PRINT : PRINT USING "#### DATA ";L%; : L% = L% + 1
190 GET #1,P%
200 X%=ASC(A$)
210 IF X%<16 THEN PRINT "0";
220 PRINT HEX$(X%);
230 P%=P%+1
240 N%=N%-1
250 Z%=Z%+1 : IF Z%=10 THEN Z%=0 ELSE IF N%>0 THEN PRINT ", ";
260 WEND
270 PRINT
```

This BASIC program reads your OBJ file and displays on screen the appropriate DATA statements to be used later. Translated to machine language via the assembler-OBJREAD route, the CLREOL routine consists of the following 24 bytes:

```
B4 0F CD 10 86 E0 32 E4 50 B4 03 CD 10 32 F6 59 2B CA B8 20 0A CD 10 CB
```

Knowing this, you can create a string 24 bytes long for this routine. Of the many ways available for creating a string, one is as good as another; pick the method you find most comfortable. In the following sample BASIC program, I have used the SPACE instruction:

```
10 ' ************************************************************
20 ' *                                                         *
30 ' * Sample program to show poking an assembly language      *
40 ' * subroutine into BASIC's string variable space.          *
50 ' *                                                         *
60 ' ************************************************************
```

```
100 CLS
110 DEF FN ADR(X$)=256*PEEK(VARPTR(X$)+2)+PEEK(VARPTR(X$)+1)
120 RESTORE 1000
130 READ NUMBYTES
140 MODULE$=SPACE$(NUMBYTES)
150 FOR J=1 TO NUMBYTES
160 READ VALUE$
170 MID$(MODULE$,J,1)=CHR$(VAL("&H"+VALUE$))
180 NEXT

190 LOCATE 10,1
200 PRINT "This line will be cleared from HERE on to the end;";
210 PRINT " press any key now.";
220 WHILE INKEY$=""
230 WEND
240 LOCATE 10,36
250 D=FN ADR(MODULE$)
260 CALL D
270 END

1000 DATA 24
1010 DATA B4,OF,CD,10,86,EO,32,E4,50,B4
1020 DATA 03,CD,10,32,F6,59,2B,CA,B8,20
1030 DATA OA,CD,10,CB
```

Notice that the byte values making up the subroutine are contained in DATA statements at the end of the program. The first DATA statement (in line 1000) indicates the number of bytes in the subroutine. These lines were created using OBJREAD.BAS.

Lines 120 through 180 read and act on the DATA statements. Line 170 stores the values into the variable space of MODULE$. These lines can be used, unchanged, to load any assembly language module into string space.

Lines 190 through 270 test the routine to show that it works. The two LOCATE statements position the cursor appropriately, and the WHILE...WEND in lines 220 and 230 provides the time delay so that you can see what is happening.

Notice line 250, which is used to determine the physical address of MODULE$. Through the use of the function definition at line 110, the address is determined by using the string descriptor (maintained by BASIC) that specifies the length and location of variables. Look again at line 110:

```
110 DEF FN ADR(X$)=256*PEEK(VARPTR(X$)+2)+PEEK(VARPTR(X$)+1)
```

VARPTR returns the address of MODULE$. In this case, because we are working with a string, the address of the string descriptor is returned. This descriptor consists of three bytes that give the string's length and address. Because the length is unimportant in this case, you need to use the first and second offset bytes at the descriptor address.

These offset bytes specify the address in memory of the first byte of MODULE$. The address is assigned (in line 250) to the numeric variable D. Because MODULE$ contains the machine language subroutine that should be called, line 260 passes control to that routine, starting at the first byte of MODULE$ (whose address is in D).

Sometimes you may want to clear a portion of the screen in a different color without using the BASIC color-setting capabilities. By slightly rewriting the routine, you can pass to assembly language a variable that specifies the color attribute to use as in the following assembly language program:

```
        Page 60,132
;       ************************************************************
;       *                                                          *
;       * File:    CLREOL2.ASM                                     *
;       * Date:    10/21/89                                        *
;       *                                                          *
;       * Descrpt: Subroutine designed to clear screen from current *
;       *          cursor position to end of line. Designed to be  *
;       *          called from interpretive BASIC.                 *
;       *                                                          *
;       * Format:  CALL D(A%)                                      *
;       *          D = Address of subroutine                       *
;       *          A% = Attribute to use when clearing             *
;       *                                                          *
;       ************************************************************

                PUBLIC  CLREOL

CODE            SEGMENT 'CODE'
                ASSUME  CS:CODE


;       ---------------------------------------------------------------
CLREOL          PROC    FAR

                PUSH    BP              ; set up stack frame
                MOV     BP,SP
                MOV     AH,OFh          ; get video mode data
                INT     10h             ; using BIOS function
```

```
        XCHG    AH,AL           ; set up COLS data
        XOR     AH,AH
        PUSH    AX              ; and save it

        MOV     AH,03h          ; get current cursor pos
        INT     10h
        XOR     DH,DH           ; ignore row
        POP     CX              ; get width back
        SUB     CX,DX           ; calc number left on line
        MOV     SI,[BP+6]       ; get address of parameter
        MOV     BL,[SS:SI]      ; get attribute byte itself
        MOV     AX,0920h        ; write char + attr, blank
        INT     10h

        POP     BP              ; release stack frame
        RET     2               ; flush off the parameter
CLREOL  ENDP
; -----------------------------------------------------------------

CODE    ENDS
        END
```

The two versions of the assembly language routine are noticeably different. This rewritten version is a dozen bytes longer, and all the added bytes of code are used to obtain the attribute value from the calling BASIC program.

The variable is passed through the stack. When the CALL statement is executed, BASIC pushes the variable's *address* on the stack. Thus, to access the parameter value, you must first retrieve the pointer from the stack and then use the pointer to load BL with the parameter value itself.

Notice also that, in this version of the assembly language routine, you must use RET (return from procedure) with a specification of the number of additional bytes to pop from the stack. In this example, you use RET 2 because the address BASIC pushed on the stack is two bytes long. If you don't use this method of return when you pass parameters, the chances of getting back to BASIC are slim.

Not quite so obvious is the change in the BIOS function call that actually writes the blanks to the screen. This call now tells the screen to use the attribute value in the BL register instead of the one already on the screen. Without this change, all the rest would be wasted.

You also must change the BASIC program that uses this routine for passing a value. The modified routine follows:

```
10 ' *************************************************************
20 ' *                                                          *
30 ' * Sample program to show poking an assembly language       *
40 ' * subroutine into BASIC's string variable space.           *
50 ' *                                                          *
60 ' *************************************************************
100 CLS
110 DEF FN ADR(X$)=256*PEEK(VARPTR(X$)+2)+PEEK(VARPTR(X$)+1)
120 RESTORE 1000
130 READ NUMBYTES
140 MODULE$=SPACE$(NUMBYTES)
150 FOR J=1 TO NUMBYTES
160 READ VALUE$
170 MID$(MODULE$,J,1)=CHR$(VAL("&H"+VALUE$))
180 NEXT

190 LOCATE 10,1
200 PRINT "This line will be cleared from HERE on to the end;";
210 PRINT " press any key now.";
220 WHILE INKEY$=""
230 WEND
240 LOCATE 10,36
250 A%=&H10
260 D=FN ADR(MODULE$)
270 CALL D(A%)
280 PRINT
290 PRINT "The clearing will be UNDERLINE if mono, or BLUE if color."

1000 DATA 36
1010 DATA 55, 8B, EC, B4, OF, CD, 10, 86, C4, 32
1020 DATA E4, 50, B4, 03, CD, 10, 32, F6, 59, 2B
1030 DATA CA, 8B, 76, 06, 36, 8A, 1C, B8, 20, 09
1040 DATA CD, 10, 5D, CA, 02, 00
```

Notice that the only modifications to the routine are in the invocation (lines 250 and 270) and in the DATA statements that begin at line 1000 (after all, this assembly language routine is longer than the first).

Some new lines are added (lines 280 and 290) to verify that control returns to BASIC properly after the routine is CALLed. If you input a delay of 0, the program will end.

In line 270 note especially that the variable being passed to the routine (A%) is an integer variable. Integer variables are extremely easy to work with in assembly language. They require only two bytes in the BASIC variable area and can be accessed as word values in assembly language. This routine would have been far more complicated had the % integer flag been left out!

Interfacing Longer Subroutines

If the subroutine is more than 255 bytes long, or if you are not comfortable placing the subroutine into a string variable, you can place it directly into memory by following these steps:

1. Determine how much space to reserve for the assembly language subroutine.

2. Use the CLEAR command to set aside the necessary memory space.

3. Poke the subroutine into the reserved area of memory.

Even though this process is particularly well-suited to subroutines longer than 255 bytes, I will use the same routine as the previous example to demonstrate the process. This routine has no coding that would render it static, and it is "*relocatable*," which means that it will function properly no matter where it is placed in memory. Interfacing is relatively easy. This type of routine gives programmers few headaches and little trouble.

To reserve memory for this routine, you use the CLEAR command with a designation specifying the highest memory address that BASIC can access. BASIC ordinarily uses a full 64K segment. (64K is essentially equivalent to FFFFh.) By subtracting (from this unlimited amount) the amount of space you want to reserve for your assembly language routines, you can determine a new ceiling limit to use in the CLEAR statement.

For example, this subroutine, which occupies 36 bytes of memory, and an additional 10 similar routines would need perhaps one full K of memory. Subtracting 400h (1K) from FFFFh results in FBFFh—the address (FBFFh, or 64511) to use with the CLEAR statement in the BASIC program. The process is shown in the following routine:

```
10 ' ***********************************************************
20 ' *                                                         *
30 ' * Sample program to show poking an assembly language      *
40 ' * subroutine into BASIC's high memory area.               *
50 ' *                                                         *
60 ' ***********************************************************
100 CLEAR ,64511
110 D=64512

120 RESTORE 1000
130 READ NUMBYTES
140 FOR J=1 TO NUMBYTES
150 READ VALUE$
160 POKE 64511+J,VAL("&H"+VALUE$)
170 NEXT

180 LOCATE 10,1
190 PRINT "This line will be cleared from HERE on to the end;";
200 PRINT " press any key now.";
210 WHILE INKEY$=""
220 WEND
230 LOCATE 10,36
240 A%=&H10
250 CALL D(A%)
260 PRINT
270 PRINT "The clearing will be UNDERLINE if mono, or BLUE if color."

1000 DATA 36
1010 DATA 55, 8B, EC, B4, 0F, CD, 10, 86, C4, 32
1020 DATA E4, 50, B4, 03, CD, 10, 32, F6, 59, 2B
1030 DATA CA, 8B, 76, 06, 36, 8A, 1C, B8, 20, 09
1040 DATA CD, 10, 5D, CA, 02, 00
```

Notice the program coding at line 160. In this method of using an assembly language routine, the POKE statement is used to transfer the routine to the appropriate memory area. Note also that the function definition is omitted because the routine's address will never change.

This type of usage has clear advantages, the greatest of which is that BASIC can access long assembly language subroutines. The other advantage is that the subroutine resides at one static location. In this example, the assembly language subroutine will always reside at FC00h (64512). Clearly, this is preferable to having to calculate the beginning address whenever you want to invoke the routine.

Compiled BASIC

Several compilers for BASIC exist, but the least expensive and apparently most popular is Microsoft's QuickBasic, which is now at version 4.5. All the different compilers vary slightly from each other; the examples in this chapter were written and tested with QuickBasic 4.5.

Although normal interpretive BASIC offers quick development time, compiled BASIC programs require a few extra steps. Earlier compilers required that you run the source programs through the compiler and linker. QuickBASIC gives you the option of doing program development within an integrated environment or of using a command-line compiler. With either option, program development takes place in an environment that makes the compiling and linking steps essentially invisible.

Compiled and interpretive BASIC differ in several ways. The most noticeable distinctions are that strings may be up to 32,767 bytes long in compiled BASIC, and that rather than poking assembly language routines into memory you can call them by their names. In the QuickBASIC environment, the routines must exist in a Quick Library QLB file before you can call them; with the command-line compiler, they can be linked to the BASIC program by using the LINK program provided with QuickBASIC.

Because longer strings are possible in compiled BASIC, the string descriptors that BASIC maintains must be of a different length than those in interpretive BASIC. Under compiled BASIC, string descriptors require not three bytes, but four: two for the length, followed by two for the starting address. During the CALL, the address of this descriptor is passed to the subroutine on the stack.

By taking into account this consideration for the string descriptors, you *can* handle assembly language subroutines as you would handle them under interpretive BASIC. They can be poked into high memory or stored in a string variable. However, a simpler, more straightforward method involves using just the name of the assembly language subroutine. The rest of the details are left up to the LINK process.

As an example of how to interface assembly language subroutines with compiled BASIC programs, consider the assembly language subroutine CLREOL previously described (the second version). To use this routine with the QuickBASIC environment, all that's necessary is to put it into a QLB file. No change to the routine itself is required.

To create a QLB file containing just the CLREOL routine, use LINK with the /QUICKLIB option switch as follows. The CLREOL routine is assumed to be in a file named EX2.OBJ, and the LINK operation will create Quick Library MINE.QLB:

```
C:\QB>LINK /Q EX2,MINE,,BQLB45;

Microsoft (R) Overlay Linker  Version 3.69
Copyright (C) Microsoft Corp 1983-1988.  All rights reserved.

LINK : warning L4045: name of output file is 'MINE.QLB'
```

Notice that LINK provided a warning message to let you know that the library name differed from that of the OBJ file. This message can be ignored; it does not indicate any kind of true error. The BQLB45 library must be specified to create a QLB file.

Once the QLB file exists, you can cause QuickBASIC to use it during a development session by typing the following:

```
C:\QB>QB /LMINE
```

This will bring the QuickBASIC environment into action, loading library file MINE.QLB into memory. Within the environment, you can type in the following QuickBASIC program. Note that, unlike the interpreter, QuickBASIC does not require line numbers:

```
' ****************************************************************
' *                                                            *
' * File:     QBCLREOL.BAS                                     *
' * Date:     10/21/89                                         *
' *                                                            *
' * Descrpt:  Demo of using assembly language within a         *
' *           QuickBASIC 4.5 program.                          *
' *                                                            *
' ****************************************************************

CLS
a% = 16
LOCATE 10, 1
PRINT "This line will be cleared from HERE";
x% = POS(0)
y% = CSRLIN
PRINT " to the end of the line."
PRINT "Press any key to continue:"
WHILE INKEY$ = ""
WEND
```

```
LOCATE y%, x%
CALL clreol(a%)
PRINT
PRINT "Control returned okay.    "
```

Note the total lack of any setup routine or DATA statements. Except for that, the only difference between this example and the corresponding one for the interpreter is that here, the POS() and CSRLIN keywords were used to automatically remember the cursor position for the second LOCATE.

If you want to verify that the attribute value is actually being passed through and used, you can change the value assigned to a% at the start of the program. On a color monitor, a value of 32 will produce a green background, 48 will create cyan, 64 will result in red, and so on up to 112, which specifies white. The code is simply 16 times the normal color value, but color values must be from 0 through 7; higher values are handled mod 8.

Notice that, because you don't need to worry about either poking or addresses, the procedure for calling assembly language subroutines in this program is a good deal simpler than the corresponding procedure for interpretive BASIC.

If you use the command-line compiler instead of the environment, you don't even need to create the QLB file. In this case, combining the assembly language subroutine with the BASIC program is accomplished through the LINK process (see Chapter 9).

Summary

Although BASIC is a readily available and extremely popular computer language, it has several shortcomings that make assembly language subroutines attractive and, in some instances, necessary to the viability of a program.

The process of interfacing assembly language subroutines depends largely on whether the BASIC program is written in interpretive or compiled BASIC. Each type of BASIC has differences that affect how the language interacts with and passes variables to assembly language subroutines.

These subroutines are invoked through the versatile, easy-to-use CALL statement. But remember that, upon returning from an assembly language subroutine, BASIC does not remove any information it has pushed on the stack before calling. When you pass parameters to your routines, you must use the modified RET instruction to remove this information. BASIC is not very tidy in its handling of assembly language subroutines.

## CHAPTER 4

Interfacing with Pascal

Pascal, a relatively new programming language that first appeared in 1970, has a loyal following of users who enjoy the language's structured approach to programming. Pascal is readily available for most computer systems at a moderate cost, and several companies (such as Borland and Microsoft) supply good, reasonably priced Pascal compilers. Such availability has added to the language's popularity.

Like any other computer language, Pascal "bogs down" in certain areas. I don't mean to imply that Pascal is unacceptable; it's just slower than assembly language in certain areas. As a result, many programmers have developed assembly language subroutines to interface with their Pascal programs.

General Interfacing Guidelines

The way to interface your assembly language subroutines with Pascal programs depends largely on your personal programming style, and to a lesser extent on the Pascal compiler that you are using. For example, using either Microsoft's QuickPascal or Borland's Turbo Pascal, you can include machine language code by means of the `inline()` statement or by automatic inclusion of OBJ files through the `{$L filename}` compiler directive (prior to version 4.0, Turbo Pascal provided only the inline() capability). The choice of methods to use is left up to you.

As an example of how the compiler itself affects the interfacing technique, many older Pascal compilers use a two-step approach to program development. After the source code is complete, it is *compiled* and then, in the second step, *linked*. If your Pascal compiler uses this two-step approach, you can only incorporate assembly language subroutines into your programs by assembling the subroutines separately and including them at the link step.

Inline Routines

When you include assembly language subroutines in Pascal programs by using the inline() capability, the subroutines must be completely "relocatable" and fully self-contained. In other words, there can be no external references in the subroutine, and all branching must be short. Although this type of structure is possible in assembly language coding, it is severely limiting.

External Procedures

If you compile the assembly language subroutine separately, whether you use the {$L filename} directive to associate the subroutine with your Pascal program or use the two-phase development process of compiling and linking, there usually is only one stipulation for interfacing with assembly language subroutines: you must use the PROCEDURE statement to define the subroutine name and the variables to be passed. The format of this statement is

```
PROCEDURE function_name(arg1,arg2,arg3, ... ,argn: dtype); EXTERNAL;
```

In this syntax, function_name is the publicly declared name of the assembly language subroutine. The arguments (1 through n) are the names of the variables whose values will be passed to the subroutine. For simplicity's sake, the parameters' data type (dtype) usually is INTEGER. (Although all parameters in our example are of the same type, these parameter types can often be mixed; see your compiler's reference manual for details.)

To indicate that pointers rather than values should be passed, the variable names can be modified with VAR prefixes. VAR indicates that only the offset address of the variable will be passed.

The Interrupt Attribute

Recent versions of Turbo Pascal (4.0 and above) and all versions of QuickPascal offer the capability of writing interrupt procedures in addition to the usual procedures and functions. When you choose the `inline()` technique for associating your assembly language module with your Pascal program, you can add the `Interrupt;` attribute to the declaration to specify that this procedure will be made suitable for servicing a machine interrupt.

Because it affects *only* the code generated automatically by the compiler, this attribute does not apply to external procedures. However, you have always had the ability to make external procedures suitable for interrupt servicing because you must provide all of their code.

When you add the `Interrupt;` attribute to the declaration of a procedure that uses `inline()` coding, then extra code is automatically generated at the procedure's entry point to save all the CPU registers and to change the DS register so that it points to your procedure's own `DATA` area. In addition, the normal `RET` instruction is replaced by an `IRET`, and all registers are restored before exit.

The extra code generated corresponds to the following typical declaration:

```
PROCEDURE intsvc( Flags,CS,IP,AX,BX,CX,DX,SI,DI,DS,ES,BP : word );
INTERRUPT;
BEGIN
.
.
.
END;
```

Your procedure can modify any of these parameters on the stack, and the changes will affect the registers upon return from the interrupt. However, because it is usually impossible to predict what the system will be doing at the instant the interrupt occurs, hardware interrupt procedures should leave the saved register values alone.

Using this feature requires relatively advanced knowledge of your system's architecture, so any simplified examples of such a procedure's use would be misleading.

Note that the `Interrupt;` attribute is not limited to assembly language routines alone; any Pascal code can be used within such a procedure. One of the most frequent applications of this feature is in the creation of serial-communications programs capable of keeping up with 1200-BPS and higher data rates. Often, these routines mix Pascal code that deals with memory use and inline assembly language to communicate with the serial port hardware.

Interfacing Subroutines without Variable Passing

To help you better understand how an assembly language subroutine is interfaced with Pascal, let's look at a sample subroutine that does not require parameter passing. Consider the following assembly language program:

```
Page 60,132
; ************************************************************
; *                                                         *
; * File:     CUROFF.ASM                                    *
; * Date:     10/20/89                                      *
; *                                                         *
; * Descrpt: Subroutine designed to turn the cursor off.    *
; *                                                         *
; ************************************************************


CODE    SEGMENT WORD PUBLIC
        ASSUME  CS:CODE


        PUBLIC  CUROFF
CUROFF  PROC    FAR
        PUSH    BP              ; save stackframe
        MOV     BP,SP
        MOV     AH,3            ; get current cursor
        XOR     BX,BX
        INT     10h
        OR      CH,20h          ; force to OFF condition
        MOV     AH,1            ; set new cursor values
        INT     10h
        POP     BP              ; restore stackframe
        RET
CUROFF  ENDP


CODE    ENDS
        END
```

This short routine turns the video cursor off, using the BIOS functions that first get the current cursor type and then set a new cursor type after forcing the cursor-off control bit to a value of 1 by means of the OR CH,20h instruction. A notable omission from both the QuickPascal and Turbo Pascal libraries is a method for controlling the cursor's visibility, so this routine is not only a simple example but will also serve a useful purpose.

To include CurOff in a program using the inline() facility, first assemble CUROFF.ASM and get a listing of the output by using the /L option switch on your assembler. Then, using your text editor's cut-and-paste facilities, move the hex code bytes from the LST file generated by the assembler into a Pascal source program so that it looks like this (note that I also included CurOn, which differs in only one statement, so that the test could turn the cursor back on before returning to DOS):

```
{ Pascal Example 1, Jim Kyle, 10/22/89 }


procedure CurOff;
begin
inline(
    $B4/$03/      { MOV     AH,3     ; get current cursor      }
    $33/$DB/      { XOR     BX,BX                              }
    $CD/$10/      { INT     10h                                }
    $80/$CD/$20/ { OR      CH,20h  ; force to OFF condition }
    $B4/$01/      { MOV     AH,1     ; set new cursor values   }
    $CD/$10);     { INT     10h                                }
end;


procedure CurOn;
begin
inline(
    $B4/$03/      { MOV     AH,3     ; get current cursor      }
    $33/$DB/      { XOR     BX,BX                              }
    $CD/$10/      { INT     10h                                }
    $80/$E5/$1F/ { AND     CH,1Fh  ; force to ON condition  }
    $B4/$01/      { MOV     AH,1     ; set new cursor values   }
    $CD/$10);     { INT     10h                                }
end;


begin
  Writeln('The cursor is now turning OFF');
  CurOff;
  ReadLn;
  Writeln('Now going back ON');
  CurOn;
end.
```

Note that both the first and last few lines of the assembly language routine (those that save and restore the stack frame, and return [RET] from the procedure) are *not* included in the inline code. These actions are done automatically by the Pascal compiler and the begin and end keywords that bracket the procedure definition.

This program was tested, with no changes, using both Turbo Pascal version 5.5 and QuickPascal version 1.0. The EXE file produced by QuickPascal was nearly twice the size of that produced by Turbo Pascal, but this reflects a difference in the way the two systems handle debugging information rather than any difference in compiler quality.

If you are using any version of Turbo Pascal earlier than 4.0, this technique is the *only* method available for you to include assembly language in your programs. Although you can also use this method with later versions (and with QuickPascal), the following option is also available. This program is somewhat simpler to type but requires that you assemble your subroutines separately so that OBJ files will be available when you compile the main program.

```
{ Pascal Example 2, Jim Kyle, 10/22/89 }

{$L CUROFF.OBJ}
{$F+}procedure CurOff; external;{$F-}

{$L CURON.OBJ}
{$F+}procedure CurOn; external;{$F-}

begin
  Writeln('The cursor is now turning OFF');
  CurOff;
  ReadLn;
  Writeln('Now going back ON');
  CurOn;
end.
```

When this technique is used, the OBJ files must contain the stack frame code and the appropriate RET; your Pascal compiler will not add anything to a procedure defined as external. The only difference in this technique and that used by older compilers that require a separate link step is the presence of the {$L} compiler directives and {$F} switches. The {$L} directives cause the OBJ file to be included in the final program, and the {$F} switches bracketing the procedure declarations indicate FAR procedures. Again, this program works, unchanged, with both Turbo Pascal and QuickPascal.

If the OBJ files are created from FAR procedures, it is absolutely essential that the procedure statements be bracketed by the {$F+} and {$F-} switches. Otherwise, although no error will be detected during compilation, the program will cause your system to lock up when it executes because it will not return properly from the first such procedure called.

Notice that there is nothing mystical or magical about the way this routine is called. The compiler or the linker makes sure that the proper routines are linked to create the executable (EXE) file. Invocation of the assembly language subroutine presupposes that the external procedures have been declared in the program header. Without the procedure statements, an error would have been generated during the compilation process.

Interfacing Subroutines with Variable Passing

Pascal is one of the high-level languages, mentioned in Chapter 2, that use the stack for passing variables to assembly language. Values, short pointers, and long pointers can be passed.

Because the preceding subroutines (CurOff and CurOn) differ in only one instruction, combining them into a single routine that could do both jobs would make much more efficient use of space. You can easily modify the routine so that a flag value specifies whether to turn the cursor off or on. The following assembly language program includes this modification:

```
Page 60,132
; ********************************************************************
; *                                                                  *
; * File:     CURSW.ASM                                              *
; * Date:     10/20/89                                               *
; *                                                                  *
; * Descrpt:  Subroutine designed to turn the cursor on or           *
; *           off.                                                    *
; *                                                                  *
; * Format:   CurSw(0) to turn cursor off                            *
; *           CurSw(1) to turn cursor on                             *
; *           The variable passed to CurSw() should be an            *
; *           integer value.                                         *
; *                                                                  *
; ********************************************************************
```

```
SWITCH  EQU     [BP+6]              ; name for parameter

CODE    SEGMENT WORD PUBLIC
        ASSUME  CS:CODE, DS:NOTHING


        PUBLIC  CURSW
CURSW   PROC    FAR
        PUSH    BP                 ; save stackframe
        MOV     BP,SP
        MOV     AX,SWITCH          ; get flag value
        OR      AX,AX              ; test zero/nonzero
        JNZ     CS1
        MOV     AX,20h             ; zero means OFF
        JMP     SHORT CS2
CS1:    MOV     AX,0               ; else turn ON
CS2:    PUSH    AX                 ; either way, save it
        MOV     AH,3               ; get current cursor
        XOR     BX,BX
        INT     10H
        POP     AX                 ; retrieve saved control
        AND     CH,1Fh             ; clear previous bit
        OR      CH,AL              ; and set in new one
        MOV     AH,1               ; set new cursor values
        INT     10H
        POP     BP
        RET     2                  ; flush off parameter
CURSW   ENDP

CODE    ENDS
        END
```

This version of the assembly language routine differs noticeably from its predecessors. CURSW tests an input value and turns the cursor off for zero or on for anything else.

Notice that the variable is passed through the stack as described in Chapter 2. On entry to this routine, Pascal pushes the variable's *value* on the stack. Because the variable is an integer (it must be declared as such in the Pascal program), it can be accessed as a word on the stack.

Notice also that you must add a specification of the number of additional bytes to pop from the stack to the RET (return from procedure) instruction. RET 2 is used in this case because Pascal pushed an integer value (2 bytes long) on the stack. If you do not use this method of return when passing parameters, the chances of getting back to Pascal are slim.

You also must change the Pascal programs that use this routine to pass a value. The modified routine for inline() code is as follows:

```
{ Pascal Example 3, Jim Kyle, 10/22/89 }

procedure CurSw( switch : integer );
begin
inline(
    $8B/$46/$06/ {        MOV   AX,SWITCH   ; get flag value          }
    $0B/$C0/     {        OR    AX,AX        ; test zero/nonzero       }
    $75/$05/     {        JNZ   CS1                                    }
    $B8/$20/$00/ {        MOV   AX,20h       ; zero means OFF          }
    $EB/$03/     {        JMP   SHORT CS2                              }
    $B8/$00/$00/ { CS1:   MOV   AX,0         ; else turn ON            }
    $50/         { CS2:   PUSH  AX           ; either way, save it     }
    $B4/$03/     {        MOV   AH,3         ; get current cursor      }
    $33/$DB/     {        XOR   BX,BX                                  }
    $CD/$10/     {        INT   10H                                    }
    $58/         {        POP   AX           ; retrieve saved control  }
    $80/$E5/$1F/ {        AND   CH,1Fh       ; clear previous bit      }
    $0A/$E8/     {        OR    CH,AL        ; and set in new one      }
    $B4/$01/     {        MOV   AH,1         ; set new cursor values   }
    $CD/$10);    {        INT   10H                                    }
end;

begin
  Writeln('The cursor is now turning OFF');
  CurSw(0);
  ReadLn;
  Writeln('Now going back ON');
  CurSw(1);
end.
```

For the external procedure version, the Pascal program is modified as follows:

```
{ Pascal Example 4, Jim Kyle, 10/22/89 }

{$L CURSW.OBJ}
{$F+}procedure CurSw( switch : integer ); external;{$F-}
```

```
begin
  Writeln('The cursor is now turning OFF');
  CurSw(0);
  ReadLn;
  Writeln('Now going back ON');
  CurSw(1);
end.
```

Notice that only a few modifications are made to the routine. The line that declares the procedure uses a name between the parentheses, and the lines that invoke the name place a constant value between the parentheses to control the routine's actions. As before, the inline() version's housekeeping is done by the compiler, but you must perform this task yourself for the external procedure.

Because it fills a void in the provided video control libraries, this routine can become a useful item in your Pascal toolbox.

Passing Variable Pointers

The preceding routine works well if the variable being passed on the stack is a value. But a pointer to a variable would cause problems for the assembly language subroutine, which is not designed to pass a pointer.

Why would passing a variable's address pointer be valuable, as opposed to passing only a value? Because if you know the variable's location in memory, you can make direct changes to the variable's value in the assembly language subroutine. This capability can be invaluable if you need to pass information back to the calling program.

One feature notably absent from most Pascal runtime libraries is a capability for reading data directly from the screen. To do so, you must pass the data being read back to the calling program. One way of doing this is to use a pointer to a string variable that is also available to the calling program. Here's the assembly language for such a module; note that it is much more complex than any example shown so far:

```
        Page 60,132
;       *************************************************************
;       *                                                           *
;       * File:     READSCRN.ASM                                    *
;       * Date:     10/22/89                                        *
;       *                                                           *
;       * Descrpt:  Subroutine designed to read data directly from  *
;       *           screen to Pascal string.                        *
;       *                                                           *
;       * Format:   READSCRN(ROW,COL,NUM:word;BFR:string);          *
;       *               ROW: Row at which to start, 0-24            *
;       *               COL: Column at which to start, 0-79         *
;       *               NUM: number of characters to read, 1-255    *
;       *               BFR: pointer to string where data will be put. *
;       *                                                           *
;       *************************************************************

                PUBLIC    READSCRN
CODE            SEGMENT   WORD PUBLIC
                ASSUME    CS:CODE


ROW             EQU       [BP+14]
COL             EQU       [BP+12]
NUM             EQU       [BP+10]
BFR             EQU       [BP+6]


;       ----------------------------------------------------------------
READSCRN        PROC      FAR
                PUSH      BP                      ;Save stack frame
                MOV       BP,SP
                PUSH      ES
                PUSH      DI

                LES       DI,BFR                  ;Get string address

                MOV       AH,0Fh                  ;Get video page in BH
                INT       10h
                MOV       AH,03                   ;Get current cursor location
                INT       10h
                PUSH      DX                      ;Save it to restore later

                MOV       AX,ROW                  ;Get row number
                CMP       AX,25
```

```
            JAE     ERROR           ;Too big, get out
            MOV     DH,AL           ;Okay, set into DH
            MOV     AX,COL          ;Get col number
            CMP     AX,80
            JB      OKAY            ;Not too big so proceed
ERROR:      XOR     AL,AL           ;Too big, set string to zero
            STOSB
            JMP     SHORT EXIT

OKAY:       MOV     DL,AL           ;Now set in column
            MOV     AH,2            ;and change cursor location
            INT     10h
            MOV     CX,NUM          ;Get length of string
            MOV     AL,CL           ;and store it as string length
            STOSB

READEM:     MOV     AH,8            ;Get char from BIOS
            INT     10h
            STOSB                   ;Put down in string
            INC     DL              ;Advance cursor
            CMP     DL,80           ;If off end of row, do wrap
            JB      R1              ;Still on row, okay
            INC     DH              ;Off end, go to next row
            XOR     DL,DL           ;at column zero
R1:         MOV     AH,2            ;Set new cursor location
            INT     10h
            LOOP    READEM          ;and go back for next

EXIT:       POP     DX              ;Restore original cursor
            MOV     AH,2
            INT     10h
            POP     DI              ;Restore saved registers
            POP     ES
            POP     BP
            RET     10              ;Remove 10 bytes pushed
READSCRN    ENDP
;      -------------------------------------------------------------
CODE        ENDS
            END
```

In this routine, the calling program passes in the row and column where the data read action is to begin and the number of characters to be read, as well as a pointer to the string variable where the data is to be placed. The assembly language code then saves the original cursor position, moves the cursor to the position where the read is to begin, and copies characters from the screen to the string until the desired number of characters have been read. The routine then restores the original cursor position and returns.

If any of the characters passed in are outside the limits of the screen, no characters are read, and the length of the string is set to zero to indicate that an error occurred.

The following Pascal code for ReadScrn works without change for both Turbo Pascal and QuickPascal. To save space, only the external procedure version is shown:

```
program RdScrn; { by Jim Kyle, 10-23-89 }

{$L READSCRN.OBJ}
{$F+} procedure ReadScrn( Row, Col, Num : integer; var Bfr : string );
      external; {$F-}

var
  Inputbuf : string;
  r, c     : integer;

begin
  Writeln('This is a test of the READSCRN capability');
  ReadScrn(0,0,20,Inputbuf);
  Writeln(Inputbuf);
  repeat
    Write('Row ');
    Readln(r);
    Write('Col ');
    Readln(c);
    ReadScrn(r,c,80,Inputbuf);
    Writeln(Inputbuf);
  until r+c = 0;
end.
```

In this test program, the string *Inputbuf*, declared at the global level, accumulates the data read from the screen. The single word *var* in the declaration of the external procedure, preceding the reference to *Inputbuf*, is what makes Pascal pass the address of the string, rather than the string itself, to the procedure.

Pointers can also be useful when you work with strings, as you can see from the following program:

```
        Page 60,132
;    ************************************************************
;    *                                                          *
;    * File:     ULCASE.ASM                                     *
;    * Date:     10/23/89                                       *
;    *                                                          *
;    * Descrpt:  Subroutine designed to convert a string to     *
;    *           upper- or lowercase.  Designed to be called    *
;    *           from Turbo Pascal or QuickPascal as EXTERNAL.  *
;    *                                                          *
;    * Format:   ULCASE(S,X)                                    *
;    *              S:  Pointer to string to be converted       *
;    *              X:  Controls conversion                     *
;    *                 0 = Convert to uppercase                 *
;    *                 ?  Any other value signifies convert to  *
;    *                     lowercase                            *
;    *                                                          *
;    ************************************************************

          PUBLIC    ULCASE

          NAME      ULCASE
CODE      SEGMENT   WORD PUBLIC
          ASSUME    CS:CODE

PARMA     EQU       8
PARMB     EQU       6


;    ------------------------------------------------------------
ULCASE    PROC      FAR
          PUSH      BP
          MOV       BP,SP
          PUSH      DI

          MOV       DI,[BP]+PARMA          ;Get string address
          INC       DI                     ;Point past length
          MOV       CX,[BP]+PARMA+2        ;Get length of string
          MOV       AX,[BP]+PARMB          ;Get action variable
          CMP       AX,0                   ;Converting to uppercase?
          JZ        UPPER                  ;Yes, so go handle

LOWER:    CMP       BYTE PTR [DI],0        ;Is this end of string?
          JE        EXIT                   ;Yes, so exit
          CMP       BYTE PTR [DI],'A'      ;Is it < A ?
```

```
              JB      L1                      ;Yes, so skip character
              CMP     BYTE PTR [DI],'Z'       ;Is it > Z ?
              JA      L1                      ;Yes, so skip character
              OR      BYTE PTR [DI],20h       ;Make lowercase (00100000b)
      L1:     INC     DI                      ;Next character
              JMP     LOWER                   ;Do it again


      UPPER:  CMP     BYTE PTR [DI],0         ;Is this end of string?
              JE      EXIT                    ;Yes, so exit
              CMP     BYTE PTR [DI],'a'       ;Is it < a ?
              JB      U1                      ;Yes, so skip character
              CMP     BYTE PTR [DI],'z'       ;Is it > z ?
              JA      U1                      ;Yes, so skip character
              AND     BYTE PTR [DI],05Fh      ;Make uppercase (01011111b)
      U1:     INC     DI                      ;Next character
              JMP     UPPER                   ;Do it again


      EXIT:   POP     DI
              POP     BP
              RET     6                       ;Remove 6 bytes pushed
      ULCASE  ENDP
;       ------------------------------------------------------------
      CODE    ENDS
              END                             ;Required by MASM 5.1
```

This simple program, which converts a string to either all upper- or all lowercase, expects two parameters to be passed from Pascal: a pointer to the string to be converted, and an integer value indicating whether the string is to be converted to upper- or lowercase.

Even though only two parameters are passed in this routine, six bytes are popped during the return sequence. This occurs because Pascal passes four bytes for a string variable when an external procedure is defined as FAR. This first pushes the two bytes representing the offset address and then pushes the segment address of the string. Notice also that the conversion process begins at the string's second character, not its first, because the first position of a string variable always contains the number of characters in the string.

If you look at the calling syntax for the subroutine

```
ULCASE(S,X)
```

you will notice that Pascal places the function parameters on the stack in their order of occurrence from left to right. Thus, the first value pushed is the offset address pointer for S, and the second is the value for X.

In the body of the program, PARMA and PARMB are used to specify the relative location of each parameter on the stack. PARMA represents the first (leftmost) parameter in the calling list; PARMB represents the second parameter.

The Pascal program that will use this subroutine follows:

```
{PROGRAM} to test the calling of ULCase()
 Date: 10/23/89
}
program UTestP;

var
   s : string;

{$L ULCASE.OBJ}
{$F+}procedure ULCase(var s:string; x:integer);
     external; {$F-}

begin
   s:='Original string value';
   While length(s)>0 do
      begin
      Write('String to convert: ');
      Readln(s);
      If length(s)>0 then
         begin
            Writeln('UPPERCASE:    ');
            ULCase(s,0);
            Writeln(s);
            Writeln('lowercase:   ');
            ULCase(s,1);
            Writeln(S);
         end;
      end;
end.
```

Using Function Subprograms

When you want an assembly language routine to return a value to your Turbo Pascal or QuickPascal program, you don't have to pass in a pointer to a variable for the routine to use. Instead, you can make the routine itself return a value to the calling program. Although doing so is a little more trouble for the programmer, it can greatly simplify the calling program.

To return a value, your assembly language routine must be declared as a *function* rather than a *procedure*, and the type of value that the routine will return must be specified. Then, within the routine, the return value must be placed where the Pascal compiler expects to find it.

This expected location varies with the type of variable involved. For values up to 32 bytes in length (byte, integer, word, and longint types) the lowest 16 bits are returned in the AX register and the highest 16 bits in DX.

For strings, the compiler allocates temporary storage space and passes a pointer to the space as the first parameter pushed onto the stack (the one with the largest offset from BP). When you return from the procedure, do not flush that pointer from the stack; the Pascal program is expecting to find the pointer there.

For other types of data, see your Pascal reference manual. Usually, you will be dealing with either numeric values or strings.

The following assembly language program for a function version of READSCRN.ASM shows the differences between using a pointer and creating a function:

```
Page 60,132
; *****************************************************************
; *                                                             *
; * File:     RSFUNC.ASM                                        *
; * Date:     10/23/89                                          *
; *                                                             *
; * Descrpt:  Function designed to read data directly from      *
; *           screen to Pascal string.                          *
; *                                                             *
; * Format:   Function READSCRN(ROW,COL,NUM:word):string;       *
; *              ROW: Row at which to start, 0-24               *
; *              COL: Column at which to start, 0-79            *
; *              NUM: number of characters to read, 1-255       *
; *                                                             *
; *****************************************************************

            PUBLIC   RSFUNC

CODE        SEGMENT  WORD PUBLIC
            ASSUME   CS:CODE
```

```
BFR         EQU     [BP+12]                 ;Temp retval area

ROW         EQU     [BP+10]                 ;Actual parameters
COL         EQU     [BP+8]
NUM         EQU     [BP+6]


;       --------------------------------------------------------------
RSFUNC      PROC    FAR
            PUSH    BP
            MOV     BP,SP
            PUSH    ES
            PUSH    DI

            LES     DI,BFR                  ;Get retval address

            MOV     AH,0Fh                  ;Get video page in BH
            INT     10h
            MOV     AH,03                   ;Get current cursor location
            INT     10h
            PUSH    DX                      ;Save it to restore later

            MOV     AX,ROW                  ;Get row number
            CMP     AX,25
            JAE     ERROR                   ;Too big, get out
            MOV     DH,AL                   ;Okay, set into DH
            MOV     AX,COL                  ;Get col number
            CMP     AX,80
            JB      OKAY                    ;Not too big so proceed
ERROR:      XOR     AL,AL                   ;Too big, set retval to zero
            STOSB
            JMP     SHORT EXIT

OKAY:       MOV     DL,AL                   ;Now set in column
            MOV     AH,2                    ;and change cursor location
            INT     10h
            MOV     CX,NUM                  ;Get length of retval
            MOV     AL,CL                   ;and store it as string length
            STOSB

READEM:     MOV     AH,8                    ;Get char from BIOS
            INT     10h
            STOSB                           ;Put down in retval
            INC     DL                      ;Advance cursor
```

```
                CMP      DL,80           ;If off end of row, do wrap
                JB       R1              ;Still on row, okay
                INC      DH              ;Off end, go to next row
                XOR      DL,DL           ;at column zero
        R1:     MOV      AH,2            ;Set new cursor location
                INT      10h
                LOOP     READEM          ;and go back for next


        EXIT:   POP      DX              ;Restore original cursor
                MOV      AH,2
                INT      10h
                POP      DI              ;Restore saved registers
                POP      ES
                POP      BP
                RET      6               ;Remove ONLY the args
        RSFUNC  ENDP                     ;leave temp pointer on stack!
        ;       -------------------------------------------------------------
        CODE    ENDS
                END
```

There are two major differences between this code and that used for
the earlier pointer version:

❑ A different sequence of EQU statements defines the parameter offsets.

❑ Only 6 bytes, rather than 10 bytes, are flushed from the stack upon
  returning.

The rest of the routine is identical to the previous example.

To use this function version, the Pascal program must be changed
somewhat:

```
{PROGRAM} to test the calling of READSCRN()
 Date: 10/23/89
}
program RSFuncTest;

{$L RSFUNC.OBJ}
{$F+} function RSFunc( Row, Col, Num : integer ) : string ;
     external; {$F-}

var
  r, c : integer;
  x : string;
```

```
begin
  Writeln('This is a test of the READSCRN capability');
  x := RSFunc( 0, 0, 20 );
  Writeln( x );
  repeat
    Write('Row ');
    Readln(r);
    Write('Col ');
    Readln(c);
    x := RSFunc ( r, c, 80 );
    Writeln( x );
  until r+c = 0;
end.
```

Notice that the external declaration, which is for a function rather than a procedure, omits mention of the string pointer. A type declaration follows the closing parenthesis of the declaration.

Within the program, the major difference is that RDScrn() is invoked by assigning its value to a string variable instead of just calling it by name. However, not having to include the buffer name as a parameter to each call makes the program's operation a bit clearer; this way, all the parameters are information passed *into* the routine.

Summary

Pascal is a popular language among many programmers. However, the ease with which you can combine assembly language subroutines with Pascal programs depends on the type of Pascal compiler you use.

Until Turbo Pascal version 4.0 became available, only the high-powered "professional" Pascal compilers that required a separate linking phase were easy to augment with assembly language modules. However, both Turbo Pascal and QuickPascal now offer a choice of several simple interfacing methods.

No matter which method you choose, you'll find that the performance of your Pascal programs can be significantly improved if you make the small effort it takes to master the assembly language interface.

CHAPTER 5

Interfacing with C

C is one of today's fastest-growing high-level languages. It has been said that over 75 percent of all commercial programs for personal computers are written in C—quite a plaudit for the popularity of the language.

Why is C so popular? Although the reasons vary from programmer to programmer, for most people C seems to provide the right mix of ease of use, access to system-level functions, and transportability. These benefits make C an attractive development language.

Eventually, most serious C programmers must face the task of interfacing assembly language subroutines with the language. Because C is a compiled language, assembly language subroutines can be linked as the final step in program development. The trick is to make sure that the interface between C and assembly language is followed strictly, to allow proper passage of variables.

Most of the popular C compilers on the market today (including Microsoft C, Lattice C, Aztec C, and Turbo C) have similar functions and implementations of the language. Any notable differences between versions are mentioned as the examples in this chapter are developed.

All tests of the examples given in this chapter were conducted using Microsoft's QuickC version 2.01 and Borland's Turbo C version 2.01. If you use other versions or another implementation of the language, check your C reference manual in case of any problems.

Memory Models

Before any general guidelines for interfacing with C programs can be developed, memory models must be discussed because they have significant impact on all guidelines.

Chapter 1 discussed how the Intel CPU chip design forces memory management to be done in segments and how each segment can address a maximum of 65,636 (64K) bytes. That's the basis of the memory model concept; it simply specifies how the segments are to be managed.

Originally, C compilers for MS-DOS addressed only one memory model, the one now known as *small*. All code procedures shared a single 64K-maximum code segment and all data had to fit into another 64K-maximum data segment. However, programmers found this far too limiting, and today's compilers support four to six memory models. The usual definitions for these models are listed in table 5.1.

Table 5.1. *Memory model definitions.*

Model	Code Segments	Data Segments
Tiny	One, also containing data	Shared with code
Small	One for all procedures	One for all data
Medium	Many	One
Compact	One	Many
Large	Many	Many (64K static)
Huge	Many	Many (>64K static)

The *tiny* model may be familiar to you as the format used by COM files in which data, code, and stack must all fit into a single 64K segment. The *small* model breaks code and data into separate segments of 64K each. In both of these models, all pointers for both procedures and data are NEAR.

In the *medium* model, each separate module of code has its own segment and each may be up to 64K, but all data is confined to a single segment. In this model, procedure pointers are usually FAR, but data pointers remain NEAR.

The reverse of the medium model is the *compact* model, where each major data structure has its own segment, but code is all contained within

64K; pointers are NEAR, and data pointers are FAR. This model is not encountered frequently.

The *large* model uses FAR pointers for both code and data, although it still confines static data storage to 64K. This model is often used when dealing with complex systems of programs; it combines the advantages of the medium and compact models.

Finally, the *huge* model removes the 64K limit on static data and enables a single data structure to span more than one segment. When you use the huge model, internal address calculations rapidly become complicated, so you should avoid using this model unless it is necessary for writing your program.

Most C programs are written using either the small or the large memory models. Both QuickC and Turbo C are configured for the small model by default, but their options can be changed to default to any desired model. When you use these compilers' command-line versions rather than the integrated development environments, the desired model is selected by an option switch.

General Interface Guidelines

To interface assembly language subroutines with C, you must follow a few general guidelines. First, you must give a specific segment name to the code segment of your assembly language subroutine. The name will vary, depending on which compiler you use. For example, Microsoft C, QuickC, and Turbo C require either the segment name _TEXT (for tiny, small, or compact memory model programs; Microsoft C does not support the tiny model) or a segment name with the suffix _TEXT (for other memory models). Aztec C requires the segment name CODESEG.

Second, your C compiler may require specific names for data segments (if the data is being referenced outside the code segment). Microsoft C, QuickC, and Turbo C require that the segment be named _DATA, whereas you must use the segment name DATASEG with Aztec C. You must use these segment names, which are specific to C, to properly link and then execute the programs.

Third, you must realize how variables are passed to assembly language subroutines through the stack. In the function-calling syntax of

```
function_name(arg1,arg2,arg3,...,argn);
```

the values of each argument are pushed on the stack in reverse order. Thus, argument n (argn) is pushed on the stack first, and argument 1 (arg1) is pushed last. An actual value, or a pointer to a variable, can be passed on the stack. Although most values and pointers are passed as word-length stack elements, the longer data elements such as long or unsigned long-type variables require 32 bits (2 words) of stack space.

If the memory model being used is compact, large, or huge, or if the data item has a segment override, data pointers also require 32 bits of stack space. Float-type variables use 64 bits (4 words) of stack space. Remember this distinction of stack usage by variable type; failure to do so can produce undesired results.

Fourth, in the assembly language source file, the assembly language routines to be called from C must begin (for Microsoft C, QuickC, or Turbo C if using its default options) or end (for Aztec C) with an underline. However, the underline is not included when the routines are invoked in C. The examples in this chapter reflect this distinction; Turbo C's option for this was left set at its default ON condition to obtain maximum compatibility in the code while testing, but can be set to OFF if you want to eliminate the need for the underline prefix.

Fifth, remember to save any special-purpose registers (such as CS, DS, SS, BP, SI, and DI) that your assembly language subroutine may disturb. Failure to save them may have undesired consequences when control is returned to the C program. This is especially important with Turbo C because it defaults to the automatic use of register variables. You do not have to save the contents of AX, BX, CX, or DX because these registers are considered to be volatile by C; that is, the language assumes that you will change them and even requires you to do so in order to return a value.

The examples in this chapter were designed to work with Microsoft C, QuickC, and Turbo C. If you are using another C compiler, the only differences you will need to deal with should be in the required segment names for code and data or in the naming of the subroutines. If you are not using QuickC or Turbo C, remember to make the appropriate changes when you enter this chapter's examples.

Interfacing Subroutines with No Variable Passing

To help you understand how an assembly language subroutine is interfaced with C, let's look at a sample subroutine that requires no parameter passing. Consider the following assembly language program:

```
        Page 60,132
;       ****************************************************************
;       *                                                              *
;       * File:      CEX1.ASM                                          *
;       * Date:      10/24/89                                          *
;       *                                                              *
;       * Descrpt:   Subroutines designed to turn the cursor on and    *
;       *            off.                                               *
;       *                                                              *
;       ****************************************************************

        PUBLIC  _CURON,_CUROFF

_TEXT   SEGMENT WORD PUBLIC 'CODE'
        ASSUME  CS:_TEXT

_CURON  PROC    NEAR                ; for small model
        PUSH    BP                  ; save stackframe
        MOV     BP,SP
        MOV     AH,3                ; get current cursor
        XOR     BX,BX
        INT     10h
        AND     CH,1Fh              ; force to ON condition
        MOV     AH,1                ; set new cursor values
        INT     10h
        POP     BP
        RET
_CURON  ENDP

_CUROFF PROC    NEAR                ; for small model
        PUSH    BP                  ; save stackframe
        MOV     BP,SP
        MOV     AH,3                ; get current cursor
        XOR     BX,BX
        INT     10h
```

```
        OR      CH,20h          ; force to OFF condition
        MOV     AH,1            ; set new cursor values
        INT     10h
        POP     BP
        RET
_CUROFF ENDP


_TEXT   ENDS
        END
```

You may recall this example from Chapter 4; note that in this version of the example both procedures have been included in a single ASM file so that only one OBJ file is necessary. This is possible because most C programs that use assembly language do so by means of OBJ files that are incorporated at link time. Pascal's methods of dealing with assembly language modules make such manipulation more difficult.

Notice also that the value of BP is saved on the stack (on entry to each subroutine) and restored at the end of the routine. Because the program does not modify the value of BP and has no variables to access, these steps are not necessary, but they are good programming practice.

The C program written to test this routine is as follows:

```
/**********************************************************/
/*                                                        */
/*  File:     CEX1S.C                                     */
/*  Date:     10/24/89                                    */
/*                                                        */
/*  Descrpt:  Example of using CURON() and CUROFF()       */
/*                                                        */
/**********************************************************/

#include <stdio.h>

void CurOn(void);
void CurOff(void);

void main()
{ printf( "%s\n", "The cursor is now turning OFF");
  CurOff();
  getchar();
  printf( "%s\n", "Now going back ON");
  CurOn();
}
```

Notice that the routines invoked as CurOn() and CurOff() in this example are called _CURON and _CUROFF in the assembly language source file. This difference (the leading underline) is important for you to remember when you write programs and subroutines.

Using QuickAssembler with QuickC

It's possible to create this entire program, both the ASM and C portions of it, without leaving the integrated development environment if you are using QuickC version 2.01, which includes QuickAssembler.

The program was initially tested using exactly that combination. It proved necessary to modify the option settings for all steps (the assembler, the compiler, and the linker) to make everything work. The key change was to turn off all debugging options and incremental linking and to make the link step ignore case sensitivity. This was necessary because the ASM file uses all-uppercase procedure names, whereas the C program uses mixed case names.

It would also have been possible to use mixed case in the ASM portion, but because all uppercase is used for all other examples, I kept it here for consistency (and to provide you an example of how to overcome problems of this type in your own code).

Using Inline ASM Coding with Turbo C

If you use Turbo C, you can include your assembly language routines as inline statements in much the same way as you can with Turbo Pascal. However, because doing so involves many extra restrictions, this is probably not worth the effort. Here's what the previous CurOn()/CurOff() example looks like using the inline-assembler capability of Turbo C:

```
/********************************************************/
/*                                                      */
/*  File:     CEX2S.C                                   */
/*  Date:     10/24/89                                  */
/*                                                      */
/*  Descrpt:  Example of using CURON() and CUROFF()     */
/*                                                      */
/********************************************************/
```

```c
#include <stdio.h>

void CurOn()
{ asm MOV AH,3;            /* get current cursor      */
  asm XOR BX,BX;
  asm INT 0x10;
  asm AND CH,0x1F          /* force to ON condition  */
  asm MOV AH,1;            /* set new cursor values  */
  asm INT 0x10;
}

void CurOff()
{ asm MOV AH,3;            /* get current cursor      */
  asm XOR BX,BX;
  asm INT 0x10;
  asm OR  CH,0x20;         /* force to OFF condition */
  asm MOV AH,1;            /* set new cursor values  */
  asm INT 0x10;
}

void main()
{ printf( "%s\n", "The cursor is now turning OFF");
  CurOff();
  getchar();
  printf( "%s\n", "Now going back ON");
  CurOn();
}
```

Notice that every line of ASM code requires its own asm keyword and that the comments follow C standards rather than those of normal assembly language.

What this example does *not* show is that the inline coding cannot be used from Turbo C's integrated environment; it works *only* with the command-line compiler. Furthermore, inline coding requires that a version of C0.ASM (contained in Borland's STARTUP.ARC package) appropriate to the memory model in use be available. Without it the linker cannot complete its work.

About the only advantage you gain by using this inline capability is that the program itself needs no changes if you decide to switch from one memory model to another. However, the C0?.OBJ file for the desired memory model must exist. Because Turbo C is the only compiler that supports this feature, and this support adds several layers of complication, you'll probably find it much easier to do everything through OBJ files and link-time inclusion.

Interfacing Subroutines with Variable Passing

As you probably remember from the discussions earlier in this chapter and in Chapter 2, variables are passed on the stack in C. This is C's normal method of variable passing.

You can easily combine the preceding subroutines and eliminate much of the extensive duplication of code by passing a variable that specifies whether to turn the cursor on or off. The following assembly language program includes this modification:

```
        Page 60,132
;       ***************************************************************
;       *                                                             *
;       * File:      CEX3.ASM                                         *
;       * Date:      10/24/89                                         *
;       *                                                             *
;       * Descrpt:   Subroutines designed to turn the cursor on and   *
;       *            off by passing a variable on the stack.          *
;       *                                                             *
;       * Format:    void CurSw( integer switch )                     *
;       *                   switch = 0; turn cursor off               *
;       *                   switch <> 0; turn cursor on               *
;       *                                                             *
;       ***************************************************************

SWITCH  EQU      [BP+6]              ; name for parameter

        PUBLIC   _CurSw
_TEXT   SEGMENT  WORD PUBLIC 'CODE'
        ASSUME   CS:_TEXT, DS:NOTHING

_CurSw  PROC     FAR                 ; large memory model
        PUSH     BP                  ; save stackframe
        MOV      BP,SP
        MOV      AX,SWITCH           ; get flag value
        OR       AX,AX               ; test zero/nonzero
        JNZ      CS1
```

```
            MOV     AX,20h              ; zero means OFF
            JMP     SHORT CS2
CS1:        MOV     AX,0                ; else turn ON
CS2:        PUSH    AX                  ; either way, save it
            MOV     AH,3                ; get current cursor
            XOR     BX,BX
            INT     10H
            POP     AX                  ; retrieve saved control
            AND     CH,1Fh              ; clear previous bit
            OR      CH,AL               ; and set in new one
            MOV     AH,1                ; set new cursor values
            INT     10H
            POP     BP
            RET                         ; caller will flush stack
_CurSw      ENDP

_TEXT       ENDS
            END
```

Notice that the variable is passed through the stack, as described earlier in this chapter and in Chapter 2. On entry to this routine, C pushes the variable's *value* on the stack. Because the variable is an integer (it must be declared as such in the C program), it can be accessed as a word on the stack.

This routine was declared as FAR for use with the large memory model in C; had it been declared NEAR, the value for SWITCH would have been [BP+4] instead of [BP+6] because a NEAR procedure has only two bytes of return-address data on the stack, not four.

Correspondence between the PROC declaration in the assembly language program and the memory model in use by C is an important detail that must always be checked. All modern assemblers provide methods to handle this automatically, which are described in Chapter 8. The essential point here is that you must fully understand the required details before trusting a program to handle them for you.

The C program that uses this routine was also changed to pass a value. The modified routine (based on the previous example, CEX2S.C) appears as follows:

```
/********************************************************/
/*                                                      */
/*  File:      CEX3S.C                                  */
/*  Date:      10/24/89                                 */
/*                                                      */
/*  Descrpt:   Example of using CurSw()                 */
/*                                                      */
/********************************************************/

#include <stdio.h>

void CurSw( int );

void main()
{ printf( "%s\n", "The cursor is now turning OFF");
  CurSw(0);
  getchar();
  printf( "%s\n", "Now going back ON");
  CurSw(1);
}
```

Notice that both the prototype and the invocations of the function now include material between the parentheses. The prototype declaration specifies that the parameter passed must be an integer, and the invocations specify integer constant values: 0 to turn the cursor off and 1 to turn it back on.

When developing from the integrated environments of QuickC and Turbo C, certain tricks are necessary to force the linker to consider the assembler module's OBJ file. Both tricks are based on the idea of the MAKE file, which Chapter 12 discusses in detail.

In QuickC, you must add the OBJ file by name to the program list for your C file, using the MAKE menu (if you have not already established a program list, you must do so first from the same menu). The MAKE file that actually drives the link process is generated automatically from this program list.

In Turbo C, you must create a PRJ file for your program. This is merely a text file that lists names of the files to be included. For the previous example, CEX3.PRJ contained

```
cex3s
cex3.obj
```

The file extension is not necessary for a C source file but is required for OBJ or LIB files. This file can be created by any text editor and should bear the file name that you want assigned to the final EXE file with the extension PRJ.

Passing Variable Pointers

It's not always enough to merely pass information into your assembly language routines. You also need to be able to get data back from them. Unlike Pascal and Basic, C keeps the calling program in full control of things, so one of the standard techniques for returning information is to pass in a pointer that contains the address of a storage area in the main program.

Returning Data via Pointers

To understand how pointers are handled, consider first this assembly language program, which was designed to read a specified number of characters from the screen:

```
        Page 60,132
;       ***********************************************************
;       *                                                         *
;       * File:     CEX4.ASM                                      *
;       * Date:     10/24/89                                      *
;       *                                                         *
;       * Descrpt:  Subroutine designed to read data directly from *
;       *           screen to C array of char.                    *
;       *                                                         *
;       * Format:   void ReadScrn(unsigned ROW,                   *
;       *                         unsigned COL,                   *
;       *                         unsigned NUM,                   *
;       *                         char far * BFR);                *
;       *           ROW: Row at which to start, 0-24              *
;       *           COL: Column at which to start, 0-79           *
;       *           NUM: number of characters to read, 1-255      *
;       *           BFR: pointer to array where data will be put. *
;       *                                                         *
;       ***********************************************************
```

```
                PUBLIC    _READSCRN
RS_TEXT         SEGMENT   WORD PUBLIC 'CODE'
                ASSUME    CS:RS_TEXT


ROW             EQU       [BP+6]
COL             EQU       [BP+8]
NUM             EQU       [BP+10]
BFR             EQU       [BP+12]


;        ------------------------------------------------------------------
_READSCRN       PROC      FAR                     ;Depends on memory model
                PUSH      BP
                MOV       BP,SP
                PUSH      ES
                PUSH      DI

                LES       DI,BFR                  ;Get string address

                MOV       AH,0Fh                  ;Get video page in BH
                INT       10h
                MOV       AH,03                   ;Get current cursor location
                INT       10h
                PUSH      DX                      ;Save it to restore later

                MOV       AX,ROW                  ;Get row number
                CMP       AX,25
                JAE       EXIT                    ;Too big, get out
                MOV       DH,AL                   ;Okay, set into DH
                MOV       AX,COL                  ;Get col number
                CMP       AX,80
                JAE       EXIT                    ;Too big, get out
                MOV       DL,AL                   ;Okay, so set column
                MOV       AH,2                    ;and change cursor location
                INT       10h
                MOV       CX,NUM                  ;Get length of string

READEM:         MOV       AH,8                    ;Get char from BIOS
                INT       10h
                STOSB                             ;Put down in string
                INC       DL                      ;Advance cursor
                CMP       DL,80                   ;If off end of row, do wrap
                JB        R1                      ;Still on row, okay
                INC       DH                      ;Off end, go to next row
                XOR       DL,DL                   ;at column zero
```

```
R1:         MOV     AH,2                ;Set new cursor location
            INT     10h
            LOOP    READEM              ;and go back for next

EXIT:       XOR     AL,AL               ;Mark end of string
            STOSB
            POP     DX                  ;Restore original cursor
            MOV     AH,2
            INT     10h
            POP     DI                  ;Restore saved registers
            POP     ES
            POP     BP
            RET                         ;Caller will flush stack
_READSCRN   ENDP
;           ------------------------------------------------------------
RS_TEXT     ENDS
            END
```

This routine is the C version of the one for use with Pascal described previously. It's instructive to compare the two and see what changes were required. The biggest change results from the reversed sequence in which C pushes parameter values onto the stack when a procedure or function is called. Other changes include adding the underline character to all PUBLIC symbols and leaving the pushed parameters on the stack to be handled by the calling program.

The following program demonstrates how ReadScrn() can be used, although its function is more than a trifle contrived:

```
/**********************************************************/
/*                                                        */
/*  File:     CEX4S.C                                     */
/*  Date:     10/24/89                                    */
/*                                                        */
/*  Descrpt:  Example of using ReadScrn()                 */
/*                                                        */
/**********************************************************/

#include <stdio.h>

void far ReadScrn( int r, int c, int n, char * b );

char Buf[81];
int r, c;
```

```
void main()
{ printf("%s\n", "This is a test of the READSCRN capability");
  ReadScrn(0,0,20,&Buf[0]);
  printf("%s\n",Buf);
  do
  { printf("%s","Row ");
    scanf( "%d", &r );
    printf("%s","Col ");
    scanf( "%d", &c );
    ReadScrn(r,c,80,&Buf[0]);
    printf("%s\n",Buf);
  } while (r+c != 0);
}
```

This program simply asks you for a row and a column, then reads 80 characters starting at that location (wrapping around the end of a line to the next line if necessary) and reports back to you what it read. The procedure continues until you reply to both prompts with 0.

Again, this example is a bit contrived for simplicity's sake. In practice, ReadScrn() would be used with other functions; for example, a mouse driver could position the mouse pointer over some data on the screen, and then a click of the left button would cause the data there to be copied by ReadScrn() into a buffer, from which a later click of the right button could stuff the data into the keyboard buffer as simulated keyboard input.

Using Pointers to Process Strings

Another reason to pass a pointer to a variable's address instead of simply passing the value is that if you know the variable's location in memory, you can directly change the value in your assembly language subroutine. This capability can be invaluable when you are working with strings, as in the following example:

```
        Page 60,132
;       ************************************************************
;       *                                                          *
;       * File:     ULCASEC.ASM                                    *
;       * Date:     10/24/89                                       *
;       *                                                          *
;       * Descrpt:  Subroutine designed to convert a string to upper-*
;       *           or lowercase.  Designed to be called from      *
;       *           Microsoft C.                                   *
;       *                                                          *
;       * Format:   ulcase(s,x)                                    *
;       *               s:  Pointer to string to be converted     *
;       *               x:  Controls conversion                   *
;       *                   0 = Convert to uppercase               *
;       *                   ?  Any other signifies convert to lower-*
;       *                      case                                *
;       *                                                          *
;       ************************************************************

                PUBLIC    _ULCASE

                NAME      ULCASE
_TEXT           SEGMENT   BYTE PUBLIC 'CODE'
                ASSUME    CS:_TEXT

PARMB           EQU       8                     ;For COMPACT model
PARMA           EQU       4


;       ------------------------------------------------------------------
_ULCASE         PROC      NEAR
                PUSH      BP
                MOV       BP,SP
                PUSH      DS
                PUSH      DI

                LDS       DI,[BP]+PARMA         ;Get string address

                MOV       AX,[BP]+PARMB         ;Get action variable
                CMP       AX,0                  ;Converting to uppercase?
                JZ        UPPER                 ;Yes, so go handle

LOWER:          CMP       BYTE PTR [DI],0       ;Is this end of string?
                JE        EXIT                  ;Yes, so exit
```

```
              CMP     BYTE PTR [DI],'A'     ;Is it < A ?
              JB      L1                    ;Yes, so skip character
              CMP     BYTE PTR [DI],'Z'     ;Is it > Z ?
              JA      L1                    ;Yes, so skip character
              OR      BYTE PTR [DI],20h     ;Make lowercase (00100000b)
      L1:     INC     DI                    ;Next character
              JMP     LOWER                 ;Do it again


      UPPER:  CMP     BYTE PTR [DI],0       ;Is this end of string?
              JE      EXIT                  ;Yes, so exit
              CMP     BYTE PTR [DI],'a'     ;Is it < a ?
              JB      U1                    ;Yes, so skip character
              CMP     BYTE PTR [DI],'z'     ;Is it > z ?
              JA      U1                    ;Yes, so skip character
              AND     BYTE PTR [DI],05Fh    ;Make uppercase (01011111b)
      U1:     INC     DI                    ;Next character
              JMP     UPPER                 ;Do it again


      EXIT:   POP     DI
              POP     DS
              POP     BP
              RET
      _ULCASE ENDP
      ;       --------------------------------------------------------------
      _TEXT   ENDS
              END
```

This simple program converts a string to either all upper- or lowercase. The program expects two parameters to be passed from C: a pointer to the string to be converted and an integer value indicating whether the string is to be converted to upper- or lowercase. This time I have defined the parameter offsets for a *compact* model, which has NEAR procedure calls and FAR data pointers, so the PROC is NEAR, but the PARMA data pointer takes four bytes.

Notice the calling syntax for the subroutine: ULCASE(S,X). Unlike some other languages, C places the function parameters onto the + stack in reverse order, from right to left. Thus, the first item pushed is the value for X, and the second item pushed is the (four-byte FAR) pointer to S.

Notice that in the body of the program PARMA and PARMB are used to specify each parameter's relative location on the stack. PARMA represents the first (leftmost) parameter in the calling list, and PARMB represents the second parameter.

The C program that uses this subroutine follows:

```
/*********************************************************/
/*                                                       */
/* File:     CEX5S.C                                     */
/* Date:     10/24/89                                    */
/*                                                       */
/* Descrpt:  Example of using ulcase()                   */
/*                                                       */
/*********************************************************/

#include <stdio.h>
#include <string.h>

void ulcase( char *, int );   /* function prototype */

unsigned char s[]="This is the original string";

void main()
{ while (strlen(s) != 0)
  { printf("String to convert: ");
    gets(s);
    if (strlen(s) != 0)
      { printf("\nUPPERCASE:\n");
        ulcase(s,0);
        printf("%s\nlowercase:\n",s);
        ulcase(s,1);
        printf("%s\n\n",s);
      }
  }
}
```

Summary

C is a popular language to which assembly language programs are easily interfaced. Although the specific interfacing syntax may vary from one compiler to another, the general guidelines are the same for all compilers. Code and data segments must conform to a specialized segment name, and public labels must adhere to a convention such as adding an underscore as a prefix or suffix.

Variables can be passed in C in many ways. You can pass variables on the stack as values or as pointers. Variables can be returned to C either by changing the variable value in the C data segment or by returning a variable in the AX register. (This second method for returning a variable is not covered in this chapter but will be demonstrated in the developmental examples in Chapter 8 and particularly in Chapter 9.)

CHAPTER 6

Interfacing with dBASE and FoxBase

One of the most widely used high-level languages for business applications of MS-DOS computers has no official name. The language originated as the command set for one of the first popular database management systems, Ashton-Tate's dBASE II. As dBASE II evolved through versions III and III+ into the current dBASE IV, other firms found a market for enhanced dBASE clones, and as a result the language and the product began to lead separate lives.

Now legal actions are moving through the courts in which Ashton-Tate claims copyright to the language, while Ashton-Tate's competitors insist that a copyright can cover only a specific implementation of a language—not the language itself.

Until the question is settled in court, many independent developers who make their living using the language have begun to refer to it as xBase to indicate its independence from any single product. Meanwhile, the different implementations of the language continue to slug it out in the marketplace.

Most of these implementations feature among their core attractions a strict compatibility with the Ashton-Tate version. One result is that most of them need a bit of help, via assembly language routines, to do such common actions as turning the cursor on and off, or saving a screen while displaying help data.

Fortunately, the xBase language provides commands that work together to provide such assistance:

❏ LOAD brings a separately assembled support procedure into memory and makes it available to the xBase program.

❏ CALL invokes execution of the LOADed program, in much the same way that the GOSUB statement operates in BASIC.

❏ RELEASE MODULE can be used to remove from memory any LOADed program that is no longer needed, freeing space for other modules. Its use is optional; the other two must be used together.

In dBASE III+ a maximum of 5 separate support files, each up to 32,000 bytes, can be LOADed into memory at the same time. Any or all of them can then be CALLed as required. Both LOAD and CALL commands can be included in PRG program files or issued interactively from the dot prompt. The number of files increases to 16 if you are using FoxBase+ or dBASE IV.

If you're an old hand at xBase, you can skip the rest of this section and go directly to the section titled "General Interfacing Guidelines." However, if you're a newcomer to the world of xBase, you may find these terms confusing. Here's a brief explanation.

All of the conventional implementations of the xBase language (such as dBASE III+ and IV, or FoxBase+) operate primarily as *interpreters* in an interactive mode. That's the same way DOS itself works. Just as DOS issues the C> prompt to let you know it's ready for a new command, the xBase program issues a dot prompt consisting of a single period at the left margin to let you know when it's ready for another instruction. And just as DOS enables you to string a sequence of commands together into a BAT file and then execute the entire stream of actions without individually typing each at the command prompt, the xBase program provides command files with the same capability. In xBase, the command file is indicated by the extension PRG, so such files are commonly called PRG files.

Other special file extensions used by xBase include MEM for files of saved memory variables (memvars) and BIN for the assembly language support routines that this chapter discusses. There are many more, but these are the only ones you need to know about in this chapter.

General Interfacing Guidelines

Certain restrictions are imposed on BIN files to ensure that they will be completely compatible with the xBase interpreters:

❏ The file must be a pure memory image, like a COM file, instead of being in the relocatable EXE format usually produced by most linker programs.

❏ All memory addresses within the file must be relative to zero. That is, the assembly language source must contain an ORG 0 statement either implicitly or explicitly; this differs from conventional COM-file usage, which requires an ORG 0100h starting point.

❏ The file is accessed by a FAR call from the interpreter, so it must use the far version of RET to return to its caller. This is most easily accomplished by making the procedure a FAR PROC construct.

❏ Both the CS and the SS registers must be returned to the caller holding the same values they had at entry. This means that if your procedure changes the registers, it must save the original values and restore them before returning. No other registers need be preserved by your routine.

❏ All code and working data storage must be contained within a single 64K segment. The procedure must not attempt to access any data maintained by the xBase program, except through the parameter-passing mechanism provided. This restriction, however, does not apply to accessing data outside of the xBase program, such as the BIOS data area, the video RAM, and so forth.

❏ The BIN file must not contain a STACK segment or make any reference to other segments that would have to be resolved when the file is linked. Failure to observe this restriction may make it impossible to convert the file to the required memory image format.

The file name used for the BIN file and the procedure name used for the internal procedure should be identical to prevent confusion. Only one lookup table is used; this table is set up to refer to the file name when you LOAD the file, then later is used to find the procedure when you CALL it. This means that only one procedure can be contained in each file.

The procedure name is actually unimportant to the system itself because that name never gets through to the xBase interpreter; only the file name is ever known to xBase. However, it's much easier for you to keep track of things when your ASM files and your PRG files use the same names for procedures.

Interfacing Subroutines without Variable Passing

To understand how the restrictions on BIN files apply in practice, consider first the simplest types of BIN files—those that simply perform a procedure without needing data from the calling program or passing any values back to it.

One such procedure, which fills a real need in dBASE III+, is a routine that turns the CRT cursor OFF when it is CALLed. Although FoxBase and other competitors added special capabilities for cursor control, dBASE III+ lacks such a feature. Example 1 supplies the capability for turning the cursor off, and Example 2 provides the other half of the feature so that you can turn the cursor back on.

Example 1—Turning the Cursor OFF

Turning the cursor on and off is actually done by the Video BIOS. The assembly language procedures call BIOS to get the current cursor condition, change it, and call BIOS again to put it back. Here's how to turn the cursor off:

```
; NOCURSOR.ASM - xBase Example 1, no parameters passed
;
;        LOAD nocursor
;        CALL nocursor    && to turn cursor OFF
;
ASSUME  CS:CODE_SEG

CODE_SEG        SEGMENT
        ORG     0

NOCURSOR PROC   FAR
        MOV     AH,03   ; Read cursor information
        INT     10h     ;   using BIOS features
        OR      CH,20h  ; Set cursor off bit
        MOV     AH,01   ; Set cursor type
```

```
        INT     10h     ;   using BIOS features
        RET             ; Return
NOCURSOR ENDP

CODE_SEG        ENDS

                END
```

This file, when assembled and linked as described later in this chapter, creates a 12-byte BIN file. If the file is named NOCURSOR.BIN, then the command LOAD NOCURSOR will bring it into memory and make it available to xBase, and a subsequent command, CALL NOCURSOR, will make the cursor vanish.

Although this example is indeed tiny, it does illustrate all the major requirements of an assembly language source file for any BIN-file routine. Everything is contained in a single segment (CODE_SEG), the program begins at zero (ORG 0), and the code is declared as PROC FAR which ensures that the proper type of RET opcode is generated.

The cursor is actually turned off by the single line OR CH,20h; this bit instructs the CRT controller on the video card to shut off the cursor until further notice. The code before that ensures that the CX register contains the proper cursor size information when the second call sends the data back to BIOS.

As expected, this example produced identical BIN files from each major assembler package tested. However, the sizes of the intermediate files varied greatly: TASM produced a 139-byte OBJ file, MASM generated one 72 bytes long, and OPTASM's output was only 65 bytes. These differences in OBJ file size reflect differing amounts of diagnostic information included. However, all that matters is the size of the final BIN file.

Example 2—Turning the Cursor ON

Now that you can turn the cursor off, you need a corresponding capability to turn the cursor back on the next time you want it to show on the screen. Example 2 provides this capability:

```
; CURSORON.ASM - xBase Example 2, no parameters passed
;
;       LOAD cursoron
;       CALL cursoron    && to turn cursor ON
;
```

```
        ASSUME  CS:CODE_SEG

CODE_SEG        SEGMENT
        ORG     0

CURSORON PROC   FAR
        MOV     AH,03    ; Read cursor information
        INT     10h      ;   using BIOS features
        AND     CH,1Fh   ; Clear cursor off bit
        MOV     AH,01    ; Set cursor type
        INT     10h      ;   using BIOS features
        RET              ; Return
CURSORON ENDP

CODE_SEG        ENDS

                END
```

The only difference between this routine and that shown in Example 1 is the line AND CH,1Fh. Where Example 1 set the cursor-off bit to 1 by ORing in a value of 20h, this routine uses the inverse operation to force that same bit to zero so that the CRT controller can enable the cursor to show once again.

With xBase you can LOAD several BIN files at once, so you can LOAD both NOCURSOR and CURSORON, then alternate CALLs to them for full cursor control.

And even though FoxBase does provide a special SYS() function that can be used to do the same thing, many developers who support several implementations of xBase prefer to use identical code for all of them, to keep the maintenance job simpler. These routines work not only with dBASE but also with FoxBase.

Interfacing Subroutines with Variable Passing

While these two preceding examples describe the techniques for creating and using BIN files, most assembly language routines you write will probably require that information be passed in from, or back to, the caller. The xBase language provides that capability, although it is somewhat restricted compared to C or Pascal.

In addition to the simple CALL statement used with the preceding examples, you can use the statement

```
CALL procedure WITH parameter
```

to pass a single parameter to your procedure. The procedure can then return any results in that same parameter.

Unfortunately, usually only one parameter can be passed (dBASE IV can pass more as explained subsequently). When your routine is entered, the segment address of that single parameter is in the DS register, and its offset is in BX. (If no parameter is passed in, BX contains 0000h.)

While the official language definitions all agree that either a character expression, or a memory variable of *any* type, can be passed in the CALL statement, it's almost universal practice to use a memvar of type "character" as the parameter. You can use such a memvar as a buffer to pass data that is not necessarily in character format.

When a parameter is passed, additional restrictions are imposed on it:

❏ The size of the parameter may not be changed by your routine; if the result takes less space than the parameter passed in, your routine must handle it by some method *other* than changing the parameter's length.

❏ If a character (or string) variable is involved, never try to save its address from one call of your routine to the next. Some implementations of xBase move such data in memory much as BASIC does. Always get such addresses immediately before they are to be used to ensure that they are correct.

The limit of only one parameter makes it necessary to pass multiple arguments as a string, which may include several fields in ASCII with commas as delimiters. Such a string cannot contain bytes that are all zeroes, and its maximum size is 254 bytes.

Example 3—Saving and Restoring the Screen

To understand the passing of data into a procedure, consider the program SCRUTL.BIN. This procedure can save and restore up to three screens. FoxBase provides this capability within its implementation, but dBASE III+ does not. SCRUTL.BIN works with both dBASE III+ and FoxBase+, and can easily be expanded to save up to 12 different screens of information. Several similar programs have been published; this example combines the best features of all:

```
; SCRUTL.ASM - xBase Example 3, with parameters passed
;
;        LOAD scrutl
;        OpCode = 'S1'              && to save screen to Area 1
;        CALL scrutl WITH OpCode
;
;        OpCode = 'R1'              && to restore screen from Area 1
;        CALL scrutl WITH OpCode
;
; Three work areas are provided but you can easily add more; the
; more you have, the more space is taken from your xBase program.
;
CODE     SEGMENT
         ASSUME  CS:CODE
         ORG     0


SCRUTL   PROC    FAR

         PUSH    BX              ; determine screen address
         MOV     AH,0Fh          ; Video display    ah=functn 0Fh
         INT     10h             ;  get state, al=mode, bh=page
         CMP     AL,7            ; test for MONO mode
         MOV     AX,0B000h       ; preset video SEG for MDA
         JE      MONO
         ADD     AH,8            ; adjust video SEG for CGA/EGA
MONO:    POP     BX
         MOV     CX,25*80        ; words to move
         MOV     DX,[BX]         ; DL = code, DH = area
         AND     DL,5Fh          ; force to uppercase
         CMP     DL,'S'
         JE      SAVE            ; is 'Save'
         CMP     DL,'R'
         JE      RESTOR          ; is 'Restore'
         JMP     SHORT WINDUP    ; neither, ignore it

SAVE:    MOV     DS,AX           ; set SRC to video RAM
         MOV     SI,0
         PUSH    CS
         POP     ES              ; set DEST to this segment
         CMP     DH,'1'          ; check area index
         JNE     NOTS1
```

```
            MOV     DI,OFFSET AREA1 ; was for area 1
            JMP     SHORT DOSAVE    ; so go move it all

NOTS1:      CMP     DH,'2'
            JNE     NOTS2
            MOV     DI,OFFSET AREA2
            JMP     SHORT DOSAVE

NOTS2:      CMP     DH,'3'
            JNE     WINDUP
            MOV     DI,OFFSET AREA3

DOSAVE:     CLD                     ; be sure of direction
            REP     MOVSW           ; then do block move
            JMP     SHORT WINDUP    ; and it's done

RESTOR:     MOV     ES,AX           ; set DEST to video RAM
            MOV     DI,0
            PUSH    CS              ; and SRC to this segment
            POP     DS
            CMP     OH,'1'
            JNE     NOTR1
            MOV     SI,OFFSET AREA1 ; Restore from area 1
            JMP     SHORT DOREST

NOTR1:      CMP     DH,'2'
            JNE     NOTR2
            MOV     SI,OFFSET AREA2
            JMP     SHORT DOREST

NOTR2:      CMP     DH,'3'
            JNE     WINDUP
            MOV     SI,OFFSET AREA3

DOREST:     CLD                     ; be sure of direction
            REP     MOVSW           ; then block move back

WINDUP:     RET

SCRUTL ENDP
```

```
AREA1    DW      2000 DUP (0)    ; screen save areas
AREA2    DW      2000 DUP (0)    ; (in SEG but not PROC)
AREA3    DW      2000 DUP (0)

CODE     ENDS

         END
```

Although much larger than the previous examples in this chapter, SCRUTL.BIN is not much more complex. It begins by determining whether it is running with a monochrome or a color monitor and placing the appropriate segment address (B000h for mono or B800h for color) of the video RAM in the AX register.

Next, the program puts the number of 16-bit words (attribute byte plus actual display character) into the CX register; note the use of assembly-time arithmetic to calculate this number in terms of rows and columns. This makes modifying the routine to support other display sizes simpler.

With the segment address and count tucked into registers, the program then uses the parameter address that is in BX to load the first two bytes of the parameter string into the DX register. The first byte goes into DL and the second into DH. This is all done by a single instruction to move a 16-bit value.

The first byte, in DL, is then masked against 5Fh to convert it from lowercase to uppercase if necessary. If the byte is not a letter or is already uppercase, this step doesn't change anything; however, this step eliminates the need to test whether it is needed, and so saves time.

If the resulting byte is S, indicating a Save command, control jumps to the label SAVE. If it is R, for Restore, it goes to RESTOR. If it is neither, then either no parameter at all or some unknown value was passed to the routine; in either case control then goes to WINDUP, which returns to the caller without doing anything else.

At SAVE, the segment address value stored in AX is moved into the DS register to become the source for the subsequent data move, and the current segment address (in CS) is copied into ES to become the destination. The offset for the source, in SI, is set to zero, and the program then goes through a three-level set of tests to determine which save-area address to load into DI for use as the destination.

The tests are run in DH, which contains the second character of the parameter passed. Only 1, 2, and 3 are acceptable values; anything else sends control directly to WINDUP to return without doing anything more. If one of these three characters is matched, the corresponding offset address is moved into DI, and control goes to DOSAVE, which performs the actual data transfer.

At DOSAVE, a CLD instruction ensures that the move will be made in the correct direction (see Chapter 17 for details of why this is needed), and a REP MOVSW instruction causes a block move of data from DS:SI to ES:DI, continuing for the number of words specified by the value in CX. After the move is finished, control goes to WINDUP, which returns to the caller. The specified area now contains an exact copy of the current content of the video RAM.

If control reaches RESTOR instead of SAVE, essentially the same actions occur, but the source and destination addresses are reversed so that data is moved from the specified area back to the video RAM.

Note that the three save areas are contained within the CODE segment although they are not inside the SCRUTL procedure itself. The 12,000 bytes of storage specified here account for most of the 12,115 bytes contained in the BIN file. Because the maximum size for a BIN file is 32,000 bytes, you could add nine more save areas. However, you would need to use letters to identify the areas because with the decoding technique used, only one character can serve as an area identifier.

Interfacing for dBASE IV

Interfacing to a BIN file with dBASE IV is a bit more complex and flexible. The main difference is that up to seven arguments can be passed rather than just one. As in the other xBase implementations, the address of the first parameter is passed in DS:BX. However, the actual number of values being passed is in the CX register, and the addresses are placed in a table of FAR (four-byte) pointers. This table begins at the address in ES:DI.

Any BIN file created to work with the older xBase implementations will work with dBASE IV; however, dBASE IV BIN files will not necessarily work with the older xBase implementations. If you want maximum portability of your routines from one version of xBase to another, you must avoid using the multiple-parameter capability. For this reason, no example of this capability is provided.

Assembling and Linking the BIN Files

Every assembly language program for use with the LOAD/CALL capability must be assembled, linked, and converted to a BIN file. The details of doing this differ, depending on the assembler and linker you use. The major differences are among the link steps.

Assembling the OBJ File

No matter which assembler you use, the technique for assembling your BIN-file routine will be the same. First, make sure that any debugging options are disabled (this applies primarily to QuickAssembler; the other assemblers leave such actions up to the linking step). Then, by invoking the assembler as described in Chapter 8, you can create an OBJ file that the linker can use.

If the assembler reports warning messages or errors, study them carefully and correct their causes before proceeding. You may need to re-assemble the program and specify that a LST file be output to find the exact spots where the errors occur. Only when the assembly step reports no problems should you proceed to the linking action.

Here are the assembler commands used with each of the major programs to generate the OBJ files for Example 3:

```
C>TASM scrutl;
C>OPTASM scrutl;
C>MASM scrutl;
```

Linking the OBJ to Make the BIN

Once your routine is successfully assembled into an OBJ file, you must convert that OBJ file into the final BIN file by using your linker program and, in some cases, other utilities. The following examples show the exact commands used when testing Example 3.

If you use Borland's TLINK, you can create the final file in a single step by using the command line:

```
C>TLINK /t scrutl,scrutl.bin;
```

which will automatically force the output file to meet the BIN-file requirements. The /t option switch is necessary.

If you are using OPTLINK from SLR, Inc., you can create the final file in two steps:

1. Link the OBJ file into a SYS file with

   `C>OPTLINK scrutl,scrutl.sys;`

   which will automatically force the output file to meet the BIN-file requirements. Optlink uses the .sys file extension rather than the /t option switch to determine that no EXE file is desired.

2. Rename the file from SYS to BIN with

   `C>REN scrutl.sys scrutl.bin`

   which completes the procedure.

If you are using Microsoft's LINK, this procedure is slightly more complex:

1. Link the OBJ file into EXE format as follows (ignore the warning message; it's normal in this case):

   ```
   C>LINK scrutl;
   LINK : warning L4021: no stack segment
   ```

2. Convert the EXE file into BIN format:

   `C>EXE2BIN scrutl`

3. Delete the intermediate file MYOBJ.EXE:

   `C>DEL scrutl.exe`

If you are using DOS 3.2 or an earlier version, you will have EXE2BIN on your DOS disk. At version 3.3, EXE2BIN was removed from the standard package and is now exclusively available (at an extra cost) with the Technical Reference Manual package. However, a free clone, EXE2COM, is available on CompuServe in the IBMNET forum group, and from many community bulletin board services. This clone works and performs the same as EXE2BIN.

Using the BIN Files

Once you have created your BIN files, you can use them in PRG files to be executed by either dBASE III+ or FoxBase+, or you can use them directly from the dot prompt in an interactive mode.

Using a BIN-file procedure is a two-step process: the file must first be LOADed into memory to make the procedure available to your program and then CALLed (possibly with a parameter) by a separate program statement. You can also use the RELEASE command to free space when a BIN module is no longer needed in memory.

LOADing the File

The first step in using your BIN file is to LOAD filename to place the BIN file's filename in memory. Keep in mind the limits on how many such files can be in memory at any one time: five for dBASE III+, 16 for Fox-Base+ or dBASE IV.

Loading another file with the same name as one that has already been loaded (even if it is a different file from a different subdirectory) will replace the first with the second. The extension (BIN) need not be entered; xBase adds it automatically.

CALLing the Procedure

Once your module has been loaded, you can CALL modulename to execute the procedure. You can also CALL modulename WITH parameter to execute, passing the single parameter. And if you are using dBASE IV and your procedure was written to accommodate it, you can CALL modulename WITH parameter-list to pass up to seven parameters.

Making Room for More

Any time a resource is limited, you will eventually need to find a way past that limit. If you need more BIN modules in a program than your xBase interpreter has room for, you can RELEASE modulename to make room for LOADing a new module.

Using the Examples

The following SCRUTL.PRG shows how all the BIN file examples in this chapter can be loaded and called. This PRG file runs identically under both dBASE III+ and FoxBase+:

```
SET STATUS OFF
SET SCOREBOARD OFF
SET TALK OFF

LOAD scrutl
LOAD nocursor
LOAD cursoron

SET COLOR TO W/B
CALL nocursor
CLEAR

i = 2
DO WHILE i < 22
   @ i, i+3 SAY 'This is a test screen for USING ASSEMBLY LANGUAGE'
   i = i+1
ENDDO

SET COLOR TO W*/N
@ 1,20 SAY " USING ASSEMBLY LANGUAGE, Second Edition "
SET COLOR TO W/N

@ 21,0 SAY ""
WAIT
@ 22,0 SAY SPACE(75)
CALL scrutl WITH "S1"
@ 5,5 CLEAR TO 10,15
@ 5,5 TO 10,15 DOUBLE
@ 6,6 SAY "This is 1"

CALL scrutl WITH "S2"
@ 21,0 SAY ""
WAIT
```

```
@ 22,0 SAY SPACE(75)
SET COLOR TO N/W
@ 7,8 CLEAR TO 20,70
@ 7,8 TO 20,70
@ 8,9 SAY "Here's 2"
SET COLOR TO W/N
@ 21,0 SAY ""
WAIT


@ 22,0 SAY SPACE(75)
CALL scrutl WITH "S3"
SET COLOR TO N/N
@ 13,25 CLEAR TO 17,55        && create the shadow
SET COLOR TO W+/B
@ 12,24 CLEAR TO 16, 54       && create the window
@ 12,24 TO 16,54 DOUBLE       && draw the border
@ 13,25 SAY "And in 3 a shadowed display"
SET COLOR TO W/N
@ 21,1 SAY ""
CALL cursoron
WAIT "Press any key to begin removing windows"

CALL scrutl WITH "R3"
@ 21,1 SAY ""
WAIT "Restored from area 3"

CALL scrutl WITH "R2"
@ 21,1 SAY ""
WAIT "Restored from area 2"

CALL scrutl WITH "R1"
@ 21,1 SAY ""
WAIT "Demo complete, press any key to return to DOS"

QUIT
```

Here's how the example works: the first three lines SET conditions so that nothing will interfere with the display, and the three LOAD commands after that bring the three BIN files into memory where they can be CALLed. Then the colors are set to white on blue, NOCURSOR is CALLed to make the cursor invisible, and the screen is cleared.

Next, a single line of text is repeated 22 times to fill the screen with details that will make the SAVE and RESTORE actions easy to see. The color is then changed to blinking white on black, and a title is displayed at the top of the screen. The color is then changed again, to white on black, and a WAIT command is issued. That command displays the message

```
Press any key to continue
```

and the next command erases the message once a key has been pressed. This pause gives you time to examine the display; note that no cursor is visible.

After you press a key, SCRUTL is called with the parameter S1 to save the screen in area 1, and then a small box is drawn from Row 5 Column 5 to Row 10 Column 15, with a double-line border and with the legend inside "This is 1". SCRUTL is called again to save the changed screen in area 2. Another WAIT command allows you to check this first change.

When the program proceeds (after you press a key), the colors are reversed to black on white, and a larger box is drawn from Row 7 Column 8 to Row 20 Column 70 in reversed colors with a single-line border. This box's label is "Here's 2". The colors are then set back to white on black, and another WAIT command allows you to check this screen.

After another call to SCRUTL to save this screen in area 3, a third box is drawn, using a shadowed technique, from Row 12 Column 24 to Row 16 Column 54, and given a double-line border and a title. Colors are then restored, and CURSORON is CALLed to make the cursor visible once more after the message

```
Press any key to begin removing windows
```

is displayed.

The rest of the program consists of a sequence of CALLs to SCRUTL. These CALLs restore the screen from the three saved areas in the reverse order in which they were originally stored, with WAIT commands after each CALL to give you time to see what is happening. After the original screen is restored, the final WAIT prompt tells you to press any key to return to DOS. When you do, QUIT ends the xBase interpreter's operation.

Although this demonstration program performs a fairly worthless task, the program structure itself demonstrates a number of techniques made possible by the BIN files described in this chapter. These techniques can be used in your production programs to add a more professional touch.

Summary

The xBase language may be the single most popular high-level language used today for business applications in the MS-DOS environment. In this chapter, you've learned how to create assembly language modules to extend the capabilities of that language and how to use those modules in your programs.

7

Interfacing with Clipper

The Clipper package from Nantucket, Inc. compiles the same DBMS language used by dBASE III+ and FoxBase+ into stand-alone programs. The Clipper programs do not require that a runtime module be furnished to the end user.

A major feature available with Clipper is that you can code just about anything you need, using either C or assembler, and then link it with the Clipper-generated OBJ file. With this capability, you can extend the language almost any way you want.

The only drawback to this feature is that it has changed at each major update to Clipper. The techniques described in this chapter are those used with the Clipper version identified as Summer '87. That version was created using Microsoft C version 5.1, and all PUBLIC symbols comply with the Microsoft C conventions. Earlier versions of Clipper used another C compiler and consequently required different usage of the PUBLIC symbols.

Clipper Version 5.0 is now nearing release. The techniques described in this chapter may work properly with the new update, but Nantucket has not made a prerelease version of its product available for testing, so nothing can be guaranteed.

Before getting into a detailed discussion of interfacing with Clipper, a definition of terms may be in order. If you are already familiar with Clipper terminology, you can skip the next two paragraphs.

Clipper source files, like source files in dBASE, are stored in PRG files. These ASCII program files ending with the extension PRG are nothing mysterious; they just hold the program source code written with the xBase language and any Clipper extensions to the language.

UDF is an acronym for *User Defined Function*. These are your external functions—written either in Clipper or in a non-xBase language—which are linked to your Clipper application when it is compiled.

General Interfacing Guidelines

When interfacing assembler routines to Clipper, you must follow a few well-defined rules. It's absolutely essential that between entry to your routine and return to Clipper you preserve unchanged the values of the DS, BP, SI, and DI registers. All other registers can be modified as needed.

To make it easy for you to meet all requirements, Clipper furnishes with the compiler a set of macros that you can use to generate all the necessary save and restore code. Some assembler packages also provide similar macro capability as part of their standard high-level-language support. Of course, you can always disregard such shortcuts and write all the necessary code yourself.

While you are learning how to interface with Clipper, this last option is recommended. Once you know what needs to be done and why it is necessary, then you can take shortcuts. However, until you know what's needed, these same shortcuts can keep you from learning!

Clipper, unlike compiled BASIC, Pascal, and C, does not generate true native machine code. An EXE file generated by Clipper consists of one call to Clipper's internal runtime interpreter for each PRG file contained in the EXE file. This is followed by a sequence of bytes in Clipper's own proprietary internal "tokenization." The runtime interpreter translates these tokens into calls to the native-code library routines.

Because of this, when you write a UDF in assembly language (or in C), you must always use the subroutines furnished with Clipper (as part of the EXTEND.LIB file) to communicate with your UDF. If your function doesn't pass information either way, you need not use EXTEND.LIB; one example of such a UDF would be a function that changes the cursor shape.

However, most useful functions either pass information in from the calling program or return data back to the calling program. Because Clipper's data storage structure is not directly accessible to your assembly language code, such functions will require routines from EXTEND.LIB to perform either of these tasks.

The techniques described in this chapter (except for one technique usable only with recent versions of MASM) work equally well with all the assemblers described in Chapter 8. However, if you use QuickAssembler, be sure that you have configured its environment to *omit* generation of CodeView information; that data embedded in the OBJ file will prevent Clipper from properly using your code.

Using Explicit Code without Macros

Although it may seem more reasonable to look at the macros provided with Clipper before seeing how to get along without them, I am first going to examine the no-macro route for two reasons:

❑ Macros really don't apply in the case of a simple routine that does not pass data to or from a UDF.

❑ Even when information must be passed through a UDF interface, you'll better understand what the macros do and when they will be helpful if you know in detail what they are actually providing.

In earlier chapters, our examples of assembly language code dealt mostly with cursor control. The examples in this chapter are no exception, although a cursor-control function is already provided by Clipper. However, rather than pursuing capabilities that only duplicate built-in Clipper functions, the example code in this chapter shows how to do something that Clipper will not do. Although many languages change the shape of the cursor to indicate whether you are operating in insert or overtype mode, Clipper does not provide this capability.

Three different examples are presented—each a bit more advanced (and therefore a little more complicated) than its predecessor:

1. The first example shows you how to interface without using any EXTEND.LIB functions. The code consists of four different functions, each of which first uses BIOS to read the current cursor information, then modifies it and puts it back. One function turns

the cursor off, and the other three turn it on. Of the three functions that turn the cursor on, one provides a line cursor, one makes it a block, and one provides a half block.

2. The second example shows how you can use the parameters to make just one procedure do the entire job. The sizes are specified by a code number passed into the function from Clipper; a code of 0 turns the cursor off, 1 makes it a line, 2 is a full block, and 3 is a half block.

3. Because both of these preceding examples go directly to BIOS to change the cursor size, Clipper's internal record will not reflect the actual cursor condition. This makes the built-in SET CURSOR function unreliable, and makes it difficult for your program to determine whether the cursor is on or off at any given instant. Therefore, the third example adds a value-return capability to the second example, so that it tells your program what the cursor condition *was* before you changed it. This is exactly like, and in fact is modeled from, the existing Clipper SETCOLOR() action.

Interfacing Subroutines without Variable Passing

First, I will code functions that require no passing of parameters although this approach requires a separate function to perform each action:

```
; ClipEx1.asm - cursor control utilities, no parameters
;
; declare as EXTERNAL CurOff, CurLine, CurBlok, CurHalf
; to turn cursor OFF:
;     use as DO CurOff
;         or CurOff()
; invoke other routines similarly to set cursor size
;
; for Clipper Summer 87 version only.


        TITLE   SETCUR

        PUBLIC  CUROFF, CURLINE, CURBLOK, CURHALF

_CSET   SEGMENT PARA 'CODE'
        ASSUME  CS:_CSET, DS:NOTHING
```

```
CUROFF  PROC    FAR
        PUSH    BP              ; save stackframe
        MOV     AH,3            ; get current cursor
        XOR     BX,BX           ; Clipper uses Page 0 only
        INT     10h             ; start in CH, end in CL
        OR      CL,20h          ; set NOCURSOR bit for BIOS
        MOV     AH,1            ; set new cursor values
        INT     10h
        POP     BP
        RET
CUROFF  ENDP

CURLINE PROC    FAR
        PUSH    BP              ; save stackframe
        MOV     AH,3            ; get current cursor
        XOR     BX,BX           ; Clipper uses Page 0 only
        INT     10h             ; start in CH, end in CL
        AND     CL,1Fh          ; be sure it's ON
        MOV     CH,CL           ; copy endline to startline
        DEC     CH              ; and back up by 1
        MOV     AH,1            ; set new cursor values
        INT     10h
        POP     BP
        RET
CURLINE ENDP

CURBLOK PROC    FAR
        PUSH    BP              ; save stackframe
        MOV     AH,3            ; get current cursor
        XOR     BX,BX           ; Clipper uses Page 0 only
        INT     10h             ; start in CH, end in CL
        AND     CL,1Fh          ; be sure it's ON
        XOR     CH,CH           ; force start to scanline 0
        MOV     AH,1            ; set new cursor values
        INT     10h
        POP     BP
        RET
CURBLOK ENDP

CURHALF PROC    FAR
        MOV     BP,SP
        MOV     AH,3            ; get current cursor
        XOR     BX,BX           ; Clipper uses Page 0 only
```

```
            INT     10h             ; start in CH, end in CL
            AND     CL,1Fh          ; be sure it's ON
            MOV     CH,CL           ; copy endline to startline
            SHR     CH,1            ; and divide start by 2
            MOV     AH,1            ; set new cursor values
            INT     10h
            POP     BP
            RET
    CURHALF ENDP

    _CSET   ENDS
            END
```

Although this looks like a lot of code, remember that it's essentially four copies of the same procedure. These procedures only vary in the values set in the CL register just before the second INT 10h call. Everything else remains unchanged from one procedure to the next.

Notice that each PROC must be declared as FAR to be usable by Clipper, and that all entry points (in this case, the four procedure names) must be declared as PUBLIC. These are essential points to remember in creating your own UDFs.

In each of these procedures, the BIOS function to read the cursor position and size (INT 10h, AH=3) is used. Upon returning, CH holds the startline value, and CL holds the endline value, and these two values together define the cursor shape. These values can then be modified and, by using the BIOS function to set the cursor size (INT 10h, AH=1), the shape of the cursor can be changed. The trick is to appropriately adjust the values in CH and CL.

To turn the cursor off, just OR 20h into the CH register. To turn it on, mask off that bit by ANDing with 1Fh. Those actions have already become familiar to you through the examples in previous chapters. Now, to create a LINE cursor, set the startline (in CH) to one less than the endline value (in CL) by MOV CH,CL followed by DEC CH. For a BLOCK, force the startline value to zero. For a half block, set the startline value (CH) to be half the value of the endline value (CL).

Now that the values have been modified, they are used to set the cursor size with the proper BIOS function, and control is passed back to the caller—in this case a Clipper program.

Interfacing Subroutines with Variable Passing

The routines in this first example illustrate the simplest possible interface of assembly language and Clipper programs, but it would be better if just one routine could do all four jobs. This can easily be done by adding a few lines of code to pass a numeric parameter from the Clipper program:

```
; ClipEx2.asm - cursor control utility in one procedure
;
; declare as EXTERNAL CurSet
;
;    codes are:
;         0 - Cursor OFF
;         1 - Line Cursor
;         2 - Block Cursor
;         3 - Half-Block Cursor
;
;      use as DO CurSet WITH 0
;           or Curset(0)
;         to turn cursor OFF (other values similar)
;
; for Clipper Summer 87 version only.


        TITLE   SETCUR

        EXTRN   __PARNI:FAR

        PUBLIC  CURSET

_CSET   SEGMENT PARA 'CODE'
        ASSUME  CS:_CSET, DS:NOTHING

CURSET  PROC    FAR
        PUSH    BP              ; save stackframe
        MOV     BP,SP
        MOV     AX,1            ; get number passed in
        PUSH    AX
        CALL    __PARNI         ; using EXTEND facility
        ADD     SP,2
        AND     AX,3            ; force to a valid value
        PUSH    AX              ; save the value
```

```
            MOV     AH,3             ; get current cursor
            XOR     BX,BX            ; Clipper uses Page 0 only
            INT     10h              ; start in CH, end in CL
            POP     AX               ; retrieve saved number
            INC     AL               ; force to range 1-4
            DEC     AL               ; easy decoder tree
            JNZ     NOT0
            OR      CH,20h           ; was 0, force OFF
            JMP     SHORT SETIT
NOT0:       AND     CL,1Fh           ; not 0, force ON
            DEC     AL
            JNZ     NOT1
            MOV     CH,CL            ; was 1, set to LINE
            DEC     CH               ; (start = end - 1)
            JMP     SHORT SETIT
NOT1:       DEC     AL
            JNZ     NOT2
            XOR     CH,CH            ; was 2, set to BLOCK
            JMP     SHORT SETIT      ; (start = 0)
NOT2:       MOV     CH,CL            ; was 3, make half block
            SHR     CH,1             ; (start = end/2)
SETIT:      MOV     AH,1             ; set new cursor values
            INT     10h
            MOV     SP,BP            ; restore stackframe
            POP     BP
            RET
CURSET      ENDP

_CSET       ENDS
            END
```

One of the first major differences you see here (besides the fact that it's only one function rather than four) is the EXTRN directive that identifies __PARNI as a FAR procedure defined in some other module. This EXTEND routine retrieves a numeric integer-format parameter passed in by Clipper, and returns the parameter in the AX register. To tell __PARNI which parameter to get, PUSH a value onto the stack before calling __PARNI. Here, the program pushes the value 1 to tell __PARNI to return the *first* parameter in the list.

The EXTEND package provides routines that accomplish the following:

❑ Determine how many parameters were passed in the call

❑ Identify the type of each parameter

❑ Retrieve the value in each of the valid types

❑ Return values in each valid type

These EXTEND package routines will be described in more detail in the sections that discuss the macro package furnished with Clipper to simplify the use of these routines. For now, let's look at the other features added to this example.

When the __PARNI routine returns a value, that value is then ANDed with 3 to force the value to one of the four values the routine is prepared to accept. This simplifies the code by making it literally impossible to provide an incorrect value; no matter what value is passed, the code is forced into the "correct" range. However, coding of this sort can lead to confusion; if you pass a value of −1 to this routine, the AND action will turn the value into 3. For maximum bullet-proofing, it would be better to test for, and ignore, values less than 0 or greater than 3; but that would unnecessarily complicate our discussion for now.

Having forced the value into range, the routine then preserves the value by pushing it onto the stack, and goes to BIOS to find out the current cursor type (as done earlier in the chapter). Here, only one such sequence suffices for all four actions. After returning, the cursor type is in the CX register. The routine then POPs the value back into AX for decoding.

Because the input was forced to be either 0, 1, 2, or 3, the routine can use a highly simplified decoding technique. First, INC AX forces the input to a nonzero value, either 1, 2, 3, or 4. Then DEC AX automatically sets the CPU flags. If the result is then zero, fall through the JNZ action into the code that turns the cursor off, then JMP ahead to set the cursor using BIOS. Otherwise take the JNZ, which goes to the AND CL,1Fh (also repeated three times in our previous example) that forces all other choices to turn the cursor on.

Now DEC again, and JNZ if the result is not zero. If it *is* zero, then the original code value must have been 1, so set CH to CL−1 for a LINE cursor, and jump to SETIT to set the cursor. If the value is nonzero, take the JNZ, and do it all over one more time. This time, zero means an original value of 2, and nonzero means 3, because those are the only choices left. In each case, CH is set appropriately.

At the label SETIT, BIOS is called by INT 10h to set the new cursor type. Finally, the procedure restores the stack frame and returns to the Clipper program that called it.

Interfacing Subroutines That Return Values

To return a value to the Clipper program that indicates what the previous cursor condition was, all that's necessary is to add one byte of storage and a few lines of code:

```
; ClipEx3.asm - cursor control utility returning old code
;
; declare as EXTERNAL CurSet
;
;    codes are:
;         0 - Cursor OFF
;         1 - Line Cursor
;         2 - Block Cursor
;         3 - Half-Block Cursor
;
;     use as OldCurVal = Curset(0)
;         to turn cursor OFF (other values similar)
;
; for Clipper Summer 87 version only.

          TITLE   SETCUR

          EXTRN   __PARNI:FAR
          EXTRN   __RETNI:FAR

          PUBLIC  CURSET

_CSET     SEGMENT PARA 'CODE'
          ASSUME  CS:_CSET, DS:NOTHING

OLDVAL    DB      1                   ; stores last value

CURSET    PROC    FAR
          PUSH    BP                  ; save stackframe
          MOV     BP,SP
          MOV     AL,CS:OLDVAL        ; get current value
          PUSH    AX                  ;    and save it for now
          MOV     AX,1                ; get number passed in
          PUSH    AX
          CALL    __PARNI             ; using EXTEND facility
```

```
        ADD     SP,2
        AND     AX,3                ; force to a valid value
        MOV     CS:OLDVAL,AL        ; save for next call
        PUSH    AX                  ; save the value
        MOV     AH,3                ; get current cursor
        XOR     BX,BX               ; Clipper uses Page 0 only
        INT     10h                 ; start in CH, end in CL
        POP     AX                  ; retrieve saved number
        INC     AL                  ; force to range 1-4
        DEC     AL                  ; easy decoder tree
        JNZ     NOT0
        OR      CH,20h              ; was 0, force OFF
        JMP     SHORT SETIT
NOT0:   AND     CL,1Fh              ; not 0, force ON
        DEC     AL
        JNZ     NOT1
        MOV     CH,CL               ; was 1, set to LINE
        INC     CH
        JMP     SHORT SETIT
NOT1:   DEC     AL
        JNZ     NOT2
        XOR     CH,CH               ; was 2, set to BLOCK
        JMP     SHORT SETIT
NOT2:   MOV     CH,CL               ; was 3, make HALF block
        SHR     CH,1
SETIT:  MOV     AH,1                ; set new cursor values
        INT     10h
        POP     AX                  ; get original OLDVAL back
        CBW                         ; extend the sign bit
        PUSH    AX                  ; push down for __RETNI
        CALL    __RETNI             ; using EXTEND facility
        ADD     SP,2
        MOV     SP,BP               ; restore stackframe
        POP     BP
        RET
CURSET  ENDP

_CSET   ENDS
        END
```

The added byte of storage, OLDVAL, is initialized to 1 because all Clipper applications start with the cursor turned on, and Clipper always sets the cursor shape to LINE.

At each call to CURSET, the current content of OLDVAL is first pushed onto the stack to save it. Then, just before the new code value is pushed onto the stack, that same new value is stored in OLDVAL for use on the next call.

Finally, after the new cursor condition has been set, the original value of OLDVAL is brought back from the stack, converted from a byte to a word, and returned to the calling procedure as the value of the function by the second EXTEND routine, __RETNI.

If you need to initialize OLDVAL to something else in any application, call CURSET with the desired initial value, at the beginning of your program, and ignore the value that it returns on that first call. Like C, Clipper lets you ignore the results of function calls.

Using the Clipper Macros

With the 14 functions Clipper provides in EXTEND.LIB, you can interface between Clipper programs and assembly language UDFs and two sets of INCLUDEable macros. The following are declarations for the 14 functions:

```
        EXTRN     __PARINFO:FAR     ; returns information

        EXTRN     __PARC:FAR        ; return parameters
        EXTRN     __PARNI:FAR
        EXTRN     __PARNL:FAR
        EXTRN     __PARND:FAR
        EXTRN     __PARDS:FAR
        EXTRN     __PARL:FAR

        EXTRN     __RETC:FAR        ; send values back to PGM
        EXTRN     __RETNI:FAR
        EXTRN     __RETNL:FAR
        EXTRN     __RETND:FAR
        EXTRN     __RETDS:FAR
        EXTRN     __RETL:FAR
        EXTRN     __RET:FAR
```

The following parameter type codes returned by __PARINFO can be used to determine what type of data is being passed:

```
;-----------------------------------
; data type equates from EXTEND.H
;-----------------------------------
UNDEF      EQU    0      ; parameter not defined
CHARACTER EQU    1      ; includes strings
NUMERIC    EQU    2
LOGICAL    EQU    4
DATE       EQU    8
ALIAS      EQU    16
```

Possibly the best way to describe how these functions are used is to show what's in the macros provided in Clipper's EXTENDA.MAC file (which has been placed in the public domain). All of these macros are made available to your program by adding the line INCLUDE EXTENDA.MAC at the beginning of the source file.

The following paragraphs describe the purpose of each macro, followed by the code that the macro generates when used. The first two macros provide information about the parameters being passed rather than dealing with values:

❏ GET_PCOUNT obtains the number of parameters being passed. Its result is returned in AX.

```
XOR      AX,AX
PUSH     AX
CALL     __PARINFO
ADD      SP,2
```

❏ GET_PTYPE <expN> obtains the type of the parameter being passed. Its result is returned in AX (as one of the parameter type codes previously described by the data type equates).

```
MOV      AX,N ; n = parameter number
PUSH     AX
CALL     __PARINFO
ADD      SP,2
```

The next six macros retrieve values of specified parameters in one of the six valid data type formats:

❏ GET_CHAR <expN> gets the requested parameter as a string. The address of the string is returned in AX:BX (segment:offset).

```
MOV      AX,N
PUSH     AX
CALL     __PARC
```

```
ADD     SP,2
MOV     BX,AX
MOV     AX,DX
```

❏ GET_INT <expN> gets the requested parameter as integer
(16 bits). Its result is returned in AX.

```
MOV     AX,N
PUSH    AX
CALL    __PARNI
ADD     SP,2
```

❏ GET_LONG <expN> gets the requested parameter as long (32 bits).
Its result is returned in AX:BX.

```
MOV     AX,N
PUSH    AX
CALL    __PARNL
ADD     SP,2
MOV     BX,AX
MOV     AX,DX
```

❏ GET_DBL <expN> gets the requested parameter as double (64-bit
floating point). Its result is returned in AX:BX:CX:DX.

```
MOV     AX,N
PUSH    AX
CALL    __PARND
ADD     SP,2
MOV     ES,DX
MOV     SI,AX
MOV     AX,ES:[SI]
MOV     BX,ES:[SI + 2]
MOV     CX,ES:[SI + 4]
MOV     DX,ES:[SI + 6]
```

❏ GET_DATESTR <expN> gets the requested parameter as a date string.
The address of the string is returned in AX:BX (segment:offset).

```
MOV     AX,N
PUSH    AX
CALL    __PARDS
ADD     SP,2
MOV     BX,AX
MOV     AX,DX
```

❑ GET_LOGICAL <expN> gets the requested parameter as logical
(1 or 0). Its result is returned in AX.

```
MOV      AX,N
PUSH     AX
CALL     __PARL
ADD      SP,2
```

The remaining six macros pass return values back to Clipper from your
assembly language code:

❑ RET_CHAR <seg_reg>,<off_reg> returns a string by providing its
address.

```
IRP      X,<REG1,REG2>
PUSH     X
ENDM
CALL     __RETC
ADD      SP,4
```

❑ RET_INT <reg> returns an integer contained in <reg>.

```
PUSH     REG1
CALL     __RETNI
ADD      SP,2
```

❑ RET_LONG <reg1>,<reg2> returns a long. Its most significant 16
bits are in <reg1>; the rest are in <reg2>.

```
IRP      X,<REG1,REG2>
PUSH     X
ENDM
CALL     __RETNL
ADD      SP,4
```

❑ RET_DBL <reg1>,<reg2>,<reg3>,<reg4> returns a double. As in the
previous macro, <reg1> is the most significant word of the 64-bit
floating-point value, and <reg4> is least significant.

```
IRP      X,<REG1,REG2,REG3,REG4>
PUSH     X
ENDM
CALL     __RETND
ADD      SP,8
```

❏ RET_DATESTR <seg_reg>,<off_reg> returns a date string. Like RET_CHAR, the string is passed as an address.

```
IRP     X,<REG1,REG2>
PUSH    X
ENDM
CALL    __RETDS
ADD     SP,4
```

❏ RET_LOGICAL <reg1> returns a logical.

```
PUSH    REG1
CALL    __RETL
ADD     SP,2
```

These macros work with each of the "big three" assemblers (MASM, OPTASM, and TASM) and also with QuickAssembler. Using EXTENDA.MAC makes it a little easier to see what your code is doing without getting tangled up in the needs of the interface. For example, here's our sample program as coded using EXTENDA.MAC:

```
; ClipEx4.asm - cursor control utility using EXTENDA.MAC
;
; declare as EXTERNAL CurSet
;
;   codes are:
;        0 - Cursor OFF
;        1 - Line Cursor
;        2 - Block Cursor
;        3 - Half-Block Cursor
;
;     use as OldCurVal = Curset(0)
;        to turn cursor OFF (other values similar)
;
; for Clipper Summer 87 version only.

        TITLE   SETCUR

INCLUDE EXTENDA.MAC

        PUBLIC  CURSET

_CSET   SEGMENT PARA 'CODE'
        ASSUME  CS:_CSET, DS:NOTHING
```

```
OLDVAL   DB       1                     ; stores last value

CURSET   PROC     FAR
         PUSH     BP                    ; save stackframe
         MOV      BP,SP
         MOV      AL,CS:OLDVAL          ; get current value
         PUSH     AX                    ;    and save it for now
         GET_INT  1                     ; get Parameter 1
         AND      AX,3                  ; force to a valid value
         MOV      CS:OLDVAL,AL          ; save for next call
         PUSH     AX                    ; save the value
         MOV      AH,3                  ; get current cursor
         XOR      BX,BX                 ; Clipper uses Page 0 only
         INT      10h                   ; start in CH, end in CL
         POP      AX                    ; retrieve saved number
         INC      AL                    ; force to range 1-4
         DEC      AL                    ; easy decoder tree
         JNZ      NOT0
         OR       CH,20h                ; was 0, force OFF
         JMP      SHORT SETIT
NOT0:    AND      CL,1Fh                ; not 0, force ON
         DEC      AL
         JNZ      NOT1
         MOV      CH,CL                 ; was 1, set to LINE
         DEC      CH                    ; (start = end - 1)
         JMP      SHORT SETIT
NOT1:    DEC      AL
         JNZ      NOT2
         XOR      CH,CH                 ; was 2, set to BLOCK
         JMP      SHORT SETIT           ; (start = 0)
NOT2:    MOV      CH,CL                 ; was 3, make HALF block
         SHR      CH,1                  ; (start = end/2)
SETIT:   MOV      AH,1                  ; set new cursor values
         INT      10h
         POP      AX                    ; get original OLDVAL back
         CBW                            ; extend the sign bit
         RET_INT  AX                    ; pass it back to Clipper
         MOV      SP,BP                 ; restore stackframe
         POP      BP
         RET
CURSET   ENDP

_CSET    ENDS
         END
```

Using Advanced Assembler Features

In addition to the relatively straightforward macros provided in EXTENDA.MAC, Clipper provides a second set, EXTENDA.INC, that almost amounts to a separate language for constructing assembly interfaces. Most of the interface requirements are coded into this second set in a way that makes them invisible to you.

The complex, nested macros in EXTENDA.INC are based on special mixed-language features that Microsoft included in MASM, and work only with MASM 5.0 or later versions. In their "normal" configurations, OPTASM spews screen after screen of error messages, and TASM quietly freezes when attempting to process this material. However, using this set of macros will include complete error-trapping into your interface (at the cost of significantly larger OBJ files), so you may find it is worth the inconvenience.

Using the EXTENDA.INC macros is simple; comprehending what they do is not. A full explanation of how they function is far beyond the scope of this book. However, so that you can see how these macros are used, here's the previous example (the CURSET function that returns the previous cursor code) as it looks when coded using EXTENDA.INC:

```
; ClipEx5.asm - cursor control utility using EXTENDA.INC
;
; declare as EXTERNAL CurSet
;
;    codes are:
;         0 - Cursor OFF
;         1 - Line Cursor
;         2 - Block Cursor
;         3 - Half-Block Cursor
;
;     use as OldCurVal = Curset(0)
;         to turn cursor OFF (other values similar)
;
; for Clipper Summer 87 version only.

INCLUDE EXTENDA.INC

CLPUBLIC CURSET
CLFUNC  INT CURSET <INT NEWVAL>
```

```
CLCODE
        MOV     AL,CS:OLDVAL        ; get current value
        PUSH    AX                  ;   and save it for now
        MOV     AX,NEWVAL           ; get number passed in
        AND     AX,3                ; force to a valid value
        MOV     CS:OLDVAL,AL        ; save for next call
        PUSH    AX                  ; save the value
        MOV     AH,3                ; get current cursor
        XOR     BX,BX               ; Clipper uses Page 0 only
        INT     10h                 ; start in CH, end in CL
        POP     AX                  ; retrieve saved number
        INC     AL                  ; force to range 1-4
        DEC     AL                  ; easy decoder tree
        JNZ     NOT0
        OR      CH,20h              ; was 0, force OFF
        JMP     SHORT SETIT


OLDVAL  DB      1                   ; data inside code segment


NOT0:   AND     CL,1Fh              ; not 0, force ON
        DEC     AL
        JNZ     NOT1
        MOV     CH,CL               ; was 1, set to LINE
        DEC     CH                  ; (start = end - 1)
        JMP     SHORT SETIT


NOT1:   DEC     AL
        JNZ     NOT2
        XOR     CH,CH               ; was 2, set to BLOCK
        JMP     SHORT SETIT         ; (start = 0)


NOT2:   MOV     CH,CL               ; was 3, make half block
        SHR     CH,1                ; (start = end/2)
SETIT:  MOV     AH,1                ; set new cursor values
        INT     10h
        POP     AX                  ; get original OLDVAL back
        CBW                         ; extend the sign bit
        CLRET   AX                  ; and return the result to Clipper


        END
```

You can see that the entire outer structure of SEGMENT/ENDS directives, and PROC/ENDP, has been replaced by the CLfunc, CLcode, and CLret macros from EXTENDA.INC.

Note also that the static storage variable OLDVAL had to be hidden after a JMP statement in the middle of the function. This helps keep the program simple by holding the variable in the code segment; otherwise the macro set would have forced DS to be changed. The OBJ file generated by MASM 5.1 for this example was 154 bytes long, compared with 91 bytes for the OBJ files generated by ClipEx4.asm, which is functionally identical. The 63-byte difference is due to the error-trapping code, which was invisibly added.

The View from Clipper's Side

No matter which of these techniques you choose, the interface from the Clipper side is exactly the same as that used for Clipper's own built-in procedures and functions.

If your routine does not return a value, you can either DO the procedure WITH its parameter list or invoke the routine by name as a function. If a value is returned, you must use the function syntax.

For example, CursorState = CurSet(0) would turn off the cursor, saving its previous condition in CursorState. Either DO CurSet WITH Cursor-State or CurSet(CursorState) would subsequently return the cursor to its original condition.

To assemble any of these examples, use your assembler as described in Chapter 8; for instance, using the source file CURSET.ASM and MASM, the command would be as follows:

```
MASM CURSET;
```

This command produces the object file CURSET.OBJ ready for linking into your Clipper programs.

To perform the linking, just add the OBJ-file name as in the following example (which assumes a main program name of YOURS.PRG and also that CLIPPER.LIB and EXTEND.LIB are accessible to your linker as described in Chapter 9):

```
LINK YOURS+CURSET,,,CLIPPER+EXTEND
```

This creates the executable file YOURS.EXE.

One last word of caution: when you use any of the example code from this chapter in your own Clipper programs, do *not* use the standard SET CURSOR ON and SET CURSOR OFF operations provided by Clipper in the same programs. Either the Clipper code or these example codes will control the cursor independently of the other; however, mixing the two sets of operations in the same program will make it impossible for that program to determine the exact cursor condition because neither set updates the invisible, internal storage locations used by the other. This is just one specific example of a problem that can always arise when you add functions to any language. To avoid such trouble, just remember to never mix similar functions.

Summary

Although Clipper uses a language that is largely compatible with dBASE and FoxBase, its operation is unlike those systems; assembly language routines for use in Clipper programs must be designed with the differences in mind.

One distinction is that in Clipper, assembly language routines can be used anywhere in the main program that an expression is acceptable. The interpretive languages require that your routines be LOADed and then CALLed. Another major feature is that the EXTEND.LIB facilities that Clipper provides *must* be used to pass information into or out of your assembly modules.

Learning to interface with Clipper is much like learning with C or with Pascal. After the first few practice runs, it's easy to do. And the results are definitely worth the effort.

Part II

Assembly Language Tools

CHAPTER 8

Choosing and Using
Your Assembler

To do any serious work with assembly language, you must have an assembler. Microsoft's MASM (Macro ASseMbler) is probably the most widely known, but there are several available alternatives that provide essentially complete compatibility with it. Still other assemblers are quite different from the Microsoft version.

To follow the instructions and examples in this chapter, you need either MASM or an assembler that has a virtually identical set of commands.

To help you choose an assembler, this chapter lists brief summaries of the advantages and disadvantages of each. But before getting into the specifics of how any one assembler operates, let's take a look at what all assemblers do.

What an Assembler Does

As the Introduction points out, an *assembler* is a program that translates assembly language instructions into machine language. In concept,

151

the assembler's job is simple. Its translation process simply converts assembly language mnemonics into a numeric equivalent that represents the proper machine language code. This sounds straightforward enough, but frequently it is not; determining what the programmer wants can be tedious and tricky. This translation or *parsing* process is what the assembler program spends the most time doing.

An assembler does not fully translate source code into machine language but creates instead an object code file, which by itself is not executable. Although the assembler program parses and translates virtually every instruction, some instructions cannot be encoded at this point. Instead, a separate pass is required to translate the object file into an executable file. (This step, called *linking*, is covered in Chapter 9.)

To translate code, an assembler must read the source file at least one time. Each read of the source file, with its associated processing, is called a *pass*. Most assemblers require two passes to create the object code file. However, some do it all in one pass, and others do even more than two.

During the first pass, the assembler does the following:

❏ Parses the source code, calculating the offset for each line

❏ Makes assumptions about undefined values

❏ Does elementary error checking, displaying error messages if necessary

❏ Generates a preliminary listing file, if requested (not all assemblers provide this action)

During the final pass, which *may* also be the first pass, the assembler does the following:

❏ Attempts to reconcile the value assumptions made during previous passes

❏ Generates the final assembly listing (LST) file, if specified

❏ Generates the object code, storing it in the object (OBJ) file

❏ Generates the cross-reference (CRF) file, if specified

❏ Completes the error-checking process, displaying error messages if necessary

The Leading Contenders

Although MASM sets the industry's standard for PC-oriented assemblers, it has stiff competition from Borland's Turbo Assembler and also from OptAsm, a product of SLR, Inc. Yet another competitor, Microsoft's own QuickAssembler, currently is available only with the QuickC package.

Let's compare these four products and see how they differ. Each has a few advantages, and each has a few problems; all are capable of excellent results. Your final choice, of course, must be based on the features that are most important to you.

One way of comparing the products is to note which features are common to two or more of them and which features are unique. For instance, table 8.1, a list of directives supported by the various assemblers, indicates where you can expect major differences between the assemblers (directives are defined and described later in this chapter).

Table 8.1. *Directives supported by major assemblers.*

Directive (Pseudo-operation)	MASM 5.1	MsQA 1.0	TASM 2.0	OptAsm 1.6
\<name\> = \<expr\>	Y	Y	Y	Y
.186	Y	Y	Y	Y
.286	Y	Y	Y	Y
.286C			Y	Y
.286P		Y	Y	Y
.287	Y	Y	Y	Y
.386	Y	Y	Y	
.386C			Y	
.386P		Y	Y	
.387		Y	Y	
.8086	Y	Y	Y	Y
.8087	Y	Y	Y	Y
ABS				Y
ALIGN	Y	Y	Y	Y
.ALPHA	Y	Y	Y	Y
ARG	Y		Y	
ASSUME	Y	Y	Y	Y
%BIN	Y		Y	
CATSTR	Y	Y	Y	Y
.CODE		Y	Y	Y
CODE	Y	Y		

Table 8.1. continues

Table 8.1. *continued*

Directive (Pseudo-operation)	MASM 5.1	MsQA 1.0	TASM 2.0	OptAsm 1.6
CODESEG		Y	Y	
COMM	Y	Y	Y	Y
COMMENT	Y	Y	Y	Y
%CONDS		Y	Y	
.CONST	Y	Y	Y	Y
CONST		Y	Y	
.CPAGE		Y		Y
.CREF	Y	Y	Y	Y
%CREF		Y	Y	
%CREFALL		Y	Y	
%CREFREF		Y	Y	
%CREFUREF		Y	Y	
%CTLS		Y	Y	
.DATA	Y	Y	Y	Y
.DATA?	Y	Y	Y	Y
DATASEG			Y	
DB	Y	Y	Y	Y
DD	Y	Y	Y	Y
%DEPTH			Y	
DF	Y	Y	Y	
DISPLAY		Y	Y	
DOSSEG	Y	Y	Y	Y
DP	Y		Y	
DQ	Y	Y	Y	Y
.DS				Y
DT	Y	Y	Y	Y
DW	Y	Y	Y	Y
ELSE	Y	Y	Y	Y
ELSEIF			Y	
EMUL			Y	
.EN				Y
END	Y	Y	Y	Y
ENDIF	Y	Y	Y	Y
ENDM	Y	Y	Y	Y
ENDP	Y	Y	Y	Y
ENDS	Y	Y	Y	Y
EQU	Y	Y	Y	Y
.ERR	Y	Y	Y	Y

Directive (Pseudo-operation)	MASM 5.1	MsQA 1.0	TASM 2.0	OptAsm 1.6
ERR			Y	
.ERR1	Y	Y	Y	Y
.ERR2	Y	Y	Y	Y
.ERRB	Y	Y	Y	Y
.ERRDEF	Y	Y	Y	Y
.ERRDIF	Y	Y	Y	Y
.ERRDIFI	Y	Y	Y	Y
.ERRE	Y	Y	Y	Y
.ERRIDN	Y	Y	Y	Y
.ERRIDNI	Y	Y	Y	Y
ERRIF			Y	
ERRIF1			Y	
ERRIF2			Y	
ERRIFB			Y	
ERRIFDEF			Y	
ERRIFDIF			Y	
ERRIFDIFI			Y	
ERRIFE			Y	
ERRIFIDN			Y	
ERRIFIDNI			Y	
ERRIFNB			Y	
ERRIFNDEF			Y	
.ERRNB	Y	Y	Y	Y
.ERRNDEF	Y	Y	Y	Y
.ERRNZ	Y	Y	Y	Y
EVEN	Y	Y	Y	Y
EVENDATA			Y	
EXITM	Y	Y	Y	Y
EXTA				Y
EXTB				Y
EXTD				Y
EXTF				Y
EXTN				Y
EXTP				Y
EXTQ				Y
EXTRN	Y	Y	Y	Y
EXTT				Y
EXTW				Y

Table 8.1. continues

Table 8.1. continued

Directive (Pseudo-operation)	MASM 5.1	MsQA 1.0	TASM 2.0	OptAsm 1.6
.FARDATA	Y	Y	Y	Y
.FARDATA?	Y	Y	Y	Y
FARDATA			Y	
GLOBAL			Y	
GROUP	Y	Y	Y	Y
IDEAL			Y	
IF ... ELSE ... ENDIF	Y	Y	Y	Y
IF1	Y	Y	Y	Y
IF2	Y	Y	Y	Y
IFB	Y	Y	Y	Y
IFCONST				Y
IFDEF	Y	Y	Y	Y
IFDIF	Y	Y	Y	Y
IFDIFI	Y	Y	Y	Y
IFE	Y	Y	Y	Y
IFIDN	Y	Y	Y	Y
IFIDNI	Y	Y	Y	Y
IFNB	Y	Y	Y	Y
IFNDEF	Y	Y	Y	Y
%INCL			Y	
INCLUDE	Y	Y	Y	Y
INCLUDELIB	Y	Y	Y	Y
INSTR			Y	Y
IRP ... ENDM	Y	Y	Y	Y
IRPC ... ENDM	Y	Y	Y	Y
JUMPS			Y	
LABEL	Y	Y	Y	Y
.LALL	Y	Y	Y	Y
.LFCOND	Y	Y	Y	Y
%LINUM			Y	
%LIST			Y	
.LIST	Y	Y	Y	Y
LOCAL	Y	Y	Y	Y
LOCALS			Y	
MACRO ... ENDM	Y	Y	Y	Y
%MACS			Y	
MASM		Y	Y	
MASM51			Y	

Directive (Pseudo-operation)	MASM 5.1	MsQA 1.0	TASM 2.0	OptAsm 1.6
.MODEL	Y	Y	Y	Y
MODEL			Y	
.MSFLOAT		Y		Y
MULTERRS			Y	
NAME	Y	Y	Y	Y
%NEWPAGE			Y	
%NOCONDS			Y	
%NOCREF			Y	
%NOCTLS			Y	
NOEMUL			Y	
%NOINCL			Y	
NOJUMPS			Y	
%NOLIST			Y	
NOLOCALS			Y	
%NOMACS			Y	
NOMASM51			Y	
NOMULTERRS			Y	
%NOSYMS			Y	
%NOTRUNC			Y	
NOWARN			Y	
ORG	Y	Y	Y	Y
%OUT	Y	Y	Y	Y
P186			Y	
P286			Y	
P286N			Y	
P286P			Y	
P287			Y	
P386			Y	
P386N			Y	
P386P			Y	
P387			Y	
P8086			Y	
P8087			Y	
PAGE	Y	Y	Y	Y
%PAGESIZE			Y	
%PCNT			Y	
PN087			Y	
POPAS				Y

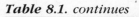

Table 8.1. *continues*

Table 8.1. continued

Directive (Pseudo-operation)	MASM 5.1	MsQA 1.0	TASM 2.0	OptAsm 1.6
%POPLCTL			Y	
PROC ... ENDP	Y	Y	Y	Y
PUBLIC	Y	Y	Y	Y
PURGE	Y	Y	Y	Y
PUSHAS				Y
%PUSHLCTL			Y	
QUIRKS			Y	
.RADIX	Y	Y	Y	Y
RADIX			Y	
RECORD	Y	Y	Y	Y
REPT ... ENDM	Y	Y	Y	Y
.SALL	Y	Y	Y	Y
SEGMENT ... ENDS	Y	Y	Y	Y
.SEQ	Y	Y	Y	Y
.SFCOND	Y	Y	Y	Y
SIZESTR		Y	Y	Y
.SOFTEXT				Y
.STACK	Y	Y	Y	Y
STACK			Y	
.STARTUP	Y	Y	Y	
STRUC .. ENDS	Y	Y	Y	Y
SUBSTR		Y	Y	Y
SUBTTL	Y	Y	Y	Y
%SUBTTL			Y	
%SYMS			Y	
%TABSIZE			Y	
%TEXT			Y	
.TFCOND	Y	Y	Y	Y
TITLE	Y	Y	Y	Y
%TITLE			Y	
%TRUNC			Y	
UDATASEG			Y	
UFARDATA			Y	
UNION			Y	
USES		Y	Y	
WARN		Y	Y	
.XALL	Y	Y	Y	Y
.XCREF	Y		Y	Y
.XLIST	Y	Y	Y	Y

As this table shows, most directives are supported by all four contenders, but Turbo Assembler has the largest number of unique, added directives. In most cases these are simply *aliases* for names of other existing, nonunique directives, such as FARDATA for .FARDATA. Such aliases are needed because in Turbo Assembler's *ideal* mode no directive can begin with a period, and in the MASM standard world nearly half of the available directives do so.

MASM from Microsoft

Microsoft's MASM is one of the most popular assemblers for assembly language. Some other assemblers, such as the one with the IBM name on it, are actually the same MASM that Microsoft publishes.

MASM is a two-pass assembler that creates relocatable object code, which can subsequently be linked and executed. It can optionally create listing files and collect cross-reference data to be processed by a separate program.

Because MASM was effectively the first assembler to achieve wide distribution and was distributed by IBM, it has become the standard against which all others are measured. This is not to say that it is perfect; from its earliest days MASM has borne a reputation for harboring strange bugs. Even in the latest version (5.1), some of MASM's actions seem a bit bizarre to many users.

Most of the true bugs in earlier versions, such as failure of some of the directives to do anything at all, have been corrected in the later releases, but in doing so Microsoft consequently made one MASM version incompatible with the next. One of the strongest valid criticisms that can be leveled against the program is that in a few cases the differences between versions are so extreme that things that are *required* to make a program work with MASM 5.0 will themselves cause the same program to *fail* under MASM 5.1.

Fortunately, virtually all such problems appear when the highly advanced techniques made possible by multilevel macro definitions are being used. Ordinary, everyday code is not nearly so touchy, and all versions of MASM seem to work well with such code.

For everyday use, one of the biggest disadvantages of MASM is its susceptibility to "phase error" problems. MASM uses this term to describe a situation where it fails to properly assign memory space during the first pass, so address references change between the first pass and the second. What makes this bug so puzzling is that it goes undetected at the point where it occurs and shows up only at the first memory location that changed, which may be many lines of code past the real error.

The only practical way to find this kind of error is to generate listings for *both* passes, then compare the two listings line by line to discover the point where the assigned memory addresses fail to match. Careful examination of the code generated by the instruction immediately preceding the first mismatch usually shows what's wrong.

Possibly the greatest advantage that MASM has over its competitors is that it *does* set the standard and therefore usually includes at least a few new features that the other products lack. That's not true at this writing, but only because MASM's current 5.1 version is nearly a year older than any of the others; since the release of 5.1, MASM's competitors have incorporated that version's new features.

Another advantage is that it's the only assembler that offers full support for OS/2.

QuickAssembler from Microsoft

The latest offering from Microsoft, QuickAssembler, is currently available only as a part of the QuickC version 2.01 package. QuickAssembler runs only as a part of QuickC.

QuickAssembler is a full implementation of 8086 assembly language but omits all support of the 80386, 80387, and OS/2 features in MASM. Although the QuickAssembler manual claims that QuickAssembler can use the "full set" of MASM 5.1 directives and operations, the manual itself only describes those directives listed in table 8.1. If you cannot find out what a directive is supposed to do, it's a bit difficult to use it.

QuickAssembler's greatest advantage is that it comes at no extra cost when you buy the latest version of the QuickC compiler. However, this advantage is counterbalanced by QuickAssembler's lack of adequate documentation. (The documentation problem is a flaw shared by all the Quick implementations, which depend a bit too much on their hypertext help system and thus fail to provide adequate printed reference data for serious users.)

By default, QuickAssembler is a single-pass assembler. This makes it faster than it otherwise would be (its speed on moderate-sized source files is astounding) but prevents features such as program-listing generation from working. You can configure QuickAssembler to operate as a two-pass system; it then works much like MASM, but with a few added directives that MASM lacks.

Because QuickAssembler is normally used only from within the QuickC environment, and because it is so similar to MASM in all other respects, it is not discussed separately in the rest of this chapter.

If you use QuickC, QuickAssembler is the simplest way to ease into the world of assembly language; otherwise you would do better with one of the separate products if only because they offer better documentation than Quick.

OptAsm from SLR, Inc.

The first major competitor to appear was OptAsm from SLR, Inc., a firm well-known in CP/M days for its fast and accurate line of program development tools. More MASM-compatible than MASM itself, this versatile program can emulate the actions of MASM versions 3, 4, and 5, and the latest OptAsm version (1.61) has added emulation of MASM 5.1. OptAsm is also easily the fastest assembler described here; assembly rates greater than 10,000 lines per minute are common with OptAsm.

However, the major advantage of OptAsm is neither its versatility nor its speed, but its accuracy. As an "n-pass" assembler, OptAsm has no strictly defined number of passes but instead processes the source file until it makes one pass in which nothing changes. Thus, it is completely free of phase errors, and that alone establishes it as the assembler of choice for many professionals.

Other features include built-in "make" and "cross-reference" actions. Both Macro Assembler and Turbo Assembler rely on other programs to perform these functions.

OptAsm has only a few serious disadvantages. Like QuickAssembler, it cannot generate special code for the 80386 and 80387, but the 80386 and 80387 can operate using the code that OptAsm *does* generate. Also, in its default configuration, OptAsm cannot handle programs that depend on some of the more esoteric features of MASM 5.1—Clipper's EXTENDA.INC macro file, for example. A lesser point against OptAsm is that because it is not nearly as well known as its competitors, it may be a bit more difficult to find.

Turbo Assembler from Borland

The other major competitor is Borland's Turbo Assembler (TASM). Turbo Assembler version 2.0 claims "100%" compatibility with full MASM; since the various versions of MASM are not compatible with each other, TASM is a useful tool when you must support several MASM versions.

The unique Turbo Assembler feature that makes such action possible is the availability of different assembly modes for existing assembly programs. To retain MASM compatibility, you have the option of using MASM, MASM51, or QUIRKS modes, either individually or in combination.

For new programs where you would prefer that the assembler not duplicate the sometimes bizarre actions of MASM but that it instead be completely consistent, you can set the mode to IDEAL. Because IDEAL mode is not compatible with the mainstream of assembly language programming, however, this chapter will not discuss the mode in detail. Although this capability is certainly a plus for Turbo Assembler, it should not be the deciding factor unless weighing other more critical advantages and disadvantages leaves you undecided.

Table 8.2, which is drawn from the Turbo Assembler HELPME!.DOC file, lists the conditions that determine which MASM-compatible mode you should use and when. Note that the default operating mode is MASM.

Table 8.2. *Turbo Assembler's conditions for selecting a MASM-compatible mode.*

Mode	Conditions for Use
Normal (MASM)	Assembles under MASM 4.00 or MASM 5.00
QUIRKS	Assembles under MASM 4.00 or MASM 5.00 but won't assemble under TASM without MASM51 or QUIRKS
MASM51	Requires MASM 5.1 for assembly
MASM51 and QUIRKS	Requires MASM 5.1 for assembly but will not assemble under TASM with only the MASM51 switch set

The differences in operation offered by each of these modes are detailed in the following paragraphs.

When used by itself, the QUIRKS mode provides the following capabilities:

❏ FAR jumps can be generated as NEAR or SHORT if ASSUME directives for CS will permit it.

❏ If present, one register can determine all instruction sizes in a binary operation.

❏ OFFSET, segment override, and other such information on = or numeric `EQU` assignments are destroyed.

❏ `EQU` assignments are forced to expressions with `PTR` or `:`, which will appear as text.

When used by itself, MASM51 mode provides the following capabilities:

❏ `Instr`, `Catstr`, `Substr`, `Sizestr`, and `\` line continuation can all be used.

❏ `EQU`s to keywords are made TEXT instead of ALIASes.

❏ Leading whitespace is not discarded on `%textmacro` in macro arguments.

When used together, MASM51 and QUIRKS modes provide the following capabilities:

❏ Each capability listed under QUIRKS is available.

❏ Each capability listed under MASM51 is available.

❏ The `@@`, `@F`, and `@B` local labels can be used.

❏ Procedure names are made PUBLIC automatically in extended MODELs.

❏ Near labels in `PROC`s can be redefined in other `PROC`s.

❏ The `::` operator can define symbols accessible outside the current `PROC`.

This versatility is one of the greatest advantages provided by Turbo Assembler. The IDEAL mode's extended syntax is an option that none of its competitors offer.

Like MASM, Turbo Assembler supports the 80386 and 80387 special instructions and provides simplified segment management directives that can greatly ease the chore of setting up the "right" interface conventions for your high-level language. If you use Turbo Pascal, Turbo Assembler's special `.MODEL TPASCAL` directive automatically sets up the correct segment definitions for TP compatibility. No other assembler provides this advantageous option.

However, Turbo Assembler also has some disadvantages. Because it is a single-pass assembler (version 2 can be configured to take as many as 5 passes), it can be confused by undeclared forward references that would be resolved automatically by a multipass assembler. Unlike MASM and OptAsm, Turbo Assembler cannot be configured by the DOS environment;

however, Turbo Assembler can achieve the same purpose by using its special TASM.CFG file, which is described in the on-line help files.

The Files Involved

No matter which one of the assemblers you choose to use, you'll be dealing with at least two different kinds of files, and probably more. The two that are always involved are the input file (the source code), which bears the file extension ASM by default, and the output file (the object code), identified by the default extension OBJ.

Others files that you may work with include MAC, INC, LST, CRF, and XRF files. The MAC and INC files can be included as part of your input data if you use INCLUDE statements in the ASM file. You also can (and usually should) request that the assembler generate the LST listing file for you and that the CRF or XRF files generate a cross-reference of all the symbol names you use.

Let's look at these different kinds of files in more detail.

The ASM Source File

Every assembly language program originally exists as an ASM source file, because these files are what all the assemblers use as their primary input. In addition to the normal ASM file, a program can also have MAC or INC files. But before looking at other files, let's see what makes up the normal ASM file. The following file descriptions apply to all four assemblers introduced in the previous section.

Format for an ASM file is relatively simple. The file must be a pure ASCII "text" file rather than a word processor document, which has embedded control characters that will confuse the assembler. Each line of the file is considered a separate record, and each line is normally divided into four fields.

These four fields contain the label, the operator, the operand(s), and any comments. Any or all of the fields may be blank; if all are blank, the record is ignored.

The label field extends from the front of the line to the first blank space (a space character or a tab). If the line begins with a blank space, the label field is empty. If the label field is not empty, but does not contain a directive, then its content is entered into the symbol table by the assembler and will eventually be translated into an address.

The operator field, which is the next field in the record, begins with the first nonblank character after the label field and extends to the next blank or to the end of the line, whichever comes first. It contains either an assembly language operator, such as `MOV` or `RET`, or a directive.

You may have noticed that *directive* has been mentioned twice, but I still have not explained what it is. A directive, sometimes called a pseudo-operator or just a pseudo for short, is an instruction to the assembler. It can appear in either the label or the operator field of a line (unless it requires a label; in that case it can appear only in the operator field). The assembler responds to a directive by performing some action, such as reserving memory in the case of the `DB` directive or noting the limits of a procedure in the case of `PROC` or `ENDP`. An operator, on the other hand, causes the generation of machine code that will perform a particular operation.

Following the operator field is the operand field, which begins with the first nonblank character and extends to the first semicolon (;) or the end of the line, whichever comes first. This field specifies what the operator or the directive is to operate on. For example, a `MOV` operator has no purpose until you tell it what to move. The line `MOV AX,1234` has no label, but contains the operator `MOV` and the operands `AX,1234`.

The final field is the comment field, which includes everything from the semicolon (if present) to the end of the line. Extended comments can also be created by using the `COMMENT` directive, which takes one character (any nonblank character) as its operand and then ignores all fields of all records until that character occurs again.

With some assemblers, an asterisk as the first character of a record will mark the entire record as a comment. However, this is not true of all assemblers; it's safest, therefore, not to rely on this method and to use the semicolon instead.

The normal assembler ASM file forces the MAC and INC types of files (if used) into it by naming them as operands for the `INCLUDE` directive, which all four assemblers recognize. The MAC extension usually identifies a macro library, which is a method for speeding up coding of repetitive tasks; the INC extension usually denotes any other type of INCLUDE file such as one containing a collection of data frequently needed. Because they become part of the ASM file at assembly time, both types of files must follow the standard ASM file formatting rules.

The OBJ Output File

This file, the most important file created by the assembler (in fact, the assembler *exists* to create this file), is basically a machine language file. But because the linking pass must be performed to resolve external references, these files are not executable. Chapter 9 discusses object files in greater detail.

The LST Listing File

It's your option whether a listing file is created or not; if created, it normally has the file extension LST. This file is the assembler's "report of operations" and contains both the source statements and the machine language instructions into which they translate. A LST file may also contain other information, such as a symbol table or, in some cases, cross-reference data.

This file and listing can be a useful tool. With it you can generate the hard copy you need to efficiently debug a program, and the listing is great for hard-copy archiving.

Here's a typical listing file output, generated by MASM from the sample file presented later in this chapter:

```
Microsoft (R) Macro Assembler Version 5.10                  12/29/89 17:12:0
                                                            Page     1-1


     1                        Page 60,132
     2                        ; **********************************************************
     3                        ; *                                                        *
     4                        ; * Date:      10/24/89                                    *
     5                        ; * File:      SUMS.ASM                                     *
     6                        ; *                                                        *
     7                        ; * Purpose:  Given an integer number X, find the sum of   *
     8                        ; *      X + (X-1) + (X-2) + (X-3) + (X-4) ... + 2 + 1      *
     9                        ; *      Designed to be called from Microsoft C.           *
    10                        ; *                                                        *
    11                        ; * Format:    SUMS(X)                                     *
    12                        ; *                                                        *
    13                        ; **********************************************************
```

```
14
15                                      PUBLIC     _SUMS
16
17                                      NAME SUMS
18 0000                   _TEXT         SEGMENT BYTE PUBLIC 'CODE'
19                                      ASSUME     CS:_TEXT
20
21 = 0004                 NUM_ADR       EQU  4
22
23 0000                   _SUMS         PROC NEAR
24 0000   55                            PUSH BP
25 0001   8B EC                         MOV  BP,SP
26
27 0003   B8 0000                       MOV  AX,0            ;Initialize to zero
28 0006   8B 5E 04                      MOV  BX,[BP]+NUM_ADR ;Get address of value
29 0009   8B 0F                         MOV  CX,[BX]         ;Get actual value
30 000B   E3 0C                         JCXZ S3             ;Num=0, no need to do
31 000D   13 C1           S1:           ADC  AX,CX           ;Add row value
32 000F   72 05                         JC   S2             ;Quit if ax overflowed
33 0011   E2 FA                         LOOP S1             ;Repeat process
34 0013   EB 04 90                      JMP  S3             ;Successful completion
35 0016   B8 0000         S2:           MOV  AX,0            ;Force a zero
36 0019   89 07           S3:           MOV  [BX],AX         ;Place back in value
37
38 001B   5D                            POP  BP
39 001C   C3                            RET
40 001D                   _SUMS         ENDP
41
42 001D                   _TEXT         ENDS
43                                      END
```

Microsoft (R) Macro Assembler Version 5.10   12/29/89 17:12:0
                                                      Symbols-1

Segments and Groups:

              N a m e   Length   Align   Combine   Class

_TEXT . . . . 001D   BYTE   PUBLIC   'CODE'

```
Symbols:

                    N a m e           Type      Value   Attr

NUM_ADR . . . . . . . . . . .         NUMBER    0004

S1 . . . . . . . . . . . . . .        L NEAR    000D    _TEXT
S2 . . . . . . . . . . . . . .        L NEAR    0016    _TEXT
S3 . . . . . . . . . . . . . .        L NEAR    0019    _TEXT

@CPU . . . . . . . . . . . .          TEXT   0101h
@FILENAME . . . . . . . . . .         TEXT   sums
@VERSION . . . . . . . . . . .        TEXT   510
_SUMS . . . . . . . . . . . . .       N PROC    0000 _TEXT Global     Length = 001D


     43 Source  Lines
     43 Total   Lines
     16 Symbols


   47336 + 323443 Bytes symbol space free

        0 Warning Errors
        0 Severe  Errors
```

The LST files created by OptAsm and by Turbo Assembler are similar to MASM's. The following excerpts from each show the major differences. First, the file produced by OptAsm is as follows:

```
SLR Systems SuperFast Optimizing Assembler              Fri, 29 Dec 89 17:13:18
                                                        OPTASM 1.61 Page   1-1


1                      ; ************************************************************
2                      ; *                                                        *
3                      ; * Date:     10/24/89                                     *
4                      ; * File:     SUMS.ASM                                     *
5                      ; *                                                        *
6                      ; * Purpose:  Given an integer number X, find the sum of   *
7                      ; *      X + (X-1) + (X-2) + (X-3) + (X-4) ... + 2 + 1      *
8                      ; *      Designed to be called from Microsoft C.           *
9                      ; *                                                        *
10                     ; * Format:   SUMS(X)                                      *
11                     ; *                                                        *
12                     ; ************************************************************
```

```
13
14                                          PUBLIC      _SUMS
15
16      0000                        _TEXT   SEGMENT BYTE PUBLIC 'CODE'
17                                          ASSUME      CS:_TEXT
18
19      = 0004                       NUM_ADR EQU  4
20
21      0000                         _SUMS   PROC NEAR
22      0000    55                           PUSH BP
23      0001    8B EC                        MOV  BP,SP
24
25      0003    B8 0000                      MOV  AX,0            ;Initialize to zero
26      0006    8B 5E 04                     MOV  BX,[BP]+NUM_ADR ;Get address of value
27      0009    8B 0F                        MOV  CX,[BX]         ;Get actual value
28      000B    E3 0B   (0018)               JCXZ S3             ;Num=0, no need to do
29      000D    13 C1               S1:      ADC  AX,CX          ;Add row value
30      000F    72 04   (0015)               JC   S2             ;Quit if ax overflowed
31      0011    E2 FA   (000D)               LOOP S1             ;Repeat process
32      0013    EB 03   (0018)               JMP  S3             ;Successful completion
33      0015    B8 0000             S2:      MOV  AX,0           ;Force a zero
34      0018    89 07               S3:      MOV  [BX],AX        ;Place back in value
35
36      001A    5D                           POP  BP
37      001B    C3                           RET
38                                  _SUMS    ENDP
39
40      001C                        _TEXT    ENDS
41                                           END
```

Groups and/or Segments:

N a m e	Size	Align	Combine	Class
$$SYMBOLS	0018	Para	None	DEBSYM
$$TYPES	000C	Para	None	DEBTYP
_TEXT	001C	Byte	Public	CODE

Other Symbols:

N a m e	Type	Value	Segment	Etc.
@CPU	Text	0101H		
@CURSEG	Text	$$TYPES		
@WORDSIZE	Text	2		
NUM_ADR	Abs	0004		
S1	Near	000D	_TEXT	
S2	Near	0015	_TEXT	
S3	Near	0018	_TEXT	
_SUMS	Near	0000	_TEXT	Public Proc Len=001C

SLR Systems SuperFast Optimizing Assembler

Fri, 29 Dec 89 17:13:19
OPTASM 1.61 Page XRF-1

Cross Reference:

N a m e	Referenced (# means Defined)			
CODE	16			
NUM_ADR	19#	26		
S1	29#	31		
S2	30	33#		
S3	28	32	34#	
_SUMS	14	21#	21#	38
_TEXT	16#	17	40	

    0 Error(s).   0 Warning(s).
   17 Symbols.   43 Lines.   3909 LPM.

The following is the listing file from Turbo Assembler:

Turbo Assembler   Version 2.0   02/15/90 18:26:51   Page 1
SUMS.ASM

```
 1                              ;**********************************************************
 2                              ; *                                                      *
 3                              ; *  Date:      10/24/89                                 *
 4                              ; *  File:      SUMS.ASM                                 *
 5                              ; *                                                      *
 6                              ; *  Purpose:   Given an integer number X, find the sum of  *
 7                              ; *             X + (X-1) + (X-2) + (X-3) + (X-4) ... + 2 + 1*
 8                              ; *             Designed to be called from Microsoft C.  *
 9                              ; *                                                      *
10                              ; *  Format:    SUMS(X)                                  *
11                              ; *                                                      *
12                              ;**********************************************************
13
14                                      PUBLIC  _SUMS
15
16                                      NAME    SUMS
17 0000                         _TEXT   SEGMENT BYTE PUBLIC 'CODE'
18                                      ASSUME  CS:_TEXT
19
20      = 0004                  NUM_ADR EQU     4
21
22 0000                         _SUMS   PROC    NEAR
23 0000  55                             PUSH    BP
24 0001  8B EC                          MOV     BP,SP
25
26 0003  B8 0000                        MOV     AX,0              ;Initialize to zero
27 0006  8B 5E 04                       MOV     BX,[BP]+NUM_ADR   ;Get address of value
28 0009  8B 0F                          MOV     CX,[BX]           ;Get actual value
29 000B  E3 0C                          JCXZ    S3                ;Num=0, no need to do
30 000D  13 C1              S1:         ADC     AX,CX             ;Add row value
31 000F  72 05                          JC      S2                ;Quit if ax overflowed
32 0011  E2 FA                          LOOP    S1                ;Repeat process
33 0013  EB 04 90                       JMP     S3                ;Successful completion
34 0016  B8 0000            S2:         MOV     AX,0              ;Force a zero
35 0019  89 07             S3:          MOV     [BX],AX           ;Place back in value
36
37 001B  5D                             POP     BP
38 001C  C3                             RET
```

```
39 001D                    _SUMS          ENDP
40
41 001D                    _TEXT          ENDS
42                                        END
```

Turbo Assembler Version 2.0   02/15/90 18:26:51   Page 2
Symbol Table

Symbol Name	Type	Value	Cref defined at #
??DATE	Text	"02/15/90"	
??FILENAME	Text	"SUMS "	
??TIME	Text	"18:26:50"	
??VERSION	Number	0200	
@CPU	Text	0101H	
@CURSEG	Text	_TEXT	#17
@FILENAME	Text	SUMS	
@WORDSIZE	Text	2	#17
NUM_ADR	Number	0004	#20 27
S1	Near	_TEXT:000D	#30 32
S2	Near	_TEXT:0016	31 #34
S3	Near	_TEXT:0019	29 33 #35
_SUMS (_SUMS)	Near	_TEXT:0000	14 #22

Groups & Segments	Bit Size Align	Combine Class	Cref defined at #
_TEXT	16 001D Byte	Public CODE	#17 18

Notice that the listing file produced by MASM included the list-control directive PAGE as its first line, but the other two files did not. Note also that both MASM and Turbo Assembler included line numbers on the listing, but OptAsm omitted the line numbers.

Aside from these rather small differences, the major variations in the listings produced by the three assemblers are in the symbol-table and error reports. I've presented these pages complete so that you can compare them. You can suppress the information (in this case, one page) by assembling the file with the /N option, no matter which assembler you use.

Not all printers print the same number of characters per line. These listing files were all formatted for 60-line pages, with 132 characters per line. The PAGE directive at the top of the ASM file controls this format. If your printer handles only 80 characters per line, you easily can change the line to

    PAGE 60,80

for a LST file formatted for 80 characters per line. How you change the line is up to you.

Other Files

In addition to the major files already listed, another file may optionally be created by the assembler. This other file is not as standardized as those already described. MASM calls it a CRF file, Turbo Assembler uses the extension XRF, and OptAsm doesn't create it at all.

No matter what the file is called or where it appears, its purpose is to enable you to generate a cross-reference that shows where each symbol in your program is defined and where each symbol is referenced in the program.

The cross-reference files created by MASM (CRF) and Turbo Assembler (XRF) contain information that other programs (supplied with the assembler) use to create the human-readable, cross-reference listing of symbols used in the source file. With OptAsm, when you specify that a cross-reference is to be created, the final listing is simply added to the end of the LST file.

By itself, a CRF or XRF file has little value. To create the actual cross-reference file, you must also run the external programs. Only the use of MASM's CREF is described in full detail here, but the TCREF utility for Turbo Assembler operates in much the same way.

CREF, like MASM, can be used interactively or on a single command line. Unlike MASM, which requires four responses, CREF requires only two: the name of the CRF file and the name of the file that CREF is to create. Thus, the entire interactive dialog for CREF is as follows:

```
C>CREF

Microsoft (R) Macro Assembler Version 5.10
Copyright (C) Microsoft Corp 1981, 1988.  All rights reserved.

Cross [.CRF]: SUMS
Listing [sums.REF]:

   49488 + 323517 Bytes symbol space free

      0 Warning Errors
      0 Severe  Errors
```

Like the MASM process, this CREF process can be shortened. At the DOS prompt, simply enter the following:

```
CREF SUMS,;
```

Either of these methods creates a file, called SUMS.REF, that contains a formatted cross-reference of the symbols in SUMS.ASM. The contents of SUMS.REF follow:

```
Microsoft Cross-Reference  Version 5.10        Fri Dec 29 17:12:03 1989


    Symbol Cross-Reference     (# definition, + modification) Cref-1

@CPU . . . . . . . . . . . . .     1#
@VERSION . . . . . . . . . . .     1#

CODE . . . . . . . . . . . . .    18

NUM_ADR. . . . . . . . . . . .    21#    28

S1 . . . . . . . . . . . . . .    31#    33
S2 . . . . . . . . . . . . . .    32     35#
S3 . . . . . . . . . . . . . .    30     34     36#

_SUMS. . . . . . . . . . . . .    15     23#    40
_TEXT. . . . . . . . . . . . .    18#    19     42


   9 Symbols
```

This listing shows each symbol with line numbers indicating where the symbol is referenced; these line numbers are the same as those shown in the LST example. If a list file is not generated, all the line numbers are number 1. A pound sign (#) appended to the line number means that the symbol was defined on that line.

Like CREF, the TCREF program for Turbo Assembler XRF files generates a REF file by default. Here's what it did for SUMS.XRF:

```
Turbo CREF  Version 1.01        02/15/90 18:27:05              Page 1


Global Symbol Name                       Cref  defined at #

_SUMS                                    # SUMS.ASM:  16  #24




Turbo CREF  Version 1.01        02/15/90 18:27:05              Page 2


Module SUMS.ASM Symbol Name              Cref  defined at #

@CURSEG                                  # SUMS.ASM:  #19
@WORDSIZE                                # SUMS.ASM:  #19
NUM_ADR                                  # SUMS.ASM:  #22  29
S1                                       # SUMS.ASM:  #32  34
S2                                       # SUMS.ASM:  33  #36
S3                                       # SUMS.ASM:  31  35  #37
_SUMS                                    # SUMS.ASM:  16  #24
_TEXT                                    # SUMS.ASM:  #19  20
```

As in the CREF-generated report, the numbers refer to line numbers in the LST file. The major difference (other than the fact that Turbo Assembler generates more predefined symbols than MASM does) is that rather than processing each file separately, the TCREF program can analyze an entire group of XRF files, so you can document a system of programs. To tell which file is which when multiple XRF files are used, TCREF adds the module name in several places.

One of the valuable ways that a cross-reference file can help make your assembly language coding more efficient is that you may be able to delete a symbol that has only one reference, the line where it is defined. Such a symbol has no meaning and just clutters the program; any symbol *used* will appear at least twice.

A Sample Program

To proceed through this chapter, you need a sample subroutine to assemble. This subroutine will be neither large nor complex, nor will it exemplify the best reasons for using assembly language. Although writing this routine in C would be easier than writing it in assembly language, I will use it to demonstrate how to assemble (and later link and debug) a subroutine.

Let's assume that you need to determine the total number of blocks in a pyramid where each ascending row contains one less block than the row beneath it, and the top row is only one block (see fig. 8.1).

Fig. 8.1. *A sample pyramid.*

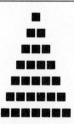

The bottom row contains 15 blocks, the next row contains 14, and so on, with only one block in the top row. Your job is to calculate the total number of blocks needed, given only the number of blocks in the bottom row. You'll use the sample program to do the job.

The program (SUMS.ASM) is designed to be called from C. The program, when passed a pointer to a 16-bit integer, calculates and returns the result in the same integer variable. The assembly language subroutine listing is as follows:

```
  Page 60,132
; *****************************************************************
; *                                                               *
; * Date:     10/24/89                                            *
; * File:     SUMS.ASM                                            *
; *                                                               *
; * Purpose:  Given an integer number X, find the sum of          *
; *       X + (X-1) + (X-2) + (X-3) + (X-4) ... + 2 + 1            *
; *       Designed to be called from Microsoft C.                 *
; *                                                               *
; * Format:   SUMS(X)                                             *
; *                                                               *
; *****************************************************************

          PUBLIC    _SUMS

          NAME SUMS
_TEXT     SEGMENT BYTE PUBLIC 'CODE'
          ASSUME    CS:_TEXT

NUM_ADR   EQU 4

_SUMS     PROC NEAR
          PUSH BP
          MOV  BP,SP

          MOV  AX,0                ;Initialize to zero
          MOV  BX,[BP]+NUM_ADR     ;Get address of value
          MOV  CX,[BX]             ;Get actual value
          JCXZ S3                  ;Num=0, no need to do
S1:       ADC  AX,CX               ;Add row value
          JC   S2                  ;Quit if ax overflowed
          LOOP S1                  ;Repeat process
          JMP  S3                  ;Successful completion
S2:       MOV  AX,0                ;Force a zero
S3:       MOV  [BX],AX             ;Place back in value

          POP  BP
          RET
_SUMS     ENDP

_TEXT     ENDS
          END
```

If the entered number results in a sum that is greater than 65,535 (the largest unsigned integer number that can be held in 16 bits), the program sets the result to 0.

To prepare for the balance of this chapter (and for Chapters 9, 10, 11, and 12), enter this subroutine as it is shown here. The controlling C program is listed in Chapter 9.

Using an Assembler

Once you have created your ASM file and checked it for typing errors, it's time to assemble the program. Because the exact commands you use to do this depend on the type of assembler you use, I will describe the assembly process separately for MASM, OptAsm, and Turbo Assembler. Therefore, you'll find that only a third (at most) of the rest of this section applies specifically to you.

Using MASM Interactively

Make sure that SUMS.ASM (the subroutine file) and MASM.EXE are in your current disk directory. If MASM.EXE is not in your current directory, it should at least be available through your current search path.

At the DOS prompt, enter

MASM

to start the assembly process. You will see a notice and prompt similar to the following:

```
Microsoft (R) Macro Assembler Version 5.10
Copyright (C) Microsoft Corp 1981, 1988.  All rights reserved.
Source filename [.ASM]: _
```

The assembler is waiting for you to indicate which file you want to assemble. (The default answer, which is shown in brackets, is accepted if you simply press the Enter key.) Enter the root name of the file to assemble, SUMS. The extension ASM is assumed. When you make this entry, the following should appear on the screen:

```
Source filename [.ASM]: SUMS
Object filename [SUMS.OBJ]: _
```

Notice that you are now prompted for the name of the OBJ file to create. Because you want to use the default suggestion of `SUMS.OBJ`, simply press the Enter key. The following prompt is displayed:

```
Object filename [SUMS.OBJ]:
Source listing  [NUL.LST]: _
```

A `Source listing` is an optional file created by the assembler as it assembles the ASM file. Notice that the default for the `Source listing` file, discussed earlier in this chapter, is `NUL.LST`. If you press Enter, no file (NUL) will be created. To create a source listing file called SUMS.LST, type **SUMS**. You will see the following prompt:

```
Source listing  [NUL.LST]: SUMS
Cross-reference [NUL.CRF]: _
```

This cross-reference file is another optional file explained elsewhere in this chapter. To indicate that you want to create the file SUMS.CRF, enter **SUMS** here.

Now that you have answered MASM's four questions, your disk drive will activate for a short time. Then you will see a message similar to the following:

```
50004 + 323001 Bytes symbol space free
```

```
  0 Warning Errors
  0 Severe  Errors
```

which indicates that the assembly process is complete. The important information here is that no errors occurred. Had there been errors, an error message indicating the type of error and the line number at which the error occurred would have appeared on the screen during assembly. The same errors also would be noted in the listing file (SUMS.LST). The number of total errors would be reflected in the final tally displayed on the screen.

If you receive any error messages, you must correct the errors before continuing. Check your source file (SUMS.ASM) against the listing file (SUMS.LST), correct any errors, and try the assembly process again. When you have corrected all the errors, you can proceed with this chapter.

Using the MASM Command Line

Instead of using MASM interactively, you can use it in another way. You can enter, directly from the MASM command line, any or all of the responses to individual prompts. For instance, entering (from DOS)

MASM SUMS,,SUMS,SUMS;

will create the same files created by the interactive method described in the preceding section.

You'll remember that MASM asks four questions. In the preceding examples, the answers to those questions are parameters to the MASM command, with commas separating the parameters and a semicolon terminating the line.

Notice the two consecutive commas, which indicate blank parameters. In this case, MASM will use the first parameter (SUMS) as the implied parameter.

To enter parameters directly from the MASM command line, use the following syntax:

```
MASM asm,obj,lst,crf
```

In this syntax, `MASM` is the command; `asm`, `obj`, `lst`, and `crf` are the file types that each parameter indicates. These file types were discussed in the preceding section.

To indicate that you do not want a particular type of file, simply use NUL as the parameter for that file type. For instance, the following commands both instruct MASM to create an OBJ file, but no LST or CRF file:

```
MASM SUMS,,NUL,NUL;
MASM SUMS;
```

Although the second command line is much shorter than the first, both have the same effect. The semicolon instructs MASM to begin processing without expecting additional parameters.

Using OptAsm Interactively

Make sure that SUMS.ASM (the subroutine file) and OPTASM.EXE are in your current disk directory. If OPTASM.EXE is not in your current directory, it should at least be available through your current search path.

At the DOS prompt, enter

OPTASM

to start the assembly process. You will see a notice and prompt similar to the following:

```
OPTASM Copyright (C) SLR Systems 1988-89 Release 1.61
All rights reserved.

Source File (C:\NUL.ASM):_
```

Here the assembler is prompting you to indicate which file you want to assemble. (The default answer, which is shown in parentheses, is accepted if you simply press the Enter key.) Enter **SUMS**, the root name of the file to assemble. The extension ASM is assumed. When you make this entry, the following should appear on the screen:

```
Source File (C:\NUL.ASM):SUMS
Object File (C:\SUMS.OBJ):_
```

Notice that you are now prompted for the name of the OBJ file to create. Because you want to use the default suggestion of SUMS.OBJ, simply press the Enter key. The following prompt is displayed:

```
Object File (C:\SUMS.OBJ):
Listing File(C:\NUL.LST):_
```

A Listing File is an optional file created by the assembler as it assembles the ASM file. Notice that the default for the Listing File, discussed later in this chapter, is NUL.LST. If you press Enter, no file (NUL) will be created. To create a listing file called SUMS.LST, type **SUMS**. You will see the following:

```
Listing File(C:\NUL.LST):SUMS
```

Now that you have answered OptAsm's questions, your disk drive will activate for a short time. Then you will see a message similar to the following:

```
0 Error(s).    0 Warning(s).
13 Symbols.    43 Lines.    11727 LPM.
```

which indicates that the assembly process is complete. The important information here is that no errors occurred. Had there been errors, an error message indicating the type of error and the line number at which the error occurred would have appeared on the screen during assembly.

The same errors also would be noted in the listing file (SUMS.LST). The number of total errors would be reflected in the final tally displayed on the screen.

If you receive any error messages, you must correct the errors before continuing. Check your source file (SUMS.ASM) against the listing file (SUMS.LST), correct any errors, and try the assembly process again. When you have corrected all the errors, you can proceed with this chapter.

Using the OptAsm Command Line

Instead of using OptAsm interactively, you can enter directly from the OptAsm command line any or all of the responses to individual prompts. For instance, entering (from DOS)

OPTASM SUMS,,SUMS;

will create the same files created by the interactive method described in the preceding section.

You'll remember that OptAsm asks three questions. In the preceding examples, the answers to those questions are parameters to the OptAsm command, with commas separating the parameters and a semicolon terminating the line.

Notice the two consecutive commas, which indicate blank parameters. In this case, OptAsm will use the first parameter (SUMS) as the implied parameter.

To enter parameters directly from the command line, use the following syntax:

```
OPTASM asm,obj,lst
```

In this syntax, `OPTASM` is the command; `asm`, `obj`, and `lst` are the file types that each parameter indicates. These file types were discussed in the preceding section.

To indicate that you do not want a particular type of file, simply use NUL as the parameter for that file type. For instance, the following commands both instruct OptAsm to create an OBJ file but no LST file:

```
OPTASM SUMS,,NUL;
OPTASM SUMS;
```

Although the second command line is much shorter than the first, both have the same effect. The semicolon instructs OptAsm to begin processing without expecting additional parameters.

Using Turbo Assembler

Unlike MASM and OptAsm, Turbo Assembler cannot be used interactively. You must enter all of the parameters directly from the command line. Use the following syntax:

```
TASM asm,obj,lst,crf
```

In this syntax, TASM is the command; asm, obj, lst, and crf are the file types that each parameter indicates. These file types were discussed in the preceding section. Thus

```
TASM SUMS,,SUMS,SUMS
```

creates all the files (OBJ, LST, and XRF).

Notice the two consecutive commas, which indicate blank parameters. In this case, Turbo Assembler uses the first parameter (SUMS) as the implied parameter for the OBJ parameter, or NUL for the others. To indicate that you do not want a particular type of file, simply use NUL as the parameter for that file type. For instance, the following commands both instruct Turbo Assembler to create an OBJ file but no LST or CRF file:

```
TASM SUMS,,NUL,NUL
TASM SUMS
```

Although the second command line is much shorter than the first, both have the same effect. Note that, unlike MASM and OptAsm, Turbo Assembler does not require a semicolon to indicate that all input is complete.

Assembler Options

All three assemblers accept several parameters (referred to as *options* or *switches* in the documentation) that alter how the program functions. You can enter these options directly from the command line or when you are running interactively.

The options, the assemblers to which they apply, and their meanings are listed alphabetically in table 8.3. Note that, like all input given on the DOS command line, the options are not case sensitive; they can appear in either upper- or lowercase.

Table 8.3. *Assembler options.*

Option	MASM 5.1	OptAsm 1.6	TASM 2.0	Meaning
/A	X	X	X	Order segments in alphabetic sequence
/Bblocks	X		X	Set buffer size (accepted by TASM, but ignored)
/C	X	X	X	Create a cross-reference file
/D	X			Create a pass 1 listing
/Dx	X	X	X	Define symbol x
/E	X	X	X	Emulate floating-point instructions
/G		X		Make all symbols GLOBAL
/H	X	X	X	Display list of valid options
/Ipath	X	X	X	Set INCLUDE file path
/Jname			X	Jam directive into effect
/KHsize			X	Set hash table capacity
/KSsize			X	Set string space capacity
/L	X	X	X	Create a listing file
/LA	X	X	X	Generate an expanded listing file
/M		X	X	Emulate MASM actions (OptAsm) Set number of passes (TASM 2.0)
ML	X	X	X	Make case of names significant
/MU	X	X	X	Make all names uppercase
/MVsize			X	Set maximum valid length for symbols
/MX	X	X	X	Make case of PUBLIC/EXTERNAL significant

Option	MASM 5.1	OptAsm 1.6	TASM 2.0	Meaning
/N	X	X	X	Exclude tables from listing file
/O			X	Generate overlay code
/P	X		X	Check purity of 286/386 code
/Q			X	Suppress OBJ records not needed for linking
/R		X	X	Create code for 8087/80287 (in MASM 4.x, not in 5.x)
/S	X	X	X	Order segments by occurrence in source code
/T	X	X	X	Suppress assembly completion messages
/V	X	X	X	Show extra assembly statistics
/W		X	X	Suppress warning messages (OptAsm); enable all warnings (TASM 2.0)
/W0	X		X	Suppress warning messages
/W1	X		X	Set warning level to Serious (MASM) or ON (TASM)
/W2	X		X	Set warning level to Advisory (MASM) or ON (TASM)
/W-xxx			X	Disable warning class xxx
/W+xxx			X	Enable warning class xxx
/X	X	X	X	List false conditional statements
/Z	X	X	X	Display error lines
/ZD	X	X	X	Add only line numbers to OBJ file
/ZI	X	X	X	Add full debugging data to OBJ file
/ZT		X		Add Turbo C line data to OBJ file

You can include assembler options at any point in the command or interactive format. Regardless of where you include them, the options affect all relevant files. The options usually are included at the end of the command line or at the end of your response to the last prompt.

You must include a delimiter before the option letter. For MASM, this delimiter can be either a slash (/), as shown in table 8.3, or a hyphen (-). MASM does not differentiate between the two symbols. For the other assemblers, use only the slash.

Some of the assembler options (/S, /MU, /C, and /L) are superficial; they are included only for compatibility with earlier versions of MASM or with other operating systems such as XENIX. Other options control the way the OBJ file is generated. Still others control interaction with the programmer. Let's look at each of the listed options.

Change from Alphabetic Segment Order (/A)

This option controls the way the assembler writes segments into the object (OBJ) file. Ordinarily, the assembler writes segments in the order in which they occur in the source file. But some assemblers write segments to the OBJ file in alphabetic order regardless of how they occur in the source file. Because these OBJ files are in alphabetic order, programs designed using such assemblers may not link and execute properly when assembled using one of the three assemblers described here. To compensate, use the /A option to force the assembler to write segments in alphabetic sequence.

Set Buffer Size (/B*blocks*)

The size of the *buffer* (the work area MASM uses in memory) was normally 32K in older versions of MASM. Depending on the amount of free RAM available on your computer, you can set the buffer size to any amount between 1K and 63K using this option. Although /B*blocks* was quietly dropped from the manual in the most recent versions of MASM, the option continues to be accepted. It is provided in Turbo Assembler only for compatibility with the older MASM versions.

If used, *blocks* is the number of 1K blocks to set aside for the buffer area. Setting aside a buffer area larger than the source file accelerates the assembly process because then all operations can occur in memory.

Create a Cross-Reference File (/C)

This option controls the creation of a cross-reference (CRF or XRF) file, described earlier in this chapter. When invoked, /C causes creation of a file with the same root name as the source file and an extension of CRF (for MASM) or XRF (for Turbo Assembler). This option, which is included mainly for compatibility with XENIX, supersedes the answer you give to the cross-reference prompt or in the command line's CRF position.

With OptAsm, this option causes the cross-reference information to be collected, processed, and added to the end of the listing file rather than written to a separate file for processing by an external program. If no listing file has been specified, this option generates one containing only the cross-reference information.

Create Pass 1 Listing (/D)

This option, available only in MASM, instructs the assembler to generate a pass 1 listing in the LST file. If you have not specified a LST file, this option simply lists pass 1 errors to the screen.

Because MASM, as a *two-pass assembler*, does two source code iterations to produce the finished object code, a pass 1 listing is beneficial if you need help locating phase errors. Phase errors are generated if MASM makes assumptions during the first pass that don't hold true in the second.

Define Symbol *x* (/D*x*)

Using the /D*x* option, you can define an assembler symbol where *x* is the symbol being defined. Because the symbol, which can be any valid assembly language symbol, is considered a null string, this option is similar to defining the symbol with an EQU directive in the source file. Older versions of MASM always defined the symbol with a value of 0; newer versions and all versions of the other assemblers permit the syntax /Dx=v where v can be any text string or integer value. This will define symbol x with value v.

Conditional assembly statements (IFDEF and IFNDEF) can use the symbol defined by this option to control how an assembly occurs. Conditional assembly statements and procedures are discussed later in this chapter.

Emulate Floating-Point Instructions (/E)

The /E option, which is the opposite of the /R option, directs the assembler to emulate the floating-point capabilities of the 8087 or 80287 numeric coprocessors. The assembler does not contain the actual emulation routines. Those routines are included when the object code is linked and a math-emulation library is used. Your high-level language (Microsoft C, for example) may include a library of this type because such libraries generally come from a third-party source.

When you use the /E option, the code that results can be executed on any compatible computer regardless of whether you have an 8087 or 80287 coprocessor.

Make All Symbols GLOBAL (/G)

This option, available only with OptAsm, tells the assembler to pass all symbols that specify memory addresses into the OBJ file as PUBLIC symbols. Its use simplifies debugging with such programs as CodeView, Turbo Debugger, or OptDebug, all of which can identify a PUBLIC symbol by name on their displays. With the other assemblers, all symbols you want treated as PUBLIC must be explicitly declared as PUBLIC.

Display List of Valid Options (/H)

All three assemblers provide concise help displays that show the command syntax and display their options list. Calling the assembler with the /H option causes this display to be shown. With Turbo Assembler, the same thing happens when you just type TASM and press Enter.

Set INCLUDE File Path (/I*path*)

This option lets you specify where the assembler should look for files to be included in the source file. You can use the option to specify, one at a time, as many as 10 different paths.

If the INCLUDE directive in the source file contains a path specification, that explicit path overrides any paths set by the /I option. If the INCLUDE directive consists of only a file name, the /I option paths will be searched in the order they are invoked.

Jam Directive into Effect (/J*name*)

This option, available only to Turbo Assembler, puts any desired Turbo Assembler directive into effect from the command line. Its major use is to establish processing modes. For instance, /JMASM is to Turbo Assembler the same as /M is to OptAsm.

Set Hash Table Capacity (/KH*size*)

This option, available only to Turbo Assembler, sets the maximum number of symbols your program can use. Without it, Turbo Assembler is limited to 8,192 different symbols; with it, you can specify any *size* you like up to 32,768. It can also reduce the space needed if you have trouble fitting everything into your available RAM.

Set String Space Capacity (/KS*size*)

This option, available only to Turbo Assembler, sets the maximum size in kilobytes that Turbo Assembler can use for string storage. The default setting is made automatically; this option is unnecessary unless you get an Out of string space message. The maximum value for *size* is 255.

Create a Listing File (/L)

This option controls creation of an assembly listing (LST) file. When invoked, the /L option creates a file with the same root name as the source file and a LST extension. (The assembly listing file is described earlier in this chapter.)

Included in MASM primarily for compatibility with XENIX and in the other assemblers for MASM compatibility, /L supersedes the answer you give to the assembly listing prompt or place in the command line's LST position.

Create an Expanded Listing File (/LA)

This option was added to MASM at version 5.1 and is in all versions of the other assemblers. It does the same as the /L option but also includes in the listing file all code generated by the simplified segment directives and high-level-language support features such as .MODEL. Without this option, code generated by such features will not appear in the listing.

Emulate MASM Actions (/M)

This option, available only in OptAsm, causes OptAsm to emulate MASM as completely as possible. The emulation may be of MASM 3.x, MASM 4.x, or MASM 5.x depending on how OptAsm's configuration was set up when you installed it.

Make Case of Names Significant (/ML)

Some programmers like to keep both upper- and lowercase in their code, and some high-level language compilers demand or expect this difference. Ordinarily, the assembler converts all symbol, variable, and label names to uppercase. This option ensures that no such conversion occurs.

Make All Names Uppercase (/MU)

The /MU option, which converts all symbol, variable, and label names to uppercase letters, is the default option. This option is included for compatibility with other assemblers and operating systems.

Make Case of PUBLIC/EXTERNAL Names Significant (/MX)

This option is similar to /ML but affects only PUBLIC and EXTERNAL names. The /MX option ensures that, instead of being converted to uppercase, any symbol, variable, or label name defined as EXTERNAL or declared PUBLIC will remain in the case it was entered.

Exclude Tables from the Listing File (/N)

Normally, the assembler includes, at the end of an assembly listing (LST) file, several tables that recap the source file's structure. You can use /N to exclude those tables without changing the rest of the listing. Using /N causes the assembler to function slightly faster.

Check Purity of 286/386 Code (/P)

MASM and Turbo Assembler can create protected-mode coding for the Intel 80286 microprocessor if the source file contains the **.286p** directive, and for the 80386 if the proper directive is present. The /P option for these assemblers specifies that the assembler should check whether the source code is "pure" (that it contains no data moved in the code segment with a CS: override). If you use this option, an additional check is done and an additional error code may be generated.

Generate Numeric Coprocessor Code (/R)

Using this option causes the assembler to generate coding that is compatible with either the 8087 or the 80287 numeric coprocessor. This generation of code affects only floating-point operations. Code created with the /R option can run only on computers that use one of these chips. The option was available in MASM 4.x but was dropped from the documentation at version 5.0 although it remains in the manual's index, and the program continues to accept it without error.

Order Segments by Occurrence in Source Code (/S)

This option, which is the opposite of /A, is the default option. It specifies that segments be written in the order they occur in the source code. This option is included for compatibility with other assemblers and operating systems.

Suppress Assembly Completion Messages (/T)

The /T (for *terse*) option suppresses all assembler messages if the assembly is successful. If at least one error occurs, the normal assembler copyright and version information will be displayed before the error is listed.

Show Extra Assembly Statistics (/V)

This option turns on the assembler's *verbose* mode, which causes additional statistics to be generated when the file is assembled. The additional information generated by the /V option varies from one assembler to another.

Control Warning Messages (/W)

All three assemblers give you control over the number and types of warning messages you receive when problems are found during assembly, and all three use variations of the /W option to do so. However, the details of this option are different for each assembler.

MASM uses /W0, /W1, or /W2 to provide the control. The /W0 option suppresses all warning messages, the /W1 option suppresses "advisory" messages but displays "serious" messages, and the /W2 option displays all messages.

OptAsm uses only the bare /W switch. Although warning and error messages are normally displayed by default, using this switch suppresses them. The levels of messages to be displayed are controlled by the configuration you establish when installing OptAsm.

Turbo Assembler uses the /W0, /W1, and /W2 options. Both /W1 and /W2 enable message display, but, as in MASM, /W0 suppresses all messages. Turbo Assembler also classifies messages into groups and uses /W- and /W+, followed by the group code, to individually disable (-) or enable (+) each group. By default, all "serious" and most "advisory" warnings are enabled.

List False Conditional Statements (/X)

If you request a listing file, and your source file includes conditional assembly directives, this option controls the listing of the code that would not normally be included in the LST file. If code were omitted from the OBJ file because the conditional assembly directives controlling that code's inclusion were FALSE, that code would normally also be excluded from the assembly listing file. However, using the /X option would enable such source code lines to be included in the listing even though no machine language code is generated.

Display Error Lines (/Z)

The assembler ordinarily indicates compilation errors by displaying an error message and the line number at which the error(s) occurred. To also display the source-code line that contains the error, use the /Z option.

Add Only Line Numbers to OBJ File (/ZD)

The /ZD option causes the assembler to write to the OBJ file data that relates each machine instruction to the line number of the ASM file that generated it. CodeView, OptDebug, Turbo Debugger, and other utilities capable of source-level debugging need this information to locate lines in the source file that correspond to the code being executed.

Add Full Debugging Data to OBJ File (/ZI)

Like /ZD, the /ZI option causes line number information to be written to the OBJ file, but /ZI also causes symbolic data about all labels and variable names to be included in the OBJ file. This provides full operation of the symbolic debuggers, including evaluation of values at runtime and replacement with new values.

Add Turbo C Line Data to OBJ File (/ZT)

The /ZT option causes OptAsm to parse certain comment lines produced by the Turbo C compiler for line number information. This line number information relates the machine instructions back to the C source file rather than to the intermediate ASM file. With this option, symbolic debuggers can retrieve the C source rather than using the intermediate ASM file generated by Turbo C's TCC command-line compiler and inline assembly material. The option is not available with either of the other assemblers, and has little usefulness for source files except those created by Turbo C.

Assembler Directives

This chapter has made frequent mention of directives without a full description of what they do. A full list of directives appears early in the chapter, in the section comparing the three assemblers. Many directives exist for each of the assemblers, but only a few of them are used often. Those directives are most easily learned by seeing how they are used in the sample programs and by studying your assembler's reference manual. Attempting to fully describe all the directives for all three assemblers, even as briefly as the options were described in the preceding section, would at least triple the size of this book.

However, two groups of directives are especially important and deserve additional emphasis here. These groups are those that control conditional assembly of code sequences, and those involved with the definition and control of macro operations.

Conditional Assembly

The conditional assembly capability is one of the powerful features common to all assemblers discussed in this chapter. Conditional assembly means that the assembler can decide, based on the values of certain symbols (or flags), whether to include specific blocks of code. This capability can greatly simplify the development process.

Table 8.4 lists the conditional assembly directives of MASM. The other assemblers have similar directives that are used in the same way. These directives are not direct assembly language commands. Rather, they are commands to the assembler that control how the source code file is processed.

Each of the conditional assembly directives listed in table 8.4 requires an expression or argument. MASM evaluates the expression or argument and, based on that evaluation, takes an appropriate action.

For instance, consider the following code segment:

```
ifdef debug
            INCLUDE DEBUG.ASM
endif
```

When this segment is coupled with the MASM command-line invocation

```
MASM FILE,,,/DDEBUG;
```

Table 8.4. *MASM's conditional assembly directives.*

Directive	Meaning
IF	Assemble if true
IF1	Assemble if pass 1
IF2	Assemble if pass 2
IFB	Assemble if blank
IFDEF	Assemble if defined
IFDIF	Assemble if different
IFDIFI	Assemble if different, ignoring case
IFE	Assemble if false
IFIDN	Assemble if identical
IFIDNI	Assemble if identical, ignoring case
IFNB	Assemble if not blank
IFNDEF	Assemble if not defined
ELSE	Used with any of the above
ENDIF	End of conditional block

the file DEBUG.ASM will be included in the object code. If you do not define DEBUG, the code will not be included. This usage lets you include debugging code easily and flexibly to facilitate the development process. To create the proper object file after debugging, you simply omit the /D option from the MASM command line.

Conditional assembly statements can be used in numerous ways. Used wisely, they can make the development process faster and less painful. Just remember that conditional assembly statements control only the assembler.

Macro Operations

If you're familiar with C, the easiest way to understand what an assembly language macro operation does is to think of it as the equivalent of the #define statement in C. Unfortunately, if your chosen language is BASIC or Pascal, that won't tell you much!

A macro operation, usually shortened to just *macro*, is a sequence of assembly language statements that has been assigned a symbolic name. Once a macro has been defined in an ASM file, you can include the entire sequence of statements simply by using the macro name as an operator. If you defined the macro to have parameters, you can also pass operands to it at each call.

In effect, the macro gives you the capability of redefining assembly language to be what you need most. You can potentially redefine assembly language until your final program is nothing but a series of macro calls, and is unreadable to any skilled assembly language programmer without the matching set of macro definitions, which are often hidden away in a separate MAC or INC file and are hardly ever printed out on the listing).

Table 8.5 lists the significant macro directives that are common to all the assemblers described in this chapter.

Table 8.5. *Assembler macro directives.*

Directive	Meaning
MACRO	Begin definition of macro
IRP	Repeat for each parameter
IRPC	Repeat for each character
REPT	Repeat sequence n times
ENDM	End sequence for all of above
LOCAL	Establish local-label list
PURGE	Remove listed definitions

The first four directives listed in table 8.5 establish the start of a macro sequence; each such sequence is ended by the ENDM directive, and sequences can be nested. Each sequence requires its own ENDM. Only the MACRO directive establishes a named sequence that can be called elsewhere; the three "repeat" directives provide an internal loop structure that can be used either in the main program or in a MACRO definition.

The syntax used by all the assemblers for the MACRO...ENDM definition sequence is

```
name MACRO list
         .
         .
         .
     ENDM
```

where *name* is the name by which the macro will be called subsequently, and *list* is an optional group of "formal parameters" that define what information can be passed into the macro when it is called.

The LOCAL directive may be used inside a MACRO...ENDM sequence to specify a list of labels to be replaced with unique symbols each time the macro is expanded. This prevents problems caused when a macro defines the same symbol to mean two different addresses.

The IRP, IRPC, and REPT directives follow a syntax similar to that used by MACRO but do not take a *name* field. Each uses a different kind of parameter *list* also.

REPT takes a single expression that must evaluate to a numeric constant and repeats the code contained within the REPT...ENDM sequence that many times.

IRP takes exactly one formal parameter, followed by an argument list enclosed in angle brackets. The assembler repeats the IRP...ENDM sequence once for each argument in the list, substituting that argument for the formal parameter wherever it occurs within the sequence.

IRPC is like IRP but instead of the angle-bracket-enclosed list of arguments requires a single text string. IRPC repeats the IRPC...ENDM sequence once for each character in that string, each time substituting that character for the formal parameter.

The PURGE directive takes as its operand a list of macro names and removes each macro from memory. PURGE normally is not required; however, if you have dozens of lengthy definitions each used only one or two times, you may need this directive to free memory for the assembler. PURGE does *not* generate any code, nor does it have any effect on your system; all it does is free some RAM for the assembler.

To show you how macros can be helpful and how to define them, here's an example. You'll recall that throughout Chapters 3-7, most of the examples dealt with manipulation of the video cursor and used functions associated with the video BIOS to do so. The following macros could have been defined to do much of this work, and you would have had fewer lines of code to type:

```
GETCUR    MACRO
          MOV  AH,3      ;; get cursor type in CX, loc in DX
          INT  10h
          ENDM


SETCUR    MACRO
          MOV  AH,1      ;; set cursor type from CX
          INT  10h
          ENDM
```

```
MOVCUR     MACRO     R,C
           MOV  DH,BYTE PTR R
           MOV  DL,BYTE PTR C
           MOV  AH,2       ;; set cursor to row R, col C
           INT  10h
           ENDM
```

Once these three macros are defined, simply delete the MOV AH,3 from
the example programs and replace the associated INT 10h with the single
word GETCUR. SETCUR is used the same way when the cursor's size or on/off
condition is to be changed.

MOVCUR, however, is a bit more complicated. This sequence illustrates
the use of formal parameters in macro definitions. The parameter list is
R,C, so each time that MOVCUR is called, the R in the MOV DH,BYTE PTR R line
is replaced with the first argument you provided as part of the call, and
the second argument you provide similarly affects the C in the next line. If
you have stored the desired row and column values in the low bytes of
16-bit variables named ROW_WORD and COL_WORD, you can call MOVCUR with
the single line

```
MOVCUR  ROW_WORD,COL_WORD
```

and the assembler will replace this with the code sequence

```
MOV    DH,BYTE PTR ROW_WORD
MOV    DL,BYTE PTR COL_WORD
MOV    AH,2                   ; set cursor to row R, col C
INT    10h
```

The BYTE and PTR operators are specifically included in this example so
that you can use *any* type or size of variable without generating an assembler error. You can omit these operators if the only locations you use
when calling MOVCUR are those defined with the DB directive; the DB definition forces the variable's type to BYTE, and therefore no BYTE PTR would
be needed.

All the assemblers have files containing collections of useful macros as
a part of the distribution packages. A few hours spent mastering macro use
will eventually save you much more time by making your programming
faster.

Using MASM through a Batch File

To make the assembly process easier, you can set up a batch file (as you can with many other development commands and programs). An example of such a file (ASM.BAT) follows:

```
ECHO OFF
CLS

:LOOP
 REM - CHECK IF NO FILES AVAILABLE ON COMMAND LINE
 IF %1/ == / GOTO DONE

 REM - CHECK IF EXTENSION (.ASM) WAS ENTERED
 IF NOT EXIST %1 GOTO CHKEXT
    ECHO Assembling ... %1
    MASM %1,; >NUL
    IF ERRORLEVEL 1 GOTO ERROR
    GOTO NEXT

:CHKEXT
 REM - CHECK FOR ROOT PLUS ASSUMED EXTENSION
 IF NOT EXIST %1.ASM GOTO NOT-FOUND
    ECHO Assembling ... %1.ASM
    MASM %1.ASM; >NUL
    IF ERRORLEVEL 1 GOTO ERROR
    GOTO NEXT

:NOT-FOUND
 REM - FILE NOT LOCATED
 ECHO File %1 Not Located or Found in Current Directory !
 GOTO NEXT

:ERROR
 ECHO Error detected while assembling %1

:NEXT
 REM - CONTINUE WITH NEXT FILE - END OF LOOP
 SHIFT
 GOTO LOOP
```

```
:DONE
REM - FINAL MESSAGE AND ALL THROUGH
ECHO ALL Files have been Assembled !M
```

This file assumes that you will enter the command line as

ASM *file1 file2 file3* ...

where *file1*, *file2*, *file3*, and so on are the names of the source code files to be assembled. You do not have to enter the ASM extension, although this batch file checks whether an extension has been entered and reacts accordingly. If none has been entered, the extension is assumed to be ASM.

If ASM.BAT can be located in your current search path, you can use it from any subdirectory. The source code file should be in the current directory, however, and the OBJ file will remain in the current directory.

With Other Assemblers, Added Files, or Options

This batch file is customized to MASM and does not create a LST or CRF file, nor does it use any of the MASM options. However, you can easily change the file. To use it with one of the other assemblers, replace all occurrences of `MASM` with the appropriate program name. To use options or to generate LST, CRF, or XRF files, you will need to change only the two lines that invoke the assembler.

With Error Codes

When MASM terminates, an error level is returned to DOS. You can use this exit code to control how the batch file will function. This exit code is used simplistically (through the `ERRORLEVEL` batch command) in the sample batch file, which checks whether an exit code of at least 1 was returned and, if it was, displays a message indicating the status. But you can be quite elaborate in your implementation of an assembler batch file. Table 8.6 lists the possible exit codes for MASM version 5.1 and their meanings (these have not changed since version 4.0):

Table 8.6. *MASM exit codes.*

Code	Meaning
0	No errors detected
1	Argument error
2	Can't open source file
3	Can't open LST file
4	Can't open OBJ file
5	Can't open CRF file
6	Can't open INCLUDE file
7	Assembly error
8	Memory allocation error
9	Unused
10	/D option error
11	Interrupted by user

For its exit code, OptAsm simply returns its count of the number of errors, which is 0 if no errors occurred. This count suffices for the level of checking performed by ASM.BAT, but does not provide for extensive error analysis. The documentation for Turbo Assembler makes no mention at all of any exit codes. Both OptAsm and Turbo Assembler are strongly oriented toward the use of MAKE files (described in Chapter 12) instead of batch files to control their operation; both provide "configurable" options to halt the MAKE operation when an error is encountered.

Summary

This chapter covered the use of the three major assembler programs: MASM from Microsoft; OptAsm from SLR, Inc.; and Turbo Assembler from Borland. (The same principles apply to the IBM Macro Assembler, also created by Microsoft.) Using the assembler properly is essential to your success in using assembly language. Even though each of these assemblers has several options available, none of these assemblers is difficult to use. You will probably use the options only in special situations.

In the next chapter, you will learn about the next step in developing assembly language routines: using the linker.

CHAPTER 9

Choosing and Using Your Linker

In Chapter 8, you learned how to use the assembler. You learned also that an assembler does not produce executable machine code. Instead, the OBJ file that the assembler creates must be *linked* successfully to work properly.

The program you use to do this task is called, curiously enough, a *linker*. You will need a copy of such a program to complete this chapter. Each of the assemblers discussed in Chapter 8 has a matching linker, but most of these linkers will work properly on OBJ files produced by any of the assemblers (or any other OBJ file that meets standard format specifications).

Unfortunately, OBJ files produced by some of the newer compilers do *not* follow the standard format specification; they go beyond it. Such OBJ files can be linked only by linkers that are designed to recognize the extensions. QuickC is one such language; its manual tells you to use only the linker furnished with it although some other versions of the Microsoft linker also work.

This chapter covers how to choose and use your linker program. Most likely, you'll simply use the program that came with your assembler or

203

high-level language, but you may find that differences in performance from one linker to another are significant enough to warrant a special purchase.

Before comparing the linkers that come with each of the assemblers, let's look at what a linker does.

What the Linker Does

A *linker* is a program that translates relocatable object code (produced by an assembler or compiler) into executable machine code. The linker performs three main tasks:

❏ Combines separate object modules into one executable file

❏ Attempts to resolve references to external variables

❏ Produces a listing (if you ask for one) showing how the object files were linked

Most people refer to these programs as linkers (as I have); others call them *linkage editors*. Whatever they are called, they do these three basic tasks. Many different linkers are available.

Choosing Your Linker

To help you decide whether to use the linker furnished with your assembler or high-level language or to purchase one elsewhere, here's a quick overview of the similarities and differences of the three major linkers: *LINK* from Microsoft, *OptLink* from SLR, Inc., and *TLINK* from Borland. However, as mentioned earlier, you may not *have* a choice as some high-level languages (most notably QuickC) require the use of the linker that was designed to match their nonstandard OBJ files.

Until recently, you had to use the Microsoft linker if you wanted to do source-level debugging (described in Chapter 10). However, this requirement no longer applies because all three linkers can now provide debugging information in their output EXE files.

LINK from Microsoft

Microsoft's LINK.EXE program is available from many sources, most noticeably Microsoft and IBM. A copy of LINK.EXE is usually included with any MS-DOS or PC DOS computer system and is always a part of the package that comes with any Microsoft language product.

As a result, you'll probably have several copies of LINK.EXE available to you, and the major question then becomes which one to use. The normal rule is to always use the most recent copy (the one with the highest version number), because Microsoft has attempted to maintain downward compatibility from one release to the next. The exception to this rule is that QuickC will require the use of the linker furnished with it, even though that version number may be lower than the version number for the linker that came with MASM or with your system.

Like its companion assembler, and for the same reasons, LINK sets the industry's standard against which other linkers are compared. Although it is not the fastest linker available, neither is it the slowest. The current version supports overlays, but does not include an overlay management routine that enables you to use them; for this reason overlays can only be used when the high-level language provides such a manager. (Although third-party overlay managers are available as shareware, they are beyond the scope of this volume.)

The major advantages of LINK can be summed up easily: it's acceptably fast, it's accurate, and it's free when you buy any Microsoft language product.

The disadvantages aren't so obvious. If you frequently link large programs (such as EXE files greater than 200K), LINK seems to drag on forever. If you are generating COM or BIN files rather than directly executable programs, LINK requires you to perform some additional steps that either of the other linkers can bypass. If your requirements call for consistent use of the option switches, the other linkers can be configured to your needs, but LINK cannot. And finally, LINK will let some of your programming errors slip by without detection (opinion is divided among professionals as to whether this is a bug or a feature).

OptLink from SLR, Inc.

OptLink, a product of SLR, Inc., is the companion linker for OptAsm although it is sold separately. An almost identical version known as Olink is provided as part of the OptAsm package; it differs from the full version only in lacking the printed manual and virtual memory support.

OptLink's major advantage is its blinding speed. Although exact comparisons are affected by the sizes of the files being produced as well as many other factors, in most cases OptLink completes its job in less than half the time required by its nearest competitors.

Other advantages include the following:

❏ The capability of creating output files in COM or SYS format directly

❏ The automatic use of expanded memory (LIM memory) if available

❏ The ability for you to configure the program, setting up the default conditions to suit your own needs

❏ Better error detection than LINK

The major disadvantage of OptLink is simply that it must be purchased as a separate program. If you buy OptAsm, however, and do not need the virtual memory support, Olink costs nothing extra.

If you are using QuickC, OptLink can generate EXE files only if you specify the /CO (CodeView) option. Without this option, the nonstandard OBJ file that QuickC generates produces a fatal error in OptLink. Using this option, however, makes the final EXE file larger although the actual program size is not affected.

TLINK from Borland

Borland's TLINK program, furnished with both Turbo C and Turbo Assembler and not available separately, falls midway between LINK and OptLink on the performance scale.

Unlike the other two programs, TLINK operates only from the command line and has no interactive mode. Although you may initially consider this a disadvantage, with practice you would probably abandon using the other programs in interactive mode anyway, so this difference would eventually lose its significance.

Borland's own description of TLINK 2.0 is "lean and mean." Features of other linkers that Borland considered superfluous were dropped to create a fast and compact utility. Thus it has the shortest list of options but also the smallest size.

I found that TLINK was completely unable to link the TEST.EXE program, used subsequently in this chapter for the examples, from the OBJ file created originally by QuickC version 2.01; TLINK could not find the routines in the QC LIB file even after the LIB had been copied to the current directory. Only after recompiling TEST.C using Turbo C could the example be linked. However, I was certainly stretching the limits of compatibility by attempting this; the QuickC manuals warn that only its own linker can be used.

Like OptLink, TLINK can generate a COM, SYS, or BIN file directly without requiring any subsequent conversion of its output.

The major advantages of TLINK are its small size, its speed, and its capability to create non-EXE files directly.

The major disadvantages of TLINK are its demonstrated incompatibility with at least some high-level languages from sources other than Borland. Also, TLINK cannot be purchased separately from Turbo Assembler or Turbo C.

If you are using the Borland high-level languages, then TLINK is probably your linker of choice because it is tailored to work efficiently with the other Borland products. For use with other languages, it does not offer enough unique advantages to warrant its purchase.

The Files Involved

Throughout this chapter I refer to the different file types that the linker creates: the *executable* and *listing* files.

Whether these files are actually created depends on how you invoke the assembler or answer the assembler's prompts. Assuming that you assembled SUMS.ASM (from Chapter 8) using MASM and requested all files, you should find the following files when you use DIR after assembly, CREF generation, and linking. Also shown are the TEST files described later in this chapter.

```
C>DIR
Volume in drive C has no label
Directory of  C:\ASSEMBLY
.            <DIR>      10-25-89    3:05p
..           <DIR>      10-25-89    3:05p
SUMS    LST     3770    10-26-89    8:37p
SUMS    ASM     1931    10-25-89   12:06p
SUMS    OBJ      102    10-26-89    8:37p
SUMS    CRF      438    10-26-89    8:37p
SUMS    REF      605    10-26-89    8:37p
TEST    OBJ     2598    10-26-89    8:36p
TEST    C        668    10-26-89    8:36p
TEST    MAP     1758    10-26-89    8:38p
TEST    EXE    13030    10-26-89    8:38p
        11 File(s)   14232832 bytes free
```

You may remember, from Chapter 8, that SUMS.ASM is the assembly language source code file. SUMS.LST, SUMS.OBJ, and SUMS.CRF were created by MASM; SUMS.REF was created by CREF.EXE; TEST.C is the C source code; and TEST.OBJ is the object code file generated by the C compiler. The remaining files, TEST.MAP and TEST.EXE, were created by the linker. Sometimes the linker also creates a temporary file, VM.TMP.

Had you used one of the other assemblers or linkers, the details might have been slightly different, but the final results would have been much the same. In particular, both the EXE and the MAP files would have been created. Before we take a look at each of the three types of files created by the linker, let's recap what the OBJ file does.

The Input File (OBJ)

The OBJ file is the output from the assembler or high-level language. In this example, you have two OBJ files: SUMS.OBJ, produced by assembling SUMS.ASM, and TEST.OBJ, created by compiling TEST.C. In actual practice you might have dozens of OBJ files, all to be combined into a single executable program.

Each OBJ file contains all the machine language code necessary to perform the corresponding portion of your program, but the bytes where memory address information must appear are left blank to be filled in by the linker when it determines what the actual address will be. This depends on where the OBJ module fits into the total program and can be determined only at link time.

In addition to the machine language data, the OBJ file contains "house-keeping" information that lets it relate names (defined in one OBJ file) and references to these names (from other OBJ files) so that everything comes together. This information is used by the linker but does not become part of the final executable program; it can easily take more space in the OBJ file than the machine code itself. For this reason the size of an OBJ file cannot be used as a reliable estimate of the size of the EXE file that will be produced from the OBJ file.

The Executable File (EXE)

The EXE file is usually the end result of the development process: an executable file. If the source files' logic and construction are correct, and no debugging or further development is needed, the EXE file is the finished program that you can invoke from DOS.

The List File (MAP)

The MAP file is the listing that the linker produced as it processed each object code file. The MAP file contains at least the beginning and ending addresses of the segments that the linker processed to create TEST.EXE and may contain even more information. LINK.EXE produces the following file, TEST.MAP:

```
Start   Stop    Length  Name        Class
00000H  02BBCH  02BBDH  _TEXT       CODE
02BBEH  02BBEH  00000H  C_ETEXT     ENDCODE
02BC0H  02C01H  00042H  NULL        BEGDATA
02C02H  02F81H  00380H  _DATA       DATA
02F82H  02F8DH  0000CH  DBDATA      DATA
02F8EH  02F9BH  0000EH  CDATA       DATA
02F9CH  02F9CH  00000H  XIFB        DATA
02F9CH  02F9CH  00000H  XIF         DATA
02F9CH  02F9CH  00000H  XIFE        DATA
02F9CH  02F9CH  00000H  XIB         DATA
02F9CH  02F9DH  00002H  XI          DATA
02F9EH  02F9EH  00000H  XIE         DATA
02F9EH  02F9EH  00000H  XPB         DATA
02F9EH  02F9FH  00002H  XP          DATA
02FA0H  02FA0H  00000H  XPE         DATA
02FA0H  02FA0H  00000H  XCB         DATA
02FA0H  02FA0H  00000H  XC          DATA
```

```
02FA0H 02FA0H 00000H XCE              DATA
02FA0H 02FA0H 00000H XCFB             DATA
02FA0H 02FA0H 00000H XCF              DATA
02FA0H 02FA0H 00000H XCFE             DATA
02FA0H 02FC1H 00022H CONST            CONST
02FC2H 02FC9H 00008H HDR              MSG
02FCAH 030E2H 00119H MSG              MSG
030E3H 030E4H 00002H PAD              MSG
030E5H 030E5H 00001H EPAD             MSG
030E6H 032BBH 001D6H _BSS             BSS
032BCH 032BCH 00000H XOB              BSS
032BCH 032BCH 00000H XO               BSS
032BCH 032BCH 00000H XOE              BSS
032C0H 034BFH 00200H c_common         BSS
034C0H 03CBFH 00800H STACK            STACK


Origin    Group
02BC:0    DGROUP


Program entry point at 0000:0166
```

When OptLink was run on the example files (exactly the same set used for the LINK example) without requesting extended map information, it produced this version of TEST.MAP:

```
Start  Stop   Length Name            Class
00000H 02BACH 02BADH _TEXT           CODE
02BAEH 02BAEH 00000H C_ETEXT         ENDCODE
02BB0H 02BF1H 00042H NULL            BEGDATA
02BF2H 02F71H 00380H _DATA           DATA
02F72H 02F7DH 0000CH DBDATA          DATA
02F7EH 02F8BH 0000EH CDATA           DATA
02F8CH 02F8CH 00000H XIFB            DATA
02F8CH 02F8CH 00000H XIF             DATA
02F8CH 02F8CH 00000H XIFE            DATA
02F8CH 02F8CH 00000H XIB             DATA
02F8CH 02F8DH 00002H XI              DATA
02F8EH 02F8EH 00000H XIE             DATA
02F8EH 02F8EH 00000H XPB             DATA
02F8EH 02F8FH 00002H XP              DATA
02F90H 02F90H 00000H XPE             DATA
02F90H 02F90H 00000H XCB             DATA
02F90H 02F90H 00000H XC              DATA
02F90H 02F90H 00000H XCE             DATA
```

```
02F90H 02F90H 00000H XCFB            DATA
02F90H 02F90H 00000H XCF             DATA
02F90H 02F90H 00000H XCFE            DATA
02F90H 02FB1H 00022H CONST           CONST
02FB2H 02FB9H 00008H HDR             MSG
02FBAH 030D2H 00119H MSG             MSG
030D3H 030D4H 00002H PAD             MSG
030D5H 030D5H 00001H EPAD            MSG
030D6H 032ABH 001D6H _BSS            BSS
032ACH 032ACH 00000H XOB             BSS
032ACH 032ACH 00000H XO              BSS
032ACH 032ACH 00000H XOE             BSS
032ACH 034ABH 00200H C_COMMON        BSS
034B0H 03CAFH 00800H STACK           STACK


Origin    Group
02BB:0    DGROUP
```

As previously noted, before TLINK could link the example files, TEST.C had to be recompiled using Turbo C, and the Turbo C libraries had to be used. Thus the following TLINK-generated TEST.MAP is not directly comparable to the other two examples:

```
Start   Stop    Length  Name             Class

00000H  01D8BH  01D8CH  _TEXT            CODE
01D90H  02341H  005B2H  _DATA            DATA
02342H  02345H  00004H  _EMUSEG          DATA
02346H  02347H  00002H  _CRTSEG          DATA
02348H  02349H  00002H  _CVTSEG          DATA
0234AH  0234FH  00006H  _SCNSEG          DATA
02350H  02395H  00046H  _BSS             BSS
02396H  02396H  00000H  _BSSEND          STACK
023A0H  0241FH  00080H  _STACK           STACK
```

Program entry point at 0000:0000

In all three example, you will notice that C automatically included a number of segments beyond those you explicitly requested. As your programs grow larger, you will find this listing file increasingly more valuable in your debugging efforts.

This simple program performs two basic tasks. First, it enables you to enter a number that is used as a value for calling SUMS(). Both the original and derived number are displayed. Second, if you enter the number 999, the program exits the interactive portion and proceeds through a loop, starting at 1, that displays values and derived values until it reaches the limit of SUMS(). You may remember from Chapter 8 that this limit is reached when the derived value is greater than 65,535. When this limit is exceeded, SUMS() returns a 0 and terminates execution of the controlling C program.

Although you can use the linker in several different ways, the principal ways are interactively or with just a command line. Let's look first at using the linker interactively.

Using LINK Interactively

These sections apply only if you use Microsoft's LINK.

Once you have the two object code files, TEST.OBJ and SUMS.OBJ, you are ready to link the files. Make sure that you have these files in your current directory. You should also have access to LINK.EXE, either in the current directory or in the search path. To start the linking process, enter the following at the DOS prompt:

LINK

When you press Enter, you'll see a notice and prompt similar to the following:

```
Microsoft (R) Overlay Linker  Version 3.64
Copyright (C) Microsoft Corp 1983-1988.  All rights reserved.
Object Modules [.OBJ]: _
```

The linker is waiting for you to specify the files to be linked. The default answer is shown in brackets; the linker accepts this answer if you simply press the Enter key. Enter the root names of the files to be linked, separated by either a space or a plus sign (+). Because the linker assumes an extension of OBJ (unless you override it), you need to specify only the root names. When you make the proper entries, the following message should appear:

```
Object Modules [.OBJ]: TEST SUMS
Run File [TEST.EXE]: _
```

Notice that the linker now is prompting you for the name of the EXE file to create. (The EXE file is the executable run file that LINK.EXE creates.) Use the default, TEST.EXE. When you press Enter to signify that you accept the default, the linker asks the following:

```
Run File [TEST.EXE]:
List File [NUL.MAP]:_
```

A list file is optional, as the default of NUL.MAP indicates. List files for the linker have the extension of MAP because they provide a "map" showing how the linker did its work. For later purposes, enter TEST to indicate that you want a list file named TEST.MAP. When you do, you will see the following prompt:

```
List File [NUL.MAP]: TEST
Libraries [.LIB]: _
```

Here LINK needs to know which library files to use for external references that cannot be resolved from within the object code files. (Libraries are covered in Chapter 11, and there are no consequential external references in this example. LINK will search automatically and use some C libraries, but again, those are covered in Chapter 11.) Simply press Enter to indicate that no explicit libraries are to be used.

LINK has now asked its four questions, and you have responded. Notice that your disk drive is active for a short time; then the DOS prompt returns. The return of the DOS prompt indicates that the linking process is complete, and no errors occurred. If an error had occurred, an error message would have appeared during linking, indicating the type of error and the source file for the error.

If you receive any error messages, you must correct the errors before continuing. Check your files against the listings in Chapter 8 and in the previous section; then try to assemble, compile, and link again. When you have corrected the errors, you can proceed with this chapter.

Using the LINK Command Line

As mentioned earlier, you also can use LINK from the DOS command line. You can enter any or all of the responses to individual prompts directly after the LINK command. For instance, entering either of the following lines produces the same results as those achieved in the last section:

```
LINK TEST SUMS,,TEST;

LINK TEST+SUMS,,;
```

Remember that LINK asks four questions during an interactive session. The parameters in either of these command lines provide answers to the questions. The parameters are separated by commas, and the line ends with a semicolon.

Notice that some parameters are left blank, as the two consecutive commas indicate. In this case, LINK uses the first parameter (TEST) as the implied parameter.

The following syntax is used to enter parameters directly from the command line:

```
LINK  obj,exe,map,lib
```

Here, *obj*, *exe*, *map*, and *lib* indicate the file type that each parameter designates. These file types were touched on in the last section and are discussed in more detail elsewhere in this chapter.

How do you indicate that you do not want a particular type of file? Simply by using NUL as the parameter for that file type. For instance, both of the following commands instruct MASM to create an EXE file but no MAP file:

```
LINK TEST SUMS,,NUL;
LINK TEST+SUMS,
```

Notice that the second command line, although shorter than the first, is effectively the same. The semicolon instructs LINK to begin processing without expecting any more parameters.

Using the LINK Response File

You can respond to the four LINK questions within a file, logically called a *response file*. This method of using LINK is beneficial when you know that you will be linking the same program over and over again during development; repeatedly typing answers to each question can be tiresome.

To use this method of providing input to LINK, create a normal ASCII text file, with any name you want, that has the answers to each question. Each question's answer should be on a separate line. For instance, using our sample programs, the response file would have only four lines:

```
TEST SUMS

TEST
;
```

LINK uses this response file to link TEST.OBJ and SUMS.OBJ, producing the default output file TEST.EXE. Also, the list file TEST.MAP is created, and no libraries are specified.

To use a response file with LINK, simply invoke LINK using the following command syntax:

```
LINK @filename.ext
```

filename.ext is the name of the response file LINK is to use. Notice the @ symbol directly before the file name. This symbol is the signal that LINK needs to differentiate between a response file and a source file.

If our sample response file is named TEST.LNK, then the following command will run LINK and provide input to LINK from our response file:

```
LINK @TEST.LNKM
```

The more you use LINK, the more you will understand the value of using response files.

Using OptLink Interactively

These sections apply only if you use OptLink.

Like LINK, OptLink can be used interactively; the process is almost identical. Make sure that you have the TEST.OBJ and SUMS.OBJ files in your current directory. You should also have access to OPTLINK.EXE, either in the current directory or in the search path. To start the linking process, enter the following at the DOS prompt:

OPTLINK

When you press Enter, you'll see a notice and prompt similar to the following:

```
OPTLINK Copyright (C) SLR Systems 1989 Release 1.00   All rights reserved.
OBJ Files: (NUL.OBJ): _
```

The linker is waiting for you to specify the files to be linked. The default answer is shown in parentheses; the linker accepts this answer if you simply press Enter. Enter the root names of the files to be linked, separated by either a space or a plus sign (+). Because the linker assumes an extension of OBJ unless you override it, you need to specify only the root names. When you make the proper entries, the following message should appear:

```
OBJ Files: (NUL.OBJ):test sums
Output File: (TEST.EXE):_
```

Notice that the linker now is prompting you for the name of the EXE file to create. (The EXE file is the executable run file that OPTLINK.EXE creates.) Use the default, TEST.EXE. When you press Enter to signify that you accept the default, the linker asks the following:

```
Output File: (TEST.EXE):
Map File: (NUL.MAP):_
```

A list file is optional, as the default of NUL.MAP indicates. List files for the linker have the extension of MAP because they provide a "map" showing how the linker did its work. For later purposes, enter TEST to indicate that you want a list file named TEST.MAP. When you do, you will see the following prompt:

```
Map File: (NUL.MAP):test
Libraries and Paths: (NUL.LIB):_
```

Here OptLink needs to know which library files to use for external references that it cannot resolve from within the object code files. Simply press Enter to indicate that no explicit libraries are to be used.

OptLink has now asked its four questions, and you have responded. Notice that your disk drive is active for a short time; then the DOS prompt returns. The return of the DOS prompt indicates that the linking process is complete, and no errors occurred. If an error had occurred, an error message would have appeared during linking, indicating the type of error and the source file for the error.

If you receive any error messages, you must correct the errors before continuing. Check your files against the listings in Chapter 8 and in the previous section; then try to assemble, compile, and link again. When you have corrected the errors, you can proceed with this chapter.

Using the OptLink Command Line

You also can use OptLink from the DOS command line. You can enter any or all of the responses to individual prompts directly after the OptLink command. For instance, entering either of the following produces the same results as those achieved in the last section:

```
OPTLINK TEST SUMS,,TEST;
OPTLINK TEST+SUMS,,;
```

Remember that OptLink asks four questions during an interactive session. The parameters in either of these command lines provide answers to the questions. The parameters are separated by commas, and the line ends with a semicolon.

The following syntax is used to enter parameters directly from the command line:

```
OPTLINK  obj,exe,map,lib
```

Here, *obj*, *exe*, *map*, and *lib* indicate the file type that each parameter designates. These file types were touched on in the last section and are discussed in more detail elsewhere in this chapter.

To indicate that you do not want a particular type of file, just use NUL as the parameter for that file type. For instance, the following command instructs OptLink to create an EXE file but no MAP file:

```
OptLink TEST SUMS,,NUL;
```

Using the OptLink Response File

You can respond to the four OptLink questions within a file, logically called a *response file*. This method of using OptLink is beneficial when you know that you will be linking the same program over and over again during development; repeatedly typing answers to each question can be tiresome.

To use this method of providing input to OptLink, create a normal ASCII text file with any name you want; use the file extension LNK to match what OptLink will use as its default. The text file should contain on a separate line the answers to each question. For instance, using the sample programs, the response file would have only four lines:

```
TEST SUMS

TEST
;
```

OptLink uses this response file to link TEST.OBJ and SUMS.OBJ, producing the default output file TEST.EXE. Also, the list file TEST.MAP is created, and no libraries are specified.

To use a response file with OptLink, simply invoke OptLink using the following command syntax:

```
OptLink @filename.ext
```

filename.ext is the name of the response file OptLink is to use. Notice the @ symbol directly before the file name. This symbol is the signal that OptLink needs to differentiate between a response file and a source file. If you omit the extension, OptLink will use LNK by default.

If our sample response file is named TEST.LNK, then the following command will run OptLink and provide input to OptLink from our response file:

```
OptLink @TEST
```

The more you use OptLink, the more you will understand the value of using response files.

Using the TLINK Command Line

These sections apply only if you use TLINK.

TLINK 2.0, the Borland linker, can be used only from the DOS command line; it has no interactive mode. You must enter all of the necessary data directly after the TLINK command. For instance, entering the following produces the files TEST.MAP and TEST.EXE. The reference to COS is required by Turbo C, and the reference to CS specifies the small-model C library. All files mentioned must be in the current directory unless you specify the complete path to the file, which is permitted; I left it out of the example for clarity.

```
TLINK COS+TEST+SUMS,TEST,TEST,CS
```

The following syntax is used:

```
TLINK  obj,exe,map,lib
```

Here, *obj*, *exe*, *map*, and *lib* indicate the file type that each parameter designates. These file types were touched on in the last section and are discussed in more detail elsewhere in this chapter. Notice that, unlike LINK and OptAsm, TLINK does not require a semicolon after the final entry to prevent it from switching into interactive mode.

To indicate that you do not want a particular type of file, just use NUL as the parameter for that file type. For instance, the following command instructs TLINK to create an EXE file but no MAP file:

```
TLINK COS+TEST+SUMS,TEST,NUL,CS
```

Using the TLINK Response File

Like both the other linkers, TLINK can receive the input parameters from a response file.

To use this method of providing input to TLINK, create a normal ASCII text file with any name you want; use the file extension LNK to match what TLINK will use as its default. The text file should contain on a separate line the data for each parameter. For instance, using the sample programs, the response file would have only four lines:

```
COS TEST SUMS
TEST
TEST
CS
```

TLINK uses this response file to link COS.OBJ (the Turbo C startup code provided with TC), TEST.OBJ, and SUMS.OBJ, producing the output file TEST.EXE. If the second line had been left blank, as it was for the Microsoft-generated C OBJ files, the output file name would have been COS.EXE.

Also, the list file TEST.MAP is created, and the Turbo C small-model library CS.LIB is specified. Both COS.OBJ and CS.LIB must be in the current directory unless you include their full paths in the response file.

To use a response file with TLINK, simply invoke TLINK using the following command syntax:

```
TLINK @filename.ext
```

filename.ext is the name of the response file TLINK is to use. Notice the @ symbol directly before the file name. This symbol is the signal that TLINK needs to differentiate between a response file and a source file. If you omit the extension, TLINK will use LNK by default.

If our sample response file is named TEST.LNK, then the following command will run TLINK and provide input to TLINK from our response file:

```
TLINK @TEST
```

The more you use TLINK, the more you will understand the value of using response files.

Using Linker Options

All linkers have several parameters that alter how the linkers function. These parameters are known as *options* or *switches*. You can enter them either directly from the command line or when you are running the linker interactively. Table 9.1 lists alphabetically the different linker options and their meanings. Note that LINK and OptLink use similar options, but TLINK's options (from TLINK 2.0) are different.

Table 9.1. *Linker options.*

Option	LINK	OptLink	TLINK	Meaning
/3			X	Enable 32-bit processing.
/BA	X	X		Operate in batch mode; do not prompt for LIBs (/B in OptLink).
/BI	X	X		Provide binary output (COM or SYS), QC Linker only.
/C			X	Make lowercase significant in symbols (same as /NOI in other linkers).
/CHECKA		X		Abort link on checksum error in OBJ file.
/CHECKE		X		Generate checksum word in EXE file.
/CHECKS		X		Check OBJ-file checksums; /CHECKA determines whether error causes warning or is fatal.
/CO	X	X		Create CodeView-compatible file.
/CP:*para*	X	X		Set maximum allocation space.
/D			X	Warn if LIBs have duplicate symbols.
/DE		X		Use default libraries specified in OBJ file.

Option	LINK	OptLink	TLINK	Meaning
/DO	X	X		Use MS-DOS segment ordering.
/DS	X	X		Place DGROUP data at high end of group.
/E	X			Pack the EXE file created by LINK.
/E			X	Ignore extended dictionary (same as LINK's /NOE).
/EC		X		Echo response-file content to screen.
/EXE		X		Interpret as LINK's /E but ignore.
/EXT		X		Use extended dictionary (opposite of /NOE).
/F	X			Convert FAR calls to NEAR where possible.
/G		X		Use group associations when setting addresses.
/HE	X	X		List LINK options.
/HI	X	X		Load program in high memory.
/I			X	Initialize all segments.
/IN		X		Display what link process is doing.
/INF	X			Display what link process is doing (same as OptLink's /IN).
/IG		X		Ignore case (opposite of /NOI).
/L	X	X	X	Include line numbers in map file.
/M	X	X	X	Include global symbol table in map file.
/N			X	Exclude default libraries.
/NOB		X		Cancel /B option if enabled.
/NOCHECKA		X		Cancel /CHECKA option if enabled.
/NOCHECKE		X		Cancel /CHECKE option if enabled.
/NOCHECKS		X		Cancel /CHECKS option if enabled.
/NOCO		X		Cancel /CO option if enabled.

Table 9.1. continues

Table 9.1. *continued*

Option	LINK	OptLink	TLINK	Meaning
/NOD	X			Exclude default libraries (same as TLINK's /N).
/NODE		X		Exclude default libraries (same as TLINK's /N).
/NODO		X		Cancel /DO option if in effect.
/NODS		X		Cancel /DS option if in effect.
/NOEC		X		Cancel /EC option if in effect.
/NOE	X			Ignore extended dictionary (same as TLINK's /E).
/NOEXT		X		Ignore extended dictionary (same as TLINK's /E).
/NOF	X	X		Do not translate FAR calls.
/NOG	X	X		Do not associate groups.
/NOH		X		Cancel /HI option if in effect.
/NOI	X	X		Do not ignore case differences.
/NOL		X		Do not include line numbers in map file.
/NOM		X		Do not produce map file.
/NOP	X			Do not pack code segments.
/NOPAC		X		Do not pack code segments (same as LINK's /NOP).
/NOPAU		X		Cancel /PAU option if in effect.
/NOX		X		Cancel /X option if in effect.
/O:*int*	X	X		Set overlay loader interrupt number.
/PAC	X	X		Pack contiguous code segments.
/PAU	X	X		Pause for disk change.
/Q	X	X		Produce Quick Library QLB file (accepted, but ignored, by OptLink).

Option	LINK	OptLink	TLINK	Meaning
/S			X	Generate detailed segment map.
/SE:*seg*	X	X		Specify maximum segments.
/ST:*size*	X	X		Override stack size.
/T			X	Create COM/SYS/BIN image file (same as LINK's /BI option).
/V			X	Include debugger data in EXE file (same as other linkers' /CO).
/X		X		Generate cross-reference data in MAP file.
/X			X	Do not produce any MAP file.

Some of the options shown for LINK may not be available in your version of LINK.EXE. Microsoft, IBM, and other software developers have distributed many different versions of LINK, each with different parameters. The group of parameters listed in table 9.1 comes with version 3.64 of LINK as distributed with MASM, version 5.1.

You can include linker options at any point in the LINK command or during the interactive format. Regardless of the inclusion point, options affect all the relevant files. Usually, you include the options at the end of the command line or at the end of your response to the last LINK prompt. You can enter the options in either upper- or lowercase.

You must include a delimiter before the actual option letter. Table 9.1 shows this delimiter as a slash, but with LINK you can also use a hyphen (-) as an equivalent delimiter; however, the other linkers accept the slash only.

Let's look at each of the listed options.

Enable 32-Bit Processing (/3)

This option, available only in Borland's TLINK, enables the linker to properly handle 32-bit code for the 80386 processor. You usually should not use this option.

Operate Linker in Batch Mode (/BA)

This option does nothing; it is accepted for compatibility with older versions of LINK.EXE, where it prevented interactive error processing. Current versions never process errors interactively.

Produce Binary Image File (/BI or /T)

With the QuickC version of LINK, the /BI option can be used to produce a binary image file (COM or SYS style) rather than an EXE file as the linker's output. With TLINK, the /T option does the same thing. OptLink uses the output file name extension to determine whether an image file or an EXE file is to be generated.

Do Not Ignore Case Differences (/C or /NOI)

The /C option causes TLINK to differentiate between upper- and lowercase letters. The /NOI option does the same thing with LINK and OptLink.

Process Checksum Errors (/CHECKA, /CHECKE, /CHECKS)

These three options, available only in OptLink, deal with how the linker treats checksum errors encountered in OBJ files, and whether it will generate a checksum in the EXE file. The /CHECKS option tells the linker to check the OBJ file checksums; the /CHECKA option tells the linker to quit linking if an error is detected. The /CHECKE option tells the linker to write a checksum to the output EXE file.

Create CodeView-Compatible File (/CO or /V)

This special option, available to both LINK and OptLink as /CO and to TLINK as /V, instructs the linker to create an EXE file that is compatible with Microsoft's CodeView debugger and other source-level debugging utilities. For more information on using CodeView, refer to Chapter 10.

Set Allocation Space (/CP:*para*)

With this option, available to both LINK and OptLink, you can specify how much memory (in paragraphs) the program is to use. MS-DOS requires that programs request a block of memory for program use so that there are no memory conflicts. Usually, the linker requests all memory, 65,535 paragraphs. Because this much memory is never available, MS-DOS returns the largest contiguous block of memory for program use.

Using this option lets you state explicitly how much memory should be requested. *para* is the number of paragraphs (16-byte memory blocks) that your program's code and data need. Because the amount of memory you designate probably will be an amount smaller than the linker normally allocates, memory will be freed for other purposes.

If *para* is smaller than the amount of memory the program actually needs, the linker ignores the *para* parameter and requests the maximum memory area.

Warn about Duplicate LIB Symbols (/D)

This option, available only in TLINK, forces TLINK to list all duplicate symbols encountered in the library files that it searches. /D is used when you have identical symbols in different LIB files for different code and want to know which file TLINK encounters first, because the code in that file will be the code that TLINK uses.

Use Default Libraries (/DE)

Some high-level languages include in the OBJ file the name(s) of default libraries for LINK to search when linking the file. This option, available only with OptLink, forces the linker to search any libraries that the language specified in the OBJ files.

Use MS-DOS Segment Ordering (/DO)

The /DO option, available to both LINK and OptLink, instructs the linker to process files using the MS-DOS segment ordering rules. These rules are as follows:

1. Segments with a class name of CODE are placed at the start of the linked file.

2. Segments with a class name of DGROUP are placed at the end of the linked file.

3. All other segments are placed after the CODE class segments but before the DGROUP class.

Normally, the linker copies segments to the file in the order that they occur in the object files.

Place DGROUP at High End (/DS)

The linker normally assigns data in DGROUP (a program's data group) to a low address, starting at an offset of 0. This option, available to both LINK and OptLink, causes the linker to start data assignments so that the last byte in DGROUP is at an offset of FFFFh, or the top of memory. Usually, this option is used with the /HI option.

Pack EXE File (/E)

The /E option causes LINK (the only linker that reacts to the option, although OptLink also recognizes it) to create an EXE file that is optimized for size. Using this option may result in a more compact EXE file. How much, if any, space this option will save through packing the executable file depends on the number of repeated bytes used in the file. If your program requires much relocation upon loading, this option causes the relocation table to be optimized for size. If the resulting EXE file is smaller, it logically will load more quickly than a file linked without this option.

If you plan to convert your EXE file to a COM file, do not use this option. If you pack your EXE file, you cannot convert it to a COM file.

Ignore Extended Dictionary (/E, /NOE, or /NOEXT)

Newer versions of the library manager utilities (discussed in Chapter 11) all can create *extended dictionaries* that the linker will then normally use to complete the linking process more rapidly. This option, known to TLINK as /E, to LINK as /NOE, and to OptLink as /NOEXT, prevents the linker from using any extended dictionary that may be available. This would normally be done only if you need every byte of memory you can get to link your program.

Echo Response File to Screen (/EC)

This option, available only to OptLink, causes each line of any response file that you use to be echoed to the screen.

Translate *FAR* Calls Where Possible (/F)

This option, implemented only in LINK but recognized and ignored by OptLink, causes CALL instructions to FAR procedures to be converted into a PUSH CS followed by a NEAR call instruction, which takes fewer bytes in your program and executes more rapidly.

Use Group Associations (/G)

This option, available only to OptLink, instructs the linker to honor the GROUP directives included in the OBJ files and combine all the named segments within a GROUP into a single segment. This is the default condition for LINK, and can be turned off by using the /NOG option. Because the defaults for OptLink can be configured with either the /G option or the /NOG option, /G is provided to choose the nondefault condition if the linker is configured to default to /NOG.

List Linker Options (/HE)

The /HE option, available to both LINK and OptLink, is the linker's help function. For example, if you enter the command

```
LINK /HE
```

LINK responds with a listing of its available options. The screen appears similar to the following:

```
Microsoft (R) Overlay Linker  Version 3.64
Copyright (C) Microsoft Corp 1983-1988.  All rights reserved.

Valid options are:
  /BATCH              /CODEVIEW
  /CPARMAXALLOC       /DOSSEG
  /DSALLOCATE         /EXEPACK
  /FARCALLTRANSLATION /HELP
```

```
/HIGH                    /INFORMATION
/LINENUMBERS             /MAP
/NODEFAULTLIBRARYSEARCH  /NOEXTDICTIONARY
/NOFARCALLTRANSLATION    /NOGROUPASSOCIATION
/NOIGNORECASE            /NOPACKCODE
/OVERLAYINTERRUPT        /PACKCODE
/PAUSE                   /QUICKLIBRARY
/SEGMENTS                /STACK
```

Notice that the verbose option names are listed. You only need to enter enough characters to differentiate your desired option from the others. OptLink displays a similar list of options.

To view the available options for TLINK, simply omit all command-line parameters:

```
TLINK
```

Load Program in High Memory (/HI)

Normally, the linker assumes that a program is to be loaded at the lowest free memory address. The /HI option, available to both LINK and OptLink, instructs the linker to load the linked program as high in memory as possible. This option typically is used with the /DS option.

Initialize All Segments (/I)

This option, available only with TLINK, causes TLINK to output all segments named in the OBJ files, even if some of them do not contain any bytes. Without this option, TLINK will not output empty segments (inserted by some high-level languages to establish segment sequence). LINK and OptLink always output all segments, so these linkers do not need this option.

Display Progress of Linking Process (/IN or /INF)

This option, available to LINK as /INF and OptLink as /IN, causes the linker to display, by STDERR, a running account of what it is doing. The display is primary used to debug problems that show up as an inability to link your OBJ files successfully.

Ignore Case (/IG)

This option, available only to OptLink, forces the linker to treat all symbols as uppercase. Because this is the default condition for both the other linkers, they have no need for the option. Although you can configure OptLink's default condition as you like, with this option you can also change the default operation as necessary without needing to reconfigure it.

Include Line Numbers in List File (/L)

If you specified a listing file, you can use the /L option (available in all three linkers) to include a list of all source code line memory addresses in the list file. Such a list is helpful when you are debugging.

This option is useful only if the OBJ file includes a line number, which depends on how the OBJ file was created. MASM does not include line numbers in the OBJ file, but many high-level languages do. If the OBJ file does not include line number information, no extra information is generated in the MAP file.

Include Global Symbol Table in List File (/M)

When you include the /M option (available in all three linkers), the linker creates a public symbol listing. This option forces a listing file to be created. The listing file will have the name of the first OBJ file and the extension MAP, unless you provide a different name on the command line or at the interactive prompt.

Do Not Use Default Libraries (/N, /NOD, or /NODE)

Some high-level languages include in the OBJ file the names of default libraries for the linker to search when linking the file. This option, known to TLINK as /N, to LINK as /NOD, and to OptLink as /NODE, overrides such specifications so that the linker ignores any libraries that the language specified in the OBJ files.

Cancel OptLink Default Condition Options (/NOB, /NOCHECKA, etc.)

These options are available only to OptLink. Each option will cancel the effects of another option configured as an OptLink default condition. For example, /NOB will cancel a default condition configured with the batch (/BA) option. The following table matches the option codes that set these default conditions with the option codes that cancel them.

Default condition option code	Option code canceling default condition
/BA	/NOB
/CHECKA	/NOCHECKA
/CHECKE	/NOCHECKE
/CHECKS	/NOCHECKS
/CO	/NOCO
/DO	/NODO
/DS	/NODS
/EC	/NOEC
/H	/NOH
/I	/NOI
/L	/NOL
/M	/NOM
/PAU	/NOPAU
/X	/NOX

You cannot configure the default conditions for LINK and TLINK, so those linkers have no need for these options.'

Do Not Translate FAR Calls (/NOF)

This option, available to both LINK and OptLink, prevents the linker from converting FAR calls into NEAR calls. Unless this option is used, LINK's default condition is to insert a PUSH CS machine instruction, then emit a NEAR call using only the CS offset. This saves both time and space but confuses debugging efforts. OptLink may be configured to have either /F or /NOF as its default (refer to the /F option). If configured for full LINK compatibility, the /NOF option does the same as in LINK.

Do Not Associate Groups (/NOG)

The /NOG option, available to both LINK and OptLink, instructs the linker to ignore GROUP associations when it assigns memory addresses for data and program code. The option is intended specifically for use with object code generated by old versions of the Microsoft FORTRAN and Pascal compilers.

Do Not Ignore Case Differences (/NOI)

The /NOI option, available to both LINK and OptLink, causes the linker to differentiate between upper- and lowercase letters.

Do Not Pack Code Segments (/NOP or /NOPAC)

This option, known to LINK as /NOP and to OptLink as /NOPAC, prevents the linker from packing contiguous code segments that have different names into a single segment for loading. Because they activate what normally is the default condition, /NOP and /NOPAC are usually not needed. However, if OptLink's default is configured for /PAC condition, or LINK is switched by an environment variable to the /PAC condition, /NOP or /NOPAC at the command line will restore the nonpacking mode.

Set Overlay Loader Interrupt Number (/O:*int*)

The /O: option, available to both LINK and OptLink, enables you to specify the interrupt number used by an overlay loader. Use this option with object code generated by compilers that support overlays, such as Microsoft C (but not MASM). *int* is the number (between 0 and 255) of the MS-DOS interrupt to use for the overlay loader.

OptLink does not process overlays, so it actually does nothing with this option but recognize it for LINK compatibility.

Pack Contiguous Code Segments (/PAC)

This option, available to both LINK and OptLink, instructs the linker to pack adjacent code segments bearing different names into a single segment and adjust offset addresses accordingly. Used with the /F option it can significantly reduce code size and increase operating speed for programs that have multiple code segments.

OptLink does not process FAR call translation, so it actually does nothing with this option but recognize it for LINK compatibility.

Pause for Disk Change (/PAU)

Using this option, available to both LINK and OptLink, causes the linker to display a message and wait for you to switch disks before the linker writes the EXE file. This option is particularly useful if you have a limited number of disk drives or disk space. When the linker has completely written the EXE file, the linker prompts you to return the original disk.

Produce QuickLibrary QLB File (/Q)

This option, available to both LINK and OptLink, instructs the linker to generate as its output a QLB file rather than a normal executable EXE file. The QLB file is suitable for use with the Microsoft Quick languages.

OptLink does not generate Quick Libraries, so it actually does nothing with this option but recognize it for LINK compatibility.

Generate Detailed Segment Map (/S)

This option, available only to TLINK, directs the linker to generate a detailed segment map as part of the listing file.

Specify Maximum Segments (/SE:*seg*)

This option, available to both LINK and OptLink, directs the linker to process no more than a specific number of segments. Typically, this option is used if the program being linked has a large number of segments. LINK, by default, handles only up to 128 segments. *seg* can be any number between 1 and 1024.

Override Stack Size (/ST:*size*)

Normally, the linker determines the stack size in the finished program based on any stack declarations in the OBJ file. The /ST:*size* option, available to both LINK and OptLink, overrides this value. To use this option you must substitute a number for *size* between 1 and 65,535, representing the desired stack size.

Generate Turbo Debugger Information (/V)

This option, available only to TLINK, instructs the linker to generate information used by Turbo Debugger in the EXE file. It is functionally similar to the /CO option that LINK and OptLink use for CodeView-compatible code generation. For more information on Using Turbo Debugger, refer to Chapter 10.

Generate Cross-References in Listing File (/X)

This option, available only to OptLink, directs the linker to generate complete cross-reference listings as a part of the MAP listing file. Take care not to confuse it with the following TLINK option that has the same name but a different meaning.

Do Not Generate Any Listing File (/X)

This option, available only to TLINK, directs the linker not to generate any listing file. Unlike the other linkers, TLINK generates a MAP file by default and must be directed not to do so if you do not want one.

Testing the Finished TEST.EXE

Now that your linker has created TEST.EXE, you can try your program to see if it works. Enter the following at the DOS prompt to start execution of the program:

TEST

The result should be a prompt asking you for an initial value. Enter an integer number, such as 7. You have just asked TEST to calculate the number of blocks in a seven-level pyramid, as shown in figure 9.1.

Fig. 9.1. *A seven-level pyramid.*

The program dialog and results should appear as follows:

```
C>TEST
Initial Value: 7
    7        28
Initial Value: _
```

Of course, this program is designed for utility, not attractiveness. The returned values indicate the original value entered (7) and the total number of blocks in the pyramid (28).

This program is designed to continue asking for values and returning results until you enter a value of 999. Then the program will generate a list showing the initial values and resulting values for pyramids between one row high and the maximum number of rows the program can handle. A partial program dialog follows:

```
C>TEST
Initial Value: 7
   7         28
Initial Value: 5
   5         15
Initial Value: 22
  22        253
Initial Value: 103
 103       5356
Initial Value: 999
   1          1
   2          3
   3          6
   4         10
   5         15
   6         21
   7         28
   8         36
   9         45
  10         55
```

(Intermediate values have been deleted to conserve space.)

```
 353      62481
 354      62835
 355      63190
 356      63546
 357      63903
 358      64261
 359      64620
 360      64980
 361      65341
 362          0

C>_
```

Notice that the upper limit the routine can handle represents a 361-row pyramid. A 362-row pyramid contains 65,703 blocks, a number too large to be stored in the unsigned integer that is used to return values from the assembly language subroutine.

Summary

The linking step is vital to completion of any program. Using a linker is easy because during ordinary use, you don't need to worry about using options or other complicating factors.

In this chapter you have compared the characteristics of the three major linkers and learned how each is used to create a sample program, TEST.EXE.

The only use of the linker that is not covered in this chapter is using it with libraries. That topic is discussed in Chapter 11. The next chapter deals with debugging programs.

10

Debugging Assembly Language Subroutines

W e all know what *bugs* are. The bane of programmers everywhere, bugs seem to crop up at the most inopportune times (such as when the program you are working on is supposed to be shipped out the door) and have been known to keep frustrated programmers from sleeping at night. The term *debugging* refers to removal of these pesky problems from your programs.

Debugging as an Art Form

If you have been programming for any length of time, you are already familiar with debugging tools for high-level languages. Anyone who has stared at program listings for hours on end knows that debugging software can make the job of debugging much faster and easier.

Assembly language programmers can benefit from this software as much as high-level-language programmers. The type and amount of programming you do are important factors in determining the type (and price) of the debugging tool you need. Hundreds of debugging tools, which run the gamut of features and prices, are available.

239

No debugging tool will, in itself, make the task of finding and removing bugs really easy. To do that, you must learn the *art* of debugging, and the only way to do that is the hard way, through experience.

You may question my statement that debugging is an art; most other programming activity is usually considered to be either a science or a craft. However, there's a true art to the good debugger's work; it's much like comparing the detective exploits of Sherlock Holmes with tedious beat-pounding police work.

Sometimes, of course, it takes the boring step-by-step trace through a program to pin down a really subtle problem. More often, though, the debug artist will absorb clues from the way the bug manifests itself. Often, the things that *don't* happen reveal more than the things that *do* happen, as Sherlock Holmes observed in *Hound of the Baskervilles* about the dog's failure to bark at night. The debug artist then leaps directly to the root cause by what looks to others as either a feat of magic or an uncommonly good guess.

To learn the art of debugging, you'll need to choose a set of debugging tools that fits the way you personally prefer to work. Yet before you can make that choice, you must learn at least the beginnings of the art. Although this may seem to be a catch-22 situation, it's just typical of everything that happens in the wacky world of debugging!

I can show you enough of the art so that you can wisely select your first set of tools. But first let's take a quick look at the tools that are available.

The Two General Classes of Tools

Software and hardware *debuggers* are development tools that simplify the task of tracking and exterminating software bugs. Software debuggers (such as DEBUG) are memory-resident and work from within memory. Hardware debuggers usually combine a hardware computer card with software to provide external debugging capabilities.

Which group of debuggers is *better* depends on the type of bugs you anticipate. If you are an applications programmer, software debuggers usually fill the bill. But for system-level programmers as well as for applications programmers who develop software designed to operate in real-time using interrupts, hardware debuggers can make life easier. The types of glitches that crop up in such programs can easily lock up a computer, rendering software debuggers useless.

Software Debuggers

Software debuggers range in price from free (DEBUG) to more than $500. Higher-priced debuggers usually offer advanced features that may make the investment worthwhile. For example, if your programming time is worth $40 an hour, just a few hours lost to manual debugging (using a free debugger) would justify the cost of a higher-priced commercial system. Many programmers have found that the time saved locating a single bug more than offsets the cost of the debugger.

Typically, software debuggers are written to monitor (in a controlled way) the operation of the target program. These debuggers load themselves in RAM and then load the program to be debugged into a work area where the debugger can control execution of the program.

Table 10.1 lists a few software debuggers in addition to those discussed in this chapter, along with the names and addresses of the companies that publish them.

Table 10.1. Software debuggers.

Product	Source
RBUG86	Answer Software Corp. 20045 Stevens Creek Blvd. Cupertino, CA 95014 (408) 253-7515
Software Source Probe	Atron Corp. 12950 Saratoga Ave. Saratoga, CA 95070 (800) 283-5933 (408) 253-5933
Soft-Scope III	Concurrent Sciences, Inc. P.O. Box 9666 Moscow, ID 83843 (208) 882-0445
DB86	Intel Corp. 3065 Bowers Ave. Santa Clara, CA 9505 (800) 548-4725

Table 10.1. continues

Table 10.1. *continued*

Product	Source
Advanced Trace86	Morgan Computing Co., Inc. 1950 Stemmons Freeway, Suite 5001 Dallas, TX 75207 (214) 991-7598
Periscope I Periscope II Periscope II-X Periscope I/MC	The Periscope Co., Inc. 1197 Peachtree St., Plaza Level Atlanta, GA 30361 (404) 875-8080
Pfix86 +	Polytron Products Division Sage Software, Inc. 1700 Northwest 167th Place Beaverton, OR 97006 (800) 547-4000 (503) 645-1150
CodeSmith-86	Visual Age 642 N. Larchmont Blvd. Los Angeles, CA 90004 (213) 534-4202

Benign observers, software debuggers ignorantly follow instructions. If you instruct the debugger to execute a section of code, it will attempt to do so, sometimes destroying itself in the process. For example, if an errant program causes a sector to be loaded from disk into RAM at the place where the debugging software resides, the debugging session will come to a screeching halt, and the debugger will do nothing to stop the error. Totally isolating a software-only debugger is impossible.

Hardware Debuggers

Hardware debuggers come in a variety of shapes, sizes, and capabilities. They typically consist of both hardware and software components. Usually, the hardware component is either a card that fits in an expansion slot of the computer, or a device that is placed between the microprocessor and the system board. The software component may be similar to the previously described software debuggers, or it may reside in ROM on the hardware board. Table 10.2 lists a few hardware debuggers and where you can get them.

Table 10.2. Hardware debuggers.

Product	Source
PDTPC PDTAT ICD286	Answer Software Corp. 20045 Stevens Creek Blvd. Cupertino, CA 95014 (408) 253-7515
286 Probe 286 Source Probe 386 Probe	Atron Corp. 12950 Saratoga Ave. Saratoga, CA 95070 (800) 283-5933 (408) 253-5933
PSCOPE-86 I²ICE ICE-286 ICE-386 MON386 ICD-486 iPAT	Intel Corp. 3065 Bowers Ave. Santa Clara, CA 95051 (800) 548-4725
hyperICE hyperSOURCE	Microcosm Inc. 15275 Southwest Koll Parkway, Suite E Beaverton, OR 97006 (503) 626-6100
Periscope III Periscope IV	The Periscope Co., Inc. 1197 Peachtree St., Plaza Level Atlanta, GA 30361 (404) 875-8080

Hardware debuggers, which are much more expensive than software debuggers, can range in price from $200 to almost $8,000. The prices vary according to the type of hardware debugger, the types of options added, and the type of computer you will use.

The more expensive systems usually require a second computer to monitor the functioning of the first. These systems are called *in-circuit emulators* or *in-circuit devices*. They are virtually isolated from the target program and include the Microcosm In-Circuit Emulator, I2ICE, and the ICD-286.

As with software debuggers, the time saved in the development process may justify the cost of a hardware debugger. Hardware debuggers are best suited for systems-level or interrupt-driven software programs, which are prone to bugs that are virtually impossible to ferret out with software debuggers only.

And hardware debuggers offer greater control over the program environment than their software-only counterparts. By using the *nonmaskable interrupt* (NMI) line of the processor, hardware debuggers usually provide a way for you to recover system control at virtually any time, even if the computer has "hung." Such a brute-force method of seizing control of the computer seldom fails to work.

Some Software Debuggers Compared

To help you get a feel for how software debuggers compare, I'll describe the commands and general usage of half a dozen. These programs should be available at no extra cost as parts of the assembler and high-level language packages. Although you are unlikely to have all of them on hand, you should have two or three from this group available, no matter what assembler and language you choose.

Built-In, High-Level Language Debuggers

If you are using QuickC, QuickPascal, Turbo C, or Turbo Pascal, your language's Integrated Development Environment (the full-screen editor and compiler combo usually used for program development) has a built-in debugging tool. This tool tracks each high-level language source statement so you can *watch* any variable that you specify.

For finding problems in the high-level language code itself these debuggers are quite useful, but they are much less useful in attempting to find problems within assembly language modules that are called from the high-level language. The reason for this is that these debuggers make it difficult or impossible to see what is going on in the CPU registers while stepping through your assembly language modules, and the register contents provide many of the clues about what is going wrong.

With Microsoft's Quick languages, you can set watch variables with the register names and see those variables change; however, Borland's Turbo languages require that you set the pseudo-variables (_AX for AX, and so forth) in the watch window so you can see what is happening. Apparently, neither language can enable you to view the result in the FLAGS register.

The major use that I have found for the built-in debuggers in this situation is to verify that the problem really *is* in the assembly language module and not elsewhere in the high-level program. However, once the trouble has been isolated to the assembly language area, you have to switch to a tool that can show you everything that is happening there. For this, you need one of the separate debugging utilities.

DEBUG, the Low-Cost Standard

You probably already have a copy of DEBUG on your DOS distribution disk. Only a few versions of DOS omit it, although the documentation for the program was moved over to the extra-cost Technical Reference Manual at version 3.3.

Although the axiom "you get what you pay for" is often true, DEBUG is a notable exception. This "free" program (free in the sense that most DOS users don't even know it's part of the package they pay for, so it comes at no extra cost) has most of the capability of any other software debugger. It can be used for just about anything except tracing the operation of DOS itself; that requires a hardware debugger and a separate system connected to it!

Once you know how to handle DEBUG, you can quickly learn just about any other software debugger. DEBUG's only serious shortcoming is that it does not provide source program display and tracking.

DEBUG recognizes two special file extensions, EXE and HEX, and treats files that have them differently from all others. The program loads any EXE file into memory just as the DOS loader would, using the file's relocation information to do the loading, and then discarding the information from the file. For this reason EXE files cannot be written back to disk; they're not all there by the time you see the first DEBUG prompt.

The other special file extension, HEX, is not often used today except with embedded systems, although in the days of CP/M, HEX files were the standard output of assemblers. Files with the HEX extension undergo a conversion similar to that of EXE files, and, like EXE files, cannot be written back to disk from DEBUG.

All other files are treated as memory images, like COM files, and are loaded at an offset of 0100h; if you debug BIN files or device drivers, both of which begin at offset 0000h, all assigned addresses will be 0100h too high.

DEBUG provides the 19 commands listed in table 10.3. Only about half of these commands are normally used during a debugging session. The most frequently used commands are indicated by an asterisk (∗) after the command letter.

Table 10.3. *The DEBUG command set.*

Command	Meaning
A ∗	Assemble
C	Compare
D ∗	Dump
E ∗	Enter
F	Fill
G ∗	Go
H ∗	Hexadecimal arithmetic
I	Input
L	Load
M	Move
N	Name
O	Output
Q ∗	Quit
P ∗	Proceed through operation
R ∗	Register
S ∗	Search
T ∗	Trace into operation
U ∗	Unassemble
W	Write

To invoke any of these commands, enter the command character in either upper- or lowercase, and then enter any parameters that the command may require. In this chapter's examples of DEBUG commands, the command and any required parameters are shown in **boldface** with optional parameters in italics.

DEBUG does not require any delimiters between commands and parameters, except when two hexadecimal numbers are entered as separate parameters. In all other instances, delimiters are optional, although you may find that using them makes the commands you enter more readable. A delimiter can be either a space or comma; use a colon as the delimiter between the segment and offset of a hexadecimal address.

Commands are executed when you press Enter, not as you type them. You can change a line by pressing the backspace key to delete what you have typed and then type the correct characters. When the command line is as you want it, press Enter to execute the entire line.

DEBUG does not detect errors until you have pressed Enter. If you make a syntax error in an entry, the command line is redisplayed with the word error added at the point at which the error was detected. If a command line contains more than one error, only the first error will be detected and indicated, and execution will cease at that point.

In case you do not have any official DEBUG documentation available to you, let's examine each of the 19 DEBUG commands. (Discussions in later sections of this chapter about the more advanced, source-level debuggers will describe only those commands needed to get through a sample debugging session.)

Assemble (A)

The Assemble command is used for entering assembly language mnemonics and for having them translated directly into machine language instructions in memory. This capability is extremely helpful for making on-the-fly changes to a program and for entering short test programs. The syntax for this command is

A *address*

address is an optional beginning address (hexadecimal) at which the assembled machine language instructions will be placed. If you do not specify an address, DEBUG will start placing the instructions either at CS:0100 or after the last machine language instruction entered through Assemble.

Virtually every assembly language mnemonic, including segment override specifiers (CS:, DS:, ES:, SS:), is supported. There are one or two differences, however, between the standard mnemonics and DEBUG's implementation of them. First, because DEBUG cannot differentiate between NEAR and FAR returns, RET is assumed to be a near return, and RETF to be a far return.

Also, when a command line you enter refers to memory locations, DEBUG cannot always determine whether you want to act on a byte or on a word at that location. In the following example:

```
DEC [42B]
```

it is not clear whether a byte or a word should be decremented at that location. To overcome this ambiguity, you must indicate explicitly which you intend. To do so, use BYTE PTR or WORD PTR, as in the following amended example:

```
DEC BYTE PTR [42B]
```

Clearly, such explicitness is not always necessary, as in this example:

```
MOV AL,[42B]
```

Because only a byte can be moved into AL, using BYTE PTR here would be redundant.

The Assemble command lets you use DB and DW (in addition to the regular 8088 and 8087 assembly language mnemonics) to define data areas.

Each line is assembled after you press Enter. If DEBUG cannot determine what you want when you enter a certain mnemonic, it flags the error and does not assemble that line.

When you have finished using the Assemble command, press Enter to return to the DEBUG dash prompt.

Compare (C)

The Compare command compares and reports on any differences between the contents of two memory blocks. The syntax for this command is

C block1 address

block1 is either both the beginning and ending addresses or, if preceded by an **l**, the beginning address and length of the first memory block. **address** is the start of the second memory block. The length of the second block is assumed to be equal to the length of the first. The memory blocks can overlap, and the second block can lie physically before the first.

The command compares the two blocks, byte-by-byte, and reports any differences in the following format:

```
address1   value1     value2   address2
```

Dump (D)

The Dump command is one you will use often. It displays the contents of a series of memory locations. The syntax for the command is

D *address1 address2*

You must specify address1, an optional starting address for the display, before you can specify *address2*, an optional ending address.

If no addresses are specified, DEBUG will start displaying memory locations either with DS:0100 or, if Dump has already been used, with the byte following the last byte displayed by the most recent Dump command.

Dump always displays 16 bytes per line, beginning with the nearest paragraph (16-byte) boundary. This display rule may differ with the first and last lines displayed, because you may have asked DEBUG to start the dump with a memory location that was not on a paragraph boundary.

If you do not specify an ending address, DEBUG always displays 128 bytes of memory. Each byte is shown in both hexadecimal and ASCII representation, as in the following example:

```
-D 2C5
126F:02C0                   OF 00 03-D1 52 57 36 FF 2E AC 04        ....RW6....
126F:02D0    58 5F 07 8B DE BE 00 05-8B 0E 40 05 3D 53 59 74    X_........@.=SYt
126F:02E0    4F 3D 48 50 74 4A 3D 49-4E 74 45 BE 54 04 8B 0E    O=HPtJ=INtE.T...
126F:02F0    51 04 3D 42 4F 74 39 26-80 3D 00 74 16 26 80 7D    Q.=BOt9&.=.t.&.}
126F:0300    01 3A 75 0F 26 8A 15 80-CA 20 80 EA 60 8A C2 FE    .:u.&.... ..'...
126F:0310    C8 EB 06 B4 19 CD 21 32-D2 04 41 AA B8 3A 5C AB    ......!2..A..:\.
126F:0320    8C C0 8E D8 87 FE B4 47-CD 21 87 FE 73 12 EB 0D    .......G.!..s...
126F:0330    83 F9 03 74 01 49 D1 E9-73 01 A4 F3 A5 32 C0 AA    ...t.I..s....2..
126F:0340    8B F3 36 FF 2E                                     ..6..
```

Reading from left to right, notice that each line shows the address of the first byte, followed by eight bytes, a hyphen, and the remaining eight bytes of the paragraph. The rightmost characters on each line are the ASCII representation of the hexadecimal values in the paragraph. Note also that if a specific hexadecimal value has no corresponding ASCII character, a period is used as a placeholder.

Enter (E)

To try temporary fixes during a session, you will frequently need to use the Enter command. It enables you to change the contents of specific memory locations. The syntax for this command is

E address *changes*

address is the beginning address for entering changes, and changes is an optional list of the changes to be made.

You can specify *changes* on the command line in any combination of hexadecimal numbers or ASCII characters. (ASCII characters must be enclosed in quotation marks.)

If you do not specify changes on the command line, DEBUG enters a special entry mode in which the values of memory locations, beginning at **address**, are displayed. You can change these values one byte at a time. (Be sure to enter the changes as hexadecimal numbers.) After each entry, press the space bar to effect the change. The next byte will then be displayed so that you can make any necessary changes. To exit entry mode and return to DEBUG command mode, press Enter.

If you enter a minus sign or hyphen as part of a change to a byte, DEBUG will go back one byte to the preceding memory location. You can then make additional changes to that byte.

If you have not made any changes to a byte, press the space bar to proceed to the next byte. The unchanged byte retains its original value.

Fill (F)

Use this command to fill a block of memory with a specific value or series of values. The syntax for this command is

F block fillvalue

block is either both the beginning and ending addresses or, if preceded by an **l**, the beginning address and length of the memory block. **fillvalue** is the byte value(s) that should be used to fill the memory block. If **fillvalue** represents fewer bytes than are needed to fill the **block**, the series is repeated until the **block** is completed.

fillvalue may be any combination of hexadecimal numbers or ASCII characters. (Any ASCII characters must be enclosed in quotation marks.)

As an example, either of the following command lines will fill (with a null value) the memory block DS:0000 through DS:00FF:

```
F DS:0000 DS:00FF 0
F DS:0000 LFF 0
```

To fill the same area with the hexadecimal equivalents of the ASCII characters "ALW", followed by a carriage return and a line feed, you would use either of the following command lines:

```
F DS:0000 DS:00FF "ALW"D A
F DS:0000 LFF "ALW"D A
```

Remember that the five values (41, 4C, 57, 0D, and 0A) will be repeated again and again until all 256 bytes have been filled.

Go (G)

The Go command, which causes machine language statements to be executed, is one of the most frequently used DEBUG commands. If you are debugging a program, this command executes the program you have loaded. It also lets you specify optional *breakpoints*, which are addresses at which program execution will stop. The syntax for the Go command is

G =*start break1 break2 ... break10*

=*start* is an optional starting address, and *break1* through *break10* are optional breakpoint addresses. If the starting address is not specified, Go will begin program execution with the current address contained in CS:IP.

If the breakpoints are not reached, execution continues until the program ends. If you specify only an offset for a breakpoint address, CS is assumed to be the segment.

To facilitate a breakpoint, DEBUG replaces the code at the breakpoint address with the hexadecimal value CC, which is the code for an interrupt. If DEBUG reaches the interrupt (the breakpoint), all breakpoints are returned to their original values, the registers are displayed (as though by the R command), and program execution stops. If DEBUG never reaches the breakpoint, the values at the breakpoints remain in their changed state.

Hexadecimal Arithmetic (H)

This convenience command does simple hexadecimal addition and subtraction. If you are using a hexadecimal calculator, you may never need to issue this command. The syntax for this command is

H value1 value2

value1 and **value2** are hexadecimal numbers. This command returns a result line that shows two values: the sum of **value1** and **value2**, and the difference between **value1** and **value2**. This command does not alter any registers or flags.

The following examples show how the **H** command is used. In the first example, AHh and BFh are added, which results in 016Dh, and then subtracted, resulting in FFEFh:

```
-H AE BF
016D  FFEF
```

The second example performs the same operations with 96h and C2h:

```
-H 96 C2
0158  FFD4
```

Input (I)

The Input command (the opposite of the Output command) fetches a byte from a port. The syntax is

I port

port is the address of the specified port to read. The Input command fetches a byte from the desired port and then displays it as a hexadecimal value. This command does not change any registers or flags.

Load (L)

The Load command (the opposite of the Write command) is used to load a file or disk sectors into memory. The syntax is

L *buffer drivenum startsector numsector*

buffer is the destination memory address for the information to be loaded. *drivenum* is an optional numeric disk-drive designator. *startsector* is the absolute disk sector (a hexadecimal number) with which to begin reading, and *numsector* is the total number of disk sectors (a hexadecimal number) to read.

drivenum, the drive specification, is such that 0 = A, 1 = B, 2 = C, and so on. In *numsector*, no more than 128 (80h) sectors can be loaded.

If you do not provide the *drivenum startsector numsector* combination, DEBUG assumes that you want to load a file, in which case the *buffer* address is optional. If you do not specify an address, DEBUG loads the file at CS:0100. Use the Name command (described shortly) to specify the name of the file.

After a file has been loaded, BX:CX contains the number of bytes successfully read, provided that the file does not have an EXE extension. If the file has an EXE extension, BX:CX is set to the size of the program.

Move (M)

The Move command moves a block of memory from one location to another. The syntax is

M block1 address

block1 is either both the beginning and ending addresses or, if preceded by an **l**, the beginning address and length of the first memory block. **address** is the destination address for the move. The destination address and the source block can overlap. The bytes from the source block are moved, one at a time, to the destination address.

Name (N)

The Name command is used to specify a file name that will be used either by the Load and Write commands or by the program you are debugging. The syntax of this command is

N filename1 *filename2*

filename1 is the complete file specification that will be parsed and placed in a file control block at CS:005C. filename2 is the complete file specification that will be parsed and placed in a file control block at CS:006C.

In addition to parsing the file specifications, DEBUG places them (as entered) at CS:0081, preceded by a byte indicating the number of bytes entered. DEBUG then sets AX to indicate the parsing status (validity) of the file specifications, with AL corresponding to the first file and AH to the second. If either file name is invalid, its corresponding byte is set to 1; otherwise, it is set to 0.

Output (O)

The Output command (the opposite of the Input command) outputs a byte to a specified port. The syntax is

O port value

port is the address of the specified port, and **value** is the hexadecimal byte to write. This command does not change any registers or flags.

Proceed (P)

The Proceed command is only available with DEBUG programs distributed with DOS 3.0 or later versions. Using this command, you can execute machine language instructions in a single step, treating a CALL or an INT as a single instruction and performing the entire action with no pause, after which the register status is displayed (as with the Register command). The syntax of the Proceed command is

P = *start count*

Both of these parameters are optional; = start is a starting address, and *count* is a hexadecimal number that signifies how many individual instructions must be traced through to execute the command. If = *start* is not specified, execution will begin with the current address contained in CS:IP. If *count* is excluded, only one machine language instruction will be executed.

The P command differs from T only in its handling of the CALL and INT instructions; P executes the entire called routine before pausing, but T executes only the transfer of control and then pauses at the first instruction of the called routine.

Quit (Q)

The Quit command is used to quit DEBUG and return control of your computer to DOS. You simply press *Q*. There are no parameters for this command, which does not save the programs on which you were working.

Register (R)

The Register command displays the microprocessor's register and flag values, and enables you to change individual register values. The command's syntax is

R *register*

register, the optional name of the register to modify, may be any of the following: AX, BX, CX, DX, SP, BP, SI, DI, DS, ES, SS, CS, IP, PC, or F. IP and PC are synonymous; both refer to the instruction pointer register. F refers to the flags register.

If you enter the Register command with no parameters, DEBUG responds by displaying a register summary similar to the following:

```
-r
AX=0000  BX=0000  CX=0000  DX=0000  SP=FFEE  BP=0000  SI=0000  DI=0000
DS=1206  ES=1206  SS=1206  CS=1206  IP=0100   NV UP EI PL NZ NA PO NC
1206:0100 FB            STI
```

If you enter a register name as a parameter, DEBUG displays the current register value and waits for you to enter a new value. If you enter a value, it is assumed to be in hexadecimal. If you do not enter a value, no change is made to the register value.

(For more information on the Register command, refer to this chapter's "Using DEBUG" section.)

Search (S)

With the Search command, you can search a block of memory for a specific sequence of values. The syntax is

S block searchvalue

block is either both the beginning and ending addresses or, if preceded by an **l**, the beginning address and length of the first memory block. **searchvalue** is the byte value(s) that you want to search for in the memory block.

The values that DEBUG searches for can be any combination of hexadecimal numbers and ASCII characters. (ASCII characters must be enclosed in quotation marks.)

If DEBUG locates any exact matches, it displays the address of the beginning of the match. If no matches are found, no message is displayed.

Trace (T)

Using the Trace command, you can execute machine language instructions in a single step, after which the register status is displayed (as with the Register command). The syntax of the Trace command is

T =*start count*

Both of these parameters are optional; =*start* is a starting address, and *count* is a hexadecimal number that signifies how many individual instructions must be traced through to execute the command. If =*start* is not specified, execution will begin with the current address contained in CS:IP. If *count* is excluded, only one machine language instruction will be executed.

The T command differs from P only in its handling of the CALL and INT instructions; T executes only the transfer of control and then pauses at the first instruction of the called routine, but P executes the entire called routine before pausing.

Unassemble (U)

The Unassemble command decodes the values of a group of memory locations into 8088 mnemonics. One of the most frequently used DEBUG commands, Unassemble enables you to view the instructions that will be executed during the DEBUG operation. The syntax is as follows:

U *address range*

address, which is optional, is the beginning address of the area to be unassembled. *range*, which is optional if *address* is specified, is either the ending address of the area or, if preceded by an *l*, the length of the area. If you specify an *address* but no *range*, approximately one screenful of data will be displayed.

If you do not specify an address or range, unassembly begins with the memory location indicated by CS:IP or (if Unassemble has already been used) with the byte following the last byte displayed by the most recent Unassemble command. The unassembly proceeds for 16 bytes. The number of instruction lines this process represents depends on the number of bytes used in each instruction line. If you specify an address and a range, all bytes within that block are unassembled.

(The Unassemble command is used extensively in this chapter's "Debugging TEST.EXE" section.)

Write (W)

The Write command (the opposite of the Load command) is used to write a file or individual disk sectors to a disk. The syntax is

W *buffer drivenum startsector numsector*

buffer is the memory address of the information to be written; *drivenum* is an optional numeric disk-drive designator; *startsector* is the absolute disk sector (a hexadecimal number) at which writing is to begin; and *numsector* is the total number of disk sectors (a hexadecimal number) to be written.

The drive specification, *drivenum*, is such that 0 = A, 1 = B, 2 = C, and so on. In *numsector*, the number of sectors loaded cannot exceed 128, or 80h.

If you do not provide the *drivenum startsector numsector* combination, DEBUG assumes that you want to write a file; the buffer address is then optional. If you do not specify an address, DEBUG assumes that the start of the file is CS:0100. (Use the Name command to specify the name of the file.)

Before a file is written, BX:CX must be set to the number of bytes to be written.

As noted previously, two types of files cannot be written back to disk: those with an extension of EXE and those with an extension of HEX. The distinction is made solely on the file name's extension; if necessary, you could use the N command to change the name and then write the file. However, the file that is written will be significantly different from the one that DEBUG read into memory. What is written will be a memory image that is no longer relocatable (if an EXE file) or in ASCII text format (if a HEX file).

CodeView from Microsoft

As you will see a bit later when you go through the debugging technique using the sample file TEST.EXE, making effective use of DEBUG with programs generated by a high-level language requires some extra effort to get past the "invisible" start-up code that all high-level languages include in their output programs.

Because of this, *source-level debuggers* have become popular. One of the first of these utilities was Microsoft's CodeView. First distributed with the Microsoft C Compiler version 4.0, it is now packed with all the upper-echelon Microsoft language products. The version used for these examples came as part of the MASM version 5.1 package.

Microsoft's manual describes CodeView as "a powerful, window-oriented tool that enables you to track down logical errors in programs." That's an accurate description. Like DEBUG, CodeView enables you to step through the execution of your program one operation at a time. Unlike DEBUG, it can also show you your actual source program in the language you wrote it in, and perform entire statements without pause; yet when you need the single-step capability, that's present too.

You can use CodeView with any executable program, either COM or EXE. However, to take full advantage of the debugger's capabilities you must create an EXE file, using the special CodeView options during all steps of its creation, to get all the symbolic information from your source programs to a place where CodeView can use it.

This means that your high-level language code and your assembly language modules should all be compiled or assembled, using the /ZI or /ZD options, to put the information into the OBJ files. Then when you do the linking, you should use the /CO option to move this information to the EXE file.

Only when you do all this, can CodeView show you your source program line by line and replace the hex memory addresses in the register window with the names of your variables. Because these options are available only to Microsoft and SLR products, you won't be able to take full advantage of CodeView if you're a Turbo user. But as you'll soon see, you're not left out in the cold, either.

Unlike DEBUG, whose 19 simple commands mostly follow the same syntax as CodeView's commands, CodeView offers an extensive list of command variations. The entries for "Commands" in the manual index take 1-1/2 pages, and those are only the major references.

However, for routine debugging you need only a few of the available commands. Those that I have found essential are listed in table 10.4. Notice that, unlike DEBUG, many of these "commands" are actually "hot-key" operations; that is, all you do is press the function key, and the command executes. You need to press Enter only for the Q (quit) action.

Table 10.4. *Essential CodeView commands.*

Key	Action
F1	Display on-line help screens
F2	Open Registers window (display registers)
F5	Go (same as DEBUG's G)
F8	Trace (same as DEBUG's T)
F9	Set breakpoint at cursor location
F10	Proceed (same as DEBUG's P)
P	Proceed (same as DEBUG)
Q	Quit
R	Register (same as DEBUG)
T	Trace (same as DEBUG)

When you call CodeView with a program file, as explained later in this chapter, CodeView automatically brings in the program's source code if the source code is available in the current directory. If the source code is not available, or the program file does not contain debugging information, then the debugger automatically goes into "machine language" mode, which provides a display much like that of DEBUG.

You can move the screen cursor by using the arrow keys or a mouse. CodeView is the only one of the external debugging utilities described here that supports a mouse automatically.

As you step through your program using either F8 or F10, the highlight bar moves with you. When you get to your assembly language module, if you use F8 so that you do not step right over the module, the display will change to show your ASM source code.

That characteristic makes CodeView much simpler to use than DEBUG, as you will see when you step through a session with DEBUG. If you have CodeView available, you may choose to use DEBUG only when you cannot spare the memory that CodeView requires.

OptDebug from SLR

OptDebug, from SLR, Inc., and Odebug, the version furnished with OptAsm, are identical except that Odebug omits virtual memory support and has no printed manual. Both, however, have extensive on-line help capability and are relatively easy to use.

Like CodeView, OptDebug requires that the EXE file contain debugging information to reach its full capability. It uses exactly the same information as CodeView, so you must prepare your files in the same way.

Also like CodeView, OptDebug offers a multitude of commands, although most of them are not used frequently. Only a few commands, which are listed in table 10.5, are needed for successful debugging. Notice that they are similar in action to, but differ in detail from, those of CodeView. Actually, you could configure OptDebug to make its interface nearly identical to CodeView, but that's beyond the scope of this book.

Table 10.5. *Essential commands for OptDebug.*

Key	Action
F1	Display on-line help screens
F8	Proceed (same as DEBUG's P)
F9	Trace (same as DEBUG's T)
Alt-F3	Establish Source + Register + Data Windows
Alt-F9	Untrace (unique; undo last action)
Q	Quit

When called with a program file, OptDebug, like CodeView, automatically brings in the program's source code if it is available. If the source code is not available, or the program file does not contain debugging information, then the debugger automatically goes into "machine language" mode, which provides a display much like that of DEBUG.

Like CodeView, OptDebug automatically switches to the appropriate source-code file as you step from one module into another during a debugging session. However, to move the cursor you must use the function keys rather than the arrow keys, and the program does not support the mouse.

Your choice between CodeView and OptDebug is more likely to be based on your choice of assembler or linker than it is on the features of the two programs; they are essentially equivalent to each other. If you like to customize things to your own way of operating, OptDebug is more configurable, but CodeView supports the mouse interface automatically. Those are just about the only significant differences between them.

Turbo Debugger from Borland

Borland describes Turbo Debugger as a state-of-the-art source-level debugger designed for Turbo language programmers and those using other languages who want a more powerful debugging environment. It *does* offer several features not present in the other programs discussed in this chapter. Among the most notable are its ability to take advantage of the 80386 chip's capability to run multiple virtual machines, and its provisions for remote debugging. Added at version 2.0 were capabilities to backtrack in the program being debugged and mouse support.

For the average DOS user, however, Turbo Debugger's major advantage is that it's designed especially for compatibility with the Turbo programming language packages, and meshes with them more easily than either of the other packages. For example, the screen layout and menu choices are similar to those found in the integrated development environments of Turbo Pascal and Turbo C.

Similarly, where possible the command and function keys serve the same purposes: F3 calls up the pick list, Alt-X exits, and so forth. The essential keys and commands needed for use of Turbo Debugger are listed in table 10.6. As in all the Turbo environments, a context-sensitive reminder bar across the bottom of the screen shows you the most essential items at all times.

Table 10.6. Essential commands for Turbo Debugger.

Key	Action
F1	Display help screen
Alt-F1	Display last help used
F2	Set breakpoint at cursor
F7	Trace (like DEBUG's T)
F8	Proceed (like DEBUG's P)
F9	Go (like DEBUG's G)
F10	Use top-of-screen menu
Alt-X	Quit to DOS

Like CodeView and OptDebug, Turbo Debugger is able to automatically display the source file for each module and to switch between source files upon entering an assembly language module if the program is compiled, assembled, and linked with all the appropriate options. These options, however, are different for Turbo Debugger than they are for the other two source-level debuggers, and EXE files prepared for the others must be processed through a TDCONVRT utility to change them to the TD format. They are then no longer compatible with CodeView or OptDebug.

This is not likely to be a major factor. You will probably choose one of the three and stick with it. Only in most unusual circumstances would you find it useful to convert repeatedly between the two debugger-data EXE-file formats.

Turbo Debugger is bundled with Turbo Assembler, and both Turbo Debugger and Turbo Assembler are bundled into the "professional" versions of Turbo Pascal and Turbo C. Therefore, if you are a Borland fan, you'll most likely choose this debugger. However, if you prefer one of the other assemblers, you'll probably choose its matching debugger. All are capable of excellent performance and appear to be equally easy to use.

The General Techniques

This section will give you enough experience with the art of debugging to make informed decisions about which debugging tool best fits your own methods of working. An example of a debugging session will lead you through a somewhat artificial problem that is, however, typical of many real-life bugs: those that are accidentally caused by a typing error, resulting in a subtle code flaw so similar to the intended code that it slips by proofreading.

The initial, step-by-step description of how to debug this error will use a tool you most likely already have, DEBUG. Then I'll go through the same exercise much more briefly using the other three debugging tools to show you how they differ from DEBUG and from each other.

Using DEBUG

You should already have DEBUG because it is normally supplied with both PC DOS and MS-DOS. This section describes the basics of using DEBUG and takes you step-by-step through a sample debugging session.

Loading DEBUG by Itself

You can begin a DEBUG session either with or without a file. The simplest way to start is without a file. At the DOS prompt, enter

DEBUG

After you enter this command, a dash will appear on the screen at the left edge of the next line. This dash, which is DEBUG's prompt character, tells you that DEBUG is awaiting your command. If you see any other message, chances are that you have misspelled DEBUG or that DEBUG.COM is not available on the current disk drive.

At the DEBUG prompt, type the letter R in either upper- or lowercase, and press Enter. The display on your screen should be similar to the following:

```
C>debug
-r
AX=0000  BX=0000  CX=0000  DX=0000  SP=FFEE  BP=0000  SI=0000  DI=0000
DS=1206  ES=1206  SS=1206  CS=1206  IP=0100    NV UP EI PL NZ NA  PO NC
1206:0100 FB              STI
-
```

This entire display is the basic DEBUG "status line." (On your screen, the numbers and letters on the line that starts with DS= may be different from those shown here.) The R that you entered is DEBUG's Register command, which causes DEBUG to display the contents of the CPU registers.

As you learned in Chapter 1, AX, BX, CX, and DX are general-purpose registers. Ordinarily, they are the ones used for direct data manipulation. The other registers (SP, BP, SI, DI, DS, ES, SS, CS, and IP) are specialized registers. When you start DEBUG, the registers AX, BX, CX, DX, BP, SI, and DI are all set to zero.

The characters NV, UP, EI, PL, NZ, NA, PO, and NC are the settings of each of the status register's status flags. Table 10.7 shows the possible display values for each flag, depending on the flag setting. Note that in the Condition column, set denotes a value of 1 in the corresponding register bit, and clear denotes a value of 0.

Table 10.7. Status flag display characteristics for DEBUG.

Status flag	Condition	Meaning	Display
Overflow	set	yes	OV
	clear	no	NV
Direction	set	decrement	DN
	clear	increment	UP
Interrupt	set	enabled	EI
	clear	disabled	DI
Sign	set	negative	NG
	clear	positive	PL
Zero	set	yes	ZR
	clear	no	NZ
Auxiliary carry	set	yes	AC
	clear	no	NA
Parity	set	even	PE
	clear	odd	PO
Carry	set	yes	CY
	clear	no	NC

The current disassembled values of the code segment and the offset are displayed in the bottom line. 1206, the value of the code segment (CS) register, is used as the segment; 0100, the value of the instruction pointer (IP) register, is used as the offset.

When you enter DEBUG without a file, the value shown for disassembly could be almost anything because you have not instructed DEBUG to initialize the memory area. In this instance, the byte at 1206:0100 contains the value FBh, which is the numeric value for the mnemonic instruction STI.

To end the DEBUG session and return to DOS, type the letter **Q** (for Quit), and press Enter.

Now let's look at the other way to start DEBUG.

Loading DEBUG with a File

The other way to begin a DEBUG session is to specify the file that you want to debug. Suppose, for example, that you want to debug a file called TEST.COM. To load DEBUG and then TEST.COM, enter the following line at the DOS prompt:

DEBUG TEST.COM

If DEBUG cannot find the specified file, you will see an error message, and DEBUG will continue as though you had not entered a file name. Should this happen, you must do either of the following:

❏ Use the Q command to exit DEBUG and then, using the proper file specification, start over (I prefer this option because it lets me verify the file specification).

❏ Use the N command to correct the file name, followed by the L command to load the correct file. (These commands were described in the previous section.)

If the program you are debugging requires command-line parameters to function, simply add the parameters to the line invoking DEBUG. For instance, if TEST.COM needed a drive specification as a parameter, you would enter:

DEBUG TEST.COM B:

After DEBUG has loaded TEST.COM, you will see the dash prompt—DEBUG is ready and waiting for a command. If you enter the Register command, the status display will be similar to the one shown in the preceding section. But this time the BX:CX register pair will be equal to the number of bytes loaded from the file TEST.COM. All other registers and flags should be equivalent to the default settings that DEBUG uses when no file has been loaded.

Debugging TEST.EXE

Now that you are familiar with starting and quitting DEBUG and with the DEBUG commands, let's see how DEBUG functions in a real-life debugging session. First, you will put a bug in the assembly language subroutine of the TEST.EXE program (developed in Chapters 8 and 9) so that there's a reason for the search. Then, using DEBUG, you will step through the faulty program to find out why it isn't working.

The bug to be introduced will be a common typing error: reversing the two register names in a MOV command. To create it, modify SUMS.ASM (refer to Chapter 8) by changing the line labeled S1. The modified listing follows:

```
Page 60,132
; ******************************************************************
; *                                                                *
; * Date:     10/24/89                                             *
; * File:     SUMS.ASM                                             *
; *                                                                *
; * Purpose:  Given an integer number X, find the sum of           *
; *      X + (X-1) + (X-2) + (X-3) + (X-4) ... + 2 + 1             *
; *      Designed to be called from Microsoft C.                   *
; *                                                                *
; * Format:   SUMS(X)                                              *
; *                                                                *
; ******************************************************************

              PUBLIC    _SUMS

              NAME SUMS
_TEXT         SEGMENT BYTE PUBLIC 'CODE'
              ASSUME    CS:_TEXT

NUM_ADR       EQU  4

_SUMS         PROC NEAR
              PUSH BP
              MOV  BP,SP

              MOV  AX,0              ;Initialize to zero
              MOV  BX,[BP]+NUM_ADR   ;Get address of value
              MOV  CX,[BX]           ;Get actual value
              JCXZ S3                ;Num=0, no need to do
S1:           ADC  CX,AX             ;Add row value
              JC   S2                ;Quit if ax overflowed
              LOOP S1                ;Repeat process
              JMP  S3                ;Successful completion
S2:           MOV  AX,0              ;Force a zero
S3:           MOV  [BX],AX           ;Place back in value

              POP  BP
              RET
```

```
_SUMS      ENDP

_TEXT      ENDS
           END
```

The change you've made will cause the routine to always return an answer of 0. From this point on, pretend that you do not know what is causing this error. Put yourself in the place of a programmer who has discovered an honest-to-goodness bug in a program.

Assemble the modified routine, and then link it to TEST.OBJ to form a new TEST.EXE. Next, test this version of TEST.EXE to see what happens. If you use the inputs shown in Chapter 9, the following results occur:

```
TEST
Initial Value: 7
     7         0
Initial Value: 5
     5         0
Initial Value: 22
    22         0
Initial Value: 103
   103         0
Initial Value: 999
     1         0


C>_
```

This is not the intent of the program! Clearly, a problem exists. But where in the program or routine is it occurring? We need to start looking. Deductively, we can determine that the SUMS routine, where the returned value always appears to be 0, is a good place to begin the search.

To begin using DEBUG with TEST.EXE, enter

DEBUG TEST.EXE

DEBUG should respond with the dash prompt, signaling that it is ready and awaiting a command. To get an idea of where you are in the program, enter the Register command (press R).

```
DEBUG TEST.EXE
-R
AX=0000  BX=0000  CX=228C  DX=0000  SP=0800  BP=0000  SI=0000  DI=0000
DS=128C  ES=128C  SS=150A  CS=129C  IP=00D4    NV UP EI PL NZ NA PO NC
129C:00D4 B430          MOV  AH,30
-
```

This display tells you that TEST.EXE has been loaded, the segment registers have been set properly, and the IP register is loaded correctly with the address of the first program instruction to be executed. Notice that the offset entry address is 00D4h, which is the entry address noted in the MAP file produced by LINK.EXE (refer to Chapter 9). Notice also the values of the segment registers, particularly CS and DS. (The values in your segment registers may be different from those shown here, depending on where in your computer's memory DEBUG has loaded the program.)

Next, use the Unassemble command so that you can look at the first portions of program code:

```
-U
129C:00D4 B430          MOV   AH,30
129C:00D6 CD21          INT   21
129C:00D8 3C02          CMP   AL,02
129C:00DA 730E          JNB   00EA
129C:00DC B80400        MOV   AX,0004
129C:00DF 50            PUSH  AX
129C:00E0 E8110B        CALL  0BF4
129C:00E3 92            XCHG  DX,AX
129C:00E4 B409          MOV   AH,09
129C:00E6 CD21          INT   21
129C:00E8 CD20          INT   20
129C:00EA BF7E14        MOV   DI,147E
129C:00ED 8B360200      MOV   SI,[0002]
129C:00F1 2BF7          SUB   SI,DI
129C:00F3 81FE0010      CMP   SI,1000
-U
129C:00F7 7203          JB    00FC
129C:00F9 BE0010        MOV   SI,1000
129C:00FC FA            CLI
129C:00FD 8ED7          MOV   SS,DI
129C:00FF 81C4BE08      ADD   SP,08BE
129C:0103 FB            STI
129C:0104 730B          JNB   0111
129C:0106 33C0          XOR   AX,AX
129C:0108 50            PUSH  AX
129C:0109 E8180B        CALL  0C24
129C:010C B8FF4C        MOV   AX,4CFF
129C:010F CD21          INT   21
129C:0111 81E4FEFF      AND   SP,FFFE
129C:0115 36            SS:
129C:0116 89265800      MOV   [0058],SP
-
```

This code is the assembly language translation of the machine language to which the C program (TEST.C) was converted. However, you have deduced that the bug probably is not in the C program; it is in the assembly language subroutine. How do you find it?

One way to find the right subroutine is to use the Search command. But first you must determine what to search for. To do so, you need to look at the contents of the file TEST.LST (shown in Chapter 8) to see what the first several bytes of machine language should be. The appropriate code follows:

```
15                              PUBLIC   _SUMS
16
17                              NAME     SUMS
18 0000             _TEXT       SEGMENT BYTE PUBLIC 'CODE'
19                              ASSUME  CS:_TEXT
20
21 = 0004           NUM_ADR     EQU      4
22
23 0000             _SUMS       PROC     NEAR
24 0000   55                    PUSH     BP
25 0001   8B EC                 MOV      BP,SP
26
27 0003   B8 0000         MOV     AX,0           ;Initialize to zero
28 0006   8B 5E 04        MOV     BX,[BP]+NUM_ADR ;Get address of value
```

Notice that, beginning in line 24, the first machine code bytes generated by the assembler were 55, 8B, EC, B8, 00, 00, 8B, 5E, and 04. You will search for these nine bytes—a combination unique enough to pinpoint the start of the SUMS subroutine.

Using the Search command, search for these bytes from the beginning of the code segment. Be sure to search an area that is at least equal to the length of the file.

When you enter

-S CS:00 L248C 55 8B EC B8 00 00 8B 5E 04

the computer responds

    129C:00A1

Sure enough, this series of bytes occurs at only one point in memory: at offset 00A1h, the entry point for the SUMS subroutine. To view the code, use the Unassemble command. When you enter **U A1**, the following code will be displayed:

```
-U A1
129C:00A1 55          PUSH   BP
129C:00A2 8BEC        MOV    BP,SP
129C:00A4 B80000      MOV    AX,0000
129C:00A7 8B5E04      MOV    BX,[BP+04]
129C:00AA 8B0F        MOV    CX,[BX]
129C:00AC E30C        JCXZ   00BA
129C:00AE 13C8        ADC    CX,AX
129C:00B0 7205        JB     00B7
129C:00B2 E2FA        LOOP   00AE
129C:00B4 EB04        JMP    00BA
129C:00B6 90          NOP
129C:00B7 B80000      MOV    AX,0000
129C:00BA 8907        MOV    [BX],AX
129C:00BC 5D          POP    BP
129C:00BD C3          RET
129C:00BE 59          POP    CX
129C:00BF 8BDC        MOV    BX,SP
-
```

This code is the unassembled SUMS routine, beginning at offset 00A1h and continuing through offset 00BDh. Following this routine, a different one begins at offset 00BEh.

However, the search technique can quickly become tedious if you have not one but a dozen or so assembly language modules. Finding just the right one can take quite a while and divert your attention from the more essential task of finding the bug inside it.

A quick way to get to the start of a specific assembly language routine is to go back and edit its source file, inserting the statement INT 3 as the first line after the PROC directive in the module to be located. Then reassemble and relink the file, and bring it into DEBUG. Instead of searching for its first few bytes, however, just press G to let the program begin executing.

When the program gets to your INT 3 operation, it will automatically pop back to the DEBUG status line displaying the INT 3 as the current operation. In the present case, the screen would look like this:

```
Initial Value: 5
AX=1098  BX=1098  CX=007A  DX=0000  SP=1094  BP=109A  SI=00A3  DI=116D
DS=147E  ES=147E  SS=147E  CS=129C  IP=00A1    NV UP EI PL NZ NA PE NC
129C:00A1 CC                INT    03
```

To get past this instruction and into the routine itself, use the RIP (Register Instruction Pointer) command

```
-rip
IP 00A1
:_
```

and reply with the next address, A2. This command will achieve the same effect attained by following the search with a breakpoint.

The RIP command works because the INT 3 instruction is actually the way that all debuggers make the breakpoint happen. By placing the command right in your source program, you have automatically put a breakpoint exactly where it needs to be.

However, using the INT 3 instruction does require that you take the time to reassemble and relink your program, so let's use the search technique for this example session. Remember that we found the one and only occurrence of the target string of bytes at location 00A1.

Now, because you want to see what happens in this routine, simply use the Go command to execute the program through the beginning of SUMS. Because the program will run normally until it reaches the breakpoint, you must answer the question asked by TEST.EXE; for test purposes, enter a 5 at the prompt for an initial value:

```
-G A1
Initial Value: 5

AX=1098  BX=1098  CX=007A  DX=0000  SP=1094  BP=109A  SI=00A3  DI=116D
DS=147E  ES=147E  SS=147E  CS=129C  IP=00A1    NV UP EI PL NZ NA PE NC
129C:00A1 55                PUSH   BP
-
```

When DEBUG reaches the specified breakpoint of CS:00A1 (the CS is assumed), program execution stops, and the register values are displayed. Now, using the Trace command to step through the routine, you can examine what is happening to the number being passed from C.

```
-T

AX=1098  BX=1098  CX=007A  DX=0000  SP=1092  BP=109A  SI=00A3  DI=116D
DS=147E  ES=147E  SS=147E  CS=129C  IP=00A2   NV UP EI PL NZ NA PE NC
129C:00A2 8BEC          MOV   BP,SP
-
```

After each Trace command is entered, DEBUG executes the previously displayed instruction, which is shown on the unassembled status line, and displays the registers again, as in the following code:

```
-T

AX=1098  BX=1098  CX=007A  DX=0000  SP=1092  BP=1092  SI=00A3  DI=116D
DS=147E  ES=147E  SS=147E  CS=129C  IP=00A4   NV UP EI PL NZ NA PE NC
129C:00A4 B80000         MOV   AX,0000
-
```

In this display, the base pointer has been set so that the passed parameters can be accessed. The next Trace instruction will result in execution of the MOV AX,0000 instruction, which simply clears the AX register. Soon, AX will be used to accumulate the count of pyramid blocks. Go ahead and Trace through the next step:

```
-T

AX=0000  BX=1098  CX=007A  DX=0000  SP=1092  BP=1092  SI=00A3  DI=116D
DS=147E  ES=147E  SS=147E  CS=129C  IP=00A7   NV UP EI PL NZ NA PE NC
129C:00A7 8B5E04         MOV   BX,[BP+04]    SS:1096=1098
-
```

AX has been cleared, and you now are ready to pull the parameter (an integer pointer) from the stack. DEBUG displays the value at SS:[BP + 04]. (Remember that DEBUG assumes the SS unless your coding explicitly overrides it.) Two additional traces result in the following:

```
-T

AX=0000  BX=1098  CX=007A  DX=0000  SP=1092  BP=1092  SI=00A3  DI=116D
DS=147E  ES=147E  SS=147E  CS=129C  IP=00AA   NV UP EI PL NZ NA PE NC
129C:00AA 8B0F           MOV   CX,[BX]    DS:1098=0005
-T

AX=0000  BX=1098  CX=0005  DX=0000  SP=1092  BP=1092  SI=00A3  DI=116D
DS=147E  ES=147E  SS=147E  CS=129C  IP=00AC   NV UP EI PL NZ NA PE NC
129C:00AC E30C           JCXZ  00BA
-
```

Executing the two instructions (MOV BX,[BP+04] and MOV CX,[BX]) placed the correct value of the parameter (5) in CX. So far, the routine is functioning properly with no problems. The next instruction (JCXZ 00BA) checks whether the parameter passed was a 0. If so, DEBUG performs no calculations.

```
-T

AX=0000  BX=1098  CX=0005  DX=0000  SP=1092  BP=1092  SI=00A3  DI=116D
DS=147E  ES=147E  SS=147E  CS=129C  IP=00AE    NV UP EI PL NZ NA PE NC
129C:00AE 13C8          ADC    CX,AX
-
```

The instruction to be executed next (ADC CX,AX) is supposed to add the row value (5, which also represents the number of blocks on the row) to the value in AX. But in the following display:

```
-T

AX=0000  BX=1098  CX=0005  DX=0000  SP=1092  BP=1092  SI=00A3  DI=116D
DS=147E  ES=147E  SS=147E  CS=129C  IP=00B0    NV UP EI PL NZ NA PE NC
129C:00B0 7205          JB     00B7
-
```

the value in AX did not change. The problem must be occurring here; the value is not being added to AX. As written, the program results in the sum of AX and CX being deposited in the wrong register, CX.

To test this hypothesis, change the coding here by using the Assemble command and entering the following code:

```
-A AE
129C:00AE ADC AX,CX
129C:00B0
-
```

Now the corrected coding is in place, but the instruction pointer register still points to the wrong location. You need to have the computer execute this newly entered instruction. The following dialog shows how to use the Register command to change the IP register and then use the command again to view the register contents:

```
-RIP
IP 00B0
:AE
-R
AX=0000  BX=1098  CX=0005  DX=0000  SP=1092  BP=1092  SI=00A3  DI=116D
```

```
DS=147E  ES=147E  SS=147E  CS=129C  IP=00AE  NV UP EI PL NZ NA PE NC
129C:00AE 11C8          ADC     AX,CX
-
```

RIP enabled the IP register to be changed to AE, the memory offset of
the instructions just entered. Finally, the Register command causes
DEBUG to display the registers so that you can verify that the computer is
indeed ready to execute the proper instruction. Now you will trace
through this step (ADC AX,CX) to verify its effect on the AX register.

In the following display, the AX register has been updated to the correct value:

```
-T

AX=0005  BX=1098  CX=0005  DX=0000  SP=1092  BP=1092  SI=00A3  DI=116D
DS=147E  ES=147E  SS=147E  CS=129C  IP=00B0  NV UP EI PL NZ NA PE NC
129C:00B0 7205          JB      00B7
-
```

Now, so that you can quit DEBUG, execute the rest of the program by
using the Go command:

```
-G
     5          15
Initial Value: 3
     3           6
Initial Value: 7
     7          28
Initial Value: 999
     1           1
     2           3
     3           6
     4          10
     5          15
*** Portion of output deleted for space ***
358     64261
359     64620
360     64980
361     65341
362         0

Program terminated normally

-Q

C>_
```

Well, you've done it! You have just used DEBUG to track down a bug in a program. This example may be simple, but the precepts are the same regardless of the complexity of the problem. Whatever the task, you must step through the coding to make sure that all is going as expected.

By the way, DEBUG did not change the source or executable files. Now that you have discovered what the problem was, you will have to change SUMS.ASM, reassemble, and then link to produce a corrected version of TEST.EXE.

Using CodeView

Now that you've seen how to locate the bug using DEBUG, let's take a look at how it's done with CodeView. The same bug will be used, but the OBJ files and the EXE file must be rebuilt to include the necessary debugging data.

First, be sure that both of the OBJ files contain the needed data by recompiling the TEST.C file and reassembling SUMS.ASM, using the /ZD switch in both cases. Then link them as before, but add the /CO switch to write the debugging information into the EXE file. Then invoke the debugger by typing

CV TEST.EXE

Be sure that both TEST.C and SUMS.ASM are in the current directory so that CodeView can find them. The debugger will load, and the first screen will look like figure 10.1.

Fig. 10.1. *Initial CodeView screen. (bottom portion of screen, 43-line mode)*

```
File  View  Search  Run  Watch  Options  Language  Calls  Help | F8=Trace F5=Go
                          test.c
1:            /* Program to test the calling of SUMS()
2:             * Date: 10/26/89
3:             */
4:
5:            #include <stdio.h>
6:
7:            extern void sums(short*);
8:            short status(short);
9:
10:           short status(short orig)
11:           { unsigned short new;
12:             new=orig;
13:             SUMS(&new);
14:             printf("%5u%10u\n",orig,new);      /* must be uppercase to match!
15:             return (new);
16:           }
17:
18:           void main()
Microsoft (R) CodeView (R)  Version 2.2
(C) Copyright Microsoft Corp. 1986-1988.  All rights reserved.
>
```

At this point the debugger is awaiting your instructions. What you see on the screen is not the machine code that DEBUG showed you at the start but rather the first portion of source file TEST.C. Notice, also, that you don't get any indication of what the CPU registers contain.

To see what is in the registers, you can enable the Register display window by pressing function key F2. When you do, the screen changes to look like figure 10.2.

Fig. 10.2. *CodeView C screen with Register window. (43-line mode)*

```
TEST       EXE    16675    1-01-90   2:29p
TEST       OBJ     2175    1-01-90   2:29p
TEST       C        623    1-01-90   2:29p
SUMS       ASM     1076    1-01-90   2:33p
FIG10-1    PIX     2953    1-01-90   3:26p
       11 File(s)     2924544 bytes free

D>e:\masm\bin\cv test.exe
```

```
File  View  Search  Run  Watch  Options  Language  Calls  Help | F8=Trace F5=Go
                              test.c
 1:          /* Program to test the calling of SUMS()           AX = 0000
 2:           * Date: 10/26/89                                  BX = 0000
 3:           */                                                CX = 0000
 4:                                                             DX = 0000
 5:          #include <stdio.h>                                 SP = 0000
 6:                                                             BP = 0000
 7:          extern void sums(short*);                          SI = 0000
 8:          short status(short);                               DI = 0000
 9:                                                             DS = 6A16
10:          short status(short orig)                           ES = 6A16
11:          { unsigned short new;                              SS = 6CEE
12:            new=orig;                                        CS = 6A26
13:            SUMS(&new);              /* must be uppercase     IP = 00E4
14:            printf("%5u%10u\n",orig,new);
15:            return (new);                                    NV UP
16:          }                                                  EI PL
17:                                                             NZ NA
18:          void main()                                        PO NC
19:          { unsigned short j, x;
20:            j=0;
21:            while (j!=999)
22:            { printf("Initial Value: ");
```

Now you can step through the program, one C statement at a time, by pressing function key F10 once for each line. This is the same as using the P key in DEBUG and fully executes any lower-level function without pausing. Therefore, when you get to the line in main() that calls the status() function, use F8 rather than F10 so that CodeView will trace into status().

Once in status(), you can continue to use F8 because it calls no lower-level functions except your machine language routine, sums(), and that's the one you want to examine. When you reach line 16 of TEST.C and press F8, the screen display will change to that shown in figure 10.3.

Fig. 10.3. CodeView MASM screen. (43-line mode)

```
TEST      EXE     16675    1-01-90   2:29p
TEST      OBJ      2175    1-01-90   2:29p
TEST      C         623    1-01-90   2:29p
SUMS      ASM      1076    1-01-90   2:33p
FIG10-1   PIX      2953    1-01-90   3:26p
        11 File(s)      2924544 bytes free

D>e:\masm\bin\cv test.exe
Initial Value: 9
```

```
File  View  Search  Run  Watch  Options  Language  Calls  Help | FH-Trace F5-Go
                     SUMS.ASM
 8:      ; *         X + (X-1) + (X-2) + (X-3) + (X-4) ... + 2 + 1  AX = 0EA0
 9:      ; *         Designed to be called from Microsoft C.        BX = 0EA0
10:      ; *                                                        CX = 0019
11:      ; *  Format:     SUMS(X)                                   DX = 0000
12:      ; *                                                        SP = 0E90
13:      ; ****************************************************      BP = 0EA2
14:                                                                 SI = 0380
15:                  PUBLIC  _SUMS                                  DI = 0380
16:                                                                 DS = 6C80
17:                  NAME    SUMS                                   ES = 6C80
18:      _TEXT       SEGMENT BYTE PUBLIC 'CODE'                     SS = 6C80
19:                  ASSUME  CS:_TEXT                               CS = 6A26
20:                                                                 IP = 00C6
21:      NUM_ADR     EQU     4
22:                                                                 NV UP
23:      _SUMS       PROC    NEAR                                   EI PL
24:                  PUSH    BP                                     NZ NA
25:                  MOV     BP,SP                                  PE MC
26:
27:                  MOV     AX,0              ;INITIALIZE TO ZE
28:                  MOV     BX,[BP]+NUM_ADR   ;GET ADDRESS OF V
29:                  MOV     CX,[BX]           ;GET ACTUAL VALUE
```

Notice how much simpler it was to reach the assembly language routine with CodeView than with DEBUG. As you continue to press F8, operation will step through the SUMS module, and when control returns to status(), the display will change back to the C source code.

When you determine that the instruction at label S1 in figure 10.3 is at fault, you then can use the arrow keys to place the cursor highlight on it, and use the A command exactly as you did with DEBUG to make a trial correction and verify that this fixes the problem.

As with DEBUG, you've actually done nothing to make a permanent fix. Once you have identified the problem and verified a fix that will work, you still have to put it into the source files.

Using OptDebug

Working essentially the same way as CodeView, OptDebug also requires that you include the debugging data in the OBJ and EXE files and have all source files in the current directory when you type

OPTDEBUG TEST

to start the debugger's operation. Unlike CodeView, OptDebug's first screen displays the end of the last source file instead of the beginning of the program. Figure 10.4 shows the first screen for the sample TEST.EXE. (Because it was newer, I used the Odebug version for this example instead of OptDebug; the displays are identical except for the program name in the prompt.)

Fig. 10.4. *Initial screen for OptDebug.*

```
35:     S2:           MOV     AX,0            ;FORCE A ZERO
36:     S3:           MOV     [BX],AX         ;PLACE BACK IN VALUE
37:
38:                   POP     BP
39:                   RET
40:     _SUMS         ENDP
41:
42:     _TEXT         ENDS
43:                   END
44:       →
```

```
Version 4.0.35 - Press F1 for Help
ODEBUG>
```

The four empty lines above the first horizontal bar are actually empty on the initial screen display. To get a more usable screen that shows the data area, the CPU registers, and the status flags, you can press Alt-F3.

Like CodeView, OptDebug uses the function keys to Trace and to Proceed through the source file one line at a time. However, different function keys are used. To proceed through a lower-level function without pausing inside it, you use F8, but to trace into a function, you use F9. For help, press F1. Figure 10.5 shows the display after Alt-F5 and then F9 have been pressed.

Using Turbo Debugger

Turbo Debugger also requires that the EXE file contain appropriate debugging data but cannot use the data from the CodeView-linked EXE file directly. A utility, TDCONVRT.EXE, is included with the package to convert CodeView files. To use it, first type

TDCONVRT TEST.EXE TDTEST.EXE

to convert the CodeView-linked TEST.EXE file into a TD-linked file TDTEST.EXE; then type

TD TDTEST

to invoke Turbo Debugger for TDTEST.EXE. The first screen displayed would look something like figure 10.6.

Fig. 10.5. *Odebug at Start of Action*

```
AX=80D3 'ç^    DS=503E SI=0380 _fpinit+C     (c) Soft Advances 1989
BX=FFFF         ES=4DCF DI=0380
CX=7FEB         CS=4DE4 IP=0047 main          P  Z  I    >=
DX=80D3         SS=503E SP=0EC6               BP=0000

15:             return (new);
16:         }
17:
18:         void main()
19:         { unsigned short j, x;
20:             j=0;
21:             while (j!=999)
22:             { printf("Initial Value: ");
23:               scanf("%u",&j);
24:               if (j!=999)
25:               { x=status(j);
26:               }

0000:0000    7901E44D 7C3C972F A5017000 5D0C7000  yΘΣM!<ù/Ñ©p ]♀p
0000:0010    5D0C7000 FA5200C0 A0C200F0 A0C200F0  ]♀p ·R ᴸá_T ≡á_T ≡
0000:0020    1C29B319 063D972F 24037000 9E037000  ⌐)|♣=ù/$♥p R♥p
0000:0030    18047000 92047000 0C057000 5D0C7000  ↑♦p ╢♦p ♀♣p ]♀p

ODEBUG>
```

Notice that, unlike the other two source-level debuggers, Turbo Debugger shows you a one-line help reference across the bottom of the screen. This reminds you that F7 is the key for tracing into a routine and that F8 is the key for stepping over a low-level routine without pausing (what I have called *Proceed* in the other descriptions).

Just like the other two debuggers, Turbo Debugger automatically switches to the appropriate source file when you trace into a new module and enables you to try various corrective actions once you have spotted the bug you are hunting. Figure 10.7 shows the result. The exact commands differ slightly, but all three of these source-level debugging utilities have the same functions. The differences between them are more related to their general look and feel than their capabilities for ordinary use.

Fig. 10.6. First screen of Turbo Debugger.

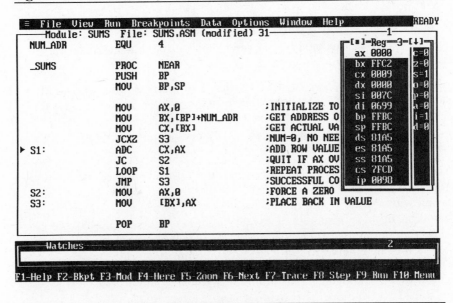

```
≡  File  View  Run  Breakpoints  Data  Options  Window  Help          READY
    ┌─Module: SUMS  File: SUMS.ASM (modified) 31─────────────────────1
    NUM_ADR        EQU     4                              ┌─[■]─Reg─3─[↓]┐
                                                          │ ax 0000   c=0
    _SUMS          PROC    NEAR                            │ bx FFC2   z=0
                   PUSH    BP                              │ cx 0009   s=1
                   MOV     BP,SP                           │ dx 0000   o=0
                                                          │ si 007C   p=0
                   MOV     AX,0            ;INITIALIZE TO  │ di 0699   a=0
                   MOV     BX,[BP]+NUM_ADR ;GET ADDRESS O  │ bp FFBC   i=1
                   MOV     CX,[BX]         ;GET ACTUAL VA  │ sp FFBC   d=0
                   JCXZ    S3              ;NUM=0, NO NEE  │ ds 81A5
  ▶ S1:            ADC     CX,AX           ;ADD ROW VALUE  │ es 81A5
                   JC      S2              ;QUIT IF AX OV  │ ss 81A5
                   LOOP    S1              ;REPEAT PROCES  │ cs 7FCD
                   JMP     S3              ;SUCCESSFUL CO  │ ip 0090
    S2:            MOV     AX,0            ;FORCE A ZERO
    S3:            MOV     [BX],AX         ;PLACE BACK IN VALUE

                   POP     BP
    ┌─Watches───────────────────────────────────────────────────2
    │
    └─────────────────────────────────────────────────────────────
F1-Help F2-Bkpt F3-Mod F4-Here F5-Zoom F6-Next F7-Trace F8 Step F9-Run F10-Menu
```

Fig. 10.7. Turbo Debugger ASM screen.

```
≡  File  View  Run  Breakpoints  Data  Options  Window  Help          READY
┌[■]=Module: TEST  File: test.c 18════════════════════════════1=[↑][↓]═┐
│         return (new);
│       }
│
▶      void main()
│      { unsigned short j, x;
│        j=0;
│        while (j!=999)
│        { printf("Initial Value: ");
│          scanf("%u",&j);
│          if (j!=999)
│          { x=status(j);
│          }
│        }
│        for (j=1, x=1; x!=0; x=status(j++))
│        ;
│      }
│
│
│
└◀────────────────────────────────────────────────────────────▶─
    ┌─Watches───────────────────────────────────────────────────2
    │
    └─────────────────────────────────────────────────────────────
Ctrl: I-Inspect W-Watch M-Module F-File P-Previous L-Line S-Search N-Next
```

Summary

In this chapter, you learned the differences between software debuggers and hardware debuggers, and saw some of the characteristics of several popular software debuggers.

You also learned how to use DEBUG. You learned what the DEBUG commands are and how to use them to help uncover errors in your subroutines. As you work with DEBUG, try to become familiar with all of the available commands so that you can make your debugging sessions as efficient and productive as possible.

Although DEBUG is helpful, it is not the answer to every debugging need. You may discover errors that completely lock up your computer, leaving you with no other alternative to regain control but to turn off the computer. In these instances, software debuggers such as DEBUG are virtually useless because they assume that you will always have some control, such as being able to enter keyboard commands.

Professional debuggers that combine hardware and software also are available. These debuggers provide a virtually independent way to monitor and debug programs. Professional debuggers may be expensive, but in many development environments they are the only viable option for effective debugging.

The ideal debugging system, regardless of type, performs as a benign observer until you instruct it to perform a task. A debugger that interferes with the operation of the program is of little use, because there will be no way to examine how the program operates without the debugger.

CHAPTER 11

Developing Libraries

When it's time to link your assembly language subroutines, the process of specifying each file name can be unwieldy if you use an increasingly large number of routines. Consider, for example, the following external declaration section from one (and *only* one) subroutine, keeping in mind that these external subroutines call other subroutines, which may call still other subroutines:

```
; ****   OUTSIDE SUBROUTINES CALLED   ****
          EXTRN     SET_DI:NEAR
          EXTRN     CURSOR_ON:NEAR
          EXTRN     CURSOR_OFF:NEAR
          EXTRN     HORIZ_LINE:NEAR
          EXTRN     PRINT_CHAR:NEAR
          EXTRN     PRINT_STRING:NEAR
          EXTRN     ERASE_LINE:NEAR
          EXTRN     BOOP:NEAR
          EXTRN     CALC_LEN:NEAR
```

As you can imagine, the list of possible subroutines can become extensive. To solve this problem, you can place your assembly language OBJ files into a *library*, a special file that is searched at linkage time.

281

The Advantages of Libraries

When the linker finds an external declaration, it looks for the external reference in the explicit OBJ file names you entered. If the external reference is not contained in one of those files, the linker searches libraries named in response to that prompt for the reference. If the reference is located, the linker extracts the OBJ module and combines it into the executable file being created.

This library concept relieves the programmer of several potential headaches (and errors) in the program development process. If you change a source file, you can simply update the library and recompile or reassemble all files that use that routine—quick, simple, and effective.

In addition, the library greatly simplifies the task of distributing all the necessary routines. In fact, without the library concept, you would not have the high-level languages as you know them today. They all depend upon their library routines to support input, output, and housekeeping requirements.

But all these advantages that libraries provide are not restricted to software publishers; you too can create your own libraries that contain your own customized routines. All you need is a library maintenance program, and most assembler packages include a library utility as part of the package.

Library Maintenance Programs

Both Microsoft's MASM and Borland's TASM provide library maintenance programs as part of the package sold with the assembler. OptLib, the library program that matches OptAsm, is an extra-cost utility. Other library management software is available from various vendors.

Many library maintenance programs are available, but to simplify our discussion this book focuses on a single system: a program called LIB.EXE, which is distributed with the Microsoft and IBM assembler packages. However, to show you how similar the other library programs are, I've also summarized the commands and operations of the programs from SLR and from Borland.

Don't be concerned if the descriptions that follow seem somewhat confusing; review them after you finish the chapter and they should seem much clearer. The actions controlled by the options, in all three programs, involve details that you're not familiar with yet.

LIB from Microsoft

The LIB program has only four options (listed in table 11.1), and three operation codes that can in some cases be combined for a total of five functional operations. The four options can be given either on the command line immediately following the word LIB and preceding the first OBJ file name, or in response to the first prompt.

Table 11.1. *LIB options.*

Option	Meaning
/Ignorecase	Force all symbols to uppercase
/NOIgnorecase	Do not change case of any symbols
/NOExtdict	Do not create extended dictionary for library
/PAgesize:	Set increment of storage space used (normally 16 bytes)

The operation codes are the plus sign (+) to add a module, the minus sign (-) to delete a module, and the asterisk (*) to copy a module out to an OBJ file. The allowable combinations are minus-plus (-+) to replace an entry by deleting the old and adding the new, and minus-asterisk (-*) or asterisk-minus (*-) to move an entry by copying and relocating the entry and then deleting the entry at its original location).

Details of the use of these options and operations are found in the subsequent sections on creating a library and maintaining a library.

OptLib from SLR

Unlike LIB, OptLib from SLR, Inc. sports 25 options, and four operation codes. Table 11.2 lists these 25 options as they appear in OptLib's /Help action. In addition, this program can be custom-configured to default to your own requirements. The additional capabilities may justify purchasing it separately if you do much assembly language library maintenance. Other advantages are speed and the ability to easily modify library symbols.

Table 11.2. *OptLib options.*

Option	Meaning
/Bmaximum:	Specify maximum number of blocks to enter in directory (/B:nnn)
/Aco:	Limit average collisions per directory entry
/Tco:	Limit total number of collisions for the entire directory
/PUblicrename:	Rename or delete a Public symbol (/PUB:*old=new*)
/EXtrnrename:	Rename or delete an External symbol (/EXT: *old=new*)
/EChoin	Echo text from indirect file to screen
/NOEchoin	Disable /EChoin
/Help	Display list of options
/Index	List all module names with offset, as well as their code and data sizes
/NOIndex	Disable /Index
/Map	List all module names and public symbols
/NOMap	Disable /Map
/CHECKSum	Check OBJ records for valid checksum
/NOCHECKSum	Disable checksum testing
/CHECKAbort	Abort on bad checksum
/NOCHECKAbort	Do not abort on checksum errors
/PAgesize:	Specify the byte where boundary modules start
/PWidth:	Specify the page width of the device output
/Stats	Print statistics at end of library build
/NOStats	Disable /Stats
/Okmultidef	Allow multiply defined Publics
/NOOkmultidef	Disable /Okmultidef
/NOUpdatetime	Preserve Time and Date stamp
/Xref	List each symbol with defining and referencing modules
/NOXref	Disable /Xref

Notice that several of these options use the same letter sequences as the options for LIB but have significantly different meanings. For instance, OptLib's /O option means the same as LIB's /NOE (multiple definitions for Public symbols are allowed), but OptLib's /NOE option disables echoing from a response file. In fact, only the /PA option has the same meaning with both programs.

OptLib's four operation codes include the three used by LIB, with the same meanings and the same possible combinations plus one additional code; The tilde () tells OptLib to replace the module named after this code if, and only if, the OBJ file has a later date/time stamp than the module in the library. For this to work, OptLib maintains the date and time for each module in the library file, unlike the other programs discussed in this chapter.

Many of OptLib's options affect what data will be included in the listing report that the program generates; of the three library maintenance programs, OptLib offers by far the greatest flexibility for controlling the listing report.

TLIB from Borland

Borland's TLIB program has the same three operation codes as LIB and uses them identically. However, TLIB offers even fewer options than LIB, providing only the following pair:

❏ /C flags case (when used, TLIB becomes case-sensitive).

❏ /E creates an extended dictionary if present.

Thus TLIB's /C option is the same as LIB's /NOI option, and TLIB's /E option is the opposite of LIB's /NOE option. If neither of its options are used, TLIB converts all public symbols to uppercase and does not create extended dictionaries.

Creating a Library

You create a library by using one of the library maintenance programs.

If you have done the examples in this book, you have created several assembly language subroutines that can be joined together into a library (see table 11.3). Be sure that the OBJ files created for these routines are available, because you will use them in this session.

Table 11.3. *Available files to be placed in a library file.*

File name	Chapter	Function
CEX3.ASM	5	C Cursor Switch
CLIPEX2.ASM	7	Clipper cursors
CLIPEX3.ASM	7	Clipper cursors
SUMS.ASM	9	Linker example for C

Using LIB or OptLib

Let's look first at how you use the software from Microsoft and IBM to create and modify libraries. Like MASM and LINK, LIB has several ways of getting its input data. Only the interactive method is discussed in this section; I explain the others later.

Make sure that you have the Microsoft LIB.EXE program on a floppy disk, in the current directory, or accessible through a search path (if you are using OptLib, the operation is almost identical, but the exact prompts differ). Then, at the DOS prompt, enter the following command:

LIB

to execute the LIB.EXE program. You will see on your screen a notice and prompt similar to the following:

```
C>LIB

Microsoft (R) Library Manager  Version 3.02
Copyright (C) Microsoft Corp 1983, 1984, 1985. All rights reserved.

Library name: _
```

If you are using the IBM version of LIB.EXE or OptLib, your screen will look a little different. However, because the prompts are similar, you should be able to follow this session. Borland's TLIB has no interactive interface; to use it, refer to the next subsection, "Using TLIB."

Now, enter TEST, the name of the library file that you want to create. Because the standard library extension [LIB] is appended automatically unless another extension is entered, the full name of this library will be TEST.LIB. When you press Enter, the following prompt is displayed:

```
Library name: TEST
Library does not exist. Create? _
```

This prompt is just a precaution, in case you misspelled the name of the library. Because you are creating a new library, press **Y**. Your screen will look like this:

```
Library does not exist. Create? Y
Operations: _
```

LIB is requesting information about the operations you want to perform with TEST.LIB. There are three basic operations: adding, deleting, and copying. By combining these basic commands, you can perform two additional operations. For instance, you can replace a library entry by deleting the old and then adding the new, or you can move the entry by deleting it at its original location and then copying the entry at a new location. Table 11.4 lists the available LIB operations.

Table 11.4. *LIB operations.*

Operation	Function
+	Add an OBJ file as a library entry
−	Delete a library entry
*	Copy a library entry
− +	Replace a library entry
− *	Move a library entry

Because you are creating a new library, you don't need to delete, copy, replace, or move an entry. You want to add OBJ files to the new library. To do so, enter the following at the Operations: prompt:

+CEX3 +CLIPEX2 +CLIPEX3 +SUMS

This entry instructs LIB to add to the newly created and still empty library the object code files you created in Chapters 5, 7, and 9: CEX3.OBJ, CLIPEX2.OBJ, CLIPEX3.OBJ, and SUMS.OBJ (OBJ is the default file extension).

If you used the BASIC examples in Chapter 3 to create your files, you should substitute the names of those files in the preceding response line. Include only those files that were developed for use with compiled BASIC, because interpretive BASIC files are not suited for use with a library. Interpretive BASIC does not go through a linkage phase in development.

In Chapter 3, only one file (CLREOL2.ASM) was developed for use with compiled BASIC. The chapter's other routines (those for interpretive BASIC) can be modified so that they work with compiled BASIC and are therefore suited for inclusion in a library.

If you used the Pascal examples in Chapter 4 to create your files, you should substitute the names of those files in the LIB response line. The appropriate file names are listed in table 11.5.

Table 11.5. *Available files to be placed in a library (for use with Pascal).*

File name	Chapter
CURSW.ASM	4
READSCRN.ASM	4
RSFUNC.ASM	4
ULCASE.ASM	4

To add these files as entries to a library, each file will require an individual command—a plus sign. Although you can use commas as command delimiters, I prefer to separate each command from the others with a space.

You can also enter the commands on individual lines as follows:

```
Operations: +CEX3 +CLIPEX2 &
Operations: +CLIPEX3 +SUMS
```

The ampersand (&) at the end of the first line signifies that more follows. Use it if you cannot fit all the desired operations onto one command line.

Finally, the following prompt will appear on your screen:

```
Operations: +CEX3 +CLIPEX2 +CLIPEX3 +SUMS
List file: _
```

A list file, which is optional, contains reference information that you may find interesting and helpful. If you do not want one, simply press Enter. But here, for the sake of illustration, enter TEST.LST as a file name. Be sure to specify the **LST** file extension because LIB does not provide a default extension for list files.

After a few moments, the DOS prompt returns to the screen, signifying that LIB has created the library TEST.LIB. If any errors occur during the process of creating a library, an error message is displayed. (In some instances, notification of the action taken by LIB is also displayed.)

In this example, because the symbol (routine name) CURSET appeared in both CLIPEX2.OBJ and CLIPEX3.OBJ, LIB refused to add the symbol the second time it was found and displayed a message saying so. This duplication of symbols makes the CLIPEX3 version inaccessible in the library. To solve this problem, go back to the CLIPEX3.ASM file, change the symbol CURSET to something else that is not duplicated, reassemble the file, and then replace the CLIPEX3 module with the changed version. In the section "Maintaining a Library" I'll detail how this is done.

To get an idea of what happened during the process of creating the library, look at the list file that was created. If you type **TEST.LST**, you should see the following display:

```
C>TYPE TEST.LST
CURSET............CLIPEX2              _CURSW............CEX3
_SUMS.............SUMS


CEX3              Offset: 00000010H  Code and data size: 25H
   _CURSW


CLIPEX2           Offset: 00000090H  Code and data size: 46H
   CURSET


CLIPEX3           Offset: 00000150H  Code and data size: 5bH


SUMS              Offset: 00000240H  Code and data size: 1dH
   _SUMS


C>_
```

The list file (in this case, TEST.LST) contains information about the newly created library: the names of the modules in the library, as well as information about where each module begins and the length of each module. From this TEST.LST file, you can see that the file SUMS (the OBJ extension is assumed) contains the public label _SUMS, that the module begins at a file offset of 240h, and that its length is 1Dh.

You can also see that while the CLIPEX3 module is in the library and occupies 5Bh bytes of space, it has no symbols by which it can ever be referenced. I'll show you how to fix this in the section on "Maintaining a Library."

Using TLIB

Because TLIB has no interactive capability, you must pass in all its input data either on the command line or in a response file. The response file method is identical to that used by the other library programs and explained later in this chapter; this section describes only the use of the command line.

Make sure that you have the TLIB.EXE program on a floppy disk, in the current directory, or accessible through a search path. Then, at the DOS prompt, enter the following command:

TLIB TEST +CEX3 +CLIPEX2 +CLIPEX3 +SUMS, TEST.LST

This tells TLIB to create or update the library TEST.LIB, adding the four OBJ modules (CEX3.OBJ, CLIPEX2.OBJ, CLIPEX3.OBJ, and SUMS.OBJ), and finally to create a listing file, TEST.LST.

After you enter the command, you'll get the following display on your screen:

```
TLIB  Version 2.0  Copyright (c) 1987, 1988 Borland International

Error: public 'CURSET' in module 'CLIPEX3' clashes with prior module 'CLIPEX2'
```

As mentioned in the previous section, this error happens because the symbol CURSET appears in both OBJ files; you can correct this error by changing the symbol in CLIPEX3 so that the clash is resolved. However, where LIB or OptLib went ahead and created TEST.LIB, simply omitting the second version of CURSET, TLIB stopped short and did not create the library at all.

To bypass the problem (so that I can use it as a maintenance example later in this chapter), just leave +CLIPEX3 off the command line, and try again:

TLIB TEST +CEX3 +CLIPEX2 +SUMS, TEST.LST

This time no error message appears, and a directory check shows that all requested files were indeed created. Here's the listing version created by TLIB:

```
Publics by module

CEX3     size = 37
    _CURSW

CLIPEX2 size = 70
    CURSET

SUMS     size = 29
    _SUMS
```

Although TLIB's listing file is much less wordy than those provided by the other programs, it gives you all the essential information: the module names, the symbol names, and the size of each module. Unlike LIB, which lists sizes in hexadecimal, the TLIB report is in decimal, which makes it much more comprehensible to the average reader.

Using a Library

Now that you've learned how to create a library using either LIB, OptLib, or TLIB, let's see how the result can be used. Again, although I mostly use Microsoft products in my examples, the following explanations apply to all three lines, except for a few specific details that I will point out as they are encountered.

Linking with a Library

As you may recall from Chapter 9, one of the LINK prompts asked which libraries to use in the linking process. Because libraries had not yet been discussed, the discussion of linking libraries was deferred to this chapter.

Now that you have created a library (TEST.LIB), you can perform the linking process again to see how TEST.LIB affects the process. Although the following examples use the Microsoft versions, the other linkers operate almost exactly the same way.

When you enter the LINK command at the DOS prompt, your screen should look like this:

```
C>LINK
Microsoft (R) Overlay Linker  Version 3.51
Copyright (C) Microsoft Corp 1983, 1984, 1985, 1986. All rights reserved.

Object Modules [.OBJ]: _
```

Enter **TEST** (the name of the object file used in Chapter 9). Then, to signify that the run file will be the default file, press Enter. Your screen should look like this:

```
Object Modules [.OBJ]: TEST
Run File [TEST.EXE]:
List File [NUL.MAP]: _
```

Because you do not need a list file for this example, simply press Enter.

Now comes the important question:

```
List File [NUL.MAP]:
Libraries [.LIB]: _
```

In response to this prompt, enter the name of the library (or libraries) that you want to use to link this file. If you enter several library names, use spaces to separate them. You don't have to include a file extension (LIB is assumed).

To continue with the sample library (TEST.LIB), simply type **TEST**, and press Enter.

LINK asks no further questions but goes to work on the tasks you specified. First, all of the specified object files are linked together (in this case, there is only one: TEST.OBJ). Then, if any unresolved external references remain, the library files are searched to see whether the references are included as public symbol declarations. Thus, when _SUMS cannot be located in TEST.OBJ, TEST.LIB is examined to ascertain whether it contains the symbol. If (as in this case) the library file contains the symbol, the module containing the symbol is extracted from TEST.LIB and linked to TEST.OBJ.

If any other unresolved external references remain (in other words, if the _SUMS routine contains any references that cannot be satisfied internally to _SUMS or in the TEST.OBJ file), the library is searched again. This search-and-include cycle continues until all possible references have been resolved. If some references cannot be resolved, LINK generates an error message, and the linkage process stops.

If an error message such as the following occurs:

```
C>LINK
Microsoft (R) Overlay Linker  Version 3.51
Copyright (C) Microsoft Corp 1983, 1984, 1985,1986. All rights reserved.

Object Modules [.OBJ]: TEST
Run File [TEST.EXE]:
List File [NUL.MAP]:
Libraries [.LIB]: TEST

Unresolved externals:

_sums in file(s):
TEST.OBJ(test.C)
```

```
There was 1 error detected

C>_
```

you know that LINK could not find the subroutine in the object file (TEST.OBJ) or in the library (TEST.LIB). Usually, this means that you have forgotten to include all necessary files in the library. Check your work again, and try the linking procedure one more time.

Creating and Using Library Response Files

With LIB, as with LINK, you can provide a file (cleverly called a *response file*) of responses to questions. Because repeatedly typing answers to each question is tiresome, this method of using LIB is beneficial when you know that you will be adjusting a library time and again during development.

To use this method of providing input to LIB, create an ASCII text file that contains the answers to each question. You can give this file whatever name you want. Just be sure to place the answer to each question on a separate line. For instance, I regularly create a new library of all my assembly language subroutines by using the following LIB response file:

```
\assemble\huge.lib
Y
+ \assemble\obj\asciibin &
+ \assemble\obj\box &
+ \assemble\obj\boxita &
+ \assemble\obj\calclen &
+ \assemble\obj\cdir &
+ \assemble\obj\clrwndow &
+ \assemble\obj\cls &
+ \assemble\obj\conascii &
+ \assemble\obj\conhex &
+ \assemble\obj\concase &
+ \assemble\obj\crc &
+ \assemble\obj\cursoff &
+ \assemble\obj\curson &
+ \assemble\obj\dait &
+ \assemble\obj\dayt &
+ \assemble\obj\direct &
+ \assemble\obj\eraselne &
```

```
+ \assemble\obj\findcard &
+ \assemble\obj\fmenu &
+ \assemble\obj\fsize &
+ \assemble\obj\getkey &
+ \assemble\obj\getline &
+ \assemble\obj\getlinea &
+ \assemble\obj\getyn &
+ \assemble\obj\horiz &
+ \assemble\obj\invert &
+ \assemble\obj\mbindiv &
+ \assemble\obj\mencom &
+ \assemble\obj\menuar &
+ \assemble\obj\menubox &
+ \assemble\obj\message &
+ \assemble\obj\motr &
+ \assemble\obj\pauztick &
+ \assemble\obj\pauztime &
+ \assemble\obj\pchar &
+ \assemble\obj\pmsg &
+ \assemble\obj\pnum &
+ \assemble\obj\pstrng &
+ \assemble\obj\pstrng2 &
+ \assemble\obj\qscreen &
+ \assemble\obj\sbox &
+ \assemble\obj\scrn &
+ \assemble\obj\scrnbas &
+ \assemble\obj\seekey &
+ \assemble\obj\setcolor &
+ \assemble\obj\setdi &
+ \assemble\obj\soundasm &
+ \assemble\obj\soundbas &
+ \assemble\obj\tbox &
+ \assemble\obj\timer &
+ \assemble\obj\vidbas &
+ \assemble\obj\viddata
\assemble\huge.lst
;
```

Notice the response on the second line of this file, the letter Y, which is there to answer the following question:

```
Library does not exist. Create? _
```

LIB asks this question if it cannot find HUGE.LIB. The construction of this response file presupposes that the original library (if any) has been deleted. The Y response causes LIB to combine into HUGE.LIB the 52 specified object code files. The ampersand (&) at the end of each line (except the final file specification line) tells LIB that additional commands follow. Finally, LIB is directed to create a list file called HUGE.LST.

If you are using TLIB, it does not ask the Create? question, so you should omit the Y line from a TLIB response file. Otherwise TLIB works exactly the same way, even though it has no interactive mode to imitate.

To use a response with LIB, simply invoke LIB with the following command syntax:

LIB @*filename.ext*

filename.ext is the name of the response file to be used. Notice the @ symbol directly before the file name. LIB needs this key symbol to differentiate between a response file and a library name.

If the sample response file were called HUGE.LRF, you could use it by issuing the following command:

LIB @HUGE.LRF

As you use LIB repeatedly, you will appreciate being able to use response files.

Maintaining a Library

Once you've gotten used to the idea of creating libraries to keep collections of similar assembly language routines together in one place, and to using them when you create your programs, you'll come face-to-face with the need to maintain your libraries. That is, you'll need to add new routines or change old ones. And you may even want to extract routines from one library to add them into another one.

This is all made simple by the library managing programs. First I'll show you how it's done, by correcting the conflict that showed up earlier as TEST.LIB was created. Then I'll discuss some techniques to help make the entire library management task easier. And in the next chapter, I'll carry those ideas even further.

Making Changes to a Library

Changing a library file is as easy as creating one. By using the commands to delete, add, copy, replace, or move, you can update an existing library to reflect current needs. For example, remember that the module CLIPEX3 in TEST.LIB contained the duplicate symbol CURSET. To enable CLIPEX2 and CLIPEX3 to both exist in the same library, you must first change the symbol in one of the modules, then reassemble that module, and replace the old module with the new one.

If you edited CLIPEX3.ASM to replace every instance of the old CURSET with the new CURSETF, and then assembled the edited CLIPEX3.ASM into a new copy of CLIPEX3.OBJ, you would update TEST.LIB by using the following dialog (for a change, this example shows OptLib in action; LIB would work exactly the same way):

```
C>OPTLIB /M TEST
OPTLIB Copyright (C) SLR Systems 1988
All rights reserved.
Operations: (NUL.OBJ):-+ clipex3
List File: (TEST.LST):
Output File:(TEST.LIB):

C>_
```

The /M option told OptLib to create the same output format of listing file that LIB created the first time. I used the LIB name on the command line, then completed the job interactively to show you how you could switch between modes.

However, the key to this dialog is the -+ operation code. This told the library manager program to first delete (-) the existing copy in the LIB file, then append (+) a new copy from file CLIPEX3.OBJ. The result is shown by the following display of the listing file TEST.LST:

```
C>TYPE TEST.LST
SLR Systems SuperFast Librarian              11:09:33 Sat, 04 Nov 89
                                    OPTLIB      PAGE SYM-1


Module Name: CEX3      lib offset: 0010H      Code & Data Size: 0025H
  _CURSW


Module Name: CLIPEX2   lib offset: 0090H      Code & Data Size: 0046H
  CURSET
```

```
Module Name: SUMS        Lib offset: 0150H        Code & Data Size: 001DH
   _SUMS


Module Name: CLIPEX3     Lib offset: 01C0H        Code & Data Size: 005BH
   CURSETF
```

This process updates TEST.LIB with the new version of CLIPEX3.OBJ. But what if the new version of the file is in another directory or on another disk? You simply provide the necessary information at the Operations: prompt, as in the following dialog:

```
C>OPTLIB TEST
OPTLIB Copyright (C) SLR Systems 1988
All rights reserved.
Operations: (NUL.OBJ):-clipex3 +b:\obj\clipex3
List File: (NUL.LST):
Output File:(TEST.LIB):


C>_
```

Notice that you indicate the deletion and addition as two separate steps. However, the result is the same as in the previous example.

To modify the library in other ways, simply specify the operation you want performed (refer to table 11.4) and the name of the file module you want to modify.

Managing a Library

As you add files to your library, you can follow either of two avenues usually taken by programmers: you can create one large library containing (in one convenient location) all of your subroutines, or you can create several smaller libraries, each representing a specialized category of subroutine.

Let's assume that you want to manage only one large library and that, from time to time, you would like to be able to update one of the subroutines in the library. Updating the library is simple if you combine the procedures that you have learned in this chapter with the capabilities of DOS batch files. You can apply the same techniques to smaller libraries, as well.

The usual process for updating a library is as follows:

1. Assemble the source file.

2. Delete the original OBJ file from the library.

3. Add the new OBJ file to the library.

Let's assume that your library is called HUGE.LIB and that, to make matters more complicated, you need to update several files. You can update your library by using the following batch file (UPDATE.BAT) to perform the three steps:

```
echo off
 cls
 del *.obj >nul
 del \assemble\hugelib.txt
 :loop
     if %1\ == \ goto exit
         echo Working on %1.asm
         echo Assembling %1.asm >>\assemble\hugelib.txt
         masm %1,; >>\assemble\hugelib.txt
         echo Adding %1.obj to HUGE.LIB >>\assemble\hugelib.txt
         lib \assemble\huge -+%1; >>\assemble\hugelib.txt
         shift
         goto loop
 :exit
 del *.obj >nul
```

This batch file assumes that MASM and LIB are in either your current directory or the search path; that the source file (ASM) is in the current directory; and that you want HUGE.LIB to be in the subdirectory ASSEMBLE.

The proper syntax for this batch file is

UPDATE *file1 file2 file3 file4 ....*

file1 is the root file name of the ASM file to be updated in the library. *file2*, *file3*, *file4*, and so on are the optional names of other source files that you want updated to the library.

After this batch file has completed its job, the dialog normally presented by MASM.EXE and by LIB.EXE will be saved (in the ASSEMBLE subdirectory) in a file called HUGELIB.TXT. Any errors will be noted in this file. Notice the use of the >> redirection symbol, rather than the usual >; this forces each stage of the process to append its messages to the end of the file. If you use the **>** symbol instead, only the report from the last LIB run will be in HUGELIB.TXT.

Summary

This chapter has shown you how to create, change, and manage libraries and how libraries fit into the linking process.

Libraries, which are intended to make the programmer's life easier, can be a headache if they are not managed properly or logically. Take time to think through your library needs. Consider how to fit library use into your normal methods for program development. Then develop some batch files (such as the one described in this chapter) that will help you make the most of libraries.

As you become adept at using libraries, you will find that they can make your tasks much easier.

CHAPTER 12

Using Makefiles

In Chapter 11, you saw one way to simplify the management of a project by creating BAT files that enter all the necessary keystrokes to completely compile, assemble, and link an application. But what do you do when you have an application that's made up of a dozen C files and twice that many assembly language modules, and you make a change to just *one* of those pieces?

Of course you *could* just run the BAT file that recompiles and reassembles everything, but over a decade ago professional system developers came up with a better way. Now that same technique is available to anyone who buys a copy of MASM, Quick-C, or Turbo Assembler (not to mention the availability of the technique in somewhat modified form with many of the other products described earlier).

The technique is usually known as *MAKE*, from the name of the first such program developed (as part of the UNIX system). In many ways it resembles the use of BAT files, but with a twist: when you execute a BAT file, nearly all the commands it contains are executed; however, when you run MAKE or one of its descendants, only those commands that are necessary get done, and the rest are bypassed.

How can MAKE know which commands are necessary and which should be bypassed at any specific run time? That's the secret of the technique, and that's the next subject.

301

What Does MAKE Do?

What the MAKE program and its descendants do, specifically, is cycle through a file that you provide which describes how the various parts of your application depend on each other. Such a file is called a *dependency file* in most MAKE documentation, but the original system's default file name, *MAKEFILE*, is also widely used in cases where a dependency file name is not specified.

A dependency file consists of several parts. Most of these parts are optional, so the various brands of available MAKE programs differ significantly. However, all dependency files share one key part in common: a list of *description blocks*.

Each description block begins with an *outfile-infile* relationship. Such a statement can be easily identified because it starts at the first column of the line and does not begin with a # character (the # denotes a comment line). This relationship statement contains at least two file names, separated by a colon (:). The first file name is that of the outfile, the output file for this block. The second is that of the input file. You can have multiple input files, but only one outfile per block.

This relationship line specifically says that outfile depends on all of the listed infiles, so if the date-time stamp of any infile is later than that of the outfile, you'll have to correct the situation, usually by rebuilding the outfile.

The remaining lines of the description block, which each start with a blank space or a tab character, are called *command lines*. They specify exactly what actions are to be performed if action is indicated by the date-time comparison.

The command lines are exactly like the individual lines in a BAT file except that the command lines are indented. If MAKE determines that the actions of this description block must be performed, the command lines are fed in strict sequence to the computer just as if they had been typed in at the keyboard.

One of the major differences between the various MAKE programs available involves the sequence in which the description blocks are evaluated. Some of them go through the dependency file in strict sequence—the first block in the file is the first one evaluated, and its actions are performed, if necessary, before the second one is examined. With this approach, the final application file must be the one described by the final description block.

However, other MAKE programs evaluate only the first description block in the file (unless another target is specified on the command line). Any actions that the block calls for may, in turn, require subsequent blocks to be evaluated (this process is similar to Chapter 11's description of how a linker searches a library file). For this approach, the ultimate application file must be the *first* one described rather than the last.

Because of the present lack of standardization, evaluation sequencing varies among MAKE programs, so a dependency file that works well with one MAKE program may not work at all with another.

Microsoft's Program Maintenance Utility

When you buy MASM at any version from 4.0 on, one of the "free" utilities you get with it is a copy of MAKE.EXE, the Microsoft program maintenance utility. Although not representative of mainstream MAKE programs, this utility is probably the simplest to comprehend, so it is described first.

This program enables one or more description blocks to be entered in each of its dependency files and evaluates each block as it is encountered. MAKE.EXE does not backtrack to see if any of its actions affected description blocks that it already processed during the current run. Thus, the final application must be the subject of the file's last block if the file's relationships are affected by any other description blocks in the file.

The file itself, and any description block, may be headed by a *comment line*. The character # indicates the start of a comment; whenever this character is encountered by the program, all subsequent characters up to the end of that line are ignored. Thus comments may be added at the end of any line, embedded within a description block, or used for headers.

For this version of MAKE, a description block always begins with an *empty* line that separates it from any preceding description block. The block may contain comment lines at any point, but normally any descriptive comment precedes the *dependency line*.

The dependency line begins with the name of the output or *target* file, including its extension but without a path. This need not be an actual file name. For example, the *pseudo-target* ALL (or any other string you like) can be used if you want to force the *command list* to be executed every time this dependency file is processed.

Following the target file name is a colon (:), and then the *infile* list. This is a list of one or more file names, again without a path. Either a comma or a blank space may be used to separate the names in the infile list.

When the dependency line is evaluated, the date-time stamp maintained by DOS for each file in the infile list is compared to that of the target. If any infile has a more recent time or date than that of the target, the command list is executed; if the target is more recent than any infile, the command list is skipped over and the next dependency block, if any, evaluated.

The command list consists of one or more DOS commands to be executed, just as in a conventional BATch file. However, to distinguish the command list lines from the rest of the dependency file content, each must begin with at least one blank space or tab character. Most dependency blocks contain at least one line in their command list although this is not required. If no commands follow the dependency line, then a default mechanism called the *inference rule* list takes over. If the dependency line fits any inference rule, the command list for that rule is executed. If not, then nothing is executed, but no error is declared either.

Thus the full syntax for a dependency block in this version of MAKE is

[# *comment*]
target : *infile*[[,] *infile*][# *comment*]
            [*command* [# *comment*]]

where the items shown within brackets are optional.

The inference rule list consists of one or more rules that tell MAKE what commands to execute when a dependency block contains no command list of its own. Each rule, like a dependency block, begins with a relationship statement, but rather than dealing with specific files by name, an inference rule applies to groups of files distinguished by their extensions. The syntax is

[# *comment*]
.*inext.outext*:
            command
            [*command*]

Notice that in the inference rule, both the inext and the outext appear in the "target" position, to the left of the colon, and nothing appears to the right of the colon. When a rule is to be applied, the time relationships have already been determined; the purpose of this line in the rule list is to let MAKE find the specific rule to apply. For instance, a typical inference rule list for assembly language programs might be

```
# default actions when assembly required, keep CODEVIEW info
.ASM.OBJ:
        MASM /Zi $*;

# default linker actions
.OBJ.EXE:
        LINK /MAP /CO $**,$@;
```

The dependency line, `test.obj : test.asm`, with no associated command list, would match the first of these rules, executing the command `MASM /Zi test;` as a result. Then a subsequent dependency line, `test.exe : test.obj mine.obj`, again with no command list, would match the second rule and execute `LINK /MAP /CO test.obj mine.obj,test.exe;` as a result.

Those strange expressions `$*`, `$**`, and `$@` in the preceding inference rule list are references to *macro definitions* built into MAKE and are defined in table 12.1. The program also provides for user-defined macros in its dependency files.

Table 12.1. *Built-in macros.*

Macro	Meaning
$*	Target name without extension
$@	Complete target name
$**	Complete list of infiles

When MAKE is processing any command list, whether from an inference rule or from a dependency block, these macros expand into the corresponding file reference as shown in the example. However, the macro capability is not limited to file name references. Macros are also commonly used to modify the options passed to the assembler, the linker, or the library manager.

To create a user-defined macro, the syntax is similar to that used at the DOS level to SET an environment string:

```
[# comment]
name[ ]=[ ][ "]text[ "]
```

MAKE ignores any blank space on either side of the equals sign (=) character. If the text string, which will replace the macro name when referenced, contains any blank spaces or "special" characters, the string must be enclosed by double quotes. Including the quotation marks never hurts and can prevent problems caused by "special" characters (that is, characters other than letters and numbers).

To indicate where MAKE should replace a macro with a text string, just reference the macro as follows:

$(*name*)

This entire string is then replaced by the *text* associated with *name*. For example, if the command line for the LINK inference rule in the previous example had been LINK $(LOPT) $**,$@; instead of LINK /MAP /CO $**,$@; , and the macro definition LOPT=../MAP /CO.. had preceded the inference rule in the file, the results would have been the same.

However, to remove the CodeView information from the output file, you only need to redefine LOPT as /MAP and that, as you will see shortly, can be done from the command line when MAKE is invoked. Thus the macro capability gives you an added dimension of freedom (and consequently a greater possibility for complications) in the use of the file.

You can also refer to environment variables as if they were macro definitions within the file. For instance, to use the environment variable PATH as part of a command line, you would simply insert $(PATH) in that command line of the dependency file. If the file actually has a macro named PATH, it will be used; if not, the content of the environment variable PATH will be used.

Be careful not to overuse the macro feature. Excessive use of macros is the major reason why most sample dependency files supplied with the various language products are incomprehensible at first glance. MAKE itself never requires such complexity.

Remember that this version of MAKE processes its dependency files in strict sequence. Thus all macro definitions must appear before the files can be referenced, and all inference rules must be defined before the files can be used. The full syntax for a dependency file used with Microsoft's MAKE is as follows:

[# *comment*]
[*macro defs*]
[# *comment*]
[*inference rules*]
[# *comment*]
[*description blocks*]

To use MAKE, invoke it from the DOS prompt with the following syntax:

MAKE [*options*] [*macrodefs*] *filename*

The only part of this syntax that isn't optional, other than the program name itself, is the file name. This must be the name of the dependency file that you want MAKE to use. If you omit the file name, MAKE gives you the following warning:

```
MAKE : warning U4014: usage : make <options> [name=value ...] file
   <options> = [/n] [/d] [/i] [/s] [/x file]
```

The options recognized by MAKE are listed and described in table 12.2. You can use any noncontradictory options simultaneously.

Table 12.2. Command-line options for Microsoft's MAKE.

Option	Meaning
/N	Commands that would be executed are displayed but are not actually executed; useful for debugging
/D	Date each file was last modified is displayed as file is scanned
/I	MAKE normally halts execution when any command it executes returns a nonzero exit or error-level code; this option causes MAKE to ignore the codes returned and continue execution
/S	This "silent" mode does not display command lines as they are executed
/X	Normally, MAKE displays all error messages to the CRT. This option, which requires a file name, separated from the option by a single blank space, redirects all error output to the named file so that you can refer to it later. If the file is read-only, error U1015 will result. This option is not present in versions of MAKE prior to those furnished with MASM 5.1

You can define macros in the command line just as they are in the dependency file. Any definition given in the command line overrides internal definitions in the dependency file itself (which, in turn, override environment variables of the same name). Therefore, in the previous example, to change the definition of the LOPT macro so that no Code-

View information is put into the EXE file, assuming that the dependency file is named sample.mak simply type

MAKE LOPT="/MAP" sample.mak

For a full example of the use of this version of MAKE, see the subsequent section on "Creating and Using a Makefile." First, though, I want to show you how the other similar utilities differ from this one.

Microsoft's NMAKE

With the release of QuickC version 2.0, Microsoft began shipping a different program maintenance utility called NMAKE.EXE. According to Microsoft, this utility resembles the original UNIX program more closely than MAKE. The differences between NMAKE and the MAKE supplied with previous Microsoft products (including MSC 5.1 and MASM 5.1) are significant, and dependency files originally written for MAKE will require some conversion effort to make them acceptable to the newer program.

The most significant of these differences involves the sequence in which the programs evaluate blocks. Unlike MAKE.EXE, which evaluates dependency blocks as they are encountered, NMAKE evaluates only the first such block automatically, and then examines the others only if their target files are in the infiles list of that first block or in the infiles list of some subsequent block that was evaluated because its target was involved in the first block. This action is similar to the way a linker program searches a library file for global references and then returns to search again just in case the new module introduced new references.

Another significant difference is that with NMAKE you can express things (macros, explicit dependencies, inference rules, and so on) many more ways, which make it easy to create a dependency file that defies human understanding (although the computer has no problems dealing with such a file). I omit many of these bells and whistles to keep the major differences clear; for a full description of all NMAKE capabilities, see pages 155 through 176 of the *Microsoft QuickC Tool Kit* manual furnished with your QuickC package.

Other differences include the following advantages offered only by NMAKE:

❏ The ability to use response files

❏ More command-line options

❏ Additional unique built-in macros

❏ Support of internal directives in the dependency file

❏ Some predefined inference rules

A response file for NMAKE, like those already described for use by linkers and library managers, contains the command-line option, definition, and file name information. Each appears in exactly the same format as it would on a command line.

The advantage of a response file is that you can type all of this information into a response file once, and then use it repeatedly thereafter without having to retype it. A secondary advantage is that the response file, unlike the DOS command line, is not limited to 127 characters; you can use the \ line-extension character to make a multiline response file acceptable to NMAKE.

If you have a response file named MYRESP.FIL to pass to NMAKE, just type

NMAKE @MYRESP.FIL

to do so. The @ character, which performs the same type of function here as it did for LINK and LIB, tells NMAKE that what follows is the name of a response file.

The command-line options recognized by NMAKE are listed and described in table 12.3. Notice that all the options recognized by MAKE are included with the same meanings, but eight more options have been added to the list.

Table 12.3. *Command-line options for Microsoft NMAKE.*

Option	Meaning
/A	Commands are executed to build all targets requested, even if those targets are not out of date.
/C	Copyright message, warnings, and nonfatal error messages are suppressed.
/D	Date each file was last modified is displayed as the file is scanned.
/E	Environment variables override internal macro definitions (opposite of normal precedence).

Table 12.3. *continues*

Table 12.3. *continued*

Option	Meaning
/F *filename*	This option command is always followed by a file name specifying the name of the dependency file to process. If this option is omitted, NMAKE searches for default file name MAKEFILE *before* searching for any other file named on the command line.
/I	NMAKE normally halts execution when any command it executes returns a nonzero exit or error-level code; this option causes NMAKE to ignore the codes returned and continue execution.
/N	Commands that would be executed are displayed, but not actually executed—useful for debugging.
/P	All macro definitions and target descriptions are printed.
/Q	Zero exit code is returned if target is up to date, and nonzero is returned if the target is out of date—useful when running NMAKE from within a BATch file.
/R	Inference rules and macro definitions contained in the TOOLS.INI file are ignored; normally, these rules and definitions provide defaults if similar rules and definitions are not contained in the dependency file.
/S	This "silent" mode does not display command lines as they are executed.
/T	Modification dates for out-of-date targets are changed to the current date and time; target file is *not* modified.
/X *filename*	Normally, NMAKE displays all error messages to the CRT; this option, which requires a file name separated from the option by a single blank space, redirects all error output to the named file so that you can refer to it later.

NMAKE recognizes 10 built-in or special macro definitions, compared to the 3 known to MAKE. These built-in macros and their meanings are listed in table 12.4.

Table 12.4. *Built-in macros for Microsoft NMAKE.*

Macro	Meaning
$*	Target name without extension (same as MAKE)
$@	Complete name of target (same as MAKE)
$**	Complete list of infiles (same as MAKE)
$<	Name of infile that triggered execution of command list (evaluated only for inference rules)
$?	List of infiles that are newer than the target—useful for updating LIB files and executing similar actions
$$@	Target currently being evaluated; can be used only in dependency lines
$(CC)	Command to invoke C compiler; preset to *cl* to invoke full MSC compiler, but must be changed if another compiler is in use (For instance, to invoke QuickC, this command must be redefined with CC=qcl.)
$(AS)	Command to invoke assembler; preset to *masm*, but like $(CC) can be redefined to invoke another program
$(MAKE)	Name with which NMAKE was invoked, used to call program recursively; causes line in which it appears to be executed even if /N option is in effect
$(MAKEFLAGS)	List of NMAKE options currently in effect; cannot be redefined, but is used with $(MAKE) to pass current option list to recursive call—for example: $(MAKE) $(MAKEFLAGS)

In NMAKE, you can control the flow of actions within a dependency file in several ways not possible with MAKE. One is by specifying a different target file on the command line. Another is by using *directives* in the dependency file. These directives are used in dependency files much as directives are used in the assemblers themselves—as commands primarily directed toward controlling the NMAKE program's actions rather than generating output. Using the NMAKE directives listed and described in table 12.5, you can change the commands that are executed based on the presence or absence of a defined macro name, or on the value of an expression. Directives also let you use INCLUDE files, output an error message, or alter the settings of the option switches.

Table 12.5. *Directives for Microsoft NMAKE.*

Directive	Meaning
!IF *expr*	If the value of *expr* is nonzero, statements in the file between this directive and the next matching !ELSE or !ENDIF are executed; otherwise, such a sequence of statements is not executed. If an !ELSE statement is the next matching directive, the statements between it and the matching !ENDIF are executed; otherwise no statements before the matching !ENDIF are executed.
!ELSE	Used only between !IF and !ENDIF statements, this directive indicates the end of a statement list to be executed if !IF is true (nonzero), and beginning of a list to be executed if the condition is false (zero).
!ENDIF	This directive marks end of an !IF sequence. !IF... !ENDIF sequences can be nested because each !IF extends to its matching !ENDIF.
!IFDEF *macro*	This directive is similar to the !IF directive, but instead of basing its decision on the value of an expression, !IFDEF executes subsequent statements only if *macro* has been defined, although the value of *macro* is immaterial. !ELSE and !ENDIF statements are executed the same as they were with !IF.
!IFNDEF *macro*	Exactly like !IFDEF, but with reversed meaning; statements are executed if *macro* has *not* been defined.
!UNDEF *macro*	After execution of this directive, *macro* is no longer defined.
!ERROR *text*	This directive causes message *text* to be printed, then halts execution of NMAKE.
!INCLUDE	Followed by a file name, this directive causes the named file to be read and evaluated before continuing processing of a current makefile. If the file name is enclosed in angle brackets (<>), paths specified by an INCLUDE macro or an environment variable will be searched for the file; otherwise, only the current directory will be searched.

`!CMDSWITCHES:`	This directive may be followed by a plus sign (+) or a minus sign (-), and must then specify one of four option indicators: /D, /I, /N, or /S. If the plus sign (+) appears, the named option is turned on; if the minus sign (-) appears, the option is turned off; if neither appears, the option is returned to the condition specified by the command line upon entering NMAKE. This directive changes the MAKEFLAGS macro, which cannot be altered directly.

Using the directives greatly complicates the design of a dependency file, but does make it possible to introduce powerful capabilities, based on choices specified by the presence or absence of only a few command-line-defined macros. However, until you are completely comfortable with the simpler ways of dealing with dependency files, you'll do best to avoid using the directives.

Unlike MAKE, NMAKE has three built-in inference rules (listed in table 12.6). These rules use some of the special macros from table 12.4 in their commands, so the actions of these rules can be modified by redefining the associated macros.

Table 12.6. *Built-in inference rules for Microsoft NMAKE.*

Rule	Command	Default action
.c.obj	$(CC) $(CFLAGS)/c $*.c	CL /c $*.c
.c.exe	$(CC) $(CFLAGS) $*.c	CL $*.c
.asm.obj	$(AS) $(AFLAGS) $*;	masm $*;

Notice that all three rules include macro names that end in *FLAGS* and are not listed in table 12.4. Because an undefined macro causes no error but simply evaluates to a zero-length text string, references like CFLAGS and AFLAGS give you the opportunity to specify special options to be invoked, either by defining them in your dependency files or on the command line.

For excellent examples of how this feature is used in practice, create a "project list" in QuickC for any of your source files, then examine the MAK file generated. (Later this chapter lists such a file, TEST.MAK.) You will see not one but four macros for CFLAGS; the first three are distinguished by added characters: _G (General), _D (Debugging), and _R (Release).

To see how the macros work, compare their contents with the options you told QuickC to employ when generating make files. Then CFLAGS itself is defined as the concatenation of CFLAGS_G with one of the other two characters, depending on whether you have flagged a Debug run or a Release run to QuickC. The built-in inference rule then passes the resulting option list to the compiler.

Another feature added to NMAKE that was not present in MAKE is the use of the command modifiers listed and described in table 12.7. When command modifiers are prefixed to commands, NMAKE changes the way those prefixed commands are executed.

Table 12.7. *Command modifiers for Microsoft NMAKE.*

Command modifier	Meaning
-	Disables error checking for the command that it modifies. If followed by a number, NMAKE halts only when the exit code returned by the command is greater than the specified number.
@	Prevents NMAKE from displaying the command as it executes. The modifier is identical in action with similar modifier for BATch files in DOS version 3.3 and later versions.
!	Causes command to be repeated for each file in the list represented by the special macro if the modified command uses one of the special macros $? or $**. On each repetition, the special macro is replaced by the next file name in the list.

In all three cases, the command modifier must immediately precede the command to which it applies.

Except for complications caused by the use of directives, the syntax for NMAKE's dependency files is identical to the dependency files for MAKE. However, the sequence in which dependency blocks appear differs.

If no target is specified on the command line, NMAKE's default condition is to evaluate only the first dependency block, so the ultimate dependency block for the file should appear *first* rather than *last*, as it must for MAKE. However, an existing file can easily be modified by adding a new dependency block before any of the others; for example, you could call for a pseudotarget such as ALL, which depends on the infile MYFILE.EXE.

The command-line syntax used with NMAKE is similar to MAKE's syntax, but with several critical differences:

NMAKE[*options*] [*macrodefs*] [*targets*] [*filename*]

The most obvious difference is that all parameters, even *filename*, are now optional. If all are omitted, NMAKE looks for a file named MAKEFILE by default, and processes it as the dependency file. In fact, unless the /F*filename* option is used to specify the dependency file's name as part of the option list, MAKEFILE will be used if it exists. The file name passed on the command line by itself is used only if MAKEFILE cannot be found.

The other obvious difference is that NMAKE can have one or more target files specified on the command line. If they are specified, their dependency lines will be evaluated regardless of where they occur in the dependency file sequence. The first-block rule applies only when no target is explicitly named; however, this is normally the case.

This description of NMAKE is far from complete; many features have been touched upon only briefly, and some have been omitted entirely to keep your introduction to NMAKE as simple, yet useful, as possible. However, you can make good use of the program with only the information given here and wait until much later before exploring its more advanced features.

Borland's Version of MAKE

Like NMAKE, the MAKE.EXE supplied with Borland's Turbo Assembler operates more like the original UNIX program than the Microsoft MAKE.EXE. In fact, Borland's MAKE is so similar to NMAKE that I'll discuss only those features where the two programs differ. So, like the NMAKE section, this section does not attempt to cover all features of the program.

The command-line syntax for the program is similar to NMAKE's, but shorter:

MAKE[*options*] [*targets*]

Notice that this version treats all file names on the command line as targets and does not provide for macro definitions as a separate kind of command-line parameter; they are still there, but as options.

The option list for MAKE is much shorter than NMAKE's list. And, unlike the Microsoft programs, this version treats the option character's case as significant: -Dmac defines a macro named mac, but -dmac is not recognized and results in a fatal error. The valid options and their meanings are listed in table 12.8.

Table 12.8. *Options recognized by Borland's MAKE.*

Option	Meaning
−a	Causes MAKE to perform an autodependency check (unfortunately neither the manuals nor the on-line help give any clue as to what this might be!)
−D*macro*	Defines a macro with no content
−D*macro* = *string*	Defines a macro containing a string; both -D options provide for command-line redefinition of macros
−f*filename*	Tells MAKE to use *filename* as its input dependency file; if *filename* cannot be found and does not contain an extension, MAKE then searches for *filename*.MAK
−I*directory*	Specifies the directory to be searched (in addition to the current directory) for files to be INCLUDEd
−n	Does not execute commands (same as Microsoft programs' /N option)
−s	Does not display command lines as they are executed (same as Microsoft programs' "silent" mode)
−U*macro*	Undefines any existing definitions of *macro*
−? or −h	Provides on-line help

Like NMAKE, MAKE will evaluate the dependency blocks for all files named on the command line as targets and, if no -f option is used, will take MAKEFILE as the default name for the dependency file to process.

Also like NMAKE, if no target files are designated on the command line, the first dependency block encountered is the only one automatically evaluated. All other blocks are evaluated *only* if their target files are in the infiles list for that first dependency block or of some subsequent block that was evaluated because its target was involved in the first block.

The list of built-in macros for MAKE is much shorter; table 12.9 lists and describes all of them. In addition to the seven macros listed in the table, all existing environment variables are automatically loaded as macros.

Table 12.9. *Built-in macros for Borland's MAKE.*

Macro	Meaning
$d(*macro*)	Expands to 1 if *macro* is defined, and to 0 if not; only valid when used in !if and !elif directives to achieve the same results as NMAKE's !IFDEF and !IFNDEF directives
$*	Expands to the base name (including the path but without the extension) of the target file
$<	Expands to the full name (including path and extension) of the target file when used in a dependency block, or to the base name plus source file extension when used in an inference rule
$:	Expands to the path name (without the file name or extension) of the target file
$.	Expands to the file name (without the path but including extension) of the target file
$&	Expands to the base name only (without the path or extension) of target file
MAKE	Expands to 1

Like NMAKE, Borland's MAKE implements directives that serve the same purpose as those used in assembly language. The list of directives is much shorter, though; table 12.10 describes all of them.

This version of MAKE has no built-in inference rules; however, you can define your own standard set and store them in a file named BUILTINS.MAK. The contents of such a file are automatically loaded by MAKE before any processing for a dependency file begins.

Only two of the three command modifiers used by NMAKE are valid for MAKE; the ! modifier is not recognized. Table 12.11 lists and describes the valid modifier characters. In both cases these characters appear as prefixes to the command being modified.

Table 12.10. *Directives for Borland's MAKE.*

Directives	Meaning
!if	As in NMAKE, this directive begins an !if...!endif sequence that may optionally include !elif and !else directives. The directive must be followed by an expression (using any of the standard C operators), which may include the $d() macro. If the expression evaluates to a nonzero value, all statements up to the next matching !elif, !else, or !endif statement are executed, and then statements are ignored until the matching !endif is reached. If the expression evaluates to zero, then statements up to the next matching !elif or !else are ignored.
!elif	This directive, which is unique to Borland's MAKE, performs another test similar to !if when previous tests have failed. Like !if, !elif is always followed by an expression. If !elif is reached by skipping over previous statements because a zero resulted earlier, the expression is evaluated in the same way as for the !if, and has the same result of executing or skipping over subsequent statements. If reached after execution of statements because of an earlier nonzero !if or !elif, the expression is not evaluated, and all subsequent statements up to the next matching !endif are skipped. As many !elif tests as you like may be placed between an !if directive and the !else directive to perform multiple, mutually exclusive tests and conditional execution.
!else	This directive can appear only between an !if or an !elif and the matching !endif, and (unlike !elif) can appear only once during the sequence. If reached after execution of statements because of a nonzero test result, !else causes all following statements, up to the matching !endif, to be skipped. If reached while skipping over statements because of a zero test result, !else causes the subsequent statements up to the matching !endif to be executed.
!endif	This directive ends an !if...!elif...!else...!endif sequence.

!undef	This directive, which must be followed by the name of a macro, causes the named macro to be forgotten by MAKE. If no such macro exists, the directive has no effect.
!include	This directive must be followed by the name of a file enclosed in double quote marks ("name"). !include causes the entire contents of the named file to be evaluated and executed before proceeding with evaluation of the current file.
!error	This directive, which must be followed by a text string, causes the text string to be displayed, and then halts execution of MAKE.

Table 12.11. *Command modifiers for Borland's MAKE.*

Command modifier	Meaning
-	Disables error checking for the command that it modifies; if followed by a number, MAKE halts only when the exit code returned by the command is greater than the specified number
@	Prevents MAKE from displaying the command as it executes; identical in action with similar modifier for BATch files in DOS version 3.3 and later versions

Except for the differences noted in this section, Borland's MAKE operates almost exactly like NMAKE.

Creating and Using a Makefile

To create a dependency file, you must first decide which modules you want it to include. All modules related to a single project should be handled by the same dependency file; if you assign that file a name that indicates a specific project, you can then update everything by simply typing

MAKE *project*

after you make any source file changes. If your dependency blocks are accurately written, all processes necessary for your update will be executed as a result.

As an example of how MAKE is typically used, the following dependency file for VIDEO.LIB (a program developed in Chapter 13) can be used with the Microsoft version of MAKE:

```
# Makefile for VIDEO.LIB - 11/12/89
#
FINDCARD.OBJ : FINDCARD.ASM
  MASM FINDCARD;

PCHAR.OBJ    : PCHAR.ASM
  MASM PCHAR;

PSTRNG.OBJ   : PSTRNG.ASM
  MASM PSTRNG;

PCHARA.OBJ   : PCHARA.ASM
  MASM PCHARA;

PSTRNGA.OBJ  : PSTRNGA.ASM
  MASM PSTRNGA;

BOX.OBJ      : BOX.ASM
  MASM BOX;

SETDI.OBJ    : SETDI.ASM
  MASM SETDI;

SCRN.OBJ     : SCRN.ASM
  MASM SCRN;

VIDEO.LIB : FINDCARD.OBJ PCHAR.OBJ PSTRNG.OBJ PCHARA.OBJ PSTRNGA.OBJ BOX.OBJ \
SETDI.OBJ SCRN.OBJ
  LIB @VIDEOLIB
```

This file, which I named VIDEO, shows the essentials of classic dependency file construction. The file contains no inference rules, nor does it use any macro definitions; none are needed, although the many repetitions of MASM ...; could have been replaced by a single inference rule. I did not do so because then the action of the file would have been much less clear.

Here's how it works.

The first eight dependency blocks in this file are identical except for the base file names in each; these blocks define the dependencies for the eight OBJ modules that make up VIDEO.LIB. In each case, if the DOS time stamp indicates that the ASM file is newer than the OBJ file, or if the OBJ file does not exist, MASM is invoked by the single command line to create an updated OBJ file.

The ninth (and final) block defines the LIB itself in terms of its OBJ components. If any OBJ file is newer than the LIB, then the entire LIB file is rebuilt using the LIB response file VIDEOLIB:

```
VIDEO
-+ FINDCARD.OBJ &
-+ PCHAR.OBJ &
-+ PSTRNG.OBJ &
-+ PCHARA.OBJ &
-+ PSTRNGA.OBJ &
-+ BOX.OBJ &
-+ SETDI.OBJ &
-+ SCRN.OBJ
```

Because Microsoft's MAKE processes the dependency blocks in strict sequence, any ASM file newer than its corresponding OBJ file will cause MASM to be run. When the final block is reached, if any other block caused a new OBJ file to be created, then at least one of the listed OBJ files will be newer than the LIB, and the whole LIB file will be updated. (With NMAKE or Borland's MAKE, you would have to move this last dependency block to be the first block; the program would then trace through the dependencies for each OBJ file named in its infile list to determine if any action was required.)

To illustrate the process, I deleted one OBJ file from the directory so that it would force rebuilding of that file, and then ran MAKE; here's the result:

```
C>MAKE VIDEO

Microsoft (R) Program Maintenance Utility  Version 4.07
Copyright (C) Microsoft Corp 1984-1988.  All rights reserved.

MAKE : warning U4000: 'PCHAR.OBJ' : target does not exist
  MASM PCHAR;
Microsoft (R) Macro Assembler Version 5.10
Copyright (C) Microsoft Corp 1981, 1988.  All rights reserved.

  49946 + 224196 Bytes symbol space free
```

```
      0 Warning Errors
      0 Severe Errors

   LIB @VIDEOLIB

Microsoft (R) Library Manager  Version 3.10
Copyright (C) Microsoft Corp 1983-1988.  All rights reserved.

Library name:VIDEO
Operations:-+ FINDCARD.OBJ &
Operations:-+ PCHAR.OBJ &
Operations:-+ PSTRNG.OBJ &
Operations:-+ PCHARA.OBJ &
Operations:-+ PSTRNGA.OBJ &
Operations:-+ BOX.OBJ &
Operations:-+ SETDI.OBJ &
Operations:-+ SCRN.OBJ
List file:
Output library:


C>_
```

If only one of the modules is likely to be updated on any particular run of the file, a more efficient file would omit the final block and, instead, invoke LIB (as a second line for each of the other eight blocks) to update only the single module affected:

```
FINDCARD.OBJ : FINDCARD.ASM
  MASM FINDCARD;
  LIB VIDEO-+FINDCARD;

PCHAR.OBJ    : PCHAR.ASM
  MASM PCHAR;
  LIB VIDEO-+PCHAR;

PSTRNG.OBJ   : PSTRNG.ASM
  MASM PSTRNG;
  LIB VIDEO-+PSTRNG;

PCHARA.OBJ   : PCHARA.ASM
  MASM PCHARA;
  LIB VIDEO-+PCHARA;
```

```
PSTRNGA.OBJ  : PSTRNGA.ASM
  MASM PSTRNGA;
  LIB VIDEO-+PSTRNGA;

BOX.OBJ      : BOX.ASM
  MASM BOX;
  LIB VIDEO-+BOX;

SETDI.OBJ    : SETDI.ASM
  MASM SETDI;
  LIB VIDEO-+SETDI;

SCRN.OBJ     : SCRN.ASM
  MASM SCRN;
  LIB VIDEO-+SCRN;
```

This second example, which cannot readily be translated for use with NMAKE or Borland's MAKE, should be followed only when it's unlikely that more than one module will be updated on a single run. This program causes the entire library to be updated for each object module instead of waiting until all OBJ files are done and then updating the LIB one file at a time to get them all.

Here's another example of how a makefile can be built; the following TEST.MAK file was created by QuickC from the integrated environment's "select list" inputs for the debugging example in Chapter 10. I then added comments explaining the purpose of each line. This file can be used with NMAKE to perform a full compilation and linking of TEST.EXE:

```
PROJ =TEST      # passes name of desired output file to 1st block
DEBUG     =1
CC   =qcl       # defines "qcl" as C compiler
AS   =qcl       # and also as the assembler
CFLAGS_G  = /AC /W3 /Ze
CFLAGS_D  = /Zi /Zr /Od
CFLAGS_R  = /Od /DNDEBUG
CFLAGS    =$(CFLAGS_G) $(CFLAGS_D) # sets up for DEBUG run
AFLAGS_G = /Cu /W2 /P1
AFLAGS_D = /Zi
AFLAGS_R = /DNDEBUG
AFLAGS    =$(AFLAGS_G) $(AFLAGS_D) # sets up for DEBUG run
LFLAGS_G  = /CP:0xfff /SE:0x80 /ST:0x800
LFLAGS_D  = /CO /M /INCR
LFLAGS_R  =
LFLAGS    =$(LFLAGS_G) $(LFLAGS_D) # sets up for DEBUG use
```

```
RUNFLAGS  =
OBJS_EXT =     sums.obj          # the assembly language module
LIBS_EXT =

.asm.obj: ; $(AS) $(AFLAGS) -c $*.asm    # redefines built-in rule

all: $(PROJ).EXE              # first dependency block, a pseudo

test.obj: test.c              # causes compilation on source change

$(PROJ).EXE:   test.obj $(OBJS_EXT)     # causes linking if OBJ changed
     echo >NUL @<(PROJ).crf
test.obj +
$(OBJS_EXT)
$(PROJ).EXE

$(LIBS_EXT);
<<
     ilink -a -e "link $(LFLAGS) @$(PROJ).crf" $(PROJ)

run: $(PROJ).EXE              # used by QC to RUN file, not used here
     $(PROJ) $(RUNFLAGS)
```

The PRJ file used by Borland's Turbo C pseudomake capability is much simpler:

```
test
sums.obj
```

This file merely lists the names of all input files involved in the generation of an output file (if no extension is given, C is assumed). If any of the input files' date-time stamp is newer than that of the output file (the first file name, with an EXE extension), then compilation and linking are performed as necessary to bring the output file up to date.

Summary

In this chapter, you've learned about makefiles and the various utilities available to process them and have seen how judicious use of these features can greatly simplify the task of maintaining your assembly language programs.

You have also seen how the various MAKE utilities differ significantly from one version to another, even from the same publisher, and have learned some methods of accounting for those differences.

Finally, you have learned how to construct and work with a makefile, using the Microsoft MAKE utility. You can use this example to maintain the library that will be developed in the next portion of this book.

Part III

Advanced Assembly
Language Topics

CHAPTER 13

Video Memory

Writing information to a video display monitor is perhaps the biggest bottleneck in most high-level languages. The sad thing is, most programmers do not even realize that it is a bottleneck.

The video display is simply a representation of what is contained in a specific area of memory. This type of display is referred to as a *memory-mapped* display; the display memory area is called a *video buffer* because it holds what will be displayed on the monitor. Changes occur constantly in the video buffer, and affect what is seen on the video display. The buffer's location in memory depends on the type of display adapter that is being used. A discussion of the buffer's location is included in this chapter's description of each display adapter type.

The original displays for the PC used an 80-column, 25-line screen. Each text screen's video buffer occupied 4,000 bytes (0FA0h) of data. How was this number derived? Each character position on the screen uses two bytes of memory—one for the character and one for the character's attribute. The *attribute byte* controls how the character will be displayed (in color, with underlining, blinking, and so on). Therefore, one text screen required 4,000 bytes (80 times 25 times 2) of memory.

With the introduction of the EGA, and later the MCGA and VGA, display capabilities became a bit more complex. With these advanced video adapter cards, you can extend the number of columns on each line to

132, and the number of lines per screen to 60. Doing so raises the buffer size requirement from 4,000 to 15,840 bytes.

You can display either individual characters or strings by using certain BIOS and DOS interrupts, but they tend to be rather slow. You can use BIOS and DOS functions to gain some (but not much) speed advantage over high-level language display techniques. You do not gain much of an advantage because, to guarantee portability and compatibility, most high-level languages ordinarily use the BIOS and DOS interrupts in their display library routines.

Because of the way the BIOS, and subsequently the DOS, routines were written, they repeat several tasks during a display operation. Although perhaps necessary to maintain the general-purpose design of the BIOS routines, this repetition can slow down display operations so much that they almost become unacceptable. For example, in more than one instance in the BIOS video routines, the individual routines that make up INT 10h call themselves to determine necessary information for completing the current task. This results in much more pushing, popping, and overhead than if the video routines had been written with a specific purpose intended. On newer PC models, with clock speeds of 8 MHz and up instead of the original 4.77 MHz speed, the delays become much less noticeable, but are nonetheless time consuming.

Because a video display is simply a representation of a special memory area, you can alter the display by altering that memory area directly. As you know, you can transfer large blocks of memory quickly from one location to another. By using the string-manipulation mnemonics, you can use the following subroutine to transfer an entire video screen in approximately 80,100 clock cycles:

```
MOVE_BLOCK      PROC    NEAR
                PUSH    CX                      ;Save all used registers
                PUSH    SI
                PUSH    DI
                PUSH    ES

                MOV     SI,OFFSET SOURCE_DAT    ;Image data to be moved
                MOV     ES,VIDEO_BUFFER         ;Segment of video buffer
                MOV     DI,0                    ;Start at beginning
                                                ; of video buffer
                MOV     CX,0FA0h                ;Size of video screen
                REP     MOVSB                   ;Move it

                POP     ES                      ;Restore all used registers
```

```
                    POP    DI
                    POP    SI
                    POP    CX
                    RET
MOVE_BLOCK          ENDP
```

Stated in clock cycles, this may sound like a long time for transferring data. However, you must remember that on a standard IBM PC, running at 4.772727 MHz, one clock cycle is only 0.0000002095238 seconds long; therefore, the entire process takes approximately 0.01678307 seconds. The speed increases significantly on a Personal Computer AT or compatible or on an 80386-based machine.

No matter which machine you use, an entire screen can be displayed in less than 1/50 of a second, which is virtually instantaneous. Compare that to a high-level language and the way you have to clear the screen and then move data elements individually to the screen!

For those of us who use high-level languages, the capability of displaying things instantaneously on the screen is one of the attractions of using assembly language.

Because the physical location of the video memory depends on which display adapter is used, let's take just a moment to examine the display adapters commonly used on IBM microcomputers.

Differences between Display Adapters

The IBM family of personal computers (and major clones) use a variety of display devices. Several have been around for years, and new ones crop up periodically. In this section, I discuss the methods and conventions used to display information on the six most popular display devices:

❏ The IBM Monochrome Display Adapter (MDA)

❏ The Hercules Graphics Adapter (HGA), which includes a monochrome graphics capability

❏ The IBM Color Graphics Adapter (CGA)

❏ The IBM Enhanced Graphics Adapter (EGA)

❏ The IBM Multi-Color Graphics Array (MCGA)

❏ The IBM Video Graphics Array (VGA)

The way you program your application largely depends on which of these display devices you use. You should do some advance research to ensure that you know which device(s) you will use. If several different display types are likely to be used, you can program your software to make intelligent choices about which type of display is currently in use. You will learn about one such method later in this chapter.

All of these display adapters (except the MDA) can display true graphics data. As I stated in the introduction, I will not delve into specific graphics routines. Rather, I will discuss the way in which each type of display adapter stores and displays textual data.

The Monochrome Display Adapter (MDA)

The IBM Monochrome Display Adapter made its debut when the IBM Personal Computer was introduced in 1981. As the name implies, the MDA displays information in monochrome (one color). Which color depends on the type of monitor you have. Most monochrome monitors display data in either green or amber, although other colors can be displayed.

The MDA offers a resolution of 720 by 350 pixels—a total of 252,000 picture elements. This total is segmented into 2,000 character cells (each with a resolution of 9 by 14 pixels) arranged in 25 rows of 80 cells each.

The contents of each character cell are stored in memory as a single byte of information. Each character cell has a corresponding attribute byte that controls the way in which the character is displayed. The composition and use of the attribute byte are discussed later in this chapter.

The video buffer used by the MDA holds a single text screen and consists of 4K of RAM, beginning at B0000h (segment address B000:0000). The characters and their attribute bytes are interlaced so that the video memory is mapped beginning at the upper left corner of the screen and proceeding across and down the display (see table 13.1).

Each character-display position can contain a value of 1 through 256, with each value equivalent to a specific character code. The character code used by the MDA is a superset of ASCII (see fig. 13.1).

The character codes shown in figure 13.1 are created by an 8K character generator on the MDA interface board. To generate a character, simply place the character in the proper memory location in the MDA buffer. The internal hardware of the MDA takes care of the rest.

Table 13.1. *Memory locations for MDA display data.*

Segment address	Character/attribute
B000:0000	Character for row 1, column 1
B000:0001	Attribute for row 1, column 1
B000:0002	Character for row 1, column 2
B000:0003	Attribute for row 1, column 2
B000:0004	Character for row 1, column 3
B000:0005	Attribute for row 1, column 3
B000:009C	Character for row 1, column 79
B000:009D	Attribute for row 1, column 79
B000:009E	Character for row 1, column 80
B000:009F	Attribute for row 1, column 80
B000:00A0	Character for row 2, column 1
B000:00A1	Attribute for row 2, column 1
B000:00A2	Character for row 2, column 2
B000:00A3	Attribute for row 2, column 2
B000:0EFC	Character for row 24, column 79
B000:0EFD	Attribute for row 24, column 79
B000:0EFE	Character for row 24, column 80
B000:0EFF	Attribute for row 24, column 80
B000:0F00	Character for row 25, column 1
B000:0F01	Attribute for row 25, column 1
B000:0F02	Character for row 25, column 2
B000:0F03	Attribute for row 25, column 2
B000:0F9C	Character for row 25, column 79
B000:0F9D	Attribute for row 25, column 79
B000:0F9E	Character for row 25, column 80
B000:0F9F	Attribute for row 25, column 80

The Hercules Graphics Adapter (HGA)

The Hercules Graphics Adapter, which is similar to the MDA, comes from a company called Hercules Computer Technology. This device is supported by a great deal of software and is the standard for monochrome graphics.

Ordinarily, the HGA behaves exactly like the MDA, except that the HGA includes a monochrome graphics capability. In bit-mapped graphics mode, the HGA provides a resolution of 720 by 348 pixels—the highest

Fig. 13.1. ASCII character code for MDA.

0=	32=	64=@	96=`	128=Ç	160=á	192=└	224=α
1=☺	33=!	65=A	97=a	129=ü	161=í	193=┴	225=β
2=☻	34="	66=B	98=b	130=é	162=ó	194=┬	226=Γ
3=♥	35=#	67=C	99=c	131=â	163=ú	195=├	227=π
4=♦	36=$	68=D	100=d	132=ä	164=ñ	196=─	228=Σ
5=♣	37=%	69=E	101=e	133=à	165=Ñ	197=┼	229=σ
6=♠	38=&	70=F	102=f	134=å	166=ª	198=╞	230=µ
7=•	39='	71=G	103=g	135=ç	167=º	199=╟	231=τ
8=◘	40=(	72=H	104=h	136=ê	168=¿	200=╚	232=Φ
9=○	41=)	73=I	105=i	137=ë	169=⌐	201=╔	233=Θ
10=◙	42=*	74=J	106=j	138=è	170=¬	202=╩	234=Ω
11=♂	43=+	75=K	107=k	139=ï	171=½	203=╦	235=δ
12=♀	44=,	76=L	108=l	140=î	172=¼	204=╠	236=∞
13=♪	45=-	77=M	109=m	141=ì	173=¡	205=═	237=φ
14=♫	46=.	78=N	110=n	142=Ä	174=«	206=╬	238=ε
15=☼	47=/	79=O	111=o	143=Å	175=»	207=╧	239=∩
16=►	48=0	80=P	112=p	144=É	176=░	208=╨	240=≡
17=◄	49=1	81=Q	113=q	145=æ	177=▒	209=╤	241=±
18=↕	50=2	82=R	114=r	146=Æ	178=▓	210=╥	242=≥
19=‼	51=3	83=S	115=s	147=ô	179=│	211=╙	243=≤
20=¶	52=4	84=T	116=t	148=ö	180=┤	212=╘	244=⌠
21=§	53=5	85=U	117=u	149=ò	181=╡	213=╒	245=⌡
22=▬	54=6	86=V	118=v	150=û	182=╢	214=╓	246=÷
23=↨	55=7	87=W	119=w	151=ù	183=╖	215=╫	247=≈
24=↑	56=8	88=X	120=x	152=ÿ	184=╕	216=╪	248=°
25=↓	57=9	89=Y	121=y	153=Ö	185=╣	217=┘	249=·
26=→	58=:	90=Z	122=z	154=Ü	186=║	218=┌	250=·
27=←	59=;	91=[	123={	155=¢	187=╗	219=█	251=√
28=∟	60=<	92=\	124=|	156=£	188=╝	220=▄	252=ⁿ
29=↔	61==	93=]	125=}	157=¥	189=╜	221=▌	253=²
30=▲	62=>	94=^	126=~	158=₧	190=╛	222=▐	254=■
31=▼	63=?	95=_	127=⌂	159=ƒ	191=┐	223=▀	255=

resolution of any adapter discussed in this book. In text mode, the HGA operates exactly like the MDA. (For additional information, refer to the section on the MDA.)

The Color Graphics Adapter (CGA)

IBM's first offering for color graphics capability on the IBM family of microcomputers, the Color Graphics Adapter, can operate in text mode (like the MDA) or in a bit-mapped graphics mode. I will focus on the display of textual data because, as I stated in the introduction, the bit-mapped graphics mode is beyond the scope of this book.

The high resolution offered by the CGA is 640 by 200 pixels, a total of 128,000 picture elements. As with the MDA, this total can be segmented into 2,000 character cells, which are arranged in 25 rows of either 40 or 80 cells each. But the resolution of each cell is significantly less with the CGA—only 8 by 8 pixels, which renders characters that are not as readable or crisp as those on the MDA.

In text mode, the CGA functions much like the MDA. This is understandable—the CGA and MDA both use the Motorola 6845 CRT Controller chip. With the CGA as with the MDA, the contents of each character cell are stored in memory as a single byte of information. Each character cell has a corresponding attribute byte that controls how the character is displayed. The composition and use of the attribute byte is different in the CGA and the MDA, as you will learn later in this chapter.

The video buffer used by the CGA consists of 16K of RAM, beginning at B8000h (segment address B800:0000). Because a 40 by 25 text screen requires only 2K of memory, the video buffer can hold as many as eight text screens, or pages. With an 80 by 25 text screen, which requires 4K of memory, as many as four video pages can be contained in the video buffer.

The currently displayed video page can be changed easily; to do so, you modify the buffer start address used by the 6845 CRTC. Normally, this address is set to point to the memory block starting at B8000h. The current video page is changed through the use of BIOS function calls (see Chapter 15).

As with the MDA, the characters and their attribute bytes are interlaced, beginning at the upper left corner of the screen and proceeding across and down the display. Table 13.2 shows how the video memory for the first page of an 80 by 25 screen is mapped.

Each character-display position can contain a value of 1 through 256, with each value equivalent to a specific character code. The character codes used by the CGA are the same as those used by the MDA, and are a superset of ASCII. The CGA also uses a ROM character generator.

The Enhanced Graphics Adapter (EGA)

IBM introduced the Enhanced Graphics Adapter in late 1984. Most software treats the EGA, in text mode, as though it were a Color Graphics Adapter. But even in text mode, there are several noticeable differences between the EGA and the Color Graphics Adapter. The following advantages are available with an EGA card:

Table 13.2. *Memory locations for first page of an 80 by 25 CGA.*

Segment address	Character/attribute
B800:0000	Character for row 1, column 1
B800:0001	Attribute for row 1, column 1
B800:0002	Character for row 1, column 2
B800:0003	Attribute for row 1, column 2
B800:0004	Character for row 1, column 3
B800:0005	Attribute for row 1, column 3
B800:009C	Character for row 1, column 79
B800:009D	Attribute for row 1, column 79
B800:009E	Character for row 1, column 80
B800:009F	Attribute for row 1, column 80
B800:00A0	Character for row 2, column 1
B800:00A1	Attribute for row 2, column 1
B800:00A2	Character for row 2, column 2
B800:00A3	Attribute for row 2, column 2
B800:0EFC	Character for row 24, column 79
B800:0EFD	Attribute for row 24, column 79
B800:0EFE	Character for row 24, column 80
B800:0EFF	Attribute for row 24, column 80
B800:0F00	Character for row 25, column 1
B800:0F01	Attribute for row 25, column 1
B800:0F02	Character for row 25, column 2
B800:0F03	Attribute for row 25, column 2
B800:0F9C	Character for row 25, column 79
B800:0F9D	Attribute for row 25, column 79
B800:0F9E	Character for row 25, column 80
B800:0F9F	Attribute for row 25, column 80

❏ More colors can be displayed

❏ Text information, displayed in color, can blink

❏ Resolution is improved

❏ More display modes are available

❏ User-defined character sets are available

Before proceeding, let's examine this last point. As you can see from table 13.3, the EGA offers 12 display modes.

Table 13.3. *EGA display modes.*

Mode number	Mode type	Display type	Pixel resolution	Characters	Box size	Colors
0	Text	Color	320 x 200	40 x 25	8 x 8	16
		Enhanced	320 x 350	40 x 25	8 x 14	16/64
1		---------- Same as mode 0 ----------				
2	Text	Color	640 x 200	80 x 25	8 x 8	16
		Enhanced	640 x 350	80 x 25	8 x 14	16/64
3		---------- Same as mode 2 ----------				
4	Graph	Clr/Enh	320 x 200	40 x 25	8 x 8	4
5		---------- Same as mode 4 ----------				
6	Graph	Clr/Enh	640 x 200	80 x 25	8 x 14	2
7	Text	Mono	720 x 350	80 x 25	9 x 14	4
13	Graph	Clr/Enh	320 x 200	40 x 25	8 x 8	16
14	Graph	Clr/Enh	640 x 200	80 x 25	8 x 8	16
15	Graph	Mono	640 x 350	80 x 25	8 x 14	4
16	Graph	Enhanced	640 x 350	80 x 25	8 x 14	varies

Notice that the resolution offered by the EGA is not quite as good as that offered by the MDA and HGA boards. EGA resolution is 640 by 350 pixels—a total of 224,000 picture elements.

The possibilities of using this resolution in a color graphics mode are quite impressive, but these capabilities are beyond the scope of this book. Because the effective use of the EGA would fill an entire book, I will focus only on using the EGA in text mode.

Like the other video adapters, the EGA normally segments the text screen into 2,000 character cells, each with a resolution of 8 by 14 pixels. These character cells are arranged in 25 rows of 80 cells each. The contents of each character cell are stored in memory as a single byte of information. Each character cell has a corresponding attribute byte that controls how the character is displayed. (The composition and use of the attribute byte are discussed later in this chapter.)

However, the EGA provides a capability for loading user-specified character sets, and when you load the 8 by 8 pixel ROM set normally used only with 40-column graphics modes, the number of rows of text rises from 25 to 43! This in turn increases the size of the video buffer to 6,880 bytes (3,440 characters plus the same number of attribute bytes).

Which video buffer is used by the EGA depends on the amount of memory available on the card. Most of the higher memory capabilities are used only in multipage graphics software or in animation. In text mode, however, the EGA is capable of emulating either the MDA or CGA in memory usage. If connected to a monochrome monitor, the video buffer begins at absolute address B0000h (segment address B000:0000), as does the MDA. If connected to a color monitor, the video buffer begins at absolute address B8000h (segment address B800:0000), as does the CGA.

As with other text screens, the characters and their attribute bytes are interlaced so that, beginning at the upper left corner of the screen and proceeding across and down the display, the video memory is mapped as shown in table 13.4. The question mark is replaced by 0 if the EGA is connected to a monochrome monitor, and by 8 if connected to a color monitor.

Table 13.4. *Memory locations for EGA display data.*

Segment address	Character/attribute
B?00:0000	Character for row 1, column 1
B?00:0001	Attribute for row 1, column 1
B?00:0002	Character for row 1, column 2
B?00:0003	Attribute for row 1, column 2
B?00:0004	Character for row 1, column 3
B?00:0005	Attribute for row 1, column 3
B?00:009C	Character for row 1, column 79
B?00:009D	Attribute for row 1, column 79
B?00:009E	Character for row 1, column 80
B?00:009F	Attribute for row 1, column 80
B?00:00A0	Character for row 2, column 1
B?00:00A1	Attribute for row 2, column 1
B?00:00A2	Character for row 2, column 2
B?00:00A3	Attribute for row 2, column 2
B?00:0EFC	Character for row 24, column 79
B?00:0EFD	Attribute for row 24, column 79
B?00:0EFE	Character for row 24, column 80
B?00:0EFF	Attribute for row 24, column 80
B?00:0F00	Character for row 25, column 1
B?00:0F01	Attribute for row 25, column 1
B?00:0F02	Character for row 25, column 2
B?00:0F03	Attribute for row 25, column 2
B?00:0F9C	Character for row 25, column 79
B?00:0F9D	Attribute for row 25, column 79
B?00:0F9E	Character for row 25, column 80
B?00:0F9F	Attribute for row 25, column 80

The EGA can display the same character set that each of the other display adapters can display. However, the characters are displayed differently. The EGA uses a RAM character generator, not one that is ROM-based. This means that you can design and download custom fonts based on your own needs. As many as four fonts of 256 characters each can be developed and subsequently used by the EGA, but only two of the fonts can be used at any given time. Detailed information on the development and use of alternate fonts is beyond the scope of this book.

The Multi-Color Graphics Array (MCGA)

When the PS/2 line was introduced, replacing the original PC products, IBM moved the video adapter functions from the traditional separate card onto the system motherboard, and changed the name from "adapter" to "array" as a result.

IBM also produced two different kinds of graphics arrays, one for the "low end" of the line (Models 25 and 30) and another for the rest of them.

The "low-end" device is the Multi-Color Graphics Array, which replaces the CGA and offers vastly improved performance. Resolution was increased to 640 by 480 pixels, and the number of colors MCGA can display is limited only by the quality of the attached monitor. In graphics mode, MCGA can display any 256 colors from a range of more than 262,000 hues, in 320 by 200 resolution. In text mode, MCGA's performance is similar to that of the high-end device, the VGA (discussed in the next section), except that MCGA's vertical resolution is limited to 350 scan lines.

The Video Graphics Array (VGA)

The Video Graphics Array is the "high-end" device for the PS/2 line of IBM systems, and is also available as an adapter card for all older IBM-compatible PCs and clones.

The VGA offers all the capability of the MCGA (and more) in graphics modes, but increases resolution up to 720 by 400 pixels in text modes, whereas the MCGA goes only to 640 by 350.

Like the EGA, both the MCGA and the VGA can be loaded with user-defined fonts. The VGA also gives you the choice of 200-line, 350-line, or

400-line vertical resolution. This choice gives you an even wider range of possible buffer sizes, because you can have up to 60 rows of text on a single screen. However, the most common choices are either 25 rows (the conventional 8x16 character box at 400 lines) or 50 rows (a 8x8 box at 400 lines).

If you will be using an MCGA or VGA with other than the conventional 25-line screen sizing, you may find the exact code developed in this chapter unusable; however, you can easily modify the code to work properly with any screen size you choose by changing the portions that convert row and column counts to absolute memory addresses.

Like the EGA, both the MCGA and the VGA automatically map their text buffer memory addresses to either the B000h or B800h range, depending upon whether a monochrome or color monitor is connected. So as long as you stick to the 80x25 screen dimensions, you can use the same assembly language routines to deal with all the displays available.

Determining the Type of Display Installed

Because the way in which text is displayed depends on the type of display adapter installed, your first task is to determine which type of adapter is installed in the computer. To communicate with the peripherals that are attached to it, the computer must know what those peripherals are—including the display adapters.

BIOS cannot display information unless it knows what type of display adapter is being used. BIOS keeps a list of video-related information beginning at memory locations 0449h through 0489h (see table 13.5).

Currently, two of the memory locations shown in table 13.5 are of interest. The byte at 0410h tells what the system board switch settings were when the POST (Power-On Self Test) was performed at booting. Each bit of the word denotes a different setting. Table 13.6 shows the bit meanings of the value at 0410h.

The value of bits 5-4 tells you what type of card (color or monochrome) is installed, according to the system board dip switch settings. But you can't tell whether the monochrome board is an MDA or HGA or whether the color board is a CGA or EGA. (The distinction is not germane to this discussion, however, because we are dealing only with textual display of data.) A monochrome adapter, such as the MDA, the HGA, or the

Table 13.5. *BIOS video-related data.*

Memory location	Length	Purpose
0410h	byte	POST equipment list 1
0411h	byte	POST equipment list 2
0449h	byte	BIOS video mode
044Ah	word	Columns
044Ch	word	Page length
044Eh	word	Page beginning
0460h	word	Cursor start/end
0462h	byte	Page number
0463h	word	Current adapter base port
0465h	byte	Mode selection
0466h	byte	Palette
0484h	byte	Rows (EGA/MCGA/VGA only)
0485h	byte	Points (EGA/MCGA/VGA only)

Table 13.6. *Meaning of bits at memory location 0410h.*

Bits 76543210	Meaning of bits
00	1 disk drive installed, if bit 0 = 1
01	2 disk drives installed, if bit 0 = 1
10	3 disk drives installed, if bit 0 = 1
11	4 disk drives installed, if bit 0 = 1
01	Initial video mode is color, 40 by 25
10	Initial video mode is color, 80 by 25
11	Initial video mode is monochrome, 80 by 25
00	64K system board RAM installed
01	128K system board RAM installed
10	192K system board RAM installed
11	256K system board RAM installed
x	Position not used
0	No disk drives installed
1	Disk drives installed, see bits 7-6

EGA, MCGA, or VGA in monochrome mode, uses a video buffer starting at B0000h; a color adapter, such as the CGA, or EGA, MCGA, or VGA in a text color mode, uses a video buffer starting at B8000h.

The other memory location of interest is 0463h, which provides the adapter's base port address. This can be either of two values as shown in table 13.7.

Table 13.7. *Adapter base port values stored at 0463h.*

Adapter	Base port
MDA	03B4h
CGA	03D4h
HGA	03B4h
EGA	03D4h
MCGA	03D4h
VGA	03D4h

Notice that the same values are stored at 0463h for the MDA/HGA and the CGA/EGA/MCGA/VGA. This information tells you which class of adapter is being used. Color-capable adapters have a base port address of 03D4h, whereas monochrome adapters have a base port address of 03B4h. Coupled with the data obtained from memory location 0410h (whether the computer is in monochrome or color mode), you easily and safely can assume which type of monitor the computer is using. It might appear that you need only one of these items to tell the monitor type; however, what if you are using a monochrome monitor connected to a VGA? For some peripherals, you need to know the type of card in addition to the type of monitor.

Now, let's use this information in a subroutine to determine the segment address that should be used for display of textual information. This routine is a "building block" that will be called by other (still to be developed) assembly language subroutines. Like all other programs in this chapter, this routine uses the new "simplified segment directives" introduced by MASM version 5 instead of the older techniques described in previous chapters:

```
;   ******************************************************************
;   *                                                                *
;   *  Date:     11/15/89                                            *
;   *  Program:  FINDCARD.ASM                                        *
;   *                                                                *
;   *  Purpose:  Determine type of video card and save info.         *
;   *            To be called from other assembly language routines. *
;   *                                                                *
;   *  Note:     All programs in this chapter use the simplified     *
;   *            segment directives introduced in MASM 5.1.          *
;   *                                                                *
;   ******************************************************************
```

```
; PUBLIC ROUTINE
          PUBLIC  FIND_CARD

; PUBLIC DATA
          PUBLIC MONITOR_ADDR
          PUBLIC STATUS_PORT

; EQUATES

MONO        EQU     0B000h          ;Mono video buffer start
COLOR       EQU     0B800h          ;Color video buffer start

.MODEL MEDIUM,BASIC
.DATA

MONITOR_ADDR DW     0000            ;Offset of video buffer
STATUS_PORT  DW     0000            ;Address of card status port
; -----------------------------------------------------------------


.CODE
FIND_CARD   PROC    FAR
            PUSH    BX              ;Store all the registers
            PUSH    DX              ;      used in this
            PUSH    ES              ;      routine

            MOV     BX,0040h        ;Look at base port value
            MOV     ES,BX           ;      03B4h = monochrome
            MOV     DX,ES:63h       ;      03D4h = color
            ADD     DX,6            ;Point to card's status port
            MOV     STATUS_PORT,DX  ;Save the status port

            MOV     MONITOR_ADDR,COLOR  ;Default to color card
            MOV     BX,ES:10h       ;Get equipment list
            AND     BX,30h          ;Only want bits 5-4
            CMP     BX,30h          ;Is it monochrome (bits=11)?
            JNE     FC1             ;No, so keep as color
            MOV     MONITOR_ADDR,MONO  ;Yes, set for monochrome

FC1:        POP     ES              ;Restore the registers
            POP     DX
            POP     BX
```

```
                    RET                            ;Return to caller
FIND_CARD    ENDP
; ------------------------------------------------------------------------

                    END
```

At the conclusion of this routine, the address of the display adapter's status port is saved in STATUS_PORT, and the segment offset for the video buffer is stored in MONITOR_ADDR. These variables are declared PUBLIC so that they can be used by the routine that actually moves a character of data to the video buffer. (You soon will find out why determining the adapter's status port location is important.)

Displaying a Character in Video Memory

The next task is to develop a routine to move a character directly into video memory. You may remember that the IBM family of computers uses a memory-mapped video display. Consequently, changing the video memory results in a display change.

You can move data directly into the video buffer area, but doing so may result in an undesirable side effect of "snow," or glitches, on the display screen. This effect, particularly objectionable on the original IBM CGA design in text color mode and in all truly faithful clones of that adapter, is caused by accessing the video memory at a time that conflicts with other demands placed on it.

All of the IBM display adapters are based on the Motorola 6845 CRT Controller chip. The chip used in the EGA is different, but is based on the 6845. This chip controls the video RAM buffer area. When conventional memory chips make up the video buffer, they can be accessed by only one other device at a time. If you try to read from or write to them at the same time that the 6845 is trying to read them for display, you will momentarily block the 6845 from accessing the RAM. That interference is visible on the CRT as multicolored snow.

The effect was well known by the time the EGA was designed, so the EGA's controller prevents snow from occurring. The MCGA and VGA are also snow-free. Even a few CGA designs avoided the problem by including more expensive dual-ported memory chips. But most CGA designs faithfully mimic the original version, including its susceptibility to interference and snow.

To compensate for this potential conflict, a routine must verify that a character is deposited only when the 6845 is not reading video memory. This "safe" time occurs during what is referred to as a horizontal retrace condition (HRC). While this condition is in effect, depositing a character in a video memory location will not result in interference.

The adapter card's status port contains information about the current state of the 6845. One factor that can be determined by reading this port is whether the adapter is currently in a horizontal retrace condition. If bit 0 is set to 0, the 6845 has video enabled and is accessing memory. If bit 0 is set to 1, a horizontal retrace condition exists and video memory is not being accessed.

The time available is extremely short; you can only move a single 16-bit word—one character and its accompanying attribute—into the buffer during a single HRC time.

To display a single character without causing a conflict, you must write a low-level routine such as PCHAR. Remember that the following is a low-level routine, designed to be called from other assembly language routines:

```
;       ****************************************************************
;       *                                                            *
;       *  Date:         11/15/89                                    *
;       *  Program:      PCHAR.ASM                                   *
;       *                                                            *
;       *  Purpose:      To print a character on the video screen.   *
;       *                                                            *
;       *  Note:         All programs in this chapter use the simplified *
;       *                segment directives introduced in MASM 5.1.  *
;       *                                                            *
;       *  Enter with: AL = ASCII value of character to print        *
;       *              DI = video buffer offset at which to place AL  *
;       *                                                            *
;       ****************************************************************

;  PUBLIC ROUTINES
            PUBLIC  PCHAR

;  EXTERNAL DATA:
            EXTRN   MONITOR_ADDR:WORD
            EXTRN   STATUS_PORT:WORD

.MODEL MEDIUM,BASIC
.CODE
```

```
;   ------------------------------------------------------------------
PCHAR       PROC    FAR
            PUSH    DX
            PUSH    ES

            MOV     ES,MONITOR_ADDR
            MOV     DX,STATUS_PORT

            CLI                          ;Don't allow interrupts
            PUSH    AX                   ;Store the character
RETRACE:    IN      AL,DX                ;Get card status
            TEST    AL,1                 ;Are we in a retrace state?
            JNZ     RETRACE              ;Yes, so check again
                                         ;On fall-through, just
                                         ;   exited retrace state

NO_RETRACE: IN      AL,DX                ;Get card status
            TEST    AL,1                 ;Are we in a retrace state?
            JZ      NO_RETRACE           ;No, so check again
                                         ;On fall-through, just
                                         ;   entered retrace state

            POP     AX                   ;Yes, get character back
            MOV     ES:[DI],AL           ;OK to write it now
            STI                          ;OK to have interrupts now

            INC     DI                   ;Point to attribute
            INC     DI                   ;Next screen location

            POP     ES
            POP     DX
            RET
PCHAR       ENDP


;   ------------------------------------------------------------------

            END
```

Notice that the 6845 status port is read in two separate loops. The first, RETRACE, tests bit 0 to determine whether an HRC currently exists. If bit 0 is equal to 1, the zero flag will be clear, and the JNZ is executed to check again for an HRC. The loop is exited only when the HRC does not exist. This may sound backwards, because I pointed out earlier that accessing video memory during the retrace is safe. It *is* safe, but the instructions to pop the character from the stack and deposit it in video memory take time—the HRC could be over by the time the character is deposited.

When this routine is entered, you have no idea how long the HRC has been in effect or when it will end. Thus, the first loop waits until any existing HRC is completed. The second loop waits for an HRC and then accesses the memory at the start of the HRC. The result is the least possible snow.

Hardware interrupts are disabled (CLI) at entry to this routine and then enabled again (STI) just after storing the byte in video RAM. This is necessary; without these instructions, a lengthy hardware interrupt might occur just as the routine decided it was safe to access the video buffer, and the HRC would be over long before the interrupt returned control to PCHAR. Once the character has been stored, interrupts can be tolerated. Any time you find it necessary to disable hardware interrupts to meet strict time requirements, be sure to enable the interrupts as soon as you can safely do so.

After verifying that an HRC has begun, PCHAR places a character at the video buffer offset position determined by DI. The following section shows how to determine the value of DI from simple X-Y coordinates.

PCHAR returns with all registers (except DI) intact. DI is incremented to point at the next character position in the video buffer. After completion of this routine, you can develop a routine (callable from a high-level language) to display a string of ASCII characters instantly at any position on the display screen.

Displaying an ASCII String

You now know what type of display adapter is installed, you have saved the segment address of the video buffer, and you know how to display a single character. All that remains is to determine the correct offset address so that you know where to begin displaying information.

From the details presented earlier in this chapter, you can easily derive a formula for determining the offset for displaying a character at any given location on the screen. This formula can be expressed as

$$[(ROW\text{-}1) * 80 + (COLUMN\text{-}1)] * 2$$

In this equation, ROW is assumed to be in the range of 1 through 25, and COLUMN is assumed to be in the range of 1 through 80. (If you change the number of rows when using an EGA, MCGA, or VGA, these formulas must change accordingly!) The offset for the attribute of any given character can be located by the formula

$$[(ROW\text{-}1) * 80 + (COLUMN\text{-}1)] * 2 + 1$$

Notice that the character addresses are always even, whereas the attribute addresses are always odd.

All you need to calculate the memory offset are the X (COLUMN) and Y (ROW) coordinates. Using this equation and the routines developed in the two preceding sections, you can write a routine that displays a string at any given position on the text screen. The following routine, which is called from QuickBASIC, will perform this task:

```
;       ***********************************************************
;       *                                                         *
;       *  Date:       11/15/89                                   *
;       *  Program:    PSTRNG.ASM                                 *
;       *                                                         *
;       *  Purpose:    To display a string directly to video memory *
;       *              from QuickBASIC.                           *
;       *                                                         *
;       *  Note:       All programs in this chapter use the simplified *
;       *              segment directives introduced in MASM 5.1. *
;       *                                                         *
;       *  Formats:    CALL PSTRNG(A$,X%,Y%)                      *
;       *                                                         *
;       *  Variables: A$:  The BASIC string to be displayed.      *
;       *             X%:  The integer column value.              *
;       *             Y%:  The integer row value.                 *
;       *                                                         *
;       ***********************************************************

; PUBLIC ROUTINES
        PUBLIC  PSTRNG

; EXTERNAL ROUTINES
        EXTRN   FIND_CARD:FAR
        EXTRN   PCHAR:FAR

; EQUATES

PARMC   EQU     10
PARMB   EQU     08
PARMA   EQU     06

.MODEL MEDIUM,BASIC

.CODE
; ---------------------------------------------------------------
```

```
PSTRNG  PROC    FAR
        PUSH    BP
        MOV     BP,SP               ;Point to stack
        PUSH    ES

        CALL    FIND_CARD           ;Locate the video buffer
        MOV     BX,[BP+PARMC]       ;Get BASIC's string pointer
        MOV     CX,[BX]             ;Get the string's length
        JCXZ    EXIT                ;No length, so don't print
        MOV     SI,[BX+2]           ;SI points to string

        MOV     BX,[BP+PARMB]       ;Get address for row
        MOV     AX,[BX]             ;Get row value
        DEC     AX                  ;Put as a zero offset
        MOV     BX,[BP+PARMA]       ;Get address for column
        MOV     DI,[BX]             ;Get column value
        DEC     DI                  ;Put as zero offset
        MOV     BX,80               ;80 characters/row
        MUL     BX                  ;Now have rows in AX
        ADD     DI,AX               ;Add to column number
        SHL     DI,1                ;Multiply by 2, DI=offset

PSLOOP: MOV     AL,[SI]             ;Get the string character
        INC     SI                  ;Point to the next character
        CALL    PCHAR               ;No, so print the character
        LOOP    PSLOOP              ;Redo for length of string

EXIT:   POP     ES
        POP     BP
        RET     3*2                 ;Return to BASIC
PSTRNG  ENDP

; -------------------------------------------------------------------
        END
```

When you pass parameters from QuickBASIC to this routine, it is important to remember that the X-Y coordinates must be integer values. Unpredictable results may occur if integers are not used.

Using the Attribute Byte

You may recall that each displayed character in the video buffer requires two bytes of information—the ASCII value of the character and the character's display attribute.

This attribute byte controls how the character is displayed. Each bit of the attribute byte has a different function and, regardless of the type of display adapter you are using, the purpose of each bit is the same. However, the *effect* produced by different settings varies according to the type of adapter.

Usually, bits 0-3 and 7 control the foreground, whereas bits 4-6 control the background. The foreground is the character itself. The background is the area of the character cell surrounding the character. Although these bits are used the same way on both color and monochrome adapters, their effect on the adapters differs. Table 13.8 lists the meanings and possible settings of the bits in each character's attribute byte on a monochrome monitor. Table 13.9 shows the same information for attribute bytes on a color monitor.

Table 13.8. *Meaning of the bits in a monochrome attribute byte.*

Bits 76543210	*Meaning of bit setting*
0	Nonblinking character
1	Blinking character
000	Black background (normal)
111	White foreground (inverse)
0	Normal intensity
1	High intensity
001	Underlined white foreground
111	White foreground (normal)
000	Black foreground (inverse)

Table 13.9. *Meaning of the bits in a color attribute byte.*

Bits 76543210	*Meaning of bit setting*
0	Normal foreground
1	Blinking foreground
bbb	Background (see table 13.10)
ffff	Foreground (see table 13.10)

You can see from table 13.10 that, with the color attribute, only the first eight colors (0-7) can be used for background values, whereas all 16 colors can be used for foreground. When you use both the monochrome and color attributes, certain combinations of foreground and background will result in invisible characters. (Invisible characters, although useless to humans, are valid to the computer.) You can test for different color combinations that you may find pleasing for different applications.

You can have bright backgrounds, as well as bright foregrounds, if you are willing to give up the capability of making the foreground color blink. However, the method used to change bit 7 from foreground blink control to background intensity control varies with the different types of video cards.

If you are using an MDA, a Hercules adapter, or a CGA, just flip the value of one bit in the CRT controller's mode control register. The values contained in this register are stored in the BIOS RAM byte at 0465h (see table 13.5), and the following code can be called from most any language to flip the control bit from BLINK to BRIGHT and then called again to flip back to BLINK:

```
.MODEL MEDIUM
.CODE

FLIP    PROC    FAR
        PUSH    ES              ; save segment register
        MOV     AX,0040h
        MOV     ES,AX           ; point it to BIOS RAM
        MOV     DX,ES:[0063h]   ; CRTC base port address
        ADD     DX,4            ; offset to control port
        MOV     AL,ES:[0065h]   ; image of current content
        XOR     AL,20h          ; flip blink-enable bit
        MOV     ES:[0065h],AL   ; put it back
        OUT     DX,AL           ; and send to CRTC too
        POP     ES
        RET                     ; to caller
FLIP    ENDP
        END
```

If you are using an EGA, MCGA, or VGA, you must go through the video BIOS routines to switch this bit; refer to Chapter 15 for details and a code example.

Table 13.10 lists the colors built into the CGA; if you use an EGA, MCGA, or VGA, you can modify the exact colors that correspond to each bit setting. With an EGA, you can select any 16 of 64 different shades;

these are composed from the three primary colors (red, blue, and green) and four levels of each color (none, 1/3, 2/3, and 3/3 brightness). Thus, black is obtained by having all three colors off, and bright white by having all three at 3/3 brightness. The MCGA/VGA cards are similar.

Table 13.10. Background and foreground colors for color attribute byte.

Bit setting	Decimal value	Color
0000	0	Black
0001	1	Blue
0010	2	Green
0011	3	Cyan
0100	4	Red
0101	5	Magenta
0110	6	Brown
0111	7	White
1000	8	Gray
1001	9	Light blue
1010	10	Light green
1011	11	Light cyan
1100	12	Light red
1101	13	Light magenta
1110	14	Yellow
1111	15	White (high intensity)

How can you apply this to enhance the routines developed in this chapter? You do not need to change the FIND_CARD routine, which simply locates the type of card and sets two variables for use in the other routines. But PCHAR and PSTRNG can be changed so that they use a specified attribute value.

PCHAR is written to display a character on either a monochrome or color monitor. If the original routine were modified so that it could make an intelligent decision about converting attribute values, the high-level program could be written to take advantage of a color monitor, but PCHAR would translate the character attribute to a display format appropriate for a monochrome display. This new implementation, PCHARA (for Attribute), is as follows:

```
;    ****************************************************************
;    *                                                              *
;    *  Date:        11/15/89                                       *
;    *  Program:     PCHARA.ASM                                     *
;    *                                                              *
;    *  Purpose:     To print a character on the video screen.      *
;    *                                                              *
;    *  Note:        All programs in this chapter use the simplified *
;    *               segment directives introduced in MASM 5.1.     *
;    *                                                              *
;    *  Enter with: AL = ASCII value of character to print          *
;    *               DI = video buffer offset at which to place AL  *
;    *               ATTRIBUTE is initialized by calling program    *
;    *                                                              *
;    *               Sets the video attribute according to the color *
;    *               table values if using a monochrome display.    *
;    *                                                              *
;    ****************************************************************

;  PUBLIC ROUTINES
          PUBLIC  PCHARA

;  PUBLIC DATA
          PUBLIC  ATTRIBUTE

;  EXTERNAL DATA
          EXTRN   MONITOR_ADDR:WORD
          EXTRN   STATUS_PORT:WORD

;  EQUATES

MONO          EQU     0B000h                  ;Mono video buffer start
COLOR         EQU     0B800h                  ;Color video buffer start

.MODEL MEDIUM,BASIC
.DATA

ATTRIBUTE    DB      00
ATTR_TEST    DB      00
COLOR_TABLE  EQU     THIS BYTE
BWT_BLK      DB      0Fh,0Fh                   ;Black background
BLU_BLK      DB      01h,01h
YEL_BLU      DB      1Eh,70h
```

```
BLU_WHT     DB      71h,70h
GRN_WHT     DB      72h,70h
CYN_WHT     DB      73h,70h
RED_WHT     DB      74h,70h
MAG_WHT     DB      75h,70h
BRN_WHT     DB      76h,70h
GRY_WHT     DB      78h,70h
LBL_WHT     DB      79h,70h
LGR_WHT     DB      7Ah,70h
LCY_WHT     DB      7Bh,70h
LRD_WHT     DB      7Ch,70h
LMG_WHT     DB      7Dh,70h
YEL_WHT     DB      7Eh,70h
BWT_WHT     DB      7Fh,70h
TABLE_END   DB      00h,07h                 ;End of table


            .CODE
; -------------------------------------------------------------------
PCHARA      PROC    FAR
            PUSH    BX
            PUSH    DX
            PUSH    SI
            PUSH    ES


            MOV     ES,MONITOR_ADDR
            MOV     DX,STATUS_PORT


; HANDLE TRANSLATION FOR MONOCHROME MONITORS


            MOV     AH,ATTRIBUTE            ;Get video attribute
            CMP     MONITOR_ADDR,COLOR     ;Is it a color monitor?
            JE      POK                    ;Yes, assume correct
            CMP     AH,ATTR_TEST           ;Is it the same as before?
            JE      POK                    ;Yes, so keep going
            MOV     SI,OFFSET COLOR_TABLE
COLOR_LOOP: MOV     BH,[SI]                ;Get the first color
            INC     SI                     ;Point to mono equivalent
            CMP     BH,0                   ;End of table?
            JE      SET_COLOR              ;Yes, so use default
            CMP     AH,BH                  ;Should we translate?
            JE      SET_COLOR              ;Yes, so set new color
            INC     SI                     ;Skip the mono equivalent
            JMP     COLOR_LOOP
```

```
SET_COLOR:   MOV     AH,[SI]              ;Get mono equivalent
             MOV     ATTR_TEST,AH         ;Reset the test byte

POK:         CLI                          ;Don't allow interrupts
             PUSH    AX                   ;Store the character
RETRACE:     IN      AL,DX                ;Get card status
             TEST    AL,1                 ;Are we in a retrace state?
             JNZ     RETRACE              ;Yes, so check again
                                          ;On fall-through, just
                                          ;   exited retrace state

NO_RETRACE:  IN      AL,DX                ;Get card status
             TEST    AL,1                 ;Are we in a retrace state?
             JZ      NO_RETRACE           ;No, so check again
                                          ;On fall-through, just
                                          ;   entered retrace state

             POP     AX                   ;Yes, get character back
             MOV     ES:[DI],AX           ;OK to write it now
             STI                          ;OK to have interrupts now

             INC     DI                   ;Point to attribute
             INC     DI                   ;Next screen location

             POP     ES
             POP     SI
             POP     DX
             POP     BX
             RET
PCHARA       ENDP


;  -------------------------------------------------------------------


             END
```

This new version of the routine is only slightly different from the earlier PCHAR. The modified routine has the additional data areas needed for the attribute and the attribute translation.

The translation table begins at the label COLOR_TABLE. Each color attribute to be translated is listed, followed by the monochrome equivalent of the attribute. For instance, the color attribute for a yellow foreground on a blue background (YEL_BLU) translates to an inverse (black on white) attribute in monochrome.

A 0 in the color attribute position signifies the end of the table. Any translation that has not been caught specifically in the table is translated to normal monochrome white on black.

This translation process is handled in PCHARA by the coding beginning at the line

```
; HANDLE TRANSLATION FOR MONOCHROME MONITORS
```

First, PCHARA checks whether a monochrome monitor is in use. If not, no translation is needed, and processing continues. If a monochrome monitor is in use, the old attribute (ATTR_TEST) is checked against the new one. If the two attributes are the same, no translation is needed, and processing continues.

If a translation is indicated, PCHARA loads the offset of COLOR_TABLE into SI. Next, the attribute byte at that location (SI) is loaded, and SI is incremented to point at the monochrome equivalent of the color attribute. Then PCHARA checks for the end-of-table flag. If the end has been reached, the routine is exited, the default attribute (white on black) is loaded, and the character is displayed. If a valid translation is needed, the new attribute is loaded from the table, and the character is displayed.

Notice that in this version of PCHARA an entire word (both the ASCII value and its attribute) is moved into the video buffer; in the earlier version of the routine, only the ASCII character was moved to memory.

The overhead associated with the changes to this routine is a small price to pay for the added value received. Now you can control not only *which* character is displayed but also *how* a character is displayed.

Notice that ATTRIBUTE is assumed to have been set before entry into PCHARA. ATTRIBUTE is a video attribute that can be set in PSTRNG with a value passed from a high-level language. You can set ATTRIBUTE using the following new version, PSTRNGA, which is written for compiled BASIC:

```
;    ******************************************************************
;    *                                                                *
;    *   Date:      11/15/89                                          *
;    *   Program:   PSTRNGA.ASM                                       *
;    *                                                                *
;    *   Purpose:   To display a string directly to video memory from *
;    *              compiled BASIC.                                   *
;    *                                                                *
;    *   Note:      All programs in this chapter use the simplified   *
;    *              segment directives introduced in MASM 5.1.        *
;    *                                                                *
```

```
;   *   Formats:    CALL PSTRNGA(A$,X%,Y%,Z%)                      *
;   *                                                             *
;   *   Variables: A$:  The BASIC string to be displayed.         *
;   *              X%:  The integer column value.                 *
;   *              Y%:  The integer row value.                    *
;   *              Z%:  The integer video attribute.              *
;   *                                                             *
;   ****************************************************************

; PUBLIC ROUTINES
            PUBLIC  PSTRNGA

; EXTERNAL ROUTINES
            EXTRN   FIND_CARD:FAR
            EXTRN   PCHARA:FAR

; EXTERNAL DATA
            EXTRN   ATTRIBUTE:BYTE

; EQUATES

PARMD       EQU     12
PARMC       EQU     10
PARMB       EQU     08
PARMA       EQU     06

.MODEL MEDIUM,BASIC

.CODE
; --------------------------------------------------------------------
PSTRNGA     PROC    FAR                 ;Always FAR PROC from BASIC
            PUSH    BP
            MOV     BP,SP               ;Point to stack
            PUSH    ES

            CALL    FIND_CARD           ;Locate the video buffer
            MOV     BX,[BP+PARMA]       ;Address of attribute value
            MOV     AX,[BX]             ;Get attribute value
            MOV     ATTRIBUTE,AL        ;Only working with a byte

            MOV     BX,[BP+PARMD]       ;Get BASIC's string pointer
            MOV     CX,[BX]             ;Get the string's length
            JCXZ    EXIT                ;No length, so don't print
            MOV     SI,[BX+2]           ;SI points to string
```

```
              MOV      BX,[BP+PARMC]      ;Get address for row
              MOV      AX,[BX]            ;Get row value
              DEC      AX                 ;Put as a zero offset
              MOV      BX,[BP+PARMB]      ;Get address for column
              MOV      DI,[BX]            ;Get column value
              DEC      DI                 ;Put as zero offset
              MOV      BX,80              ;80 characters/row
              MUL      BX                 ;Now have rows in AX
              ADD      DI,AX              ;Add to column number
              SHL      DI,1               ;Multiply by 2, DI=offset

PSLOOP:       MOV      AL,[SI]            ;Get the string character
              INC      SI                 ;Point to the next character
              CALL     PCHARA             ;Print the character
              LOOP     PSLOOP             ;Redo for length of string

EXIT:         POP      ES
              POP      BP
              RET      4*2                ;Return to BASIC
PSTRNGA       ENDP

; ------------------------------------------------------------------

              END
```

There is only one difference between this and the earlier version of PSTRNG. With this version you can pass an additional variable by BASIC to specify the attribute of the string being printed. This attribute is placed in the variable ATTRIBUTE for subsequent use by PCHARA.

Notice that even though a word (16-bit integer) is passed from BASIC, only the lower byte of the word is used for the attribute. As you will recall from the memory-mapped display of the IBM computer family, only one byte is used to specify a character's attribute.

Creating Text-Based Graphics Routines

Now that you know how information is stored on the screen and how the appearance of the information is controlled, you can use these building blocks to create routines for handling text-based graphics. Such routines are helpful when you create attractive menus or data-input screens. Using assembly language, you can paint appealing screens and display them instantaneously to enhance the image of your program. In addition, you can create the screens and menus with one call from your high-level language.

In the ASCII character set of the IBM family of microcomputers, several characters are well suited for ASCII graphics. These characters were specifically designed for creating screen forms and display outlines. Figure 13.2 shows the different groups of ASCII graphics characters.

Fig. 13.2. *ASCII graphics characters.*

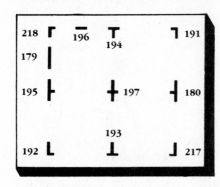

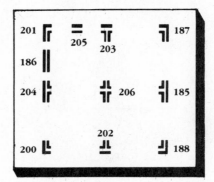

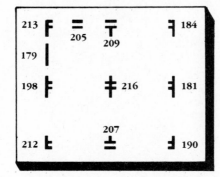

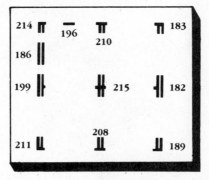

Let's create a routine that uses some of these ASCII graphics characters to display a double-lined box anywhere on the screen. All you have to do is pass the coordinates for the upper left and lower right corners of the box, along with the display attribute to use when creating the box. This routine, named BOX, is coded as follows when called from compiled BASIC:

```
;   ******************************************************************
;   *                                                                *
;   *   Date:      11/16/89                                          *
;   *   Program:   BOX.ASM                                           *
;   *                                                                *
;   *   Purpose:   To display a string directly to video memory      *
;   *              from compiled QuickBASIC 4.5.                      *
;   *                                                                *
;   *   Note:      All programs in this chapter use the simplified    *
;   *              segment directives introduced in MASM 5.1.         *
;   *                                                                *
;   *   Formats:   CALL BOX(TLC%,BRC%,Z%)                             *
;   *                                                                *
;   *   Variables: TLC%:  The top left screen coordinate.             *
;   *              BRC%:  The bottom right screen coordinate.         *
;   *              Z%:    The integer video attribute.                *
;   *                                                                *
;   ******************************************************************


; PUBLIC ROUTINES
            PUBLIC  BOX

; EXTERNAL ROUTINES
            EXTRN   FIND_CARD:FAR
            EXTRN   SET_DI:FAR
            EXTRN   PCHARA:FAR

; EXTERNAL DATA
            EXTRN   ATTRIBUTE:BYTE



; EQUATES

PARMC       EQU     10
PARMB       EQU     08
PARMA       EQU     06
```

```
.MODEL MEDIUM,BASIC
.DATA

BOX_CHAR     DB      ⌐ ⌐ ╠

BOX_ULC      EQU     THIS WORD
UL_COL       DB      00
UL_ROW       DB      00
BOX_LRC      EQU     THIS WORD
LR_COL       DB      00
LR_ROW       DB      00

; -----------------------------------------------------------------
.CODE
BOX          PROC    FAR
             PUSH    BP
             MOV     BP,SP               ;Get addressability

             MOV     BX,[BP+PARMA]       ;Get address of attribute
             MOV     AX,[BX]             ;Get value of attribute
             MOV     ATTRIBUTE,AL        ;Store the attribute
             MOV     BX,[BP+PARMB]       ;Get address of BRC
             MOV     AX,[BX]             ;Get value of BRC
             MOV     BOX_LRC,AX          ;Store the value
             MOV     BX,[BP+PARMC]       ;Get address of TLC
             MOV     AX,[BX]             ;Get value of TLC
             MOV     BOX_ULC,AX          ;Store the value

             CALL    FIND_CARD           ;Locate the monitor info

; PRINT SIDES OF BOX, TOP TO BOTTOM

             MOV     BH,UL_ROW           ;Get upper left (row only)
             INC     BH                  ;Start next row down
             MOV     AL,BOX_CHAR+4       ;Character for side of box
             MOV     CH,UL_ROW           ;Top row
             MOV     CL,LR_ROW           ;Bottom row
             SUB     CL,CH               ;Height is left in CL
             SUB     CH,CH               ;Zero out CH
             DEC     CX                  ;Adjust for actual height
V1:          MOV     BL,UL_COL           ;Set left column
             CALL    SET_DI              ;Position offset
             CALL    PCHARA
```

```
                MOV     BL,LR_COL               ;Set right column
                CALL    SET_DI                  ;Position offset
                CALL    PCHARA
                INC     BH                      ;Next row
                LOOP    V1

; PRINT TOP OF BOX

                MOV     BX,BOX_ULC              ;Get upper left column
                INC     BX                      ;Next space right
                CALL    SET_DI                  ;Position offset
                MOV     AL,BOX_CHAR+5           ;Top/bottom character
                MOV     CL,LR_COL               ;Left column
                MOV     CH,UL_COL               ;Right column
                SUB     CL,CH
                SUB     CH,CH                   ;Zero out
                DEC     CX                      ;Width of box is in CX
                PUSH    CX                      ;Store width for later
TB1:            CALL    PCHARA
                LOOP    TB1                     ;Do it again

; PRINT BOTTOM OF BOX

                MOV     BH,LR_ROW
                MOV     BL,UL_COL               ;Now have bottom left corner
                INC     BX                      ;Next space right
                CALL    SET_DI                  ;Position offset
                POP     CX                      ;Get width back
                MOV     AL,BOX_CHAR+5           ;Top/bottom character
TB2:            CALL    PCHARA
                LOOP    TB2                     ;Do it again

; PRINT CORNERS

                MOV     BX,BOX_ULC              ;Upper left
                CALL    SET_DI                  ;Position offset
                MOV     AL,BOX_CHAR+2           ;Upper left character
                CALL    PCHARA

                MOV     BX,BOX_LRC              ;Upper right
                CALL    SET_DI                  ;Position offset
                MOV     AL,BOX_CHAR+3           ;Lower right character
                CALL    PCHARA
```

```
            MOV     BH,UL_ROW
            MOV     BL,LR_COL               ;Upper right
            CALL    SET_DI                  ;Position offset
            MOV     AL,BOX_CHAR             ;Upper right character
            CALL    PCHARA


            MOV     BH,LR_ROW
            MOV     BL,UL_COL               ;Lower left
            CALL    SET_DI                  ;Position offset
            MOV     AL,BOX_CHAR+1          ;Lower left character
            CALL    PCHARA


            POP     BP
            RET     2*3                     ;Return to BASIC
BOX         ENDP


;   --------------------------------------------------------------


            END
```

This routine displays a double-lined box at the specified location on the video screen without erasing the area within the box. Using the following equation, the controlling program—in QuickBASIC—passes the coordinates through an integer variable that contains the row/column coordinates:

COORD% = ROW * 256 + COLUMN

The controlling program's use of this equation results in less need for number manipulation during the execution of this routine. Using this equation, the coordinates are passed in a format that places the row in the upper byte of the integer parameter, and the column in the lower byte.

This routine is designed so that you can easily change the type of border used for the box. To draw a different type of box, you simply change the contents of BOX_CHAR to the six appropriate drawing bytes.

The FIND_CARD and PCHARA subroutines are both used in this routine, as well as another subroutine, SET_DI. The SET_DI subroutine converts a row/column coordinate, which is held in BX, into an offset into the video buffer. The code for SET_DI follows:

```
;     ******************************************************************
;     *                                                                *
;     * Date:      11/15/89                                            *
;     * Program:   SETDI.ASM                                           *
;     *                                                                *
;     * Purpose:   To set DI from BX. On entry, BX contains the        *
;     *            desired screen row/column. On exit, DI contains     *
;     *            the screen memory offset. All other registers       *
;     *            are unchanged.                                      *
;     *                                                                *
;     * Note:      All programs in this chapter use the simplified     *
;     *            segment directives introduced in MASM 5.1.          *
;     *                                                                *
;     ******************************************************************

; PUBLIC ROUTINES:
                PUBLIC  SET_DI

.MODEL MEDIUM,BASIC
.CODE


; -----------------------------------------------------------------------
SET_DI          PROC    FAR

                PUSH    DX
                PUSH    BX                      ;Save row/column
                PUSH    AX

                MOV     AH,0                    ;Don't need AH now
                MOV     AL,BH                   ;Move the row
                MOV     BH,0                    ;And zero it out
                MOV     DI,BX                   ;Move the column
                MOV     BX,80                   ;columns per row
                MUL     BX                      ;AX = row * 80
                ADD     DI,AX                   ;Add to column
                SHL     DI,1                    ;Multiply by 2

                POP     AX                      ;Restore all registers
                POP     BX
                POP     DX
```

```
                      RET
SET_DI                ENDP


;  --------------------------------------------------------------


                      END
```

By studying BOX, you can see how easily you can place graphics on the video screen. Using ASCII characters, you can change the routine to create any type of screen graphics you want. The speed with which assembly language paints entire screens may surprise you.

Using Window Techniques: Saving and Restoring Windows

Now that you know how to create boxes, you can take the next logical step—creating routines that can generate pop-up windows from compiled BASIC.

To create pop-up windows, you need to follow these steps:

❑ Determine the rectangular coordinates of the area to contain the window.

❑ Save the current screen contents within that area.

❑ Clear the defined area.

❑ Draw a box around the area.

Perhaps the most important step is that of saving the video information under the pop-up window. A complete routine must not only save this information but also be able to restore previous video information. Recreating the entire screen after the user is finished with the window is unacceptable—and, in many cases, impossible.

The routines described in this section will perform all of these tasks. With these routines you can use a "window stack" to save and create multiple windows. Using this stack concept, you can remove the windows from the screen in reverse order.

The following listing includes two callable routines. SAVSCRN, which is similar to the process used in BOX, requires the passing of the upper left corner and lower right corner of the window area; GETSCRN removes the previously created window. The listing is as follows:

```
;       *****************************************************************
;       *                                                               *
;       *  Date:      11/16/89                                          *
;       *  Program:   SCRN.ASM                                         *
;       *                                                               *
;       *  Purpose:   To save and restore a portion of the screen to a  *
;       *             buffer from QuickBASIC 4.5.                        *
;       *                                                               *
;       *  Note:      All programs in this chapter use the simplified    *
;       *             segment directives introduced in MASM 5.1.         *
;       *                                                               *
;       *  Format:    CALL SAVSCRN(TLC%,BRC%)                           *
;       *             CALL GETSCRN                                       *
;       *                                                               *
;       *****************************************************************

; PUBLIC ROUTINES
                PUBLIC  SAVSCRN
                PUBLIC  GETSCRN

; EXTERNAL ROUTINES
                EXTRN   SET_DI:FAR
                EXTRN   PCHARA:FAR

; EXTERNAL DATA
                EXTRN   MONITOR_ADDR:WORD
                EXTRN   STATUS_PORT:WORD

; EQUATES

PARMB           EQU     08
PARMA           EQU     06


.MODEL MEDIUM,BASIC
.DATA

TEMP            DW      0000
WND_WIDTH       DW      0000

BOX_CHAR        DB      ┐  └┘ ╠


BOX_ULC         EQU     THIS WORD
UL_COL          DB      00
```

```
UL_ROW          DB       00
BOX_LRC         EQU      THIS WORD
LR_COL          DB       00
LR_ROW          DB       00


SCREENS         DB       4 DUP(1024 DUP(0))   ;Screen stack space
END_SCREENS     DB       00                   ;End of screen stack space

.CODE
; ----------------------------------------------------------------------
SAVSCRN         PROC     FAR
                PUSH     BP
                MOV      BP,SP                 ;Get addressability
                PUSH     ES

                MOV      BX,[BP+PARMA]         ;Get address of BRC
                MOV      AX,[BX]               ;Get BRC value
                MOV      BOX_LRC,AX            ;Save it
                MOV      BX,[BP+PARMB]         ;Get address of TLC
                MOV      AX,[BX]               ;Get TLC value
                MOV      BOX_ULC,AX            ;Save it

                CALL     CALCSIZE              ;Calculate space for save
                CALL     FINDFREE              ;Find free space in screen
                                              ;   stack area
                JNC      SS_CONT               ;Continue
                JMP      SS_EXIT               ;Sorry, no space left

SS_CONT:        PUSH     SI                    ;Save area
                ADD      SI,6                  ;Set past pointer area
                MOV      AX,BOX_ULC            ;Move upper left corner
                MOV      TEMP,AX               ;   into work area
SS_LOOP:        MOV      BX,TEMP
                CALL     SET_DI                ;Set offset
                MOV      ES,MONITOR_ADDR
                MOV      CX,WND_WIDTH
SS_L2:          MOV      AX,ES:[DI]            ;Get character/attribute
                MOV      [SI],AX               ;Place into screen stack
                INC      DI                    ;Point to next display set
                INC      DI
                INC      SI                    ;Increment stack pointer
                INC      SI
                LOOP     SS_L2                 ;Do for entire line
```

```
        ADD     TEMP,0100h          ;Proceed to next line
        MOV     AX,TEMP
        MOV     BX,BOX_LRC
        CMP     AH,BH               ;Are we too far down?
        JLE     SS_LOOP             ;No, so continue

        MOV     BX,SI               ;Get end of screen in stack
        POP     SI                  ;Get start of area
        MOV     AX,BOX_ULC          ;Store upper left corner
        MOV     [SI],AX             ;   coordinates
        INC     SI                  ;Point to next coordinate
        INC     SI                  ;   location
        MOV     AX,BOX_LRC          ;Store lower right corner
        MOV     [SI],AX             ;   coordinates
        INC     SI                  ;Point to next coordinate
        INC     SI                  ;   location
        MOV     [SI],BX             ;Store pointer to start of
                                    ;   stack free space

; PRINT SIDES OF BOX, TOP TO BOTTOM

        MOV     BH,UL_ROW           ;Get upper left (row only)
        INC     BH                  ;Start next row down
        MOV     AL,BOX_CHAR+4       ;Character for side of box
        MOV     CH,UL_ROW           ;Top row
        MOV     CL,LR_ROW           ;Bottom row
        SUB     CL,CH               ;Height is left in CL
        SUB     CH,CH               ;Zero out CH
        DEC     CX                  ;Adjust for actual height
V1:     MOV     BL,UL_COL           ;Set left column
        CALL    SET_DI              ;Position offset
        CALL    PCHARA
        MOV     BL,LR_COL           ;Set right column
        CALL    SET_DI              ;Position offset
        CALL    PCHARA
        INC     BH                  ;Next row
        LOOP    V1

; PRINT TOP OF BOX

        MOV     BX,BOX_ULC          ;Get upper left column
        INC     BX                  ;Next space right
        CALL    SET_DI              ;Position offset
        MOV     AL,BOX_CHAR+5       ;Top/bottom character
```

```
                MOV     CL,LR_COL           ;Left column
                MOV     CH,UL_COL           ;Right column
                SUB     CL,CH
                SUB     CH,CH               ;Zero out
                DEC     CX                  ;Width of box is in CX
                PUSH    CX                  ;Store width for later
TB1:            CALL    PCHARA
                LOOP    TB1                 ;Do it again

; PRINT BOTTOM OF BOX

                MOV     BH,LR_ROW
                MOV     BL,UL_COL           ;Now have bottom left corner
                INC     BX                  ;Next space right
                CALL    SET_DI              ;Position offset
                POP     CX                  ;Get width back
                MOV     AL,BOX_CHAR+5       ;Top/bottom character
TB2:            CALL    PCHARA
                LOOP    TB2                 ;Do it again

; PRINT CORNERS

                MOV     BX,BOX_ULC          ;Upper left
                CALL    SET_DI              ;Position offset
                MOV     AL,BOX_CHAR+2       ;Upper left character
                CALL    PCHARA

                MOV     BX,BOX_LRC          ;Upper right
                CALL    SET_DI              ;Position offset
                MOV     AL,BOX_CHAR+3       ;Lower right character
                CALL    PCHARA

                MOV     BH,UL_ROW
                MOV     BL,LR_COL           ;Upper right
                CALL    SET_DI              ;Position offset
                MOV     AL,BOX_CHAR         ;Upper right character
                CALL    PCHARA
                MOV     BH,LR_ROW
                MOV     BL,UL_COL           ;Lower left
                CALL    SET_DI              ;Position offset
                MOV     AL,BOX_CHAR+1       ;Lower left character
                CALL    PCHARA
```

```
                    MOV     CX,BOX_ULC          ;Upper left corner
                    ADD     CX,0101h            ;Don't erase box
                    MOV     DX,BOX_LRC          ;Bottom right corner
                    SUB     DX,0101h            ;Don't erase box

                    MOV     BH,07h              ;Normal white/black
                    MOV     AH,6                ;Clear upwards
                    MOV     AL,0                ;Clear the window
                    INT     10h                 ;Call BIOS interrupt

                    CLC                         ;No errors

SS_EXIT:            POP     ES
                    POP     BP
                    RET     2*2                 ;Return to BASIC
SAVSCRN             ENDP
; -------------------------------------------------------------------
GETSCRN             PROC    FAR
                    PUSH    BP
                    MOV     BP,SP               ;Get addressability
                    PUSH    ES

                    CALL    FINDLAST            ;Find last saved screen
                    JC      GS_EXIT             ;Sorry, none there

                    PUSH    SI
                    MOV     AX,[SI]             ;Get upper left corner
                    MOV     BOX_ULC,AX          ;Store in this area
                    MOV     TEMP,AX             ;Store in work area
                    INC     SI                  ;Point to next coordinate
                    INC     SI                  ;  location

                    MOV     AX,[SI]             ;Get lower right corner
                    MOV     BOX_LRC,AX          ;  and store it
                    INC     SI                  ;Point to next coordinate
                    INC     SI                  ;  location

                    MOV     AX,[SI]             ;Get pointer to next area
                    PUSH    AX                  ;Save temporarily
                    INC     SI                  ;Point to next coordinate
                    INC     SI                  ;  location
```

```
                 CALL    CALCSIZE             ;This will set the width
GS_LOOP:         MOV     BX,TEMP
                 CALL    SET_DI               ;Position cursor there
                 MOV     CX,WND_WIDTH
GS_L2:           MOV     AX,[SI]              ;Get from stack area
                 CALL    MCHAR                ;Move the character
                 INC     SI                   ;Point to next character
                 INC     SI                   ;  group
                 LOOP    GS_L2                ;Repeat for entire line
                 ADD     TEMP,0100h           ;Point to next line
                 MOV     AX,TEMP
                 MOV     BX,BOX_LRC
                 CMP     AH,BH                ;Are we too far down?
                 JLE     GS_LOOP              ;No, so continue

                 POP     BX                   ;Get back next area pointer
                 POP     SI                   ;Get back start
                 SUB     BX,SI                ;Size of area
                 INC     BX
                 MOV     AX,0                 ;Zero out entire area
                 MOV     CX,BX
FL:              MOV     [SI],AL
                 INC     SI
                 LOOP    FL
                 CLC                          ;Set for no errors

GS_EXIT:         POP     ES
                 POP     BP
                 RET                          ;Return to BASIC
GETSCRN          ENDP


; ----------------------------------------------------------------------
; SUBROUTINES FOR SAVSCRN AND GETSCRN
; ----------------------------------------------------------------------


; ----------------------------------------------------------------------
; FINDFREE - FIND A BLOCK ON SCREEN STACK LARGE ENOUGH TO HOLD WINDOW
;            ENTER WITH CX SET TO SIZE NEEDED, IN BYTES
; ----------------------------------------------------------------------

FINDFREE         PROC    NEAR
                 LEA     SI,SCREENS           ;Start of screen stack
```

```
FF_LOOP:        MOV     BX,[SI+4]           ;Get pointer to next area
                CMP     BX,0                ;Is there anything here?
                                            ;  BX equal to 1 past end
                                            ;  of saved screen if so
                JE      FOUND_FREE          ;Nothing here
                MOV     SI,BX               ;Point to next screen set
                JMP     FF_LOOP             ;Keep looking

FOUND_FREE:     MOV     AX,SI               ;Set to beginning of entry
                ADD     AX,12               ;Add enough for two sets of
                                            ;  pointers
                ADD     AX,CX               ;Add length of save
                LEA     DX,END_SCREENS      ;End of screen stack
                CMP     AX,DX               ;Are we past end of stack?
                JGE     FF_NOPE             ;Yes, too big (can't save)
                CLC                         ;Return without error
                JNC     FF_EXIT
FF_NOPE:        STC
FF_EXIT:        RET                         ;Return to caller
FINDFREE        ENDP

; ----------------------------------------------------------------------
; CALCSIZE - CALCULATE THE SPACE NEEDED FOR THE WINDOW AREA
;           RETURNS WITH CX SET TO NUMBER OF BYTES
; ----------------------------------------------------------------------
CALCSIZE        PROC    NEAR
                MOV     AX,BOX_ULC          ;Get upper left corner
                MOV     BX,BOX_LRC          ;Lower right corner
                SUB     BX,AX               ;Absolute rows/columns

                ADD     BX,0101h            ;Set to actual numbers
                MOV     AX,0
                MOV     AL,BH               ;Number of rows in AX
                MOV     BH,0                ;Number of columns in BX
                MOV     WND_WIDTH,BX        ;Save width for later use
                MUL     BX                  ;Character positions in AX
                SHL     AX,1                ;Number of bytes in block
                MOV     CX,AX               ;Put in proper register
                RET                         ;Return to caller
CALCSIZE        ENDP

; ----------------------------------------------------------------------
; FINDLAST - LOCATES THE LAST SAVED SCREEN ON THE SCREEN STACK
; ----------------------------------------------------------------------
```

```
FINDLAST        PROC    NEAR
                LEA     SI,SCREENS
                MOV     AX,0
                PUSH    AX              ;Save original pointer
FL_LOOP:        MOV     BX,[SI+4]       ;Get pointer to next area
                CMP     BX,0            ;Is there anything here?
                                        ;  BX equal to 1 past end
                                        ;  of saved screen if so

                JE      FOUND_LAST      ;Nothing here, at end
                POP     AX              ;Get back old pointer
                PUSH    SI              ;Save where we are now
                MOV     SI,BX           ;Point to next screen set
                JMP     FL_LOOP         ;Keep looking


FOUND_LAST:     POP     SI              ;Get back the good pointer
                CMP     SI,0            ;Was it zero (nothing to
                                        ;   restore)?
                JE      FL_NOPE         ;Yes, so error
                CLC                     ;Return without error
                JNC     FL_EXIT
FL_NOPE:        STC
FL_EXIT:        RET
FINDLAST        ENDP


; ----------------------------------------------------------------------
; MCHAR - MOVE A CHARACTER INTO THE VIDEO BUFFER (SIMILAR TO PCHAR)
; ----------------------------------------------------------------------
MCHAR           PROC    NEAR
                PUSH    ES
                PUSH    DX

                MOV     ES,MONITOR_ADDR
                MOV     DX,STATUS_PORT

                CLI                     ;Don't allow interrupts
                PUSH    AX              ;Store the character
RETRACE:        IN      AL,DX           ;Get card status
                TEST    AL,1            ;Are we in a retrace state?
                JNZ     RETRACE         ;Yes, so check again
                                        ;On fall-through, just
                                        ;   exited retrace state
```

```
NO_RETRACE:     IN      AL,DX               ;Get card status
                TEST    AL,1                ;Are we in a retrace state?
                JZ      NO_RETRACE          ;No, so check again
                                            ;On fall-through, just
                                            ;   entered retrace state

                POP     AX                  ;Yes, get character back
                MOV     ES:[DI],AX          ;OK to write it now
                STI                         ;OK to have interrupts now

                INC     DI                  ;Point to attribute
                INC     DI                  ;Next screen location

                POP     DX
                POP     ES
                RET
MCHAR           ENDP
; ----------------------------------------------------------------------

                END
```

This set of routines is an example of the point made at the beginning of this book—that source code for assembly language routines takes a great deal of space. When assembled, however, the resulting object code is significantly smaller than a similar routine written entirely in BASIC.

Notice that these routines, particularly SAVSCRN, do not use the SI and DI registers in the usual manner; in these routines, DI points to the source, whereas SI points to the destination. I did this so that maximum use could be made of existing routines, such as SET_DI. I hope that the purists among you will not become incensed.

As much as 4K of screen data (the size of the entire screen) can be saved using SAVSCRN. Because most pop-up windows do not use the whole screen, you can save several windows. If you find that you need a larger screen stack area, you can increase the area by changing the number of bytes defined by SCREENS.

Notice that GETSCRN uses a subroutine called MCHAR. You will find, on examination, that MCHAR seems similar to PCHAR, the routine developed earlier in this chapter. Right you are! The routines are similar because they do almost the same thing: they store information into the video buffer. A new routine was warranted because, instead of using the default ATTRIBUTE (as PCHARA does), you are retrieving data one word at a time.

If you want to collect these routines into a library for use with Quick-BASIC's command-line compiler capability, you can use the makefile VIDEO shown in Chapter 12 to do so. The following QuickBASIC program demonstrates most of the library's functions:

```
REM   This is a test routine that verifies actions of
REM   VIDEO.LIB/VIDEO.QLB when run under QuickBASIC version 4.5

CLS
FOR r% = 2 TO 24
a% = r% - 1
a$ = "This is a Test: Attr =" + STR$(a%)
c% = 2 * r%
CALL PSTRNGA(a$, r%, c%, a%)
NEXT r%
PRINT "First Test"
LINE INPUT a$
tlc% = 5 * 256 + 5
brc% = 20 * 256 + 75
CALL SAVSCRN(tlc%, brc%)
PRINT "Second Test"
LINE INPUT a$
tlc% = 10 * 256 + 20
brc% = 15 * 256 + 60
a% = 10
CALL BOX(tlc%, brc%, a%)
PRINT "Third Phase"
LINE INPUT a$
CALL GETSCRN
PRINT "Test Complete"
```

Summary

The wide range of display adapters and monitors available for the IBM family of microcomputers can all be classified in one of two categories—monochrome or color. Because the classification of display devices can be determined by software, you can write routines that quickly display video data on either category of display adapter.

Video display routines written in assembly language execute faster and take less object code space than those written in high-level languages. Adding assembly language display subroutines to a high-level language program increases the overall speed of the program, especially one that is heavily screen-dependent.

The routines in this chapter have all been written for compiled BASIC. These routines could have been written just as easily for any other high-level language. If you change the parameter passing coding, the routines should work with C and Pascal as well as with compiled BASIC.

14

Accessing Hardware
Ports

To communicate with peripheral devices, the CPU in your PC (whether it is an 8086/8088, 80286, or an even newer design) uses *hardware ports*. These ports are areas that the 8086/8088 accesses by using special assembly language instructions. This chapter discusses specific hardware ports and the assembly language instructions that apply to them. In addition, the chapter covers several significant hardware port addresses, addresses that are important because they are used for direct control of such computer devices as the keyboard, the video monitor, and the speaker.

The 8086/8088 chip family can address as many as 65,536 hardware ports. However, because of the way the IBM PC microcomputers were implemented, the microprocessor uses only the first 1K of I/O addresses (hardware I/O port addresses 0 through 3FFh).

As the designs progressed through the XT, the IBM Personal Computer AT, and the PS/2 models, the same group of port addresses was retained although some usage details changed.

These addresses (memory locations) are accessible to both the microprocessor and the I/O device. Before we see how the I/O ports are used, let's look at the specific manner in which the ports are accessed.

The *IN* and *OUT* Assembly Language Instructions

The IN and OUT assembly language instructions handle the transfer of data to and from hardware ports. By using these mnemonics, you can transfer a single byte of information to or from a port address.

Because the I/O ports greatly resemble specialized memory locations, you may wonder why you cannot use the MOV instruction to transfer the appropriate information. There is a good reason: the architecture of the Intel CPU designs does not mix these two kinds of addresses—RAM and I/O port memory are kept separate. The IN and OUT instructions cause different pins of the microprocessor to be activated for the data transfer. Therefore, when the 8086/8088 microprocessor executes the instructions, it "knows" to access the specialized I/O hardware.

If the peripheral device were designed to interface through main RAM, the IN and OUT instructions would not be needed. (Several other manufacturers produce popular microprocessor chips, not used in the IBM line or its clones, that do in fact use such a "memory-mapped" approach to dealing with hardware ports; as you saw in Chapter 13, even the IBM designs mix the approaches when dealing with video displays.)

How, then, do you access these individual I/O ports? If the address of the port you are accessing is less than 256, you can code the address explicitly into the instruction, as in the following example:

```
IN          AL,50           ;Get a byte from the port
```

Notice that the byte is read from the port address specified by the source operand (50) and placed in the destination operand, or AL register. All IN and OUT instructions assume that the data transfer will be between the port address and the AL register. Attempting to transfer data to a different register results in an error during the assembly process because the CPU cannot perform such a transfer to or from any other register.

Because the IBM can directly access more than 256 I/O addresses, there must be a way to access these other ports. That method is to use the DX register to specify the port address. For example, the following code facilitates writing a byte to a port with a higher address:

```
                 MOV        DX,CS:STATUS_PORT

                 CLI                           ;Don't allow interrupts
                 PUSH       AX                 ;Store the character
RETRACE:         IN         AL,DX              ;Get card status
```

You may recognize this code as a section from the listings in Chapter 13. The I/O port address, which is assumed to be larger than 255, is loaded into DX and then used (in the RETRACE line) to fetch a byte from that port and place the byte into the AL register.

OUT works the same way as IN except that the data flows in the other direction; data is transferred from the source operand (AL) to the destination operand (the I/O port address). As you can see from the following examples, port addresses that are lower than 256 can be coded explicitly; those that are higher than 255 must be specified in the DX register:

```
OUT        50,AL
OUT        DX,AL
```

The IN and OUT statements are analogous to the MOV statement; they all transfer information. The main difference is that the MOV statement works on RAM memory, whereas the IN and OUT statements work with I/O addresses.

IN and OUT attempt to transfer information, regardless of the meaning of the port address supplied. Even if no device is using the port address, IN places a byte of information in AL, and OUT writes a byte of information from AL. The statements do not check whether a device is at the port address or whether the specified information was written successfully to a device. Because a peripheral device ordinarily uses more than one port address (perhaps one for input, one for output, and one for status), you can check different ports to verify the success of any interfacing. (A tip: because the IBM PC data bus *pulls up* to binary 1 when no hardware is enabled, an attempt to IN data from an address that has no device connected will usually return a value of 0FFh.)

There is no standard among devices to stipulate how the interfacing will occur. For instance, the procedure for communicating with the monochrome display adapter is different from the procedure for communicating with the asynchronous communications adapter. Each adapter or device uses different combinations of ports and addresses for different purposes.

When transferring data to or from a port, remember that not all external port devices can respond fast enough to keep pace with modern processor chips; this problem will continue to grow as processor speeds increase, and port hardware becomes more complicated. To safeguard against problems caused by slow port devices, always follow any IN or OUT instruction with a do-nothing JMP $+2 statement.

For a modern high-speed processor such as the 80286 or 80386, the effect of such a statement is much greater than you might think. Because RAM access is usually the limiting factor for CPU speed, these chips use a *lookahead queue* built into the chip itself, which contains the next several bytes of program code. The chips "cheat" by reading more than one byte per memory access. This lets the CPU decode the next instruction at the same time that it is executing the present one and possibly fetching the second, third, or fourth into the queue.

Obviously, execution of any JMP instruction makes all the data in the queue meaningless; the next instruction has to come from somewhere else, so the CPU flushes out and ignores everything in the lookahead area. It does so even if "somewhere else" is the exact same memory location from which the queue was loaded, as it is for JMP $+2. Thus, in addition to the actual time it takes to perform the JMP itself, this instruction slows the CPU down by the time required to reload the queue.

It may seem wasteful to buy a high-speed CPU and then deliberately slow it down by such coding tricks. However, keep in mind that you need only do this for the relatively few statements that move data to or from a hardware port. And if you are *certain* that the port can respond rapidly enough (as was the case with the video routines in Chapter 13) you need not do it at all. But as a general rule, it's the best policy to follow.

The I/O Port Map

IBM has defined some of the I/O port addresses for specific I/O purposes. The first 256 I/O ports (0-FFh) are reserved for use by the system board. Peripheral devices that control such areas as memory refresh, timers, interrupt controllers, and coprocessor utilization are linked to the main system at these ports.

The remaining I/O ports (100h-3FFh) are used for other general-purpose I/O, with some areas set aside for specialized usage. Table 14.1 details the currently defined hardware I/O addresses.

Table 14.1. *Hardware I/O port addresses and their usage.*

I/O Port range	Use/purpose
0-0Fh	8237—A Direct Memory Access (DMA) controller
10h	Manufacturing test point (10h-1Fh are additional DMA controllers in PS/2)
20h-23h	8259 Interrupt Controller (controller 1 in PC-AT and PS/2)
30h-3Fh	8259 Interrupt Controller 1 in AT
40h-43h	8253 timer (AT uses 8254, PS/2 uses 40h, 42h-44h, and 47h)
50h-5Fh	8253 timer (AT uses 8254)
60h-6Fh	8255 programmable peripheral interface on PC and XT, 8042 Keyboard interface on AT and PS/2
70h-71h	Real Time Clock and NMI mask on AT and PS/2
80h-8Fh	DMA page registers (all models)
90h-97h	DMA page registers (PC, XT, and AT) I/O Channel (PS/2)
A0h-AFh	Nonmaskable interrupt registers (PC and XT); 8259 Interrupt Controller 2 (AT and PS/2)
B0h-BFh	8259 Interrupt Controller 2 (AT only)
C0h-DFh	8237 DMA controller 2 (AT and PS/2)
E0h-EFh	Reserved for system use
F0h-FFh	Numeric coprocessor usage
100h-1EFh	AT I/O channel, PS/2 uses 100-107 for programmable option select registers
1F0h-1F8h	AT fixed disk interface
200h-20Fh	Game controller (PC, XT, and AT only)
210h-217h	Expansion unit (PC and XT only)
220h-26Fh	Reserved (available for I/O on AT)
278h-27Fh	LPT2: (PC, XT, and AT); LPT3: (PS/2)
280h-2AFh	Reserved (available for I/O on AT)
2B0h-2DFh	Alternate EGA (PC, XT, and AT only)
2E0h-2E3h	GPIB 0 (AT only)
2E8h-2EFh	COM4:
2F0h-2F7h	Reserved
2F8h-2FFh	COM2:
300h-31Fh	Prototype cards (PC, XT, and AT only)
320h-32Fh	XT fixed disk interface
360h-377h	AT Network (low address)
378h-37Fh	LPT2: (not on video card; PC, XT, and AT)

Table 14.1. *continues*

Table 14.1. *continued*

I/O Port range	Use/purpose
380h-38Ch	SDLC/secondary bi-sync interface (PC, XT, and AT)
390h-39Fh	AT cluster adapter
3A0h-3A9h	Primary bi-sync interface (PC, XT, and AT)
3B0h-3BBh	Monochrome display or PS/2 video
3BCh-3BFh	LPT1: (on video card)
3C0h-3CFh	EGA display control or PS/2 video
3D0h-3DFh	Color/graphics display or PS/2 video
3E8h-3EFh	COM3:
3F0h-3F7h	Floppy disk controller
3F8h-3FFh	COM1:

Areas that are not shown as defined or in use in table 14.1 are available for other I/O devices. Some third-party interface devices may use other I/O addresses that are not shown. However, port addresses below 256 (FFh) are reserved for exclusive use by the system board.

Because there is no real standard for communicating with external devices, and because such interfacing varies according to the type of device, the use of most I/O ports is not well documented in the IBM literature. In some cases, specialized books or manuals from either Intel or the specific peripheral manufacturer may contain relevant information. In the next few sections, I give you a brief look at some of the specific ports.

Some Significant Hardware Ports

Several hardware port addresses are significant to assembly language programmers—those for the ports most often accessed through assembly language programs.

Some hardware ports are used predominantly by the internal workings of BIOS and DOS routines (see Chapters 15 and 16). Other ports are available for different interface devices. Although the exact way in which all of these ports may interact with your program is beyond the scope of this book, a quick look at some of the hardware port addresses may be helpful.

The 8259 Interrupt Controller

The computer uses the 8259 Programmable Interrupt Controller to control interrupts. The Interrupt Controller handles as many as eight interrupts, according to their priority sequence, presenting them to the microprocessor in prioritized order.

As you can see from table 14.1, the 8259 Interrupt Controller uses four port addresses (20h through 23h). Although IBM documentation indicates that these four port addresses are reserved for the 8259, only the two lower ports (20h and 21h) are documented as usable by programmers. The other two ports (22h and 23h) are used only when reprogramming the 8259 for special dedicated systems that operate in modes not compatible with normal IBM PC operation.

I/O address 20h is referred to as the 8259 command port because it is used to send commands to the 8259. Programmers most commonly use this port with interrupt handlers—assembly language routines that control how the computer will react when presented with a system interrupt. Before issuing an IRET, the programmer is responsible for informing the system that it can process other interrupts. To do so, a 20h is sent to I/O address 20h in the following manner:

```
MOV       AL,20h              ;Signal other interrupts OK
OUT       20h,AL
```

Port 21h is the interrupt mask register for the 8259. Specific interrupts can be either enabled or disabled, depending on the settings of the bits in this register. Table 14.2 lists the meaning of the bits at the port.

The 8253 Timer

The IBM PC family of microcomputers uses an 8253 timer chip to control certain system functions. This chip, which operates at a frequency of 1.19318 MHz, provides for three independent timer channels and six separate operation modes.

The 8253 is interfaced through I/O port addresses 40h through 43h. Port 40h is used for timer channel 0 I/O, port 41h for timer channel 1 I/O, and port 42h for timer channel 2 I/O. Port 43h is used for mode control (see table 14.3).

Table 14.2. *Meaning of 8259 interrupt mask register bits for I/O port 21h.*

Bits 76543210	Meaning
0	IRQ 7 (parallel printer) interrupt enabled
1	IRQ 7 (parallel printer) interrupt disabled
0	IRQ 6 (floppy disk controller) interrupt enabled
1	IRQ 6 (floppy disk controller) interrupt disabled
0	IRQ 5 (XT fixed disk controller) interrupt enabled
1	IRQ 5 (XT fixed disk controller) interrupt disabled
0	IRQ 4 (COM1:) interrupt enabled
1	IRQ 4 (COM1:) interrupt disabled
0	IRQ 3 (COM2:) interrupt enabled
1	IRQ 3 (COM2:) interrupt disabled
0	IRQ 2 Reserved interrupt enabled
1	IRQ 2 Reserved interrupt disabled
0	IRQ 1 (keyboard) interrupt enabled
1	IRQ 1 (keyboard) interrupt disabled
0	IRQ 0 (system timer) interrupt enabled
1	IRQ 0 (system timer) interrupt disabled

Table 14.3. *Meaning of 8253 mode control bits for I/O port 43h.*

Bits 76543210	Meaning
00	Channel 0
01	Channel 1
10	Channel 2
00	Latch present counter value
01	Read/write only MSB
10	Read/write only LSB
11	Read/write LSB followed by MSB
000	Operation mode 0
001	Operation mode 1
010	Operation mode 2
011	Operation mode 3
100	Operation mode 4
101	Operation mode 5
0	Binary counter operation
1	BCD counter operation

The 8253's three timer channels are used for different purposes within the computer. Each channel has an associated divisor (one word long) that indicates how often the channel generates an interrupt. This divisor may range from 1 to 65,536. A divisor of 0 is equivalent to 65,536. To derive the channel interrupt frequency, you divide 1,193,180 (the chip operating frequency) by the divisor.

Channel 0, which is used for the system timer, uses a divisor of 0. The resulting interrupt (INT 8, IRQ0) frequency of 1,193,180/65,536 is approximately 18.2065 times per second, or once every 54.9 milliseconds. This channel is used to update the BIOS clock counter and the controls that turn off the floppy disk drive motor. This channel operates in mode 3, which signifies that the timer generates a square wave.

Channel 1 is used for DMA memory-refresh operations. It uses a divisor of 18, resulting in a frequency of 1,193,180/18, or approximately 66,287.7778 times per second. This is equivalent to a DMA interrupt being generated approximately once every 15.086 microseconds. Operation of this channel is in mode 2, which signifies that a pulse is generated once every period.

Channel 2, which is available for general use, is used most often with the speaker port. A specific example of this type of use is covered in the following section.

The 8255 Programmable Peripheral Interface (PPI)

The 8255A Programmable Peripheral Interface (PPI) is used to control the keyboard, the speaker, and the configuration switches. Four port addresses, 60h through 63h, (or more, depending on the computer) are associated with this device.

Because the use of each of these port addresses varies by computer, be sure to check your computer's technical documentation if you plan to program the addresses directly. This section provides some general information and direction but should not be accepted as "the gospel truth."

I/O port 60h is used for keyboard input and (on some versions of the IBM) for reading the configuration switches from the system board. If port 60h is used for reading the configuration switches, bit 7 of I/O port 61h should be set. If this bit is cleared, port 60h is used strictly for keyboard input. This port and port 61h are used in the examples shown later in this section.

I/O port 61h is used for configuration information for various devices, most notably the keyboard. Table 14.4 lists the meaning of the bit settings for this port.

Table 14.4. *Meaning of I/O port 61h bit settings.*

Bits 76543210	Meaning
0	Keyboard enabled
1	PC—Read configuration switches
1	XT—Keyboard acknowledge
0	Keyboard click off
1	Keyboard click on
0	Parity errors from expansion ports enabled
1	Parity errors from expansion ports disabled
0	RAM parity errors enabled (used for speed control on some Turbo clones)
1	RAM parity errors disabled (used for speed control on some Turbo clones)
0	PC—Cassette motor on (used for speed control on some Turbo clones)
1	PC—Cassette motor off (used for speed control on some Turbo clones)
0	XT—Read high nibble, configuration switches, port 62h
1	XT—Read low nibble, configuration switches, port 62h
0	PC—Read spare switches, port 62h
1	PC—Read RAM size switches, port 62h
x	XT—Unused
0	Speaker off
1	Speaker on
0	Direct speaker control through bit 1
1	Speaker control through 8253 timer (channel 2)

You use I/O port 62h to input a variety of system information (see table 14.5).

Table 14.5. *Meaning of I/O port 62h bit settings.*

Bits 76543210	Meaning
1	RAM parity error
1	Expansion slot error
?	8253 timer channel 2 output
?	PC—Cassette data input
x	XT—Unused
????	PC—Input according to bit 2, port 61h
????	XT—Input according to bit 3, port 61h

I/O port 63h is used as a mode-control register to control the other three I/O ports for this device. Table 14.6 details the individual bit settings and their meaning.

Table 14.6. *Meaning of I/O port 63h bit settings.*

Bits 76543210	Meaning
0	Port active
1	Port inactive
00	Port 60h mode 0
01	Port 60h mode 1
10	Port 60h mode 2
0	Port 60h used for output
1	Port 60h used for input
0	Port 62h, bits 7-4 used for output
1	Port 62h, bits 7-4 used for input
0	Port 61h mode 0
1	Port 61h mode 1
0	Port 61h used for output
1	Port 61h used for input
0	Port 62h, bits 3-0 used for output
1	Port 62h, bits 3-0 used for input

I/O port 64h is used as a status port for the keyboard on the IBM Personal Computer AT, as you will learn in the following section.

Controlling the Keyboard

Controlling hardware devices directly (through I/O ports) is possible. Because the process generally entails more work than most programmers choose to tackle, programmers usually elect to use either BIOS or DOS functions to control standard devices (see Chapters 16 and 17). Nevertheless, you should be aware that direct control of hardware devices is possible. Some programmers may even need to use direct control programming for specific applications.

This section includes an example of such programming—a program that directly controls the keyboard. I chose this particular device because not every reader may have a speaker or a video monitor, but you're sure to be able to get your hands on a keyboard.

The following sample program reads the information presented by the keyboard and then outputs the information as a decimal scan code (originally contained in the AL register).

Although this particular example is written as a stand-alone assembly language program, you can convert and modify it easily if you want to run it as a subroutine of a high-level language.

```
        page 60,132
;       *****************************************************************
;       *                                                               *
;       *    Date:    06/29/87                                          *
;       *  Program:  KEYHARD.COM                                        *
;       *                                                               *
;       *  Purpose:  This intercepts and prints the value returned by the *
;       *            keyboard each time a key is pressed.  Once installed, *
;       *            the only way out of this program is to turn off      *
;       *            the computer.                                        *
;       *                                                               *
;       *****************************************************************

CODE            SEGMENT BYTE PUBLIC 'CODE'
                ORG     100H
; ----------------------------------------------------------------------
KEYHARD         PROC    FAR

                ASSUME  CS:CODE,DS:CODE
                JMP     KEY_BEGIN               ;Starts the program
```

```
KB_DATA          EQU     60h
STATUS_PORT      EQU     64h
INPT_BUF_FULL    EQU     02h
DIS_KBD          EQU     0ADh
ENA_KBD          EQU     0AEh


KEY_NORMAL       DD      0                       ;Holds the normal keyboard
                                                 ;  interrupt vector address
OK_MSG           DB      'Program is installed$'


; --------------------------------------------------------------------
PNUM             PROC    NEAR
                 PUSH    AX
                 PUSH    BX
                 PUSH    CX
                 PUSH    DX

                 MOV     CX,0FFFFh               ;Push our ending flag
                 PUSH    CX
                 MOV     CX,10                   ;Always dividing by 10
DIVLP:           MOV     DX,0
                 DIV     CX
                 ADD     DX,30h                  ;Change to ASCII character
                 PUSH    DX                      ;Save remainder
                 CMP     AX,0
                 JA      DIVLP

NPLOOP:          POP     AX                      ;Get number back
                 CMP     AX,0FFFFh               ;Is it our ending flag?
                 JE      PNUM_EXIT               ;Yes, so go on our way
                 CALL    PCHAR                   ;Go print the character
                 JMP     NPLOOP                  ;Do next one

PNUM_EXIT:       POP     DX
                 POP     CX
                 POP     BX
                 POP     AX
                 RET
PNUM             ENDP
```

```
; ------------------------------------------------------------------
PCHAR           PROC    NEAR
                PUSH    AX
                PUSH    BX

                MOV     BH,0
                MOV     AH,0Eh              ;Display character
                INT     10h                ;BIOS interrupt

                POP     BX
                POP     AX
                RET
PCHAR           ENDP

; ------------------------------------------------------------------
SEND_IT         PROC    NEAR
                PUSH    AX                 ;Save byte to send
                CLI                        ;Disable interrupts
SIO:            IN      AL,STATUS_PORT     ;Get keyboard status
                TEST    AL,INPT_BUF_FULL   ;Is the coding complete?
                LOOPNZ  SIO                ;No, so continue waiting
                POP     AX                 ;Retrieve byte to send
                OUT     STATUS_PORT,AL     ;Send the byte
                STI                        ;Enable interrupts
                RET
SEND_IT         ENDP

; ------------------------------------------------------------------
NEW_KBD_INT:    PUSHF                      ;Save the flags
                PUSH    AX                 ;Only messing with AX

                MOV     AL,DIS_KBD
                CALL    SEND_IT            ;Go disable keyboard

                CLI                        ;Disable interrupts
GET_KB_STAT:    IN      AL,STATUS_PORT     ;Get keyboard status
                TEST    AL,INPT_BUF_FULL   ;Is the coding complete?
                LOOPNZ  GET_KB_STAT        ;No, so continue waiting
                IN      AL,KB_DATA         ;Yes, so get code
                STI                        ;Enable interrupts

                TEST    AL,80h             ;Is it an acknowledgment?
                JNZ     END_IT             ;Yes, so ignore it
```

```
            PUSH    AX                      ;Save code
            MOV     AL,'A'                  ;Print 'AL='
            CALL    PCHAR
            MOV     AL,'L'
            CALL    PCHAR
            MOV     AL,'='
            CALL    PCHAR
            POP     AX                      ;Retrieve code

            MOV     AH,0                    ;Only want AL
            CALL    PNUM                    ;Print decimal value
            MOV     AL,13                   ;Print carriage return
            CALL    PCHAR
            MOV     AL,10                   ;Print line feed
            CALL    PCHAR

END_IT:     MOV     AL,20h                  ;Signify end of interrupt
            OUT     20h,AL

            MOV     AL,ENA_KBD
            CALL    SEND_IT                 ;Go enable keyboard again

            POP     AX                      ;Restore AX register
            POPF                            ;  and the flags
            IRET

; -----------------------------------------------------------------
KEY_BEGIN:  MOV     AL,9h                   ;Get keyboard interrupt
            MOV     AH,35h
            INT     21h
            MOV     SI,OFFSET KEY_NORMAL    ;Store it here
            MOV     [SI],BX                 ;Offset address
            MOV     [SI+2],ES               ;Segment address
            MOV     AX,CS                   ;New segment address
            MOV     DS,AX
            MOV     DX,OFFSET NEW_KBD_INT   ;New offset address
            MOV     AL,9h                   ;Change keyboard vector
            MOV     AH,25h                  ;  to point to NEW_KBD_INT
            INT     21h
```

```
          MOV    DX,OFFSET OK_MSG      ;Installation complete
          MOV    AH,9                  ;Print message at DS:DX
          INT    21h
          MOV    DX,OFFSET KEY_BEGIN   ;End of resident portion
          INT    27h                   ;Terminate but stay resident

KEYHARD   ENDP
; ------------------------------------------------------------------
CODE      ENDS
          END    KEYHARD
```

After it has been entered, assembled, and executed, this program takes control of the keyboard by redirecting the keyboard interrupt vector to the new interrupt handler, NEW_KBD_INT. This handler intercepts and prints the decimal value of every keystroke; thus, every key on the keyboard returns a code, with no intervening translation by BIOS.

Because this routine prints the keyboard scan code for *every* key without exception, the only way to disable the program is to turn off the computer. This routine, although of limited value and usefulness, does give you a rudimentary way to control the keyboard.

Notice that this program directly reads and interprets signals from I/O ports 60h and 64h. Because the program was designed to work on an IBM Personal Computer AT or COMPAQ 386, the address values may be different if you are using a different type of computer.

Controlling the Speaker

This example, which shows how you can control the speaker directly, uses both the 8253 timer and the 8255 PPI. The WARBLE subroutine provides a good sound for error routines; BOOP provides a gentle sound when the wrong key is pressed.

You can call these routines directly from C. To modify them so that they work with compiled BASIC or Pascal, simply remove the underscores that precede the labels, and change WARBLE and BOOP from NEAR to FAR routines.

```
          page 60,132
;         ****************************************************************
;     *                                                                  *
;     *      Date:    7/21/87                                            *
;     *  Program:    SOUND.COM                                          *
;     *                                                                  *
;     *  Purpose:  Provide common error sounds from C.                  *
;     *                                                                  *
;     * Subroutines:                                                    *
;     *      WARBLE - Sound used in error routines                      *
;     *      BOOP - Sound used when wrong key pressed                   *
;     *                                                                  *
;         ****************************************************************

                    PUBLIC    _WARBLE
                    PUBLIC    _BOOP

                    NAME      SOUND
_TEXT               SEGMENT   BYTE PUBLIC 'CODE'
                    ASSUME    CS:_TEXT


; ----------------------------------------------------------------------
_WARBLE             PROC      NEAR
                    PUSH      BP
                    MOV       BP,SP

                    IN        AL,61h          ;Save speaker port contents
                    PUSH      AX

                    MOV       DX,0Bh
MAIN:               MOV       BX,477          ;1,193,180 / 2500
                    CALL      WARBCOM
                    MOV       CX,2600h
DELAY1:
                    LOOP      DELAY1
                    MOV       BX,36           ;1,193,180 / 32767
                    CALL      WARBCOM
                    MOV       CX,1300h
DELAY2:
                    LOOP      DELAY2
                    DEC       DX
                    JNZ       MAIN
```

```
                    POP     AX              ;Restore speaker port
                    OUT     61h,AL          ;   contents (turn it off)

                    POP     BP
                    RET
_WARBLE             ENDP
; ------------------------------------------------------------------
_BOOP               PROC    NEAR
                    PUSH    BP
                    MOV     BP,SP
                    PUSH    AX
                    PUSH    BX
                    PUSH    CX

                    IN      AL,61h          ;Save speaker port contents
                    PUSH    AX

                    MOV     BX,6818         ;1,193,180 / 175
                    CALL    WARBCOM
                    MOV     CX,4B4Bh
DELAY3:
                    LOOP    DELAY3

                    POP     AX              ;Restore speaker port
                    OUT     61h,AL          ;   contents (turn it off)

                    POP     CX
                    POP     BX
                    POP     AX
                    POP     BP
                    RET
_BOOP               ENDP
; ------------------------------------------------------------------
WARBCOM             PROC    NEAR
                    MOV     AL,10110110b    ;Channel 2, write LSB/MSB,
                    OUT     43h,AL          ;   operation mode 3, binary
                    MOV     AX,BX           ;Send counter LSB
                    OUT     42h,AL
                    MOV     AL,AH           ;Send counter MSB
                    OUT     42h,AL
                    IN      AL,61h          ;Get 8255 port contents
                    OR      AL,00000011b    ;Enable speaker and use
                    OUT     61h,AL          ;   clock channel 2 for input
```

```
                    RET
WARBCOM             ENDP
; --------------------------------------------------------------------

_TEXT               ENDS
                    END
```

The root of these subroutines is the procedure WARBCOM, which turns on the speaker at a specific frequency, specified in BX. The procedure sets channel 2 of the 8253 timer chip (ports 42h and 43h) and then ties timer output to speaker input through the 8255 PPI (port 61h).

Unlike many other port addresses (which may change with succeeding generations of computers), the port addresses used in SOUND.ASM have been left unchanged by IBM. Because of this, the routines should work on any IBM PC or true compatible.

Video Controller Ports

The addresses of the video controller ports vary, depending on the adapter card you are using (see table 14.7).

Table 14.7. Port address ranges for adapter cards.

Adapter card	Port address range
Monochrome	3B0h-3BBh
CGA	3D0h-3DCh
EGA or VGA	3B0h-3DFh

Your programs can determine which card is in use and modify their behavior accordingly. This section simply outlines some of the specific port uses—monochrome and color. (For an in-depth discussion of this process, refer to Chapter 13.)

The Monochrome Adapter

Although IBM lists the port addresses from 3B0h to 3BBh as being reserved for the monochrome adapter, the only ports used to control the monochrome display adapter are 3B4h, 3B5h, 3B8h, and 3BAh. The adapter does not use 3B0h through 3B3h, 3B6h, and 3B7h, and ports 3B9h and 3BBh are reserved.

Port 3B4h, the index register, is used to specify the register to be accessed through port 3B5h. You use the OUT instruction to output the desired register (0 through 17) to this port.

Port 3B5h, the data register, is used for communication with the adapter's internal registers. The desired register is specified through port 3B4h. Table 14.8 details the individual adapter registers.

Table 14.8. *The internal monochrome display adapter registers.*

Register	Use/meaning
0	Total horizontal characters
1	Total displayed horizontal characters
2	Horizontal sync position
3	Horizontal sync width
4	Total vertical rows
5	Vertical scan line adjust value
6	Total displayed vertical rows
7	Vertical sync position
8	Interlace mode
9	Maximum scan line address
10	Scan line at which cursor starts
11	Scan line at which cursor ends
12	High-byte start address
13	Low-byte start address
14	High-byte cursor address
15	Low-byte cursor address
16	Light pen (high byte)
17	Light pen (low byte)

Port 3B8h, the CRT control port, is set during power-up and should never be changed. Only three bits are significant (see table 14.9).

Port 3BAh, the CRT status port, is a read-only address. This byte has only two significant bits, with bit 0 (when clear) indicating that video is enabled. Bit 3 is set when a vertical retrace condition exists.

The Color/Graphics Adapter

IBM lists the port addresses from 3D0h to 3DFh as being reserved for the color/graphics adapter. But, as with the monochrome adapter, the color/graphics adapter uses only some of these ports; 3D4h, 3D5h, and 3D8h through 3DCh are the only ports used to control the color/graphics adapter.

Table 14.9. *Bit meanings in monochrome adapter mode-control register, port 3B8h.*

Bits 76543210	Meaning
xx	Not used
0	Disable blink
1	Enable blink
x	Not used
0	Video disable
1	Video enable
xx	Not used
1	80 x 25 display mode

Port 3D4h, the index register, is used to specify the register to be accessed through port 3D5h. The desired register (0 through 17) is output to this port.

Port 3D5h, the data register, is used for communication with the adapter's internal registers. The desired register is specified through port 3D4h.

Because both adapters use the same chip for display control, the register meanings for the color/graphics adapter are identical to those for the monochrome display adapter (see table 14.8).

Port 3D8h is the mode-control register. Only six bits in the byte are significant (see table 14.10).

Table 14.10. *Bit meanings in color/graphics adapter mode-control register, port 3D8h.*

Bits 76543210	Meaning
xx	Not used
0	Disable blink
1	Enable blink
0	Normal resolution
1	High resolution (640 x 200)
0	Video disabled
1	Video enabled
0	Color mode
1	Black-and-white mode
0	Alphanumeric mode

Table 14.10. *continues*

Table 14.10. *continued*

Bits 76543210	Meaning
1	320 x 200 graphics mode
0	40 x 25 alphanumeric display mode
1	80 x 25 alphanumeric display mode

Port 3D9h, the color-select register, is used to specify the colors used in various display modes. Only the lower six bits are significant (see table 14.11).

Table 14.11. *Bit meanings in color/graphics adapter color-select register, port 3D9h.*

Bits 76543210	Meaning
xx	Not used
1	Selects cyan/magenta/white color set
0	Selects green/red/brown color set
1	Selects intensified color set in graphics modes, or background colors in alphanumeric display mode
1	Selects intensified border color in 40 x 25 alphanumeric display mode, intensified background color in 320 x 200 graphics mode, or red foreground color in 640 x 200 graphics mode
1	Selects red border color in 40 x 25 alphanumeric display mode, red background color in 320 x 200 graphics mode, or red foreground color in 640 x 200 graphics mode
1	Selects green border color in 40 x 25 alphanumeric display mode, green background color in 320 x 200 graphics mode, or green foreground color in 640 x 200 graphics mode
1	Selects blue border color in 40 x 25 alphanumeric display mode, blue background color in 320 x 200 graphics mode, or blue foreground color in 640 x 200 graphics mode

Port 3DAh, a read-only address, is the CRT status port. This byte has only four significant bits, which are shown in table 14.12.

Table 14.12. *Bit meanings in color/graphics adapter status register, port 3DAh.*

Bits 76543210	Meaning
xxxx	Not used
1	Vertical retrace condition
0	Light pen triggered
1	Light pen not triggered
1	Light pen trigger set
0	Video disabled
1	Video enabled

Port 3DBh, a strobe, is used to clear the light pen latch; any writing to this port clears bit 1 at port 3DAh. Port 3DCh is a strobe used to preset the light pen latch.

Printer Ports

The line-printer interface ports vary according to the number of printer interface cards installed in the system. Normally, the three printer ports are addressed as indicated in table 14.13.

Table 14.13. *Normal printer-port addressing.*

Designation	Port address range
LPT1:	3BCh-3BFh
LPT2:	378h-37Fh
LPT3:	278h-27Fh

The addresses shown in table 14.13 are general guidelines, and will vary from installation to installation. For example, if instead of installing a printer interface that uses the addresses normally assigned to LPT1:, you install an interface card that uses one of the other port ranges, that card becomes known to the system as LPT1:.

The first port in each address range (3BCh, 378h, or 278h) is used to output information to the printer. The bits of information are output directly on the parallel port. Bit 0 corresponds to pin 2, bit 1 to pin 3, and so on through bit 7, which corresponds to pin 9 of the parallel connector.

Port 3BDh (or 379h, or 279h) is the printer-status register. The bits at this port indicate the status of various line signals for the parallel connector. The meaning of each bit is indicated in table 14.14.

Table 14.14. *Bit meanings for parallel printer adapter status register, port 3BDh/379h/279h.*

Bits 76543210	*Meaning*
0	Printer busy
0	Acknowledged
1	Out of paper
1	On-line (printer selected)
1	Printer error
xx	Not used
1	Time out

Port 3BEh (or 37Ah, or 27Ah) is the printer-control register. The bits at this port are used to control the printer, as indicated in table 14.15.

Table 14.15. *Bit meanings for parallel printer adapter control register, port 3BEh/37Ah/27Ah.*

Bits 76543210	*Meaning*
xxx	Not used
1	Enable IRQ7 interrupt for printer acknowledge
1	Printer reads output
1	Initialize printer
1	Enable auto-linefeed
1	Output data to printer (strobe)

The remaining ports (3BFh, 37Bh through 37Fh, and 27Bh through 27Fh) are not used by the parallel interface.

Asynchronous Communications Ports

The serial communications interface ports vary according to the number of asynchronous interface cards installed in the system. Ordinarily, BIOS and DOS allow no more than two communications ports to be used (see table 14.16).

Table 14.16. *Normal printer-port addressing.*

Designation	Port address range
COM1:	3F8h-3FFh
COM2:	2F8h-2FFh
COM3:	3E8h-3EFh
COM4:	2E8h-2EFh

Notice that table 14.16 lists the addresses for four communications ports. Although neither BIOS nor DOS supports the addresses for COM3: and COM4:, many communications devices do support four communications ports; software can be written to enable use of the two additional ports.

Because the intricacies and complexities of programming for asynchronous communications are astounding, a detailed explanation of the communications ports, their use, programming, and functions is best left for another book. The balance of this section simply details the meanings of the ports used by asynchronous communications devices.

Port 3F8h, which ordinarily is used to transmit and receive data, can be used also (if bit 7 of port 3FBh is set) to specify the low-order byte of the baud-rate divisor.

The baud-rate divisor is used to specify the baud rate of the communications device; the divisor is a number that, divided into the clock speed of a specific device, results in the proper number of bits-per-second for the baud rate of that device.

Port 3F9h also is used for different purposes. If bit 7 of port 3FBh is set, this port is used to specify the high-order byte of the baud-rate divisor.

Table 14.17 details several popular baud rates and their proper baud-rate divisor settings. The port addresses shown are for COM1:. Other communications ports should use the corresponding port addresses of 2F9h/2F8h, 3E9h/3E8h, or 2E9h/2E8h.

The proper procedure for setting the baud rate is to set bit 7 of port 3FBh, output the proper divisors to the appropriate ports, and then clear bit 7 of port 3FBh.

If bit 7 of port 3FBh is clear, port 3F9h serves as the interrupt-enable register. The interrupt-enable register lets you specify which communications events will generate interrupts to the microprocessor. The bit meanings for this register are indicated in table 14.18.

Table 14.17. *Baud-rate divisor settings for standard 1.8432 MHz clock speed.*

Baud-rate divisor		
MSB 3F9h	LSB 3F8h	Resulting baud rate—bps
4	17h	110
1	80h	300
0	60h	1,200
0	30h	2,400
0	18h	4,800
0	0Ch	9,600
0	06h	19,200
0	01h	115,200 (maximum possible)

Table 14.18. *Bit meanings for the interrupt-enable register, port 3F9h (or 2F9h, 3E9h, or 2E9h).*

Bits 76543210	Meaning
0000	Not used, set to 0
1	Enable interrupt on modem status change
1	Enable interrupt on receive line status change
1	Enable interrupt on transmit holding register empty
1	Enable interrupt on data available

Port 3FAh is the interrupt identification register. When the microprocessor receives an interrupt generated by the communications device, the program reads this register to determine exactly caused the interrupt. Only the three least significant bits are meaningful (see table 14.19).

Table 14.19. *Bit meanings for the interrupt-identification register, port 3FAh (or 2FAh, 3EAh, or 2EAh).*

Bits 76543210	Meaning
00000	Not used, set to 0
11	Receiver line status interrupt
10	Received data available
01	Transmitter holding register empty
00	Modem status change
1	Interrupt not pending
0	Interrupt pending

Port 3FBh, the line-control register, is used to specify the format of the data that is transmitted and received through the communications port. Table 14.20 lists the meanings of the bit settings for this register.

Table 14.20. *Bit meanings for the line-control register, port 3FBh (or 2FBh, 3EBh, or 2EBh).*

Bits 76543210	Meaning
0	Normal access to ports 3F8h/3F9h
1	Use ports 3F8h/3F9h to specify baud-rate divisor
0	Normal operation
1	Transmit break condition (constant SPACE)
0	Parity held at value in bit 4
1	Parity operates normally
0	Odd parity
1	Even parity
0	Parity disabled
1	Parity enabled
0	1 stop bit
1	2 stop bits (1.5 if bits 0-1 are clear)
00	5-bit data length
01	6-bit data length
10	7-bit data length
11	8-bit data length

Port 3FCh, the modem-control register, is used to control the modem interface. The bit meanings for this register are detailed in table 14.21.

Table 14.21. *Bit meanings for the modem-control register, port 3FCh (or 2FCh, 3ECh, or 2ECh).*

Bits 76543210	Meaning
000	Not used, set to 0
0	Normal modem functioning
1	Operate in loop-back test mode
1	"User 2" bit, must be "1" for operation of 8250 interrupt signals
0	"User 1" bit, forces modem reset if "1"
0	RTS clear
1	RTS set
0	DTR clear
1	DTR set

Port 3FDh, the line-status register, is used to indicate the condition of data transfer. The bit meanings in this register are detailed in table 14.22.

Table 14.22. *Bit meanings for the line-status register, port 3FDh (or 2FDh, 3EDh, or 2DCh).*

Bits 76543210	Meaning
0	Not used, set to 0
0	Transmitter shift register full
1	Transmitter shift register empty
0	Transmitter holding register full
1	Transmitter holding register empty
1	Break condition detected
1	Framing error detected
1	Parity error detected
1	Overrun error detected
0	No character ready
1	Received character ready

Port 3FEh, the modem-status register, is used to reflect the state of the modem-control lines. Table 14.23 shows its bit meanings.

Table 14.23. *Bit meanings for the modem-status register, port 3FEh (or 2FEh, 3EEh, or 2DEh).*

Bits 76543210	Meaning
1	Receive line signal detected
1	Ring detected
1	DSR set
1	CTS set
1	Change in receive line signal detect state
1	Change in ring indicator state
1	Change in DSR state
1	Change in CTS state

Ordinarily, the communications device uses port 3FFh internally as a "scratch pad."

Summary

The organization and use of hardware ports were discussed in this chapter. Hardware ports are necessary for computers to be able to communicate with outside devices such as video monitors, keyboards, printers, mice, and so on. By writing software, you can access these hardware devices directly (through the IN and OUT mnemonic instructions).

To use hardware ports properly, you must know which ports are used by the device you want to control. Certain devices, such as the keyboard, speaker, and video monitors, use standardized hardware port addresses that can be readily accessed and programmed through assembly language.

Such intimate control of the individual device has drawbacks, however. Future releases of DOS or future generations of computers may abandon the currently accepted standard I/O addresses in favor of a different standard. In that event, software that directly controls devices through I/O ports would have to be changed. The BIOS and DOS services in Chapters 16 and 17 insulate programmers from such vagaries of change.

Part IV

Reference

CHAPTER 15

Accessing BIOS Services

BIOS (Basic Input/Output System) is the lowest software level for communicating with hardware. Because the BIOS software usually is contained in the computer's read-only memory (ROM), BIOS is often referred to as ROM-BIOS.

The BIOS contains a series of functions that are easily accessible to an outside program—such as one you may develop. These functions, which are nothing more than callable subroutines, are invoked through software interrupts. Interrupts are generated by the assembly language instruction INT, which causes the microprocessor to use an address fetched from an interrupt table in low memory as the address for this special type of subroutine.

Specifically, INT pushes the flag(s) register on the stack and then resets the interrupt and trap flags. The full return address (CS:IP) is placed on the stack and then the desired interrupt vector (address) is retrieved from the interrupt table and placed in CS:IP. Execution of the interrupt then continues until an IRET instruction is encountered, at which point the return address is popped from the stack and placed in CS:IP. The flags register is then restored from the stack, and program execution continues from the point at which the interrupt was invoked.

409

Notice that the number of the interrupt being invoked determines which interrupt address is fetched from the interrupt table. Thus, the full syntax for calling an interrupt is

```
INT XX
```

where XX represents the number of the appropriate interrupt.

This chapter covers the BIOS interrupt services, listing in detail the different BIOS interrupt numbers and the tasks they perform. (Chapter 16 covers the DOS interrupt services.)

As you will recall, Chapter 14 describes how to access the computer's hardware ports directly. Ordinarily, BIOS does most of this direct accessing. The concept of allowing BIOS to perform hardware interfacing, instead of performing the interfacing in your software, is readily justifiable. Although the chips that make up the computer hardware (or their related port address) may change or vary from one computer to another, the BIOS interfaces should not change. Any given BIOS function should produce identical results, regardless of which computer you're using. The way BIOS performs a task will differ, depending on the hardware. But because of the insulation provided by BIOS, this difference does not affect you, the programmer.

The universality of the BIOS applies only to the world of IBM micro-computers or close clones. Some computers that are purported to be IBM compatible are not. And there are different levels of compatibility; some computers are hardware compatible, some are DOS compatible, and others are BIOS compatible. The BIOS services listed in this chapter should work on any machine that is BIOS-compatible with the IBM.

The interface layer that BIOS introduces between the hardware and software levels has definite benefits. The primary benefit should be immediately apparent—software development time is greatly enhanced, so programmers can develop software more efficiently. Because of the BIOS, you don't have to develop a different interface for every possible hardware combination. Other benefits include the security of knowing that your software will work on a variety of hardware configurations.

The BIOS Service Categories

The services offered by BIOS can be divided into several broad categories. Generally, these categories are determined by the I/O devices supported by the BIOS functions. Some categories, however, contain BIOS functions that deal with the internal workings of the computer rather than an external peripheral. (As used in this chapter, the interrupt itself is a function; a subfunction, or subinterrupt—such as AH = ?—is a service.)

The BIOS function categories include

❏ Video services

❏ Keyboard services

❏ Disk services

❏ Printer services

❏ Communications services

❏ Date/time services

❏ Cassette tape services

❏ System services

This section's descriptions of services apply to all IBM-compatible BIOS versions except as noted in the individual write-ups. However, I can't verify each and every clone design and BIOS, so it's possible that your own system's services may vary from these descriptions. If you are using a PS/2, note that significant additions were made to the video BIOS service, and that the service originally used as a tape cassette interface was changed extensively, when the PS/2 line was introduced.

The BIOS Services

The rest of this chapter is designed as a convenient reference. Each BIOS function call is described in detail, with the following information listed:

❏ **Function name.** A name based on the BIOS function names selected and listed by IBM in various technical documentation. Where appropriate, names have been modified or expanded to more accurately reflect the true purpose of the service.

❏ **Category.** The general classification of the function.

❏ **Registers on entry.** BIOS function parameters generally are passed through registers. The expected register settings are detailed here.

❏ **Registers on return.** Knowing how registers are affected by interrupts is important for proper operation of software. Because BIOS functions frequently return values through registers, such information is detailed here. For most BIOS operations, all registers (except the AX and flags registers) remain intact.

❏ **Memory areas affected.** Some BIOS functions modify memory. Any affected memory is detailed here.

❏ **Syntax for calling.** A coding section that shows the proper method for calling the interrupt.

❏ **Description.** Details of the purpose, benefits, and special considerations of the function.

The functions are arranged in ascending numerical order. Each function can be identified by the primary interrupt number and a service number. (Each service number is specified by the contents of the AH register.) In this notation scheme, any BIOS service can be denoted by a hexadecimal number pair, *II/SS*, in which *II* is the interrupt number and *SS* is the service number. For example, the service used to set video mode, service 10/0, has an interrupt number of 10h, and a service number (specified through AH) of 0.

Print Screen (Interrupt 5)

Category: Printer services

Registers on Entry: Not significant

Registers on Return: Unchanged

Memory Affected: None

Syntax:

```
INT     5h          ;BIOS print screen interrupt
```

Description: To invoke this BIOS interrupt, press PrtSc (to access PrtSc, you may need to press the Shift key). The interrupt causes the ASCII contents of the video screen to be sent to the printer.

Because most programs do not need a verbatim copy of the screen being sent to the printer, this interrupt normally is not called by a user program. However, the interrupt is designed for this type of use, and there is no problem in calling it from software control. The effect is the same as if the user had pressed the PrtSc key.

By changing the vector for this interrupt, you can create a custom version of the print screen service or disable it completely. For information on changing an interrupt vector, see DOS service 21/25 (Chapter 16).

When you call this interrupt, the contents of the registers are not significant; they remain unchanged on return. This routine does not change the position of the video cursor.

The status of this operation, which is contained in the single byte at memory address 50:0, is 1 while printing is in progress. The status is 0 if the print operation was successful, and 0FFH if an error occurred during the last print screen operation.

Set Video Mode (Interrupt 10h, service 0)

Category: Video services

Registers on Entry:

AH: 0
AL: Desired video mode

Registers on Return: Unchanged

Memory Affected: Ordinarily, the video memory area for the desired mode is cleared unless the high-order bit of AL is set and an Enhanced Graphics Adapter card is in use.

Syntax:

```
MOV    AH,0              ;Specify service 0
MOV    AL,3              ;80x25 color, TEXT (CGA display adapter)
INT    10h               ;BIOS video interrupt
```

Description: This service is used to set a specific video mode. The acceptable modes will vary, depending on the type of display adapter installed in the computer. Table 15.1 shows the possible settings for video modes.

Normally, setting the video mode causes the video buffer to be cleared. If you are using an EGA or VGA card, however, you can add the value 128 to any video mode value to indicate that the video display memory should not be cleared. Adding 128 is equivalent to setting the high-order bit of AL.

As new types of display adapters become available, the list of video modes listed in table 15.1 will probably change or grow. Depending on the amount of RAM available to the display adapter, the colors available with the EGA or VGA card in the various video modes will vary.

Table 15.1. *Video mode settings for BIOS service 10/0.*

Mode number	Mode type	Display adapter	Pixel resolution	Characters	Colors
0	Text	CGA	320 x 200	40 x 25	16(gray)
		EGA	320 x 350	40 x 25	16(gray)
		MCGA	320 x 400	40 x 25	16
		VGA	360 x 400	40 x 25	16
1	Text	CGA	320 x 200	40 x 25	16
		EGA	320 x 350	40 x 25	16/64
		MCGA	320 x 400	40 x 25	16
		VGA	360 x 400	40 x 25	16
2	Text	CGA	640 x 200	80 x 25	16(gray)
		EGA	640 x 350	80 x 25	16(gray)
		MCGA	640 x 400	80 x 25	16
		VGA	720 x 400	80 x 25	16
3	Text	CGA	640 x 200	80 x 25	16
		EGA	640 x 350	80 x 25	16/64
		MCGA	640 x 400	80 x 25	16
		VGA	720 x 400	80 x 25	16
4	Graph	CGA/EGA/ MCGA/VGA	320 x 200	40 x 25	4
5	Graph	CGA/EGA/ MCGA/VGA	320 x 200 320 x 200	40 x 25 40 x 25	4(gray) 4
6	Graph	CGA/EGA/ MCGA/VGA	640 x 200	80 x 25	2
7	Text	MDA/EGA	720 x 350	80 x 25	Mono
		VGA	720 x 400	80 x 25	Mono
8	Graph	PCjr	160 x 200	20 x 25	16
9	Graph	PCjr	320 x 200	40 x 25	16
10	Graph	PCjr	640 x 200	80 x 25	4
13	Graph	CGA/EGA/VGA	320 x 200	40 x 25	16
14	Graph	CGA/EGA/VGA	640 x 200	80 x 25	16
15	Graph	EGA/VGA	640 x 350	80 x 25	Mono
16	Graph	EGA/VGA	640 x 350	80 x 25	16
11h	Graph	MCGA/VGA	640 x 480	80 x 30	2
12h	Graph	VGA	640 x 480	80 x 30	16
13h	Graph	MCGA/VGA	320 x 200	40 x 25	256

If you use a mode that is not supported by the display adapter that you are using, the results can be unpredictable, although the usual result is that no characters are displayed.

Set Cursor Size (Interrupt 10h, service 1)

Category: Video services

Registers on Entry:

AH: 1
CH: Beginning scan line of cursor
CL: Ending scan line of cursor

Registers on Return: Unchanged

Memory Affected: None

Syntax:

```
MOV    AH,1           ;Specify service 1
MOV    CH,0           ;Start on scan line 0
MOV    CL,7           ;End on scan line 7
INT    10h            ;BIOS video interrupt
```

Description: Depending on the type of display adapter used, the number of scan lines used by a text character can vary. The MDA and EGA adapters use characters that are 14 pixels high. The CGA uses a character box that is 8 pixels high. Each of these pixels corresponds to a scan line (the horizontal path traced by the electron beam that paints a character on the video monitor).

This service allows you to specify where in the character box the cursor should start and end. These positions, which are the beginning and ending scan lines, can vary from 0 to 7 lines (for the CGA) or from 0 to 13 lines (for the MDA and EGA). Within the valid numeric range, you can specify any combination of beginning and ending scan lines. If the beginning scan line is greater than the ending scan line, the cursor will wrap around the bottom of the character box, resulting in an apparent two-part cursor. A normal cursor occupies only the bottom one or two scan lines in the character box.

With the MCGA and VGA cards, this service operates a bit differently than with either EGA, CGA, or MDA. You usually can treat these cards the same way you use the EGA so long as you are using the normal 80 x 25 text screens; however, if you change display sizes, you must also change cursor sizes using the character height in pixels (stored in the BIOS RAM area at address 0:0485h, or returned by service 11) to determine the ending stop line. The start value can be the same (for a single line cursor) or 0 (for a block).

Set Cursor Position (Interrupt 10h, service 2)

Category: Video services

Registers on Entry:

AH: 2
BH: Video page number
DH: Cursor row
DL: Cursor column

Registers on Return: Unchanged

Memory Affected: None

Syntax:

```
MOV     AH,2            ;Specify service 2
MOV     DH,0            ;Place cursor at top left
MOV     DL,0            ;  corner of screen (0,0)
MOV     BH,0            ;Primary text page
INT     10h             ;BIOS video interrupt
```

Description: This service, which sets the position of the video cursor, is based on a screen-coordinate system. Generally, the cursor row, stored in DH, can vary from 0 to 24. The cursor column, stored in DL, normally varies from 0 to 79. However, the exact range of positions depends on the type of display adapter you are using and the current video mode.

If you are using graphics mode, the video page number stored in BH should be set for 0. In text modes, which can accommodate more than one video page, the number usually varies from 0 to 3. If you are operating in 40-column mode, the video page number can vary from 0 to 7. The cursor position for each video page is independent of the other pages.

Read Cursor Position and Size (Interrupt 10h, service 3)

Category: Video services

Registers on Entry:

AH: 3
BH: Video page number

Registers on Return:

BH: Video page number
CH: Beginning scan line of cursor
CL: Ending scan line of cursor
DH: Cursor row
DL: Cursor column

Memory Affected: None

Syntax:

```
MOV    AH,3                ;Specify service 3
MOV    BH,0                ;Primary text page
INT    10h                 ;BIOS video interrupt
MOV    CUR_SIZE,CX         ;Save current cursor size
MOV    CUR_POSITION,DX     ;Save current position
```

Description: Use this service to determine the cursor's current status. Be sure to save the values so that, after manipulation, the program can restore the cursor condition.

If you are using graphics mode, the video page number stored in BH should be set for 0. In text modes, which can accommodate more than one video page, the video page number usually varies from 0 to 3. If you are operating in 40-column mode, the video page can vary from 0 to 7. The cursor position for each video page is independent of the other pages.

In this service (which is the opposite of services 10/1 and 10/2) the cursor size and position for a desired video page number are returned in CX and DX.

Ordinarily, the scan lines returned in CH and CL will vary from 0 to 7 (for the CGA adapter) or from 0 to 13 (for the MDA and EGA adapters). For additional information on scan line designations, refer to service 10/1.

The cursor row returned in DH normally varies from 0 to 24, and the cursor column returned in DL varies either from 0 to 39 or from 0 to 79, depending on which video mode currently is set.

Read Light Pen Position (Interrupt 10h, service 4)

Category: Video services

Registers on Entry:

AH: 4

Registers on Return:

AH: Light pen trigger status
BX: Pixel column
CX: Raster line (pixel row)
DH: Light pen row
DL: Light pen column

Memory Affected: None

Syntax:

```
MOV     AH,4            ;Specify service 4
INT     10h             ;BIOS video interrupt
```

Description: If you have a light pen attached to your computer, this service allows you to determine the status of the light pen. Even though the hardware for using a light pen exists on the MDA, its use effectively is defeated by the long retention time of the phosphor used in monochrome monitors.

On return from this interrupt, you should check the value in AH. If the value is 0, the light pen has not been triggered. Because the other values will be meaningless, do not attempt further analysis and action based on the light pen's status.

If the value in AH is 1, the light pen has been triggered and two sets of coordinates (pixel and text) are returned. The video mode you are using determines which set of coordinates you should use: the pixel coordinates are appropriate for graphics screens; the text coordinates, for text screens.

The register pair CX:BX contains the set of pixel coordinates. CX is the *raster line*, or vertical pixel position, which varies from 0 to 199 or, for some EGA modes, from 0 to 349. BX (the horizontal pixel position) can vary from 0 to 319 or from 0 to 639, depending on the resolution of the video adapter used in the computer.

The accuracy of the pixel coordinates returned by this BIOS service varies. Because the vertical (raster line) coordinate is always a multiple of 2, only even lines are returned, even if an odd number line triggered the pen. Similarly, if the video mode currently allows for a horizontal resolution of 320 pixels, the horizontal coordinate returned is a multiple of 2. If the horizontal resolution is 640 pixels, the horizontal coordinate is a multiple of 4. Thus, this BIOS function precludes use of a light pen for precise graphics work.

If you are working in text mode, you will want to use the other set of light pen coordinates: the row (DH) and column (DL) coordinates. The row coordinate normally varies from 0 to 24; the column coordinate varies either from 0 to 39, or from 0 to 80, depending on the video adapter. 0,0 is the coordinate for the upper left corner of the display area.

Select Active Display Page (Interrupt 10h, service 5)

Category: Video services

Registers on Entry:

AH: 5
AL: Desired display page

Registers on Return: Unchanged

Memory Affected: This service determines which area of video memory is displayed.

Syntax:

```
MOV     AH,5              ;Specify service 5
MOV     AL,1              ;Want page 1 video
INT     10h               ;BIOS video interrupt
```

Description: Depending on the current display mode and the video adapter you are using, you can use multiple, independent display pages. This BIOS service allows you to specify which video page is to be active, or displayed.

The desired display page is specified in AL. This value will vary within a range determined by the current display mode and the type of adapter you are using (see table 15.2). The video mode numbers indicated in table 15.2 correlate directly to those shown in table 15.1.

Notice that you can set the active display page only if you are operating in text mode. The contents of the different display pages are not modified if you switch between pages.

Table 15.2. *Video display pages for various display modes and video adapters.*

Mode number	Display adapter	Page range
0	all	0-7
1	all	0-7
2	CGA	0-3
	EGA/MCGA/VGA	0-7
3	CGA	0-3
	EGA/MCGA/VGA	0-7
7	MDA	0
	CGA/EGA/VGA	0-7
13	EGA/VGA	0-7
14	EGA/VGA	0-3
15	EGA/VGA	0-1
16	EGA/VGA	0-1

Scroll Window Up (Interrupt 10h, service 6)

Category: Video services

Registers on Entry:

AH: 6
AL: Number of lines to scroll
BH: Display attribute for blank lines
CH: Row for upper left corner of window
CL: Column for upper left corner of window
DH: Row for lower right corner of window
DL: Column for lower right corner of window

Registers on Return: Unchanged

Memory Affected: This service modifies the desired video buffer area of the active display page.

Syntax:

```
MOV     AH,6            ;Specify service 6
MOV     AL,3            ;Want to scroll 3 lines
MOV     BH,7            ;Normal white-on-black
MOV     CH,5            ;Upper left = 5,5
MOV     CL,5
```

```
MOV     DH,15               ;Lower right = 15,74
MOV     DL,74
INT     10h                 ;BIOS video interrupt
```

Description: Use this service (which is the opposite of service 10/7) to selectively scroll up portions of the text screen. Only the currently active text display page is affected. The number of lines to scroll, contained in AL, is set for the desired value. If this value is set to 0, or to a value greater than the height of the specified window, the entire window area is cleared. (Using a value 1 greater than the window height will clear the window area more quickly than if you use zero, because the routine loops until AL decrements to zero regardless of its value at entry.)

CX and DX should contain the upper left and lower right coordinates for the window, respectively. The high byte of each register is the row, normally in the range of 0 to 24. The low byte is the column, normally either 0 to 39 or 0 to 79, depending on the current display mode. If the rectangle specified is inverted so that the value in CX is greater than the value in DX, the results will be unpredictable.

The information scrolled off the top of the window is lost. The blank lines scrolled on the bottom of the window consist of spaces with the character attribute specified by the byte value in BH. Table 15.3 lists the character attributes available for a CGA or EGA video adapter; other values may be available, depending on which video adapter card you use.

Table 15.3. *Character attribute byte values.*

Foreground	Background	Hex value	Decimal value
Blue	Black	01h	1
Green	Black	02h	2
Cyan	Black	03h	3
Red	Black	04h	4
Magenta	Black	05h	5
Brown	Black	06h	6
White	Black	07h	7
Gray	Black	08h	8
Light blue	Black	09h	9
Light green	Black	0Ah	10
Light cyan	Black	0Bh	11
Light red	Black	0Ch	12
Light magenta	Black	0Dh	13
Yellow	Black	0Eh	14
Bright white	Black	0Fh	15

Table 15.3. continues

Table 15.3. *continued*

Foreground	Background	Hex value	Decimal value
Black	Blue	10h	16
Green	Blue	12h	18
Cyan	Blue	13h	19
Red	Blue	14h	20
Magenta	Blue	15h	21
Brown	Blue	16h	22
White	Blue	17h	23
Gray	Blue	18h	24
Light blue	Blue	19h	25
Light green	Blue	1Ah	26
Light cyan	Blue	1Bh	27
Light red	Blue	1Ch	28
Light magenta	Blue	1Dh	29
Yellow	Blue	1Eh	30
Bright white	Blue	1Fh	31
Black	Green	20h	32
Blue	Green	21h	33
Cyan	Green	23h	25
Red	Green	24h	26
Magenta	Green	25h	27
Brown	Green	26h	28
White	Green	27h	29
Gray	Green	28h	40
Light blue	Green	29h	41
Light green	Green	2Ah	42
Light cyan	Green	2Bh	43
Light red	Green	2Ch	44
Light magenta	Green	2Dh	45
Yellow	Green	2Eh	46
Bright white	Green	2Fh	47
Black	Cyan	30h	48
Blue	Cyan	31h	49
Green	Cyan	32h	50
Red	Cyan	34h	52
Magenta	Cyan	35h	53
Brown	Cyan	36h	54
White	Cyan	37h	55
Gray	Cyan	38h	56
Light blue	Cyan	39h	57
Light green	Cyan	3Ah	58

Foreground	Background	Hex value	Decimal value
Light cyan	Cyan	3Bh	59
Light red	Cyan	3Ch	60
Light magenta	Cyan	3Dh	61
Yellow	Cyan	3Eh	62
Bright white	Cyan	3Fh	63
Black	Red	40h	64
Blue	Red	41h	65
Green	Red	42h	66
Cyan	Red	43h	67
Magenta	Red	45h	69
Brown	Red	46h	70
White	Red	47h	71
Gray	Red	48h	72
Light blue	Red	49h	73
Light green	Red	4Ah	74
Light cyan	Red	4Bh	75
Light red	Red	4Ch	76
Light magenta	Red	4Dh	77
Yellow	Red	4Eh	78
Bright white	Red	4Fh	79
Black	Magenta	50h	80
Blue	Magenta	51h	81
Green	Magenta	52h	82
Cyan	Magenta	53h	83
Red	Magenta	54h	84
Brown	Magenta	56h	86
White	Magenta	57h	87
Gray	Magenta	58h	88
Light blue	Magenta	59h	89
Light green	Magenta	5Ah	90
Light cyan	Magenta	5Bh	91
Light red	Magenta	5Ch	92
Light magenta	Magenta	5Dh	93
Yellow	Magenta	5Eh	94
Bright white	Magenta	5Fh	95
Black	Brown	60h	96
Blue	Brown	61h	97
Green	Brown	62h	98
Cyan	Brown	63h	99
Red	Brown	64h	100

Table 15.3. *continues*

Table 15.3. *continued*

Foreground	Background	Hex value	Decimal value
Magenta	Brown	65h	101
White	Brown	67h	103
Gray	Brown	68h	104
Light blue	Brown	69h	105
Light green	Brown	6Ah	106
Light cyan	Brown	6Bh	107
Light red	Brown	6Ch	108
Light magenta	Brown	6Dh	109
Yellow	Brown	6Eh	110
Bright white	Brown	6Fh	111
Black	White	70h	112
Blue	White	71h	113
Green	White	72h	114
Cyan	White	73h	115
Red	White	74h	116
Magenta	White	75h	117
Brown	White	76h	118
Gray	White	78h	120
Light blue	White	79h	121
Light green	White	7Ah	122
Light cyan	White	7Bh	123
Light red	White	7Ch	124
Light magenta	White	7Dh	125
Yellow	White	7Eh	126
Bright white	White	7Fh	127

Scroll Window Down (Interrupt 10h, service 7)

Category: Video services

Registers on Entry:

AH: 7
AL: Number of lines to scroll
BH: Display attribute for blank lines
CH: Row for upper left corner of window
CL: Column for upper left corner of window
DH: Row for lower right corner of window
DL: Column for lower right corner of window

Registers on Return: Unchanged

Memory Affected: This service modifies the desired video buffer area of the active display page.

Syntax:

```
MOV   AH,7          ;Specify service 7
MOV   AL,5          ;Want to scroll 5 lines
MOV   BH,7          ;Normal white-on-black
MOV   CH,10         ;Upper left = 10,5
MOV   CL,5
MOV   DH,20         ;Lower right = 20,74
MOV   DL,74
INT   10h           ;BIOS video interrupt
```

Description: Use this service, which is the opposite of service 10/6, to selectively scroll down portions of the text screen. Only the currently active text display page is affected. The number of lines to scroll, contained in AL, is set for the desired value. If this value is set to 0, or to a value greater than the height of the specified window, the entire window area is cleared. (Using a value 1 greater than the window height will clear the window area more quickly than using zero, because the routine loops until AL decrements to zero regardless of its value at entry.)

CX and DX should contain the upper left and lower right coordinates for the window, respectively. The high byte of each register is the row, normally in the range of 0 to 24. The low byte is the column, normally either 0 to 39 or 0 to 79, depending on the current display mode. If the rectangle specified is inverted so that the value in CX is greater than that in DX, the results will be unpredictable.

The information scrolled off the bottom of the window is lost, and the blank lines scrolled on the top of the window consist of spaces with the character attribute specified by the value in BH. (Some of the possible video attributes are listed in table 15.3.)

Read Character and Attribute (Interrupt 10h, service 8)

Category: Video services

Registers on Entry:

AH: 8
BH: Video page number

Registers on Return:

AH: Attribute byte
AL: ASCII character code

Memory Affected: None

Syntax:

```
; POSITION CURSOR AT DESIRED LOCATION PRIOR TO USING THIS SERVICE
; (SEE SERVICE 10/2)
MOV     AH,2                    ;Specify service 2
MOV     DH,0                    ;Place cursor at top left
MOV     DL,0                    ;  corner of screen (0,0)
MOV     BH,0                    ;Primary text page
INT     10h                     ;BIOS video interrupt


; NOW USE SERVICE 10/8 TO READ THE CHARACTER/ATTRIBUTE WORD

MOV     AH,8                    ;Specify service 8
MOV     BH,0                    ;Primary text page
INT     10h                     ;BIOS video interrupt
```

Description: Because this service reads (from any display page) the character and attribute at the cursor's current position, you are not limited to the currently visible display page.

This service works in both text and graphics modes, although the character attribute has significance only in text mode. In text mode, the value returned in AH represents the character's video attribute (refer to table 15.3). In graphics mode, the color of the character is returned in AH. NULL (ASCII 0) is returned in AL if the character at the cursor's current position (in graphics mode) does not match any valid ASCII character.

Write Character and Attribute (Interrupt 10h, service 9)

Category: Video services

Registers on Entry:

AH: 9
AL: ASCII character code
BH: Video page number
BL: Video attribute of character in AL
CX: Number of character/attribute words to display

Registers on Return: Unchanged

Memory Affected: This service modifies the desired area of the active display page's video buffer.

Syntax:

```
MOV    AH,9        ;Specify service 9
MOV    AL,'-'      ;Want to display a dash
MOV    BH,0        ;Primary text page
MOV    BL,0Eh      ;Yellow on black attribute
MOV    CX,50h      ;Print 80 characters
INT    10h         ;BIOS video interrupt
```

Description: This service displays a specific number of characters at the cursor's current position on any valid video page.

The character in AL is displayed with the video attribute specified in BL, which is valid only for text modes. (For a list of possible video attributes, refer to table 15.3.) In graphics modes, the color of the character (foreground) should be specified in BL. If bit 7 of BL is set to 1, then the color in BL is XORed with the background color where the character is to be displayed. If the same character (AL) is displayed at the same position with the same color (BL) and bit 7 of BL set, the character will be erased and the background will remain undisturbed.

The character displayed by this service can be displayed on any valid video page, not just on the currently visible one. By using this service and service 10/0Ah, you can create a page of text on a background (not displayed) page, and then display the entire page at once through service 10/5.

This service can be used to display any number of characters from 1 through 65,536. Setting the value in CX to 0 signifies 65,536 characters, the ultimate number of character repetitions. In text mode, if the number being displayed extends beyond the right margin, the characters progress from line to line. In graphics mode, however, no line-wrap occurs; only those characters on the current line are displayed.

Even though this service displays a specified number of characters at the current cursor position, the cursor position does not advance. To subsequently change the cursor position, use service 10/2.

Write Character (Interrupt 10h, service 0Ah)

Category: Video services

Registers on Entry:

AH: 0Ah
AL: ASCII character code
BH: Video page number
BL: Color of character in AL (only in graphics modes)
CX: Number of character/attribute words to display

Registers on Return: Unchanged

Memory Affected: This service modifies the desired area of the active display page's video buffer.

Syntax:

```
MOV     AH,0Ah          ;Specify service 0Ah
MOV     AL,'*'          ;Want to display an asterisk
MOV     BH,0            ;Primary text page
MOV     CX,1            ;Print only 1 character
INT     10h             ;BIOS video interrupt
```

Description: This service is effectively the same as service 10/9, but uses the existing video attribute values. In graphics modes, the color of the character (foreground) should be specified in BL. If bit 7 of BL is set to 1, the color in BL is XORed with the background color where the character will be displayed. If the same character (AL) is displayed at the same position with the same color (BL) and bit 7 of BL set, the character will be erased, and the background will remain undisturbed.

The character can be displayed on any valid video page (not just on the currently visible video page). Using this service and service 10/9, you can create a page of text on a background (not displayed) page, and then display the entire page at once through service 10/5.

This service can be used to display any number of characters from 1 through 65,536. Setting the value in CX to 0 signifies 65,536 characters, the ultimate number of character repetitions. In text mode, if the number being displayed extends beyond the right margin, the characters progress from line to line. In graphics mode, however, no line wrap occurs; only those characters on the current line are displayed.

Even though this service displays a specified number of characters at the current cursor position, the cursor position does not advance. To subsequently change the cursor position, use service 10/2.

Set Color Palette (Interrupt 10h, service 0Bh)

Category: Video services

Registers on Entry:

AH: 0Bh
BH: Palette ID
BL: Palette ID color value

Registers on Return: Unchanged

Memory Affected: None

Syntax:

```
MOV    AH,0Bh              ;Specify service 0Bh
MOV    BH,1               ;Setting palette
MOV    BL,0               ;Green/red/brown palette
INT    10h                ;BIOS video interrupt
```

Description: This service, which is used primarily to set the color palette used by medium-resolution graphics services, has significance only in a few video modes, most notably mode 4. (For more information on video modes, see the service 10/0 description.)

This service does not affect the video memory. It only changes the way that the 6845 CRT Controller chip on the CGA board interprets and displays pixel values already in video memory.

If BH contains 0, the value of BL is used as both the background and border colors. If BH contains a 1, the value in BL specifies which color palette to use; BL can be set to any value, but only the contents of the low bit are significant. This bit value determines one or the other of the following palettes:

Value	Palette
0	Green, red, and brown
1	Cyan, magenta, and white

Notice the colors for palette 0. The technical specifications for the CGA card and the 6845 CRT Controller show that these are the proper colors although the system BIOS reference in the *IBM Technical Reference* manual states that the colors for this palette are green, red, and yellow.

A palette specifies the display colors to be used for various bit combinations. Changing the palette changes the screen display immediately.

Rapidly using this service and alternately changing the palette can result in a flashing screen. The pixel bit determination is as follows:

Pixel value	Palette 0 color	Palette 1 color
00	Background	Background
01	Green	Cyan
10	Red	Magenta
11	Brown	White

You can use this service also to set the border color in text mode. In text mode, if BH is 0, the value in BL is used as the border color.

Write Pixel Dot (Interrupt 10h, service 0Ch)

Category: Video services

Registers on Entry:

AH: 0Ch
AL: Pixel value
CX: Pixel column
DX: Raster line (pixel row)

Registers on Return: Unchanged

Memory Affected: This service modifies the desired area of the active display page's video buffer.

Syntax:

```
MOV     AH,0Ch              ;Specify service 0Ch
MOV     AL,11b              ;Pixel value to use
MOV     CX,A0h              ;Position at 100,160
MOV     DX,64h
INT     10h                 ;BIOS video interrupt
```

Description: This general-purpose graphics plotting service (the opposite of service 10/0Dh) works in either medium- or high-resolution graphics modes although the effects in each are different.

In medium-resolution graphics modes on the CGA, the contents of AL can vary from 0 to 3. The display effect of these pixel values depends on the color palette in use (see service 10/0Bh). The results of the various setting of AL are

Pixel value	Palette 0 color	Palette 1 color
00	Background	Background
01	Green	Cyan
10	Red	Magenta
11	Brown	White

In high-resolution graphics modes on the CGA, the value of AL can vary between 0 and 1. These values correspond to whether the pixel is off (black) or on (white).

If the high-order bit of AL is set (1), the pixel color is XORed with the pixel's current contents. Because of the behavior of XORing values, this capability provides a quick way to display a pixel and then to erase it by again writing the same pixel value to the location. If the high-order bit of AL is set (0), the pixel value is written to the pixel location.

The register pair DX:CX contains the pixel's plotting coordinates. DX is the *raster line*, or vertical pixel position; its value can range from 0 to 199, or from 0 to 349 for some EGA video modes. The value of CX (the horizontal pixel position) can range either from 0 to 319 (medium-resolution) or from 0 to 639 (high-resolution). Coordinates are numbered from top to bottom and from left to right; 0,0 is the top left screen corner, and either 199,319 or 199,639 is the bottom right corner, depending on the resolution of the video mode. If you specify coordinates outside the legal range for the current graphics mode, the results can be unpredictable.

Read Pixel Dot (Interrupt 10h, service 0Dh)

Category: Video services

Registers on Entry:

AH: 0Dh
CX: Pixel column
DX: Raster line (pixel row)

Registers on Return:

AL: Pixel value
CX: Pixel column
DX: Raster line (pixel row)

Memory Affected: None

Syntax:

```
MOV     AH,0Dh          ;Specify service 0Dh
MOV     CX,A0h          ;Want pixel value at
MOV     DX,64h          ; coordinate 100,160
INT     10h             ;BIOS video interrupt
```

Description: This service (the opposite of 10/0Ch) is used in either medium- or high-resolution graphics modes to determine the pixel value of the pixel at any given screen location.

The desired pixel coordinates are specified in the register pair DX:CX. DX is the *raster line*, or vertical pixel position; its value can range from 0 to 199, or from 0 to 349 for some EGA video modes. The value of CX (the horizontal pixel position) can range either from 0 to 319 (medium-resolution) or from 0 to 639 (high-resolution). Notice that this horizontal resolution is in a 16-bit register but that the other coordinate is in an 8-bit register. Coordinates are numbered from top to bottom and from left to right; 0,0 is the top left screen corner, and either 199,319, 199,639, or 349,639 is the bottom right corner, depending on the resolution of the video mode. If you specify coordinates outside the legal range for the current graphics mode, the results can be unpredictable.

The pixel value returned in AL depends on the current video mode. In medium-resolution graphics modes on the CGA, the value of AL can vary from 0 to 3. In high-resolution graphics modes on the CGA, the value of AL can vary between 0 and 1. (For more information about pixel values, see the description for service 10/0Ch.)

TTY Character Output (Interrupt 10h, service 0Eh)

Category: Video services

Registers on Entry:

AH: 0Eh
AL: ASCII character code
BH: Video page number
BL: Character color (graphics foreground)

Registers on Return: Unchanged

Memory Affected: This service modifies the desired area of the active display page's video buffer.

Syntax:

```
MOV     AH,0Eh          ;Specify service 0Eh
MOV     AL,'.'          ;Output a period
MOV     BH,0            ;Primary video page
INT     10h             ;BIOS video interrupt
```

Description: This service is similar to service 10/9, except that the output is in *Teletype* mode (a limited amount of character processing is performed on the output). The ASCII codes for bell (07), backspace (08), linefeed (10), and carriage return (13) are all intercepted and translated to the appropriate actions. Line wrap and scrolling are performed if the printed characters exceed the right display margin or the bottom display line.

Because the ASCII value of the character to be output is loaded in AL, and the video page number loaded in BH, this output service can be used for display pages other than the current one. By using this service and service 10/0Ah, you can create a page of text on a background (not displayed) page, and then display the entire page at once through service 10/5. If output is to a background page, the processing of the bell character (ASCII 07) will still result in the familiar "beep."

The foreground color, which is specified in BL, has significance only in graphics modes. Notice that the syntax example for this service does not specify BL. In text mode, the current video attributes for the screen location are used. With this service, you cannot specify a video attribute other than the current one.

You can use this service, which advances the cursor position, to display multiple characters in series. With this service, you do not have to set the cursor position before displaying each character.

Get Current Video State (Interrupt 10h, service 0Fh)

Category: Video services

Registers on Entry:

AH: 0Fh

Registers on Return:

AH: Screen width
AL: Display mode
BH: Active display page

Memory Affected: None

Syntax:

```
MOV    AH,OFh          ;Specify service OFh
INT    10h             ;BIOS video interrupt
MOV    COLUMNS,AH      ;Save number of columns
MOV    MODE,AL         ;Save display mode
MOV    PAGE,BH         ;Save display page
```

Description: This service, which is used to determine the current video state of the computer, returns three pieces of information: the width in columns of the display screen (AH), the current video display mode (AL), and the current video display page (BH). Table 15.1 (service 10/0) lists possible video-mode settings.

EGA/VGA Palette Registers (Interrupt 10h, service 10h)

Category: Video services

Registers on Entry:

AH: 10h

AL: 00h, Set palette register
BH: Color value
BL: Palette register to set

AL: 01h, Set border color register
BH: Color value

AL: 02h, Set all registers and border
DX: Offset address of 17-byte color list
ES: Segment address of 17-byte color list

AL: 03h, Toggle blink/intensity (EGA only)
BL: Blink/intensity bit
    00h = Enable intensity
    01h = Enable blinking

AL: 07h, Read palette register (PS/2 only)
BL: Palette register to read (0-15)

AL: 08h, Read overscan register (PS/2 only)

AL: 09h, Read palette registers and border (PS/2 only)
DX: Offset address of 17-byte table for values
ES: Segment address of 17-byte table for values

AL: 10h, Set individual color register
BX: Color register to set
CH: Green value to set
CL: Blue value to set
DH: Red value to set

AL: 12h, Set block of color registers
BX: First color register to set
CX: Number of color registers to set
DX: Offset address of color values
ES: Segment address of color values

AL: 13h, Select color page
BL: 00h, Select paging mode
BH: Paging mode
      00h = 4 register blocks of 64 registers
      01h = 16 register blocks of 16 registers

AL: 13h, Select color page
BL: 01h, Select page
BH: Page number
      00-03h = 64 register blocks
      00-0Fh = 16 register blocks

AL: 15h, Read color register (PS/2 only)
BX: Color register to read

AL: 17h, Read block of color registers
BX: First color register to read
CX: Number of color registers to read
DX: Offset address of buffer to hold color values
ES: Segment address of buffer to hold color values

AL: 1Ah, Read color page state

AL: 1Bh, Sum color values to gray shades
BX: First color register to sum
CX: Number of color registers to sum

Registers on Return:

Subfunctions 07h-08h
BH: Value read

Subfunction 09h
DX: Offset address of 17-byte table
ES: Segment address of 17-byte table

Subfunction 15h
CH: Green value read
CL: Blue value read
DH: Red value read

Subfunction 17h
DX: Offset address of color table
ES: Segment address of color table

Subfunction 1Ah
BL: Current paging mode
CX: Current page

Memory Affected: Varies by subfunction

Syntax: Varies by subfunction

Description: On the MCGA, EGA, and VGA display systems, this function controls the correspondence of colors to pixel values. Although listed as reserved in the IBM Personal Computer AT BIOS, this function is an extension to the BIOS, applicable to EGA/VGA display systems. Some subfunctions, designated by the contents of AL when calling this function, are not available on the PS/2 Model 30 system. These include subfunctions 01h, 02h, 07h, 08h, 09h, 13h, and 1Ah.

EGA/VGA Character Generator (Interrupt 10h, service 11h)

Category: Video services

Registers on Entry:

AH: 11h
AL: 00h, User alpha load
BH: Number of bytes per character
BL: Block to load
CX: Count to store

DX: Character offset into table
BP: Offset address of user table
ES: Segment address of user table

AL: 01h, ROM monochrome set
BL: Block to load

AL: 02h, ROM 8*8 double dot
BL: Block to load

AL: 03h, Set block specifier
BL: Character-generator block selection

AL: 10h, User alpha load
BH: Number of bytes per character
BL: Block to load
CX: Count to store
DX: Character offset into table
BP: Offset address of user table
ES: Segment address of user table

AL: 11h, ROM monochrome set
BL: Block to load

AL: 12h, ROM 8*8 double dot
BL: Block to load

AL: 20h, Set user graphics characters pointer at 1Fh
BP: Offset address of user table
ES: Segment address of user table

AL: 21h, Set user graphics characters pointer at 43h
BL: Row specifier
CX: Bytes per character
BP: Offset address of user table
ES: Segment address of user table

AL: 22h, ROM 8*14 set
BL: Row specifier

AL: 23h, ROM 8∗8 double dot
BL: Row specifier

AL: 30h, System information
BH: Font pointer

Registers on Return: Varies by subfunction

Memory Affected: Varies by subfunction

Syntax: Varies by subfunction

Description: This service, which contains 14 subfunctions, supports the character-generator functions of the EGA, MCGA, and VGA, enabling a program to set up its own character-generator tables. The service also makes it easy to change the number of rows displayed. Some subfunctions, designated by the contents of AL when this service is called, are not available on the PS/2 Model 30 system. These include subfunctions 01h, 10h, 11h, 12h, and 22h.

Subfunctions 11h, 12h, and 14h are particularly useful because they reprogram the CRT controller to display more than 25 rows of text. The exact number displayed varies between EGA and VGA; for a VGA, the number depends on how many scan lines were chosen (service 10/12).

Alternate Video Select (Interrupt 10h, service 12h)

Category: Video services

Registers on Entry:

AH: 12h

BL: 10h, Return EGA information

BL: 20h, Select alternate print-screen routine

BL: 30h, Select number of scan lines
AL: 00h = 200 lines
    01h = 350 lines
    02h = 400 lines

BL: 31h, Load palette when setting mode
AL: 00h = enable
    01h = disable

BL: 32h, Video on/off
AL: 00h = enable
    01h = disable

BL: 33h, Sum color to grayscale
AL: 00h = enable
    01h = disable

BL: 34h, Cursor emulation on/off
AL: 00h = enable
    01h = disable

Registers on Return:

Subfunction 10h (setting in BL):
    BH: BIOS video mode (0 color/1 mono)
    BL: Size of EGA RAM (0=64K to 3=256K)

In all cases AL = 12h if service was valid.

Memory Affected: None

Syntax:

```
MOV     AX,1202h      ;Service 10/12, set 400 scan lines
MOV     BL,30h
INT     10h           ;BIOS video services interrupt
```

Description: This service and its various subfunctions are effective only for the EGA, MCGA, and VGA adapters.

Write String (Interrupt 10h, service 13h)

Category: Video services

Registers on Entry:

AH: 13h
AL: Mode
BH: Video page number
BL: Character attribute (depending on AL)
CX: Length of string
DH: Cursor row where string is to be displayed
DL: Cursor column where string is to be displayed
BP: Offset address of string
ES: Segment address of string

Registers on Return: Unchanged

Memory Affected: This service modifies the desired area of the active display page's video buffer.

Syntax:

```
MOV     BH,0                    ;Primary video page
MOV     BL,07h                  ;Normal attributes
MOV     DH,5                    ;Display string at
MOV     DL,5                    ;   coordinates 5,5
PUSH    DS                      ;Make ES same as DS
POP     ES
MOV     BP,OFFSET ES:MSG_1      ;Point to message offset
MOV     CX,10h                  ;Standard string length
MOV     AH,13h                  ;Specify service 13h
INT     10h                     ;BIOS video interrupt
```

Description: *This service is available only on PC XTs with BIOS dates of 1/10/86 or later, on the Personal Computer AT, and on machines in the PS/2 family.* Use this service, which is a logical extension of the BIOS character display functions, to display an entire string on any video page.

The mode specified in AL determines how BIOS will treat the string that is to be displayed. Table 15.4 lists this service's four modes.

Table 15.4. *Modes for service 10/13.*

Mode	Cursor	Attribute	String composition (C = character, A = attribute)
0	Not moved	in BL	CCCCCCC...CC
1	Moved	in BL	CCCCCCC...CC
2	Not moved	in string	CACACACA...CA
3	Moved	in string	CACACACA...CA

Notice that the display attributes can be specified either in BL or in the string, depending on the contents of AL. If you are using mode 2 or 3, the contents of BL are not significant. The mode also determines whether the cursor is moved when the string is displayed.

The string's address is specified in ES:BP. CX contains the length of the string. The service displays the string until CX reaches 0. Do not use a length of 0. If you do, 65,536 characters will be displayed, and the effects of displaying this number of characters probably will be undesirable.

Because this service makes limited use of BIOS service 10/0E, some character processing is performed on the individual string characters. The ASCII codes for bell (07), backspace (08), linefeed (10), and carriage return (13) are all intercepted and directed to service 10/0E, where they are translated to the appropriate actions. Line wrap and scrolling are performed if the printed characters exceed the right display margin or the bottom display line. If the string character is not a bell, backspace, linefeed, or carriage return, it is displayed by service 10/9.

Although this service is neither particularly fast nor efficient, it is convenient. The routines in Chapter 13 result in faster displays but entail more work for the programmer. Only you can decide which to use.

Get Equipment Status (Interrupt 11h)

Category: System services

Registers on Entry: Not significant

Registers on Return:

AX: Equipment status

Memory Affected: None

Syntax:

```
INT    11h              ;Invoke BIOS interrupt
```

Description: Use this rudimentary service, which returns a minimal amount of information, to determine what equipment is attached to the computer. The equipment status word is set up during the booting process and does not change. The meaning of each bit in the returned word is shown in table 15.5.

Depending on the computer you are using, certain portions of this equipment status word may not be significant. If you are using an IBM Personal Computer AT, for example, the value of bits 2 and 3 have no meaning. These bits are relics of the days when 64K of RAM was considered as much as anyone could possibly want in a microcomputer.

You can see that the register contents on entry are not significant and that AX is the only register changed on return.

Table 15.5. *Bit meanings for equipment status word returned by interrupt 11.*

Bits		
FEDCBA98	76543210	*Meaning of bits*
xx		Number of printers attached
x		Not used
0		Game adapter not installed
1		Game adapter installed
xxx		Number of serial cards attached
x		Not used
	00	1 disk drive attached (if bit 0 = 1)
	01	2 disk drives attached (if bit 0 = 1)
	10	3 disk drives attached (if bit 0 = 1)
	11	4 disk drives attached (if bit 0 = 1)
	01	Initial video mode—40 x 25 BW/color card
	10	Initial video mode—80 x 25 BW/color card
	11	Initial video mode—80 x 25 BW/mono card
	00	16K system board RAM
	01	32K system board RAM
	10	48K system board RAM
	11	64K system board RAM
	1	Math coprocessor installed
	0	No disk drives installed (bits 6-7 insignificant)
	1	Disk drives installed (bits 6-7 significant)

Get Memory Size (Interrupt 12h)

Category: System services

Registers on Entry: Not significant

Registers on Return:

    AX: Memory blocks

Memory Affected: None

Syntax:

```
INT     12h                  ;Invoke BIOS interrupt
```

Description: Use this service to return the number of contiguous 1K blocks of memory installed in the computer. The memory size, which is determined when you power-up the computer, is returned in AX.

Notice that the number of contiguous memory blocks is returned. If the power-on self test (POST) determines that defective RAM chips are installed in the computer, the value returned by this interrupt will be equal to the number of 1K blocks counted before the defective memory area was encountered.

On entry of this interrupt, the register contents are not significant. AX is the only register changed on return.

The method used to determine available memory depends on the system, but usually consists of an attempt to read and write to a memory block. As soon as the write/read cycle fails, the end of memory is assumed to have been reached.

When there is more than 640K of memory, service 15/88 must be called to determine extended memory size.

On PS/2 systems, this interrupt returns a maximum amount of memory of up to 640K, minus the amount of memory set aside for the extended BIOS data area (EBDA). The EBDA may be as little as 1K. (See service 15/ C1 for more information.)

Reset Disk Drives (Interrupt 13h, service 0)

Category: Disk services

Registers on Entry:

AH: 0

DL: Drive number (0 based)
    bit 7 = 0 for a diskette

Registers on Return: Unchanged

Memory Affected: None

Syntax:

```
MOV     AH,0            ;Specify service 0
MOV     DL,82h          ;for drive C
INT     13h             ;BIOS disk interrupt
```

Description: Use this service to reset the disk drive controller. (The service works on the NEC series of floppy disk drive controllers that IBM specifies as standard equipment, and in most implementations performs the same function for any hard disk drive controllers present.)

Calling this service has no apparent effect on the disk drives. The recalibrate command is sent directly to the floppy drive controller in use, and a reset flag is set to recalibrate all the drives the next time they are used. This recalibration retracts the read/write head to track 0, causing the familiar "grinding" sound often heard after a disk error. The read/write head is forced to track 0 and then must seek out the desired track.

Used primarily in routines that handle critical errors on disks, this service forces the controller to recalibrate itself on the subsequent operation. If a critical error occurs, the service is necessary for reliable disk operation; it forces the disk controller to make no assumptions about its position or condition—assumptions that may be wrong because of the critical error condition.

Get Floppy Disk Status (Interrupt 13h, service 1)

Category: Disk services

Registers on Entry:

> AH: 1
> DL: Drive number (0 based)
> > bit 7 = 0 for a diskette

Registers on Return:

> AL: Status byte

Memory Affected: None

Syntax:

```
MOV     AH,1             ;Specify service 1
MOV     DL,82h           ;for drive C
INT     13h              ;BIOS disk interrupt
```

Description: This service returns the status of the disk drive controller. The status, which is set after each disk operation (such as reading, writing, or formatting), is returned in AL. The meaning of each bit in the returned status byte is shown in table 15.6.

Table 15.6. *Meaning of the status byte returned by service 13/1.*

Bits 76543210	Hex	Decimal	Meaning of bits
1	80	128	Time out—drive did not respond
1	40	64	Seek failure—couldn't move to requested track
1	20	32	Controller malfunction
1	10	16	Bad CRC detected on disk read
1 1	9	9	DMA error—64K boundary crossed
1	8	8	DMA overrun
1	4	4	Bad sector/sector not found
11	3	3	Write protect error
1	2	2	Bad sector ID (address) mark
1	1	1	Bad command

Read Disk Sectors (Interrupt 13h, service 2)

Category: Disk services

Registers on Entry:

AH: 2
AL: Number of sectors
BX: Offset address of data buffer
CH: Track
CL: Sector
DH: Head (side) number
DL: Drive number
ES: Segment address of data buffer

Registers on Return:

AH: Return code

Memory Affected: RAM buffer area specified by address starting at ES:BX is overwritten by sectors requested from disk.

Syntax:

```
MOV     AL,1              ;Reading 1 sector
MOV     CH,TRACK          ;Specify track
MOV     CL,SECTOR         ;  and sector
MOV     DH,SIDE           ;Specify side
MOV     DL,DRIVE          ;Specify drive
```

```
PUSH    DS                      ;Point ES to proper
POP     ES                      ;   segment address
MOV     BX,OFFSET ES:BUFFER     ;Offset of buffer area
MOV     AH,2                    ;Specify service 2
INT     13h                     ;BIOS disk interrupt
```

Description: Use this service to control reading from the disk. This service is the opposite of service 13/3, which controls writing to the disk.

To use this service, you must specify the precise physical location on the disk at which you want to begin reading. The drive is specified in DL (A = 0, B = 1, C = 2, etc., or bit 7 is set if the drive is a hard disk). The side, or head, is specified in DH and can be 0 or 1. CH and CL contain the track and sector, respectively. These values will vary depending on the type of disk drive in use. The number of sectors to be read is specified in AL.

The final registers to be set up specify which RAM area will be used as a buffer for the sectors that are read. This address is specified in ES:BX. You need to know the size of each disk sector ahead of time because this information determines how large the RAM buffer should be. For instance, if each disk sector contains 512 bytes, and you are going to read 4 sectors, the length of your buffer should be 2K, or 2048 bytes.

This service checks parameters only on the requested drive number (DL); all other passed parameters are not checked for validity. If you pass invalid parameters, the results are unpredictable. Table 15.7 shows some typical parameter ranges for this service.

Table 15.7. *Parameter ranges for service 13/2 using a 360K disk.*

Parameter	Register	Valid range
# of sectors	AL	1 through 9
Track	CH	0 through 39
Sector	CL	1 through 9
Head (side)	DH	0 or 1
Drive	DL	0 = A, 1 = B, 2 = C, etc.

On return from this service, the carry flag signifies whether an error occurred. If the carry flag is not set, AH will contain a zero (0). If the carry flag is set, AH will contain the disk status byte described under service 13/1 (refer to table 15.6). If an error occurs during reading, use service 13/0 to reset the disk system before you attempt another read.

Note: In this service and service 13/3, a particularly confusing error may occur. DMA boundary error (AH=9) means that an illegal boundary was crossed when the information was placed into RAM. Direct Memory Access (DMA) is used by the disk service routines to place information into RAM. If a memory offset address ending in three zeros (ES:1000, ES:2000, ES:3000, etc.) falls in the middle of the area being overlaid by a sector, this error will occur. You must calculate and read a much smaller chunk so that this type of memory boundary corresponds with a sector boundary. I don't know why this happens; it is simply frustrating as heck to a programmer.

Write Disk Sectors (Interrupt 13h, service 3)

Category: Disk services

Registers on Entry:

AH: 3
AL: Number of sectors
BX: Offset address of data buffer
CH: Track
CL: Sector
DH: Head (side) number
DL: Drive number
ES: Segment address of data buffer

Registers on Return:

AH: Return code

Memory Affected: None

Syntax:

```
MOV     AL,9                      ;Write entire track
MOV     CH,TRACK                  ;Specify track
MOV     CL,SECTOR                 ;  and sector
MOV     DH,SIDE                   ;Specify side
MOV     DL,DRIVE                  ;Specify drive
PUSH    DS                        ;Point ES to proper
POP     ES                        ;  segment address
MOV     BX,OFFSET ES:BUFFER       ;Offset of buffer area
MOV     AH,3                      ;Specify service 3
INT     13h                       ;BIOS disk interrupt
```

Description: This service, which controls writing to the disk, is the opposite of service 13/2, which controls reading from the disk.

To use this service, you must specify (in ES:BX) which RAM area will be used as the buffer for the sectors that are written. This buffer area must contain all of the information that you want written to the disk. You must know the size of the sectors being written on the disk because this service calculates, based on the sector size and the number of sectors to write (AH), the amount of RAM to read and subsequently write. The preceding example requires a buffer of 4068 bytes (4.5K), assuming that each sector requires 512 bytes.

By setting up the other registers, you determine the precise physical location on the disk at which you wish to begin writing. The drive is specified in DL (A = 0, B = 1, C = 2, etc., or bit 7 is set if the drive is a hard disk). The side, or head, is specified in DH, which can be 0 or 1. CH and CL contain the track and sector, respectively. (These values will vary, depending on the type of disk drive in use.) In AL, specify the number of sectors to be written.

This service checks parameters only on the requested drive number (DL); all other passed parameters are not checked for validity. If you pass invalid parameters, the results are unpredictable and may result in errors or damaged disks. (Some typical parameter ranges for this service are listed in table 15.7.)

On return from this service, the carry flag signifies whether an error occurred. If the carry flag is not set, AH contains a zero (0). If the carry flag is set, AH contains the disk status byte as detailed in service 13/1 (refer to table 15.6). If an error occurs during the writing operation, use service 13/0 to reset the disk system before you attempt another write operation.

Note: In this service and service 13/2, a particularly confusing error may occur. DMA boundary error (AH=9) means that an illegal boundary was crossed when the information was placed into RAM. Direct Memory Access (DMA) is used by the disk service routines to place information into RAM. This error will occur if a memory offset address ending in three zeros (ES:1000, ES:2000, ES:3000, etc.) is crossed before this service completes reading an entire sector of information. You must calculate and reread so that this type of memory boundary corresponds with a sector boundary.

Verify Disk Sectors (Interrupt 13h, service 4)

Category: Disk services

Registers on Entry:

AH: 4
AL: Number of sectors
CH: Track
CL: Sector
DH: Head (side) number
DL: Drive number

Registers on Return:

AH: Return code

Memory Affected: None

Syntax:

```
MOV    AL,9           ;Verify entire track
MOV    CH,TRACK       ;Specify track
MOV    CL,SECTOR      ;  and sector
MOV    DH,SIDE        ;Specify side
MOV    DL,DRIVE       ;Specify drive
MOV    AH,4           ;Specify service 4
INT    13h            ;BIOS disk interrupt
```

Description: Use this service to verify the address fields of the specified disk sectors. No data is transferred to or from the disk during this operation. Disk verification, which takes place on the disk, does not (as some people believe) involve verification of the data on the disk against the data in memory. Notice that this function has no buffer specification. This function does not read or write a disk; rather, it causes the system to read the data in the designated sector or sectors and to check its computed Cyclic Redundancy Check (CRC) against data stored on the disk.

The CRC is a sophisticated checksum that detects a high percentage of any errors that may occur. When a sector is written to disk, an original CRC is calculated and written along with the sector data. The verification service reads the sector, recalculates the CRC, and compares the recalculated CRC with the original CRC. If they agree, there is a high probability that the data is correct; if they disagree, an error condition is generated.

You set up the registers to determine the precise physical location on the disk at which you wish to begin verification. The drive is specified in DL (A = 0, B = 1, C = 2, etc.). The side, or head, is specified in DH and can be 0 or 1. CH and CL contain the track and sector, respectively. These values will vary, depending on the type of disk drive in use. Specify in AL the number of sectors to be verified.

This service checks parameters only on the requested drive number (DL); all other passed parameters are not checked for validity. If you pass invalid parameters, the results are unpredictable and may result in errors or damaged disks. (For some typical parameter ranges for this service, refer to table 15.7.)

On return from this service, the carry flag signifies whether an error occurred. If the carry flag is not set, AH contains a zero (0). If the carry flag is set, AH contains the disk status bits as detailed in service 13/1 (refer to table 15.6). If an error occurs during the writing operation, use service 13/0 to reset the disk system before attempting another read, write, or verify operation.

Format Disk Track (Interrupt 13h, service 5)

Category: Disk services

Registers on Entry:

AH: 5
BX: Offset address of track address fields
CH: Track
DH: Head (side) number
DL: Drive number
ES: Segment address of track address fields

Registers on Return:

AH: Return code

Memory Affected: None

Syntax:

```
MOV     CH,TRACK                    ;Specify track
MOV     DH,SIDE                     ;Specify side
MOV     DL,DRIVE                    ;Specify drive
PUSH    DS                          ;Point ES to proper
POP     ES                          ;  segment address
MOV     BX,OFFSET ES:ADR_FIELD      ;Offset of address fields
MOV     AH,5                        ;Specify service 5
INT     13h                         ;BIOS disk interrupt
```

Description: Use this service to format a specific track on a disk. To format an entire disk, you must "step through" each track, invoking this service for each track.

The registers to be set up specify the disk track to be formatted (CH) and the side, or head. Specify the side (which can be 0 or 1) in DH. Specify the drive in DL (A = 0, B = 1, C = 2, etc.). Because an entire track is formatted at one time, this service does not require a specification for the starting sector or the number of sectors.

Notice that ES:BX contains the address of an area referred to as the *track address fields*, a collection of fields that indicate specific information about each sector on the track. Some of this information is written to the sector header so that the sector being formatted can subsequently be located with read, write, or verify operations.

The track address fields consist of four bytes for each sector on the track. These four bytes detail the following information in the following order:

Cylinder (track)
Head (side)
Record (sector number)
Size code

In common computerese, the *cylinder*, *head*, and *record* information are the track, side, and sector numbers, respectively. Clearly, the sector number will vary. But the track and side numbers are the same for all of the track address fields. These numbers do not have to be in sequential order; they can be interleaved to enhance disk performance or for some other special purpose. Regardless of the order denoted by this entry (the record field) into the track address fields, the sectors are placed physically on the disk in the order indicated by the position of the address field. Although this description may sound confusing, it corresponds to physical and logical placement of sectors on the disk.

Physically, the sectors are always arranged in sequential order (for example, from 1 through 9 for a 360K DS/DD disk). Logically, however, physical sector 1 may have a sector address mark that is not 1. The following example shows two typical interleave schemes in which consecutive logical sectors are placed physically either two or five sectors apart. The logical numbers are those entered in the address fields.

Physical order	1	2	3	4	5	6	7	8	9
Logical order	1	6	2	7	3	8	4	9	5
Logical order	1	3	5	7	9	2	4	6	8

IBM microcomputers read sectors from the disk logically (by their sector address), not physically (by their placement on the disk).

The *size code* is nothing more than an indicator of the number of bytes the sector will contain. The size code may vary from 0 to 3 (see table 15.8).

Table 15.8. *Valid size codes for use in service 13/5 track address fields.*

Size code	Bytes per sector
0	128
1	256
2	512
3	1024

If you understand the makeup of the track address fields, you easily can compose the 36 bytes necessary for formatting a 360K DS/DD disk. If you were writing the sectors in sequential order on side 0 of track 5, the bytes would appear as follows (for clarity, an extra space has been inserted between every four bytes):

5012 5022 5032 5042 5052 5062 5072 5082 5092

If you were constructing the same track address fields for an interleaved track with an interleave factor of 5, the bytes would appear as follows:

5012 5032 5052 5072 5092 5022 5042 5062 5082

On return from this service, the carry flag signifies whether an error occurred. If the carry flag is not set, AH contains a zero (0). If the carry flag is set, AH contains the disk status bits as detailed in service 13/1 (refer to table 15.6). If an error occurs during the formatting operation, use service 13/0 to reset the disk system before you attempt to reformat the track.

The following stripped-down, bare-bones routine to format any given track of a disk was written to format a DS/DD 360K disk on an IBM PC, PC XT, or compatible computer. To format different types of disks, you would have to change the data beginning at ADR_FIELD, as well as the logic that changes this area and controls the formatting of both sides of the disk.

To format a DS/DD 360K disk on an IBM Personal Computer AT or compatible, you must use additional BIOS services to ensure that the parameters are set properly for the formatting operation. To do this setup work and to perform the formatting properly, you would call the subroutine FMT_AT_TRK.

Note: The following routine is a subroutine only; you must incorporate it into another program.

```
TRUE            EQU     -1
FALSE           EQU     0

FMT_TYPE        DB      01                  ;1=360K in 360K drive
                                            ;2=360K in 1.2M drive
                                            ;3=1.2M in 1.2M drive
                                            ;4=720K in 720K drive


CUR_DISK        DB      00
CUR_TRACK       DB      00
RETRY_CNT       DB      00

RECOVERABLE     DB      00                  ;Flag: TRUE=recoverable
                                            ;      FALSE=not recoverable
BAD_SPOT_FLAG   DB      00                  ;FLAG: TRUE=bad spots
                                            ;      FALSE=none bad

ADR_FIELD       DW      0000                ;Track/side
                DB      01                  ;Sector number
                DB      02                  ;Size code=512 bytes/sector

                DW      0000                ;Track/side
                DB      02                  ;Sector number
                DB      02                  ;Size code=512 bytes/sector

                DW      0000                ;Track/side
                DB      03                  ;Sector number
                DB      02                  ;Size code=512 bytes/sector

                DW      0000                ;Track/side
                DB      04                  ;Sector number
                DB      02                  ;Size code=512 bytes/sector

                DW      0000                ;Track/side
                DB      05                  ;Sector number
                DB      02                  ;Size code=512 bytes/sector
```

```
            DW       0000                    ;Track/side
            DB       06                      ;Sector number
            DB       02                      ;Size code=512 bytes/sector

            DW       0000                    ;Track/side
            DB       07                      ;Sector number
            DB       02                      ;Size code=512 bytes/sector

            DW       0000                    ;Track/side
            DB       08                      ;Sector number
            DB       02                      ;Size code=512 bytes/sector

            DW       0000                    ;Track/side
            DB       09                      ;Sector number
            DB       02                      ;Size code=512 bytes/sector

; ----------------------------------------------------------------
; HANDLE FORMATTING A SINGLE TRACK ON AN AT - 360K DS/DD
;        BEFORE CALLING, MAKE SURE FMT_TYPE IS SET TO THE PROPER
;        VALUE BASED ON THE TYPE OF DRIVE BEING USED TO FORMAT
;        THE 360K DISK
; ----------------------------------------------------------------

FMT_AT_TRK      PROC     NEAR
                PUSH     AX
                PUSH     BX
                PUSH     DX
                PUSH     ES

                MOV      AL,FMT_TYPE             ;Set DASD for drive
                MOV      DL,CUR_DISK             ;Set for drive
                MOV      AH,17h                  ;Set for function 17h
                INT      13h                     ;Call BIOS disk service

                MOV      AH,35h                  ;Get interrupt vector
                MOV      AL,1Eh                  ;Disk base table vector
                INT      21h                     ;DOS service to get vector
                ADD      BX,7                    ;Offset to format gap length
                MOV      AL,ES:[BX]              ;Get current gap length
                PUSH     AX                      ;Store original value
                MOV      BYTE PTR ES:[BX],50h    ;Set TO appropriate gap
                DEC      BX                      ;Point to proper field:
                DEC      BX                      ;  last sector (sectors
```

```
            DEC     BX                      ;  per track)
            MOV     AL,ES:[BX]              ;Get current last sector
            PUSH    AX                      ;Store original value
            MOV     BYTE PTR ES:[BX],9      ;Set for 9 sectors/track
            PUSH    BX                      ;Save offset address
            PUSH    ES                      ;Save segment address

            CALL    FMT_TRACK               ;Go format the track

            POP     ES                      ;Get segment back
            POP     BX                      ;Get offset back
            POP     AX                      ;Get original value back
            MOV     ES:[BX],AL              ;Restore last sector value
            INC     BX                      ;Point to proper field:
            INC     BX                      ;  format gap length
            INC     BX                      ;
            POP     AX                      ;Get original value back
            MOV     ES:[BX],AL              ;Restore last sector value

            POP     ES
            POP     DX
            POP     BX
            POP     AX
            RET

FMT_AT_TRK  ENDP


; ----------------------------------------------------------------
; HANDLE FORMATTING A SINGLE TRACK - 360K DS/DD
; ----------------------------------------------------------------

FMT_TRACK   PROC    NEAR
            PUSH    AX
            PUSH    BX
            PUSH    CX
            PUSH    DX
            PUSH    ES

            PUSH    CS                      ;Data and code segments
            POP     ES                      ;  are the same

            MOV     AL,CUR_TRACK            ;Move track number
            MOV     AH,1                    ;Counter for heads done
```

```
FD_A:          MOV     DH,AH                  ;Formatting two sides
               MOV     RETRY_CNT,3            ;Allow 3 retries/track

               MOV     CX,9                   ;Want to do 9 fields
               MOV     BX,OFFSET ADR_FIELD    ;Starting here
FD_B:          MOV     [BX],AX
               ADD     BX,4                   ;Point at next field
               LOOP    FD_B

FD_C:          MOV     BX,OFFSET ADR_FIELD    ;Data area for formatting
               MOV     DL,CUR_DISK            ;Set for drive
               MOV     CH,CUR_TRACK           ;Move track number
               MOV     CL,1
               MOV     AH,5                   ;Want to format a track
               INT     13h                    ;ROM BIOS diskette services
               JC      FMT_ERROR              ;If error, go handle

               MOV     AX,ADR_FIELD           ;Get current track/head
               DEC     AH                     ;Decrement head
               JZ      FD_A                   ;If zero, loop

FD_EXIT:       POP     ES
               POP     DX
               POP     CX
               POP     BX
               POP     AX
               RET

FMT_ERROR:     CALL    DO_ERROR
               CMP     RECOVERABLE,TRUE       ;Was the error recoverable?
               JE      FD_C                   ;Yes, do it again
               DEC     RETRY_CNT_FMT
               JNZ     FD_C
               MOV     BAD_SPOT_FLAG,TRUE     ;Set flag for bad spots
               JMP     FD_EXIT

FMT_TRACK      ENDP


; ----------------------------------------------------------------
; HANDLE ERRORS THAT OCCUR DURING FORMATTING A TRACK
; ----------------------------------------------------------------
```

```
DO_ERROR        PROC    NEAR
                MOV     RECOVERABLE,FALSE     ;Assume non-recoverable
                PUSH    AX                    ;Save current status byte
                XOR     AX,AX                 ;Zero out, reset disk system
                INT     13h                   ;ROM BIOS diskette services
                POP     AX                    ;Get status byte back
                CMP     AH,03h                ;Was it a write protect?
                JE      DE_C                  ;Yes, go handle
                CMP     AH,80h                ;Was it time out?
                JNE     DE_EXIT               ;No, so exit
DE_C:           MOV     RECOVERABLE,TRUE      ;Recoverable error

DE_EXIT:        RET
DO_ERROR        ENDP
```

If an error is detected during formatting, the routine DO_ERROR is called. This routine can be improved. For example, although DO_ERROR considers write-protect and timeout errors as recoverable, no allowance is made for the program to pause while the operator corrects the source of the errors. You can easily add a pause in your programs.

(For additional information about the disk base table, see Appendix B.)

Return Drive Parameters (Interrupt 13h, service 8)

Category: Disk services

Registers on Entry:

AH: 8

DL: drive number (0 based)
    bit 7 is set if fixed disk

Registers on Return:

CH: Number of tracks/side
CL: Number of sectors/track
DH: Number of sides
DL: Number of consecutive drives attached

Memory Affected: None

Syntax:

```
MOV    DL,80h              ;Use first hard disk drive
MOV    AH,8               ;Specify service 8
INT    13h                ;BIOS disk interrupt
```

Description: Use this service to retrieve disk parameters for a disk drive. *(This service is available only on the IBM Personal Computer AT.)*

Notice that when you call this service, you will specify the disk drive number in DL (80h for the first fixed disk, 81h for the second, etc.). These numbers do not correspond to the standard BIOS disk-number scheme. If you attempt the service with any out-of-range *fixed* disk drive numbers (those below 80h), an error will be returned.

On return from this service, the carry flag signifies whether an error occurred. If the carry flag is not set, AH contains a zero (0). If the carry flag is set, AH contains the disk status bits as detailed in service 13/1 (refer to table 15.6).

Initialize Fixed Disk Table (Interrupt 13h, service 9)

Category: Disk services

Registers on Entry:

AH: 9
DL: Fixed disk drive number

Registers on Return: Unchanged

Memory Affected: None

Syntax:

```
MOV    DL,80h              ;Use first disk drive
MOV    AH,9               ;Specify service 9
INT    13h                ;BIOS disk interrupt
```

Description: Use this service to initialize the fixed disk parameter tables for a specific drive. *(This service is available only on the IBM Personal Computer AT and works only with fixed disks.)*

Notice that when you call this service, you will specify the fixed disk drive number in DL (80h for the first fixed disk, 81h for the second, etc.) These numbers do not correspond to the standard BIOS disk numbering scheme. If you attempt the service with any out-of-range fixed disk drive numbers (those below 80h), an error will be returned.

On return from this service, the carry flag signifies whether an error occurred. If the carry flag is not set, AH contains a zero (0). If the carry flag is set, AH contains the disk status byte as detailed in service 13/1 (refer to table 15.6).

The fixed disk parameter tables for as many as two fixed disks are contained in RAM at the memory addresses pointed to by interrupt vectors 41h and 46h.

Read Long Sectors (Interrupt 13h, service 0Ah)

Category: Disk services

Registers on Entry:

AH: 0Ah
AL: Number of sectors
BX: Offset address of data buffer
CH: Track
CL: Sector
DH: Head (side) number
DL: Fixed disk drive number
ES: Segment address of data buffer

Registers on Return:

AH: Return code

Memory Affected: RAM data buffer starting at memory address ES:BX is overwritten by sectors requested from the fixed disk.

Syntax:

```
MOV     AL,1                    ;Reading 1 sector
MOV     CH,LOW_TRACK            ;Specify low-order track
MOV     CL,HIGH_TRACK           ;Specify high-order track
MOV     BL,6                    ;Want to shift 6 bits
SHL     CL,BL                   ;   left, place in bits 6/7
OR      CL,SECTOR               ;Place sector in bits 0-5
MOV     DH,SIDE                 ;Specify side
MOV     DL,80h                  ;Use first disk drive
PUSH    DS                      ;Point ES to proper
POP     ES                      ;   segment address
MOV     BX,OFFSET ES:BUFFER     ;Offset of buffer area
MOV     AH,0Ah                  ;Specify service 0Ah
INT     13h                     ;BIOS disk interrupt
```

Description: Use this service to control reading long sectors from the IBM Personal Computer AT's 20M fixed disk drive. (This service, *which is available only on the IBM Personal Computer AT and works only with fixed disks*, is the opposite of service 13/0B, which controls writing long sectors to the fixed disk.) A long sector consists of a regular sector of data and four bytes of error-correction information used to verify the information that is read from the fixed disk.

To use this service, you must specify the precise physical location on the fixed disk at which you want to begin reading. In DL, specify the fixed disk drive number (80h for the first fixed disk, 81h for the second, etc.). These numbers do not correspond to the standard BIOS disk numbering scheme. If you attempt the service with any out-of-range fixed disk drive numbers (those below 80h), an error will be returned.

In DH, specify the side, or head, which may vary from 0 to 15. CH and CL contain the track and sector, respectively. These values, which will vary depending on the size of fixed disk used, are normally in the range specified in table 15.9. Track (CH) and sector (CL) information in the table are encoded according to the description for this service.

Table 15.9. *Parameter ranges for service 13/A on an IBM Personal Computer AT.*

Parameter	Register	Valid range
# of sectors	AL	1-121
Track	CH/CL	0-1023
Sector	CL	1-17
Head (side)	DH	0-15
Drive	DL	80 = first, 81 = second, etc.

As you can see, the track range (CH) can be greater than 255, the largest number that can be contained in a single byte. Actually, the track is specified as a 10-bit number, with the two high-order bits stored in bits 7 and 6 of CL. The sector specification is stored in bits 0 through 5 of CL.

The final registers to be set up specify which RAM area will be used as a buffer for the sectors that are read. This address is specified in ES:BX. To determine the size of the RAM buffer, you must know ahead of time how large each disk sector is. For instance, if each disk sector contains 512 bytes, and you are going to read four sectors, your buffer should be 2048 bytes (2K) long.

This service checks parameters on the requested drive number (DL) only; all other passed parameters are not checked for validity. If you pass invalid parameters, the results are unpredictable.

On return from this service, the carry flag signifies whether an error occurred. If the carry flag is not set, AH will contain a zero (0). If the carry flag is set, AH will contain the disk status bits as detailed in service 13/1 (refer to table 15.6). If an error occurs during the reading operation, use service 13/0, with the fixed disk drive number in DL, to reset the fixed disk system before you attempt another read operation.

Note: In this service, a particularly confusing error may occur. DMA boundary error (AH=9) means that an illegal boundary was crossed when the information was placed into RAM. Direct Memory Access (DMA) is used by the disk service routines to place information into RAM. This error will occur if a memory offset address ending in three zeros (ES:1000, ES:2000, ES:3000, etc.) falls in the middle of the area being overlaid by a sector. You must calculate and reread so that this type of memory boundary corresponds with a sector boundary. I don't know why this happens, but it is frustrating as all get out to a programmer. (This error code consideration applies also to services 13/2, 13/3, and 13/0Bh.)

Write Long Sectors (Interrupt 13h, service 0Bh)

Category: Disk services

Registers on Entry:

AH: 0Bh
AL: Number of sectors
BX: Offset address of data buffer
CH: Track
CL: Sector
DH: Head (side) number
DL: Fixed disk drive number
ES: Segment address of data buffer

Registers on Return:

AH: Return code

Memory Affected: None

Syntax:

```
MOV    AL,17                  ;Writing entire track
MOV    CH,LOW_TRACK           ;Specify low-order track
MOV    CL,HIGH_TRACK          ;Specify high-order track
MOV    BL,6                   ;Want to shift 6 bits
SHL    CL,BL                  ;  left, place in bits 6/7
OR     CL,SECTOR              ;Place sector in bits 0-5
MOV    DH,SIDE                ;Specify side
MOV    DL,80h                 ;Use first disk drive
PUSH   DS                     ;Point ES to proper
POP    ES                     ;  segment address
MOV    BX,OFFSET ES:BUFFER    ;Offset of buffer area
MOV    AH,0Bh                 ;Specify service 0Bh
INT    13h                    ;BIOS disk interrupt
```

Description: This service, which controls writing long sectors to the IBM Personal Computer AT 20M fixed disk drive, *is available only on the IBM Personal Computer AT and works only with fixed disks.* (It is the opposite of service 13/0Ah, which controls reading long sectors from the fixed disk.) A long sector consists of a regular sector of data and four bytes of error-correction information, which is used to verify the information that is read from the fixed disk.

To use this service, you must specify (in ES:BX) which RAM area is used as the buffer for the sectors written. The area should be initialized with the desired data in the right amount. Because this service calculates the amount of RAM to read and subsequently write based on the number of sectors to write (AH) and the sector size, you must know the size of the sectors being written on the disk. Assuming that each sector requires 512 bytes, the example shown in the syntax section requires a buffer of 8,704 bytes (8.5K).

You set up other registers to determine the precise physical location on the fixed disk at which you wish to begin writing. Specify the fixed disk drive number in DL (80h for the first fixed disk, 81h for the second, etc.). These numbers do not correspond to the standard BIOS disk numbering scheme. If you attempt the service with any out-of-range fixed disk drive numbers (those below 80h), an error will be returned.

The side, or head, is specified in DH and may vary from 0 to 15. CH and CL contain the track and sector, respectively. These values, which will vary depending on the size of fixed disk used, are normally in the range specified in table 15.9 (refer to service 13/0Ah).

The track range (CH) can be greater than 255, the largest number that can be contained in a single byte. Actually, the track is specified as a 10-bit number, with the two high-order bits stored in bits 7 and 6 of CL. The sector specification is stored in bits 0 through 5 of CL.

This service checks parameters on the requested drive number (DL) only; all other passed parameters are not checked for validity. If you pass invalid parameters, the results are unpredictable.

On return from this service, the carry flag signifies whether an error occurred. If the carry flag is not set, AH contains a zero (0). If the carry flag is set, AH contains the disk status bits as detailed in service 13/1 (refer to table 15.6). If an error occurs during the reading operation, use service 13/0, with the fixed disk drive number in DL, to reset the fixed disk system before you attempt another write operation.

Note: In this service (and services 13/2, 13/3, and 13/0Ah) a particularly confusing error may occur. DMA boundary error (AH=9) means that an illegal boundary was crossed as the information was read from the RAM buffer. Direct Memory Access (DMA) is used by the disk service routines to place information into RAM. This error will occur if a memory offset address ending in three zeros (ES:1000, ES:2000, ES:3000, etc.) is crossed before this service completes reading an entire sector of information. You must calculate and reread so that this type of memory boundary corresponds with a sector boundary.

Seek Cylinder (Interrupt 13h, service 0Ch)

Category: Disk services

Registers on Entry:

AH: 0Ch
CH: Low-order track
CL: High-order track
DH: Head (side) number
DL: Fixed disk drive number

Registers on Return:

AH: Return code

Memory Affected: None

Syntax:

```
MOV    CH,LOW_TRACK        ;Specify low-order track
MOV    CL,HIGH_TRACK       ;Specify high-order track
MOV    BL,6                ;Want to shift 6 bits
SHL    CL,BL               ;  left, place in bits 6/7
MOV    DH,SIDE             ;Specify side
MOV    DL,80h              ;Use first disk drive
MOV    AH,0Ch              ;Specify service 0Ch
INT    13h                 ;BIOS disk interrupt
```

Description: Use this service to move the read/write heads of the fixed disk drive to a specific track (cylinder). *This service is available only on the IBM Personal Computer AT and works only with fixed disks.*

To use this service, you must specify the fixed disk drive number (80h for the first fixed disk, 81h for the second, etc.) in DL. These numbers do not correspond to the standard BIOS disk numbering scheme. If you attempt the service with any out-of-range fixed disk drive numbers (those below 80h), an error will be returned.

The side, or head, is specified in DH and may vary from 0 to 15. CH and CL contain the track and sector, respectively. These values, which will vary depending on the size of fixed disk used, are normally in the range specified in table 15.9 (refer to service 13/0Ah).

The track range (CH) can be greater than 255, the largest number that can be contained in a single byte. Actually, the track is specified as a 10-bit number, with the two high-order bits stored in bits 7 and 6 of CL.

This service checks parameters on the requested drive number only (DL); all other passed parameters are not checked for validity. If you pass invalid parameters, the results are unpredictable.

On return from this service, the carry flag signifies whether an error occurred. If the carry flag is not set, AH contains a zero (0). If the carry flag is set, AH contains the disk status byte as detailed in service 13/1 (refer to table 15.6).

Alternate Reset (Interrupt 13h, service 0Dh)

Category: Disk services

Registers on Entry:

AH: 0Dh
DL: Fixed disk drive number

Registers on Return:

AH: Return code

Memory Affected: None

Syntax:

```
MOV    DL,80h        ;Use first disk drive
MOV    AH,0Dh        ;Specify service Dh
INT    13h           ;BIOS disk interrupt
```

Description: This service, *which is available only on the IBM Personal Computer AT*, resets the fixed disk drive.

The IBM Personal Computer AT BIOS shows that, after compensating for the fixed disk drive specification, this service is hard-coded to the same routine address as service 13/0; there is absolutely no difference between the two services. This service apparently was included for future expansion—for the day when identical reset routines could not be used for both fixed and floppy disks.

To use this service, you must specify the fixed disk drive number (80h for the first fixed disk, 81h for the second, etc.) in DL. These numbers do not correspond to the standard BIOS disk numbering scheme. If you attempt the service with any out-of-range fixed disk drive numbers (those below 80h), an error will be returned.

When this service is called, its effect on the fixed disk drive is not apparent. The recalibrate command is sent directly to the fixed disk controller, and a reset flag is set to recalibrate the drive the next time it is used. (This recalibration consists primarily of retracting the read/write head to track 0.)

Used primarily in routines that handle critical errors, this service forces the controller to recalibrate itself on the subsequent operation. If a critical error occurs, this service is necessary for reliable operation of the fixed disk. The service forces the controller to make no assumptions about its position or condition—assumptions that may be wrong because of the previously experienced critical-error condition.

On return from this service, the carry flag signifies whether an error occurred. If the carry flag is not set, AH will contain a zero (0). If the carry flag is set, AH contains the disk status byte as detailed in service 13/1 (refer to table 15.6).

Unused (Interrupt 13H, services Eh, Fh)

These services, which are listed as unused in the IBM Personal Computer AT BIOS, will more than likely be used as peripherals as capabilities are added.

Read DASD Type (Interrupt 13h, service 15h)

Category: Disk services

Registers on Entry:

AH: 15h
DL: Drive number

Registers on Return:

AH: Return code
CX: High byte—number of fixed disk sectors
DX: Low byte—number of fixed disk sectors

Memory Affected: None

Syntax:

```
MOV    DL,0          ;Use drive A:
MOV    AH,15h        ;Specify service 15h
INT    13h           ;BIOS disk interrupt
```

Description: This service, *which is available only on the PC XT (BIOS dated 1/10/86 or later), PC XT 286, IBM Personal Computer AT, or PS/2 line*, is used to determine the Direct Access Storage Device (DASD) type of a given disk drive.

DL can contain either a normal BIOS disk drive number (0 = A, 1 = B, 2 = C, etc.) or a fixed disk drive number (80h for the first fixed disk, 81h for the second, etc.).

On return from this service, the carry flag signifies whether an error occurred. If the carry flag is set, AH contains the disk status byte as detailed in service 13/1 (refer to table 15.6). If an error occurs, use service 13/0 to reset the disk system before you attempt to use this service again.

If the carry flag is clear, the return code in AH indicates the DASD type of the drive. Table 15.10 lists the possible return codes and their meanings.

Table 15.10. DASD types for service 13/15.

Code	Meaning
0	The drive requested (DL) is not present
1	Drive present, cannot detect disk change
2	Drive present, can detect disk change
3	Fixed disk

If the return code indicates a DASD type of 3 (fixed disk), the register pair CX:DX will indicate the number of sectors on the fixed disk.

Read Disk Change Line Status (Interrupt 13h, service 16h)

Category: Disk services

Registers on Entry:

AH: 16h
DL: Drive number

Registers on Return:

AH: Return code

Memory Affected: None

Syntax:

```
MOV   DL,0      ;Use drive A:
MOV   AH,16h    ;Specify service 16h
INT   13h       ;BIOS disk interrupt
```

Description: Use this service, *which is available only on the PC XT (BIOS dated 1/10/86 or later), PC XT 286, IBM Personal Computer AT, or PS/2 line*, to determine whether the disk in a drive has been changed.

The result code in AH will be either a zero (0) or a 6. A 0 means that the disk has not been changed; a 6 means that it has. If the disk has not been changed, the carry flag will be clear; if the disk has been changed, the carry flag will be set.

The use of the carry flag can have strange consequences in this service. The carry flag is set not only if an error has occurred but also if the disk has been changed. Because having two uses for the carry flag can be confusing, be sure to check the contents of AH for the true result code. If AH is 0, and the carry flag is set, you know that an error has occurred. AH can

Part IV: Reference

then be assumed to contain the disk status byte as detailed in service 13/1 (refer to table 15.6).

Even if there is no disk in the drive, this service works and does not generate an error. The drive is activated and checked, and if no disk is present, a result of 6 is returned. If this service is called several times with no intervening disk access, the same result code is returned repetitively. For instance, if you request a disk's directory and then invoke this service, a result code of 0 will be returned. If you then change the disk, a result code of 6 is generated. If you leave the same disk in the drive and again call this service, a result code of 6 will again be returned. A result code of 0, indicating that there has been no change, will be returned only after the disk has been read.

Set DASD Type for Format (Interrupt 13h, service 17h)

Category: Disk services

Registers on Entry:

AH: 17h
AL: DASD format type
DL: Drive number

Registers on Return: Unchanged

Memory Affected: None

Syntax:

```
MOV    AL,3        ;Set DASD for 1.2M
MOV    DL,0        ;Set drive A:
MOV    AH,17h      ;Specify service 17h
INT    13h         ;BIOS disk interrupt
```

Description: Use this service with service 13/5 to format a disk. You must use this service, *which is available only on the PC XT (BIOS dated 1/10/86 or later), PC XT 286, IBM Personal Computer AT, or PS/2 line,* to specify not only the type of disk to format but also the type of drive in which that disk will be formatted.

The DASD format type specified in AL can be a number from 1 to 3 (see table 15.11).

Table 15.11. DASD format types for service 13/17.

Type	Meaning
1	Formatting a 320/360K disk in a 320/360K drive
2	Formatting a 320/360K disk in a 1.2M drive
3	Formatting a 1.2M disk in a 1.2M drive

For more information on the proper use of this service, see the discussion and sample routines for service 13/5.

Set Media Type for Format (Interrupt 13h, service 18h)

Category: Disk services

Registers on Entry:

AH: 18h
CH: Number of tracks
CL: Sectors per track
DL: Drive number (zero based)

Registers on Return:

DI: Offset address of 11-byte parameter table
ES: Segment address of 11-byte parameter table

Memory Affected: None

Syntax:

```
MOV     CH,39       ;Set for 40 tracks
MOV     CL,9        ;Set 9 sectors
MOV     DL,0        ;Set drive A:
MOV     AH,18h      ;Specify service 18h
INT     13h         ;BIOS disk interrupt
```

Description: This service, *which is available only on the PC XT (BIOS dated 1/10/86 or later), PC XT 286, IBM Personal Computer AT, or PS/2 line*, specifies to the formatting routines the number of tracks and sectors per track to be placed on the media. You will not normally use this service; it makes possible the creation of nonstandard track layouts.

Park Heads (Interrupt 13h, service 19h)

Category: Disk services

Registers on Entry:

> AH: 19h
> DL: Drive number, zero based and HD coded

Registers on Return: Not significant

Memory Affected: None

Syntax:

```
MOV    DL,80h    ;First fixed drive (C:)
MOV    AH,19h    ;Request park heads service
INT    13h       ;BIOS disk service interrupt
```

Description: This service, *which is available only on the PC XT (BIOS dated 1/10/86 or later), PC XT 286, IBM Personal Computer AT, or PS/2 line*, moves the heads of the specified fixed disk drive to a "safe" storage position.

Format ESDI Unit (Interrupt 13h, service 1Ah)

Category: Disk services

Registers on Entry:

> AH: 1Ah
> AL: 0 = no defect table
>   <> 0 = use defect table
> ES: Segment address of defect table
> BX: Offset address of defect table
> CL: modifier bits:

Bits	
76543210	*Meaning*
1	Ignore primary defect map
1	Ignore secondary defect map
1	Update secondary defect map
1	Perform extended surface analysis
1	Turn periodic interrupts ON
xxx	Reserved

> DL: Drive number (zero based)

Registers on Return: Not significant

Memory Affected: None

Description: This service, *which is available only on the PS/2 line models 50, 60, and 80*, reformats an ESDI disk unit. You should never need to use it.

Initialize Communications Port (Interrupt 14h, service 0)

Category: Communications services

Registers on Entry:

AH: 0
AL: Initialization parameter
DX: Communications port

Registers on Return:

AH: Line status
AL: Modem status

Memory Affected: None

Syntax:

```
MOV     AL,10000011b        ;Set for 1200/N/8/1
MOV     DX,0                ;Set COM1:
MOV     AH,0                ;Specify service 0
INT     14h                 ;BIOS comm. interrupt
```

Description: This service is used to initialize the communications (RS-232) port specified in DX. The contents of DX can vary from 0 to 3 (corresponding to COM1:, COM2:, COM3:, and COM4:).

In AL, you specify how the communications port should be initialized. This service allows you to set the baud rate, parity, data length, and stop bits. Specify these settings through the bits of register AL, according to the coding scheme shown in table 15.12.

This service returns two values, which correspond to the asynchronous chip's line status (AH) and modem status (AL) registers. These return values, which indicate the status and condition of the asynchronous communications adapter, are the same as those returned in service 14/3. The meaning of each bit of the line status register is shown in table 15.13; table 15.14 lists the meaning of the modem status register.

Table 15.12. *Meaning of AL bits for service 14/0.*

Bits 76543210	Meaning
000	110 baud
001	150 baud
010	300 baud
011	600 baud
100	1200 baud
101	2400 baud
110	4800 baud
111	9600 baud
00	No parity
01	Odd parity
10	No parity
11	Even parity
0	1 stopbit
1	2 stopbits
10	7-bit data length
11	8-bit data length

Table 15.13. *The line status register bit meanings.*

Bits 76543210	Meaning
1	Time-out error
1	Transfer shift register (TSR) empty
1	Transfer holding register (THR) empty
1	Break interrupt detected
1	Framing error
1	Parity error
1	Overrun error
1	Data ready

Table 15.14 The modem status register bit meanings.

Bits 76543210	Meaning
1	Receive line signal detect
1	Ring indicator
1	Data set ready (DSR)
1	Clear to send (CTS)
1	Delta receive line signal detect
1	Trailing edge ring detector
1	Delta data set ready (DDSR)
1	Delta clear to send (DCTS)

Note that the value in AH, which corresponds to the line status register, has an added bit. Although the meaning of bit 7 in the line status register ordinarily is undefined, BIOS uses this bit to signal that an excessive amount of time has passed since a character has been received.

Although this book does not attempt to explain the purpose, use, and interpretation of each bit in these registers, many books on asynchronous communications are available.

Transmit Character (Interrupt 14h, service 1)

Category: Communications services

Registers on Entry:

AH: 1
AL: ASCII character
DX: Communications port

Registers on Return:

AH: Return code

Memory Affected: None

Syntax:

```
MOV    AL,'T'          ;Send the letter 'T'
MOV    DX,0            ;Set COM1:
MOV    AH,1            ;Specify service 1
INT    14h            ;BIOS comm. interrupt
```

Description: This service sends a character to the communications (RS-232) port specified in DX. The contents of DX can vary from 0 to 3 (corresponding to COM1:, COM2:, COM3:, and COM4:). Before calling this service for the first time, make sure that service 14/0 has been used to initialize the communications port.

The character to be sent should be loaded in AL. The transmission was successful if the high-order bit of AH is clear (AH < 80h) on return. Table 15.13 shows the balance of the bits in AH after a successful transmission.

If the transmission was unsuccessful, the high-order bit will be set (AH > 7Fh) and the balance of AH will appear as in table 15.13.

Receive Character (Interrupt 14h, service 2)

Category: Communications services

Registers on Entry:

> AH: 2
> DX: Communications port

Registers on Return:

> AH: Return code

Memory Affected: None

Syntax:

```
MOV    DX,0        ;Set COM1:
MOV    AH,2        ;Specify service 2
INT    14h         ;BIOS comm. interrupt
```

Description: This service is used to receive a character from the communications (RS-232) port specified in DX. The contents of DX can vary from 0 to 3 (corresponding to COM1:, COM2:, COM3:, and COM4:). Before calling this service for the first time, make sure that you have used service 14/0 to initialize the communications port.

Because this service waits for a character, other computer processing is suspended until the character is received or until the communications port returns an error.

On return, AH contains a return code. In this return code, which is analogous to the line control register's return values of service 14/3, only the error bits are used (refer to table 15.13).

If you set AL to 0 before calling this service, you can quickly test whether a character was received. Because most receiving software discards NULL characters (ASCII value of 0), no action need be taken even if a null character is received; your routine can continue to await an incoming character.

Get Communications Port Status (Interrupt 14h, service 3)

Category: Communications services

Registers on Entry:

AH: 3
DX: Communications port

Registers on Return:

AH: Line status
AL: Modem status

Memory Affected: None

Syntax:

```
MOV    DX,0         ;Set COM1:
MOV    AH,3         ;Specify service 3
INT    14h          ;BIOS comm. interrupt
```

Description: Use this service to check the status of the communications line and the modem. The communications (RS-232) port is specified in DX. The contents of DX can vary from 0 to 3 (corresponding to COM1:, COM2:, COM3:, and COM4:).

This service returns two values, which correspond to the asynchronous chip's line status (AH) and modem status (AL) registers. The meaning of each line status register bit is shown in table 15.13; that of each modem status register bit, in table 15.14.

Notice that the value in AH, which corresponds to the line status register, has an added bit. Although the meaning of bit 7 in the line status register is undefined, BIOS uses this bit to signal that too much time has passed since a character has been received.

Although this book does not attempt to explain the purpose, use, and interpretation of each bit in these registers, many books on asynchronous communications are available.

Extended Communications Port Initialization (Interrupt 14h, service 4)

Category: Communications services

Registers on Entry:

```
AH: 04h
AL: 00h = no break
    01h = break
BH: 00h = no parity
    01h = odd parity
    02h = even parity
    03h = mark parity
    04h = space parity
BL: 00h = one stop bit
    01h = two stop bits
CH: 00h = 5 data bits
    01h = 6 data bits
    02h = 7 data bits
    03h = 8 data bits
CL: 00h = 110 BPS
    01h = 150 BPS
    02h = 300 BPS
    03h = 600 BPS
    04h = 1200 BPS
    05h = 2400 BPS
    06h = 4800 BPS
    07h = 9600 BPS
    08h = 19200 BPS
DX: Serial port (0 = COM1, etc.)
```

Registers on Return:

```
AH: Port status (table 15.13)
AL: Modem status (table 15.14)
```

Memory Affected: None

Syntax:

```
MOV     AH,04h      ;extended initialization function
MOV     AL,0        ;no break
MOV     BH,2        ;even parity
MOV     BL,0        ;1 stop bit
MOV     CH,2        ;7 data bits
```

```
MOV     CL,4        ;1200 BPS
MOV     DX,0        ;COM1
INT     14h         ;communications service
```

Description: This service, *available only on the PS/2 line*, greatly simplifies the initialization of the communications ports.

Extended Communications Port Control (Interrupt 14h, service 5)

Category: Communications services

Registers on Entry:

AH: 05h
AL: 00h, Read modem control register
    01h, Write modem control register
BL: New MCR content if AL=01h
DX: Serial port (0 = COM1, etc.)

Registers on Return:

AH: Port status (table 15.13)
AL: Modem status (table 15.14)
BL: Modem control register (see Chapter 14):

Bits	
76543210	*Meaning*
1	Data terminal ready (DTR)
1	Request to send (RTS)
1	User 1
1	User 2
1	Loopback test
xxx	Reserved

Memory Affected: None

Syntax:

```
MOV     AH,05h      ;extended MCR control function
MOV     AL,0        ;read MCR
MOV     DX,0        ;COM1
INT     14h         ;communications service
```

Description: This service, *available only on the PS/2 line*, greatly simplifies modem control through the communications ports.

Turn On Cassette Motor (Interrupt 15h, service 0)

Category: Cassette services

Registers on Entry:

AH: 0

Registers on Return:

AH: Return code

Memory Affected: None

Syntax:

```
MOV   AH,0        ;Specify service 0
INT   15h         ;BIOS cassette interrupt
```

Description: This service (the opposite of service 15/1) turns on the cassette motor. Because this service works only on older models of the PC, using it on the IBM PC XT or Personal Computer AT causes the return of an 86h in AH and sets the carry flag.

Turn Off Cassette Motor (Interrupt 15h, service 1)

Category: Cassette services

Registers on Entry:

AH: 1

Registers on Return:

AH: Return code

Memory Affected: None

Syntax:

```
MOV   AH,1        ;Specify service 1
INT   15h         ;BIOS cassette interrupt
```

Description: This service (the opposite of service 15/0) turns off the cassette motor. Because this service works only on older models of the PC, using it on the IBM PC XT or Personal Computer AT causes the return of an 86h in AH and sets the carry flag.

Read Data Blocks from Cassette (Interrupt 15h, service 2)

Category: Cassette services

Registers on Entry:

AH: 2
BX: Offset address of data buffer
CX: Number of bytes to read
ES: Segment address of data buffer

Registers on Return:

AH: Return code
DX: Number of bytes read

Memory Affected: RAM buffer area specified by address starting at ES:BX is overwritten with bytes requested from cassette.

Syntax:

```
MOV    CX,NUM_BYTES          ;Read this many bytes
PUSH   DS                    ;Point ES to proper
POP    ES                    ;  segment address
MOV    BX,OFFSET ES:BUFFER   ;Offset of buffer area
MOV    AH,2                  ;Specify service 2
INT    15h                   ;BIOS cassette interrupt
```

Description: This service reads data from the cassette tape port. Because this service works only on older models of the PC, using it on the IBM PC XT or Personal Computer AT causes the return of an 86h in AH and sets the carry flag.

Information is read from the cassette in 256-byte blocks, but only the number of bytes requested in CX are transferred to the memory address pointed to by ES:BX.

On completion, DX is set to the number of bytes actually read. If no error occurred, the carry flag is clear; if an error occurred, the carry flag is set and AH will contain an error code. The error codes shown in table 15.15 are valid only if the carry flag is set.

Table 15.15. *Error codes returned in AH for service 15/2.*

AH	Meaning
0h	Invalid command
1h	CRC error
2h	Data transitions lost
3h	No data located on tape
86h	No cassette port available

Write Data Blocks to Cassette (Interrupt 15h, service 3)

Category: Cassette services

Registers on Entry:

AH: 3
BX: Offset address of data buffer
CX: Number of bytes to write
ES: Segment address of data buffer

Registers on Return:

AH: Return code

Memory Affected: None

Syntax:

```
MOV    CX,NUM_BYTES          ;Write this many bytes
PUSH   DS                    ;Point ES to proper
POP    ES                    ;  segment address
MOV    BX,OFFSET ES:BUFFER   ;Offset of buffer area
MOV    AH,3                  ;Specify service 3
INT    15h                   ;BIOS cassette interrupt
```

Description: This service writes data to the cassette tape port. Because this service works only on older models of the PC, using it on the IBM PC XT or Personal Computer AT causes the return of an 86h in AH and sets the carry flag.

Information is written to the cassette in 256-byte blocks, but only the number of bytes indicated in CX are transferred from the memory address pointed to by ES:BX.

If an error is detected when this service is invoked, the carry flag is set and AH will contain an error code (see table 15.16). These error codes, which are valid only if the carry flag is set, indicate only syntactical errors. Neither of the errors returned indicates that information was written improperly to the cassette.

Table 15.16. Error codes returned in AH for service 15/3.

AH	Meaning
0h	Invalid command
86h	No cassette port available

ESDI Format Hook (Interrupt 15h, service 0Fh)

Category: PS/2 services

Registers on Entry:

AH: 0Fh
AL: 01h = Surface analysis
02h = Formatting
Other values reserved

Registers on Return:

Carry flag set if formatting is to stop
AH: 86h if service not available

Memory Affected: None

Description: This service, *available only on the PS/2 line*, is called by the ESDI format service after each cylinder is formatted or analyzed. If you want to perform some action at that time, you can set the INT 15h vector to your own routine, trap the condition of AH = 0Fh, and chain on to the existing BIOS code for all other conditions. Most programmers will never use this service.

If called on older PC models, this service will set the carry flag and return 86h in AH (or 80h on original PC and PCjr models) to indicate that the service is invalid on the model.

On return from this service, the carry flag signifies one of two things: If the carry flag is set and AH contains 86h, then the service is not available; if AH contains some other value, then formatting is to stop.

Keyboard Intercept Hook (Interrupt 15h, service 4Fh)

Category: Keyboard

Registers on Entry:

AH: 4Fh
AL: Keyboard scan code

Registers on Return:

AL: New scan code if changed, original code otherwise

Memory Affected: None

Description: This service, *available only on the PS/2 line (except Model 30)*, is called by the BIOS routine that services INT 09h each time that a scan code is received from the keyboard. If you want to provide special processing, you can intercept this service to do so. Normally, this service is never called by a programmer.

If called on older PC models, this service will set the carry flag and return 86h in AH (or 80h on original PC and PCjr models) to indicate that the service is invalid on the model.

Device Open (Interrupt 15h, service 80h)

Category: System

Registers on Entry:

AH: 80h
BX: Device ID code
CX: Process ID code

Registers on Return: Unchanged

Memory Affected: None

Syntax:

```
MOV     BX,DEVID        ;device affected
MOV     CX,PROCID       ;process owning device
MOV     AH,80h          ;service code
INT     15h             ;BIOS extension interrupt
```

Description: This service, available only on systems dated since 11/08/82, is part of the networking and multitasking interface; and as such, its use is beyond the scope of this book.

If called on older PC models, this service will set the carry flag and return 86h in AH (or 80h on original PC and PCjr models) to indicate that the service is invalid on the model.

Device Close (Interrupt 15h, service 81h)

Category: System

Registers on Entry:

AH: 81h
BX: Device ID code
CX: Process ID code

Registers on Return: Unchanged

Memory Affected: None

Syntax:

```
MOV     BX,DEVID        ;device affected
MOV     CX,PROCID       ;process owning device
MOV     AH,81h          ;service code
INT     15h             ;BIOS extension interrupt
```

Description: This service, available only on systems dated since 11/08/82, is part of the networking and multitasking interface; its use is beyond the scope of this book.

If called on older PC models, this service will set the carry flag and return 86h in AH (or 80h on original PC and PCjr models) to indicate that the service is invalid on the model.

Terminate Program (Interrupt 15h, service 82h)

Category: System

Registers on Entry:

AH: 82h
BX: Process ID code

Registers on Return: Unchanged

Memory Affected: None

Syntax:

```
MOV     BX,PROCID           ;process to terminate
MOV     AH,82h              ;service code
INT     15h                 ;BIOS extension interrupt
```

Description: This service, available only on systems dated since 11/08/82, is part of the networking and multitasking interface; its use is beyond the scope of this book.

If called on older PC models, this service will set the carry flag and return 86h in AH (or 80h on original PC and PCjr models) to indicate that the service is invalid on the model.

Event Wait (Interrupt 15h, service 83h)

Category: System

Registers on Entry:

AH: 83h
AL: 00h = set interval
  01h = cancel interval already set (PS/2 only)
BX: Offset address of byte to set when time expires
CX: High-order value of microseconds until posting
DX: Low-order value of microseconds until posting
ES: Segment address of byte to set when type expires

Registers on Return: Unchanged

Memory Affected: High-order bit of byte addressed by ES:BX will be set as soon as possible after requested time interval expires. Maximum time that can be set is approximately 70 minutes ($2**32$ microseconds).

Syntax:

```
MOV     AH,83h              ;service code
MOV     AL,00h              ;set an interval
MOV     BX,OFFSET RByte
PUSH    DS
POP     ES
MOV     CX,0                ;high word of time count
MOV     DX,10000            ;wait 1/100 second
INT     15h                 ;BIOS extension interrupt
```

Description: This service, available only on systems dated since 11/08/82, is part of the networking and multitasking interface; its use is beyond the scope of this book.

If called on older PC models, this service will set the carry flag and return 86h in AH (or 80h on original PC and PCjr models) to indicate that the service is invalid for the model.

Joystick Support (Interrupt 15h, service 84h)

Category: Miscellaneous services

Registers on Entry:

AH: 84h
DX: 00h = read switches
  01h = read joystick position

Registers on Return:

If reading switches (DX=0):
 AL = switch settings (bits 4-7)
If reading position (DX=1):
 AX = A(X) value
 BX = A(Y) value
 CX = B(X) value
 DX = B(Y) value

Memory Affected: None

Syntax:

```
MOV     AH,84h      ;joystick service
MOV     DX,1        ;read position
INT     15h         ;BIOS extension interrupt
```

Description: With this service, *which is available on all IBM PC and PS/2 systems released since 1983*, you can read either the joystick switch settings (called with AL=0) or the joystick position.

If called on older PC models, this service will set the carry flag and return 86h in AH (or 80h on original PC and PCjr models) to indicate that the service is invalid for the model.

SYSREQ Key Pressed (Interrupt 15h, service 85h)

Category: Keyboard

Registers on Entry:

AH: 85h
AL: 00h = SYSREQ key pressed
  01h = SYSREQ key released

Registers on Return: Unchanged

Memory Affected: None

Description: This service, *available only on IBM PC and PS/2 systems released since 1983*, is meaningful only when the keyboard includes the SYSREQ key (84-key and later designs). BIOS calls the service when either a press or release of the SYSREQ key is detected by INT 09h. Normally, this service is never called by a programmer.

To provide special action when the key is pressed, your program must replace the existing INT 15h service routine with a new one that traps the condition AH = 85h and passes control on to the original routine for all other cases. Your routine can then determine whether the key was pressed or released by testing the content of the AL register. Be sure to remove your special routine before returning to DOS.

On return from this service, the carry flag signifies whether an error occurred. If the carry flag is set and contains 86h, then this service is not available.

Delay (Interrupt 15h, service 86h)

Category: System

Registers on Entry:

    AH: 86h
    CX: High-order value of delay time in microseconds
    DX: Low-order value of delay time in microseconds

Registers on Return: Unchanged

Memory Affected: None

Syntax:

```
MOV    AH,86h      ;delay service
MOV    CX,0        ;high 16 bits of value
MOV    DX,10000    ;wait 1/100 second
INT    15h         ;BIOS extension interrupt
```

Description: This service, *which is available only on the IBM Personal Computer AT and PS/2 lines*, pauses a specified length of time before returning to its caller. The service is intended for system use only, not for general application.

If called on older PC models, the service will set the carry flag and return 86h in AH (or 80h on original PC and PCjr models) to indicate that service is invalid on the model.

Move Block to/from Extended Memory (Interrupt 15h, service 87h)

Category: System

Registers on Entry:

AH: 87h
CX: Number of words to move
ES: Segment address of GDT (see table 15.17)
SI: Offset address of GDT (see table 15.17)

Registers on Return: Unchanged

Memory Affected: As described by GDT values

Syntax:

```
MOV     AH, 87h          ;move block
MOV     CX, 40           ;80 bytes
MOV     ES, SEG GDT      ;set table address
MOV     SI, OFFSET GDT
INT     15h              ;BIOS extension interrupt
```

Description: This service, *available only on the IBM Personal Computer AT and PS/2 lines*, moves data to or from extended memory as described by the global descriptor table (GDT) (see table 15.17). This service cannot transfer more than 64K bytes of data at one call.

If called on older PC models, this service will set the carry flag and return 86h in AH (or 80h on original PC and PCjr models) to indicate that the service is invalid on the model.

Table 15.17. *Global descriptor table format.*

Offset	Description
00h	Dummy, set to zero
08h	GDT data segment location, set to zero
10h	Source GDT, points to 8-byte GDT for source memory block
18h	Target GDT, points to 8-byte GDT for target memory block
20h	Pointer to BIOS code segment, initially zero
28h	Pointer to BIOS stack segment, initially zero

Source/target GDT layouts

00h	Segment limit
02h	24-bit segment physical address
05h	Data access rights (set to 93h)
06h	Reserved word, must be zero

Size Extended Memory (Interrupt 15h, service 88h)

Category: System

Registers on Entry:

AH: 88h

Registers on Return:

AX: Number of contiguous 1K blocks of RAM above 10000h

Memory Affected: None

Syntax:

```
MOV    AH,88h        ;get extended RAM size service
INT    15h           ;BIOS extension interrupt
```

Description: This service, *available only on the IBM Personal Computer AT and PS/2 lines*, returns the amount of "extended" memory available above the normal 1-megabyte limit. The service is meaningful only for machines equipped with the 80286 or later CPU chip.

If called on older PC models, this service will set the carry flag and return 86h in AH (or 80h on original PC and PCjr models) to indicate that the service is invalid on the model.

Protected Mode Switch (Interrupt 15h, service 89h)

Category: System

Registers on Entry:

AH: 89h
BL: IRQ0 vector offset
BH: IRQ8 vector offset
CX: Offset into protected mode CS to jump to
ES: Segment address of GDT (see table 15.17)
SI: Offset address of GDT (see table 15.17)

Registers on Return: Unchanged

Memory Affected: None

Description: This service, *available only on the IBM Personal Computer AT and PS/2 lines*, switches the CPU into protected mode operation so that you can directly access the full 16-megabyte address range. The service is meaningful only for machines equipped with the 80286 or later CPU chip.

You are not likely to use this service with any DOS programs you write because DOS cannot use protected mode operation.

If called on older PC models, this service will set the carry flag and return 86h in AH (or 80h on original PC and PCjr models) to indicate that the service is invalid on the model.

Get System Configuration (Interrupt 15h, service C0h)

Category: System

Registers on Entry:

AH: C0h

Registers on Return:

BX: Offset address of system configuration table
ES: Segment address of system configuration table

Memory Affected: None

Syntax:

```
MOV     AH,C0h      ;request get configuration service
INT     15h         ;BIOS extension interrupt
```

Description: This service, which is available only on PC and PS/2 models dated after 01/10/84, returns a pointer to the system descriptor table. Table 15.18 shows the layout of this area; tables 15.19 and 15.20 provide more detail.

Table 15.18. *System descriptor table.*

Offset	Meaning
00h	Byte count of subsequent data (minimum 8)
02h	Model byte (see table 15.20 for meaning)
03h	Submodel byte (see table 15.20 for meaning)
04h	BIOS revision level (00 = first release)
05h	Feature information (see table 15.19 for meaning)
06-09h	Reserved

Table 15.19. *Feature information byte.*

Bits 76543210	Hex	Decimal	Meaning of bits
1	80	128	DMA channel 3 used by hard disk BIOS
1	40	64	Second interrupt chip present
1	20	32	Real-time clock present
1	10	16	Keyboard intercept called by INT 09h
1	8	8	Wait for external event is supported
1	4	4	Extended BIOS data area allocated
1	2	2	Micro channel architecture
0			PC bus I/O channel
x			Reserved

Table 15.20. *System model identification.*

Computer type	Model byte (offset 02h)	Submodel (offset 03h)	BIOS revision (offset 04h)	BIOS date
PC	FFh			
PC XT	FEh			
PC XT	FBh	00h	01h	1/10/86
PC XT	FBh	00h	02h	5/09/86
PCjr	FDh			
AT	FCh			
AT	FCh	00h	01h	6/10/85
AT, COMPAQ 286	FCh	01h	00h	11/15/85
PC XT 286	FCh	02h	00h	
PC Convertible	F9h	00h	00h	
PS/2 Model 30	FAh	00h	00h	
PS/2 Model 50	FCh	04h	00h	
PS/2 Model 60	FCh	05h	00h	
PS/2 Model 80	F8h	00h	00h	

If called on older PC models, this service will set the carry flag and return 86h in AH (or 80h on original PC and PCjr models) to indicate that the service is invalid on the model.

Get Extended BIOS Address (Interrupt 15h, service C1h)

Category: PS/2 services

Registers on Entry:

AH: C1h

Registers on Return:

ES: Extended BIOS Data Area's segment address

Memory Affected: None

Syntax:

```
MOV     AH,C1h      ;request service
INT     15h         ;BIOS extension interrupt
```

Description: This service, *available only on the PS/2 line*, sets the ES register to point to the Extended BIOS Data Area's segment address; it is meaningful only if the feature information byte (table 15.19) of service 15/C0 indicates that such an area has been allocated.

If called on older PC models, this service will set the carry flag and return 86h in AH (or 80h on original PC and PCjr models) to indicate that the service is invalid on the model.

Pointing Device Interface (Interrupt 15h, service C2h)

Category: PS/2 services

Registers on Entry:

```
AH: C2h
AL: 00h = enable/disable device
    01h = reset device
    02h = set sampling rate for device
    03h = set resolution of device
    04h = read device type
    05h = initialize device interface
    06h = indicate extended commands for device
    07h = initialize FAR call device
BH: 00h = enable (if AL=0)
    01h = disable (if AL=0)
```

Registers on Return: Unchanged

Memory Affected: None

Syntax:

```
MOV    AL,00h      ;enable/disable subfunction
MOV    BH,00h      ;enable pointing device
MOV    AH,C2h      ;request service
INT    15h         ;BIOS extension interrupt
```

Description: This service, *available only on the PS/2 line*, need never be called by your programs; the standard mouse interface of INT 33h uses this service, if applicable, so that your programs can communicate with pointing devices by using the INT 33h interface.

If called on older PC models, this service will set the carry flag and return 86h in AH (or 80h on original PC and PCjr models) to indicate that the service is invalid with the model.

Watchdog Timer (Interrupt 15h, service C3h)

Category: PS/2 services

Registers on Entry:

AH: C3

AL: 00h = disable timer
01h = enable timer

BX: Timer count (1-255)

Registers on Return: Unchanged

Memory Affected: None

Syntax:

```
MOV     BX,182      ;set alarm for 182 ticks (approx 10 sec)
MOV     AH,C3h      ;request service
MOV     AL,01h      ;enable timer
INT     15h         ;BIOS extension interrupt
; .
; .     do something that must complete within 10 seconds
; .
MOV     AH,C3h      ;request service
MOV     AL,00h      ;disable timer
INT     15h         ;BIOS extension interrupt
```

Description: This service, *available only on the PS/2 line*, sets a "watch-dog" alarm based on the 18.2-tick/second main timer cycle. If you call this service to enable the timer with a count from 1 to 255 in the BX register and fail to call the service again before the count reaches zero, a nonmaskable interrupt (INT 02h) is generated. The count decrements by one at each timer tick.

If called on older PC models, this service will set the carry flag and return 86h in AH (or 80h on original PC and PCjr models) to indicate that the service is invalid on the model.

Programmable Option Select (Interrupt 15h, service C4h)

Category: PS/2 services

Registers on Entry:

AH: C4h

AL: 00h = return base POS register address
01h = enable slot for setup
02h = enable adapter

Registers on Return:

DL: base POS register port address (if AL=0)
BL: slot number (if AL=1)

Memory Affected: None

Syntax:

```
MOV    AL,00h       ;get address to DL
MOV    AH,C4h       ;request service
INT    15h          ;BIOS extension interrupt
```

Description: This service, available only on the PS/2 line, eliminates the need to set DIP switches. Instead, programmable registers accessed by this service establish options for the various plug-in boards.

Note: Using this service improperly can cause physical damage to some plug-in boards. Be sure that you know exactly what your program is doing, and why, before attempting to use this service.

If called on older PC models, this service will set the carry flag and return 86h in AH (or 80h on original PC and PCjr models) to indicate that the service is invalid on the model.

Read Keyboard Character (Interrupt 16h, service 0)

Category: Keyboard services

Registers on Entry:

AH: 0

Registers on Return:

AH: Keyboard scan code
AL: ASCII value of keystroke

Memory Affected: None

Syntax:

```
MOV    AH,0              ;Specify service 0
INT    16h              ;BIOS keyboard interrupt
MOV    SCAN_CODE,AH     ;Store scan code
MOV    ASCII_KEY,AL     ;Store ASCII value
```

Description: This service, which is similar to service 16/1, examines the keyboard buffer to determine whether a keystroke is available. If no keystroke is available, the service waits until a key is pressed; otherwise the service returns the ASCII value of the keystroke in AL and the scan code value in AH.

Several keys or key combinations on a standard IBM PC keyboard do not have a corresponding ASCII value. If these keys are pressed, this service returns a 0 (zero) in AL; the value in AH still represents the appropriate scan code value. (For a list of keyboard scan codes and ASCII values, see Appendix C.)

You cannot use this service to return a scan code for every possible keystroke on the keyboard. It does not return scan codes for some keys (such as the Shift, Ctrl, and Alt keys) that cause modification to the key(s) which follow. When these keys alone are pressed, no scan code is returned. However, key combinations such as Alt-T or Ctrl-A cause scan code/ASCII combinations to be returned.

Some keys (such as SysRq, PrtSc, and Ctrl-Alt-Del) also cause an interrupt to occur. This service does not trap and return these keys.

Through this service, any ASCII value from 0 to 255 can be derived by combining the Alt key with the numeric keypad. For example, holding the Alt key while pressing 153 on the keypad, and then releasing the Alt key, causes 0 to be returned in AH (scan code) and 153 to be returned in AL (ASCII value). Pressing a keypad number larger than 255 while holding the Alt key causes the value returned in AL to be the modulo of that number divided by 256. For example, if you use the preceding Alt-key procedure but press 8529 on the keypad, a value of 81 (the remainder when 8529 is divided by 256) will be returned in AL.

Read Keyboard Status (Interrupt 16h, service 1)

Category: Keyboard services

Registers on Entry:

AH: 1

Registers on Return:

AH: Keyboard scan code
AL: ASCII value of keypress

Memory Affected: None

Syntax:

```
        MOV     AH,1            ;Specify service 1
        INT     16h             ;BIOS keyboard interrupt
        JZ      NO_KEY          ;No key available
        MOV     SCAN_CODE,AH    ;Store scan code
        MOV     ASCII_KEY,AL    ;Store ASCII value
NO_KEY:
```

Description: This service, which is similar to service 16/0, examines the keyboard buffer to determine whether a keystroke is available. If a key is available, the zero flag is cleared, the ASCII value of the keystroke is returned in AL, and the scan code value is returned in AH. If no keystroke is waiting, the zero flag is set on return; the contents of AH and AL are not significant.

Several keys or key combinations on a standard IBM PC keyboard do not have a corresponding ASCII value. If these keys are pressed, this service returns a 0 (zero) in AL; the value in AH still represents the appropriate scan code value. (For a list of keyboard scan codes and ASCII values, see Appendix C.)

You cannot use this service to return a scan code for every possible keystroke on the keyboard. It does not return scan codes for some keys (such as the Shift, Ctrl, and Alt keys) that cause modification to the key(s) which follow. When these keys alone are pressed, no scan code is returned. However, key combinations such as Alt-T or Ctrl-A cause scan code/ASCII combinations to be returned.

Some keys (such as SysRq, PrtSc, and Ctrl-Alt-Del) also cause an interrupt to occur. This service does not trap and return these keys.

Through this service, any ASCII value from 0 to 255 can be derived by combining the Alt key with the numeric keypad. For example, holding the Alt key while pressing 153 on the keypad, and then releasing the Alt key, causes 0 to be returned in AH (scan code) and 153 to be returned in AL (ASCII value). Pressing a keypad number larger than 255 while holding the Alt key causes the value returned in AL to be the modulo of that number divided by 256. For example, if you use the preceding Alt-key procedure but press 8529 on the keypad, a value of 81 (the remainder when 8529 is divided by 256) will be returned in AL.

Read Keyboard Shift Status (Interrupt 16h, service 2)

Category: Keyboard services

Registers on Entry:

AH: 2

Registers on Return:

AL: Shift status (table 15.21)

Memory Affected: None

Syntax:

```
MOV   AH,2        ;Specify service 2
INT   16h         ;BIOS keyboard interrupt
```

Description: This service returns (in AL) the keyboard's current shift status. Each bit of the returned value represents the state of a specific keyboard shift key (see table 15.21).

Table 15.21. Keyboard shift status values returned by service 16/2.

Bits 76543210	Hex	Decimal	Meaning of bits
1	80	128	Insert on
1	40	64	Caps Lock on
1	20	32	Num Lock on
1	10	16	Scroll Lock on
1	8	8	Alt key down
1	4	4	Ctrl key down
1	2	2	Left Shift key down
1	1	1	Right Shift key down

Your programs can use this function to check for exotic key combinations that serve as a signal to perform a certain task. For instance, you may want to minimize the possibility of accidentally exiting your program. Instead of using the Esc key (which is easy to press accidentally) to exit the program, you can set up your program so that the user can exit only by pressing the Ctrl-Alt-Left Shift key combination. It is unlikely that this combination will be entered by accident.

The BIOS controls the setting of this status byte through the keyboard interrupt. Whenever someone presses the Ins, Shift, Ctrl, Alt, Num Lock, or Scroll Lock key, BIOS changes the appropriate bits in the keyboard status byte and resumes waiting for another key to be pressed.

Adjust Repeat Rate (Interrupt 16h, service 03h)

Category: Extended keyboard services

Registers on Entry:

AH: 03h

AL: 00h = restore default values (PCjr only)
01h = increase initial delay (PCjr only)
02h = cut repeat rate in half (PCjr only)
03h = do both 01 and 02 (PCjr only)
04h = turn off keyboard repeat (PCjr only)
05h = set repeat rate and delay (Personal Computer
        AT and PS/2 only)
BH: Repeat delay (0-3 x 250 ms; Personal Computer
     AT and PS/2 only)
BL: Repeat rate (0-31, lower values are faster;
     Personal Computer AT and PS/2 only)

Registers on Return: Not significant

Memory Affected: None

Syntax:

```
MOV     AH,03h          ;request service
MOV     AL,05h          ;for AT
MOV     BX,0307h        ;delay=750 ms, rate code=7
INT     16h             ;BIOS keyboard interrupt
```

Description: This service, *available only on the PCjr and on the IBM Personal Computer AT and PS/2 lines*, modifies both the initial delay before repeats begin, and the repeat rate, of the keyboard.

Key-Click Control (Interrupt 16h, service 04h)

Category: Extended keyboard services

Registers on Entry:

AH: 04h
AL: 00h = silent
    01h = click sounds

Registers on Return: Not significant

Memory Affected: None

Syntax:

```
MOV     AH,04h          ;request service
MOV     AL,00h          ;be quiet!
INT     16h             ;BIOS keyboard interrupt
```

Description: This service, available only on the PCjr, silences or re-enables the built-in, key-click generator. The service has no effect on other models, but generates no error code.

Write to Keyboard Buffer (Interrupt 16h, service 05h)

Category: Extended keyboard services

Registers on Entry:

AH: 05h
CH: Scan code to write
CL: ASCII code to write

Registers on Return: Not significant

Memory Affected: None

Syntax:

```
            MOV     CX,0FFFFh       ;write test codes
            MOV     AH,05h          ;into keyboard buffer
            INT     16h             ;BIOS keyboard interrupt
            MOV     CX,16           ;set loop count
GET_CODES:  MOV     AH,10h          ;read test codes back
            INT     16h             ;BIOS keyboard interrupt
            CMP     AX,0FFFFh       ;test to see if test code came back
            JE      HAVE_101        ;found it, enhanced KB present
            LOOP    GET_CODES       ;else keep looking until buffer empty
            JMP     NO_101          ;enhanced KB not present
```

Description: This service, *available only on the IBM Personal Computer AT and PS/2 lines*, is meaningful only when the enhanced 101-key keyboard is being used, because older designs lack buffers into which the service can write.

The syntax example shows a method for using this service together with service 16/10 to determine whether the enhanced 101-key keyboard is installed.

Get Extended Keystroke (Interrupt 16h, service 10h)

Category: Extended keyboard services

Registers on Entry:

AH: 10h

Registers on Return: Same as for service 16/0

Memory Affected: None

Syntax:

```
MOV     AH,10h      ;request service
INT     16h         ;BIOS keyboard interrupt
```

Description: This service, *available only on the IBM Personal Computer AT and PS/2 lines*, operates exactly like service 16/0; however, unlike service 16/0, this service also recognizes the keys added to the 101-key keyboard and can distinguish between them.

Check Extended Keyboard Status (Interrupt 16h, service 11h)

Category: Extended keyboard services

Registers on Entry:

AH: 11h

Registers on Return: Same as for service 16/1

Memory Affected: None

Syntax:

```
MOV     AH,11h      ;request service
INT     16h         ;BIOS keyboard interrupt
```

Description: This service, *available only on the IBM Personal Computer AT and PS/2 lines*, operates exactly like service 16/1; however, unlike service 16/1, this service also recognizes the keys added to the 101-key keyboard and can respond to them.

Get Extended Keyboard Status Flags (Interrupt 16h, service 12h)

Category: Extended keyboard services

Registers on Entry:

AH: 12h

Registers on Return: Same as for service 16/2

Memory Affected: None

Syntax:

```
MOV     AH,12h      ;request service
INT     16h         ;BIOS keyboard interrupt
```

Description: This service, *available only on the IBM Personal Computer AT and PS/2 lines*, operates exactly like service 16/2; however, unlike service 16/2, this service also recognizes the keys added to the 101-key keyboard, and can respond to them.

Print Character (Interrupt 17h, service 0)

Category: Printer services

Registers on Entry:

AH: 0
AL: Character to print
DX: Printer to be used

Registers on Return:

AH: Printer status (table 15.22)

Memory Affected: None

Syntax:

```
MOV     AL,'*'      ;Print an asterisk
MOV     DX,0        ;Use first printer
MOV     AH,0        ;Specify service 0
INT     17h         ;BIOS printer interrupt
```

Description: This service outputs a character to a printer port. The character to be printed is loaded in AL; the printer to use is designated in DX. A printer designation of 0 to 2 is valid (0 corresponds to LPT1:, 1 to LPT2:, and 2 to LPT3:).

The value that this service returns in AH is the printer status byte. (Services 17/1 and 17/2 also return the printer status byte in AH.) Table 15.22 lists the meaning of the bits in this returned byte.

Table 15.22. Meaning of bits returned in AH for services 17/0, 17/1, and 17/2.

Bits 76543210	Meaning of bits
1	Printer not busy
0	Printer busy
1	Printer acknowledgment
1	Out of paper
1	Printer selected
1	I/O error
??	Unused
1	Time-out

Initialize Printer (Interrupt 17h, service 1)

Category: Printer services

Registers on Entry:

AH: 1
DX: Printer to be used

Registers on Return:

AH: Printer status

Memory Affected: None

Syntax:

```
MOV     DX,0        ;Use first printer
MOV     AH,1        ;Specify service 1
INT     17h         ;BIOS printer interrupt
```

Description: The outputs from this service initialize the IBM- or EPSON-compatible printer connected to the port specified in DX. A printer designation of 0 to 2 is valid (0 corresponds to LPT1:, 1 to LPT2:, and 2 to LPT3:).

Two values (08h and 0Ch) are output to initialize the printer. The printer interprets these values as a command to perform a reset. Note that this series works only on IBM- and EPSON-compatible printers. Other printers may not understand this series and may produce unwanted results.

The value that this service returns in AH is the printer status byte. (Refer to table 15.22 for the meaning of the bits in this returned byte.)

Get Printer Status (Interrupt 17h, service 2)

Category: Printer services

Registers on Entry:

AH: 2
DX: Printer to be used

Registers on Return:

AH: Printer status

Memory Affected: None

Syntax:

```
MOV    DX,0        ;Use first printer
MOV    AH,2        ;Specify service 2
INT    17h         ;BIOS printer interrupt
```

Description: This service retrieves the status of the printer specified in DX. A printer designation of 0 to 2 is valid (0 corresponds to LPT1:, 1 to LPT2:, and 2 to LPT3:).

The value that this service returns in AH is the printer status byte. (Refer to table 15.22 for the meaning of the bits in this returned byte.)

Warm Boot (Interrupt 19h)

Category: System services

Registers on Entry: Not significant

Registers on Return: Not applicable (no return)

Memory Affected: Contents of memory after invocation will reflect normal memory conditions after a warm-booting procedure. The contents of any given free memory area are unpredictable.

Syntax:

```
INT    19h        ;BIOS warm boot
```

Description: This interrupt, which performs a warm reboot of the computer system, is functionally the same as pressing Ctrl-Alt-Del or turning off the computer and then turning it back on.

There are differences between this method and the other methods of starting the computer system, however. This interrupt does not go through the power-on self test (POST) procedures, nor does it reset the equipment status word in memory (refer to Interrupt 11h).

Get Clock Counter (Interrupt 1Ah, service 0)

Category: Date/time services

Registers on Entry:

AH: 0

Registers on Return:

AL: Midnight flag
CX: Clock count high-order word
DX: Clock count low-order word

Memory Affected: None

Syntax:

```
MOV    AH,0       ;Specify service 0
INT    1Ah        ;BIOS date/time interrupt
```

Description: This service retrieves the current value of the system software clock counter. This value is a double word register that is incremented approximately 18.2065 times per second, starting from 0 (midnight). Midnight is assumed when the value of the counter reaches 1800B0h or when the counter has been incremented 1,573,040 times. Dividing this counter value by 18.2065 indicates that this clock count represents 86,399.9121 seconds (a fairly accurate representation of a full day, because there are 86,400 seconds in a 24-hour period).

AL is set to 1 if midnight has been passed since the last read of the clock. If midnight has not been passed, AL is set to 0 (zero). Invoking this service always causes the midnight flag to be reset to 0.

Set Clock Counter (Interrupt 1Ah, service 1)

Category: Date/time services

Registers on Entry:

H: 1
CX: Clock count high-order word
DX: Clock count low-order word

Registers on Return: Unchanged

Memory Affected: None

Syntax:

```
MOV    CX,HIGH_COUNT        ;Clock high-order word
MOV    DX,LOW_COUNT         ;Clock low-order word
MOV    AH,1                 ;Specify service 1
INT    1Ah                  ;BIOS date/time interrupt
```

Description: This service sets the current value of the system software clock counter. This value is a double word register that is incremented approximately .2065 times per second, starting from 0 (midnight).

To determine the proper settings for any given time of the day, simply determine the number of seconds since midnight and then multiply this number by 18.2065. For instance, the clock value for 14:22:17.39 (military time) would be determined as follows:

14 hours =	14 * 60 * 60	= 50400	seconds
22 minutes =	22 * 60	= 1320	seconds
17.39 seconds =	17.39	= 17.39	seconds
		—————	
Total:		51737.39	seconds
Clock ticks per second =		18.2065	ticks
		—————	
Ticks represented:		941956.7910	ticks

Because fractional ticks cannot be represented, the number of ticks is rounded to 941,957 (0E5F85h). CX is loaded with 0Eh; DX, with 5F85h.

Be careful. Because this service performs no range checks on the values you specify in CX and DX, you can inadvertently specify an invalid time without any indication from BIOS that you have done so. (An invalid time is any value greater than 1800B0h, the number of ticks in a full 24-hour period.)

Read Real-Time Clock (Interrupt 1Ah, service 2)

Category: Date/time services

Registers on Entry:

AH: 2

Registers on Return:

CH: Hours (BCD)
CL: Minutes (BCD)
DH: Seconds (BCD)

Memory Affected: None

Syntax:

```
MOV     AH,2            ;Specify service 2
INT     1Ah             ;BIOS date/time interrupt
MOV     HOUR,CH         ;Save current hour
MOV     MINUTE,CL       ;Save current minute
MOV     SECOND,DH       ;Save current second
```

Description: This service, *which is available only on the IBM Personal Computer AT*, retrieves the value of the real-time clock. Remember that the values returned in CH, CL, and DH are in *binary coded decimal* (BCD) and that you must make allowances for subsequent calculations that use these return values.

If the clock is not functioning, the carry flag is set on return; otherwise, the carry flag is clear.

Set Real-Time Clock (Interrupt 1Ah, service 3)

Category: Date/time services

Registers on Entry:

AH: 3
CH: Hours (BCD)
CL: Minutes (BCD)
DH: Seconds (BCD)
DL: Daylight saving time

Registers on Return: Unchanged

Memory Affected: None

Syntax:

```
MOV     CH,HOUR          ;Get current hour
MOV     CL,MINUTE        ;Get current minute
MOV     DH,SECOND        ;Get current second
MOV     DL,0             ;Normal time
MOV     AH,3             ;Specify service 3
INT     1Ah              ;BIOS date/time interrupt
```

Description: This service, *which is available only on the IBM Personal Computer AT*, sets the real-time clock. Remember that the values specified in CH, CL, and DH should be in *binary coded decimal* (BCD).

DL should be set to indicate whether the time being set is daylight saving time. If DL is 0 (zero), standard time is indicated; if DL is 1, daylight saving time is indicated.

Read Date from Real-Time Clock (Interrupt 1Ah, service 4)

Category: Date/time services

Registers on Entry:

AH: 4

Registers on Return:

CH: Century (BCD)
CL: Year (BCD)
DH: Month (BCD)
DL: Day (BCD)

Memory Affected: None

Syntax:

```
MOV     AH,4      ;Specify service 4
INT     1Ah       ;BIOS date/time interrupt
```

Description: This service, *which is available only on the IBM Personal Computer AT*, retrieves the date from the real-time clock. Remember that all values returned are in *binary coded decimal* (BCD) and that you must make allowances for subsequent calculations which use these return values.

For instance, if the date is July 1, 1987, the value returned in CH is 19h, the value in CL is 87h, the value in DH is 07h, and the value in DL is 01h.

If the clock is not functioning, the carry flag is set on return; otherwise, the carry flag is clear.

Set Date of Real-Time Clock (Interrupt 1Ah, service 5)

Category: Date/time services

Registers on Entry:

AH: 5
CH: Century (BCD, 19 or 20)
CL: Year (BCD)
DH: Month (BCD)
DL: Day (BCD)

Registers on Return: Unchanged

Memory Affected: None

Syntax:

```
MOV     CX,1986h    ;Year in BCD
MOV     DH,12h      ;December (BCD)
MOV     DL,25h      ;Day in BCD
MOV     AH,5        ;Specify service 5
INT     1Ah         ;BIOS date/time interrupt
```

Description: This service, *which is available only on the IBM Personal Computer AT*, sets the date of the real-time clock. Remember that all values used by this service should be in *binary coded decimal* (BCD).

Because no range checking is performed on the registers for this service, all range checking should be performed by the user program.

Set Alarm (Interrupt 1Ah, service 6)

Category: Date/time services

Registers on Entry:

AH: 6
CH: Hours (BCD)
CL: Minutes (BCD)
DH: Seconds (BCD)

Registers on Return: Unchanged

Memory Affected: None

Syntax:

```
MOV    CH,01h       ;1 hour
MOV    CL,30h       ;30 minutes (BCD)
MOV    DH,0         ;0 seconds
MOV    AH,6         ;Specify service 6
INT    1Ah          ;BIOS date/time interrupt
```

Description: This service, *which is available only on the IBM Personal Computer AT*, sets the BIOS alarm function. Remember that all values used by this service are expected to be in *binary coded decimal* (BCD). The time specified in the registers (CH, CL, DH) is the elapsed time before the alarm will occur. In the preceding syntax example, the alarm will occur 1 hour, 30 minutes, 0 seconds from the time the service is invoked.

The BIOS alarm function simply generates an interrupt signal after the appropriate period of time has elapsed. The address of the routine that you want to perform should be vectored to Interrupt 4Ah.

Because no range checking is performed on the registers for this service, all range checking should be performed by the user program.

If the clock is not functioning or if the alarm is already enabled, the carry flag is set on return; otherwise, the carry flag is clear. To reset the alarm to another time, you must first disable the alarm by invoking service 1A/7; then reset the alarm.

Disable Alarm (Interrupt 1Ah, service 7)

Category: Date/time services

Registers on Entry:

AH: 7

Registers on Return: Unchanged

Memory Affected: None

Syntax:

```
MOV    AH,7         ;Specify service 7
INT    1Ah          ;BIOS date/time interrupt
```

Description: This service, *which is available only on the IBM Personal Computer AT*, disables an alarm interrupt enabled through service 1A/6. This service must be called before the alarm can be reset.

Read Alarm (Interrupt 1Ah, service 9)

Category: Date/time services

Registers on Entry:

AH: 9

Registers on Return:

CH: BCD hours
CL: BCD minutes
DH: BCD seconds
DL: Alarm status:
    00 = not enabled
    01 = enabled, no power on
    02 = enabled, will power system on when alarm triggers

Memory Affected: None

Syntax:

```
MOV    AH,9      ;Specify service 9
INT    1Ah       ;BIOS date/time interrupt
```

Description: This service, *which is available only on the PC Convertible and the PS/2 Model 30*, reports the setting and status of the alarm interrupt enabled through service 1A/6.

Get Day Count (Interrupt 1Ah, service 0Ah)

Category: Date/time services

Registers on Entry:

AH: 0Ah

Registers on Return:

CX: Total count of days since 01/01/80

Memory Affected: None

Syntax:

```
MOV   AH,0Ah      ;Specify service 0Ah
INT   1Ah         ;BIOS date/time interrupt
```

Description: This service, *which is available only on the PC XT with BIOS dated 01/10/86 or later and on the PS/2 line*, reports the number of days that have elapsed since January 1, 1980 (the internal storage format for the date functions).

Set Day Count (Interrupt 1Ah, service 0Bh)

Category: Date/time services

Registers on Entry:

AH: 0Bh
CX: Total count of days since 01/01/80

Registers on Return: Not significant

Memory Affected: None

Syntax:

```
MOV   AH,0Bh      ;Specify service 0Ah
MOV   CX,1761     ;day count for Jan. 1, 1984
INT   1Ah         ;BIOS date/time interrupt
```

Description: This service, *which is available only on the PC XT with BIOS dated 01/10/86 or later and on the PS/2 line*, sets into memory the value in CX as the number of days that have elapsed since January 1, 1980 (the internal storage format for the date functions).

Control-Break Handler (Interrupt 1Bh)

Category: Custom service

Registers on Entry: Not known

Registers on Return: Unchanged

Memory Affected: None

Description: This service is called automatically from INT 09h if the Ctrl-Break keystroke combination is detected and response is enabled. DOS normally points this interrupt to a routine which treats it much the same as a Ctrl-C interrupt. If you want to control all break processing in your program, you can change the service for this interrupt to one of your own choosing. If you do, however, be sure to save the original address and restore it before your program finishes.

CHAPTER 16

Accessing DOS Services

D OS is an acronym for Disk Operating System. In this book, DOS is also short for MS-DOS (distributed by Microsoft) or PC DOS (distributed by IBM). Because both operating systems are effectively the same, with the same assembly language function calls available through both, this book refers to either dialect as DOS.

DOS, like BIOS, contains a series of functions that are accessible to outside programs. You invoke these functions (callable subroutines) through the use of software *interrupts*, which are generated through the INT assembly language instruction. INT causes the microprocessor to use an address from an interrupt table in low memory as the address for this special type of subroutine.

Specifically, INT pushes the flags register on the stack and then resets the interrupt and trap flags. The full return address (CS:IP) is placed on the stack, at which point the desired interrupt vector (address) is retrieved from the interrupt table and placed in CS:IP. Execution of the interrupt then continues until an IRET instruction is encountered. At this point, the return address is popped from the stack and placed in CS:IP. The flags register is then restored from the stack, and program execution continues from the point at which the interrupt was invoked.

Notice that the interrupt address is fetched from the interrupt table based on the number of the interrupt being invoked. The full syntax for calling an interrupt is

```
INT XX
```

where XX is replaced by the number of the appropriate interrupt.

The preceding chapter detailed many BIOS functions that are callable through various interrupts. This chapter provides the same kind of information for DOS services.

The DOS Service Categories

The interrupts and services offered by DOS can be divided into several broad categories, which generally are specified by the task classification of the function. The DOS function categories include

❏ I/O services

❏ Printer services

❏ Disk services

❏ System services

❏ Network services

❏ Date/time services

Some of these categories may look familiar to readers who have referred to Chapter 15. Although the categories are similar to the BIOS services, the operations may vary considerably. The largest single category of DOS services is, understandably, the disk services; after all, these services are Disk Operating System services.

The number of DOS services available depends necessarily on the version of DOS you are using. The services explained in this chapter work with DOS version 4.0. Earlier versions of DOS may not include all the functions detailed, although I have tried to indicate these cases in the individual service descriptions. If you have questions, consult your DOS technical manual.

The DOS Services

The rest of this chapter forms a convenient reference section. Each DOS service is described in detail in an organized manner. The following information is provided for each service:

❏ **Service name.** This name is based on the DOS function names selected by IBM or Microsoft and listed in various technical documentation. Where appropriate, the name has been modified or expanded to reflect more accurately the purpose of the service.

❏ **Service category.** The general classification of the service, as previously listed.

❏ **Registers on entry.** DOS service parameters generally are passed through registers. The expected register settings are given here.

❏ **Registers on return.** For proper operation of software, you must know how registers are affected by interrupts. Frequently, DOS functions return values through registers. Such information is detailed here.

❏ **Memory areas affected.** Some DOS functions modify memory based on the desired service. Any affected memory is given.

❏ **Syntax for calling.** A coding section showing the proper method for calling the interrupt is shown.

❏ **Description.** The purpose, benefits, and special considerations of the service are given in this section.

The services are arranged in ascending numerical order. Each service can be identified by the primary interrupt number and an individual service number. The service number is specified by the contents of the AH register. In this notation scheme, any DOS service can be denoted by a hexadecimal number pair, *II/SS*, where *II* is the interrupt number and *SS* is the service number. For instance, the service used to remove a subdirectory, service 21/3A, has an interrupt number of 21h, and a service number (specified through register AH) of 3Ah.

Other services may be specified as *II/SS/FF,* where the appended *FF* indicates the function number. For instance, the service used to read from a block device, service 21/44/4, has an interrupt number of 21h, a service number (specified through register AH) of 44h, and a function number (specified through register AL) of 4.

Terminate Program (Interrupt 20h)

Category: System services

Registers on Entry: Not significant

Registers on Return: Unspecified (does not return)

Memory Affected: None

Syntax:

```
INT    20h    ;Terminate program
```

Description: You can use this interrupt to terminate a program and return control to DOS. Internally, DOS restores several critical vector addresses (Ctrl-C and critical error handlers), flushes the file buffers, and transfers control to the termination handler address. This interrupt is equivalent to service 21/0.

This service does not allow you to pass a return code to DOS or to a parent program. For that capability, see services 21/31 and 21/4C.

Terminate Program (Interrupt 21h, service 0)

Category: System services

Registers on Entry:

AH: 0
CS: Segment address of program's PSP

Registers on Return: Unspecified (does not return)

Memory Affected: None

Syntax:

```
MOV    AH,0    ;Want service 0
INT    21h     ;DOS services interrupt
```

Description: You can use this service to terminate a program and return control to DOS. Internally, DOS restores several critical vector addresses (Ctrl-C and critical error handlers), flushes the file buffers, and transfers control to the termination handler address. This service is equivalent to issuing an INT 20h.

AH is the only functional register that you need to load before calling this service. Because CS, in all likelihood, will not have changed since the program began, CS should already be set to the proper value.

This service does not allow you to pass a return code to DOS or to a parent program. For that capability, see services 21/31 and 21/4C.

Character Input with Echo (Interrupt 21h, service 1)

Category: I/O services

Registers on Entry:

AH: 1

Registers on Return:

AL: Character

Memory Affected: The appropriate areas of video memory are altered to reflect the displayed (echoed) character.

Syntax:

```
MOV   AH,1    ;Want service 1
INT   21h     ;DOS services interrupt
```

Description: Originally, this service was designed to fetch a character from the keyboard and display that character on the video monitor. Intermediate versions of DOS, however, have modified this service so that I/O redirection is possible. If the standard input device or console has been redirected, this service fetches a character from the specified device. Regardless of the device, the character is echoed to the video monitor.

Even though this service waits for a character to be returned by the keyboard (or redirected I/O device), the service differs significantly from the BIOS keyboard routines in that only one character code is returned in AL. If an extended ASCII code is generated by the keyboard (such as codes generated by the function keys or cursor-control keys), interrupt 21h, service 1 returns a zero in AL. If you invoke the service again, it returns the scan code in AL.

Output Character (Interrupt 21h, service 2)

Category: I/O services

Registers on Entry:

AH: 2
DL: Character (ASCII value)

Registers on Return: Unchanged

Memory Affected: If I/O has not been redirected, the appropriate areas of video memory are altered to reflect the displayed character.

Syntax:

```
MOV    DL,'*'      ;Output an asterisk
MOV    AH,2        ;Want service 2
INT    21h         ;DOS services interrupt
```

Description: Originally, this service was designed to output a character to the video monitor. Intermediate versions of DOS, however, have modified this service so that I/O redirection is possible. If the standard output device has been redirected, this service sends a character to the specified device.

Auxiliary Input (Interrupt 21h, service 3)

Category: I/O services

Registers on Entry:

AH: 3

Registers on Return:

AL: Character

Memory Affected: None

Syntax:

```
MOV    AH,3        ;Want service 3
INT    21h         ;DOS services interrupt
```

Description: This service returns a character from the standard auxiliary device, which, if not redirected, is set to be COM1:.

This service is a poor way to read the communications port. More precise and error-free communication is possible through the BIOS communications functions (services 14/0–14/2) or, better yet, through a custom interrupt-driven communications interface. This interface, however, is beyond the scope of this book.

Auxiliary Output (Interrupt 21h, service 4)

Category: I/O services

Registers on Entry:

AH: 4
DL: Character (ASCII value)

Registers on Return: Unchanged

Memory Affected: None

Syntax:

```
MOV    DL,'_'          ;Output an underscore
MOV    AH,4            ;Want service 4
INT    21h             ;DOS services interrupt
```

Description: This service sends a character to the standard auxiliary device, which, if not redirected, is set to COM1:.

This service is a poor way to control the communications port. More precise and error-free communication is possible through the BIOS communications functions (services 14/0–14/2), or better yet through a custom interrupt-driven communications interface. This interface, however, is beyond the scope of this book.

Printer Output (Interrupt 21h, service 5)

Category: Printer services

Registers on Entry:

AH: 5
DL: Character (ASCII value)

Registers on Return: Unchanged

Memory Affected: None

Syntax:

```
MOV    DL,'_'          ;Print an underscore
MOV    AH,5            ;Want service 5
INT    21h             ;DOS services interrupt
```

Description: This service sends a character to the standard list device. Unless redirected, this device is LPT1:.

Direct Console I/O (Interrupt 21h, service 6)

Category: I/O services

Registers on Entry:

AH: 6
DL: Character (ASCII value) or input flag

Registers on Return:

AL: Input character

Memory Affected: If the service is outputting a character to the video monitor, the appropriate video memory areas are changed to reflect the character being displayed.

Syntax:

```
INP_LOOP:    MOV    DL,0FFh           ;Want to input
             MOV    AH,6              ;Want service 6
             INT    21h               ;DOS services interrupt
             JZ     NO_CHAR           ;No character ready
             CMP    AL,0              ;Was it extended ASCII?
             JNE    GOT_CHAR          ;No, treat as character
             MOV    EXTEND_FLAG,1     ;Yes, so set appropriately
             JMP    INP_LOOP          ;Get scan code
GOT_CHAR:    MOV    CHAR,AL           ;Store character
```

Description: You can use this service for character input or output, depending on the contents of DL. If DL is a value between 0 and 254 (0FEh), the contents of DL are sent to the console (unless redirected, the video screen). If DL contains 255 (0FFh), input is fetched from the console (unless redirected, the keyboard).

When you request input through this service, the zero flag is set on return to indicate the presence of a character. Zero in AL means that a key generating an extended ASCII code has been pressed, and this service should be invoked again to retrieve the scan code.

Direct Character Input without Echo (Interrupt 21h, service 7)

Category: I/O services

Registers on Entry:

AH: 7

Registers on Return:

AL: Character

Memory Affected: None

Syntax:

```
MOV   AH,7        ;Want service 7
INT   21h         ;DOS services interrupt
```

Description: Originally, this service was designed simply to fetch a character from the keyboard. Intermediate versions of DOS, however, have modified this service so that I/O redirection is possible. If the standard input device or console has been redirected, this service fetches a character from the specified device.

Even though this service waits for a character to be returned by the keyboard (or redirected I/O device), the service differs significantly from the BIOS keyboard routines in that only one character code is returned in AL. If the keyboard generates an extended ASCII code (such as codes generated by the function keys or cursor-control keys), this service returns a 0 in AL. A second invocation returns the scan code in AL.

Character Input without Echo (Interrupt 21h, service 8)

Category: I/O services

Registers on Entry:

AH: 8

Registers on Return:

AL: Character

Memory Affected: None

Syntax:

```
MOV   AH,8        ;Want service 8
INT   21h         ;DOS services interrupt
```

Description: Originally, this service was designed simply to fetch a character from the keyboard. Intermediate versions of DOS, however, have modified this service so that I/O redirection is possible. If the standard input device or console has been redirected, this service fetches a character from the specified device.

Even though this service waits for a character to be returned by the keyboard (or redirected I/O device), the service differs significantly from the BIOS keyboard routines in that only one character code is returned in AL. If the keyboard generates an extended ASCII code (such as codes generated by the function keys or cursor-control keys), this service returns a 0 in AL. A second invocation returns the scan code in AL.

This service differs from 21/7 in that it performs some interpretation on the characters received. For instance, if Ctrl-C and Ctrl-Break are received, they are translated and acted on by this service.

Output Character String (Interrupt 21h, service 9)

Category: I/O services

Registers on Entry:

AH: 9
DX: Offset address of string
DS: Segment address of string

Registers on Return: Unchanged

Memory Affected: If output is directed to the video display, the contents of the video memory buffers are changed appropriately to reflect the characters displayed.

Syntax:

```
PUSH   CS                    ;Code segment and
POP    DS                    ;  data segment are same
MOV    DX,OFFSET MSG_1       ;Offset address of string
MOV    AH,9                  ;Want service 9
INT    21h                   ;DOS services interrupt
```

Description: This service displays (or outputs) a string on the standard output device. If I/O has been redirected, the string is sent to the specified device.

Each character of the string at DS:DX—up to (but not including) the first occurrence of a dollar sign (ASCII 36)—is displayed by this service. Because of this strange convention (a carryover from CP/M), you cannot display the dollar sign when you are using this service.

Buffered Input (Interrupt 21h, service 0Ah)

Category: I/O services

Registers on Entry:

AH: 0Ah
DX: Offset address of buffer
DS: Segment address of buffer

Registers on Return: Unchanged

Memory Affected: The memory area beginning at DS:DX is overlaid with characters input from the standard input device.

Syntax:

```
PUSH    CS              ;Code segment and
POP     DS              ;  data segment are same
MOV     DX,OFFSET BUFFER ;Offset address of buffer
MOV     AH,0Ah          ;Want service 0Ah
INT     21h             ;DOS services interrupt
```

Description: This service allows the input of a specified number of characters from the standard input device. You can change the device, which originally is the keyboard, through I/O redirection.

The input characters are stored at the buffer specified by DS:DX. The value of the first byte of this buffer must indicate the maximum number of characters the buffer can contain. DOS sets the value of the second byte to indicate the number of characters this service returns. Therefore, if your maximum input length is 80 characters, you should set aside 82 bytes for the buffer.

This service does not return until you press Enter. If the buffer is filled before the service detects the carriage return, the extra characters are ignored, and the bell sounds with each extra keypress. Remember that each extended ASCII character (function keys, etc.) occupies two bytes in the buffer area.

Check for Character Waiting (Interrupt 21h, service 0Bh)

Category: I/O services

Registers on Entry:

AH: 0Bh

Registers on Return:

AL: Waiting flag

Memory Affected: None

Syntax:

```
KEY_LOOP:    MOV    AH,OBh        ;Want service OBh
             INT    21h           ;DOS services interrupt
             CMP    AL,0          ;Was there a keypress?
             JE     KEY_LOOP      ;No, continue to wait
```

Description: This service simply checks the status of the standard input device (usually the keyboard) to determine whether a character is available for input. If a character is available, AL equals FFh. If no character is available, AL equals 0.

Clear Buffer and Get Input (Interrupt 21h, service 0Ch)

Category: I/O services

Registers on Entry:

AH: 0Ch
AL: Desired input service
DX: Offset address of buffer
DS: Segment address of buffer

Registers on Return:

AL: Character (ASCII value)

Memory Affected: If AL is loaded with 0Ah, the memory area beginning at DS:DX is overlaid with characters input from the standard input device. Otherwise, memory is not affected.

Syntax:

```
PUSH    CS                     ;Code segment and
POP     DS                     ;  data segment are same
MOV     DX,OFFSET BUFFER       ;Offset address of buffer
MOV     AL,0Ah                 ;Want input service OAh
MOV     AH,0Ch                 ;Want service OCh
INT     21h                    ;DOS services interrupt
```

Description: This compound service forms a gateway to input services 21/1, 21/6, 21/7, 21/8, and 21/A. You invoke any of these input services by loading the desired service number (1, 6, 7, 8, Ah) into AL. After the type-ahead buffer is cleared, the specified service is invoked.

If AL is set to 0Ah, DS:DX must point to a buffer that is constructed in the fashion described under service 21/A. If AL is set to one of the other services, the contents of DS:DX are not significant.

If AL is set to 1, 6, 7, or 8, on return AL contains the ASCII value of the character fetched. The other characteristics of these DOS services are maintained. Please refer to the appropriate service descriptions for further information.

Reset Disk (Interrupt 21h, service 0Dh)

Category: Disk services

Registers on Entry:

AH: 0Dh

Registers on Return: Unchanged

Memory Affected: None

Syntax:

```
MOV    AH,0Dh           ;Want service 0Dh
INT    21h              ;DOS services interrupt
```

Description: This service flushes the DOS disk buffers. If a DOS file buffer contains information to be written to a disk file, that information is written to disk. The service does not close the files.

This service does not change the default drive and has no physical effect on the disk drives or their controllers.

Set Default Drive (Interrupt 21h, service 0Eh)

Category: Disk services

Registers on Entry:

AH: 0Eh
DL: Drive wanted

Registers on Return:

AL: Logical drives

Memory Affected: None

Syntax:

```
MOV    DL,2             ;Set for drive C:
MOV    AH,OEh           ;Want service OEh
INT    21h              ;DOS services interrupt
```

Description: This service has two purposes: (1) to set the default drive designation by specifying the desired drive in DL, where 0 = A, 1 = B, 2 = C, etc.; (2) to find out how many logical disk drives are connected to the computer.

Logical disk drives include RAM disks, disk emulators, and multisegmented hard disk drives. For instance, if you have two floppy drives (A: and B:), a 40M hard disk that is partitioned to two disks (C: and D:), and a RAM disk (E:), this service returns a value of 5 in AL even though only three physical drives are connected to the computer.

Clearly, knowing how many logical drives are connected to a computer without actually changing the default disk drive may be beneficial. You can get this information by determining the current default drive (through service 21/19) and then using that information to call this service. The following code segment performs this task:

```
MOV    AH,19h           ;Want service 19h
INT    21h              ;DOS services interrupt
MOV    CUR_DRIVE,AL     ;Store current drive (0-?)
MOV    DL,AL            ;Set for default drive
MOV    AH,OEh           ;Want service OEh
INT    21h              ;DOS services interrupt
MOV    NUM_DRIVES,AL    ;Store number of drives
```

For more information about service 21/19, refer to the description for that service.

Open File, Using FCB (Interrupt 21h, service 0Fh)

Category: Disk services

Registers on Entry:

AH: 0Fh
DX: Offset address of FCB
DS: Segment address of FCB

Registers on Return:

AL: Status byte

Memory Affected: If the service opens the file successfully, DOS fills in the FCB area specified by DS:DX to reflect the status of the file opened.

Syntax:

```
PUSH    CS                      ;Code segment and
POP     DS                      ;  data segment are same
MOV     DX,OFFSET FCB_1         ;Offset address of FCB
MOV     AH,OFh                  ;Want service OFh
INT     21h                     ;DOS services interrupt
```

Description: This service opens a disk file, based on a *file control block,* or FCB. The FCB is a block of information that is set initially by the programmer and then completed by DOS. The FCB consists of 44 bytes constructed in the following manner:

```
FCB_PRE       DB      OFFh            ;Extension flag
              DB      5 DUP(0)        ;Unused
              DB      00              ;File attribute
FCB_1         DB      00              ;Set for default drive
FILE_ROOT     DB      'FILENAME'      ;File name root
FILE_EXT      DB      'EXT'           ;File name extension
BLOCK_NUM     DW      0000            ;Current block number
REC_SIZE      DW      0000            ;Record size
FILE_SIZE     DD      00000000        ;File size
FILE_DATE     DW      0000            ;File date
FILE_TIME     DW      0000            ;File time
              DB      8 DUP(0)        ;DOS work area
REC_NUM       DB      00              ;Current record number
RANDOM_REC    DD      00000000        ;Random record number
```

The offset address of FCB_1 is the address you specify in DS:DX when you invoke this service. If you are using an extended FCB, use the offset address of FCB_PRE. To call this service, the values for FCB_1 (the drive designator), FILE_ROOT, and FILE_EXT must be specified. Notice that the drive designator is different from the normal method for DOS and BIOS drive designation: 0 equals the default drive, and 1 = A, 2 = B, 3 = C, etc.

If the open operation is successful, DOS returns a 0 in AL and sets FCB_1 to reflect the drive number (1 = A, 2 = B, 3 = C, etc.). DOS also sets BLOCK_NUM to 0; REC_SIZE to 80h; and FILE_SIZE, FILE_DATE, and FILE_TIME to the equivalent of the directory entry for the file. If the open operation is unsuccessful, DOS returns FFh in AL, and the FCB is not filled in.

Notice that this service allows you to use only FCBs. Because FCB file encoding does not allow for path names, any file operations must be performed in the current disk subdirectory. With floppy disks, this limitation may not be a problem. With fixed disks, however, the limitation can be serious. Refer to service 21/3D for a file-opening method that does not have this limitation.

Close File, Using FCB (Interrupt 21h, service 10h)

Category: Disk services

Registers on Entry:

AH: 10h
DX: Offset address of FCB
DS: Segment address of FCB

Registers on Return:

AL: Status byte

Memory Affected: None

Syntax:

```
PUSH   CS              ;Code segment and
POP    DS              ;  data segment are same
MOV    DX,OFFSET FCB_1 ;Offset address of FCB
MOV    AH,10h          ;Want service 10h
INT    21h             ;DOS services interrupt
```

Description: This service closes a disk file, based on a file control block, or FCB. The FCB consists of 44 bytes constructed in the following manner:

```
FCB_PRE     DB    0FFh          ;Extension flag
            DB    5 DUP(0)      ;Unused
            DB    00            ;File attribute
FCB_1       DB    00            ;Set for default drive
FILE_ROOT   DB    'FILENAME'    ;File name root
FILE_EXT    DB    'EXT'         ;File name extension
BLOCK_NUM   DW    0000          ;Current block number
REC_SIZE    DW    0000          ;Record size
FILE_SIZE   DD    00000000      ;File size
FILE_DATE   DW    0000          ;File date
FILE_TIME   DW    0000          ;File time
            DB    8 DUP(0)      ;DOS work area
REC_NUM     DB    00            ;Current record number
RANDOM_REC  DD    00000000      ;Random record number
```

The offset address of FCB_1 is the address you specify in DS:DX when you invoke this service. If you are using an extended FCB, use the offset address of FCB_PRE. To call this service, you must specify the values for FCB_1 (the drive designator), FILE_ROOT, and FILE_EXT. Notice that the drive designator is different from the normal method for DOS and BIOS drive designation. In this instance, 0 equals the default drive, and 1 = A, 2 = B, 3 = C, etc.

If the close operation is successful, DOS returns a 0 in AL; if the operation is unsuccessful, AL contains FFh.

Notice that this service allows you to use only FCBs. Because FCB file encoding does not allow for path names, any file operations must be performed in the current disk subdirectory. With floppy disks, this limitation may not be a problem. With fixed disks, however, the limitation can be serious. (Service 21/3E, another method of closing files, does not have this limitation.)

Search for First File Name Match, Using FCB (Interrupt 21h, service 11h)

Category: Disk services

Registers on Entry:

AH: 11h
DX: Offset address of FCB
DS: Segment address of FCB

Registers on Return:

AL: Status byte

Memory Affected: If a file name match is located, DOS fills in the memory area specified as the disk transfer area (DTA) so that it reflects a completed FCB for the file. DOS alters the original FCB area to allow subsequent searching with service 21/12.

Syntax:

```
PUSH   CS                    ;Code segment and
POP    DS                    ;  data segment are same
MOV    DX,OFFSET FCB_1       ;Offset address of FCB
MOV    AH,11h                ;Want service 11h
INT    21h                   ;DOS services interrupt
```

Description: This service locates a file with a specified name in the current directory of a disk drive, based on a file control block, or FCB. The FCB consists of 44 bytes constructed in the following manner:

```
FCB_PRE      DB    0FFh              ;Extension flag
             DB    5 DUP(0)          ;Unused
FILE_ATTR    DB    00                ;File attribute
FCB_1        DB    00                ;Set for default drive
FILE_ROOT    DB    'FILENAME'        ;File name root
FILE_EXT     DB    '???'             ;File name extension
BLOCK_NUM    DW    0000              ;Current block number
REC_SIZE     DW    0000              ;Record size
FILE_SIZE    DD    00000000          ;File size
FILE_DATE    DW    0000              ;File date
FILE_TIME    DW    0000              ;File time
             DB    8 DUP(0)          ;DOS work area
REC_NUM      DB    00                ;Current record number
RANDOM_REC   DD    00000000          ;Random record number
```

The offset address of FCB_1 is the address you specify in DS:DX when you invoke this service. If you are using an extended FCB, you should use the offset address of FCB_PRE. To call the service, you must specify the values for FCB_1 (the drive designator), FILE_ROOT, and FILE_EXT. Notice that the drive designator is different from the normal method for DOS and BIOS drive designation. In this instance, 0 equals the default drive, and 1 = A, 2 = B, 3 = C, etc.

One useful feature of this service is that you can use the question mark (?) as a wild card in the file name specification of the FCB. In the sample FCB, any file with the name FILENAME and any extension constitutes a match.

If you are searching for non-normal files (that is, hidden, system, etc.), you must use an extended FCB, which is the sample portion beginning with FCB_PRE. FCB_PRE is set to FFh, signaling that the FCB extension is active. You set the FILE_ATTR file attribute to specify the combination of file attributes you want to search for. Table 16.1 shows possible settings of this byte.

If the search is successful, DOS returns a 0 in AL and constructs a full FCB (either normal or extended) at the DTA location specified through service 21/1A. If the search is unsuccessful, AL contains FFh and the DTA remains undisturbed.

Notice that this service allows you to use only FCBs. Because FCB file encoding does not allow for path names, any file operations must be per-

Table 16.1. Extended FCB attribute byte settings for service 21/11.

Value	Types of files searched
0	Normal files
2	Normal and hidden files
4	Normal and system files
6	Normal, system, and hidden files
8	Volume labels only
16	Directory files

formed in the current disk subdirectory. With floppy disks, this limitation may not be a problem. With fixed disks, however, the limitation can be serious. Refer to service 21/4E, another method of searching for files, which does not have this limitation.

Search for Next File Name Match, Using FCB (Interrupt 21h, service 12h)

Category: Disk services

Registers on Entry:

AH: 12h
DX: Offset address of FCB
DS: Segment address of FCB

Registers on Return:

AL: Status byte

Memory Affected: If a file name match is located, DOS fills in the memory area specified as the DTA so that it reflects a completed FCB for the file. DOS alters the original FCB area to allow subsequent searching with service 21/12.

Syntax:

```
PUSH  CS              ;Code segment and
POP   DS              ;  data segment are same
MOV   DX,OFFSET FCB_1 ;Offset address of FCB
MOV   AH,12h          ;Want service 12h
INT   21h             ;DOS services interrupt
```

Description: Use this service to locate (in the current directory of a disk drive) a file with a specified name, based on a file control block, or FCB. Before you invoke this service, you must set the FCB by a call to service

21/11. If the FCB is not set, the results can be unpredictable. For more information, see the description for service 21/11.

Because any given directory must contain unique file names, this service is useless if the file specification for which you are searching does not contain the question-mark wild card (?).

Delete File Using FCB (Interrupt 21h, service 13h)

Category: Disk services

Registers on Entry:

AH: 13h
DX: Offset address of FCB
DS: Segment address of FCB

Registers on Return:

AL: Status byte

Memory Affected: None

Syntax:

```
PUSH   CS                      ;Code segment and
POP    DS                      ;  data segment are same
MOV    DX,OFFSET FCB_1         ;Offset address of FCB
MOV    AH,13h                  ;Want service 13h
INT    21h                     ;DOS services interrupt
```

Description: Use this service to delete files by means of a file control block, or FCB. The FCB consists of 44 bytes constructed in the following manner:

```
FCB_PRE      DB    OFFh           ;Extension flag
             DB    5 DUP(0)       ;Unused
FILE_ATTR    DB    00             ;File attribute
FCB_1        DB    00             ;Set for default drive
FILE_ROOT    DB    'FILENAME'     ;File name root
FILE_EXT     DB    '???'          ;File name extension
BLOCK_NUM    DW    0000           ;Current block number
REC_SIZE     DW    0000           ;Record size
FILE_SIZE    DD    00000000       ;File size
FILE_DATE    DW    0000           ;File date
FILE_TIME    DW    0000           ;File time
             DB    8 DUP(0)       ;DOS work area
```

```
REC_NUM        DB     00               ;Current record number
RANDOM_REC     DD     00000000         ;Random record number
```

When you invoke this service, specify the offset address of FCB_1 in DS:DX. If you are using an extended FCB, use the offset address of FCB_PRE. To call this service, you must specify the values for FCB_1 (the drive designator), FILE_ROOT, and FILE_EXT. Notice that the drive designator is different from the normal method for DOS and BIOS drive designation. In this instance, 0 equals the default drive, and 1 = A, 2 = B, 3 = C, etc.

A useful feature of this service is that you can use the question mark (?) as a wild card in the file name specification of the FCB. In the sample FCB, any file with the name FILENAME and any extension is deleted.

Notice that this service allows you to use only FCBs. Because FCB file encoding does not allow for path names, any files deleted must reside in the current disk subdirectory. With floppy disks, this limitation may not be a problem, but with fixed disks, the limitation can be serious. Refer to service 21/41, a method of deleting files that does not have this limitation.

Sequential Read Using FCB (Interrupt 21h, service 14h)

Category: Disk services

Registers on Entry:

AH: 14h
DX: Offset address of FCB
DS: Segment address of FCB

Registers on Return:

AL: Status byte

Memory Affected: The memory area designated as DTA is overwritten with information read from the disk.

Syntax:

```
PUSH   CS                  ;Code segment and
POP    DS                  ; data segment are same
MOV    DX,OFFSET FCB_1     ;Offset address of FCB
MOV    AH,14h              ;Want service 14h
INT    21h                 ;DOS services interrupt
```

Description: This service is used to read a block of information from a file that has been opened to the DTA. You designate the block size through the file control block, or FCB. The FCB consists of 44 bytes constructed in the following manner:

```
FCB_PRE      DB    OFFh              ;Extension flag
             DB    5 DUP(0)          ;Unused
FILE_ATTR    DB    00                ;File attribute
FCB_1        DB    00                ;Set for default drive
FILE_ROOT    DB    'FILENAME'        ;File name root
FILE_EXT     DB    'DAT'             ;File name extension
BLOCK_NUM    DW    0000              ;Current block number
REC_SIZE     DW    0000              ;Record size
FILE_SIZE    DD    00000000          ;File size
FILE_DATE    DW    0000              ;File date
FILE_TIME    DW    0000              ;File time
             DB    8 DUP(0)          ;DOS work area
REC_NUM      DB    00                ;Current record number
RANDOM_REC   DD    00000000          ;Random record number
```

When you invoke this service, specify the offset address of FCB_1 in DS:DX. If you are using an extended FCB, use the offset address of FCB_PRE. Before you open the file, set the values for FCB_1 (the drive designator), FILE_ROOT, and FILE_EXT. Specify the size of the block to be read in the REC_SIZE field. The values in BLOCK_NUM and REC_NUM designate where in the file the read is to begin; these fields are incremented automatically after a successful read.

When the service is completed, the value of AL indicates the status of the operation. If AL is 0, the read was successful. If AL is 1, no data was read because the end of file was already reached. If AL is 2, the DTA crossed a segment boundary (a memory address ending in 000), which resulted in an error condition. If AL is 3, the end of file had already been reached when the read began and the service could not read the entire block (the partial block was read and placed in the DTA area).

Sequential Write Using FCB (Interrupt 21h, service 15h)

Category: Disk services

Registers on Entry:

AH: 15h
DX: Offset address of FCB
DS: Segment address of FCB

Registers on Return:

AL: Status byte

Memory Affected: None

Syntax:

```
PUSH   CS                    ;Code segment and
POP    DS                    ; data segment are same
MOV    DX,OFFSET FCB_1       ;Offset address of FCB
MOV    AH,15h                ;Want service 15h
INT    21h                   ;DOS services interrupt
```

Description: This service is used to write a block of information from the DTA to an open file. You designate the block size through the file control block, or FCB. The FCB consists of 44 bytes constructed in the following manner:

```
FCB_PRE      DB    OFFh         ;Extension flag
             DB    5 DUP(0)     ;Unused
FILE_ATTR    DB    00           ;File attribute
FCB_1        DB    00           ;Set for default drive
FILE_ROOT    DB    'FILENAME'   ;File name root
FILE_EXT     DB    'DAT'        ;File name extension
BLOCK_NUM    DW    0000         ;Current block number
REC_SIZE     DW    0000         ;Record size
FILE_SIZE    DD    00000000     ;File size
FILE_DATE    DW    0000         ;File date
FILE_TIME    DW    0000         ;File time
             DB    8 DUP(0)     ;DOS work area
REC_NUM      DB    00           ;Current record number
RANDOM_REC   DD    00000000     ;Random record number
```

You specify the offset address of FCB_1 in DS:DX when you invoke this service. If you are using an extended FCB, you should use the offset address of FCB_PRE. You should set the values for FCB_1 (the drive designator), FILE_ROOT, and FILE_EXT before you open the file. You specify the size of the block to be written in the REC_SIZE field. The values in BLOCK_NUM and REC_NUM designate where in the file the writing is to begin. After a successful write, these fields are incremented automatically.

When the service is completed, the value of AL indicates the status of the operation. If AL is 0, the write was successful. If AL is 1, a disk-full error was detected during the write. If AL is 2, the DTA crossed a segment boundary (a memory address ending in 000), and an error was generated.

Create File Using FCB (Interrupt 21h, service 16h)

Category: Disk services

Registers on Entry:

AH: 16h
DX: Offset address of FCB
DS: Segment address of FCB

Registers on Return:

AL: Status byte

Memory Affected: If the file is created successfully, DOS fills in the FCB area (specified by DS:DX) to reflect the status of the file.

Syntax:

```
PUSH    CS              ;Code segment and
POP     DS              ;  data segment are same
MOV     DX,OFFSET FCB_1 ;Offset address of FCB
MOV     AH,16h          ;Want service 16h
INT     21h             ;DOS services interrupt
```

Description: This service uses the information in the file control block, or FCB, to create or truncate a disk file. This FCB is a block of information that the programmer initially sets and DOS subsequently completes. The FCB consists of 44 bytes constructed in the following manner:

```
FCB_PRE      DB     0FFh        ;Extension flag
             DB     5 DUP(0)    ;Unused
             DB     00          ;File attribute
FCB_1        DB     00          ;Set for default drive
FILE_ROOT    DB     'FILENAME'  ;File name root
FILE_EXT     DB     'EXT'       ;File name extension
BLOCK_NUM    DW     0000        ;Current block number
REC_SIZE     DW     0000        ;Record size
FILE_SIZE    DD     00000000    ;File size
FILE_DATE    DW     0000        ;File date
FILE_TIME    DW     0000        ;File time
             DB     8 DUP(0)    ;DOS work area
REC_NUM      DB     00          ;Current record number
RANDOM_REC   DD     00000000    ;Random record number
```

You specify the offset address of FCB_1 in DS:DX when you invoke this service. If you are using an extended FCB, you should use the offset address of FCB_PRE. To call this service, you must specify the values for FCB_1 (the drive designator), FILE_ROOT, and FILE_EXT. Notice that the drive designator is different from the normal method for DOS and BIOS drive designation. In this instance, 0 equals the default drive, and 1 = A, 2 = B, 3 = C, etc.

If you use the FCB extension area, you can specify the attribute of the file being created. In the example, the extended FCB begins with the area shown as FCB_PRE. FCB_PRE is set to FFh, signaling that the FCB extension is active. The FILE_ATTR file attribute is set to specify the file attribute for the new file.

If the file name specified in the FCB already exists in the current directory, the file is opened and its length is truncated to 0.

If the file is created successfully, DOS returns a 0 in AL. In addition, the service sets FCB_1 to reflect the drive number (1 = A, 2 = B, 3 = C, etc.), and sets BLOCK_NUM to 0, REC_SIZE to 80h, and FILE_SIZE, FILE_DATE, and FILE_TIME to their appropriate values for the new file. If the open operation is unsuccessful, DOS returns FFh in AL and does not fill in the FCB.

When this service is completed, the specified file is left open. You do not need to open the file, but you must remember to close it.

Notice that this service allows you to use only FCBs. Because FCB file encoding does not allow for path names, any file operations must be performed in the current disk subdirectory. With floppy disks, this limitation may not be a problem. With fixed disks, however, the limitation can be serious. Refer to service 21/3C; this method of creating files does not have this limitation.

Rename File Using FCB (Interrupt 21h, service 17h)

Category: Disk services

Registers on Entry:

AH: 17h
DX: Offset address of modified FCB
DS: Segment address of modified FCB

Registers on Return:

AL: Status byte

Memory Affected: None

Syntax:

```
PUSH  CS              ;Code segment and
POP   DS              ; data segment are same
MOV   DX,OFFSET FCB_1 ;Offset address of FCB
MOV   AH,17h          ;Want service 17h
INT   21h             ;DOS services interrupt
```

Description: This service uses information contained in a modified file control block, or FCB, to rename a file in the current directory. This modified FCB consists of 44 bytes constructed in the following manner:

```
MOD_FCB   DB   00         ;Set for default drive
OLD_ROOT  DB   'OLD_FILE'  ;Original file root
OLD_EXT   DB   'EXT'       ;Original file extension
          DB   5 DUP(0)    ;DOS work area
NEW_ROOT  DB   'NEW_FILE'  ;New file root
NEW_EXT   DB   'EXT'       ;New file extension
          DB   16 DUP(0)   ;DOS work area
```

You specify the offset address of MOD_FCB in DS:DX when you invoke this service. To call this service, you must specify the values for MOD_FCB (the drive designator), OLD_ROOT, and OLD_EXT. Notice that the drive designator is different from the normal method for DOS and BIOS drive designation. In this instance, 0 equals the default drive, and 1=A, 2=B, 3=C, etc.

If the renaming operation is successful, DOS returns a 0 in AL. If the operation is unsuccessful, DOS returns FFh in AL.

This service does not allow you to rename files outside of the current directory. With floppy disks, this limitation may not be a problem. With fixed disks, however, the limitation can be serious. Refer to service 21/56; this method of creating files does not have this limitation.

Reserved (Interrupt 21h, service 18h)

Description: IBM and Microsoft list this service as reserved for the internal use of DOS. According to the original author of the operating system, the service—which is not publicized or documented—was included for exact compatibility with the older CP/M system for 8-bit hardware and referred to a function that did not apply in this system.

Get Current Drive (Interrupt 21h, service 19h)

Category: Disk services

Registers on Entry:

AH: 19h

Registers on Return:

AL: Drive code

Memory Affected: None

Syntax:

```
MOV    AH,19h            ;Want service 19h
INT    21h               ;DOS services interrupt
MOV    CUR_DRIVE,AL      ;Store drive designator
```

Description: This service is used to determine the current default disk drive. The service has no calling parameters, and the returned value in AL is a drive code in which $0 = A$, $1 = B$, $2 = C$, etc.

Generally, the default disk drive is the drive from which the computer was booted or the drive last set with service 21/0E.

Set Disk Transfer Area (DTA) (Interrupt 21h, service 1Ah)

Category: Disk services

Registers on Entry:

AH: 1Ah
DX: Offset address of DTA
DS: Segment address of DTA

Registers on Return: Unchanged

Memory Affected: None

Syntax:

```
PUSH   CS                ;Code segment and
POP    DS                ; data segment are same
MOV    DX,OFFSET FCB_1   ;Offset address of FCB
MOV    AH,1Ah            ;Want service 1Ah
INT    21h               ;DOS services interrupt
```

Description: When DOS works with file control blocks (FCBs), DOS transfers information to and from the disk through a block of memory called the DTA.

Normally, this DTA is set as a 128-byte memory area at offset 80h in the program segment prefix (PSP). You can, however, set aside for the DTA an area of memory within your program. If the size of the blocks you will be reading and writing is larger than 128 bytes, you need to specify your own DTA through this service.

Get FAT (File Allocation Table) Information for Default Drive (Interrupt 21h, service 1Bh)

Category: Disk services

Registers on Entry:

AH: 1Bh

Registers on Return:

AL: Sectors per cluster
BX: Offset address of FAT ID byte
CX: Bytes per sector
DX: Clusters per disk
DS: Segment address of FAT ID byte

Memory Affected: None

Syntax:

```
MOV    AH,1Bh          ;Want service 1Bh
INT    21h             ;DOS services interrupt
```

Description: This service returns basic information about the disk in the default drive. The information includes the number of bytes per sector (CX), the number of sectors per cluster (AL), the number of clusters per disk (DX), and the address of the File Allocation Table identification (ID) byte (DS:BX).

Once you know this information, deriving other valuable information is easy. For instance, to determine the byte capacity of the disk, you simply multiply CX by AL by DX.

The File Allocation Table (FAT) identification byte to which DS:BX points indicates the type of disk in use. Actually, this byte indicates only how the disk was formatted. Table 16.2 shows some possible values for the FAT ID byte.

Table 16.2. *Some possible FAT ID byte values.*

Value	Disk characteristics
F0	Not identifiable
F8	Fixed disk
F9	Double sided, 15 sectors/track
F9	Double sided, 9 sectors/track (720K)
FC	Single sided, 9 sectors/track
FD	Double sided, 9 sectors/track (360K)
FE	Single sided, 8 sectors/track
FF	Double sided, 8 sectors/track

Get FAT Information for Drive (Interrupt 21h, service 1Ch)

Category: Disk services

Registers on Entry:

   AH: 1Ch
   DL: Drive code

Registers on Return:

   AL: Sectors per cluster
   BX: Offset address of FAT ID byte
   CX: Bytes per sector
   DX: Clusters per disk
   DS: Segment address of FAT ID byte

Memory Affected: None

Syntax:

```
MOV   DL,0        ;Drive A:
MOV   AH,1Ch      ;Want service 1Ch
INT   21h         ;DOS services interrupt
```

Description: This service returns basic information about the disk in the drive specified by DL. The drive number is specified as A = 0, B = 1, C = 2, etc.

The information returned by this service is identical to that for service 21/1B. The information includes the number of bytes per sector (CX), the number of sectors per cluster (AL), the number of clusters per disk (DX), and the address of the File Allocation Table ID byte (DS:BX).

Once you know this information, deriving other valuable information is easy. For instance, to determine the byte capacity of the disk, you simply multiply CX by AL by DX.

The FAT ID byte to which DS:BX points indicates the type of disk in use. Actually, this byte indicates only how the disk was formatted. (Refer to table 16.2 for some possible values for the FAT ID byte.)

Reserved (Interrupt 21h, services 1Dh, 1Eh, 1Fh, 20h)

Description: IBM and Microsoft list these services as reserved for the internal use of DOS. According to the original author of the operating system, the services (except for service 1Fh, which was documented in the original version), which are not publicized or documented, were included for exact compatibility with the older CP/M system for 8-bit hardware, and referred to functions that did not apply in this system.

Random Read, Using FCB (Interrupt 21h, service 21h)

Category: Disk services

Registers on Entry:

AH: 21h
DX: Offset address of FCB
DS: Segment address of FCB

Registers on Return:

AL: Status byte

Memory Affected: The memory area designated as DTA is overwritten with information read from the disk.

Syntax:

```
PUSH  CS              ;Code segment and
POP   DS              ;  data segment are same
MOV   DX,OFFSET FCB_1 ;Offset address of FCB
MOV   AH,21h          ;Want service 21h
INT   21h             ;DOS services interrupt
```

Description: This service is used to read a data record from an open file and place the information in the DTA. You designate the record size through the file control block, or FCB. The FCB consists of 44 bytes constructed in the following manner:

```
FCB_PRE      DB    0FFh            ;Extension flag
             DB    5 DUP(0)        ;Unused
FILE_ATTR    DB    00              ;File attribute
FCB_1        DB    00              ;Set for default drive
FILE_ROOT    DB    'FILENAME'      ;File name root
FILE_EXT     DB    'DAT'           ;File name extension
BLOCK_NUM    DW    0000            ;Current block number
REC_SIZE     DW    0000            ;Record size
FILE_SIZE    DD    00000000        ;File size
FILE_DATE    DW    0000            ;File date
FILE_TIME    DW    0000            ;File time
             DB    8 DUP(0)        ;DOS work area
REC_NUM      DB    00              ;Current record number
RANDOM_REC   DD    00000000        ;Random record number
```

You specify the offset address of FCB_1 in DS:DX when you invoke this service. If you are using an extended FCB, you should use the offset address of FCB_PRE. You should set the values for FCB_1 (the drive designator), FILE_ROOT, and FILE_EXT before the file is opened. You specify the file's record size in the REC_SIZE field. The area set aside as the DTA should be as large as a record. The values in REC_SIZE and RANDOM_REC specify where the file read is to begin. After a successful read, the values in BLOCK_NUM and REC_NUM are updated to the proper values. RANDOM_REC, which is not incremented by this service, remains the same as before the invocation.

When this service is completed, the value of AL indicates the status of the operation. If AL is 0, the read was successful. If AL is 1, no data was read because the end of file was already reached. If AL is 2, the DTA crossed a segment boundary (a memory address ending in 000) which resulted in an error condition. If AL is 3, the system reached the end of file during the read and could not read an entire block (the partial block was read and placed in the DTA area).

Random Write Using FCB (Interrupt 21h, service 22h)

Category: Disk services

Registers on Entry:

AH: 22h
DX: Offset address of FCB
DS: Segment address of FCB

Registers on Return:

AL: Status byte

Memory Affected: Certain FCB values are modified.

Syntax:

```
PUSH    CS                      ;Code segment and
POP     DS                      ; data segment are same
MOV     DX,OFFSET FCB_1         ;Offset address of FCB
MOV     AH,22h                  ;Want service 22h
INT     21h                     ;DOS services interrupt
```

Description: This service is used to write a data record to a previously opened file. The information to be written is contained in the DTA. The record size is designated through the file control block, or FCB. The FCB consists of 44 bytes constructed in the following manner:

```
FCB_PRE     DB      OFFh            ;Extension flag
            DB      5 DUP(0)        ;Unused
FILE_ATTR   DB      00              ;File attribute
FCB_1       DB      00              ;Set for default drive
FILE_ROOT   DB      'FILENAME'      ;File name root
FILE_EXT    DB      'DAT'           ;File name extension
BLOCK_NUM   DW      0000            ;Current block number
REC_SIZE    DW      0000            ;Record size
FILE_SIZE   DD      00000000        ;File size
FILE_DATE   DW      0000            ;File date
FILE_TIME   DW      0000            ;File time
            DB      8 DUP(0)        ;DOS work area
REC_NUM     DB      00              ;Current record number
RANDOM_REC  DD      00000000        ;Random record number
```

You specify the offset address of FCB_1 in DS:DX when you invoke this service. If you are using an extended FCB, you should use the offset address of FCB_PRE. You should set the values for FCB_1 (the drive designator), FILE_ROOT, and FILE_EXT before the file is opened. You specify the file's record size in the REC_SIZE field. This size is the number of bytes that will be written by this service. The values in REC_SIZE and RANDOM_REC specify the location in the file at which writing is to begin. After a successful write, the values in BLOCK_NUM and REC_NUM are updated to the proper values. RANDOM_REC, which is not incremented by this service, remains the same as before the invocation.

When this service is completed, the value of AL indicates the status of the operation. If AL is 0, the write was successful. If AL is 1, a disk-full error was detected during the write. If AL is 2, the DTA crossed a segment boundary (a memory address ending in 000), and an error was generated.

Get File Size Using FCB (Interrupt 21h, service 23h)

Category: Disk services

Registers on Entry:

AH: 23h
DX: Offset address of FCB
DS: Segment address of FCB

Registers on Return:

AL: Status byte

Memory Affected: Certain FCB values are modified.

Syntax:

```
PUSH    CS              ;Code segment and
POP     DS              ;  data segment are same
MOV     DX,OFFSET FCB_1 ;Offset address of FCB
MOV     AH,23h          ;Want service 23h
INT     21h             ;DOS services interrupt
CMP     AL,0FFh         ;Was the file found?
JE      FILE_ERR        ;No, so handle error
```

Description: This service searches for a specific file name in the current directory and returns the number of records in that file. You specify the file name to be used in the file control block, or FCB. The FCB consists of 44 bytes constructed in the following manner:

```
FCB_PRE     DB      0FFh        ;Extension flag
            DB      5 DUP(0)    ;Unused
FILE_ATTR   DB      00          ;File attribute
FCB_1       DB      00          ;Set for default drive
FILE_ROOT   DB      'FILENAME'  ;File name root
FILE_EXT    DB      'DAT'       ;File name extension
BLOCK_NUM   DW      0000        ;Current block number
REC_SIZE    DW      0000        ;Record size
FILE_SIZE   DD      00000000    ;File size
FILE_DATE   DW      0000        ;File date
```

```
FILE_TIME      DW    0000          ;File time
               DB    8 DUP(0)      ;DOS work area
REC_NUM        DB    00            ;Current record number
RANDOM_REC     DD    00000000      ;Random record number
```

You specify the offset address of FCB_1 in DS:DX when you invoke this service. If you are using an extended FCB, you should use the offset address of FCB_PRE. To use this service, you should set the values for FCB_1 (the drive designator), FILE_ROOT, and FILE_EXT. The value in REC_SIZE indicates the record size in the file and has a direct bearing on the returned value. If this field is set to 1, the value returned by this service is equal to the number of bytes in the file.

On return, the value of AL indicates the status of the operation. If AL is 0, the file was located, and the value in RANDOM_REC indicates the number of records (of size REC_SIZE) in the file. If AL is FFh, the requested file could not be located, and the FCB values are not significant.

Set Random Record Field in FCB (Interrupt 21h, service 24h)

Category: Disk services

Registers on Entry:

AH: 24h
DX: Offset address of FCB
DS: Segment address of FCB

Registers on Return: Unchanged

Memory Affected: Certain FCB values are modified.

Syntax:

```
PUSH   CS                 ;Code segment and
POP    DS                 ;  data segment are same
MOV    DX,OFFSET FCB_1    ;Offset address of FCB
MOV    AH,24h             ;Want service 24h
INT    21h                ;DOS services interrupt
```

Description: This service modifies the contents of the random record field in the file control block (FCB) of an open file. The FCB is a 44-byte area constructed as follows:

```
FCB_PRE        DB    0FFh          ;Extension flag
               DB    5 DUP(0)      ;Unused
FILE_ATTR      DB    00            ;File attribute
```

```
FCB_1           DB      00                  ;Set for default drive
FILE_ROOT       DB      'FILENAME'          ;File name root
FILE_EXT        DB      'DAT'               ;File name extension
BLOCK_NUM       DW      0000                ;Current block number
REC_SIZE        DW      0000                ;Record size
FILE_SIZE       DD      00000000            ;File size
FILE_DATE       DW      0000                ;File date
FILE_TIME       DW      0000                ;File time
                DB      8 DUP(O)            ;DOS work area
REC_NUM         DB      00                  ;Current record number
RANDOM_REC      DD      00000000            ;Random record number
```

You specify the offset address of FCB_1 in DS:DX when you invoke this service. If you are using an extended FCB, you should use the offset address of FCB_PRE. Before you call the service, set the values for FCB_1 (the drive designator), FILE_ROOT, and FILE_EXT for the open file. Also set the values in REC_SIZE, REC_NUM, and BLOCK_NUM before calling this service. These values are used to compute the value in RANDOM_REC.

Set Interrupt Vector (Interrupt 21h, service 25h)

Category: System services

Registers on Entry:

AH: 25h
AL: Interrupt number
DX: Offset address of new interrupt handler
DS: Segment address of new interrupt handler

Registers on Return: Unchanged

Memory Affected: The values in the interrupt vector table in low memory are altered.

Syntax:

```
PUSH    DS                          ;Save current data segment
MOV     AL,5                        ;Print-screen interrupt
PUSH    CS                          ;Code segment and
POP     DS                          ;  data segment are same
MOV     DX,OFFSET PS_HANDLER        ;Offset address of handler
MOV     AH,25h                      ;Want service 25h
INT     21h                         ;DOS services interrupt
POP     DS                          ;Restore data segment
```

Description: This service provides a uniform method for altering the interrupt vector table in low memory. Such a method is useful if you want to alter or replace the way the system currently handles interrupts.

An important consideration is that, once changed, the old interrupt vector is lost. You can use service 21/35 to determine the current vector so that you can save the vector before changing it. Then, on program completion, you can reset the vector to the original value.

Create Program Segment Prefix (PSP) (Interrupt 21h, service 26h)

Category: System services

Registers on Entry:

AH: 26h
DX: Segment address of new PSP

Registers on Return: Unchanged

Memory Affected: The 256 bytes of memory at the desired segment address are altered.

Syntax:

```
MOV    DX,OFFSET CS:PROG_END    ;Point to end of program
MOV    AH,26h                   ;Want service 26h
INT    21h                      ;DOS services interrupt
```

Description: This service, which is used to facilitate overlays and subprograms to the current program, copies the current PSP contents to the desired paragraph and then sets the PSP vector contents to match the contents of the interrupt vector table.

The current DOS technical reference manuals (those supplied with DOS versions released since version 3.0) recommend that this service not be used; instead, they recommend using service 21/4B.

Read Random Record(s) Using FCB (Interrupt 21h, service 27h)

Category: Disk services

Registers on Entry:

AH: 27h
CX: Number of records to read
DX: Offset address of FCB
DS: Segment address of FCB

Registers on Return:

AL: Status byte
CX: Number of records read

Memory Affected: The memory designated by DTA is overlaid with information read from the disk.

Syntax:

```
PUSH    CS                      ;Code segment and
POP     DS                      ;  data segment are same
MOV     DX,OFFSET FCB_1         ;Offset address of FCB
MOV     CX,8                    ;Read 8 records
MOV     AH,27h                  ;Want service 27h
INT     21h                     ;DOS services interrupt
```

Description: This service is used to read a specified number of data records from a previously opened file and to place the information in the DTA. You specify the number of records to read in CX. Designate the record size through the file control block, or FCB. The FCB consists of 44 bytes constructed in the following manner:

```
FCB_PRE     DB      0FFh            ;Extension flag
            DB      5 DUP(0)        ;Unused
FILE_ATTR   DB      00              ;File attribute
FCB_1       DB      00              ;Set for default drive
FILE_ROOT   DB      'FILENAME'      ;File name root
FILE_EXT    DB      'DAT'           ;File name extension
BLOCK_NUM   DW      0000            ;Current block number
REC_SIZE    DW      0000            ;Record size
FILE_SIZE   DD      00000000        ;File size
FILE_DATE   DW      0000            ;File date
FILE_TIME   DW      0000            ;File time
            DB      8 DUP(0)        ;DOS work area
REC_NUM     DB      00              ;Current record number
RANDOM_REC  DD      00000000        ;Random record number
```

You specify the offset address of FCB_1 in DS:DX when you invoke this service. If you are using an extended FCB, you should use the offset address of FCB_PRE. You set the values for FCB_1 (the drive designator), FILE_ROOT, and FILE_EXT before the file is opened. You specify the file's record size in the REC_SIZE field. The area set aside as the DTA should be large enough to contain the number of records being requested. The values in REC_SIZE and RANDOM_REC specify the location in the file at which the read is to begin. After a successful read, the service updates the values in BLOCK_NUM, REC_NUM, and RANDOM_REC.

When this service is completed, the value of AL indicates the status of the operation. If AL is 0, the read was successful. If AL is 1, no data was read because the end of file was already reached. If AL is 2, the DTA crossed a segment boundary (a memory address ending in 000) which resulted in an error condition. If AL is 3, the end of file was reached during the read; the service could not read an entire block (the partial block is still read and placed in the DTA area). CX contains the number of records read.

Write Random Record(s) Using FCB (Interrupt 21h, service 28h)

Category: Disk services

Registers on Entry:

AH: 28h
CX: Number of records to write
DX: Offset address of FCB
DS: Segment address of FCB

Registers on Return:

AL: Status byte
CX: Number of records written

Memory Affected: Certain FCB values are modified.

Syntax:

```
PUSH    CS                  ;Code segment and
POP     DS                  ;  data segment are same
MOV     DX,OFFSET FCB_1     ;Offset address of FCB
MOV     CX,8                ;Write 8 records
MOV     AH,28h              ;Want service 28h
INT     21h                 ;DOS services interrupt
```

Description: This service is used to write a specific number of data records to a previously opened file. The information to be written is contained in the DTA. You specify the number of records to be written in CX. You designate the record size through the file control block, or FCB. The FCB consists of 44 bytes constructed in the following manner:

```
FCB_PRE      DB    OFFh          ;Extension flag
             DB    5 DUP(0)      ;Unused
FILE_ATTR    DB    00            ;File attribute
FCB_1        DB    00            ;Set for default drive
FILE_ROOT    DB    'FILENAME'    ;File name root
FILE_EXT     DB    'DAT'         ;File name extension
BLOCK_NUM    DW    0000          ;Current block number
REC_SIZE     DW    0000          ;Record size
FILE_SIZE    DD    00000000      ;File size
FILE_DATE    DW    0000          ;File date
FILE_TIME    DW    0000          ;File time
             DB    8 DUP(0)      ;DOS work area
REC_NUM      DB    00            ;Current record number
RANDOM_REC   DD    00000000      ;Random record number
```

You specify the offset address of FCB_1 DS:DX when you invoke this service. If you are using an extended FCB, you should use the offset address of FCB_PRE. You set the values for FCB_1 (the drive designator), FILE_ROOT, and FILE_EXT before the file is opened. Specify the file's record size in the REC_SIZE field. The values in REC_SIZE and RANDOM_REC specify the location in the file at which the writing is to begin. After a successful write, the service updates the values in BLOCK_NUM, REC_NUM, and RANDOM_REC.

When this service is completed, the value of AL indicates the status of the operation. If AL is 0, the write was successful. If AL is 1, a disk-full error was detected during the write. If AL is 2, the DTA crossed a segment boundary (a memory address ending in 000), and an error was generated. CX contains the number of records written.

Parse File Name Using FCB (Interrupt 21h, service 29h)

Category: Disk services

Registers on Entry:

AH: 29h
AL: Parsing control byte
SI: Offset address of string to be parsed
DI: Offset address of FCB
DS: Segment address of string to be parsed
ES: Segment address of FCB

Registers on Return:

AL: Status byte

SI: Offset address of first character following parsed
 string

DI: Offset address of FCB

DS: Segment address of first character following parsed
 string

ES: Segment address of FCB

Memory Affected: Certain values in the FCB are altered.

Syntax:

```
PUSH   DS                    ;Save data segment
PUSH   ES                    ;Save extra segment
MOV    AX,CS                 ;Code, data, and extra
MOV    DS,AX                 ;  segments are all
MOV    ES,AX                 ;  the same
MOV    SI,OFFSET INPUT       ;Offset address of string
MOV    DI,OFFSET FCB_1       ;Offset address of FCB
MOV    AL,00001111b          ;Set proper parse control
MOV    AH,29h                ;Want service 29h
INT    21h                   ;DOS services interrupt
POP    ES                    ;Restore extra segment
POP    DS                    ;Restore data segment
```

Description: This service is used to parse (translate) a text string to pick
out a valid drive designator, file name, and file extension. The service
parses for simple drive/file name designations only, not for path names.

DS:SI points to the text string to be parsed, and ES:DI points to the
memory area that will hold the constructed FCB. This area should be at
least 44 bytes in length.

The four low-order bits of AL control how the text string is parsed.
Table 16.3 details the meanings of the bit settings.

This service correctly translates wild card characters ($*$ and ?) to the
appropriate FCB values.

On return, AL indicates the parsing status. If AL = 0, no wild card characters were located in the text string. If AL = 1, the text string contained
wild card characters. If AL = FFh, the drive specifier was invalid. In all
instances, ES:DI points to the first byte of the new FCB.

Table 16.3. Bit settings for AL register, service 21/29.

Bits 76543210	*Meaning*
0000	Reserved—must be set to 0
0	File extension in FCB is set either to parsed value or blanks.
1	File extension in FCB is set only if 1 is detected in the text string, and the parsed file name is valid.
0	File name in FCB is set either to parsed value or blanks.
1	File name in FCB is set only if a valid file name exists in the text string.
0	Drive ID byte is set either to parsed value or 0.
1	Drive ID byte is set only if a valid drive designator is parsed in the text string.
0	Leading separators are not ignored.
1	Leading separators are ignored.

Get System Date (Interrupt 21h, service 2Ah)

Category: Date/time services

Registers on Entry:

    AH: 2Ah

Registers on Return:

    AL: Day of week
    CX: Year
    DH: Month
    DL: Day

Memory Affected: None

Syntax:

```
MOV    AH,2Ah              ;Want service 2Ah
INT    21h                 ;DOS services interrupt
```

Description: This service, which returns the system date, returns the month (DH), day (DL), and year (CX), along with the day of the week for this date. The day of the week is returned in AL as 0 = Sunday, 1 = Monday, 2 = Tuesday, etc.

Set System Date (Interrupt 21h, service 2Bh)

Category: Date/time services

Registers on Entry:

AH: 2Bh
CX: Year (1980-2099)
DH: Month (1-12)
DL: Day (1-31)

Registers on Return:

AL: Status byte

Memory Affected: None

Syntax:

```
            MOV     DH,MONTH        ;Get current month
            MOV     DL,DAY          ;Get current day
            MOV     CX,YEAR         ;Get current year
            CMP     CX,100          ;Does CX include century?
            JA      OK_GO           ;Yes, so continue
            ADD     CX,1900         ;No, so adjust
OK_GO:      MOV     AH,2Bh          ;Want service 2Bh
            INT     21h             ;DOS services interrupt
            CMP     AL,0            ;Was there an error?
            JNE     DATE_ERROR      ;Yes, go handle
```

Description: This service allows the DOS date (system software clock) to be set but does not set the real-time hardware clock on the IBM Personal Computer AT or compatibles.

To use this service, you must load a valid month, day, and year into DH, DL, and CX, respectively. On return, AL contains either a 0 (indicating that the date was valid and has been set) or FFh (indicating that the specified date is invalid).

Get System Time (Interrupt 21h, service 2Ch)

Category: Date/time services

Registers on Entry:

AH: 2Ch

Registers on Return:

CH: Hour
CL: Minute
DH: Second
DL: Hundredths of a second

Memory Affected: None

Syntax:

```
MOV    AH,2Ch          ;Want service 2Ch
INT    21h             ;DOS services interrupt
```

Description: This service converts the value of the computer's system-software clock counter to values that humans readily understand: hours (CH), minutes (CL), seconds (DH), and hundredths of seconds (DL). The hours (CH), which are returned in military time, range from 0 to 23.

Set Time (Interrupt 21h, service 2Dh)

Category: Date/time services

Registers on Entry:

AH: 2Dh
CH: Hour (0-23)
CL: Minute (0-59)
DH: Second (0-59)
DL: Hundredths of a second (0-99)

Registers on Return:

AL: Status byte

Memory Affected: None

Syntax:

```
MOV    CH,HOUR          ;Get current hour
MOV    CL,MINUTE        ;Get current minute
MOV    DH,SECOND        ;Get current second
MOV    DL,0             ;Hundredths doesn't matter
MOV    AH,2Dh           ;Want service 2Dh
INT    21h              ;DOS services interrupt
CMP    AL,0             ;Was there an error?
JNE    TIME_ERROR       ;Yes, go handle
```

Description: This service converts a specified time to the corresponding number of clock ticks and stores the resulting value in the computer's software clock counter. This service does not reset the real-time clock on the IBM Personal Computer AT or compatibles.

This service determines, through a series of multiplications, the number of clock ticks represented by the specified time. The entered values are converted to a total number of seconds, which then is multiplied by 18.2065 (the approximate number of clock ticks per second). For example, if you are setting the time to 14:22:17.39 (military time), the computer goes through conversions similar to the following:

14 hours =	14 * 60 * 60	=	50400	seconds
22 minutes =	22 * 60	=	1320	seconds
17.39 seconds =		17.39 =	17.39	seconds
Total:			51737.39	seconds
Clock ticks per second =			18.2065	ticks
Ticks represented:			941956.7910	ticks

Because fractional ticks cannot be represented, the total number is rounded to 941,957 ticks. The system software clock is then set to this value. The same type of process sets the system clock with the BIOS date/time services (refer to Chapter 15, service 1A/4). As a programmer, you can easily see the added value of some of these DOS services.

On return, AL contains either a 0 (indicating that the time was valid and has been set) or FFh (indicating that the specified time is invalid).

Set Verify Flag (Interrupt 21h, service 2Eh)

Category: Disk services

Registers on Entry:

AH: 2Eh
AL: Verify setting
DL: 0

Registers on Return: Unchanged

Memory Affected: None

Syntax:

```
MOV    AL,1           ;Set verify on
MOV    DL,0
MOV    AH,2Eh         ;Want service 2Eh
INT    21h            ;DOS services interrupt
```

Description: This service sets the system flag that determines whether DOS performs a verify operation after each disk write to ensure that the information has been recorded accurately. In most applications, the reliability of DOS operations is such that you safely can leave the verify flag set to off (the default setting).

The setting of DL is not important if you are working with DOS 3.0 or later versions but, for earlier versions, DL must be set to 0. This is an undocumented necessity; no reason is given for this setting.

If you are working with a network system, verification is not supported; the setting has no meaning.

Get Disk Transfer Area (Interrupt 21h, service 2Fh)

Category: Disk services

Registers on Entry:

AH: 2Fh

Registers on Return:

BX: Offset address of DTA
ES: Segment address of DTA

Memory Affected: None

Syntax:

```
MOV   AH,2Fh        ;Want service 2Fh
INT   21h           ;DOS services interrupt
```

Description: This service returns the address of the current DOS disk transfer area (DTA). DOS uses this area to transfer information between the computer and the disk. The address is returned in ES:BX.

Note that all services with numbers lower than 2Fh are available in all distributed versions of DOS; however, this service, and all that numerically follow it up to service 58h, became available only with the release of DOS version 2.

Get DOS Version Number (Interrupt 21h, service 30h)

Category: System services

Registers on Entry:

AH: 30h

Registers on Return:

AL: Major version number
AH: Minor version number
BX: 0
CX: 0

Memory Affected: None

Syntax:

```
MOV     AH,30h          ;Want service 30h
INT     21h             ;DOS services interrupt
CMP     AL,2            ;At least version 2.0?
JB      DOS_BAD         ;No, so exit early
```

Description: This service determines the version number of the DOS that is operating within the computer (the DOS used during booting).

The major purpose of this service is to allow programs to determine whether the proper version of DOS is in use for certain functions and services. AL contains the major version number (2 or 3). If AL contains 0, the DOS version is earlier than 2.0. The minor version number returned in AH is the number to the right of the decimal point (to two decimal places). BX and CX are also set to 0, suggesting that future versions of DOS may use this service to return expanded or additional information.

Terminate and Stay Resident (Interrupt 21h, service 31h)

Category: System services

Registers on Entry:

AH: 31h
AL: Return code
DX: Memory paragraphs to reserve

Registers on Return: Indeterminable (does not return)

Memory Affected: The available free memory is decreased by the number of paragraphs specified in DX.

Syntax:

```
MOV     AL,0            ;Return code of 0
MOV     DX,100h         ;Reserve 4K of info
MOV     AH,31h          ;Want service 31h
INT     21h             ;DOS services interrupt
```

Description: This service is used to exit a program, leaving all or part of the program's memory intact. The service is used by a wide variety of TSR (terminate and stay resident) programs such as SideKick, ProKey, etc.

The return code you specify in AL when you invoke this service is passed to the parent program or to DOS. From DOS command level, the return code is available through the ERRORLEVEL batch command; from programs, the return code can be determined through service 21/4D.

The number of paragraphs requested in DX are reserved by DOS and unavailable to other programs.

Reserved (Interrupt 21h, service 32h)

Description: IBM and Microsoft list this service as reserved for the internal use of DOS. The service, which is not publicized or documented, is subject to modification in future versions of DOS.

Ctrl-Break Flag Control (Interrupt 21h, service 33h)

Category: System services

Registers on Entry:

AH: 33h
AL: Get/set flag
DL: Ctrl-Break flag setting

Registers on Return:

DL: Ctrl-Break flag setting

Memory Affected: None

Syntax:

```
MOV    AL,1        ;Setting flag
MOV    DL,0        ;Turn off Ctrl-Break check
MOV    AH,33h      ;Want service 33h
INT    21h         ;DOS services interrupt
```

Description: This service gets or sets the flag that controls how often DOS checks whether the Ctrl-Break key combination has been pressed. Other documentation for this service implies that this flag turns Ctrl-Break checking on or off completely. Not true; this flag controls only the frequency of checking. Even with this flag set to off, checking is performed during certain DOS operations, such as performing video output.

To set the Ctrl-Break flag, load AL with 1 and DL with the desired state of the flag. If DL is 0, Ctrl-Break checking is at the minimum. If DL is 1, checking is more frequent: during virtually every DOS operation.

To get the current state of the flag, load AL with 0. On return, DL contains 0 or 1, depending on whether the flag is off or on.

Reserved (Interrupt 21h, service 34h)

Description: IBM and Microsoft list this service as reserved for the internal use of DOS. The service, which is not publicized or documented, is subject to modification in future versions of DOS.

Get Interrupt Vector (Interrupt 21h, service 35h)

Category: System services

Registers on Entry:

AH: 35h
AL: Interrupt number

Registers on Return:

BX: Offset address of interrupt handler
ES: Segment address of interrupt handler

Memory Affected: None

Syntax:

```
PUSH    ES                      ;Save registers
PUSH    BX
MOV     AL,5                    ;Print-screen interrupt
MOV     AH,35h                  ;Want service 35h
INT     21h                     ;DOS services interrupt
MOV     I5_SEG_OLD,ES           ;Store old segment
MOV     I5_OFF_OLD,BX           ;Store old offset
POP     BX                      ;Restore registers
POP     ES
```

Description: This service allows a uniform method for retrieving the address of an interrupt handler from the interrupt vector table in low memory. This service is used to determine current values so that they can be saved before changing; then service 21/25 can be used to alter the vector.

Get Disk Free Space (Interrupt 21h, service 36h)

Category: Disk services

Registers on Entry:

AH: 36h
DL: Drive code

Registers on Return:

AX: Sectors per cluster
BX: Available clusters
CX: Bytes per sector
DX: Clusters per drive

Memory Affected: None

Syntax:

```
MOV    AH,36h          ;Want service 36h
INT    21h             ;DOS services interrupt
CMP    AX,0FFFFh       ;Was there an error?
JE     ERROR           ;Yes, so go handle
PUSH   AX              ;Save sectors/cluster
MUL    DX              ;AX=sectors/drive
MUL    CX              ;DX:AX=bytes/drive
MOV    BPD_HI,DX       ;Save high word
MOV    BPD_LO,AX       ;Save low word
POP    AX              ;Get back sectors/cluster
MUL    BX              ;AX=free sectors/drive
MUL    CX              ;DX:AX=free bytes/drive
MOV    FBPD_HI,DX      ;Save high word
MOV    FBPD_LO,AX      ;Save low word
```

Description: This service returns basic information about space on the disk in the drive specified by DL. Notice that the drive code is different from the normal method for DOS and BIOS drive designation. In this instance, 0 equals the default drive, and 1 = A, 2 = B, 3 = C, etc.

On return from this service, the calling program checks AX to determine whether an error has occurred. If AX contains FFFFh, the drive code is invalid, and the balance of the registers are undefined.

If AX does not indicate an error, the information this service returns is similar to that provided by services 21/1B and 21/1C. This information includes the number of bytes per sector (CX), the number of sectors per cluster (AX), the number of clusters per disk (DX), and the number of free clusters on the disk (BX).

Once you know this information, deriving other valuable information is easy. For instance, to determine the byte capacity of the disk, you simply multiply CX by AX by DX.

Reserved (Interrupt 21h, service 37h)

Description: IBM and Microsoft list this service as reserved for the internal use of DOS. The service, which is not publicized or documented, is subject to modification in future versions of DOS.

Get/Set Country-Dependent Information (Interrupt 21h, service 38h)

Category: System services

Registers on Entry:

AH: 38h
AL: Country specifier
BX: Country specifier
DS: Segment address of information block
DX: Offset address of information block

Registers on Return: Unchanged

AX: Error code
BX: Country specifier
DS: Segment address of information block
DX: Offset address of information block

Memory Affected: If country information is retrieved, the memory block to which DS:DX points is overwritten with the country-dependent information.

Syntax:

```
MOV    AL,0                     ;Info for current country
PUSH   CS                       ;Code segment and
POP    DS                       ;  data segment are same
MOV    DX,OFFSET INFO_BLOCK     ;Offset address of block
MOV    AH,38h                   ;Want service 38h
INT    21h                      ;DOS services interrupt
```

Description: This powerful service allows you to retrieve or set a great deal of system information. The purposes and function of this service have changed over the course of several different versions of DOS. The description here conforms with the function of the service according to DOS 3.00.

DOS uses the country information governed by this service to control elements such as the display of dates and numbers. This service allows a program great flexibility in handling display formats, flexibility that is particularly useful if the software is being used for a market other than the United States. However, because most computers sold in the United States come configured for this country, this service may have little value for programmers whose sole market is the United States.

To get country-dependent information, simply load DS:DX with the segment:offset address of the 34-byte memory block that will be used to store the retrieved information. Load AL with the country code to be retrieved, as indicated in table 16.4.

Table 16.4. Country codes.

Country	Code
Currently installed	0
United States	1
Netherlands	31
Belgium	32
France	33
Spain	34
Italy	39
Switzerland	41
United Kingdom	44
Denmark	45
Sweden	46
Norway	47
Germany	49
Australia	61
Finland	358
Israel	972

If the country code is greater than 255 (as it is for Finland and Israel), you enter FFh in AL and set BX to the country code value. If AL is less than FFh, the contents of BX are not significant. Notice that if AL is 0, the country information table reflects the current country's information. If a different country is selected, that country's information is returned with no effect on the currently configured country.

On return, the carry flag indicates whether an error has occurred. If the carry flag is set, AX contains the error code, which can be handled through service 21/59. If the carry is clear, DS:DX points to the information table.

The following code segment illustrates a typical pattern for setting up the information table area. The code segment details the fields of the returned information:

```
COUNTRY_TABLE   EQU   THIS BYTE
DATE_FORMAT     DW    0000        ;Numeric code
CURRENCY_SYM    DB    5 DUP(0)    ;ASCIIZ-zero terminated
THOUSANDS_SEP   DB    00          ;ASCIIZ-zero terminated
                DB    00          ;  this byte will be nul
DECIMAL_SEP     DB    00          ;ASCIIZ-zero terminated
                DB    00          ;  this byte will be nul
DATE_SEP        DB    00          ;ASCIIZ-zero terminated
                DB    00          ;  this byte will be nul
TIME_SEP        DB    00          ;ASCIIZ-zero terminated
                DB    00          ;  this byte will be nul
CURRENCY_FMT    DB    00          ;Numeric code
CURRENCY_SD     DB    00          ;Sig. decimals in currency
TIME_FMT        DB    00          ;0=normal, 1=military
MAP_CALL        DD    00000000    ;Map call address
DATALIST_SEP    DB    00          ;ASCIIZ-zero terminated
                DB    00          ;  this byte will be nul
                DB    5 DUP(0)    ;Reserved area
```

To use this code segment, load DS:DX with the segment:offset of COUNTRY_TABLE before calling this service. On return, the information table is filled in, and individual fields can be addressed by field name.

DATE_FMT is a numeric code indicating the format to be used to display the date. Table 16.5 gives the possible values for this field. Notice also that this field is one word long, which may indicate significant expansion in future versions of DOS.

Table 16.5. *Date format codes and their meanings.*

Code	Date format	Country affiliation
0	mm dd yy	United States
1	dd mm yy	Europe
2	yy mm dd	Japan and the Far East

Now, refer again to the code segment. CURRENCY_SYM is a nul-terminated string that indicates the currency symbol for the country. This symbol can be no more than four characters long because the last character has a value of 0 (thus the designation nul-terminated, or *ASCIIZ* string).

THOUSANDS_SEP, DECIMAL_SEP, DATE_SEP, TIME_SEP, and DATALIST_SEP also are ASCIIZ strings. They indicate, respectively, the characters to be used to separate thousands in number displays, to indicate the decimal point, to separate date components, to separate time components, and to separate items in a data list. Each field is two bytes long, with the second byte set to nul. Why the writers of DOS felt that a single-byte string needed to be set up as an ASCIIZ string is a mystery.

CURRENCY_FMT is a numeric code indicating the format to be used to display the currency. Table 16.6 gives the possible values for this field.

Table 16.6. *Currency format codes and their meanings.*

Code	Meaning
0	Currency symbol immediately precedes currency value
1	Currency symbol immediately follows currency value
2	Currency symbol and space immediately precede currency value
3	Currency symbol and space immediately follow currency value
4	Currency symbol replaces decimal separator

CURRENCY_SD indicates the number of significant decimal places in the country's currency displays.

Bit 0 of TIME_FMT indicates how the hours of a time display are handled. If bit 0 is 0, a 12-hour clock is used. If bit 0 is 1, a military (or 24-hour) clock is used.

MAP_CALL is the full segment:offset address of a DOS subroutine that converts foreign ASCII lowercase characters to their uppercase equivalents. This routine is intended for ASCII codes with values greater than 7Fh. The original ASCII code is specified in AL; then this routine is called, and the converted ASCII code is returned in AL.

This service returns the country code in BX as well as the information in the country table. This code is meaningful only if you invoked the service with AL set to 0. In this way, you can determine the country for which the computer is configured.

To set country-dependent information, simply load DX with FFFFh, the signal that informs DOS that the country-dependent information is being set. You load AL with the country code (refer to table 16.4) to be retrieved. If the country code is greater than 255 (as for Finland and Israel), you enter FFh in AL and set BX to the country code value. If AL is less than FFh, the contents of BX are not significant.

On return, the carry flag indicates whether an error has occurred. If the carry flag is set, AX contains the error code, which can be handled through service 21/59. If the carry is clear, no error has occurred, and the contents of AX are not significant.

Create Subdirectory (Interrupt 21h, service 39h)

Category: Disk services

Registers on Entry:

AH: 39h
DX: Offset address of path name
DS: Segment address of path name

Registers on Return:

AX: Error code

Memory Affected: None

Syntax:

```
PUSH   CS                      ;Code segment and
POP    DS                      ;  data segment are same
MOV    DX,OFFSET PATH_NAME     ;Offset address of path
MOV    AH,39h                  ;Want service 39h
INT    21h                     ;DOS services interrupt
JC     ERROR                   ;Carry set, handle error
```

Description: This service (the opposite of service 21/3A) allows the creation of a subdirectory. The result is the same as the result of using the DOS command MKDIR, or MD. On entry, DS:DX points to an ASCIIZ (nul-terminated ASCII) string that contains the name of the directory.

On return, if the carry flag is set, an error has occurred, and the error code is in AX. Service 21/59 can be used to get detailed error information. If the carry flag is not set, the operation was successful, and AX is undefined.

Remove Subdirectory (Interrupt 21h, service 3Ah)

Category: Disk services

Registers on Entry:

> AH: 3Ah
> DX: Offset address of path name
> DS: Segment address of path name

Registers on Return:

> AX: Error code

Memory Affected: None

Syntax:

```
PUSH   CS                      ;Code segment and
POP    DS                      ;  data segment are same
MOV    DX,OFFSET PATH_NAME     ;Offset address of path
MOV    AH,3Ah                  ;Want service 3Ah
INT    21h                     ;DOS services interrupt
JC     ERROR                   ;Carry set, handle error
```

Description: This service (the opposite of service 21/39) is used to remove existing subdirectories. The result is the same as the result of using the DOS command RMDIR, or RD. On entry, DS:DX points to an ASCIIZ (nul-terminated ASCII) string that contains the name of the directory.

On return, if the carry flag is set, an error has occurred, and the error code is in AX. Service 21/59 can be used to get detailed error information. If the carry flag is not set, the operation was successful, and AX is undefined.

Set Directory (Interrupt 21h, service 3Bh)

Category: Disk services

Registers on Entry:

> AH: 3Bh
> DX: Offset address of path name
> DS: Segment address of path name

Registers on Return:

> AX: Error code

Memory Affected: None

Syntax:

```
PUSH   CS                    ;Code segment and
POP    DS                    ;  data segment are same
MOV    DX,OFFSET PATH_NAME   ;Offset address of path
MOV    AH,3Bh                ;Want service 3Bh
INT    21h                   ;DOS services interrupt
JC     ERROR                 ;Carry set, handle error
```

Description: This service is used to change the default directory setting. The result is the same as that of using the DOS command CHDIR, or CD. On entry, DS:DX points to an ASCIIZ (nul-terminated ASCII) string that contains the name of the directory.

On return, if the carry flag is set, an error has occurred, and the error code is in AX. Service 21/59 can be used to get detailed error information. If the carry flag is not set, the operation was successful, and AX is undefined.

Create File (Interrupt 21h, service 3Ch)

Category: Disk services

Registers on Entry:

AH: 3Ch
CX: File attribute
DX: Offset address of path name
DS: Segment address of path name

Registers on Return:

AX: Return code

Memory Affected: None

Syntax:

```
PUSH   CS                    ;Code segment and
POP    DS                    ;  data segment are same
MOV    DX,OFFSET PATH_NAME   ;Offset address of path
MOV    CX,0                  ;File attribute is normal
MOV    AH,3Ch                ;Want service 3Ch
INT    21h                   ;DOS services interrupt
JC     ERROR                 ;Carry set, handle error
MOV    FILE_HANDLE,AX        ;Store returned handle
```

Description: This service is used to create or truncate a disk file. On entry, DS:DX points to an ASCIIZ (nul-terminated ASCII) string that contains the full name of the file, including any applicable path name. CX is set equal to the desired attribute for the file.

This service is identical to service 21/5B except that if the file name specified in the ASCIIZ string already exists, the file is opened, and its length is truncated to 0.

On return, if the carry flag is set, an error has occurred, and the error code is in AX. Service 21/59 can be used to get detailed error information. If the carry flag is not set, the operation was successful, and AX contains the file handle for the newly opened file. This number (file handle) can be used in many other DOS file operations.

When this service is completed, the specified file is left open. You do not need to open the file, but you must remember to close it.

Open File (Interrupt 21h, service 3Dh)

Category: Disk services

Registers on Entry:

AH: 3Dh
AL: Open code
DX: Offset address of path name
DS: Segment address of path name

Registers on Return:

AX: File handle or error code

Memory Affected: None

Syntax:

```
PUSH    CS                      ;Code segment and
POP     DS                      ;  data segment are same
MOV     DX,OFFSET PATH_NAME     ;Offset address of path
MOV     AL,11000010b            ;Set proper open mode
MOV     AH,3Dh                  ;Want service 3Dh
INT     21h                     ;DOS services interrupt
JC      ERROR                   ;Carry set, handle error
MOV     FILE_HANDLE,AX          ;Save file handle
```

Description: This service opens a disk file. On entry, DS:DX points to an ASCIIZ (nul-terminated ASCII) string that contains the full name of the file, including any applicable path name. AL is set to equal the mode to be used for the open file. Each bit in AL has significance. Table 16.7 gives detailed information.

Table 16.7. *Open mode bit settings for service 21/3D.*

Bits 76543210	*Meaning*
0	File is inherited by a child process
1	File is not inherited by a child process
000	Sharing mode—allow compatible access
001	Sharing mode—exclusive access
010	Sharing mode—deny others write access
011	Sharing mode—deny others read access
100	Sharing mode—allow others full access
0	Reserved—set to 0
000	Open for read access
001	Open for write access
010	Open for read/write access

On return, if the carry flag is set, an error has occurred, and the error code is in AX. Service 21/59 can be used to get detailed error information. If the carry flag is not set, the operation was successful, and AX contains the file handle for the newly opened file. This number (file handle) can be used in many other DOS file operations.

Close File (Interrupt 21h, service 3Eh)

Category: Disk services

Registers on Entry:

AH: 3Eh
BX: File handle

Registers on Return:

AX: Error code

Memory Affected: None

Syntax:

```
MOV    BX,FILE_HANDLE      ;Get file handle
MOV    AH,3Eh              ;Want service 3Eh
INT    21h                 ;DOS services interrupt
JC     ERROR               ;Carry set, handle error
```

Description: This service closes a previously opened file. The file handle must be loaded in BX.

On return, if the carry flag is set, an error has occurred, and the error code is in AX. Service 21/59 can be used to get detailed error information. If the carry flag is not set, the operation was successful.

Read File (Interrupt 21h, service 3Fh)

Category: Disk services

Registers on Entry:

AH: 3Fh
BX: File handle
CX: Bytes to read
DX: Offset address for buffer
DS: Segment address for buffer

Registers on Return:

AX: Return code

Memory Affected: The memory area specified by DS:DX is overlaid with information read from the disk.

Syntax:

```
MOV    BX,FILE_HANDLE       ;Get file handle
PUSH   CS                   ;Code segment and
POP    DS                   ;  data segment are same
MOV    DX,OFFSET BUFFER     ;Offset address of buffer
MOV    CX,1000h             ;Read 4K of info
MOV    AH,3Fh               ;Want service 3Fh
INT    21h                  ;DOS services interrupt
JC     ERROR                ;Carry set, handle error
```

Description: This service reads information from a disk file. The file handle is specified in BX, with DS:DX pointing to the input buffer. CX is set to the number of bytes to be read.

Reading from the file is done based on the value of the file pointer. If the file has just been opened, reading begins from the beginning of the file. Subsequent reads begin at the point where the last read finished.

On return, if the carry flag is set, an error has occurred, and the error code is in AX. Service 21/59 can be used to get detailed error information.

If the carry flag is not set, the operation was successful, and AX contains the number of bytes actually read.

Write File (Interrupt 21h, service 40h)

Category: Disk services

Registers on Entry:

AH: 40h
BX: File handle
CX: Bytes to write
DX: Offset address for buffer
DS: Segment address for buffer

Registers on Return:

AX: Return code

Memory Affected: None

Syntax:

```
MOV    BX,FILE_HANDLE        ;Get file handle
PUSH   CS                    ;Code segment and
POP    DS                    ;  data segment are same
MOV    DX,OFFSET BUFFER      ;Offset address of buffer
MOV    CX,1000h              ;Write 4K of info
PUSH   CX                    ;Save for later reference
MOV    AH,40h                ;Want service 40h
INT    21h                   ;DOS services interrupt
JC     ERROR                 ;Carry set, handle error
POP    CX                    ;Get original bytes back
CMP    AX,CX                 ;Are they the same?
JNE    ERROR                 ;No, go handle
```

Description: This service writes information to a disk file. The file handle is specified in BX, with DS:DX pointing to the buffer area. CX is set to the number of bytes to be copied from the buffer to the disk.

Writing is done based on the value of the file pointer. If the file has just been opened, writing begins at the front of the file. Subsequent writes begin at the point where the last write finished.

On return, if the carry flag is set, an error has occurred, and the error code is in AX. Service 21/59 can be used to get detailed error information. If the carry flag is not set, the operation was successful, and AX contains the number of bytes actually written. If AX does not equal the number of bytes that should have been written, an error (such as the disk being full) has occurred, even though the carry flag is not set.

Delete File (Interrupt 21h, service 41h)

Category: Disk services

Registers on Entry:

AH: 41h
DX: Offset address of path name
DS: Segment address of path name

Registers on Return:

AX: Error code

Memory Affected: None

Syntax:

```
PUSH   CS                    ;Code segment and
POP    DS                    ;  data segment are same
MOV    DX,OFFSET PATH_NAME   ;Offset address of path
MOV    AH,41h                ;Want service 41h
INT    21h                   ;DOS services interrupt
JC     ERROR                 ;Carry set, handle error
```

Description: This service deletes a disk file. On entry, DS:DX points to an ASCIIZ (nul-terminated ASCII) string that contains the full name of the file, including any applicable path name. Wild cards cannot be used in the file designation. If the file being deleted has a read-only attribute, this service returns an error.

On return, if the carry flag is set, an error has occurred, and the error code is in AX. Service 21/59 can be used to get detailed error information. If the carry flag is not set, the operation was successful.

Move File Pointer (Interrupt 21h, service 42h)

Category: Disk services

Registers on Entry:

AH: 42h
AL: Movement code
BX: File handle

CX: High-order word of distance to move
DX: Low-order word of distance to move

Registers on Return:

AX: Low-order word of new pointer location or error code
DX: High-order word of new pointer location

Memory Affected: None

Syntax:

```
MOV     BX,FILE_HANDLE        ;Get file handle
MOV     AL,0                  ;Relative to start of file
MOV     CX,DIST_HIGH          ;Distance to move
MOV     DX,DIST_LOW           ;
MOV     AH,42h                ;Want service 42h
INT     21h                   ;DOS services interrupt
JC      ERROR                 ;Carry set, handle error
```

Description: This service causes the file pointer to move to a new location. The file handle is specified in BX, and the distance to move (in bytes) is specified in CX:DX. A movement code is specified in AL (see table 16.8).

***Table 16.8.** Movement code for service 21/42.*

Value	Meaning
0	Move relative to beginning of file
1	Move relative to current pointer location
2	Move relative to end of file

If the offset specified in CX:DX is too large, you can move the file pointer past the beginning or the end of the file. Doing so does not generate an immediate error but does cause an error when reading or writing is attempted later.

On return, if the carry flag is set, an error has occurred, and the error code is in AX. Service 21/59 can be used to get detailed error information. If the carry flag is not set, the operation was successful, and DX:AX contains the new file pointer value.

Get/Set File Attributes (Interrupt 21h, service 43h)

Category: Disk services

Registers on Entry:

AH: 43h
AL: Function code
CX: Desired attribute
DX: Offset address of path name
DS: Segment address of path name

Registers on Return:

AX: Error code
CX: Current attribute

Memory Affected: None

Syntax:

```
MOV     AL,0                  ;Get current attribute
PUSH    CS                    ;Code segment and
POP     DS                    ;  data segment are same
MOV     DX,OFFSET PATH_NAME   ;Offset address of PATH
MOV     AH,43h                ;Want service 43h
INT     21h                   ;DOS services interrupt
JC      ERROR                 ;Go handle error
```

Description: This service allows you to determine or set a file's attribute. The desired function is specified in AL. If AL = 0, the file attribute is retrieved; if AL = 1, the file attribute is set.

DS:DX should point to an ASCIIZ (nul-terminated ASCII) string that contains the full name of the file, including any applicable path name. Wild cards cannot be used in the file designation. If you are setting the file attribute (AL = 1), place the desired value in CX. Actually, because the file attribute is only a byte in length, the new setting is placed in CL, and CH is set to 0. Table 16.9 shows the possible file attribute settings. In this table, a 1 in a bit position indicated by an *x* means that the attribute is selected; a 0 means that the attribute is not selected.

You cannot change the volume label or subdirectory bits of the file attribute. If you attempt to do so or if these bits are not set to 0, an error is generated. If you are retrieving the file attribute (AL = 0), the contents of CX are not significant.

Table 16.9. *Bit settings for file attribute, service 21/43.*

Bits 76543210	*Meaning*
00	Reserved—set to 0
x	Archive
0	Subdirectory—set to 0 for this service
0	Volume label—set to 0 for this service
x	System
x	Hidden
x	Read-only

On return, if the carry flag is set, an error has occurred, and the error code is in AX. Service 21/59 can be used to get detailed error information. If the carry flag is not set, the operation was successful. If you were retrieving the file attribute, CX contains the requested information.

Device I/O Control (Interrupt 21h, service 44h)

Description: This service controls I/O with DOS device drivers. It has 16 individual functions, which are selected by the value in AL (prior to DOS version 3, only the first eight existed; two more were added at version 3.0, two at version 3.1, and four at version 3.2). The following several service/function sections describe the functions for this service.

Get Device Information (Interrupt 21h, service 44h, function 0)

Category: System services

Registers on Entry:

AH: 44h
AL: 0
BX: Device handle

Registers on Return:

DX: Device information

Memory Affected: None

Syntax:

```
MOV    AL,0              ;Want function 0
MOV    BX,DEVICE_HANDLE  ;Use this handle
MOV    AH,44h            ;Want service 44h
INT    21h              ;DOS services interrupt
```

Description: This function retrieves information about the device. On calling, AL should contain 0, and BX should contain the device handle. On return, DX contains the requested information, as given in table 16.10.

Table 16.10. *Device information returned by function 21/44/0.*

Bits FEDCBA98 76543210	*Meaning*
?	Reserved
0	Control strings not allowed for services 21/44/2, 21/44/3, 21/44/4, and 21/44/5. This bit is significant only if bit 7 is 1.
1	Control strings acceptable for services 21/44/2, 21/44/3, 21/44/4, and 21/44/5. This bit is significant only if bit 7 is 1.
??????	Reserved
0	This channel is a disk file.
1	This channel is a device.
0	End of file
1	Not end of file
0	Using binary mode
1	Using ASCII mode
0	Not a clock device
1	Clock device
0	Normal device
1	Null device
0	Not console output device
1	Console output device
0	Not console input device
1	Console input device

This function is not supported on network devices.

Set Device Information (Interrupt 21h, service 44h, function 1)

Category: System services

Registers on Entry:

AH: 44h
AL: 1
BX: Device handle
DH: 0
DL: Device information

Registers on Return: Unchanged

Memory Affected: None

Syntax:

```
MOV    AL,1              ;Want function 1
MOV    DH,0              ;Must be set to 0
MOV    DL,DEVICE_INFO    ;Desired configuration
MOV    BX,DEVICE_HANDLE  ;For this device
MOV    AH,44h            ;Want service 44h
INT    21h               ;DOS services interrupt
```

Description: This function is used to set information about the device. On calling, AL should contain 1, BX should contain the device handle, and DL should contain the device information, as given in table 16.11. DH must be set to 0.

This function is not supported on network devices.

Character Device Read (Interrupt 21h, service 44h, function 2)

Category: System services

Registers on Entry:

AH: 44h
AL: 2
BX: Device handle
CX: Bytes to read
DX: Offset address of buffer
DS: Segment address of buffer

Table 16.11. *Device information for function 21/44/1.*

Bits 76543210	Meaning
0	This channel is a disk file.
1	This channel is a device.
0	End of file
1	Not end of file
0	Using binary mode
1	Using ASCII mode
0	Not a clock device
1	Clock device
0	Normal device
1	Null device
0	Not console output device
1	Console output device
0	Not console input device
1	Console input device

Registers on Return:

AX: Bytes read

Memory Affected: The buffer area at DS:DX is overwritten with information read from the device driver.

Syntax:

```
PUSH    CS                    ;Code segment and
POP     DS                    ;  data segment are same
MOV     DX,OFFSET BUFFER      ;Address of input buffer
MOV     AL,2                  ;Want function 2
MOV     BX,DEVICE_HANDLE      ;Want this device
MOV     CX,NUM_BYTES          ;Read this many bytes
MOV     AH,44h                ;Want service 44h
INT     21h                   ;DOS services interrupt
```

Description: This function reads a control string from the device. The buffer specified by DS:DX stores the information from device BX. Only CX bytes are read from the device.

For this function to be usable, bit 14 of the device information word (as returned in the DX register through service 21/44/0) must be 1.

(Refer to table 16.10 for the makeup of the device information word.) This service is not supported on network devices.

Character Device Write (Interrupt 21h, service 44h, function 3)

Category: System services

Registers on Entry:

AH: 44h
AL: 3
BX: Device handle
CX: Bytes to write
DX: Offset address of buffer
DS: Segment address of buffer

Registers on Return:

AX: Bytes written

Memory Affected: None

Syntax:

```
PUSH    CS                      ;Code segment and
POP     DS                      ;  data segment are same
MOV     DX,OFFSET BUFFER        ;Address of input buffer
MOV     BX,DEVICE_HANDLE        ;Want this device
MOV     CX,NUM_BYTES            ;Write this many bytes
PUSH    CX                      ;Store for later check
MOV     AL,3                    ;Want function 3
MOV     AH,44h                  ;Want service 44h
INT     21h                     ;DOS services interrupt
POP     CX                      ;Get back original number
CMP     AX,CX                   ;Was everything written?
JE      ERROR                   ;No, go handle
```

Description: This function writes a control string to a device. CX bytes of information stored at the buffer address specified by DS:DX are written to device BX.

For this function to be usable, bit 14 of the device information word (as returned in the DX register through service 21/44/0) must be 1. (Refer to table 16.10 for the makeup of the device information word.) This service is not supported on network devices.

Block Device Read (Interrupt 21h, service 44h, function 4)

Category: System services

Registers on Entry:

AH: 44h
AL: 4
BL: Drive number
CX: Bytes to read
DX: Offset address of buffer
DS: Segment address of buffer

Registers on Return:

AX: Bytes read

Memory Affected: The buffer area at DS:DX is overwritten with information read from the drive.

Syntax:

```
PUSH    CS                      ;Code segment and
POP     DS                      ;  data segment are same
MOV     DX,OFFSET BUFFER        ;Address of input buffer
MOV     AL,4                    ;Want function 4
MOV     BL,DRIVE                ;Want this drive
MOV     CX,NUM_BYTES            ;Read this many bytes
MOV     AH,44h                  ;Want service 44h
INT     21h                     ;DOS services interrupt
```

Description: This function reads a control string from a block device, typically a disk drive. BL is used to specify which drive to use, where 0 = default, 1 = A, 2 = B, 3 = C, etc. The information is stored at the buffer specified by DS:DX. Only CX bytes are read.

For this function to be usable, bit 14 of the device information word (as returned in the DX register through service 21/44/0) must be 1. (Refer to table 16.10 for the makeup of the device information word.) This service is not supported on network devices.

Block Device Write (Interrupt 21h, service 44h, function 5)

Category: System services

Registers on Entry:

AH: 44h
AL: 5
BL: Drive number
CX: Bytes to write
DX: Offset address of buffer
DS: Segment address of buffer

Registers on Return:

AX: Bytes written

Memory Affected: None

Syntax:

```
PUSH   CS                    ;Code segment and
POP    DS                    ;  data segment are same
MOV    DX,OFFSET BUFFER      ;Address of input buffer
MOV    BL,DRIVE              ;Want this drive
MOV    CX,NUM_BYTES          ;Write this many bytes
PUSH   CX                    ;Store for later check
MOV    AL,5                  ;Want function 5
MOV    AH,44h                ;Want service 44h
INT    21h                   ;DOS services interrupt
POP    CX                    ;Get back original number
CMP    AX,CX                 ;Was everything written?
JE     ERROR                 ;No, go handle
```

Description: This function writes a control string to a block device, typically a disk drive. BL is used to specify which drive to use, where 0 = default, 1 = A, 2 = B, 3 = C, etc. CX bytes of information stored at the buffer address specified by DS:DX are written.

For this function to be usable, bit 14 of the device information word (as returned in the DX register through service 21/44/0) must be 1. (Refer to table 16.10 for the makeup of the device information word.) This service is not supported on network devices.

Get Input Status (Interrupt 21h, service 44h, function 6)

Category: System services

Registers on Entry:

AH: 44h
AL: 6
BX: Device handle

Registers on Return:
AL: Status

Memory Affected: None

Syntax:

```
MOV     BX,DEVICE_HANDLE      ;Use this device
MOV     AL,6                  ;Want function 6
MOV     AH,44h                ;Want service 44h
INT     21h                   ;DOS services interrupt
```

Description: This service determines whether the device is ready for input. If the device is ready, AL returns 0Fh. If the device is not ready, AL returns 0.

If the device specified in BX is a file, AL always returns FFh until the end of file is reached, at which point AL is equal to 0.

This function is not supported on network devices.

Get Output Status (Interrupt 21h, service 44h, function 7)

Category: System services

Registers on Entry:

AH: 44h
AL: 7
BX: Device handle

Registers on Return:

AL: Status

Memory Affected: None

Syntax:

```
MOV    BX,DEVICE_HANDLE        ;Use this device
MOV    AL,7                    ;Want function 7
MOV    AH,44h                  ;Want service 44h
INT    21h                     ;DOS services interrupt
```

Description: This service determines whether the device is ready for output. If the device is ready, AL returns 0Fh. If the device is not ready, AL returns 0.

If the device specified in BX is a file, AL always returns FFh until the end of file is reached, at which point AL is equal to 0.

This function is not supported on network devices.

Block Device Changeable? (Interrupt 21h, service 44h, function 8)

Category: System services

Registers on Entry:

AH: 44h
AL: 8
BL: Drive number

Registers on Return:

AX: Status

Memory Affected: None

Syntax:

```
MOV    BL,0                    ;Check on default drive
MOV    AL,8                    ;Want function 8
MOV    AH,44h                  ;Want service 44h
INT    21h                     ;DOS services interrupt
CMP    AX,1                    ;Is it fixed?
JE     FIXED                   ;Yes, so treat accordingly
```

Description: This function (not available before DOS version 3.0) enables your program to determine whether the block device (typically a disk drive) supports removable media. BL is used to specify which drive to check (0 = default, 1 = A, 2 = B, 3 = C, and so on).

On return, AX is equal to 0 if removable media is supported, and equal to 1 if the media is not removable (fixed disk). If AX is equal to 0Fh, the value specified in BL is an invalid drive.

This function is not supported on network devices.

Logical Device Local/Remote Determination (Interrupt 21h, service 44h, function 9)

Category: System services

Registers on Entry:

AH: 44h
AL: 9
BL: Drive number

Registers on Return:

DX: Status

Memory Affected: None

Syntax:

```
MOV     BL,0            ;Check on default drive
MOV     AL,9            ;Want function 9
MOV     AH,44h          ;Want service 44h
INT     21h             ;DOS services interrupt
```

Description: This function (not available before DOS version 3.1) is used in a networking environment to determine whether the block device (usually a disk drive) specified in BL is local or remote. BL is used to specify which drive to check (0=default, 1=A, 2=B, 3=C, and so on).

On return, bit 12 of DX is set if the device is remote. If the device is local or if redirection is paused, bit 12 is clear.

Handle Local/Remote Determination (Interrupt 21h, service 44h, function 0Ah)

Category: System services

Registers on Entry:

    AH: 44h
    AL: 0Ah
    BX: File handle

Registers on Return:

    DX: Status

Memory Affected: None

Syntax:

```
MOV    BX,FILE_HANDLE      ;Checking this file
MOV    AL,0Ah              ;Want function 0Ah
MOV    AH,44h              ;Want service 44h
INT    21h                 ;DOS services interrupt
```

Description: This function (not available before DOS version 3.1) is used in a networking environment to determine whether a given file handle (specified in BX) represents a local or a remote file.

On return, bit 15 of DX is set if the device is remote. If the device is local, bit 15 is clear.

Set Sharing Retry Count (Interrupt 21h, service 44h, function 0Bh)

Category: System services

Registers on Entry:

    AH: 44h
    AL: 0Bh
    CX: Delay loop counter
    DX: Retries

Registers on Return:

    AX: Error code

Memory Affected: None

Syntax:

```
MOV    CX,3      ;3 delay loops
MOV    DX,8      ;8 retries
```

```
MOV     AL,OBh              ;Want function OBh
MOV     AH,44h              ;Want service 44h
INT     21h                 ;DOS services interrupt
JC      ERROR               ;Error, go handle
```

Description: This function (not available before DOS version 3.0) is used in a networking environment to specify the number of attempts at file access and the delay between retries. If a file is locked or if a sharing conflict exists, DOS attempts to access the file three times with one delay loop between attempts before returning an error.

On return, the carry flag indicates an error if one has occurred. If the carry flag is set, AX contains the error code, which can be handled through service 21/59.

Handle Generic Code Page Switching (Interrupt 21h, service 44h, function 0Ch)

Category: System services

Registers on Entry:

AH: 44h
AL: 0Ch
BX: Device handle
CH: Major subfunction code
CL: Minor subfunction code
DX: Offset address of parameter block
DS: Segment address of parameter block

Registers on Return:

AX: Error code

Memory Affected: This function can have various effects on memory, depending on the major and minor subfunctions requested.

Syntax:

```
PUSH    CS                      ;Code segment and
POP     DS                      ;  data segment are same
MOV     DX,OFFSET PARM_BLOCK    ;Address of parameter block
MOV     BX,DEVICE_HANDLE        ;Device handle in use
MOV     CH,MAJOR                ;Major subfunction desired
MOV     CL,MINOR                ;Minor subfunction desired
MOV     AL,OCh                  ;Want function Ch
```

```
MOV     AH,44h                  ;Want service 44h
INT     21h                     ;DOS services interrupt
```

Description: This service (not available in this form before DOS version 3.3) allows device driver support for subfunctions that enable code page switching. You specify the device handle in BX, a major subfunction code in CH, and a minor code in CL. Currently, the service has four major codes and five minor codes, for a total of 20 possible combinations of major/minor codes. Each minor code requires a different set of parameters, which are passed through a parameter block. DS:DX points to this parameter block.

On return, the carry flag indicates an error if one has occurred. If the carry flag is set, AX contains the error code, which can be handled through service 21/59.

Because of the detail and complexity involved with this function, its discussion is best left to another publication. Detailed information about this function is available in the DOS 3.3 *Technical Reference Manual*.

Generic IOCTL Block Device Request (Interrupt 21h, service 44h, function 0Dh)

Category: System services

Registers on Entry:

AH: 44h
AL: 0Dh
BL: Drive number
CH: Major subfunction code
CL: Minor subfunction code
DX: Offset address of parameter block
DS: Segment address of parameter block

Registers on Return:

AX: Error code

Memory Affected: This function can have various effects on memory, depending on the major and minor subfunctions requested.

Syntax:

```
PUSH    CS                      ;Code segment and
POP     DS                      ;  data segment are same
```

```
MOV     DX,OFFSET PARM_BLOCK    ;Address of parameter block
MOV     BL,0                    ;Check on default drive
MOV     CH,8                    ;Always 8
MOV     CL,MINOR                ;Minor subfunction desired
MOV     AL,0Dh                  ;Want function Dh
MOV     AH,44h                  ;Want service 44h
INT     21h                     ;DOS services interrupt
```

Description: This service (not available before DOS version 3.2) allows uniform device support for a number of block device functions—typically, disk drive functions. The drive number is specified in BL (0 = default, 1 = A, 2 = B, 3 = C, and so on).

A major subfunction code is specified in CH, which is always 8 (as of DOS 3.3). A minor subfunction code is specified in CL. The possible minor codes are detailed in table 16.12.

Table 16.12. Minor subfunction codes (CL) for service 21/44/D.

Value	Meaning
40h	Set device parameters
41h	Write logical device track
42h	Format and verify logical device track
60h	Get device parameters
61h	Read logical device track
62h	Verify logical device track

Each minor code requires a different set of parameters, which are passed through a parameter block. DS:DX points to this parameter block.

On return, the carry flag indicates whether an error has occurred. If the carry flag is set, AX contains the error code, which can be handled through service 21/59.

Because of the detail and complexity involved with this function, its discussion is best left to another publication. Detailed information about this function, its subfunctions, and the parameter setup is available in the DOS 3.3 *Technical Reference Manual*.

Get Logical Device Map (Interrupt 21h, service 44h, function 0Eh)

Category: System services

Registers on Entry:

AH: 44h
AL: 0Eh
BL: Drive number

Registers on Return:

AX: Return code

Memory Affected: None

Syntax:

```
MOV    BL,0          ;Use default drive
MOV    AL,0Eh        ;Want function 0Eh
MOV    AH,44h        ;Want service 44h
INT    21h           ;DOS services interrupt
```

Description: This function (not available before DOS version 3.2) determines whether a block device (typically, a disk drive) has more than one logical drive assigned to it. Use BL to specify which drive to check (0 = default, 1 = A, 2 = B, 3 = C, and so on).

On return, the carry flag indicates whether an error has occurred. If the carry flag is set, AX contains the error code, which can be handled through service 21/59. If the carry flag is not set, AL contains the result code. If AL is 0, the block device has only one logical drive assigned. If AL contains another number, that number represents the drive letter last used to reference the device. In this case, 1 = A, 2 = B, 3 = C, etc.

Set Logical Device Map (Interrupt 21h, service 44h, function 0Fh)

Category: System services

Registers on Entry:

AH: 44h
AL: 0Fh
BL: Drive number

Registers on Return:

AX: Return code

Memory Affected: None

Syntax:

```
MOV   BL,0            ;Use default drive
MOV   AL,0Fh          ;Want function 0Fh
MOV   AH,44h          ;Want service 44h
INT   21h             ;DOS services interrupt
```

Description: This function (not available before DOS version 3.2) assigns a logical drive letter to a block device (typically a disk drive). Use BL to specify the drive letter (1 = A, 2 = B, 3 = C, and so on). You use this function where more than one logical drive letter can be assigned to a single physical block device. An example is a system with a single floppy drive. Even though the system has only one block device (the floppy drive), that device can be addressed logically as two devices (drives A: and B:). This function causes DOS to view the system as either A: or B: in subsequent I/O functions.

On return, the carry flag indicates whether an error has occurred. If the carry flag is set, AX contains the error code, which can be handled through service 21/59.

Duplicate File Handle (Interrupt 21h, service 45h)

Category: Disk services

Registers on Entry:

AH: 45h
BX: File handle

Registers on Return:

AX: Return code

Memory Affected: None

Syntax:

```
MOV   BX,FILE_HANDLE_1    ;Use current file handle
MOV   AH,45h              ;Want service 45h
INT   21h                 ;DOS services interrupt
JC    ERROR               ;Go handle error
MOV   FILE_HANDLE_2,AX    ;Save new handle
```

Description: This service, which duplicates a file handle, results in two handles that point to the same file at the same file position.

There is no clear need or use for this function; you simply can use two different handles to refer to one file. These handles operate in tandem, not independently, because any change that you make to the file pointer by using one of the handles is reflected in the other handle. The most common use for this function is with service 21/46, where you duplicate a handle before reassigning it. This use allows redirection at a later time.

On return, the carry flag indicates whether an error has occurred. If the carry flag is set, AX contains the error code, which can be handled through service 21/59.

Force Handle Duplication (Interrupt 21h, service 46h)

Category: Disk services

Registers on Entry:

    AH: 46h
    BX: File handle
    CX: File handle to be forced

Registers on Return:

    AX: Error code

Memory Affected: None

Syntax:

```
MOV    BX,FILE_HANDLE      ;Original handle
MOV    CX,4                ;Standard printer handle
MOV    AH,46h              ;Want service 46h
INT    21h                 ;DOS services interrupt
JC     ERROR               ;Branch if error
```

Description: This service forces one file handle to point to the same device (file, etc.) as another handle. In the syntax example, BX represents an open file. CX is loaded with the standard printer handle, and through this service handle 4 is made to point to the open file. Anything sent to handle 4 (normally sent to the printer) is sent to the open file.

On return, the carry flag indicates whether an error has occurred. If the carry flag is set, AX contains the error code, which can be handled through service 21/59.

Get Directory Path (Interrupt 21h, service 47h)

Category: Disk services

Registers on Entry:

AH: 47h
DL: Drive number
SI: Offset address of buffer area
DS: Segment address of buffer area

Registers on Return: Unchanged

AX: Error code
SI: Offset address of buffer area
DS: Segment address of buffer area

Memory Affected: The memory area pointed to by DS:SI is overwritten with the requested directory information.

Syntax:

```
PUSH    CS                      ;Code segment and
POP     DS                      ;  data segment are same
MOV     SI,OFFSET DIR_BUFFER    ;Address of 64-byte buffer
MOV     DL,0                    ;Use default drive
MOV     AH,47h                  ;Want service 47h
INT     21h                     ;DOS services interrupt
```

Description: This service determines the ASCIIZ string path for the current directory of the drive specified in DL, where 0 = default, 1 = A, 2 = B, 3 = C, etc.

The returned string is not the complete path name because the drive designator and root directory backslash are not returned. These characters, however, can be added to the beginning of the string to create a complete path for the directory. Because an ASCIIZ string is returned, it ends with an ASCII 0 (nul).

Because path names can be as many as 64 bytes long, a good practice is to make sure that the buffer area to which DS:SI points is 64 bytes long.

On return, the carry flag indicates whether an error has occurred. If the carry flag is set, AX contains the error code, which can be handled through service 21/59. If the carry flag is not set, the address to which DS:SI points is the start of the returned ASCIIZ string.

Allocate Memory (Interrupt 21h, service 48h)

Category: System services

Registers on Entry:

AH: 48h
BX: Paragraphs to allocate

Registers on Return:

AX: Return code
BX: Maximum paragraphs available

Memory Affected: Although the contents of the requested memory are not changed, the amount of free memory is reduced by the requested number of paragraphs.

Syntax:

```
MOV    BX,100h            ;Request 4K block of memory
MOV    AH,48h             ;Want service 48h
INT    21h                ;DOS services interrupt
JC     ERROR              ;Branch if error
MOV    BLOCK_SEG,AX       ;Save segment address
```

Description: This service is used to set aside blocks of memory for program use. You specify the number of contiguous paragraphs required in BX.

On return, the carry flag indicates whether an error has occurred. If the carry flag is set, AX contains the error code, which can be handled through service 21/59. If an error has occurred, BX contains the maximum number of contiguous paragraphs available.

If the carry flag is not set, AX points to the paragraph or segment address where the memory block begins. This memory block must later be freed (before program completion) through service 21/49.

Free Allocated Memory (Interrupt 21h, service 49h)

Category: System services

Registers on Entry:

AH: 49h
ES: Segment address of memory block

Registers on Return:

AX: Error code

Memory Affected: Although the contents of the requested memory are not changed, the amount of free memory is increased by the size of the block being relinquished.

Syntax:

```
PUSH    ES                  ;Save current segment
MOV     ES,BLOCK_SEG        ;Set to segment to free
MOV     AH,49h              ;Want service 49h
INT     21h                 ;DOS services interrupt
POP     ES                  ;Get register back
JC      ERROR               ;Branch if error
MOV     BLOCK_SEG,0         ;Zero out variable
```

Description: This service frees memory blocks allocated through service 21/48. You specify the segment address of the block in ES.

On return, the carry flag indicates whether an error has occurred. If the carry flag is set, AX contains the error code, which can be handled through service 21/59.

Change Memory Block Allocation (Interrupt 21h, service 4Ah)

Category: System services

Registers on Entry:

AH: 4Ah
BX: Total paragraphs to allocate
ES: Segment address of memory block

Registers on Return:

AX: Error code
BX: Maximum paragraphs available

Memory Affected: Although the contents of the requested memory are not changed, the amount of free memory is reduced by the difference between the number of paragraphs already allocated to the block and the requested number of paragraphs.

Syntax:

```
MOV     BX,200h              ;Change to 8K block
MOV     AH,4Ah               ;Want service 4Ah
INT     21h                  ;DOS services interrupt
JC      ERROR                ;Branch if error
MOV     BLOCK_SEG,AX         ;Save segment address
```

Description: This service changes the size of a previously allocated memory block (through service 21/48). You specify the segment address of the existing block in ES.

On return, the carry flag indicates whether an error has occurred. If the carry flag is set, AX contains the error code, which can be handled through service 21/59. If an error has occurred and an increase in block size was requested, BX contains the maximum number of contiguous paragraphs available; however, the original block allocation is not changed.

Load or Execute Program (Interrupt 21h, service 4Bh)

Category: System services

Registers on Entry:

AH: 4Bh
AL: Function code
BX: Offset address of parameter block
DX: Offset address of path name
DS: Segment address of path name
ES: Segment address of parameter block

Registers on Return:

AX: Error code

Memory Affected: The desired file, if located, is loaded into memory, overwriting previous memory contents.

Syntax:

```
MOV     AX,CS                     ;Code segment is same as
MOV     DS,AX                     ;  data segment and
MOV     ES,AX                     ;  extra segment
MOV     DX,OFFSET FILE_PATH       ;Offset address of path
MOV     BX,OFFSET LOAD_EXECUTE    ;Offset address of parameters
MOV     AL,0                      ;Load and execute
```

```
MOV     AH,4Bh                  ;Want service 4Bh
INT     21h                     ;DOS services interrupt
```

Description: This service allows a disk file to be loaded, or loaded and executed. You specify the desired function in AL; the only valid functions are indicated by a 0 or a 3. If AL=0, the file is loaded and executed; if AL=3, the file is only loaded. This last function is valuable when you use program overlays.

DS:DX should point to an ASCIIZ (nul-terminated ASCII) string that contains the full name of the file, including any applicable path name. Wild cards cannot be used in the file designation.

ES:BX should point to a parameter block that provides necessary information for loading the file. The two possible parameter blocks are organized as follows:

```
LOAD_EXECUTE    DW      SEG ENV_STRING      ;Environment string segment
                DW      OFFSET CMD_LINE     ;Offset of default command
                DW      SEG CMD_LINE        ;Segment of default command
                DW      OFFSET FCB_1        ;Offset of default FCB 1
                DW      SEG FCB_1           ;Segment of default FCB 1
                DW      OFFSET FCB_2        ;Offset of default FCB 2
                DW      SEG FCB_2           ;Segment of default FCB 2


LOAD_ONLY       DW      SEG LOAD_POINT      ;Segment of loading point
                DW      0000                ;Relocation factor for file
```

Notice that the parameter table for the load-and-execute function (AL=0) is significantly larger than that for the load-only function (AL=3).

The loaded file or program is called a child of the original program, which is referred to as the *parent*. All open files (except files with their inheritance bit set) are available for the child program. Because this service destroys all registers, remember to save all registers before using this service and restore them after returning.

On return, the carry flag indicates whether an error has occurred. If the carry flag is set, AX contains the error code, which can be handled through service 21/59.

Process Terminate (Interrupt 21h, service 4Ch)

Category: System services

Registers on Entry:

AH: 4Ch
AL: Return code

Registers on Return: Undefined (does not return)

Memory Affected: Although not altered, the memory area used by the program is made available to future programs.

Syntax:

```
MOV    AL,RETURN_CODE        ;Return code to pass
MOV    AH,4Ch                ;Want service 4Ch
INT    21h                   ;DOS services interrupt
```

Description: This service terminates a program and returns control to either a parent program or DOS. This service allows passing a return code to the parent or to DOS. If the program invoking this service is a child program, the return code is retrievable (by the parent program) through service 21/4D. If control is returned to DOS, the return code is available through the ERRORLEVEL batch-file command.

Get Return Code of a Subprocess (Interrupt 21h, service 4Dh)

Category: System services

Registers on Entry:

AH: 4Dh

Registers on Return:

AX: Return code

Memory Affected: None

Syntax:

```
MOV    AH,4Dh                ;Want service 4Dh
INT    21h                   ;DOS services interrupt
```

Description: This service retrieves the return code that a child program passes through service 21/4C. A reliable return code can be retrieved only once.

The returned value, in AX, is divided into two parts. AL contains the value passed by the child program, and AH contains one of the values shown in table 16.13.

Table 16.13. *AH return codes for service 21/4D.*

Value	Termination meaning
0	Normal
1	Ctrl-Break
2	Critical error
3	Terminate and stay resident (TSR)

Search for First File Name Match (Interrupt 21h, service 4Eh)

Category: Disk services

Registers on Entry:

AH: 4Eh
CX: File attribute
DX: Offset address of file name
DS: Segment address of file name

Registers on Return:

AX: Error code

Memory Affected: If the service locates a file name match, DOS fills the memory area specified as the DTA with 43 bytes of file information.

Syntax:

```
PUSH  CS                  ;Code segment and
POP   DS                  ;  data segment are same
MOV   DX,OFFSET PATH_NAME ;Offset address of path
MOV   AH,4Eh              ;Want service 4Eh
INT   21h                 ;DOS services interrupt
JC    ERROR               ;Branch if error
```

Description: This service locates a file with a specified file name. DS:DX should point to an ASCIIZ (nul-terminated ASCII) string that contains the full name of the file, including any applicable path name. Wild cards can be used in the file designation.

You place the desired file attribute value in CX. Actually, because the file attribute is only one byte long, you should place the new setting in CL, and set CH to 0. Table 16.14 shows bit meanings of the file attribute byte. In this table, a *1* in a bit position indicated by an x means that the attribute is selected; a *0* means that the attribute is not selected.

Table 16.14. Bit settings for file attribute, service 21/43.

Bits 76543210	Meaning
00	Reserved—set to 0
0	Archive—does not apply to this service
x	Subdirectory
x	Volume label
x	System
x	Hidden
0	Read-only—does not apply to this service

DOS follows a peculiar logic when searching for files with matching attributes. If CX is set to 0, DOS locates normal files (files with no special attributes). Selecting an attribute byte with any combination of subdirectory, system, or hidden bits set results in those files and normal files being selected. If the volume label bit is set, only files with a volume label attribute match.

On return, the carry flag indicates whether an error has occurred. If the carry flag is set, AX contains the error code, which can be handled through service 21/59. If the carry flag is not set, the service fills in the DTA with 43 bytes of information about the located file. This information is detailed as follows:

```
           DB    21 DUP(0)      ;Reserved-used by DOS
FILE_ATTR  DB    00             ;File attribute
FILE_TIME  DW    0000           ;File time
FILE_DATE  DW    0000           ;File date
FILE_SIZE  DD    00000000       ;File size
FILE_NAME  DB    13 DUP(0)      ;ASCIIZ of file name
```

The file name returned in FILE_NAME is left-justified with a period between the root and extension.

Search for Next File Name Match (Interrupt 21h, service 4Fh)

Category: Disk services

Registers on Entry:

AH: 4Fh

Registers on Return:

AX: Error code

Memory Affected: If the service locates a file name match, DOS fills in the memory area specified as the DTA with 43 bytes of file information.

Syntax:

```
MOV    AH,4Fh        ;Want service 4Fh
INT    21h           ;DOS services interrupt
JC     ERROR         ;Branch if error
```

Description: This service locates the next file with a specified file name. Before you invoke this service, the DTA must be set by a call to service 21/4E. Otherwise, the results can be unpredictable. For more information, see the description for service 21/4E.

Because any given directory must contain unique file names, this service is useless if the file specification for which you are searching does not contain the question-mark (?) wild card.

Reserved (Interrupt 21h, services 50h, 51h, 52h, 53h)

Description: IBM and Microsoft list these services as reserved for the internal use of DOS. Because their purpose and use are not publicized or documented, these services are subject to modification in future versions of DOS.

Get Verify Setting (Interrupt 21h, service 54h)

Category: System services

Registers on Entry:

AH: 54h

Registers on Return:

AL: Verify flag

Memory Affected: None

Syntax:

```
MOV   AH,54h               ;Want service 54h
INT   21h                  ;DOS services interrupt
```

Description: This service returns the system flag that specifies whether DOS verifies after each disk write to ensure that the information has been recorded accurately. The return value, in AL, signifies the state of the verify flag. If AL = 0, the verify flag is off. If AL = 1, the verify flag is on.

If you are working with a network system, verification is not supported; therefore, the return value has no meaning.

Reserved (Interrupt 21h, service 55h)

Description: IBM and Microsoft list this service as reserved for the internal use of DOS. The service, which is not publicized or documented, is subject to modification in future versions of DOS.

Rename File (Interrupt 21h, service 56h)

Category: Disk services

Registers on Entry:

AH: 56h
DX: Offset address of old file name
DI: Offset address of new file name
DS: Segment address of old file name
ES: Segment address of new file name

Registers on Return:

AX: Error code

Memory Affected: None

Syntax:

```
MOV   AX,CS                ;Code segment is same as
MOV   DS,AX                ;  data segment and
MOV   ES,AX                ;  extra segment
MOV   DX,OFFSET OLD_FILE   ;Offset address of old file
MOV   DI,OFFSET NEW_FILE   ;Offset address of new file
MOV   AH,56h               ;Want service 56h
INT   21h                  ;DOS services interrupt
```

Description: This service allows you to rename files, using ASCIIZ strings. DS:DX should point to an ASCIIZ (nul-terminated ASCII) string that contains the full name of the old file, including any applicable path name. ES:DI should point to a similar string for the new file.

Because the directory paths for the files may differ, you can rename files across directories. The only restriction is that both files must reside on the same drive.

On return, the carry flag indicates whether an error has occurred. If the carry flag is set, AX contains the error code, which can be handled through service 21/59.

Get/Set File Date and Time (Interrupt 21h, service 57h)

Category: Disk services

Registers on Entry:

AH: 57h
AL: Function code
BX: File handle
CX: New file time
DX: New file date

Registers on Return:

AX: Error code
CX: File time
DX: File date

Memory Affected: None

Syntax:

```
MOV    AL,0                ;Get file date and time
MOV    BX,FILE_HANDLE      ;Use this handle
MOV    AH,57h              ;Want service 57h
INT    21h                 ;DOS services interrupt
```

Description: This service allows you to retrieve or set the date and time for an open file, based on the function code in AL. If AL=0, the service retrieves the file date and time; if AL=1, the service sets the file date and time.

If you are setting the file date and time, specify the time in CX and the date in DX.

On return, the carry flag indicates whether an error has occurred. If the carry flag is set, AX contains the error code, which can be handled through service 21/59. If the carry flag is clear and AL=0, CX and DX reflect, on return, the file time and date, respectively.

Reserved (Interrupt 21h, service 58h)

Description: IBM lists this service as reserved for the internal use of DOS. The service, which is not publicized or documented, is subject to modification in future versions of DOS.

Microsoft, however, documents the service as a means of specifying to DOS the strategy to use for memory allocation. This was the highest-numbered service provided in version 2 of either DOS; all higher-numbered services were introduced with version 3 or later versions.

Because this service is only partially documented, and any change to the memory allocation strategy could adversely affect the functioning of all other programs, I'm following IBM's lead and omitting the service from this discussion. If you want details about this function (or any of the other undocumented functions), refer to the *DOS Programmer's Reference, 2nd Edition*, also published by Que Corporation.

Get Extended Error Information (Interrupt 21h, service 59h)

Category: System services

Registers on Entry:

AH: 59h
BX: 0

Registers on Return:

AX: Extended error code
BH: Error class
BL: Suggested remedy
CH: Locus

Memory Affected: None

Syntax:

```
ERROR:      PUSH   AX            ;Store all registers
            PUSH   BX
            PUSH   CX
            PUSH   DX
```

```
PUSH    DI
PUSH    SI
PUSH    ES
PUSH    DS
MOV     BX,0
MOV     AH,59h              ;Want service 59h
INT     21h                 ;DOS services interrupt
MOV     ERROR_CODE,AX       ;Store returned values
MOV     ERROR_CLASS,BH
MOV     ACTION,BL
MOV     LOCUS,CH
POP     DS                  ;Restore all registers
POP     ES
POP     SI
POP     DI
POP     DX
POP     CX
POP     BX
POP     AX
```

Description: This service, not available before DOS version 3.0, returns detailed information on system errors that have occurred. The service is used for DOS service calls that return errors through use of the carry flag.

The *error code* is the general system error code. The *classes* provide further information about the error classification. The suggested *actions* provide remedies that DOS "thinks" are appropriate for the type of error and the circumstances of its occurrence. The *locus* is the general hardware area where the error occurred.

Because this service destroys virtually all registers, you should save all the registers if you need their contents.

The error code returned in AX is one of the values shown in table 16.15. The possible error classes returned in BH are shown in table 16.16; possible suggested actions returned in BL are shown in table 16.17; and table 16.18 details the locus returned in CH.

Table 16.15. *Possible extended error codes returned in AX for service 21/59.*

Value	Meaning
1	Invalid function
2	File not found
3	Path not found
4	Too many file handles open
5	Access denied
6	Invalid handle
7	Memory control blocks destroyed
8	Insufficient memory
9	Invalid memory block address
10	Invalid environment
11	Invalid format
12	Invalid access code
13	Invalid data
14	Reserved
15	Invalid drive
16	Attempt to remove current directory
17	Not same device
18	No more files
19	Disk write-protected
20	Unknown unit
21	Drive not ready
22	Unknown command
23	CRC error
24	Bad request structure length
25	Seek error
26	Unknown media type
27	Sector not found
28	Out of paper
29	Write fault
30	Read fault
31	General failure
32	Sharing violation
33	Lock violation
34	Invalid disk change
35	FCB unavailable
36	Sharing buffer overflow
37	Reserved
38	Unable to complete file operation
39	Reserved

Value	Meaning
40	Reserved
41	Reserved
42	Reserved
43	Reserved
44	Reserved
45	Reserved
46	Reserved
47	Reserved
48	Reserved
49	Reserved
50	Network request not supported
51	Remote computer not listening
52	Duplicate name on network
53	Network name not found
54	Network busy
55	Network device no longer exists
56	Net BIOS command limit exceeded
57	Network adapter error
58	Incorrect network response
59	Unexpected network error
60	Incompatible remote adapter
61	Print queue full
62	Not enough space for print file
63	Print file deleted
64	Network name deleted
65	Access denied
66	Network device type incorrect
67	Network name not found
68	Network name limit exceeded
69	Net BIOS session limit exceeded
70	Temporarily paused
71	Network request not accepted
72	Print or disk redirection is paused
73	Reserved
74	Reserved
75	Reserved
76	Reserved
77	Reserved
78	Reserved
79	Reserved
80	File exists

Table 16.15. continues

Table 16.15. *continued*

Value	Meaning
81	Reserved
82	Cannot make directory entry
83	Fail on INT 24
84	Too many redirections
85	Duplicate redirection
86	Invalid password
87	Invalid parameter
88	Network data fault
89	Function not supported by network
90	Required system component not installed

Table 16.16. *Possible error classes returned in BH for service 21/59.*

Value	Meaning
1	Out of resource
2	Temporary situation
3	Authorization
4	Internal
5	Hardware failure
6	System failure
7	Application program error
8	Not found
9	Bad format
10	Locked
11	Media
12	Already exists
13	Unknown

Table 16.17. *Possible suggested actions returned in BL for service 21/59.*

Value	Meaning
1	Retry
2	Delay then retry
3	Reconsider user input
4	Abort with cleanup
5	Immediate exit without cleanup
6	Ignore
7	Retry after action taken

Table 16.18. *Possible locus values returned in CH for service 21/59.*

Value	Meaning
1	Unknown
2	Block device
3	Network
4	Serial device
5	Memory

Create Temporary File (Interrupt 21h, service 5Ah)

Category: Disk services

Registers on Entry:

AH: 5Ah
CX: File attribute
DX: Offset address of path name
DS: Segment address of path name

Registers on Return:

AX: Return code
DX: Offset address of completed path name
DS: Segment address of completed path name

Memory Affected: The ASCIIZ string specified by DS:DX is appended with the file name of the unique file created.

Syntax:

```
PUSH    CS              ;Code segment and
POP     DS              ;  data segment are same
MOV     DX,OFFSET PATH_NAME   ;Offset address of path
MOV     CX,0            ;Normal file
MOV     AH,5Ah          ;Want service 5Ah
INT     21h             ;DOS services interrupt
JC      ERROR           ;Branch if error
MOV     FILE_HANDLE,AX  ;Store returned handle
```

Description: This service, not available before DOS version 3.0, causes a file with a unique file name to be created in the specified directory. DS:DX should point to an ASCIIZ (nul-terminated ASCII) string that contains the path name of the directory which will contain the file. This path name should end with a backslash.

You should place the file attribute in CX. Actually, because the file attribute is only one byte long, place the new setting in CL, and set CH to 0. Table 16.19 shows the possible file attribute settings. In this table, a *1* in a bit position indicated by an *x* means that the attribute is selected; a *0* means that the attribute is not selected.

Table 16.19. Bit settings for file attribute, service 21/43.

Bits 76543210	*Meaning*
00	Reserved—set to 0
x	Archive
0	Subdirectory—set to 0 for this service
0	Volume label—set to 0 for this service
x	System
x	Hidden
x	Read-only

This service is helpful for programs that need temporary files for program purposes. It generates a unique file name and opens the file for read/write operations. The file stays open until you close it and is not deleted unless you delete it.

On return, the carry flag indicates whether an error has occurred. If the carry flag is set, AX contains the error code, which can be handled through service 21/59. If the carry flag is clear, AX contains the file handle for the newly created file, and DS:DX points to an ASCIIZ string that represents the full path name of the created file.

Create File (Interrupt 21h, service 5Bh)

Category: Disk services

Registers on Entry:

AH: 5Bh
CX: File attribute
DX: Offset address of path name
DS: Segment address of path name

Registers on Return:

AX: Return code

Memory Affected: None

Syntax:

```
PUSH    CS                      ;Code segment and
POP     DS                      ;  data segment are same
MOV     DX,OFFSET PATH_NAME     ;Offset address of path
MOV     CX,0                    ;File attribute is normal
MOV     AH,5Bh                  ;Want service 5Bh
INT     21h                     ;DOS services interrupt
JC      ERROR                   ;Carry set, handle error
MOV     FILE_HANDLE,AX          ;Store returned handle
```

Description: This service, not available before DOS version 3.0, creates a disk file. On entry, DS:DX points to an ASCIIZ (nul-terminated ASCII) string that contains the full name of the file, including any applicable path name. You set CX to equal the desired attribute for the file.

This service is identical to service 21/3C except that if the file name specified in the ASCIIZ string already exists, an error code is returned.

On return, if the carry flag is set, an error has occurred, and the error code is in AX. Service 21/59 can be used to get detailed error information. If the carry flag is not set, the operation was successful, and AX contains the file handle for the newly opened file. This number (file handle) can be used in many other DOS file operations.

When this service is completed, the specified file is left open. You do not need to open the file, but you must remember to close it.

File Access Control (Interrupt 21h, service 5Ch)

Category: Disk services

Registers on Entry:

AH: 5Ch
AL: Function code
BX: File handle
CX: Region offset high
DX: Region offset low
DI: Region length low
SI: Region length high

Registers on Return:

AX: Error code

Memory Affected: None

Syntax:

```
MOV    AL,0                ;Lock region
MOV    BX,FILE_HANDLE      ;Use this file
MOV    CX,PTR_HIGH         ;Offset into file
MOV    DX,PTR_LOW
MOV    SI,0                ;Only lock 1 record
MOV    DI,REC_LEN
MOV    AH,5Ch              ;Want service 5Ch
INT    21h                 ;DOS services interrupt
JC     ERROR               ;Branch if error
```

Description: This service, not available before DOS version 3.0, provides a simple access-limitation convention for files. The user can lock or unlock regions of a file, thereby limiting or expanding access to the file contents. This service is most useful in networked or multitasking environments.

AL should contain either a 0 or a 1. AL = 0 means to lock the file specified in BX; AL = 1 means to unlock the file. CX:DX contains a byte offset into the file that specifies the start of the region to be locked. SI:DI contains the length of the region to be locked.

On return, if the carry flag is set, an error has occurred, and the error code is in AX. Service 21/59 can be used to get detailed error information.

Before exiting a program, be sure to remember to unlock any regions that have been locked. Failure to do so can have unpredictable results.

Reserved (Interrupt 21h, service 5Dh)

Description: IBM and Microsoft list this service as reserved for the internal use of DOS. The service, which is not publicized or documented, is subject to modification in future versions of DOS.

Get Machine Name (Interrupt 21h, service 5Eh, function 0)

Category: Network services

Registers on Entry:

AH: 5Eh
AL: 0
DX: Offset address of buffer
DS: Segment address of buffer

Registers on Return:

AX: Error code
CH: Indicator flag
CL: NETBIOS number
DX: Offset address of buffer
DS: Segment address of buffer

Memory Affected: The memory area specified by DS:DX is overwritten with the returned string.

Syntax:

```
MOV    AL,0                 ;Get machine name
PUSH   CS                   ;Code segment and
POP    DS                   ;  data segment are same
MOV    DX,OFFSET BUFFER     ;Offset address of buffer
MOV    AH,5Eh               ;Want service 5Eh
INT    21h                  ;DOS services interrupt
JC     ERROR                ;Branch if error
```

Description: You use this function, not available before DOS version 3.1, when you are working under local area network (LAN) software. This function returns a 15-byte string indicating the name of the computer on which the software is operating. The string is padded with spaces and is nul-terminated, rendering 16 bytes in total.

On return, if the carry flag is set, an error has occurred, and the error code is in AX. Service 21/59 can be used to get detailed error information.

If the carry is clear, CH contains a flag to indicate whether the name is actually returned. If CH is 0, no name has been defined for this computer. If CH <> 0, DS:DX defines and points to the name. CL then contains a number that represents the NETBIOS number for the name at DS:DX.

Set Printer Setup (Interrupt 21h, service 5Eh, function 2)

Category: Network services

Registers on Entry:

AH: 5Eh
AL: 2
BX: Redirection list index
CX: Setup string length
SI: Offset address of buffer
DS: Segment address of buffer

Registers on Return:

AX: Error code

Memory Affected: None

Syntax:

```
MOV     AL,2                    ;Set printer setup
PUSH    CS                      ;Code segment and
POP     DS                      ;   data segment are same
MOV     SI,OFFSET SETUP_STR     ;Offset of setup string
MOV     CX,SETUP_LENGTH         ;Length of setup string
MOV     BX,INDEX                ;Redirection list
MOV     AH,5Eh                  ;Want service 5Eh
INT     21h                     ;DOS services interrupt
JC      ERROR                   ;Branch if error
```

Description: You use this service, not available before DOS version 3.1, when you are operating under local area network (LAN) software. This service allows you to specify a string to precede all files sent from the local node to a network printer. The designed purpose of the string is to allow the printer to be set up according to individual node requirements. DS:SI points to the string, which can be up to 64 bytes in length (length specified in CX). BX contains the redirection list index pointer, which is determined through service 21/5F/2.

On return, if the carry flag is set, an error has occurred, and the error code is in AX. Service 21/59 can be used to get detailed error information.

Get Printer Setup (Interrupt 21h, service 5Eh, function 3)

Category: Network services

Registers on Entry:

AH: 5Eh
AL: 3
BX: Redirection list index
DI: Offset address of buffer
ES: Segment address of buffer

Registers on Return:

AX: Error code
CX: Setup string length

DI: Offset address of buffer
ES: Segment address of buffer

Memory Affected: The memory area specified by ES:DI is overwritten with the requested network information.

Syntax:

```
MOV     AL,3                    ;Get printer setup
PUSH    CS                      ;Code segment and
POP     ES                      ;  extra segment are same
MOV     DI,OFFSET SETUP_STR     ;Offset of setup string
MOV     BX,INDEX                ;Redirection list
MOV     AH,5Eh                  ;Want service 5Eh
INT     21h                     ;DOS services interrupt
JC      ERROR                   ;Branch if error
```

Description: You use this service, not available before DOS version 3.1, when you are operating under local area network (LAN) software. This service returns the printer setup string specified with service 21/5E/2. The returned value, which is stored at the buffer specified by ES:DI, may be up to 64 bytes in length. Be sure that you set aside a large enough buffer area. BX contains the redirection list index pointer, which is determined through service 21/5F/2.

On return, if the carry flag is set, an error has occurred, and the error code is in AX. Service 21/59 can be used to get detailed error information. If the carry flag is not set, the buffer area to which ES:DI points contains the printer setup string, with CX set to the string length.

Get Redirection List Entry (Interrupt 21h, service 5Fh, function 2)

Category: Network services

Registers on Entry:

AH: 5Fh
AL: 2
BX: Redirection list index
DI: Offset address of network name buffer
SI: Offset address of local name buffer
DS: Segment address of local name buffer
ES: Segment address of network name buffer

Registers on Return:

AX: Error code
BH: Device status
BL: Device type
CX: Parameter value
DI: Offset address of network name buffer
SI: Offset address of local name buffer
DS: Segment address of local name buffer
ES: Segment address of network name buffer

Memory Affected: The buffers to which DS:SI and ES:DI point are over-written with the requested network information.

Syntax:

```
MOV     AX,CS               ;Code segment is same as
MOV     DS,AX               ;  data segment and
MOV     ES,AX               ;  extra segment
MOV     SI,OFFSET LOCAL_BUF ;Offset address of buffer
MOV     DI,OFFSET NET_BUF   ;Offset address of buffer
MOV     BX,1                ;Start with this entry
MOV     AL,2                ;Get list entry
MOV     AH,5Fh              ;Want service 5Fh
INT     21h                 ;DOS services interrupt
JC      ERROR               ;Branch if error
```

Description: You use this service, not available before DOS version 3.1, when you are operating under local area network (LAN) software. This service returns an entry from the redirection list, which is set up by service 21/5F/3. The buffers to which DS:SI and ES:DI point should each be 128 bytes in length.

On return, if the carry flag is set, an error has occurred, and the error code is in AX. Service 21/59 can be used to get detailed error information. If the carry flag is not set, DS:SI and ES:DI point to ASCIIZ strings of the requested information; and BH, BL, and CX all contain additional device information. This function destroys DX and BP.

Redirect Device (Interrupt 21h, service 5Fh, function 3)

Category: Network services

Registers on Entry:

AH: 5Fh
AL: 3

BL: Device type
CX: Caller value
DI: Offset address of network path
SI: Offset address of device name
DS: Segment address of device name
ES: Segment address of network path

Registers on Return:

AX: Error code

Memory Affected: None

Syntax:

```
MOV    AX,CS              ;Code segment is same as
MOV    DS,AX              ;  data segment and
MOV    ES,AX              ;  extra segment
MOV    SI,OFFSET DEVICE   ;Offset of device name
MOV    DI,OFFSET NET_PATH ;Offset of network path
MOV    AL,3               ;Redirect
MOV    AH,5Fh             ;Want service 5Fh
INT    21h                ;DOS services interrupt
JC     ERROR              ;Branch if error
```

Description: You use this service, not available before DOS version 3.1, when you are operating under local area network (LAN) software. The service allows you to add devices to the network redirection list. DS:SI and ES:DI both specify ASCIIZ strings.

On return, if the carry flag is set, an error has occurred, and the error code is in AX. Service 21/59 can be used to get detailed error information.

Cancel Redirection (Interrupt 21h, service 5Fh, function 4)

Category: Network services

Registers on Entry:

AH: 5Fh
AL: 4
SI: Offset address of device name/path
DS: Segment address of device name/path

Registers on Return:

AX: Error code

Memory Affected: None

Syntax:

```
PUSH   CS                        ;Code segment and
POP    DS                        ;  data segment are same
MOV    SI,OFFSET DEVICE          ;Offset of device name
MOV    AL,4                      ;Get list entry
MOV    AH,5Fh                    ;Want service 5Fh
INT    21h                       ;DOS services interrupt
JC     ERROR                     ;Branch if error
```

Description: You use this service, not available before DOS version 3.1, when you are operating under local area network (LAN) software. The service allows for deleting devices from the network redirection list. DS:SI specifies an ASCIIZ string.

On return, if the carry flag is set, an error has occurred, and the error code is in AX. Service 21/59 can be used to get detailed error information.

Reserved (Interrupt 21h, service 60h, 61h)

Description: IBM and Microsoft list these services as reserved for the internal use of DOS. Their purpose and use, which are not publicized or documented, are subject to modification in future versions of DOS.

Get Program Segment Prefix (PSP) Address (Interrupt 21h, service 62h)

Category: System services

Registers on Entry:

AH: 62h

Registers on Return:

BX: PSP segment address

Memory Affected: None

Syntax:

```
MOV    AH,62h                    ;Want service 62h
INT    21h                       ;DOS services interrupt
```

Description: This service, not available before DOS version 3.0, returns the program segment prefix (PSP) address for the current program. The PSP segment address is returned in BX.

Reserved (Interrupt 21h, service 63h, 64h)

Description: IBM and Microsoft list these services as reserved for the internal use of DOS. Their purpose and use, which are not publicized or documented, are subject to modification in future versions of DOS.

Get Extended Country Information (Interrupt 21h, service 65h)

Category: System services

Registers on Entry:

AH: 65h
AL: Information code
BX: Code page
CX: Length of information to return
DX: Country ID
DI: Offset address of buffer
ES: Segment address of buffer

Registers on Return:

AX: Error code
DI: Offset address of buffer
ES: Segment address of buffer

Memory Affected: The buffer area to which ES:DI points is overlaid with the requested country information.

Syntax:

```
MOV    AL,1                  ;Want country info
MOV    BX,-1                 ;Use current console device
MOV    DX,-1                 ;Use current country
MOV    CX,41                 ;Want all the information
PUSH   CS                    ;Code segment and
POP    ES                    ;  Extra segment are same
MOV    DI,OFFSET BUFFER      ;Offset address of buffer
MOV    AH,63h                ;Want service 63h
INT    21h                   ;DOS services interrupt
```

Description: This service, not available before DOS version 3.3, returns information similar to that provided by service 21/38. With service 63/64, you specify the information to be returned in AL and the destination in

ES:DI. Because the amount of information is specified in CX, only partial information retrieval is possible.

The country code is specified in DX, as shown in table 16.20.

Table 16.20. *Country codes.*

Country	Code
Currently installed	− 1
United States	1
Netherlands	31
Belgium	32
France	33
Spain	34
Italy	39
Switzerland	41
United Kingdom	44
Denmark	45
Sweden	46
Norway	47
Germany	49
Australia	61
Finland	358
Israel	972

If the country code (DX) does not match the code page (BX) or if either is invalid, an error is generated and returned in AX.

You request the desired information in AL. This information code can be 1, 2, 4, or 6. The possible amount of information returned by each information type specifier varies, but you can limit the information to no less than five bytes by the value placed in CX. Tables 16.21 through 16.24 detail the information returned at ES:DI by each possible value for AL. Notice, in table 16.21, the similarities to information returned by service 21/38.

Table 16.21. *Information returned for service 21/65 if AL = 1.*

Bytes	Purpose
1	Information specifier (1)
2	Size
2	Country ID
2	Code page
2	Date format

Bytes	Purpose
5	Currency symbol
2	Thousands separator
2	Decimal separator
2	Date separator
2	Time separator
1	Currency format
1	Currency decimal digits
1	Time format
4	Map call address
2	Data list separator
10	Nul bytes

Table 16.22. *Information returned for service 21/65 if AL = 2.*

Bytes	Purpose
1	Information specifier (2)
4	Uppercase table address

Table 16.23. *Information returned for service 21/65 if AL = 4.*

Bytes	Purpose
1	Information specifier (4)
4	File name uppercase table address

Table 16.24. *Information returned for service 21/65 if AL = 6.*

Bytes	Purpose
1	Information specifier (6)
4	Collate table address

Get/Set Global Code Page (Interrupt 21h, service 66h)

Category: System services

Registers on Entry:

AH: 66h
AL: Function code
BX: Code page

Registers on Return:

>   AX: Error code
>   BX: Code page
>   DX: Boot code page

Memory Affected: None

Syntax:

```
MOV    AL,1            ;Get global code page
MOV    AH,66h          ;Want service 66h
INT    21h             ;DOS services interrupt
JC     ERROR           ;Branch if error
```

Description: This service, not available before DOS version 3.3, retrieves or changes the code page for the currently selected country information. If AL = 1, the code page is retrieved. If AL = 2, the code page is set.

If you are retrieving the code page (AL = 1), the contents of BX are not significant on service entry. BX and DX return the requested information.

If you are setting the code page (AL = 2), you specify the desired code page in BX. The only return value when setting the code page is the error code in AX (if the carry flag is set).

On return, if the carry flag is set, an error has occurred, and the error code is in AX. Service 21/59 can be used to get detailed error information.

Change Handle Count (Interrupt 21h, service 67h)

Category: System services

Registers on Entry:

>   AH: 67h
>   BX: Number of handles

Registers on Return:

>   AX: Error code

Memory Affected: None

Syntax:

```
MOV   BX,50          ;Want 50 handles
MOV   AH,67h         ;Want service 67h
INT   21h            ;DOS services interrupt
```

Description: This service, not available before DOS version 3.3, allows you to specify the number of file handles available to DOS. You specify this number, which must be between 20 and 65,535, in BX. The number can be larger than 255, which is the maximum definable in the CONFIG.SYS file.

On return, if the carry flag is set, an error has occurred, and the error code is in AX. Service 21/59 can be used to get detailed error information.

Flush Buffer (Interrupt 21h, service 68h)

Category: Disk services

Registers on Entry:

AH: 68h
BX: File handle

Registers on Return:

AX: Error code

Memory Affected: None

Syntax:

```
MOV   BX,FILE_HANDLE   ;Use this file
MOV   AH,68h           ;Want service 68h
INT   21h              ;DOS services interrupt
JC    ERROR            ;Branch if error
```

Description: With this service, not available before DOS version 3.0, the file buffer of the specified file (BX) is written to disk.

On return, if the carry flag is set, an error has occurred, and the error code is in AX. Service 21/59 can be used to get detailed error information.

This was the highest-numbered service provided with any of the version 3.x releases of DOS. All services with higher numbers first appeared at version 4.0 or later.

Reserved (Interrupt 21h, services 69h, 6Ah, 6Bh)

Description: IBM and Microsoft list these services as reserved for the internal use of DOS. Their purpose and use, which are not publicized or documented, are subject to modification in future versions of DOS.

Extended Open/Create File (Interrupt 21h, service 6Ch)

Category: Disk services

Registers on Entry:

AH: 6Ch
AL: 00h (required)
BX: Access mode (table 16.25)
CX: File attributes (table 16.26)
DX: Action flags (table 16.27)

Registers on Return:

AX: File handle
CX: Action taken:
        00 = file existed and was opened
        01 = did not exist, was created
        02 = existed, was replaced

Memory Affected: None

Syntax:

```
MOV     AX,6C00h        ;Want service 6Ch
MOV     BX,0            ;read only, compatible, DOS defaults
MOV     CX,0            ;open as normal file
MOV     DX,1            ;fail if file does not exist
INT     21h             ;DOS services interrupt
JC      ERROR           ;bail out on error
MOV     MY_HANDLE,AX    ;save handle to refer to file
```

Description: This function, not available before DOS version 4.0, combines functions previously provided by service 21/3C, 21/3D, and 21/5B into a single, multipurpose facility that opens and creates files.

On return, if the carry flag is set, an error has occurred, and the error code is in AX. Service 21/59 can be used to get detailed error information.

The values available for registers upon entry to service 21/6C (the access modes in BX, the file attributes in CX, and the action codes in DX) are listed in tables 16.25, 16.26, and 16.27, respectively.

Table 16.25. *Access modes for service 21/6C (in BX).*

FEDCBA98 76543210	Meaning
000	Read-only access
001	Write-only access
010	Read/Write access
011	Not used
1xx	Not used
x	Not used
000	Compatibility mode
001	Deny all sharing
010	Deny write sharing
011	Deny read sharing
100	Deny none
101	Not used
110	Not used
111	Not used
0	Child inherits handles
1	Child does not get handles
xxxxx	Not used
0	Use INT 24h handler
1	Return error only
0	Buffered writes
1	Immediate writes
x	Not used

Table 16.26. *File attributes for service 21/6C (in CX).*

FEDCBA98 76543210	Meaning
0	Read/write
1	Read only
0	Visible
1	Hidden
0	Normal user file
1	System file
0	Not volume label
1	Volume label
x	Not used
0	Not modified
1	Modified (archive bit)
xxxxxxxx xx	Not used

Table 16.27. *Action flags for service 21/6C (in DX).*

FEDCBA98 76543210	Meaning
0000	Fail if file exists
0001	Open if file exists
0010	Replace if file exists
0011	Not used
01xx	Not used
1xxx	Not used
0000	Fail if file does not exist
0001	Create file if it does not exist
001x	Not used
01xx	Not used
1xxx	Not used
xxxxxxxx	Not used

Terminate Address (Interrupt 22h)

Description: This is not a serviceable interrupt but rather a vector to the termination handler for DOS. Control passes to this address when a program ends.

Ctrl-Break Handler Address (Interrupt 23h)

Description: This is not a serviceable interrupt but rather a vector to the address of the routine that receives control from DOS when a Ctrl-Break key combination is detected.

Critical Error Handler Address (Interrupt 24h)

Description: This is not a serviceable interrupt but rather a vector to the address of the routine that receives control from DOS when a critical error is detected.

Absolute Disk Read (Interrupt 25h)

Category: Disk services

Registers on Entry:

AL: Drive number
BX: Offset address of buffer (or parameter block if CX = −1)
CX: Sectors to read (−1 indicates extended format for DOS 4)
DX: Logical starting sector
DS: Segment address of buffer (or parameter block if CX = −1)

Registers on Return: Unchanged

Memory Affected: The buffer area specified by DS:BX (or by the parameter block pointed to, if extended format is used) is overlaid with information read from the disk.

Syntax:

```
MOV    AL,2                    ;Drive C:
MOV    DX,0                    ;Starting with sector 0
MOV    CX,3                    ;Read 3 sectors
MOV    BX,OFFSET DS:BUFFER     ;Offset of buffer area
INT    25h                     ;Read sectors
POP    DX                      ;Clean up stack
JC     ERROR                   ;Branch if error
```

Description: This interrupt, which allows DOS to read any sector from the disk, is the opposite of interrupt 26h (and similar to BIOS service 13/2).

To use this service, you must specify the precise physical location on the disk at which you want to begin reading. Specify the drive in AL, where A = 0, B = 1, C = 2, etc. DX is the logical starting sector. (All sectors on the disk are numbered logically in sequential order, starting with 0.) CX is the number of sectors to read. The final registers to be set up specify which RAM area will be used as a buffer for the sectors that are read. This address is specified in DS:BX.

With the introduction of DOS version 4, an extended format capable of dealing with 32-bit logical sector numbers was added to this interrupt. If CX is set to − 1 rather than to a positive value, then DS:BX is a far pointer to a 10-byte parameter block with the following information:

Offset	Length	Contents
00h	Double word	Logical sector number, zero based
04h	Word	Number of sectors to transfer
06h	Double word	Far pointer to data buffer

On return, if the carry flag is set, this indicates an error has occurred, and the error code is in AX. You must realize that, on return from this interrupt, the flags are still on the stack. They must be removed from the stack before the program continues.

Absolute Disk Write (Interrupt 26h)

Category: Disk services

Registers on Entry:

>AL: Drive number
>BX: Offset address of buffer (or parameter block if CX = −1)
>CX: Sectors to write (−1 indicates extended format for DOS 4)
>DX: Logical starting sector
>DS: Segment address of buffer (or parameter block if CX = −1)

Registers on Return: Unchanged

Memory Affected: None

Syntax:

```
MOV   AL,2                       ;Drive C:
MOV   DX,0                       ;Starting with sector 0
MOV   CX,3                       ;Write 3 sectors
MOV   BX,OFFSET DS:BUFFER        ;Offset of buffer area
INT   26h                        ;Write sectors
POP   DX                         ;Clean up stack
JC    ERROR                      ;Branch if error
```

Description: This interrupt, which is the opposite of interrupt 25h (and similar to BIOS service 13/3), allows DOS to write any sector to the disk.

To use this service, you must specify the precise physical location on the disk at which you want to begin writing. You specify the drive in AL, where A = 0, B = 1, C = 2, etc. DX is the logical starting sector. (All sectors on the disk are logically numbered in sequential order starting with 0.) CX is the number of sectors to write. The final registers to be set up specify the RAM area from which to take the information to be written. This address is specified in DS:BX.

With the introduction of DOS version 4, an extended format capable of dealing with 32-bit logical sector numbers was added to this interrupt. If CX is set to −1 rather than to a positive value, then DS:BX is a far pointer to a 10-byte parameter block with the following information:

Offset	Length	Contents
00h	Double word	Logical sector number, zero based
04h	Word	Number of sectors to transfer
06h	Double word	Far pointer to data buffer

On return, if the carry flag is set, an error has occurred, and the error code is in AX. You must realize that, on return from this interrupt, the flags are still on the stack. They must be removed from the stack before the program continues.

Terminate and Stay Resident (Interrupt 27h)

Category: System services

Registers on Entry:

DX: Pointer to last byte of program

Registers on Return: Unknown (does not return)

Memory Affected: None

Syntax:

```
MOV    DX,OFFSET CS:END_BYTE   ;Point to end of program
INT    27h                     ;TSR
```

Description: This interrupt, which is similar to the preferred TSR service of 21/31, allows the program to exit to DOS without freeing the program memory space.

Because only one register is used to point to the program end point, the maximum usable program size for this interrupt is obviously 64K. Any files created or opened by the program remain open after this interrupt is invoked.

Reserved (Interrupts 28h, 29h, 2Ah, 2Bh, 2Ch, 2Dh, 2Eh)

Description: IBM and Microsoft list these interrupts as reserved for the internal use of DOS. Their purpose and use, which are not publicized or documented, are subject to modification in future versions of DOS.

Multiplex Interrupt (Interrupt 2Fh)

Category: System services

Registers on Entry: Varies

Registers on Return: Varies

Memory Affected: Varies

Description: This interrupt allows user-defined routines to share the space set aside for special DOS programs such as PRINT, ASSIGN, and SHARE.

The use and function of this interrupt are beyond the scope of this book. For more information, please refer to the DOS *Technical Reference Manual*.

Reserved (Interrupts 30h through 3Fh)

Description: IBM and Microsoft list these interrupts as reserved for the internal use of DOS. Their purpose and use, which are not publicized or documented, are subject to modification in future versions of DOS.

CHAPTER 17

Processor
Instruction Sets

The heart of your computer is the microprocessor. In IBM PC or PS/2 and compatibles, this is usually the Intel family of microprocessors. Your system may contain a numeric coprocessor, which Intel refers to as a *Numeric Processing Extension*, or NPX. The numeric coprocessor is used to aid in advanced mathematic operations.

The instruction sets for both Intel microprocessors and NPXs are covered in this chapter. These include the following:

❏ 8086/8088

❏ 80286

❏ 80386

❏ 80486

❏ 8087

❏ 80287

❏ 80387

Notice that there is no corresponding NPX for the 80486 microprocessor. This is because the 80486 included all of the capabilities of an

631

NPX. In the case of the 80486, these collective advanced mathematic operations are handled by the *Floating Point Unit*, or FPU.

Programming Models

Intel describes the instruction sets of its processors in terms of a *programming model*, which defines all those parts of the processor that are visible to the programmer; those portions of the device which cannot be affected directly by the program are omitted. To use the instructions, it is helpful to know the corresponding programming model. Let's take a look at the programming model for each chip. The microprocessors will be examined first, followed by the NPXs.

8086/8088

The 8086 and 8088 processors are internally identical, although the 8086 has a full 16-bit data bus and the 8088 has an 8-bit bus automatically multiplexed to perform 16-bit transfers.

The programming model for these processors consists of the register set described in Chapter 1.

80286

The 80286 processor added a number of special-purpose registers to the 8086 programming model. These include the global descriptor table (GDT) register, the interrupt descriptor table (IDT) register, the local descriptor table (LDT) register, the machine status word (MSW), and the task register.

All of these additional registers are used only when programming for *protected mode* operation. Because DOS cannot operate in protected mode (all DOS operations run in *real mode*, the other operating mode of the 80286), you are unlikely to find these registers useful.

The two descriptor table registers make it possible to access 16 megabytes of memory address space rather than the 1-megabyte limit of the 8086/8088 designs, but again this capability is available only when operating in protected mode. If programmed for compatibility with DOS, the 80286 is little more than a faster version of the 8086/8088 programming model.

80386

Unlike its 8-bit and 16-bit predecessors, the 80386 is a 32-bit micro-processor. The registers in the 80386 reflect this enlarged structure. The 80386 still uses the same general-purpose registers as the 8086/8088 and the 80286 (AX, BX, CX, and DX), but the registers' full 32-bit counter-parts are addressed by using the E (extended) prefix. EAX, EBX, ECX, and EDX are 32-bit general-purpose registers. Without the E, only the lower 16 bits of each register are accessed. Using the traditional AL, AH, BL, BH, CL, CH, DL, or DH gives you access to 8-bit chunks of the lower 16 bits of the registers.

This use of the E prefix to denote 32-bit register size also applies to other microprocessor registers, such as BP, SI, DI, and SP, which become EBP, ESI, EDI, and ESP, respectively.

The other segment registers—CS, DS, SS, and ES—are intact as imple-mented in earlier Intel microprocessors. These registers are still 16-bits wide. They are joined, however, by two additional segment registers (also 16-bits wide): the FS and GS registers, which operate the same as the ES register.

As in earlier microprocessors, the 80386 uses a flags register, but it is also 32-bits wide. This flags register will be examined later in this chapter.

80486

Like the 80386, the 80486 is a 32-bit microprocessor, but includes much more functionality within itself than any previous member of the Intel microprocessor family.

In addition to adding six more instructions to the set, the 80486 design moved the NPX functions onto the main chip. Thus, there is no 80487; all functions previously handled by an NPX were assumed by the FPU por-tion of the 80486. The chip also contains an 8K cache memory and a built-in *Memory Management Unit* (MMU).

Despite these significant changes in design, the chip retains full com-patibility with the 80386 and 80387 operations, and three of the six added instructions deal with strictly system-level programming. For all programming purposes, the 80486 processor is just a faster version of a combined 80386 and 80387.

8087

The first generation Intel NPX is truly that—an extension to the functionality of the main microprocessor. The 8087 appears virtually transparent to programmers. The instruction and register sets of the 8086/8088 simply seem to be expanded.

No special assembler directives are needed to use the 8087 mnemonic instructions with the Microsoft Macro Assembler. The assembler's default instruction set can properly translate the 8086/8088 and 8087 source code. However, you may want to study Chapter 8 to learn about assembler options, particularly the /R option.

In design philosophy, the 8087 is a bit different from the 8086/8088. It uses a floating stack for all operations, whereas the 8086/8088 uses general-purpose registers. The 8087 uses 8 internal stack registers, each of which is 80-bits wide. These stack registers are numbered 0 through 7, with most operations able to address these registers directly as ST, ST(1), ST(2), ST(3), and so on, through ST(7).

Besides this stack-oriented design, the 8087 uses several other registers to reflect the condition of this stack and to control NPX operation. The status word and control word will be described later in this chapter.

80287

The function and operation of the 80287 are similar to those of the 8087. This second-generation NPX can operate at levels demanded by the 80286, the microprocessor with which it should be paired. Several mnemonic instructions were added to take advantage of the expanded capabilities of the 80286.

The design structure of the 80287 is virtually equivalent to that of the 8087. The 80287 changes the definition of several bits in the control word, but otherwise nothing changes.

80387

As you might expect, the 80387 is the numeric processor extension for the 80386 microprocessor. The 80387 added only a few new commands not present in the 80287 and defined one additional bit in the status word. All other operations and structure remain the same as for the earlier generations of NPXs.

Instruction Sets

Because the NPX functions are an extension of the instructions offered by the microprocessor, these functions are considered an integral part of the overall instruction set of the Intel family.

The overall instruction set can be divided according to the purpose of the individual instruction. The nine general classifications of instructions (six for CPUs and three more for numeric coprocessors) are as follows:

❏ Data transfer

❏ Arithmetic

❏ Numeric transcendental

❏ Numeric constant

❏ Bit manipulation

❏ Numeric comparison

❏ String manipulation

❏ Control transfer

❏ Flag and processor control

Let's take a look at the processing instructions in each area.

Data Transfer Instructions

This group of instructions is used to move data. The movement can be between registers, between registers and memory, or between memory locations. The following 86 instructions are included:

BSWAP	INSB	LLDT	OUTSW
FBLD	INSD	LMSW	POP
FBSTP	INSW	LSL	POPA
FILD	LAHF	LSS	POPAD
FIST	LAR	LTR	POPF
FISTP	LDS	MOV	POPFD
FLD	LEA	MOVSX	PUSH
FST	LES	MOVZX	PUSHA
FSTP	LFS	OUT	PUSHAD
FXCH	LGDT	OUTS	PUSHF
IN	LGS	OUTSB	PUSHFD
INS	LIDT	OUTSD	SAHF

SETA	SETNA	SETNO	SETZ
SETAE	SETNAE	SETNP	SGDT
SETB	SETNB	SETNS	SIDT
SETBE	SETNBE	SETNZ	SLDT
SETC	SETNC	SETO	SMSW
SETE	SETNE	SETP	STR
SETG	SETNG	SETPE	XADD
SETGE	SETNGE	SETPO	XCHG
SETL	SETNL	SETS	XLAT
SETLE	SETNLE		

Not all of these instructions are available on all microprocessors or NPXs. Later, this chapter specifies which instructions work on which chips. You can also refer to the detailed instructions at the end of the chapter for more information.

Arithmetic Instructions

This classification of instruction includes the simplest of mathematic operations. These instructions are used for operations like conversions, BCD math, integer math, and simple floating-point math. Included in this grouping are the following 49 instructions:

AAA	DAS	FIDIV	FSUB
AAD	DEC	FIDIVR	FSUBP
AAM	DIV	FIMUL	FSUBR
AAS	FABS	FISUB	FSUBRP
ADC	FADD	FISUBR	FXTRACT
ADD	FADDP	FMUL	IDIV
CBW	FCHS	FMULP	IMUL
CDQ	FDIV	FPREM	INC
CMP	FDIVP	FPREM1	MUL
CMPXCHG	FDIVR	FRNDINT	NEG
CWD	FDIVRP	FSCALE	SBB
CWDE	FIADD	FSQRT	SUB
DAA			

Numeric Transcendental Instructions

This group of instructions is performed only by the NPX/FPU chips. It includes instructions that implement basic calculations for the following common functions:

❏ Trigonometric

❏ Inverse trigonometric

❏ Hyperbolic

❏ Inverse hyperbolic

❏ Logarithmic

❏ Exponential

These tasks can be time consuming. The eight instructions that make up this group are the following:

F2XM1	FPATAN	FSIN	FYL2X
FCOS	FPTAN	FSINCOS	FYL2XP1

Numeric Constant Instructions

This instruction group operates only on the NPX/FPU chips. It results in common mathematic constants being pushed on the stack (as used within the NPX/FPU). Because they are specialized and do not actually transfer data, these instructions are categorized separately from the data transfer instructions. The top stack register is simply set to be a constant value predefined by the instruction used.

The seven instructions in this group are the following:

FLD1	FLDL2T	FLDLN2	FLDZ
FLDL2E	FLDLG2	FLDPI	

Bit Manipulation Instructions

These instructions do just what they say: they manipulate the bits within individual registers. The result of this (besides changed register values for some instructions) is that the flags register is changed to reflect the outcome of the operation. Program execution can then be modified based upon the outcome. The 22 instructions in this grouping are

AND	BTR	ROL	SHLD
ARPL	BTS	ROR	SHR
BSF	NOT	SAL	SHRD
BSR	OR	SAR	TEST
BT	RCL	SHL	XOR
BTC	RCR		

Numeric Comparison Instructions

The NPX/FPU uses these instructions to set flags within the status word register. As with other instructions, the results of these instructions can alter program execution. These 10 instructions are the following:

FCOM	FICOM	FUCOM	FUCOMPP
FCOMP	FICOMP	FUCOMP	FXAM
FCOMPP	FTST		

String Manipulation Instructions

This instruction group operates on strings within memory. These are not strings in the same sense as the term is used in high-level languages. These are simply instructions that manipulate contiguous blocks of memory. When combined with repetition instructions, which are included in this instruction group, string manipulation instructions are powerful for moving or comparing large blocks of information. This group contains the following 20 instructions:

CMPSB	LODSW	REPE	SCASD
CMPSD	MOVSB	REPNE	SCASW
CMPSW	MOVSD	REPNZ	STOSB
LODSB	MOVSW	REPZ	STOSD
LODSD	REP	SCASB	STOSW

Control Transfer Instructions

These instructions are used to change the order in which a program is executed. They directly affect the program counter, loading a different memory address into this register. After the instruction is encountered, program execution then continues from a different location.

Many of these instructions are conditional; that is, they take effect after matching a condition determined by the instruction. Usually the condition pertains to flags within the flags register or status word. These 43 instructions are the following:

CALL	JAE	JE	JLE
INT	JB	JECXZ	JMP
INTO	JBE	JG	JNA
IRET	JC	JGE	JNAE
JA	JCXZ	JL	JNB

JNBE	JNLE	JP	LOOPE
JNC	JNO	JPE	LOOPNE
JNE	JNP	JPO	LOOPNZ
JNG	JNS	JS	LOOPZ
JNGE	JNZ	JZ	RET
JNL	JO	LOOP	

Flag and Processor Control Instructions

This final instruction group contains instructions that directly affect the flags register, status word, or control word. It includes the following 46 instructions:

BOUND	FFREE	FNSTENV	INVLPG
CLC	FINCSTP	FNSTSW	LEAVE
CLD	FINIT	FRSTOR	LOCK
CLI	FLDCW	FSAVE	NOP
CLTS	FLDENV	FSETPM	STC
CMC	FNCLEX	FSTCW	STD
ENTER	FNDISI	FSTENV	STI
ESC	FNENI	FSTSW	VERR
FCLEX	FNINIT	FWAIT	VERW
FDECSTP	FNOP	HLT	WAIT
FDISI	FNSAVE	INVD	WBINVD
FENI	FNSTCW		

The Complete Instruction Set

Now that you know which instructions fall within each group, let's take a quick look at the entire Intel family instruction set along with the chips that use the instructions. Table 17.1 details this information. Even more detailed information is available later in this chapter.

Table 17.1. *Instructions for the Intel family.*

Instruction	Meaning	88	286	386	Chips 486	87	287	387
AAA	ASCII adjust for addition	X	X	X	X			
AAD	ASCII adjust for division	X	X	X	X			
AAM	ASCII adjust for multiplication	X	X	X	X			
AAS	ASCII adjust for subtraction	X	X	X	X			
ADC	Add with carry	X	X	X	X			
ADD	Add	X	X	X	X			
AND	Logical AND	X	X	X	X			
ARPL	Adjust RPL field of selector		X	X	X			
BOUND	Check array index against bounds		X	X	X			
BSF	Bit scan forward			X	X			
BSR	Bit scan reverse			X	X			
BSWAP	Swap 32-bit byte order				X			
BT	Bit test			X	X			
BTC	Bit test and complement			X	X			
BTR	Bit test and reset			X	X			
BTS	Bit test and set			X	X			
CALL	Perform subroutine	X	X	X	X			
CBW	Convert byte to word	X	X	X	X			
CDQ	Convert doubleword to quadword			X	X			
CLC	Clear carry flag	X	X	X	X			
CLD	Clear direction flag	X	X	X	X			
CLI	Clear interrupt flag	X	X	X	X			
CLTS	Clear task switched flag		X	X	X			
CMC	Complement carry flag	X	X	X	X			
CMP	Compare	X	X	X	X			
CMPSB	Compare strings by byte	X	X	X	X			
CMPSD	Compare strings by doubleword			X	X			
CMPSW	Compare strings by word	X	X	X	X			
CMPXCHG	Atomic compare/exchange				X			
CWD	Convert word to doubleword	X	X	X	X			
CWDE	Convert word to extended doubleword			X	X			
DAA	Decimal adjust for addition	X	X	X	X			
DAS	Decimal adjust for subtraction	X	X	X	X			
DEC	Decrement	X	X	X	X			
DIV	Divide	X	X	X	X			
ENTER	Make stack frame		X	X	X			
ESC	Escape	X	X	X	X			
F2XM1	2^x-1				X	X	X	X

Instruction	Meaning	88	286	386	Chips 486	87	287	387
FABS	Absolute value				X	X	X	X
FADD	Add real				X	X	X	X
FADDP	Add real and POP				X	X	X	X
FBLD	BCD load				X	X	X	X
FBSTP	BCD store and POP				X	X	X	X
FCHS	Change sign				X	X	X	X
FCLEX	Clear exceptions with WAIT				X	X	X	X
FCOM	Compare real				X	X	X	X
FCOMP	Compare real and POP				X	X	X	X
FCOMPP	Compare real and POP twice				X	X	X	X
FCOS	Cosine				X			X
FDECSTP	Decrement stack pointer				X	X	X	X
FDISI	Disable interrupts with WAIT					X		
FDIV	Divide real				X	X	X	X
FDIVP	Divide real and POP				X	X	X	X
FDIVR	Divide real reversed				X	X	X	X
FDIVRP	Divide real reversed and POP				X	X	X	X
FENI	Enable interrupts with WAIT					X		
FFREE	Free register				X	X	X	X
FIADD	Integer add				X	X	X	X
FICOM	Integer compare				X	X	X	X
FICOMP	Integer compare and POP				X	X	X	X
FIDIV	Integer divide				X	X	X	X
FIDIVR	Integer divide reversed				X	X	X	X
FILD	Integer load				X	X	X	X
FIMUL	Integer multiply				X	X	X	X
FINCSTP	Increment stack pointer				X	X	X	X
FINIT	Initialize processor with WAIT				X	X	X	X
FIST	Integer store				X	X	X	X
FISTP	Integer store and POP				X	X	X	X
FISUB	Integer subtract				X	X	X	X
FISUBR	Integer subtract reversed				X	X	X	X
FLD	Load real				X	X	X	X
FLD1	Load 1.0				X	X	X	X
FLDCW	Load control word				X	X	X	X
FLDENV	Load environment				X	X	X	X
FLDL2E	Load $\log_2 e$				X	X	X	X
FLDL2T	Load $\log_2 10$				X	X	X	X
FLDLG2	Load $\log_{10} 2$				X	X	X	X

Table 17.1. continues

Table 17.1. *continued*

Instruction	Meaning	88	286	386	Chips 486	87	287	387
FLDLN2	Load log$_e$2				X	X	X	X
FLDPI	Load pi				X	X	X	X
FLDZ	Load 0.0				X	X	X	X
FMUL	Multiply real				X	X	X	X
FMULP	Multiply real and POP				X	X	X	X
FNCLEX	Clear exceptions				X	X	X	X
FNDISI	Disable interrupts					X		
FNENI	Enable interrupts					X		
FNINIT	Initialize processor				X	X	X	X
FNOP	No operation				X	X	X	X
FNSAVE	Save state				X	X	X	X
FNSTCW	Store control word				X	X	X	X
FNSTENV	Store environment				X	X	X	X
FNSTSW	Store status word				X	X	X	X
FPATAN	Partial arctangent				X	X	X	X
FPREM	Partial remainder				X	X	X	X
FPREM1	IEEE partial remainder				X			X
FPTAN	Partial tangent				X	X	X	X
FRNDINT	Round to integer				X	X	X	X
FRSTOR	Restore state				X	X	X	X
FSAVE	Save state with WAIT				X	X	X	X
FSCALE	Scale				X	X	X	X
FSETPM	Set protected mode						X	
FSIN	Sine				X			X
FSINCOS	Sine and cosine				X			X
FSQRT	Square root				X	X	X	X
FST	Store real				X	X	X	X
FSTCW	Store control word with WAIT				X	X	X	X
FSTENV	Store environment with WAIT				X	X	X	X
FSTP	Store Real and POP				X	X	X	X
FSTSW	Store status word with WAIT				X	X	X	X
FSUB	Subtract real				X	X	X	X
FSUBP	Subtract real and POP				X	X	X	X
FSUBR	Subtract real reversed				X	X	X	X
FSUBRP	Subtract real reversed and POP				X	X	X	X
FTST	Test				X	X	X	X
FUCOM	Unordered compare				X			X
FUCOMP	Unordered compare and POP				X			X
FUCOMPP	Unordered compare and POP twice				X			X

Instruction	Meaning	88	286	386	Chips 486	87	287	387
FWAIT	CPU wait				X	X	X	X
FXAM	Examine				X	X	X	X
FXCH	Exchange registers				X	X	X	X
FXTRACT	Extract exponent and significand				X	X	X	X
FYL2X	$Y*\log_2 X$				X	X	X	X
FYL2XP1	$Y*\log_2(X+1)$				X	X	X	X
HLT	Halt	X	X	X	X			
IDIV	Integer divide	X	X	X	X			
IMUL	Integer multiply	X	X	X	X			
IN	Input from port	X	X	X	X			
INC	Increment	X	X	X	X			
INS	Input string from port		X	X	X			
INSB	Input string byte from port		X	X	X			
INSD	Input string doubleword from port			X	X			
INSW	Input string word from port		X	X	X			
INT	Software interrupt	X	X	X	X			
INTO	Interrupt on overflow	X	X	X	X			
INVD	Invalidate full cache				X			
INVLPG	Invalidate TLB entry				X			
IRET	Return from interrupt	X	X	X	X			
JA	Jump if above	X	X	X	X			
JAE	Jump if above or equal	X	X	X	X			
JB	Jump if below	X	X	X	X			
JBE	Jump if below or equal	X	X	X	X			
JC	Jump on carry	X	X	X	X			
JCXZ	Jump if $CX=0$	X	X	X	X			
JE	Jump if equal	X	X	X	X			
JECXZ	Jump if $ECX=0$			X	X			
JG	Jump if greater	X	X	X	X			
JGE	Jump if greater or equal	X	X	X	X			
JL	Jump if less	X	X	X	X			
JLE	Jump if less or equal	X	X	X	X			
JMP	Jump	X	X	X	X			
JNA	Jump if not above	X	X	X	X			
JNAE	Jump if not above or equal	X	X	X	X			
JNB	Jump if not below	X	X	X	X			
JNBE	Jump if not below or equal	X	X	X	X			
JNC	Jump on no carry	X	X	X	X			
JNE	Jump if not equal	X	X	X	X			

Table 17.1. continues

Table 17.1. *continued*

Instruction	Meaning	88	286	386	Chips 486	87	287	387
JNG	Jump if not greater	X	X	X	X			
JNGE	Jump if not greater or equal	X	X	X	X			
JNL	Jump if not less	X	X	X	X			
JNLE	Jump if not less or equal	X	X	X	X			
JNO	Jump on no overflow	X	X	X	X			
JNP	Jump on no parity	X	X	X	X			
JNS	Jump on not sign	X	X	X	X			
JNZ	Jump on not zero	X	X	X	X			
JO	Jump on overflow	X	X	X	X			
JP	Jump on parity	X	X	X	X			
JPE	Jump on parity even	X	X	X	X			
JPO	Jump on parity odd	X	X	X	X			
JS	Jump on sign	X	X	X	X			
JZ	Jump on zero	X	X	X	X			
LAHF	Load AH with flags	X	X	X	X			
LAR	Load access-rights byte		X	X	X			
LDS	Load DS register	X	X	X	X			
LEA	Load effective address	X	X	X	X			
LEAVE	High-level procedure exit		X	X	X			
LES	Load ES register	X	X	X	X			
LFS	Load FS register			X	X			
LGDT	Load GDT register		X	X	X			
LGS	Load GS register			X	X			
LIDT	Load IDT register			X	X	X		
LLDT	Load LDT register		X	X	X			
LMSW	Load machine status word		X	X	X			
LOCK	Lock bus	X	X	X	X			
LODSB	Load byte from string to AL	X	X	X	X			
LODSD	Load doubleword from string to EAX			X	X			
LODSW	Load word from string to AX	X	X	X	X			
LOOP	Loop	X	X	X	X			
LOOPE	Loop while equal	X	X	X	X			
LOOPNE	Loop while not equal	X	X	X	X			
LOOPNZ	Loop while not zero	X	X	X	X			
LOOPZ	Loop while zero	X	X	X	X			
LSL	Load segment limit		X	X	X			
LSS	Load SS register			X	X			
LTR	Load task register		X	X	X			
MOV	Move	X	X	X	X			

Instruction	Meaning	88	286	386	Chips 486	87	287	387
MOVSB	Move string byte-by-byte	X	X	X	X			
MOVSD	Move string doubleword-by-doubleword			X	X			
MOVSW	Move string word-by-word	X	X	X	X			
MOVSX	Move with sign extended			X	X			
MOVZX	Move with zero extended			X	X			
MUL	Multiply	X	X	X	X			
NEG	Negate	X	X	X	X			
NOP	No operation	X	X	X	X			
NOT	Logical NOT	X	X	X	X			
OR	Logical OR	X	X	X	X			
OUT	Output to port	X	X	X	X			
OUTS	Output string to port		X	X	X			
OUTSB	Output string byte to port		X	X	X			
OUTSD	Output string doubleword to port			X	X			
OUTSW	Output string word to port		X	X	X			
POP	Remove data from stack	X	X	X	X			
POPA	POP all general registers		X	X	X			
POPAD	POP all general doubleword registers			X	X			
POPF	Remove flags from stack	X	X	X	X			
POPFD	Remove extended flags from stack			X	X			
PUSH	Place data on stack	X	X	X	X			
PUSHA	Push all general registers		X	X	X			
PUSHAD	Push all general doubleword registers			X	X			
PUSHF	Place flags on stack	X	X	X	X			
PUSHFD	Place extended flags on stack			X	X			
RCL	Rotate left through carry	X	X	X	X			
RCR	Rotate right through carry	X	X	X	X			
REP	Repeat	X	X	X	X			
REPE	Repeat if equal	X	X	X	X			
REPNE	Repeat if not equal	X	X	X	X			
REPNZ	Repeat if not zero	X	X	X	X			
REPZ	Repeat if zero	X	X	X	X			
RET	Return from subroutine	X	X	X	X			
ROL	Rotate left	X	X	X	X			
ROR	Rotate right	X	X	X	X			
SAHF	Store AH into flags register	X	X	X	X			
SAL	Arithmetic shift left	X	X	X	X			
SAR	Arithmetic shift right	X	X	X	X			

Table 17.1. continues

Table 17.1. continued

Instruction	Meaning	88	286	386	Chips 486	87	287	387
SBB	Subtract with carry	X	X	X	X			
SCASB	Scan string for byte	X	X	X	X			
SCASD	Scan string for doubleword			X	X			
SCASW	Scan string for word	X	X	X	X			
SETA	Set byte if above			X	X			
SETAE	Set byte if above or equal			X	X			
SETB	Set byte if below			X	X			
SETBE	Set byte if below or equal			X	X			
SETC	Set byte on carry			X	X			
SETE	Set byte if equal			X	X			
SETG	Set byte if greater			X	X			
SETGE	Set byte if greater or equal			X	X			
SETL	Set byte if less			X	X			
SETLE	Set byte if less or equal			X	X			
SETNA	Set byte if not above			X	X			
SETNAE	Set byte if not above or equal			X	X			
SETNB	Set byte if not below			X	X			
SETNBE	Set byte if not below or equal			X	X			
SETNC	Set byte on no carry			X	X			
SETNE	Set byte if not equal			X	X			
SETNG	Set byte if not greater			X	X			
SETNGE	Set byte if not greater or equal			X	X			
SETNL	Set byte if not less			X	X			
SETNLE	Set byte if not less or equal			X	X			
SETNO	Set byte on no overflow			X	X			
SETNP	Set byte on no priority			X	X			
SETNS	Set byte on not sign			X	X			
SETNZ	Set byte if not zero			X	X			
SETO	Set byte on overflow			X	X			
SETP	Set byte on parity			X	X			
SETPE	Set byte on parity even			X	X			
SETPO	Set byte on parity odd			X	X			
SETS	Set byte on sign			X	X			
SETZ	Set byte if zero			X	X			
SGDT	Store GDT register		X	X	X			
SHL	Shift left	X	X	X	X			
SHLD	Shift left, double precision			X	X			
SHR	Shift right	X	X	X	X			
SHRD	Shift right, double precision			X	X			

Instruction	Meaning	88	286	386	Chips 486	87	287	387
SIDT	Store IDT register			X	X	X		
SLDT	Store LDT register			X	X	X		
SMSW	Store machine status word			X	X	X		
STC	Set carry flag	X	X	X	X			
STD	Set direction flag	X	X	X	X			
STI	Set interrupt flag	X	X	X	X			
STOSB	Store byte in AL at string	X	X	X	X			
STOSD	Store doubleword in EAX at string			X	X			
STOSW	Store word in AX at string	X	X	X	X			
STR	Store task register			X	X	X		
SUB	Subtract	X	X	X	X			
TEST	Test bits	X	X	X	X			
VERR	Verify segment for reading			X	X	X		
VERW	Verify segment for writing			X	X	X		
WAIT	Wait	X	X	X	X			
WBINVD	Invalidate cache and write back				X			
XADD	Exchange and add to memory				X			
XCHG	Exchange	X	X	X	X			
XLAT	Translate	X	X	X	X			
XOR	Logical XOR	X	X	X	X			

Specialized Registers: Flags, Control, and Status

The majority of instructions either control or change the status of the bits in any of several specialized registers used by either the microprocessor or the NPX/FPU. These specialized registers include the following:

❑ Flags register

❑ Control word

❑ Status word

The flags register applies to the microprocessors, and the status and control words apply to the NPX/FPU. Which bits are actually affected by each instruction depends on the instruction and results of the instruction.

The Flags Register

Each of the Intel microprocessors uses a flags register to indicate the status of operations. These flags can be tested to control program execution, or they can be set to control certain tasks performed by the microprocessor.

The size of the flags register depends on the microprocessor. For instance, the 8086/8088 and 80286 use a 16-bit flags register, but the 80386 and 80486 both use 32-bit flags registers. However, not every bit is always used. Table 17.2 details how each bit is used by each microprocessor.

Table 17.2. The flags register.

| Bits | Code | Use | Microprocessor | | | |
			88	286	386	486
0	CF	Carry	X	X	X	X
2	PF	Parity	X	X	X	X
4	AF	Auxiliary carry	X	X	X	X
6	ZF	Zero	X	X	X	X
7	SF	Sign	X	X	X	X
8	TF	Trap	X	X	X	X
9	IF	Interrupt	X	X	X	X
10	DF	Direction	X	X	X	X
11	OF	Overflow	X	X	X	X
12-13	IOPL	I/O privilege level		X	X	X
14	NT	Nested task		X	X	X
16	RF	Resume			X	X
17	VM	Virtual mode			X	X
18	AC	Alignment check enabled				X

Notice that although the 8086/8088 defines only nine bits, with each succeeding generation of microprocessor Intel found it necessary to define more bits; the 80286 uses 11, the 80386 uses 13, and the 80486 uses 14 bits. All other bits within the flags register remain reserved and undefined by Intel.

Table 17.3 details which instructions affect which bits within the flags register. Instructions which have no effect on the flags are omitted from this table.

Table 17.3. How instructions affect the flags register.

Instruction	Meaning	0 CF	2 PF	4 AF	6 ZF	7 SF	8 TF	9 IF	10 DF	11 OF	12/13 IOPL	14 NT	16 RF	17 VM	18 AC
AAA	ASCII adjust for addition	X	?	X	?	?				?					
AAD	ASCII adjust for division	?	X	?	X	X				?					
AAM	ASCII adjust for multiplication	?	X	?	X	X				?					
AAS	ASCII adjust for subtraction	X	?	X	?	?				?					
ADC	Add with carry	X	X	X	X	X				X					
ADD	Add	X	X	X	X	X				X					
AND	Logical AND	X	X	?	X	X				X					
ARPL	Adjust RPL field of selector				X										
BSF	Bit scan forward				X										
BSR	Bit scan reverse				X										
BT	Bit test	X													
BTC	Bit test and complement	X													
BTR	Bit test and reset	X													
BTS	Bit test and set	X													
CLC	Clear carry flag	X													
CLD	Clear direction flag								X						
CLI	Clear interrupt flag							X							
CMC	Complement carry flag	X													
CMP	Compare	X	X	X	X	X				X					
CMPSB	Compare strings by byte	X	X	X	X	X				X					
CMPSD	Compare strings by doubleword	X	X	X	X	X				X					
CMPSW	Compare strings by word	X	X	X	X	X				X					
CMPXCHG	Compare and Exchange	X	X	X	X	X				X					
DAA	Decimal adjust for addition	X	X	X	X	X				?					
DAS	Decimal adjust for subtraction	X	X	X	X	X				?					
DEC	Decrement		X	X	X	X				X					
DIV	Divide	?	?	?	?	?				?					
IDIV	Integer divide	?	?	?	?	?				?					
IMUL	Integer multiply	X	?	?	?	?				X					
INC	Increment		X	X	X	X				X					
INT	Software interrupt						X	X							

Table 17.3. continues

***Table 17.3.** continued*

Instruction	Meaning	0 CF	2 PF	4 AF	6 ZF	7 SF	8 TF	9 IF	10 DF	11 OF	12/13 IOPL	14 NT	16 RF	17 VM	18 AC
IRET	Return from interrupt	X	X	X	X	X	X	X	X	X	X	X	X	X	X
MUL	Multiply	X	?	?	?	?				X					
NEG	Negate	X	X	X	X	X				X					
OR	Logical OR	X	X	?	X	X				X					
POPF	Remove flags from stack	X	X	X	X	X	X	X	X	X	X	X			
POPFD	Remove extended flags from stack	X	X	X	X	X	X	X	X	X	X	X			
RCL	Rotate left through carry	X								X					
RCR	Rotate right through carry	X								X					
ROL	Rotate left	X								X					
ROR	Rotate right	X								X					
SAHF	Store AH into flags register	X	X	X	X	X									
SAL	Arithmetic shift left	X	X	?	X	X				X					
SAR	Arithmetic shift right	X	X	?	X	X				X					
SBB	Subtract with carry	X	X	X	X	X				X					
SCASB	Scan string for byte	X	X	X	X	X				X					
SCASD	Scan string for doubleword	X	X	X	X	X				X					
SCASW	Scan string for word	X	X	X	X	X				X					
SHL	Shift left	X	X	?	X	X				X					
SHLD	Shift left double precision	X	X	?	X	X				?					
SHR	Shift right	X	X	?	X	X				X					
SHRD	Shift right double precision	X	X	?	X	X				?					
STC	Set carry flag	X													
STD	Set direction flag								X						
STI	Set interrupt flag							X							
SUB	Subtract	X	X	X	X	X				X					
TEST	Test bits	X	?	?	X	X				X					
VERR	Verify a segment for reading				X										
VERW	Verify a segment for writing				X										
XADD	Exchange and add to memory	X	X	X	X	X				X					
XOR	Logical exclusive-or	X	X	?	X	X				X					

The Control Word

All the Intel NPX chips (including the FPU on the 80486) use a control word to govern how the chip works. Each of the 16 bits in this word has a different use. Table 17.4 details how each bit is used within each type of NPX or FPU.

Table 17.4. *The NPX/FPU control word.*

Bits	Code	Use	NPX/FPU 87	287	387	486
0	IM	Invalid operation	X	X	X	X
1	DM	Denormalized operand	X	X	X	X
2	ZM	Zero divide	X	X	X	X
3	OM	Overflow	X	X	X	X
4	UM	Underflow	X	X	X	X
5	PM	Precision	X	X	X	X
6		Reserved				
7	IEM	Interrupt enable mask	X			
		0 = Enabled				
		1 = Disabled				
8-9	PC	Precision control	X	X	X	X
		00 = 24 bits	X	X	X	X
		01 = Reserved	X	X	X	X
		10 = 53 bits	X	X	X	X
		11 = 64 bits	X	X	X	X
10-11	RC	Rounding control	X	X	X	X
		00 = Nearest or even				
		01 = Down				
		10 = Up				
		11 = Truncate				
12	IC	Infinity control	X	X		
		0 = Projective				
		1 = Affine				
13-15		Reserved				

To change the values in this word, you must construct it in memory and then use specific mnemonic instructions to direct it to be stored in the NPX/FPU. These instructions will be covered later in this section.

The Status Word

The NPX/FPU family uses a *status word* to describe the current condition of the coprocessor. This 16-bit register contains a series of bits that reflect the result of recent numeric operations. The first 6 bits (0 through 5) are exception flags; they are set when an exception occurs. Compare these flags to the similar flags in the NPX/FPU control word that govern whether exceptions for the individual conditions are trapped.

Table 17.5 defines the status word and how it is used among the members of the NPX/FPU family.

Table 17.5. *The NPX/FPU status word.*

	Status word		NPX/FPU			
Bits	Code	Use	87	287	387	486
0	IE	Invalid operation	X	X	X	X
1	DE	Denormalized operand	X	X	X	X
2	ZE	Zero divide	X	X	X	X
3	OE	Overflow	X	X	X	X
4	UE	Underflow	X	X	X	X
5	PE	Precision	X	X	X	X
6	SF	Stack flag			X	X
7	IR	Interrupt request	X			
7	ES	Error summary status		X	X	X
8	C0	Condition code 0	X	X	X	X
9	C1	Condition code 1	X	X	X	X
10	C2	Condition code 2	X	X	X	X
11-13	ST	Stack-top pointer	X	X	X	X
14	C3	Condition code 3	X	X	X	X
15	B	Busy signal	X	X	X	X

Notice the different use of bits across generations of NPX/FPU. In particular, the use of bits 6 and 7 has changed. For the 8087 and 80287, bit 6 was considered reserved; it was defined starting with the 80387. The designation and use of bit 7 changed entirely from the 8087 to the 80287.

Regardless of how the NPX/FPU uses it, the status word cannot be examined directly. To analyze the status word, you must first transfer it to memory.

The bits of the 8087, 80287, 80387, and 80486 numeric processor status words are affected by various instructions as shown in table 17.6. Bits 6 and 7 of this word are defined differently from one model of numeric processor to the next, thus there are two columns for bit 7.

Table 17.6. How instructions affect the status word.

Status word bits

Instruction	Meaning	0 IE	1 DE	2 ZE	3 OE	4 UE	5 PE	6 SF	7 IR/ES	8 C0	9 C1	10 C2	11/13 ST	14 C3	15 B
F2XM1	2^x-1	X				X	X								
FABS	Absolute value	X													
FADD	Add real	X	X		X	X	X								
FADDP	Add real and POP	X	X		X	X	X								
FBLD	BCD load	X													
FBSTP	BCD store and POP	X													
FCHS	Change sign	X													
FCLEX	Clear exceptions with WAIT	X	X	X	X	X	X		X						X
FCOM	Compare real	X	X							X	X	X		X	
FCOMP	Compare real and POP	X	X							X	X	X		X	
FCOMPP	Compare real and POP twice	X	X							X	X	X		X	
FCOS	Cosine	X	X			X	X								
FDECSTP	Decrement stack pointer												X		
FDIV	Divide real	X	X	X	X	X	X								
FDIVP	Divide real and POP	X	X	X	X	X	X								
FDIVR	Divide real reversed	X	X	X	X	X	X								
FDIVRP	Divide real reversed and POP	X	X	X	X	X	X								
FIADD	Integer add	X	X		X	X	X								
FICOM	Integer compare	X	X							X	X	X		X	
FICOMP	Integer compare and POP	X	X							X	X	X		X	
FIDIV	Integer divide	X	X	X	X	X	X								
FIDIVR	Integer divide reversed	X	X	X	X	X	X								
FILD	Integer load	X													
FIMUL	Integer multiply	X	X		X	X	X								
FINCSTP	Increment stack pointer												X		
FIST	Integer store	X					X								
FISTP	Integer store and POP	X					X								
FISUB	Integer subtract	X	X		X	X	X								
FISUBR	Integer subtract reversed	X	X		X	X	X								

Table 17.6. continues

Table 17.6. *continued*

		Status word bits														
		0	1	2	3	4	5	6	7	7	8	9	10	11/13	14	15
Instruction	*Meaning*	IE	DE	ZE	OE	UE	PE	SF	IR	ES	C0	C1	C2	ST	C3	B
FLD	Load real	X	X													
FLD1	Load 1.0	X														
FLDENV	Load environment	X	X	X	X	X	X	X		X	X	X	X	X	X	X
FLDL2E	Load log$_2$e	X														
FLDL2T	Load log$_2$10	X														
FLDLG2	Load log$_{10}$2	X														
FLDLN2	Load log$_e$2	X														
FLDPI	Load pi	X														
FLDZ	Load 0.0	X														
FMUL	Multiply real	X	X	X	X	X	X					X				
FMULP	Multiply real and POP	X	X	X	X	X	X					X				
FNCLEX	Clear exceptions	X	X	X	X	X	X		X							X
FPATAN	Partial arctangent					X	X					X				
FPREM	Partial remainder	X	X			X	X				X	X	X		X	
FPREM1	Partial remainder, IEEE version	X	X			X	X				X	X	X		X	
FPTAN	Partial tangent	X					X					X	X			
FRNDINT	Round to integer	X					X					X				
FRSTOR	Restore state	X	X	X	X	X	X	X		X	X	X	X	X	X	X
FSCALE	Scale	X	X		X	X	X					X				
FSIN	Sine	X	X			X	X					X	X			
FSINCOS	Sine and cosine	X	X			X	X					X	X			
FSQRT	Square root	X	X				X					X				
FST	Store real	X			X	X	X					X				
FSTP	Store real and POP	X			X	X	X					X				
FSUB	Subtract real	X	X		X	X	X					X				
FSUBP	Subtract real and POP	X	X		X	X	X					X				
FSUBR	Subtract real reversed	X	X		X	X	X					X				
FSUBRP	Subtract real reversed and POP	X	X		X	X	X					X				
FTST	Test	X	X								X	X	X		X	

Status word bits

Instruction	Meaning	0 IE	1 DE	2 ZE	3 OE	4 UE	5 PE	6 SF	7 IR	7 ES	8 C0	9 C1	10 C2	11/13 ST	14 C3	15 B
FUCOM	Unordered compare	X	X								X		X		X	
FUCOMP	Unordered compare and POP	X	X								X		X		X	
FUCOMPP	Unordered compare and POP twice	X	X								X		X		X	
FXAM	Examine										X	X	X		X	
FXCH	Exchange registers	X														
FXTRACT	Extract exponent and significand	X														
FYL2X	Y∗log$_2$X						X									
FYL2XP1	Y∗log$_2$(X+1)						X									

Detailed Instruction Information

In the remainder of this chapter, each member of the Intel instruction set is described in detail. The following information is given for each instruction:

❏ **Instruction name.** This name is based on the standard mnemonic code designed by Intel.

❏ **Applicable processors.** This paragraph lists the processors that perform the instruction.

❏ **Instruction category.** The general classification for the instruction is provided.

❏ **Flags affected.** The majority of the instructions change the status of the bits in the flags register (or the status word in the case of numeric processor instructions). The individual flags affected are listed in this section.

❏ **Coding examples.** Brief examples of the use of the instruction are given.

❏ **Description.** A narrative description of each instruction is provided.

The instructions are arranged in ascending alphabetical order.

AAA: ASCII Adjust for Addition

Applicable processors: 8086/8088, 80286, 80386, 80486

Category: Arithmetic instructions

Flags affected: AF, CF, OF (undefined), PF (undefined), SF (undefined), ZF (undefined)

Coding example:

```
AAA
```

Description: AAA changes the contents of AL to a valid unpacked decimal number with the high-order nibble zeroed.

AAD: ASCII Adjust for Division

Applicable processors: 8086/8088, 80286, 80386, 80486

Category: Arithmetic instructions

Flags affected: AF (undefined), CF (undefined), OF (undefined), PF, SF, ZF

Coding example:

```
AAD
```

Description: AAD multiplies the contents of AH by 10, adds the result to the contents of AL, and places the result in AL. The instruction then sets AH to 0. You use this instruction before you divide unpacked decimal numbers.

AAM: ASCII Adjust for Multiplication

Applicable processors: 8086/8088, 80286, 80386, 80486

Category: Arithmetic instructions

Flags affected: AF (undefined), CF (undefined), OF (undefined), PF, SF, ZF

Coding example:

```
AAM
```

Description: After multiplying two unpacked decimal numbers, you use AAM to correct the result to an unpacked decimal number. For the instruction to work properly, each number multiplied must have had its high-order nibbles set to 0.

AAS: ASCII Adjust for Subtraction

Applicable processors: 8086/8088, 80286, 80386, 80486

Category: Arithmetic instructions

Flags affected: AF, CF, OF (undefined), PF (undefined), SF (undefined), ZF (undefined)

Coding example:

```
AAS
```

Description: AAS corrects the result of a previous unpacked decimal subtraction so that the value in AL is a true unpacked decimal number.

ADC: Add with Carry

Applicable processors: 8086/8088, 80286, 80386, 80486

Category: Arithmetic instructions

Flags affected: AF, CF, OF, PF, SF, ZF

Coding examples:

```
ADC      AX,BX            ;AX=AX+BX+CF
ADC      AX,TEMP          ;AX=AX+TEMP+CF
ADC      SUM,BX           ;SUM=SUM+BX+CF
ADC      CL,10            ;CL=CL+10+CF
ADC      AX,TEMP[BX]      ;Indirect address example
```

Description: ADC adds the contents of the source operand to (and stores the result in) the destination operand. If the carry flag is set, the result changes in increments of 1. In this routine, the values being added are assumed to be binary.

ADD: Add

Applicable processors: 8086/8088, 80286, 80386, 80486

Category: Arithmetic instructions

Flags affected: AF, CF, OF, PF, SF, ZF

Coding examples:

```
ADD      AX,BX            ;AX=AX+BX
ADD      AX,TEMP          ;AX=AX+TEMP
ADD      SUM,BX           ;SUM=SUM+BX
ADD      CL,10            ;CL=CL+10
ADD      AX,TEMP[BX]      ;Indirect address example
```

Description: ADD adds the contents of the source operand to (and stores the result in) the destination operand. In this routine the values being added are assumed to be binary.

AND: Logical AND on Bits

Applicable processors: 8086/8088, 80286, 80386, 80486

Category: Bit manipulation instructions

Flags affected: AF (undefined), CF, OF, PF, SF, ZF

Coding examples:

```
AND       AX,BX          ;
AND       AX,TEMP        ;TEMP must be a word
AND       SUM,BX         ;SUM must be a word
AND       CL,00001111b   ;Zero high nibble
AND       AX,TEMP[BX]    ;Indirect address example
```

Description: This instruction performs a logical AND of the operands and stores the result in the destination operand. Each bit of the resultant byte or word is set to 1 only if the corresponding bit of each operand is set to 1.

ARPL: Adjust RPL Field of Selector

Applicable processors: 80286, 80386, 80486

Category: Bit manipulation instructions

Flags affected: ZF

Coding examples:

```
ARPL      SELECTOR,AX
ARPL      AX,CX
```

Description: ARPL compares the RPL bits (bits 0 and 1) of the first operand with those of the second. If the RPL bits of the first operand are less than those of the second, the two bits of the first operand are set equal to the two bits of the second, and the zero flag is set. Otherwise, the zero flag is cleared. This instruction is used only in operating system software, not in applications software.

BOUND: Check Array Index against Bounds

Applicable processors: 80286, 80386, 80486

Category: Flag and processor control instructions

Flags affected: None

Coding example:

```
BOUND     BX,LIMITS
```

Description: BOUND determines whether the signed value in the first operand falls between the two boundaries specified by the second operand. The word at the second operand is assumed to be the lower boundary, and the following word is assumed to be the upper boundary. An interrupt 5 occurs if the value in the first operand is less than the lower limit or greater than the upper limit.

BSF: Bit Scan Forward

Applicable processors: 80386, 80486

Category: Bit manipulation instructions

Flags affected: ZF

Coding examples:

```
BSF        EAX,TEMP
BSF        CX,BX
```

Description: BSF scans the bits of the second operand (starting with bit 0) to see whether any are set. If all bits are clear (second operand is 0), the first operand is not changed, and the zero flag is set. If any bit is set, the zero flag is cleared, and the first operand is set equal to the bit number of the bit that is set.

BSR: Bit Scan Reverse

Applicable processors: 80386, 80486

Category: Bit manipulation instructions

Flags affected: ZF

Coding examples:

```
BSR        EAX,TEMP
BSR        CX,BX
```

Description: BSR scans the bits of the second operand (starting with the high-order bit) to see whether any are set. If all bits are clear (second operand is 0), the first operand is not changed, and the zero flag is set. If any bit is set, the zero flag is cleared, and the first operand is set equal to the bit number of the bit that is set.

BSWAP: Swap 32-Bit Byte Order

Applicable processors: 80486

Category: Data transfer instructions

Flags affected: None

Coding examples:

```
BSWAP      EAX
BSWAP      EDX
```

Description: This instruction uses an extended (32-bit) register as an operand. It reverses the byte order in the register. Byte 0 is swapped with byte 3, and byte 1 is swapped with byte 2.

BT: Bit Test

Applicable processors: 80386, 80486

Category: Bit manipulation instructions

Flags affected: CF

Coding examples:

```
BT    TEMP,EAX
BT    BX,CX
BT    TEMP,3          ;Test 3rd bit
```

Description: BT uses the value of the second operand as a bit index into the value of the first operand. The bit at the indexed position of the first operand is copied into the carry flag.

BTC: Bit Test and Complement

Applicable processors: 80386, 80486

Category: Bit manipulation instructions

Flags affected: CF

Coding examples:

```
BTC      TEMP,EAX
BTC      BX,CX
BTC      TEMP,3         ;Opposite of 3rd bit
```

Description: BTC uses the value of the second operand as a bit index into the value of the first operand. The opposite value of the bit at the indexed position of the first operand is copied into the carry flag.

BTR: Bit Test and Reset

Applicable processors: 80386, 80486

Category: Bit manipulation instructions

Flags affected: CF

Coding examples:

```
BTR     TEMP,EAX
BTR     BX,CX
BTR     TEMP,3          ;Value of 3rd bit
```

Description: BTR uses the value of the second operand as a bit index into the value of the first operand. The bit at the indexed position of the first operand is copied into the carry flag, and then the original bit value is cleared.

BTS: Bit Test and Set

Applicable processors: 80386, 80486

Category: Bit manipulation instructions

Flags affected: CF

Coding examples:

```
BTS     TEMP,EAX
BTS     BX,CX
BTS     TEMP,3          ;Value of 3rd bit
```

Description: BTS uses the value of the second operand as a bit index into the value of the first operand. The bit at the indexed position of the first operand is copied into the carry flag, and then the original bit value is set.

CALL: Perform Subroutine

Applicable processors: 8086/8088, 80286, 80386, 80486

Category: Control transfer instructions

Flags affected: None

Coding examples:

```
CALL    WHIZ_BANG    ;WHIZ_BANG is a subroutine
CALL    [BX]         ;Perform subroutine with
                     ;  address at [BX]
CALL    AX           ;Subroutine address in AX
```

Description: CALL does the following:

❑ Pushes offset address of following instruction on the stack

❏ If procedure being called is declared as FAR, pushes segment address of following instruction on the stack

❏ Loads IP with the offset address of the procedure being called

❏ If procedure being called is declared as FAR, loads CS with the segment address of the procedure being called

Execution then continues at the newly loaded CS:IP address until a RET instruction is encountered.

CBW: Convert Byte to Word

Applicable processors: 8086/8088, 80286, 80386, 80486

Category: Arithmetic instructions

Flags affected: None

Coding example:

```
CBW
```

Description: CBW converts the byte value in AL to a word value in AX by extending the high-order bit value of AL through all bits of AH.

CDQ: Convert Doubleword to Quadword

Applicable processors: 80386, 80486

Category: Arithmetic instructions

Flags affected: None

Coding example:

```
CDQ
```

Description: CDQ converts the doubleword value in EAX to a quadword value in EDX:EAX by extending the high-order bit value of EAX through all bits of EDX.

CLC: Clear Carry Flag

Applicable processors: 8086/8088, 80286, 80386, 80486

Category: Flag and processor control instructions

Flags affected: CF

Coding example:

```
CLC
```

Description: CLC clears the flags register's carry flag by setting it to 0.

CLD: Clear Direction Flag

Applicable processors: 8086/8088, 80286, 80386, 80486

Category: Flag and processor control instructions

Flags affected: DF

Coding example:

```
CLD
```

Description: CLD clears the direction flag of the flags register by setting the flag to 0.

CLI: Clear Interrupt Flag

Applicable processors: 8086/8088, 80286, 80386, 80486

Category: Flag and processor control instructions

Flags affected: IF

Coding example:

```
CLI
```

Description: CLI clears the interrupt flag of the flags register by setting the flag to 0. While the interrupt flag is cleared, the CPU recognizes no maskable interrupts.

CLTS: Clear Task Switched Flag

Applicable processors: 80286, 80386, 80486

Category: Flag and processor control instructions

Flags affected: None

Coding example:

```
CLTS
```

Description: CLTS clears the task switched flag of the machine status word (MSW). This instruction is used only in operating system software, not in applications software.

CMC: Complement Carry Flag

Applicable processors: 8086/8088, 80286, 80386, 80486

Category: Flag and processor control instructions

Flags affected: CF

Coding example:

```
CMC
```

Description: CMC switches the carry flag of the flags register to the opposite of the flag's current setting.

CMP: Compare

Applicable processors: 8086/8088, 80286, 80386, 80486

Category: Arithmetic instructions

Flags affected: AF, CF, OF, PF, SF, ZF

Coding examples:

```
CMP   AX,BX          ;
CMP   AX,TEMP        ;TEMP must be a word
CMP   SUM,EBX        ;SUM must be a doubleword
CMP   CL,3           ;Compare to constant
CMP   AX,TEMP[BX]    ;Indirect address example
```

Description: CMP is considered an arithmetic instruction because the source operand is subtracted from the destination operand. The result, however, is used for setting the flags; it is not stored anywhere. You can use subsequent testing of the flags for program control.

CMPSB: Compare Strings, Byte-for-Byte

Applicable processors: 8086/8088, 80286, 80386, 80486

Category: String manipulation instructions

Flags affected: AF, CF, OF, PF, SF, ZF

Coding examples:

```
CMPSB           ;Compare strings
REPE CMPSB      ;Repeat a comparison loop
```

Description: CMPSB compares strings, byte-by-byte. DI and SI change in increments or decrements of 1, depending on the setting of the direction flag. Ordinarily, this instruction is used with the REPE, REPNE, REPNZ, or REPZ instructions to repeat the comparison for a maximum of CX number of bytes. Intel lists this command as CMPS, but the Microsoft Macro Assembler makes the byte (CMPSB) and word (CMPSW) distinctions. This instruction affects only the flags; no changes are made to the operands.

CMPSD: Compare Strings, Doubleword-for-Doubleword

Applicable processors: 80386, 80486

Category: String manipulation instructions

Flags affected: AF, CF, OF, PF, SF, ZF

Coding examples:

```
CMPSD           ;Compare strings
REPE CMPSD      ;Repeat a comparison loop
```

Description: CMPSD compares strings, doubleword-for-doubleword. EDI and ESI change in increments or decrements of four, depending on the setting of the direction flag. Usually, this instruction is used with REPE, REPNE, REPNZ, or REPZ instructions to repeat the comparison for the number of times specified in ECX. This instruction affects only the flags; no changes are made to the operands.

CMPSW: Compare Strings, Word-for-Word

Applicable processors: 8086/8088, 80286, 80386, 80486

Category: String manipulation instructions

Flags affected: AF, CF, OF, PF, SF, ZF

Coding examples:

```
CMPSW           ;Compare strings
REPE CMPSW      ;Repeat a comparison loop
```

Description: CMPSW compares strings, word-for-word. DI and SI change in increments or decrements of two, depending on the setting of the direction flag. Ordinarily, this instruction is used along with REPE, REPNE, REPNZ, or REPZ instructions to repeat the comparison for the number of times specified in CX. Intel lists this command as CMPS, but the Microsoft Macro Assembler makes the byte (CMPSB) and word (CMPSW) distinctions. This instruction affects only the flags; no changes are made to the operands.

CMPXCHG: Compare and Exchange

Applicable processors: 80486

Category: Arithmetic instructions

Flags affected: AF, CF, OF, PF, SF, ZF

Coding examples:

```
CMPXCHG    ECX,EBX,EAX
CMPXCHG    CL,CH,AL
```

Description: As you can see from the coding examples, this instruction uses three operands. All three operands must be the same size. The operands are (in order) the source, destination, and accumulator operands. This instruction tests the destination against the accumulator, and if they are equal, then the value of the source is loaded into the destination. If they are unequal, then nothing is changed (except ZF is cleared).

CWD: Convert Word to Doubleword

Applicable processors: 8086/8088, 80286, 80386, 80486

Category: Arithmetic instructions

Flags affected: None

Coding example:

```
CWD
```

Description: CWD converts the word value in AX to a doubleword value in DX:AX by extending the high-order bit value of AX through all bits of DX.

CWDE: Convert Word to Extended Doubleword

Applicable processors: 80386, 80486

Category: Arithmetic instructions

Flags affected: None

Coding example:

```
CWDE
```

Description: CWDE converts the word value in AX to a doubleword value in EAX by extending the high-order bit value of AX through the remaining bits of EAX.

DAA: Decimal Adjust for Addition

Applicable processors: 8086/8088, 80286, 80386, 80486

Category: Arithmetic instructions

Flags affected: AF, CF, OF (undefined for all processors through 80286, not affected beginning with 80386), PF, SF, ZF

Coding example:

```
DAA
```

Description: DAA corrects the result (AL) of a previous binary-coded decimal (BCD) addition operation.

DAS: Decimal Adjust for Subtraction

Applicable processors: 8086/8088, 80286, 80386, 80486

Category: Arithmetic instructions

Flags affected: AF, CF, OF (undefined for all processors through 80286, not affected beginning with 80386), PF, SF, ZF

Coding example:

```
DAS
```

Description: DAS corrects the result (AL) of a previous binary-coded decimal (BCD) subtraction operation.

DEC: Decrement

Applicable processors: 8086/8088, 80286, 80386, 80486

Category: Arithmetic instructions

Flags affected: AF, OF, PF, SF, ZF

Coding examples:

```
DEC     AX
DEC     ECX
DEC     SUM
DEC     CL
DEC     TEMP[SI]
```

Description: DEC changes, in decrements of 1, the contents of the operand. The operand is assumed to be an unsigned binary value.

DIV: Divide

Applicable processors: 8086/8088, 80286, 80386, 80486

Category: Arithmetic instructions

Flags affected: AF (undefined), CF (undefined), OF (undefined), PF (undefined), SF (undefined), ZF (undefined)

Coding examples:

```
DIV      BX              ;AX=DX:AX/BX
DIV      WORD_TEMP       ;AX=DX:AX/WORD_TEMP
DIV      BYTE_SUM        ;AL=AX/BYTE_SUM
DIV      DWORD_SUM       ;EAX=EDX:EAX/DWORD_SUM
DIV      WORD_TBL[BX]    ;Indirect address example
```

Description: If the operand is a byte value, DIV divides the contents of AX by the contents of the operand and stores the result in AL and the remainder in AH. If the operand is a word value, DIV divides the contents of DX:AX by the contents of the operand and stores the result in AX and the remainder in DX.

For the 80386 and 80486, if the operand is a doubleword value, DIV divides the contents of EDX:EAX by the contents of the operand and stores the result in EAX and the remainder in EDX.

This instruction treats numbers as unsigned binary values.

ENTER: Make Stack Frame for Procedure Parameters

Applicable processors: 80286, 80386, 80486

Category: Flag and processor control instructions

Flags affected: None

Coding examples:

```
ENTER     PPTR,3
ENTER     DS:BX,0
```

Description: ENTER modifies the stack appropriately for entry to a high-level language procedure. The first operand specifies the number of bytes of storage to be allocated on the stack; the second operand specifies the nesting level of the routine. The effects of this instruction are undone by the LEAVE instruction.

ESC: Escape

Applicable processors: 8086/8088, 80286, 80386, 80486

Category: Flag and processor control instructions

Flags affected: None

Coding examples:

```
ESC        6,TEMP
ESC        15,CL
```

Description: ESC provides a means for coprocessors (such as the NPX/FPU) to access data in the microprocessor data stream. When this instruction is encountered, it causes the microprocessor to place the operand on the data bus and perform an NOP internally.

F2XM1: 2x-1

Applicable processors: 8087, 80287, 80387, 80486

Category: Transcendental instruction

Status affected: PE, UE

Coding example:

```
F2XM1
```

Description: F2XM1 calculates $Y = 2^x-1$, where X is the top stack element (ST). The result (Y) replaces X as the top stack element (ST). This instruction performs no validation checking of the input value. The program ensures that $0 <= X <= 0.5$.

FABS: Absolute Value

Applicable processors: 8087, 80287, 80387, 80486

Category: Arithmetic instruction

Status affected: IE

Coding example:

```
FABS
```

Description: FABS changes the top stack element (ST) to its absolute value.

FADD: Add Real

Applicable processors: 8087, 80287, 80387, 80486

Category: Arithmetic instruction

Status affected: DE, IE, OE, PE, UE

Coding examples:

```
FADD      TEMP              ;ST=ST+TEMP
FADD      TEMP,ST(3)        ;TEMP=TEMP+ST(3)
```

Description: FADD adds two numbers together and stores them at the destination operand. If no destination operand is given (only one operand is specified), ST is the assumed destination.

FADDP: Add Real and POP

Applicable processors: 8087, 80287, 80387, 80486

Category: Arithmetic instruction

Status affected: DE, IE, OE, PE, UE

Coding examples:

```
FADDP     TEMP              ;ST=ST+TEMP
FADDP     TEMP,ST(3)        ;TEMP=TEMP+ST(3)
```

Description: FADDP adds two numbers together, stores them at the destination operand, and pops the stack. If no destination operand is given (only one operand is specified), ST is the assumed destination.

FBLD: BCD Load

Applicable processors: 8087, 80287, 80387, 80486

Category: Data transfer instruction

Status affected: IE

Coding example:

```
FBLD      TEMP
```

Description: FBLD converts the BCD number at the operand address to a temporary real and pushes on the stack.

FBSTP: BCD Store and POP

Applicable processors: 8087, 80287, 80387, 80486

Category: Data transfer instruction

Status affected: IE

Coding example:

```
FBSTP     TEMP
```

Description: FBSTP converts the top stack element (ST) to a BCD integer, stores it at the operand address, and pops the stack.

FCHS: Change Sign

Applicable processors: 8087, 80287, 80387, 80486

Category: Arithmetic instruction

Status affected: IE

Coding example:

```
FCHS
```

Description: FCHS changes the sign of the top stack element (ST).

FCLEX: Clear Exceptions with WAIT

Applicable processors: 8087, 80287, 80387, 80486

Category: Flag and processor control instructions

Status affected: B, DE, IE, IR, OE, PE, UE, ZE

Coding example:

```
FCLEX
```

Description: FCLEX clears the exception flags, interrupt request, and busy flags of the NPX/FPU status word. A CPU wait prefix precedes this instruction. See also FNCLEX.

FCOM: Compare Real

Applicable processors: 8087, 80287, 80387, 80486

Category: Comparison instruction

Status affected: C0, C2, C3, DE, IE

Coding examples:

```
FCOM                    ;Compare ST to ST(1)
FCOM        ST(4)       ;Compare ST to ST(4)
FCOM        TEMP        ;Compare ST to memory
```

Description: The top stack element (ST) is compared to either the second stack element (ST(1)) or another specified operand. Condition codes are affected accordingly.

FCOMP: Compare Real and POP

Applicable processors: 8087, 80287, 80387, 80486

Category: Comparison instruction

Status affected: C0, C2, C3, DE, IE

Coding examples:

```
FCOMP                   ;Compare ST to ST(1)
FCOMP       ST(4)       ;Compare ST to ST(4)
FCOMP       TEMP        ;Compare ST to memory
```

Description: The top stack element (ST) is compared to either the second stack element (ST(1)) or another specified operand; the stack then is popped. Condition codes are affected accordingly.

FCOMPP: Compare Real and POP Twice

Applicable processors: 8087, 80287, 80387, 80486

Category: Comparison instruction

Status affected: C0, C2, C3, DE, IE

Coding example:

```
FCOMPP                  ;Compare ST to ST(1)
```

Description: The top stack element (ST) is compared to the second stack element (ST(1)) and the stack is popped twice. Condition codes are affected accordingly.

FCOS: Cosine

Applicable processors: 80387, 80486

Category: Transcendental instruction

Status affected: DE, IE, PE, UE

Coding example:

```
FCOS      ;Replace value in radians with cosine
```

Description: The top stack element (ST) is replaced with its cosine, considering the element to be an angle in radians. Condition codes are affected accordingly.

FDECSTP: Decrement Stack Pointer

Applicable processors: 8087, 80287, 80387, 80486

Category: Flag and processor control instructions

Status affected: ST

Coding example:

```
FDECSTP
```

Description: FDECSTP decrements the stack pointer of the NPX/FPU status word.

FDISI: Disable Interrupts with WAIT

Applicable processors: 8087

Category: Flag and processor control instructions

Status affected: None

Coding example:

```
FDISI
```

Description: FDISI sets the interrupt-enable mask of the 8087 control word, thus preventing the 8087 from initiating an interrupt. A CPU wait prefix precedes this instruction. See also FNDISI.

FDIV: Divide Real

Applicable processors: 8087, 80287, 80387, 80486

Category: Arithmetic instruction

Status affected: DE, IE, OE, PE, UE, ZE

Coding examples:

```
FDIV      TEMP            ;ST=TEMP/ST
FDIV      TEMP,ST(3)      ;TEMP=ST(3)/TEMP
```

Description: FDIV divides the destination by the source operand and stores the result at the destination operand. If no destination operand is given (only one operand is specified), ST is the assumed destination.

FDIVP: Divide Real and POP

Applicable processors: 8087, 80287, 80387, 80486

Category: Arithmetic instruction

Status affected: DE, IE, OE, PE, UE, ZE

Coding examples:

```
FDIVP     TEMP           ;ST=TEMP/ST
FDIVP     TEMP,ST(3)     ;TEMP=ST(3)/TEMP
```

Description: FDIVP divides the destination by the source operand, stores the result at the destination operand, and pops the stack. If no destination operand is given (only one operand is specified), ST is the assumed destination.

FDIVR: Divide Real Reversed

Applicable processors: 8087, 80287, 80387, 80486

Category: Arithmetic instruction

Status affected: DE, IE, OE, PE, UE, ZE

Coding examples:

```
FDIVR     TEMP           ;ST=ST/TEMP
FDIVR     TEMP,ST(3)     ;TEMP=TEMP/ST(3)
```

Description: FDIVR divides the source by the destination operand and stores the result at the destination operand. If no destination operand is given (only one operand is specified), ST is the assumed destination.

FDIVRP: Divide Real Reversed and POP

Applicable processors: 8087, 80287, 80387, 80486

Category: Arithmetic instruction

Status affected: DE, IE, OE, PE, UE, ZE

Coding examples:

```
FDIVRP    TEMP           ;ST=ST/TEMP
FDIVRP    TEMP,ST(3)     ;TEMP=TEMP/ST(3)
```

Description: FDIVRP divides the source by the destination operand, stores the result at the destination operand, and pops the stack. If no destination operand is given (only one operand is specified), ST is the assumed destination.

FENI: Enable Interrupts with WAIT

Applicable processors: 8087

Category: Flag and processor control instructions

Status affected: None

Coding example:

```
FENI
```

Description: FENI clears the interrupt-enable mask of the 8087 control word, so that the 8087 can initiate interrupts. A CPU wait prefix precedes this instruction. See also FNENI.

FFREE: Free Register

Applicable processors: 8087, 80287, 80387, 80486

Category: Flag and processor control instructions

Status affected: None

Coding example:

```
FFREE     ST(3)
```

Description: FFREE changes the tag for the specified stack register to indicate that the stack register is empty.

FIADD: Integer Add

Applicable processors: 8087, 80287, 80387, 80486

Category: Arithmetic instruction

Status affected: DE, IE, OE, PE

Coding examples:

```
FIADD     TEMP          ;ST=ST+TEMP
FIADD     TEMP,ST(3)    ;TEMP=TEMP+ST(3)
```

Description: FIADD adds two numbers together as integers and stores them at the destination operand. If no destination operand is given (only one operand is specified), ST is the assumed destination.

FICOM: Integer Compare

Applicable processors: 8087, 80287, 80387, 80486

Category: Comparison instruction

Status affected: C0, C2, C3, DE, IE

Coding example:

```
FICOM    TEMP_INT       ;Compare memory to ST
```

Description: FICOM converts the operand (assumed to be an integer) to a temporary real and compares it to the top stack element (ST). Condition codes are set accordingly.

FICOMP: Integer Compare and POP

Applicable processors: 8087, 80287, 80387, 80486

Category: Comparison instruction

Status affected: C0, C2, C3, DE, IE

Coding example:

```
FICOMP    TEMP_INT       ;Compare memory to ST
```

Description: FICOMP converts the operand (assumed to be an integer) to a temporary real, compares it to the top stack element (ST), and then pops the stack. Condition codes are set accordingly.

FIDIV: Integer Divide

Applicable processors: 8087, 80287, 80387, 80486

Category: Arithmetic instruction

Status affected: DE, IE, OE, PE, UE, ZE

Coding examples:

```
FIDIV    TEMP           ;ST=TEMP/ST
FIDIV    TEMP,ST(3)     ;TEMP=ST(3)/TEMP
```

Description: FIDIV divides the destination by the source operand, as integers, and stores the result at the destination operand. If no destination operand is given (only one operand is specified), ST is the assumed destination.

FIDIVR: Integer Divide Reversed

Applicable processors: 8087, 80287, 80387, 80486

Category: Arithmetic instruction

Status affected: DE, IE, OE, PE, UE, ZE

Coding examples:

```
FIDIVR    TEMP           ;ST=ST/TEMP
FIDIVR    TEMP,ST(3)     ;TEMP=TEMP/ST(3)
```

Description: FIDIVR divides the destination by the source operand, as integers, and stores the result at the destination operand. If no destination operand is given (only one operand is specified), ST is the assumed destination.

FILD: Integer Load

Applicable processors: 8087, 80287, 80387, 80486

Category: Data transfer instruction

Status affected: IE

Coding example:

```
FILD      TEMP
```

Description: FILD converts the binary integer number at the operand address to a temporary real and pushes it on the stack.

FIMUL: Integer Multiply

Applicable processors: 8087, 80287, 80387, 80486

Category: Arithmetic instruction

Status affected: DE, IE, OE, PE

Coding examples:

```
FIMUL     TEMP           ;ST=ST*TEMP
FIMUL     TEMP,ST(3)     ;TEMP=TEMP*ST(3)
```

Description: FIMUL multiplies the source by the destination operand, as integers, and stores the result at the destination operand. If no destination operand is given (only one operand is specified), ST is the assumed destination.

FINCSTP: Increment Stack Pointer

Applicable processors: 8087, 80287, 80387, 80486

Category: Flag and processor control instructions

Status affected: ST

Coding example:

```
FINCSTP
```

Description: FINCSTP increments the stack pointer of the NPX/FPU status word.

FINIT: Initialize Processor with WAIT

Applicable processors: 8087, 80287, 80387, 80486

Category: Flag and processor control instructions

Status affected: None

Coding example:

```
FINIT
```

Description: FINIT initializes the NPX/FPU. This action is functionally equivalent to performing a hardware RESET. A CPU wait prefix precedes this instruction. See also FNINIT.

FIST: Integer Store

Applicable processors: 8087, 80287, 80387, 80486

Category: Data transfer instruction

Status affected: IE, PE

Coding example:

```
FIST    TEMP
```

Description: FIST rounds the top stack element (ST) to a binary integer number and stores it at the operand address.

FISTP: Integer Store and POP

Applicable processors: 8087, 80287, 80387, 80486

Category: Data transfer instruction

Status affected: IE, PE

Coding example:

```
FISTP      TEMP
```

Description: FISTP rounds the top stack element (ST) to a binary integer number, stores it at the operand address, and pops ST from the stack.

FISUB: Integer Subtract

Applicable processors: 8087, 80287, 80387, 80486

Category: Arithmetic instruction

Status affected: DE, IE, OE, PE

Coding examples:

```
FISUB      TEMP            ;ST=ST-TEMP
FISUB      TEMP,ST(3)      ;TEMP=TEMP-ST(3)
```

Description: FISUB subtracts the source from the destination operand, as integers, and stores the result at the destination operand. If no destination operand is given (only one operand is specified), ST is the assumed destination.

FISUBR: Integer Subtract Reversed

Applicable processors: 8087, 80287, 80387, 80486

Category: Arithmetic instruction

Status affected: DE, IE, OE, PE

Coding examples:

```
FISUBR     TEMP            ;ST=TEMP-ST
FISUBR     TEMP,ST(3)      ;TEMP=ST(3)-TEMP
```

Description: FISUBR subtracts the destination from the source operand, as integers, and stores the result at the destination operand. If no destination operand is given (only one operand is specified), ST is assumed to be the destination.

FLD: Load Real

Applicable processors: 8087, 80287, 80387, 80486

Category: Data transfer instruction

Status affected: DE, IE

Coding examples:

```
FLD     ST(3)
FLD     TEMP
```

Description: FLD pushes the value of the source operand on the stack.

FLD1: Load 1.0

Applicable processors: 8087, 80287, 80387, 80486

Category: Constant instruction

Status affected: IE

Coding example:

```
FLD1
```

Description: FLD1 pushes the value +1.0 on the stack. This value becomes ST.

FLDCW: Load Control Word

Applicable processors: 8087, 80287, 80387, 80486

Category: Flag and processor control instructions

Status affected: None

Coding example:

```
FLDCW   MEM_CW          ;Transfer control word
```

Description: FLDCW loads the NPX/FPU control word with the word value pointed to by the source operand.

FLDENV: Load Environment

Applicable processors: 8087, 80287, 80387, 80486

Category: Flag and processor control instructions

Status affected: B, C0, C1, C2, C3, DE, ES, IE, IR, OE, PE, SF, ST, UE, ZE

Coding example:

```
FLDENV  SAVE_AREA
```

Description: FLDENV restores all environment variables of the NPX/FPU from the 14-word memory location specified by the operand.

FLDL2E: Load $\log_2 e$

Applicable processors: 8087, 80287, 80387, 80486

Category: Constant instruction

Status affected: IE

Coding example:

```
FLDL2E
```

Description: FLDL2E pushes the value of $LOG_2 e$ on the stack. This value becomes ST.

FLDL2T: Load $\log_2 10$

Applicable processors: 8087, 80287, 80387, 80486

Category: Constant instruction

Status affected: IE

Coding example:

```
FLDL2T
```

Description: FLDL2T pushes the value of $LOG_2 10$ on the stack. This value becomes ST.

FLDLG2: Load $\log_{10} 2$

Applicable processors: 8087, 80287, 80387, 80486

Category: Constant instruction

Status affected: IE

Coding example:

```
FLDLG2
```

Description: FLDLG2 pushes the value of $LOG_{10} 2$ on the stack. This value becomes ST.

FLDLN2: Load $\log_e 2$

Applicable processors: 8087, 80287, 80387, 80486

Category: Constant instruction

Status affected: IE

Coding example:

```
FLDLN2
```

Description: FLDLN2 pushes the value of LOG_e2 on the stack. This value becomes ST.

FLDPI: Load Pi

Applicable processors: 8087, 80287, 80387, 80486

Category: Constant instruction

Status affected: IE

Coding example:

```
FLDPI
```

Description: FLDPI pushes the value of pi on the stack. This value becomes ST.

FLDZ: Load 0.0

Applicable processors: 8087, 80287, 80387, 80486

Category: Constant instruction

Status affected: IE

Coding example:

```
FLDZ
```

Description: FLDZ pushes the value 0.0 on the stack. This value becomes ST.

FMUL: Multiply Real

Applicable processors: 8087, 80287, 80387, 80486

Category: Arithmetic instruction

Status affected: DE, IE, OE, PE, UE

Coding examples:

```
FMUL     TEMP         ;ST=ST*TEMP
FMUL     TEMP,ST(3)   ;TEMP=TEMP*ST(3)
```

Description: FMUL multiplies the source by the destination operand and stores the result at the destination operand. If no destination operand is given (only one operand is specified), ST is the assumed destination.

FMULP: Multiply Real and POP

Applicable processors: 8087, 80287, 80387, 80486

Category: Arithmetic instruction

Status affected: DE, IE, OE, PE, UE

Coding examples:

```
FMULP     TEMP              ;ST=ST*TEMP
FMULP     TEMP,ST(3)        ;TEMP=TEMP*ST(3)
```

Description: FMULP multiplies the source by the destination operand, stores the result at the destination operand, and pops the stack. If no destination operand is given (only one operand is specified), ST is the assumed destination.

FNCLEX: Clear Exceptions

Applicable processors: 8087, 80287, 80387, 80486

Category: Flag and processor control instructions

Status affected: B, DE, IE, IR, OE, PE, UE, ZE

Coding example:

```
FNCLEX
```

Description: FNCLEX clears the exception flags, interrupt request, and busy flags of the NPX/FPU status word. This instruction is not preceded by a CPU wait prefix. See also FCLEX.

FNDISI: Disable Interrupts

Applicable processors: 8087

Category: Flag and processor control instructions

Status affected: None

Coding example:

```
FNDISI
```

Description: FNDISI sets the interrupt-enable mask of the 8087 control word, thus preventing the 8087 from initiating an interrupt. This instruction is not preceded by a CPU wait prefix. See also FDISI.

FNENI: Enable Interrupts

Applicable processors: 8087

Category: Flag and processor control instructions

Status affected: None

Coding example:

    FNENI

Description: FNENI clears the interrupt-enable mask of the 8087 control word so the 8087 can initiate interrupts. This instruction is not preceded by a CPU wait prefix. See also FENI.

FNINIT: Initialize Processor

Applicable processors: 8087, 80287, 80387, 80486

Category: Flag and processor control instructions

Status affected: None

Coding example:

    FNINIT

Description: FNINIT initializes the NPX/FPU. This action is functionally equivalent to performing a hardware RESET. This instruction is not preceded by a CPU wait prefix. See also FINIT.

FNOP: No Operation

Applicable processors: 8087, 80287, 80387, 80486

Category: Flag and processor control instructions

Status affected: None

Coding example:

    FNOP

Description: FNOP does nothing but take time and space; the NPX/FPU performs no operation.

FNSAVE: Save State

Applicable processors: 8087, 80287, 80387, 80486

Category: Flag and processor control instructions

Status affected: None

Coding example:

```
FNSAVE    SAVE_AREA
```

Description: FNSAVE saves, at the memory location specified by the operand, all registers and environment variables of the NPX/FPU. This save requires 94 words of memory. After the save, the NPX/FPU is initialized as though the FINIT or FNINIT instructions had been issued. This instruction (FNSAVE) is not preceded by a CPU wait prefix. See also FSAVE.

FNSTCW: Store Control Word

Applicable processors: 8087, 80287, 80387, 80486

Category: Flag and processor control instructions

Status affected: None

Coding example:

```
FNSTCW    MEM_CW    ;Transfer control word
```

Description: FNSTCW copies the NPX/FPU control word to the word value pointed to by the source operand. This instruction is not preceded by a CPU wait prefix. See also FSTCW.

FNSTENV: Store Environment

Applicable processors: 8087, 80287, 80387, 80486

Category: Flag and processor control instructions

Status affected: None

Coding example:

```
FNSTENV    SAVE_AREA
```

Description: FNSTENV saves, at the memory location specified by the operand, all environment variables of the NPX/FPU. This save requires 14 words of memory. After the save, this instruction sets the exception masks of the NPX/FPU control word. This instruction is not preceded by a CPU wait prefix. See also FSTENV.

FNSTSW: Store Status Word

Applicable processors: 8087, 80287, 80387, 80486

Category: Flag and processor control instructions

Status affected: None

Coding example:

```
FNSTSW    MEM_SW    ;Transfer status word
```

Description: FNSTSW copies the NPX/FPU status word to the word value pointed to by the source operand. This instruction is not preceded by a CPU wait prefix. See also FSTSW.

FPATAN: Partial Arctangent

Applicable processors: 8087, 80287, 80387, 80486

Category: Transcendental instruction

Status affected: PE, UE

Coding example:

```
FPATAN
```

Description: FPATAN computes ;gV = ARCTAN(Y/X), where X is the top stack element (ST), and Y is the second stack element (ST(1)). Both stack elements are popped, and the result (0) is pushed on the stack and becomes ST. This instruction performs no validation checking of the input value. The program ensures that $0 < Y < X < \$\tilde{}$.

FPREM: Partial Remainder

Applicable processors: 8087, 80287, 80387, 80486

Category: Arithmetic instruction

Status affected: C0, C1, C3, DE, IE, UE

Coding example:

```
FPREM
```

Description: FPREM calculates the modulo of the two top stack elements. By successively subtracting ST(1) from ST, this instruction calculates an exact remainder and remains in ST.

FPREM1: Partial Remainder, IEEE version

Applicable processors: 80387, 80486

Category: Arithmetic instruction

Status affected: C0, C1, C2, C3, DE, IE, UE

Coding example:

    FPREM1

Description: FPREM1 calculates the modulo of the two top stack elements. Formula used is ST = ST − (ST(1) ∗ *quotient*), where *quotient* is the integer nearest the exact value ST/ST(1). If two integers are equally close, the even one is used. This different formula is the only difference between FPREM1 and FPREM.

FPTAN: Partial Tangent

Applicable processors: 8087, 80287, 80387, 80486

Category: Transcendental instruction

Status affected: IE, PE

Coding example:

    FPTAN

Description: FPTAN computes Y/X = TAN(;gV), where ;gV is the top stack element (ST). The top stack element is replaced by the computed Y, and the computed X is pushed on the stack. Thus, at the end of this operation, ST(1) = Y and ST = X. This instruction performs no validation checking of the input value. The program ensures that $0 <= ;gV <= pi4$.

FRNDINT: Round to Integer

Applicable processors: 8087, 80287, 80387, 80486

Category: Arithmetic instruction

Status affected: IE, PE

Coding example:

    FRNDINT

Description: FRNDINT rounds the number in the top stack element (ST) to an integer.

FRSTOR: Restore State

Applicable processors: 8087, 80287, 80387, 80486

Category: Flag and processor control instructions

Status affected: B, C0, C1, C2, C3, DE, ES, IE, IR, OE, PE, SF, ST, UE, ZE

Coding example:

```
FRSTOR     SAVE_AREA
```

Description: FRSTOR restores all registers and environment variables of the NPX/FPU from the 94-word memory location specified by the operand.

FSAVE: Save State with WAIT

Applicable processors: 8087, 80287, 80387, 80486

Category: Flag and processor control instructions

Status affected: None

Coding example:

```
FSAVE     SAVE_AREA
```

Description: FSAVE saves, at the memory location specified by the operand, all registers and environment variables of the NPX/FPU. This save requires 94 words of memory. After the save, the NPX/FPU is initialized as though the FINIT or FNINIT instructions had been issued. This instruction (FSAVE) is preceded by a CPU wait prefix. See also FNSAVE.

FSCALE: Scale

Applicable processors: 8087, 80287, 80387, 80486

Category: Arithmetic instruction

Status affected: IE, OE, UE

Coding example:

```
FSCALE
```

Description: FSCALE calculates $X = X*2Y$, where X is the value of the top stack element (ST), and Y is the value of the second stack element (ST(1)).

FSETPM: Set Protected Mode

Applicable processors: 80287

Category: Flag and processor control instructions

Status affected: None

Coding example:

```
FSETPM
```

Description: FSETPM causes the 80287 to operate in protected mode. Ordinarily, the operation mode is of no concern to programmers of applications software created in the real mode.

FSIN: Sine

Applicable processors: 80387, 80486

Category: Transcendental instruction

Status affected: DE, IE, PE, UE

Coding example:

```
FSIN       ;Replace value in radians with sine
```

Description: The top stack element (ST) is replaced with its sine, considering the element to be an angle in radians. Condition codes are affected accordingly.

FSINCOS: Sine and Cosine

Applicable processors: 80387, 80486

Category: Transcendental instruction

Status affected: DE, IE, PE, UE

Coding example:

```
FSINCOS    ;Replace value in radians with sine and cosine
```

Description: The top stack element (ST) is replaced with its sine, considering the element to be an angle in radians, and then the cosine is calculated and pushed onto the stack. Condition codes are affected accordingly.

FSQRT: Square Root

Applicable processors: 8087, 80287, 80387, 80486

Category: Arithmetic instruction

Status affected: DE, IE, PE

Coding example:

```
FSQRT
```

Description: FSQRT calculates the square root of the top stack element (ST) and stores it as the new ST. The old ST is lost.

FST: Store Real

Applicable processors: 8087, 80287, 80387, 80486

Category: Data transfer instruction

Status affected: IE, OE, PE, UE

Coding examples:

```
FST     ST(3)
FST     TEMP
```

Description: FST copies the value of the top stack element (ST) to the operand or operand address.

FSTCW: Store Control Word with WAIT

Applicable processors: 8087, 80287, 80387, 80486

Category: Flag and processor control instructions

Status affected: None

Coding example:

```
FSTCW    MEM_CW    ;Transfer control word
```

Description: FSTCW copies the NPX/FPU control word to the word value pointed to by the source operand. A CPU wait prefix precedes this instruction. See also FNSTCW.

FSTENV: Store Environment with WAIT

Applicable processors: 8087, 80287, 80387, 80486

Category: Flag and processor control instructions

Status affected: None

Coding example:

```
FSTENV    SAVE_AREA
```

Description: FSTENV saves, at the memory location specified by the operand, all environment variables of the NPX/FPU. This save requires 14 words of memory. After the save, this instruction sets the exception masks of the NPX/FPU control word. A CPU wait prefix precedes this instruction. See also FNSTENV.

FSTP: Store Real and POP

Applicable processors: 8087, 80287, 80387, 80486

Category: Data transfer instruction

Status affected: IE, OE, PE, UE

Coding examples:

```
FSTP      ST(3)
FSTP      TEMP
```

Description: FSTP copies the value of the top stack element (ST) to the operand or operand address and pops the stack.

FSTSW: Store Status Word with WAIT

Applicable processors: 8087, 80287, 80387, 80486

Category: Flag and processor control instructions

Status affected: None

Coding example:

```
FSTSW     MEM_SW      ;Transfer status word
```

Description: FSTSW copies the NPX/FPU status word to the word value pointed to by the source operand. A CPU wait prefix precedes this instruction. See also FNSTSW.

FSUB: Subtract Real

Applicable processors: 8087, 80287, 80387, 80486

Category: Arithmetic instruction

Status affected: DE, IE, OE, PE, UE

Coding examples:

```
FSUB      TEMP            ;ST=ST-TEMP
FSUB      TEMP,ST(3)      ;TEMP=TEMP-ST(3)
```

Description: FSUB subtracts the source from the destination operand, and stores the result at the destination operand. If no destination operand is given (only one operand is specified), ST is the assumed destination.

FSUBP: Subtract Real and POP

Applicable processors: 8087, 80287, 80387, 80486

Category: Arithmetic instruction

Status affected: DE, IE, OE, PE, UE

Coding examples:

```
FSUBP     TEMP            ;ST=ST-TEMP
FSUBP     TEMP,ST(3)      ;TEMP=TEMP-ST(3)
```

Description: FSUBP subtracts the source from the destination operand, stores the result at the destination operand, and pops the stack. If no destination operand is given (only one operand is specified), ST is the assumed destination.

FSUBR: Subtract Real Reversed

Applicable processors: 8087, 80287, 80387, 80486

Category: Arithmetic instruction

Status affected: DE, IE, OE, PE, UE

Coding examples:

```
FSUBR     TEMP            ;ST=TEMP-ST
FSUBR     TEMP,ST(3)      ;TEMP=ST(3)-TEMP
```

Description: FSUBR subtracts the destination from the source operand and stores the result at the destination operand. If no destination operand is given (only one operand is specified), ST is the assumed destination.

FSUBRP: Subtract Real Reversed and POP

Applicable processors: 8087, 80287, 80387, 80486

Category: Arithmetic instruction

Status affected: DE, IE, OE, PE, UE

Coding examples:

```
FSUBRP    TEMP           ;ST=TEMP-ST
FSUBRP    TEMP,ST(3)     ;TEMP=ST(3)-TEMP
```

Description: FSUBRP subtracts the destination from the source operand, stores the result at the destination operand, and pops the stack. If no destination operand is given (only one operand is specified), ST is the assumed destination.

FTST: Test

Applicable processors: 8087, 80287, 80387, 80486

Category: Comparison instruction

Status affected: C0, C2, C3, DE, IE

Coding example:

```
FTST
```

Description: FTST compares the top stack element (ST) to zero and sets the condition codes accordingly.

FUCOM: Unordered Compare

Applicable processors: 80387, 80486

Category: Comparison instruction

Status affected: C0, C2, C3, DE, IE

Coding examples:

```
FUCOM            ;default comparison
FUCOM    ST(2)   ;compare top and ST(2)
```

Description: FUCOM compares the specified source with the top stack element (ST). If no operand is specified, FUCOM compares ST and ST(1). This instruction differs from FCOM in that FUCOM does not cause an invalid operation exception if one of the operands is a NaN. Condition codes are affected accordingly.

FUCOMP: Unordered Compare and POP

Applicable processors: 80387, 80486

Category: Comparison instruction

Status affected: C0, C2, C3, DE, IE

Coding examples:

```
FUCOMP                  ;default comparison
FUCOMP     ST(2)        ;compare top and ST(2)
```

Description: FUCOMP compares the specified source with the top stack element (ST). If no operand is specified, FUCOMP compares ST and ST(1). This instruction differs from FCOM in that FUCOMP does not cause an invalid operation exception if one of the operands is a NaN. Condition codes are affected accordingly. The stack is then popped one time.

FUCOMPP: Unordered Compare and POP Twice

Applicable processors: 80387, 80486

Category: Comparison instruction

Status affected: C0, C2, C3, DE, IE

Coding example:

```
FUCOMPP     ;compare ST and ST(1)
```

Description: FUCOMPP compares the specified source with the top stack element (ST). If no operand is specified, FUCOMPP compares ST and ST(1). This instruction differs from FCOM in that FUCOMPP does not cause an invalid operation exception if one of the operands is a NaN. Condition codes are affected accordingly. The stack is then popped twice.

FWAIT: CPU Wait

Applicable processors: 8087, 80287, 80387, 80486

Category: Flag and processor control instructions

Status affected: None

Coding example:

```
FWAIT
```

Description: FWAIT is effectively the same as the WAIT command. This instruction enables the synchronization of the microprocessor and the

NPX/FPU. FWAIT causes the microprocessor to suspend operation until it receives a signal indicating that the NPX/FPU has completed the last operation.

FXAM: Examine

Applicable processors: 8087, 80287, 80387, 80486

Category: Comparison instruction

Status affected: C0, C1, C2, C3

Coding example:

```
FXAM
```

Description: FXAM examines the top stack element (ST) and reports (in the condition codes) the condition, or attributes, of the value.

FXCH: Exchange Registers

Applicable processors: 8087, 80287, 80387, 80486

Category: Data transfer instruction

Status affected: IE

Coding examples:

```
FXCH      ST(3)
FXCH      TEMP
```

Description: FXCH switches the value of the top stack element (ST) with the value of the operand.

FXTRACT: Extract Exponent and Significand

Applicable processors: 8087, 80287, 80387, 80486

Category: Arithmetic instruction

Status affected: IE

Coding example:

```
FXTRACT
```

Description: FXTRACT removes the top stack element (ST) and converts it to two numbers: the exponent and significand of the original number. The exponent is pushed on the stack, followed by the significand, which results in ST = significand and ST(1) = exponent.

FYL2X: $Y_*\log_2 X$

Applicable processors: 8087, 80287, 80387, 80486

Category: Transcendental instruction

Status affected: PE

Coding example:

    FYL2X

Description: FYL2X calculates $Z = Y_*LOG_2 X$, where X is the top stack element (ST), and Y is the second stack element (ST(1)). Both stack elements are popped, and the result (Z) is pushed on the stack and becomes the new ST. This instruction performs no validation checking of the input value. The program ensures that $0 < X < \$\tilde{}$ and $-\$\tilde{} < Y < +\$\tilde{}$.

FYL2XP1: $Y_*\log_2(X+1)$

Applicable processors: 8087, 80287, 80387, 80486

Category: Transcendental instruction

Status affected: PE

Coding example:

    FYL2XP1

Description: FYL2XP1 calculates $Z = Y_*LOG_2(X = 1)$, where X is the top stack element (ST), and Y is the second stack element (ST(1)). Both stack elements are popped, and the result (Z) is pushed on the stack and becomes the new ST. This instruction performs no validation checking of the input value. The program ensures that $0 < |X| < (1 - (\$\sqrt{2}/2))$ and $-\$\tilde{} < Y < +\$\tilde{}$.

HLT: Halt

Applicable processors: 8086/8088, 80286, 80386, 80486

Category: Flag and processor control instructions

Flags affected: None

Coding example:

    HLT

Description: HLT causes the microprocessor to stop execution and leaves the CS:IP registers pointing to the instruction following the HLT. This halt condition is terminated only after the system receives an interrupt or after the RESET line is activated.

IDIV: Integer Divide

Applicable processors: 8086/8088, 80286, 80386, 80486

Category: Arithmetic instructions

Flags affected: AF (undefined), CF (undefined), OF (undefined), PF (undefined), SF (undefined), ZF (undefined)

Coding examples:

```
IDIV      BX                ;AX=DX:AX/BX
IDIV      WORD_TEMP         ;AX=DX:AX/WORD_TEMP
IDIV      BYTE_SUM          ;AL=AX/BYTE_SUM
IDIV      DWORD_SUM         ;EAX=EDX:EAX/DWORD_SUM
IDIV      WORD_TBL[BX]      ;Indirect address example
```

Description: If the operand is a byte value, IDIV divides the contents of AX by the contents of the operand, and stores the result in AL and the remainder in AH. If the operand is a word value, IDIV divides the contents of DX:AX by the contents of the operand and stores the result in AX and the remainder in DX.

On the 80386 and 80486, if the operand is a doubleword value, IDIV divides the contents of EDX:EAX by the contents of the operand, and stores the result in EAX and the remainder in EDX.

This instruction treats numbers as signed binary values.

IMUL: Integer Multiply

Applicable processors: 8086/8088, 80286, 80386, 80486

Category: Arithmetic instructions

Flags affected: AF (undefined), CF, OF, PF (undefined), SF (undefined), ZF (undefined)

Coding examples:

```
IMUL      BX                  ;DX:AX=AX*BX
IMUL      WORD_TEMP           ;DX:AX=AX*WORD_TEMP
IMUL      BYTE_SUM            ;AX=AL*BYTE_SUM
IMUL      WORD_TBL[BX]        ;Indirect address example
IMUL      ECX,DWORD_TEMP,10   ;ECX=DWORD_TEMP*10
```

Description: The results of this operation depend on the number of operands specified. Processors other than the 80386 and 80486 require exactly one operand for this instruction.

If only one operand is given, it is multiplied by either AL, AX, or EAX. If the operand is a byte value, IMUL multiplies the contents of AL by the contents of the operand and stores the result in AX. If the operand is a word value, IMUL multiplies the contents of AX by the contents of the operand and stores the result in DX:AX.

If two operands are given, IMUL multiplies the first operand by the second one and stores the result in the first operand. Both operands must agree in size.

If three operands are given and the third operand is an immediate value, IMUL multiplies the second operand by the third one and stores the result in the first operand.

This instruction treats numbers as signed binary values.

IN: Input from Port

Applicable processors: 8086/8088, 80286, 80386, 80486

Category: Data transfer instructions

Flags affected: None

Coding examples:

```
IN      AL,64h
IN      AX,DX
IN      EAX,DX
```

Description: IN loads a byte, word, or doubleword to AL, AX, or EAX, respectively, from the specified hardware I/O port address. A port number below 256 may be specified as a constant or as a variable in the DX register. A port number above 255, however, *must* be specified in the DX register.

INC: Increment

Applicable processors: 8086/8088, 80286, 80386, 80486

Category: Arithmetic instructions

Flags affected: AF, OF, PF, SF, ZF

Coding examples:

```
INC     AX
INC     SUM
INC     CL
INC     EDI
INC     TEMP[SI]
```

Description: INC changes, by increments of 1, the contents of the operand. The operand is assumed to be an unsigned binary value.

INS: Input String from Port

Applicable processors: 80286, 80386, 80486

Category: Data transfer instructions

Flags affected: None

Coding examples:

```
INS     CX,DX       ;Load word
INS     BL,DX       ;Load byte
INS     EAX,DX      ;Load doubleword
```

Description: INS loads a byte, word, or doubleword from the specified hardware I/O port address (indicated by the value in DX) to the destination operand. The size of the destination operand determines whether a byte, word, or doubleword is transferred. If the destination operand is an offset address, that address is relative to the ES register. No segment override is possible.

INSB: Input String Byte from Port

Applicable processors: 80286, 80386, 80486

Category: Data transfer instructions

Flags affected: None

Coding example:

```
INSB
```

Description: Upon receiving a byte from the hardware I/O port address specified in DX, INSB loads that byte to the address specified by ES:[DI]. The port number can range from 0 to 65,535. After the transfer, DI changes in an increment or decrement of 1, depending on the setting of the direction flag.

INSD: Input String Doubleword from Port

Applicable processors: 80386, 80486

Category: Data transfer instructions

Flags affected: None

Coding example:

```
INSD
```

Description: INSD loads a doubleword from the hardware I/O port address specified in DX to the address specified by ES:[EDI]. After the transfer, EDI changes in increments or decrements of four, depending on the setting of the direction flag.

INSW: Input String Word from Port

Applicable processors: 80286, 80386, 80486

Category: Data transfer instructions

Flags affected: None

Coding example:

```
INSW
```

Description: INSW loads a word from the hardware I/O port address specified in DX to the address specified by ES:[DI]. The port number can range from 0 to 65,535. After the transfer, DI changes in increments or decrements of two, depending on the setting of the direction flag.

INT: Software Interrupt

Applicable processors: 8086/8088, 80286, 80386, 80486

Category: Control transfer instructions

Flags affected: IF, TF

Coding examples:

```
INT        10h
INT        13h
```

Description: INT initiates a software interrupt of the CPU, and starts the following functions:

❏ Pushing the flags on the stack

❏ Clearing the TF and IF flags

❏ Pushing the value of CS on the stack

❏ Loading CS with the segment address of the interrupt being invoked (this segment address is found at the calculated address in the interrupt vector table)

❏ Pushing the value of IP on the stack

❏ Loading IP with the offset address of the interrupt being invoked (this offset address is found at the calculated address in the interrupt vector table)

Execution then continues at the newly loaded CS:IP address until an IRET instruction is encountered.

INTO: Interrupt on Overflow

Applicable processors: 8086/8088, 80286, 80386, 80486

Category: Control transfer instructions

Flags affected: None

Coding example:

```
INTO
```

Description: If the overflow flag (OF) is set, INTO executes an interrupt 4 and control proceeds as though an INT 4 had been issued. Be aware that, in this case, the flags register is affected as described for the INT instruction.

INVD: Invalidate Data Cache

Applicable processors: 80486

Category: Processor control instructions

Flags affected: None

Coding example:

```
INVD
```

Description: This instruction causes the information in the on-chip cache to be flushed. It also causes a special-function bus cycle to be issued which can be used as an indicator to external caches (those on on the 80486) to flush as well.

INVLPG: Invalidate TLB Entry if Present

Applicable processors: 80486

Category: Processor control instructions

Flags affected: None

Coding example:

```
INVLPG          TLB_LOC
```

Description: This instruction is used to invalidate an entry in the cache used for table entries (the TLB). If the address of the operand is a valid entry in the TLB (one that has not previously been invalidated), then it is marked as invalid.

IRET: Return from Interrupt

Applicable processors: 8086/8088, 80286, 80386, 80486

Category: Control transfer instructions

Flags affected: AC, AF, CF, DF, IF, IOPL, NT, OF, PF, RF, SF, TF, VM, ZF

Coding example:

```
IRET
```

Description: IRET terminates an interrupt procedure and, by popping the values of IP, CS, and the flags register from the stack, returns control to the point at which the interrupt occurred.

JA: Jump if Above

Applicable processors: 8086/8088, 80286, 80386, 80486

Category: Control transfer instructions

Flags affected: None

Coding example:

```
JA   NEXT_STEP
```

Description: JA causes program execution to branch to the operand address if the carry and zero flags are both clear. This instruction is functionally the same as JNBE.

JAE: Jump if Above or Equal

Applicable processors: 8086/8088, 80286, 80386, 80486

Category: Control transfer instructions

Flags affected: None

Coding example:

```
JAE   NEXT_STEP
```

Description: JAE causes program execution to branch to the operand address if the carry flag is clear. This instruction is functionally the same as JNB or JNC.

JB: Jump if Below

Applicable processors: 8086/8088, 80286, 80386, 80486

Category: Control transfer instructions

Flags affected: None

Coding example:

```
JB    NEXT_STEP
```

Description: JB causes program execution to branch to the operand address if the carry flag is set. This instruction is functionally the same as JC or JNAE.

JBE: Jump if Below or Equal

Applicable processors: 8086/8088, 80286, 80386, 80486

Category: Control transfer instructions

Flags affected: None

Coding example:

```
JBE   NEXT_STEP
```

Description: JBE causes program execution to branch to the operand address if either the carry or zero flag is set. This instruction is functionally the same as JNA.

JC: Jump on Carry

Applicable processors: 8086/8088, 80286, 80386, 80486

Category: Control transfer instructions

Flags affected: None

Coding example:

```
JC    NEXT_STEP
```

Description: JC causes program execution to branch to the operand address if the carry flag is set. This instruction is functionally the same as JB or JNAE.

JCXZ: Jump if CX=0

Applicable processors: 8086/8088, 80286, 80386, 80486

Category: Control transfer instructions

Flags affected: None

Coding example:

```
JCXZ      SKIP_LOOP
```

Description: JCXZ causes program execution to branch to the operand address if the value of CX is 0.

JE: Jump if Equal

Applicable processors: 8086/8088, 80286, 80386, 80486

Category: Control transfer instructions

Flags affected: None

Coding example:

```
JE    NEXT_STEP
```

Description: JE causes program execution to branch to the operand address if the zero flag is set. This instruction is functionally the same as JZ.

JECXZ: Jump if ECX=0

Applicable processors: 80386, 80486

Category: Control transfer instructions

Flags affected: None

Coding example:

```
JECXZ    SKIP_LOOP
```

Description: JECXZ causes program execution to branch to the operand address if the value of ECX is 0. Although functionally the same as JCXZ, JECXZ works with the 32-bit ECX register.

JG: Jump if Greater

Applicable processors: 8086/8088, 80286, 80386, 80486

Category: Control transfer instructions

Flags affected: None

Coding example:

```
JG   NEXT_STEP
```

Description: JG causes program execution to branch to the operand address if the sign flag equals the overflow flag or if the zero flag is clear. This instruction is functionally the same as JNLE.

JGE: Jump if Greater or Equal

Applicable processors: 8086/8088, 80286, 80386, 80486

Category: Control transfer instructions

Flags affected: None

Coding example:

```
JGE      NEXT_STEP
```

Description: JGE causes program execution to branch to the operand address if the sign flag equals the overflow flag. This instruction is functionally the same as JNL.

JL: Jump if Less

Applicable processors: 8086/8088, 80286, 80386, 80486

Category: Control transfer instructions

Flags affected: None

Coding example:

```
JL    NEXT_STEP
```

Description: JL causes program execution to branch to the operand address if the sign flag does not equal the overflow flag. This instruction is functionally the same as JNGE.

JLE: Jump if Less or Equal

Applicable processors: 8086/8088, 80286, 80386, 80486

Category: Control transfer instructions

Flags affected: None

Coding example:

```
JLE       NEXT_STEP
```

Description: JLE causes program execution to branch to the operand address if the sign flag does not equal the overflow flag or if the zero flag is set. This instruction is functionally the same as JNG.

JMP: Jump

Applicable processors: 8086/8088, 80286, 80386, 80486

Category: Control transfer instructions

Flags affected: None

Coding examples:

```
JMP       EXIT_CODE
JMP       [BX]            ;Jump to address at [BX]
JMP       AX              ;Jump to address in AX
```

Description: JMP initiates program execution at the designated operand address, affecting the CS and IP registers as necessary to cause this unconditional branch.

JNA: Jump if Not Above

Applicable processors: 8086/8088, 80286, 80386, 80486

Category: Control transfer instructions

Flags affected: None

Coding example:

```
JNA        NEXT_STEP
```

Description: JNA causes program execution to branch to the operand address if either the carry or zero flag is set. This instruction is functionally the same as JBE.

JNAE: Jump if Not Above or Equal

Applicable processors: 8086/8088, 80286, 80386, 80486

Category: Control transfer instructions

Flags affected: None

Coding example:

```
JNAE       NEXT_STEP
```

Description: JNAE causes program execution to branch to the operand address if the carry flag is set. This instruction is functionally the same as JB or JC.

JNB: Jump if Not Below

Applicable processors: 8086/8088, 80286, 80386, 80486

Category: Control transfer instructions

Flags affected: None

Coding example:

```
JNB        NEXT_STEP
```

Description: JNB causes program execution to branch to the operand address if the carry flag is clear. This instruction is functionally the same as JAE or JNC.

JNBE: Jump if Not Below or Equal

Applicable processors: 8086/8088, 80286, 80386, 80486

Category: Control transfer instructions

Flags affected: None

Coding example:

```
JNBE       NEXT_STEP
```

Description: JNBE causes program execution to branch to the operand address if both the carry and zero flags are clear. This instruction is functionally the same as JA.

JNC: Jump on No Carry

Applicable processors: 8086/8088, 80286, 80386, 80486

Category: Control transfer instructions

Flags affected: None

Coding example:

```
JNC        NEXT_STEP
```

Description: JNC causes program execution to branch to the operand address if the carry flag is clear. This instruction is functionally the same as JAE or JNB.

JNE: Jump if Not Equal

Applicable processors: 8086/8088, 80286, 80386, 80486

Category: Control transfer instructions

Flags affected: None

Coding example:

```
JNE        NEXT_STEP
```

Description: JNE causes program execution to branch to the operand address if the zero flag is clear. This instruction is functionally the same as JNZ.

JNG: Jump if Not Greater

Applicable processors: 8086/8088, 80286, 80386, 80486

Category: Control transfer instructions

Flags affected: None

Coding example:

```
JNG        NEXT_STEP
```

Description: JNG causes program execution to branch to the operand address if the sign flag does not equal the overflow flag or if the zero flag is set. This instruction is functionally the same as JLE.

JNGE: Jump if Not Greater or Equal

Applicable processors: 8086/8088, 80286, 80386, 80486

Category: Control transfer instructions

Flags affected: None

Coding example:

```
JNGE      NEXT_STEP
```

Description: JNGE causes program execution to branch to the operand address if the sign flag does not equal the overflow flag. This instruction is functionally the same as JL.

JNL: Jump if Not Less

Applicable processors: 8086/8088, 80286, 80386, 80486

Category: Control transfer instructions

Flags affected: None

Coding example:

```
JNL       NEXT_STEP
```

Description: JNL causes program execution to branch to the operand address if the sign flag equals the overflow flag. This instruction is functionally the same as JGE.

JNLE: Jump if Not Less or Equal

Applicable processors: 8086/8088, 80286, 80386, 80486

Category: Control transfer instructions

Flags affected: None

Coding example:

```
JNLE      NEXT_STEP
```

Description: JNLE causes program execution to branch to the operand address if the sign flag equals the overflow flag or the zero flag is clear. This instruction is functionally the same as JG.

JNO: Jump on No Overflow

Applicable processors: 8086/8088, 80286, 80386, 80486

Category: Control transfer instructions

Flags affected: None

Coding example:

```
JNO        NEXT_STEP
```

Description: JNO causes program execution to branch to the operand address if the overflow flag is clear.

JNP: Jump on No Parity

Applicable processors: 8086/8088, 80286, 80386, 80486

Category: Control transfer instructions

Flags affected: None

Coding example:

```
JNP        NEXT_STEP
```

Description: JNP causes program execution to branch to the operand address if the parity flag is clear. This instruction is functionally the same as JPO.

JNS: Jump on Not Sign

Applicable processors: 8086/8088, 80286, 80386, 80486

Category: Control transfer instructions

Flags affected: None

Coding example:

```
JNS        NEXT_STEP
```

Description: JNS causes program execution to branch to the operand address if the sign flag is clear.

JNZ: Jump on Not Zero

Applicable processors: 8086/8088, 80286, 80386, 80486

Category: Control transfer instructions

Flags affected: None

Coding example:

```
JNZ        NEXT_STEP
```

Description: JNZ causes program execution to branch to the operand address if the zero flag is clear. This instruction is functionally the same as JNE.

JO: Jump on Overflow

Applicable processors: 8086/8088, 80286, 80386, 80486

Category: Control transfer instructions

Flags affected: None

Coding example:

```
JO   NEXT_STEP
```

Description: JO causes program execution to branch to the operand address if the overflow flag is set.

JP: Jump on Parity

Applicable processors: 8086/8088, 80286, 80386, 80486

Category: Control transfer instructions

Flags affected: None

Coding example:

```
JP   NEXT_STEP
```

Description: JP causes program execution to branch to the operand address if the parity flag is set. This instruction is functionally the same as JPE.

JPE: Jump on Parity Even

Applicable processors: 8086/8088, 80286, 80386, 80486

Category: Control transfer instructions

Flags affected: None

Coding example:

```
JPE       NEXT_STEP
```

Description: JPE causes program execution to branch to the operand address if the parity flag is set. This instruction is functionally the same as JP.

JPO: Jump on Parity Odd

Applicable processors: 8086/8088, 80286, 80386, 80486

Category: Control transfer instructions

Flags affected: None

Coding example:

```
JPO      NEXT_STEP
```

Description: JPO causes program execution to branch to the operand address if the parity flag is clear. This instruction is functionally the same as JNP.

JS: Jump on Sign

Applicable processors: 8086/8088, 80286, 80386, 80486

Category: Control transfer instructions

Flags affected: None

Coding example:

```
JS   NEXT_STEP
```

Description: JS causes program execution to branch to the operand address if the sign flag is set.

JZ: Jump on Zero

Applicable processors: 8086/8088, 80286, 80386, 80486

Category: Control transfer instructions

Flags affected: None

Coding example:

```
JZ   NEXT_STEP
```

Description: JZ causes program execution to branch to the operand address if the zero flag is set. This instruction is functionally the same as JE.

LAHF: Load AH Register with Flags

Applicable processors: 8086/8088, 80286, 80386, 80486

Category: Data transfer instructions

Flags affected: None

Coding example:

    LAHF

Description: LAHF copies the low-order byte of the flags register to AH. After execution of this instruction, bits 7, 6, 4, 2, and 1 of AH are equal to SF, ZF, AF, PF, and CF, respectively.

LAR: Load Access-Rights Byte

Applicable processors: 80286, 80386, 80486

Category: Data transfer instructions

Flags affected: ZF

Coding example:

    LAR   AX,SELECT

Description: Based on the selection in the second operand, the high byte of the destination register is overwritten by the value of the access-rights byte, and the low byte is zeroed. The loading is done only if the descriptor is visible at the current privilege level and at the selector RPL. The zero flag is set if the loading operation is successful.

LDS: Load DS Register

Applicable processors: 8086/8088, 80286, 80386, 80486

Category: Data transfer instructions

Flags affected: None

Coding example:

    LDS   SI,SOURCE_BUFFER

Description: LDS performs two distinct operations: it loads DS with the segment address of the source operand and loads the destination operand with the offset address of the source operand.

LEA: Load Effective Address

Applicable processors: 8086/8088, 80286, 80386, 80486

Category: Data transfer instructions

Flags affected: None

Coding example:

```
LEA      AX,MESSAGE_1
```

Description: LEA transfers the offset address of the source operand to the destination operand. The destination operand must be a general word register.

LEAVE: High-Level Procedure Exit

Applicable processors: 80286, 80386, 80486

Category: Flag and processor control instructions

Flags affected: None

Coding example:

```
LEAVE
```

Description: LEAVE undoes the changes performed by the ENTER instruction. This instruction is used for exiting high-level language subroutines.

LES: Load ES Register

Applicable processors: 8086/8088, 80286, 80386, 80486

Category: Data transfer instructions

Flags affected: None

Coding example:

```
LES      DI,DEST_BUFFER
```

Description: LES performs two distinct operations: it loads ES with the segment address of the source operand and loads the destination operand with the offset address of the source operand.

LFS: Load FS Register

Applicable processors: 80386, 80486

Category: Data transfer instructions

Flags affected: None

Coding example:

```
LFS      DI,DEST_BUFFER
```

Description: LFS performs two distinct operations: it loads FS with the segment address of the source operand and then loads the destination operand with the offset address of the source operand.

LGDT: Load GDT Register

Applicable processors: 80286, 80386, 80486

Category: Data transfer instructions

Flags affected: None

Coding example:

```
LGDT     TEMP[BX]
```

Description: LGDT loads the six bytes associated with the global descriptor table (GDT) from the memory address specified in the operand. This instruction is for use in protected-mode operating system software; it is not used in applications software.

LGS: Load GS Register

Applicable processors: 80386, 80486

Category: Data transfer instructions

Flags affected: None

Coding example:

```
LGS      DI,DEST_BUFFER
```

Description: LGS performs two distinct operations: it loads GS with the segment address of the source operand and then loads the destination operand with the offset address of the source operand.

LIDT: Load IDT Register

Applicable processors: 80286, 80386, 80486

Category: Data transfer instructions

Flags affected: None

Coding example:

```
LIDT     TEMP[BX]
```

Description: LIDT loads the six bytes associated with the interrupt descriptor table (IDT) from the memory address specified in the operand. This instruction is for use in protected-mode operating system software; it is not used in applications software.

LLDT: Load LDT Register

Applicable processors: 80286, 80386, 80486

Category: Data transfer instructions

Flags affected: None

Coding example:

```
LLDT    AX
```

Description: Based on the selector specified in the operand, LLDT transfers the valid global descriptor table entry to the local descriptor table (LDT). This instruction is used in protected-mode operating system software but not used in applications software.

LMSW: Load Machine Status Word

Applicable processors: 80286, 80386, 80486

Category: Data transfer instructions

Flags affected: None

Coding example:

```
LMSW    AX
```

Description: LMSW copies the value of the operand to the machine status word. This instruction is for use only in operating system software, not in applications software.

LOCK: Lock Bus

Applicable processors: 8086/8088, 80286, 80386, 80486

Category: Flag and processor control instructions

Flags affected: None

Coding example:

```
LOCK XLAT
```

Description: LOCK prohibits interference from any other coprocessors during the execution of the next instruction issued. LOCK is a prefix to be used with other operations.

LODSB: Load a Byte from String into AL

Applicable processors: 8086/8088, 80286, 80386, 80486

Category: String manipulation instructions

Flags affected: None

Coding example:

```
LODSB
```

Description: LODSB loads AL with the contents of the address pointed to by SI. SI then changes in increments or decrements of 1, depending on the setting of the direction flag. Intel lists this command as LODS; however, the Microsoft Macro Assembler distinguishes between byte (LODSB) and word (LODSW).

LODSD: Load a Doubleword from String into EAX

Applicable processors: 80386, 80486

Category: String manipulation instructions

Flags affected: None

Coding example:

```
LODSD
```

Description: LODSD loads EAX with the contents of the address pointed to by ESI. ESI then changes in increments or decrements of four, depending on the setting of the direction flag.

LODSW: Load a Word from String into AX

Applicable processors: 8086/8088, 80286, 80386, 80486

Category: String manipulation instructions

Flags affected: None

Coding example:

```
LODSW
```

Description: LODSW loads AX with the contents of the address pointed to by SI. SI then changes in increments or decrements of two, depending on the setting of the direction flag. Intel lists this command as LODS; however, the Microsoft Macro Assembler distinguishes between byte (LODSB) and word (LODSW).

LOOP: Loop

Applicable processors: 8086/8088, 80286, 80386, 80486

Category: Control transfer instructions

Flags affected: None

Coding example:

```
LOOP      PRINT_LOOP
```

Description: Based on the contents of CX, program execution branches to the address of the destination operand. If CX does not equal 0, CX changes in decrements of 1, and the branch occurs. If CX is 0, no decrements or branching occurs, and execution proceeds to the next instruction.

LOOPE: Loop While Equal

Applicable processors: 8086/8088, 80286, 80386, 80486

Category: Control transfer instructions

Flags affected: None

Coding example:

```
LOOPE     TEST_LOOP
```

Description: Based on the contents of CX and the zero flag, program execution branches to the address of the destination operand. If CX does not equal 0 and the zero flag is set, CX changes in decrements of 1, and the branch occurs. If CX is 0 or the zero flag is clear, no decrements or branching occurs, and execution proceeds to the next instruction. This instruction is functionally equivalent to LOOPZ.

LOOPNE: Loop While Not Equal

Applicable processors: 8086/8088, 80286, 80386, 80486

Category: Control transfer instructions

Flags affected: None

Coding example:

```
LOOPNE TEST_LOOP
```

Description: Based on the contents of CX and the zero flag, program execution branches to the address of the destination operand. If CX does not equal 0 and the zero flag is clear, CX changes in decrements of 1, and the branch occurs. If CX is 0 or the zero flag is set, no decrements or branching occurs, and execution proceeds to the next instruction. This instruction is functionally equivalent to LOOPNZ.

LOOPNZ: Loop While Not Zero

Applicable processors: 8086/8088, 80286, 80386, 80486

Category: Control transfer instructions

Flags affected: None

Coding example:

```
LOOPNZ TEST_LOOP
```

Description: Based on the contents of CX and the zero flag, program execution branches to the address of the destination operand. If CX does not equal 0 and the zero flag is clear, CX changes in decrements of 1, and the branch occurs. If CX is 0 or the zero flag is set, no decrements or branching occurs, and execution proceeds to the next instruction. This instruction is functionally equivalent to LOOPNE.

LOOPZ: Loop While Zero

Applicable processors: 8086/8088, 80286, 80386, 80486

Category: Control transfer instructions

Flags affected: None

Coding example:

```
LOOPZ  TEST_LOOP
```

Description: Based on the contents of CX and the zero flag, program execution branches to the address of the destination operand. If CX does not equal 0 and the zero flag is set, CX changes in decrements of 1, and the branch occurs. If CX is 0 or the zero flag is clear, no decrements or branching occurs, and execution proceeds to the next instruction. This instruction is functionally equivalent to LOOPE.

LSL: Load Segment Limit

Applicable processors: 80286, 80386, 80486

Category: Data transfer instructions

Flags affected: ZF

Coding example:

```
LSL     AX,SELECTOR
```

Description: Based on the selector specified in the source operand, LSL loads the descriptor's limit field into the target operand (register). The descriptor denoted by the selector must be visible. If the loading is successful, the zero flag is set; otherwise, it is cleared.

LSS: Load SS Register

Applicable processors: 80386, 80486

Category: Data transfer instructions

Flags affected: None

Coding example:

```
LSS     DI,DEST_BUFFER
```

Description: LSS performs two distinct operations: it loads SS with the segment address of the source operand and then loads the destination operand with the offset address of the source operand.

LTR: Load Task Register

Applicable processors: 80286, 80386, 80486

Category: Data transfer instructions

Flags affected: None

Coding examples:

```
LTR     DX
LTR     TEMP[BX]
```

Description: LTR loads the task register from the value of the source operand. This instruction is for use in operating system software only and is not used in applications software.

MOV: Move

Applicable processors: 8086/8088, 80286, 80386, 80486

Category: Data transfer instructions

Flags affected: None

Coding examples:

```
MOV     AX,BX           ;AX=BX
MOV     EAX,TEMP        ;EAX=TEMP (doubleword)
MOV     SUM,BX          ;SUM=BX (SUM is a word)
MOV     CL,57           ;CL=57
MOV     DECIMAL,10      ;DECIMAL=10
MOV     AX,TEMP[BX]     ;Indirect address example
```

Description: MOV copies the contents of the source operand to the destination operand. When the source operand is not an immediate value, both operands must agree in length. If the source or destination operand is a doubleword register, the other register can be a special register, such as CR0, CR2, CR3, DR0, DR1, DR2, DR3, DR6, DR7, TR6, or TR7.

MOVSB: Move String, Byte-by-Byte

Applicable processors: 8086/8088, 80286, 80386, 80486

Category: String manipulation instructions

Flags affected: None

Coding examples:

```
MOVSB
REP MOVSB       ;Repeat a move loop
```

Description: MOVSB moves strings, byte-by-byte. The values of SI and DI change in increments or decrements of 1, depending on the setting of the direction flag. Usually, this instruction is used with the REP instruction to repeat the move for a maximum of CX bytes. Intel lists this command as MOVS; however, the Microsoft Macro Assembler makes the byte/word distinctions.

MOVSD: Move String, Doubleword-by-Doubleword

Applicable processors: 80386, 80486

Category: String manipulation instructions

Flags affected: None

Coding examples:

```
MOVSD
REP MOVSD     ;Repeat a move loop
```

Description: MOVSD moves strings, doubleword-by-doubleword. The values of ESI and EDI change in increments or decrements of four, depending on the setting of the direction flag. Usually, this instruction is used with the REP instruction to repeat the move for a maximum of ECX words.

MOVSW: Move String, Word-by-Word

Applicable processors: 8086/8088, 80286, 80386, 80486

Category: String manipulation instructions

Flags affected: None

Coding examples:

```
MOVSW
REP MOVSW     ;Repeat a move loop
```

Description: MOVSW moves strings, word-by-word. The values of SI and DI change in increments or decrements of two, depending on the setting of the direction flag. Usually, this instruction is used with the REP instruction to repeat the move for a maximum number of CX words. Intel lists this command as MOVS; however, the Microsoft Macro Assembler makes the byte/word distinctions.

MOVSX: Move with Sign Extended

Applicable processors: 80386, 80486

Category: Data transfer instructions

Flags affected: None

Coding examples:

```
MOVSX    EAX,BX     ;EAX=BX
MOVSX    EAX,TEMP   ;EAX=TEMP (TEMP is a word)
MOVSX    CX,AL      ;CX=AL
```

Description: MOVSX moves the source operand to the destination operand and extends the high-order bit to the balance of the bits in the destination operand. The source operand must be smaller than the destination operand.

MOVZX: Move with Zero Extended

Applicable processors: 80386, 80486

Category: Data transfer instructions

Flags affected: None

Coding examples:

```
MOVZX    EAX,BX     ;EAX=BX
MOVZX    EAX,TEMP   ;EAX=TEMP (TEMP is a word)
MOVZX    CX,AL      ;CX=AL
```

Description: MOVZX moves the source operand to the destination operand and clears the remaining bits in the destination operand. The source operand must be smaller than the destination operand.

MUL: Multiply

Applicable processors: 8086/8088, 80286, 80386, 80486

Category: Arithmetic instructions

Flags affected: AF (undefined), CF, OF, PF (undefined), SF (undefined), ZF (undefined)

Coding examples:

```
MUL      BX              ;DX:AX=AX*BX
MUL      ECX             ;EDX:EAX=EAX*ECX
MUL      WORD_TEMP       ;DX:AX=AX*WORD_TEMP
MUL      BYTE_SUM        ;AX=AL*BYTE_SUM
MUL      WORD_TBL[BX]    ;Indirect address example
```

Description: If the operand is a byte value, MUL multiplies the contents of AL by the contents of the operand and stores the result in AX. If the operand is a word value, MUL multiplies the contents of AX by the contents of the operand and stores the result in DX:AX. If the operand is a doubleword value, MUL multiplies the contents of EAX by the contents of the operand and stores the result in EDX:EAX. This instruction treats numbers as unsigned binary values.

NEG: Negate

Applicable processors: 8086/8088, 80286, 80386, 80486

Category: Arithmetic instructions

Flags affected: AF, CF, OF, PF, SF, ZF

Coding examples:

```
NEG     TEMP
NEG     CL
NEG     EAX
```

Description: NEG calculates the two's complement of the destination operand and stores the result in the destination operand. This calculation is effectively the same as subtracting the destination operand from zero.

NOP: No Operation

Applicable processors: 8086/8088, 80286, 80386, 80486

Category: Flag and processor control instructions

Flags affected: None

Coding example:

```
NOP
```

Description: NOP simply takes space and time. It causes the CPU to do nothing. The instruction is primarily used when patching executable files to block out instructions already in place.

NOT: Logical NOT

Applicable processors: 8086/8088, 80286, 80386, 80486

Category: Bit manipulation instructions

Flags affected: None

Coding examples:

```
NOT     CL
NOT     BYTE_SUM        ;Use byte value
NOT     WORD_SUM        ;Use word value
NOT     DWORD_SUM       ;Use doubleword value
NOT     AX
NOT     EBX
```

Description: NOT inverts the bits in the destination operand (0 becomes 1, and 1 becomes 0) and stores the inverted bits in the destination operand.

OR: Logical OR

Applicable processors: 8086/8088, 80286, 80386, 80486

Category: Bit manipulation instructions

Flags affected: AF (undefined), CF, OF, PF, SF, ZF

Coding examples:

```
OR      AL,BL
OR      AL,10000000b
OR      EAX,0FFFFh
OR      DX,TEMP
OR      AX,CX
```

Description: OR performs a logical OR of the operands and stores the result in the destination operand. Each bit of the resultant byte or word is set to 1 if either or both of the corresponding bits of each operand are set to 1.

OUT: Output to Port

Applicable processors: 8086/8088, 80286, 80386, 80486

Category: Data transfer instructions

Flags affected: None

Coding examples:

```
OUT     64h,AL
OUT     DX,AX
OUT     DX,EAX
```

Description: OUT sends a byte (AL), word (AX), or doubleword (EAX) to the specified hardware I/O port address. A port number lower than 256 may be specified as a constant or as a variable in the DX register. A port number higher than 255, however, *must* be specified in the DX register.

OUTS: Output String to Port

Applicable processors: 80286, 80386, 80486

Category: Data transfer instructions

Flags affected: None

Coding examples:

```
OUTS    DX,CX    ;Output word
OUTS    DX,BL    ;Output byte
```

Description: OUTS sends a byte or a word (length is specified by the size of the source operand) to the hardware I/O port address specified in DX. The port number can range from 0 to 65,535.

OUTSB: Output String Byte to Port

Applicable processors: 80286, 80386, 80486

Category: Data transfer instructions

Flags affected: None

Coding example:

```
OUTSB
```

Description: OUTSB sends a byte from the address specified by DS:[SI] to the hardware I/O port address specified in DX. The port number can range from 0 to 65,535. After the transfer, DI changes in an increment or decrement of 1, depending on the setting of the direction flag.

OUTSD: Output String Doubleword to Port

Applicable processors: 80386, 80486

Category: Data transfer instructions

Flags affected: None

Coding example:

```
OUTSD
```

Description: OUTSD sends a word from the address specified by DS:[ESI] to the hardware I/O port address specified in DX. After the transfer, DI changes in increments or decrements of four, depending on the setting of the direction flag.

OUTSW: Output String Word to Port

Applicable processors: 80286, 80386, 80486

Category: Data transfer instructions

Flags affected: None

Coding example:

```
OUTSW
```

Description: OUTSW sends a word from the address specified by DS:[SI] to the hardware I/O port address specified in DX. The port number can range from 0 to 65,535. After the transfer, DI changes in increments or decrements of two, depending on the setting of the direction flag.

POP: Remove Data from Stack

Applicable processors: 8086/8088, 80286, 80386, 80486

Category: Data transfer instructions

Flags affected: None

Coding examples:

```
POP        AX
POP        DS
POP        GS
POP        HOLD_REG
```

Description: POP removes a word or a doubleword (depending on the size of the operand) from the stack and places that word or doubleword in the desired destination operand.

POPA: POP All General Registers

Applicable processors: 80286, 80386, 80486

Category: Data transfer instructions

Flags affected: None

Coding example:

```
POPA
```

Description: POPA removes the general-purpose registers and loads them from the stack in this order: DI, SI, BP, SP, BX, DX, CX, AX. The SP register is discarded when it is popped.

POPAD: POP All General Doubleword Registers

Applicable processors: 80386, 80486

Category: Data transfer instructions

Flags affected: None

Coding example:

```
POPAD
```

Description: POPAD removes and loads the general-purpose registers from the stack in this order: EDI, ESI, EBP, ESP, EBX, EDX, ECX, EAX. The ESP register is discarded when it is popped.

POPF: Remove Flags from Stack

Applicable processors: 8086/8088, 80286, 80386, 80486

Category: Data transfer instructions

Flags affected: AC, AF, CF, DF, IF, IOPL, NT, OF, PF, SF, TF, ZF

Coding example:

```
POPF
```

Description: POPF removes a word from the stack and places the word in the flags register.

POPFD: Remove Extended Flags from Stack

Applicable processors: 80386, 80486

Category: Data transfer instructions

Flags affected: AF, CF, DF, IF, IOPL, NT, OF, PF, SF, TF, ZF

Coding example:

```
POPFD
```

Description: POPFD removes a doubleword from the stack and places that doubleword in the extended flags register.

PUSH: Place Data on Stack

Applicable processors: 8086/8088, 80286, 80386, 80486

Category: Data transfer instructions

Flags affected: None

Coding examples:

```
PUSH    AX
PUSH    EBX
```

```
PUSH    DS
PUSH    HOLD_REG
PUSH    50h                    ;WILL NOT WORK ON 8086/8088
```

Description: PUSH places a copy of the operand's value on the stack. For the 8086/8088, only the values of registers (byte or word) can be pushed. For all other microprocessors, immediate values can also be pushed.

PUSHA: Push All General Registers

Applicable processors: 80286, 80386, 80486

Category: Data transfer instructions

Flags affected: None

Coding example:

```
PUSHA
```

Description: The general-purpose registers are pushed on the stack in this order: AX, CX, DX, BX, SP, BP, SI, DI. The SP value that is pushed is the value existing before this instruction is executed.

PUSHAD: Push All General Doubleword Registers

Applicable processors: 80386, 80486

Category: Data transfer instructions

Flags affected: None

Coding example:

```
PUSHAD
```

Description: PUSHAD pushes the general-purpose doubleword registers on the stack in this order: EAX, ECX, EDX, EBX, ESP, EBP, ESI, EDI. The ESP value pushed is the value existing before this instruction is executed.

PUSHF: Place Flags on Stack

Applicable processors: 8086/8088, 80286, 80386, 80486

Category: Data transfer instructions

Flags affected: None

Coding example:

```
PUSHF
```

Description: PUSHF places a copy of the flags register on the stack.

PUSHFD: Place Extended Flags on Stack

Applicable processors: 80386, 80486

Category: Data transfer instructions

Flags affected: None

Coding example:

```
PUSHFD
```

Description: PUSHFD places a copy of the extended flags register on the stack.

RCL: Rotate Left through Carry

Applicable processors: 8086/8088, 80286, 80386, 80486

Category: Bit manipulation instructions

Flags affected: CF, OF

Coding examples:

```
RCL      AX,1
RCL      BL,3
RCL      EDX,16
RCL      TEMP,CL
```

Description: RCL rotates all bits in the destination operand to the left by the number of places specified in the source operand. The rotation is performed through the carry flag in an order that rotates the most significant bit of the destination operand to the carry flag and rotates the carry flag to the least significant bit of the destination operand.

RCR: Rotate Right through Carry

Applicable processors: 8086/8088, 80286, 80386, 80486

Category: Bit manipulation instructions

Flags affected: CF, OF

Coding examples:

```
RCR      AX,1
RCR      BL,3
RCR      EDX,16
RCR      TEMP,CL
```

Description: RCR rotates all bits in the destination operand to the right by the number of places specified in the source operand. The rotation is performed through the carry flag in an order that rotates the least significant bit of the destination operand to the carry flag and rotates the carry flag to the most significant bit of the destination operand.

REP: Repeat

Applicable processors: 8086/8088, 80286, 80386, 80486

Category: String manipulation instructions

Flags affected: None

Coding example:

```
REP MOVSB
```

Description: REP causes string-manipulation instructions to be repeated the number of iterations specified in CX (if working with byte or word operands) or ECX (if working with doubleword operands).

REPE: Repeat if Equal

Applicable processors: 8086/8088, 80286, 80386, 80486

Category: String manipulation instructions

Flags affected: None

Coding example:

```
REPE CMPSW
```

Description: REPE causes string-manipulation instructions to be repeated the number of iterations specified in CX (if working with byte or word operands) or ECX (if working with doubleword operands). When used with CMPSB, CMPSW, SCASB, or SCASW, this instruction repeats only while the zero flag is set. REPE is functionally equivalent to REPZ.

REPNE: Repeat if Not Equal

Applicable processors: 8086/8088, 80286, 80386, 80486

Category: String manipulation instructions

Flags affected: None

Coding example:

```
REPNE CMPSW
```

Description: REPNE causes string-manipulation instructions to be repeated the number of iterations specified in CX (if working with byte or word operands) or ECX (if working with doubleword operands). When used with CMPSB, CMPSW, SCASB, or SCASW, this instruction repeats only while the zero flag is clear. This instruction is functionally equivalent to REPNZ.

REPNZ: Repeat if Not Zero

Applicable processors: 8086/8088, 80286, 80386, 80486

Category: String manipulation instructions

Flags affected: None

Coding example:

```
REPNZ CMPSW
```

Description: REPNZ causes string-manipulation instructions to be repeated the number of iterations specified in CX (if working with byte or word operands) or ECX (if working with doubleword operands). When used with CMPSB, CMPSW, SCASB, or SCASW, this instruction repeats only while the zero flag is clear. REPNZ is functionally equivalent to REPNE.

REPZ: Repeat if Zero

Applicable processors: 8086/8088, 80286, 80386, 80486

Category: String manipulation instructions

Flags affected: None

Coding example:

```
REPZ CMPSW
```

Description: REPZ causes string-manipulation instructions to be repeated the number of iterations specified in CX (if working with byte or word operands) or ECX (if working with doubleword operands). When used with CMPSB, CMPSW, SCASB, or SCASW, this instruction repeats only while the zero flag is set. REPZ is functionally equivalent to REPE.

RET: Return from Subroutine

Applicable processors: 8086/8088, 80286, 80386, 80486

Category: Control transfer instructions

Flags affected: None

Coding examples:

```
RET
RET       2
```

Description: By popping IP from the stack, RET transfers program control back to the point where a CALL was issued. If the CALL was to a FAR procedure, both CS:IP are popped from the stack.

If the RET has a specified return value (two, in the coding example), the stack is adjusted by that number of bytes. The coding example shows that a word is discarded from the stack after either IP or CS:IP is popped.

ROL: Rotate Left

Applicable processors: 8086/8088, 80286, 80386, 80486

Category: Bit manipulation instructions

Flags affected: CF, OF

Coding examples:

```
ROL       AX,1
ROL       BL,3
ROL       DX,16
ROL       TEMP,CL
```

Description: ROL rotates all bits in the destination operand to the left by the number of places specified in the source operand.

ROR: Rotate Right

Applicable processors: 8086/8088, 80286, 80386, 80486

Category: Bit manipulation instructions

Flags affected: CF, OF

Coding examples:

```
ROR       AX,1
ROR       BL,3
ROR       DX,16
ROR       TEMP,CL
```

Description: ROR rotates all bits in the destination operand to the right by the number of places specified in the source operand.

SAHF: Store AH into Flags Register

Applicable processors: 8086/8088, 80286, 80386, 80486

Category: Data transfer instructions

Flags affected: AF, CF, PF, SF, ZF

Coding example:

```
SAHF
```

Description: SAHF copies the contents of AH to the low-order byte of the flags register. After execution of this instruction, SF, ZF, AF, PF, and CF are equal to bits 7, 6, 4, 2, and 1 of AH, respectively.

SAL: Arithmetic Shift Left

Applicable processors: 8086/8088, 80286, 80386, 80486

Category: Bit manipulation instructions

Flags affected: AF (undefined for all processors through 80286, not affected beginning with 80386), CF, OF, PF, SF, ZF

Coding examples:

```
SAL      AX,1
SAL      BL,3
SAL      DX,16
SAL      TEMP,CL
```

Description: SAL shifts all bits in the destination operand to the left by the number of places specified in the source operand. High-order bits are lost, and low-order bits are cleared.

SAR: Arithmetic Shift Right

Applicable processors: 8086/8088, 80286, 80386, 80486

Category: Bit manipulation instructions

Flags affected: AF (undefined for all processors through 80286, not affected beginning with 80386), CF, OF, PF, SF, ZF

Coding examples:

```
SAR      AX,1
SAR      BL,3
SAR      DX,16
SAR      TEMP,CL
```

Description: SAR shifts all bits in the destination operand to the right by the number of places specified in the source operand. Low-order bits are lost, and high-order bits are set equal to the existing high-order bit.

SBB: Subtract with Carry

Applicable processors: 8086/8088, 80286, 80386, 80486

Category: Arithmetic instructions

Flags affected: AF, CF, OF, PF, SF, ZF

Coding examples:

```
SBB      AX,BX         ;AX=AX-BX-CF
SBB      AX,TEMP       ;AX=AX-TEMP-CF
SBB      SUM,EBX       ;SUM=SUM-EBX-CF
SBB      CL,10         ;CL=CL-10-CF
SBB      AX,TEMP[BX]   ;Indirect address example
```

Description: SBB subtracts the contents of the source operand from (and stores the result in) the destination operand. If the carry flag is set, the result changes in a decrement of 1. In this instruction, the values being added are assumed to be binary.

SCASB: Scan String for Byte

Applicable processors: 8086/8088, 80286, 80386, 80486

Category: String manipulation instructions

Flags affected: AF, CF, OF, PF, SF, ZF

Coding examples:

```
SCASB
REPNZ SCASB      ;Repeat a scan loop
```

Description: SCASB subtracts the destination operand string byte (pointed to by DI) from the value of AL. The result is not stored, but the flags are updated. Then, the value of DI changes in increments or decrements of 1, depending on the setting of the direction flag. Usually, this instruction is used with the REPE, REPNE, REPNZ, or REPZ instructions to repeat the scan for a maximum of CX bytes, or until SCASB finds a match or difference. Intel lists this command as SCAS; however, the Microsoft Macro Assembler makes the byte/word distinctions.

SCASD: Scan String for Doubleword

Applicable processors: 80386, 80486

Category: String manipulation instructions

Flags affected: AF, CF, OF, PF, SF, ZF

Coding examples:

```
SCASD
REPNZ SCASD    ;Repeat a scan loop
```

Description: SCASD subtracts the destination operand string word (pointed to by EDI) from the value of EAX. The result is not stored, but the flags are updated. Then the value of EDI changes in increments or decrements of four, depending on the setting of the direction flag. Usually, this instruction is used with the REPE, REPNE, REPNZ, or REPZ instructions to repeat the scan for a maximum of CX bytes or until a match or difference is found.

SCASW: Scan String for Word

Applicable processors: 8086/8088, 80286, 80386, 80486

Category: String manipulation instructions

Flags affected: AF, CF, OF, PF, SF, ZF

Coding examples:

```
SCASW
REPNZ SCASW    ;Repeat a scan loop
```

Description: SCASW subtracts the destination operand string word (pointed to by DI) from the value of AX. The result is not stored, but the flags are updated. Then, the value of DI changes in increments or decrements of two, depending on the setting of the direction flag. Usually, this instruction is used with the REPE, REPNE, REPNZ, or REPZ instructions to repeat the scan for a maximum of CX bytes, or until SCASW finds a match or difference. Intel lists this command as SCAS; however, the Microsoft Macro Assembler makes the byte/word distinctions.

SETA: Set Byte if Above

Applicable processors: 80386, 80486

Category: Data transfer instructions

Flags affected: None

Coding example:

```
SETA    CL
```

Description: SETA stores a one in the operand if the carry and zero flags both are clear. If this condition is not met, a zero is stored in the operand. The operand must be a byte-length register or memory location. This instruction is functionally the same as SETNBE.

SETAE: Set Byte if Above or Equal

Applicable processors: 80386, 80486

Category: Data transfer instructions

Flags affected: None

Coding example:

```
SETAE   CL
```

Description: SETAE stores a one in the operand if the carry flag is clear. If this condition is not met, a zero is stored in the operand. The operand must be a byte-length register or memory location. This instruction is functionally the same as SETNB or SETNC.

SETB: Set Byte if Below

Applicable processors: 80386, 80486

Category: Data transfer instructions

Flags affected: None

Coding example:

```
SETB    CL
```

Description: SETB stores a one in the operand if the carry flag is set. If this condition is not met, a zero is stored in the operand. The operand must be a byte-length register or memory location. This instruction is functionally the same as SETC or SETNAE.

SETBE: Set Byte if Below or Equal

Applicable processors: 80386, 80486

Category: Data transfer instructions

Flags affected: None

Coding example:

```
SETBE   CL
```

Description: SETBE stores a one in the operand if either the carry or zero flag is set. If this condition is not met, a zero is stored in the operand. The operand must be a byte-length register or memory location. This instruction is functionally the same as SETNA.

SETC: Set Byte on Carry

Applicable processors: 80386, 80486

Category: Data transfer instructions

Flags affected: None

Coding example:

```
SETC   CL
```

Description: SETC stores a one in the operand if the carry flag is set. If this condition is not met, a zero is stored in the operand. The operand must be a byte-length register or memory location. This instruction is functionally the same as SETB or SETNAE.

SETE: Set Byte if Equal

Applicable processors: 80386, 80486

Category: Data transfer instructions

Flags affected: None

Coding example:

```
SETE   CL
```

Description: SETE stores a one in the operand if the zero flag is set. If this condition is not met, a zero is stored in the operand. The operand must be a byte-length register or memory location. This instruction is functionally the same as SETZ.

SETG: Set Byte if Greater

Applicable processors: 80386, 80486

Category: Data transfer instructions

Flags affected: None

Coding example:

```
SETG   CL
```

Description: SETG stores a one in the operand if the sign flag equals the overflow flag or if the zero flag is clear. If neither condition is met, a zero is stored in the operand. The operand must be a byte-length register or memory location. This instruction is functionally the same as SETNLE.

SETGE: Set Byte if Greater or Equal

Applicable processors: 80386, 80486

Category: Data transfer instructions

Flags affected: None

Coding example:

```
SETGE   CL
```

Description: SETGE stores a one in the operand if the sign flag equals the overflow flag. If this condition is not met, a zero is stored in the operand. The operand must be a byte-length register or memory location. This instruction is functionally the same as SETNL.

SETL: Set Byte if Less

Applicable processors: 80386, 80486

Category: Data transfer instructions

Flags affected: None

Coding example:

```
SETL   CL
```

Description: SETL stores a one in the operand if the sign flag does not equal the overflow flag. If this condition is not met, a zero is stored in the operand. The operand must be a byte-length register or memory location. This instruction is functionally the same as SETNGE.

SETLE: Set Byte if Less or Equal

Applicable processors: 80386, 80486

Category: Data transfer instructions

Flags affected: None

Coding example:

```
SETLE  CL
```

Description: SETLE stores a one in the operand if the sign flag does not equal the overflow flag or if the zero flag is set. If neither condition is met, a zero is stored in the operand. The operand must be a byte-length register or memory location. This instruction is functionally the same as SETNG.

SETNA: Set Byte if Not Above

Applicable processors: 80386, 80486

Category: Data transfer instructions

Flags affected: None

Coding example:

```
SETNA  CL
```

Description: SETNA stores a one in the operand if either the carry or zero flag is set. If neither condition is met, a zero is stored in the operand. The operand must be a byte-length register or memory location. This instruction is functionally the same as SETBE.

SETNAE: Set Byte if Not Above or Equal

Applicable processors: 80386, 80486

Category: Data transfer instructions

Flags affected: None

Coding example:

```
SETNAE CL
```

Description: SETNAE stores a one in the operand if the carry flag is set. If this condition is not met, a zero is stored in the operand. The operand must be a byte-length register or memory location. This instruction is functionally the same as SETB or SETC.

SETNB: Set Byte if Not Below

Applicable processors: 80386, 80486

Category: Data transfer instructions

Flags affected: None

Coding example:

```
SETNB  CL
```

Description: SETNB stores a one in the operand if the carry flag is clear. If this condition is not met, a zero is stored in the operand. The operand must be a byte-length register or memory location. This instruction is functionally the same as SETAE or SETNC.

SETNBE: Set Byte if Not Below or Equal

Applicable processors: 80386, 80486

Category: Data transfer instructions

Flags affected: None

Coding example:

```
SETNBE CL
```

Description: SETNBE stores a one in the operand if both the carry and zero flags are clear. If this condition is not met, a zero is stored in the operand. The operand must be a byte-length register or memory location. This instruction is functionally the same as SETA.

SETNC: Set Byte on No Carry

Applicable processors: 80386, 80486

Category: Data transfer instructions

Flags affected: None

Coding example:

```
SETNC  CL
```

Description: SETNC stores a one in the operand if the carry flag is clear. If this condition is not met, a zero is stored in the operand. The operand must be a byte-length register or memory location. This instruction is functionally the same as SETAE or SETNB.

SETNE: Set Byte if Not Equal

Applicable processors: 80386, 80486

Category: Data transfer instructions

Flags affected: None

Coding example:

```
SETNE  CL
```

Description: SETNE stores a one in the operand if the zero flag is clear. If this condition is not met, a zero is stored in the operand. The operand must be a byte-length register or memory location. This instruction is functionally the same as SETNZ.

SETNG: Set Byte if Not Greater

Applicable processors: 80386, 80486

Category: Data transfer instructions

Flags affected: None

Coding example:

```
SETNG  CL
```

Description: SETNG stores a one in the operand if the sign flag does not equal the overflow flag or the zero flag is set. If neither condition is met, a zero is stored in the operand. The operand must be a byte-length register or memory location. This instruction is functionally the same as SETLE.

SETNGE: Set Byte if Not Greater or Equal

Applicable processors: 80386, 80486

Category: Data transfer instructions

Flags affected: None

Coding example:

```
SETNGE CL
```

Description: SETNGE stores a one in the operand if the sign flag does not equal the overflow flag. If this condition is not met, a zero is stored in the operand. The operand must be a byte-length register or memory location. This instruction is functionally the same as SETL.

SETNL: Set Byte if Not Less

Applicable processors: 80386, 80486

Category: Data transfer instructions

Flags affected: None

Coding example:

```
SETNL  CL
```

Description: SETNL stores a one in the operand if the sign flag equals the overflow flag. If this condition is not met, a zero is stored in the operand. The operand must be a byte-length register or memory location. This instruction is functionally the same as SETGE.

SETNLE: Set Byte if Not Less or Equal

Applicable processors: 80386, 80486

Category: Data transfer instructions

Flags affected: None

Coding example:

```
SETNLE CL
```

Description: SETNLE stores a one in the operand if the sign flag equals the overflow flag or the zero flag is clear. If neither condition is met, a zero is stored in the operand. The operand must be a byte-length register or memory location. This instruction is functionally the same as SETG.

SETNO: Set Byte on No Overflow

Applicable processors: 80386, 80486

Category: Data transfer instructions

Flags affected: None

Coding example:

```
SETNO  CL
```

Description: SETNO stores a one in the operand if the overflow flag is clear. If this condition is not met, a zero is stored in the operand. The operand must be a byte-length register or memory location.

SETNP: Set Byte on No Parity

Applicable processors: 80386, 80486

Category: Data transfer instructions

Flags affected: None

Coding example:

```
SETNP  CL
```

Description: SETNP stores a one in the operand if the parity flag is clear. If this condition is not met, a zero is stored in the operand. The operand must be a byte-length register or memory location. This instruction is functionally the same as SETPO.

SETNS: Set Byte on Not Sign

Applicable processors: 80386, 80486

Category: Data transfer instructions

Flags affected: None

Coding example:

```
SETNS  CL
```

Description: SETNS stores a one in the operand if the sign flag is clear. If this condition is not met, a zero is stored in the operand. The operand must be a byte-length register or memory location.

SETNZ: Set Byte if Not Zero

Applicable processors: 80386, 80486

Category: Data transfer instructions

Flags affected: None

Coding example:

```
SETNZ  CL
```

Description: SETNZ stores a one in the operand if the zero flag is clear. If this condition is not met, a zero is stored in the operand. The operand must be a byte-length register or memory location. This instruction is functionally the same as SETNE.

SETO: Set Byte on Overflow

Applicable processors: 80386, 80486

Category: Data transfer instructions

Flags affected: None

Coding example:

```
SETO    CL
```

Description: SETO stores a one in the operand if the overflow flag is set. If this condition is not met, a zero is stored in the operand. The operand must be a byte-length register or memory location.

SETP: Set Byte on Parity

Applicable processors: 80386, 80486

Category: Data transfer instructions

Flags affected: None

Coding example:

```
SETP    CL
```

Description: SETP stores a one in the operand if the parity flag is set. If this condition is not met, a zero is stored in the operand. The operand must be a byte-length register or memory location. This instruction is functionally the same as SETPE.

SETPE: Set Byte on Parity Even

Applicable processors: 80386, 80486

Category: Data transfer instructions

Flags affected: None

Coding example:

```
SETPE   CL
```

Description: SETPE stores a one in the operand if the parity flag is set. If this condition is not met, a zero is stored in the operand. The operand must be a byte-length register or memory location. This instruction is functionally the same as SETP.

SETPO: Set Byte on Parity Odd

Applicable processors: 80386, 80486

Category: Data transfer instructions

Flags affected: None

Coding example:

```
SETPO    CL
```

Description: SETPO stores a one in the operand if the parity flag is clear. If this condition is not met, a zero is stored in the operand. The operand must be a byte-length register or memory location. This instruction is functionally the same as SETNP.

SETS: Set Byte on Sign

Applicable processors: 80386, 80486

Category: Data transfer instructions

Flags affected: None

Coding example:

```
SETS     CL
```

Description: SETS stores a one in the operand if the sign flag is set. If this condition is not met, a zero is stored in the operand. The operand must be a byte-length register or memory location.

SETZ: Set Byte if Zero

Applicable processors: 80386, 80486

Category: Data transfer instructions

Flags affected: None

Coding example:

```
SETZ     CL
```

Description: SETZ stores a one in the operand if the zero flag is set. If this condition is not met, a zero is stored in the operand. The operand must be a byte-length register or memory location. This instruction is functionally the same as SETE.

SGDT: Store GDT Register

Applicable processors: 80286, 80386, 80486

Category: Data transfer instructions

Flags affected: None

Coding example:

```
SGDT    TEMP[BX]
```

Description: SGDT transfers the six bytes of the global descriptor table to the memory address specified in the operand. This instruction is used in protected-mode operating system software but not in applications software.

SHL: Shift Left

Applicable processors: 8086/8088, 80286, 80386, 80486

Category: Bit manipulation instructions

Flags affected: AF (undefined for all processors through 80286, not affected beginning with 80386), CF, OF, PF, SF, ZF

Coding examples:

```
SHL     AX,1
SHL     BL,3
SHL     DX,16
SHL     TEMP,CL
```

Description: SHL shifts all bits in the destination operand to the left by the number of places specified in the source operand. High-order bits are lost, and low-order bits are cleared.

SHLD: Shift Left, Double Precision

Applicable processors: 80386, 80486

Category: Bit manipulation instructions

Flags affected: AF (undefined), CF, OF (undefined), PF, SF, ZF

Coding examples:

```
SHLD    AX,BX,4
SHLD    DWORD_TEMP,EAX,16
```

Description: SHLD shifts all bits in the first operand to the left by the number of places specified in the third operand. High-order bits are lost, and low-order bits are copied from the second operand, starting with the second operand's low-order bit. The result is stored in the first operand.

SHR: Shift Right

Applicable processors: 8086/8088, 80286, 80386, 80486

Category: Bit manipulation instructions

Flags affected: AF (undefined for all processors through 80286, not affected beginning with 80386), CF, OF, PF, SF, ZF

Coding examples:

```
SHR     AX,1
SHR     BL,3
SHR     DX,16
SHR     TEMP,CL
```

Description: SHR shifts all bits in the destination operand to the right by the number of places specified in the source operand. Low-order bits are lost, and high-order bits are cleared.

SHRD: Shift Right, Double Precision

Applicable processors: 80386, 80486

Category: Bit manipulation instructions

Flags affected: AF (undefined), CF, OF (undefined), PF, SF, ZF

Coding examples:

```
SHRD    AX,BX,4
SHRD    DWORD_TEMP,EAX,16
```

Description: SHRD shifts all bits in the first operand to the right by the number of places specified in the third operand. Low-order bits are lost, and high-order bits are copied from the second operand, starting with the second operand's high-order bit. The result is stored in the first operand.

SIDT: Store Interrupt Descriptor Table Register

Applicable processors: 80286, 80386, 80486

Category: Data transfer instructions

Flags affected: None

Coding example:

```
SIDT    TEMP[BX]
```

Description: SIDT transfers the six bytes of the interrupt descriptor table to the memory address specified in the operand. This instruction is used in protected-mode operating system software but not in applications software.

SLDT: Store Local Descriptor Table Register

Applicable processors: 80286, 80386, 80486

Category: Data transfer instructions

Flags affected: None

Coding examples:

```
SLDT    AX
SLDT    LDT_TEMP
```

Description: SLDT copies the contents of the local descriptor table to the two bytes of the operand. This instruction is used in protected-mode operating system software but not in applications software.

SMSW: Store Machine Status Word

Applicable processors: 80286, 80386, 80486

Category: Data transfer instructions

Flags affected: None

Coding examples:

```
SMSW    AX
SMSW    MSW_TEMP
```

Description: SMSW copies the value of machine status word to the operand. This instruction is used in operating system software only, not in applications software.

STC: Set Carry Flag

Applicable processors: 8086/8088, 80286, 80386, 80486

Category: Flag and processor control instructions

Flags affected: CF

Coding example:

```
STC
```

Description: STC sets the carry flag regardless of the flag's present condition.

STD: Set Direction Flag

Applicable processors: 8086/8088, 80286, 80386, 80486

Category: Flag and processor control instructions

Flags affected: DF

Coding example:

```
STD
```

Description: STD sets the direction flag regardless of the flag's present condition. This setting affects the string instructions.

STI: Set Interrupt Flag

Applicable processors: 8086/8088, 80286, 80386, 80486

Category: Flag and processor control instructions

Flags affected: IF

Coding example:

```
STI
```

Description: STI sets the interrupt flag regardless of the flag's present condition. While this flag is set, the CPU responds to maskable interrupts.

STOSB: Store Byte in AL at String

Applicable processors: 8086/8088, 80286, 80386, 80486

Category: String manipulation instructions

Flags affected: None

Coding example:

```
STOSB
```

Description: STOSB copies the contents of AL to the byte address pointed to by DI. DI then changes in increments or decrements of 1, depending on the setting of the direction flag. Intel lists this command as STOS; however, the Microsoft Macro Assembler makes the byte/word distinctions.

STOSD: Store Doubleword in EAX at String

Applicable processors: 80386, 80486

Category: String manipulation instructions

Flags affected: None

Coding example:

```
STOSD
```

Description: STOSD copies the contents of EAX to the word address pointed to by EDI. DI then changes in increments or decrements of four, depending on the setting of the direction flag.

STOSW: Store Word in AX at String

Applicable processors: 8086/8088, 80286, 80386, 80486

Category: String manipulation instructions

Flags affected: None

Coding example:

```
STOSW
```

Description: STOSW copies the contents of AX to the word address pointed to by DI. DI then changes in increments or decrements of two, depending on the setting of the direction flag. Intel lists this command as STOS; however, the Microsoft Macro Assembler makes the byte/word distinctions.

STR: Store Task Register

Applicable processors: 80286, 80386, 80486

Category: Data transfer instructions

Flags affected: None

Coding examples:

```
STR      AX
STR      MSW_TEMP
```

Description: STR copies the value of the task register to the operand. This instruction is used in operating system software only but is not used in applications software.

SUB: Subtract

Applicable processors: 8086/8088, 80286, 80386, 80486

Category: Arithmetic instructions

Flags affected: AF, CF, OF, PF, SF, ZF

Coding examples:

```
SUB     AX,BX           ;AX=AX-BX
SUB     AX,TEMP         ;AX=AX-TEMP
SUB     SUM,EBX         ;SUM=SUM-EBX
SUB     CL,10           ;CL=CL-10
SUB     AX,TEMP[BX]     ;Indirect address example
```

Description: SUB subtracts the contents of the source operand from (and stores the result in) the destination operand. In this instruction, the values being added are assumed to be binary.

TEST: Test Bits

Applicable processors: 8086/8088, 80286, 80386, 80486

Category: Bit manipulation instructions

Flags affected: AF (undefined for all processors through 80286, not affected beginning with 80386), CF, OF, PF, SF, ZF

Coding examples:

```
TEST    AX,BX           ;
TEST    AX,TEMP         ;TEMP must be a word
TEST    SUM,EBX         ;SUM must be a doubleword
TEST    CL,00001111b    ;
TEST    AX,TEMP[BX]     ;Indirect address example
```

Description: TEST performs a logical AND of the operands, but the result is not stored. Only the flags are affected. Each bit of the resultant byte or word is set to 1 only if the corresponding bit of each operand is set to 1.

VERR: Verify a Segment for Reading

Applicable processors: 80286, 80386, 80486

Category: Flag and processor control instructions

Flags affected: ZF

Coding examples:

```
VERR    TEMP
VERR    AX
```

Description: VERR determines whether the selector specified in the oper-
and is visible at the current privilege level and is readable. The zero flag is
set if the selector is accessible.

VERW: Verify a Segment for Writing

Applicable processors: 80286, 80386, 80486

Category: Flag and processor control instructions

Flags affected: ZF

Coding examples:

```
VERW    TEMP
VERW    AX
```

Description: VERW determines whether the selector specified in the oper-
and is visible at the current privilege level and can be written. The zero
flag is set if the selector is accessible.

WAIT: Wait

Applicable processors: 8086/8088, 80286, 80386, 80486

Category: Flag and processor control instructions

Flags affected: None

Coding example:

```
WAIT
```

Description: WAIT causes the CPU to wait for an external interrupt on the
TEST line before continuing.

WBINVD: Invalidate Cache and Write Back

Applicable processors: 80486

Category: Processor control instructions

Flags affected: None

Coding example:

```
WBINVD
```

Description: This instruction is similar to the INVD instruction. It results in the internal (on-chip) data cache being flushed, but the special-function bus cycles that follow are different. Two of the bus cycles are actually issued; the first is an instruction to external caches to write their information back to main memory, the second instructs the caches to flush their contents (same as INVD).

XADD: Exchange and Add to Memory

Applicable processors: 80486

Category: Data transfer instructions

Flags affected: AF, CF, OF, PF, SF, ZF

Coding example:

```
XADD        EAX,EBX
```

Description: Exchanges the values in the two operands before doing an addition. Functionally equivalent to exchanging and adding with multiple instructions.

XCHG: Exchange

Applicable processors: 8086/8088, 80286, 80386, 80486

Category: Data transfer instructions

Flags affected: None

Coding examples:

```
XCHG        AX,BX               ;Swap AX with BX
XCHG        EAX,DWORD_TEMP      ;Swap EAX with DWORD_TEMP
XCHG        CL,CH               ;Swap CL with CH
XCHG        AX,TEMP             ;Swap AX with TEMP (word)
```

Description: XCHG swaps the contents of the source and destination operands. The length of both operands must agree.

XLAT: Translate

Applicable processors: 8086/8088, 80286, 80386, 80486

Category: Data transfer instructions

Flags affected: None

Coding example:

```
XLAT
```

Description: Assuming that the offset address of a 256-byte translation table is contained in BX, this instruction uses the value in AL as a zero-based offset into the table, and subsequently loads AL with the byte value at that calculated offset. This instruction is helpful for translation tables.

XOR: Logical Exclusive-Or

Applicable processors: 8086/8088, 80286, 80386, 80486

Category: Bit manipulation instructions

Flags affected: AF (undefined), CF, OF, PF, SF, ZF

Coding examples:

```
XOR     AX,BX           ;
XOR     EAX,TEMP        ;TEMP must be a doubleword
XOR     SUM,BX          ;SUM must be a word
XOR     CL,00001111b    ;
XOR     AX,TEMP[BX]     ;Indirect address example
```

Description: XOR performs a logical XOR of the operands and stores the result in the destination operand. Each bit of the resultant byte or word is set to 1 only if the corresponding bit of each operand contains opposite values.

The ASCII Character Set

Hex	Dec	Screen	Ctrl	Key	Hex	Dec	Screen	Ctrl	Key
00h	0		NUL	^@	1Ah	26	→	SUB	^Z
01h	1	☺	SOH	^A	1Bh	27	←	ESC	^[
02h	2	●	STX	^B	1Ch	28	∟	FS	^\
03h	3	♥	ETX	^C	1Dh	29	↔	GS	^]
04h	4	♦	EOT	^D	1Eh	30	▲	RS	^^
05h	5	♣	ENQ	^E	1Fh	31	▼	US	^_
06h	6	♠	ACK	^F	20h	32			
07h	7	●	BEL	^G	21h	33	!		
08h	8	◘	BS	^H	22h	34	"		
09h	9	○	HT	^I	23h	35	#		
0Ah	10	◙	LF	^J	24h	36	$		
0Bh	11	♂	VT	^K	25h	37	%		
0Ch	12	♀	FF	^L	26h	38	&		
0Dh	13	♪	CR	^M	27h	39	'		
0Eh	14	♫	SO	^N	28h	40	(		
0Fh	15	☼	SI	^O	29h	41	)		
10h	16	►	DLE	^P	2Ah	42	*		
11h	17	◄	DC1	^Q	2Bh	43	+		
12h	18	↕	DC2	^R	2Ch	44	,		
13h	19	‼	DC3	^S	2Dh	45	-		
14h	20	¶	DC4	^T	2Eh	46	.		
15h	21	§	NAK	^U	2Fh	47	/		
16h	22	▬	SYN	^V	30h	48	0		
17h	23	↨	ETB	^W	31h	49	1		
18h	24	↑	CAN	^X	32h	50	2		
19h	25	↓	EM	^Y	33h	51	3		

Hex	Dec	Screen	Hex	Dec	Screen	Hex	Dec	Screen
34h	52	4	62h	98	b	90h	144	É
35h	53	5	63h	99	c	91h	145	æ
36h	54	6	64h	100	d	92h	146	Æ
37h	55	7	65h	101	e	93h	147	ô
38h	56	8	66h	102	f	94h	148	ö
39h	57	9	67h	103	g	95h	149	ò
3Ah	58	:	68h	104	h	96h	150	û
3Bh	59	;	69h	105	i	97h	151	ù
3Ch	60	<	6Ah	106	j	98h	152	ÿ
3Dh	61	=	6Bh	107	k	99h	153	Ö
3Eh	62	>	6Ch	108	l	9Ah	154	Ü
3Fh	63	?	6Dh	109	m	9Bh	155	¢
40h	64	@	6Eh	110	n	9Ch	156	£
41h	65	A	6Fh	111	o	9Dh	157	¥
42h	66	B	70h	112	p	9Eh	158	₧
43h	67	C	71h	113	q	9Fh	159	ƒ
44h	68	D	72h	114	r	A0h	160	á
45h	69	E	73h	115	s	A1h	161	í
46h	70	F	74h	116	t	A2h	162	ó
47h	71	G	75h	117	u	A3h	163	ú
48h	72	H	76h	118	v	A4h	164	ñ
49h	73	I	77h	119	w	A5h	165	Ñ
4Ah	74	J	78h	120	x	A6h	166	a
4Bh	75	K	79h	121	y	A7h	167	o
4Ch	76	L	7Ah	122	z	A8h	168	¿
4Dh	77	M	7Bh	123	{	A9h	169	⌐
4Eh	78	N	7Ch	124	|	AAh	170	¬
4Fh	79	O	7Dh	125	}	ABh	171	½
50h	80	P	7Eh	126	~	ACh	172	¼
51h	81	Q	7Fh	127	Δ	ADh	173	¡
52h	82	R	80h	128	Ç	AEh	174	«
53h	83	S	81h	129	ü	AFh	175	»
54h	84	T	82h	130	é	B0h	176	░
55h	85	U	83h	131	â	B1h	177	▒
56h	86	V	84h	132	ä	B2h	178	▓
57h	87	W	85h	133	à	B3h	179	│
58h	88	X	86h	134	å	B4h	180	┤
59h	89	Y	87h	135	ç	B5h	181	╡
5Ah	90	Z	88h	136	ê	B6h	182	╢
5Bh	91	[	89h	137	ë	B7h	183	╖
5Ch	92	\	8Ah	138	è	B8h	184	╕
5Dh	93	]	8Bh	139	ï	B9h	185	╣
5Eh	94	^	8Ch	140	î	BAh	186	║
5Fh	95	_	8Dh	141	ì	BBh	187	╗
60h	96	`	8Eh	142	Ä	BCh	188	╝
61h	97	a	8Fh	143	Å	BDh	189	╜

Hex	Dec	Screen
BEh	190	┙
BFh	191	┐
C0h	192	└
C1h	193	┴
C2h	194	┬
C3h	195	├
C4h	196	─
C5h	197	┼
C6h	198	╞
C7h	199	╟
C8h	200	╚
C9h	201	╔
CAh	202	╩
CBh	203	╦
CCh	204	╠
CDh	205	═
CEh	206	╬
CFh	207	╧
D0h	208	╨
D1h	209	╤
D2h	210	╥
D3h	211	╙

Hex	Dec	Screen
D4h	212	╘
D5h	213	╒
D6h	214	╓
D7h	215	╫
D8h	216	╪
D9h	217	┘
DAh	218	┌
DBh	219	█
DCh	220	▄
DDh	221	▌
DEh	222	▐
DFh	223	▀
E0h	224	α
E1h	225	β
E2h	226	Γ
E3h	227	π
E4h	228	Σ
E5h	229	σ
E6h	230	μ
E7h	231	τ
E8h	232	Φ
E9h	233	θ

Hex	Dec	Screen
EAh	234	Ω
EBh	235	δ
ECh	236	∞
EDh	237	ϕ
EEh	238	$\in$
EFh	239	$\cap$
F0h	240	$\equiv$
F1h	241	$\pm$
F2h	242	$\geq$
F3h	243	$\leq$
F4h	244	$\lceil$
F5h	245	$\rfloor$
F6h	246	$\div$
F7h	247	$\approx$
F8h	248	$\circ$
F9h	249	$\bullet$
FAh	250	$\cdot$
FBh	251	$\sqrt{}$
FCh	252	^{n}
FDh	253	^{2}
FEh	254	■
FFh	255	

B

The Disk Base Table

The disk base table is a set of parameters that controls the operation of a disk drive. Most of these parameters help directly govern the drive controller.

The location of the disk base table can be determined from the vector at interrupt 1Eh. This vector points to the RAM address where the table begins. In the early days of DOS (Version 1.0), the disk base table was contained in ROM. Now, this table is constructed and vectored when you load DOS so that system changes in DOS can be reflected in the disk operation.

Table B.1 details the makeup of the disk base table. The values in this table will differ according to the needs of your particular version of DOS or the disk drives you use in your computer.

Table B.1. *The Disk base table for controlling disk drives*

Byte	Meaning
0	Step rate/head unload time in milliseconds
1	Head load time, DMA mode in milliseconds
2	Motor turn-off delay in clock ticks
3	Bytes/sector code
	0 = 128 bytes/sector
	1 = 256 bytes/sector

Table B.1. continues

Table B.1. *continued*

Byte	Meaning
	2 = 512 bytes/sector
	3 = 1024 bytes/sector
4	Sectors per track
5	Inter-sector gap length for read/write operations
6	Data length (if sector length not specified)
7	Inter-sector gap length for formatting
8	Initial data value for newly formatted sectors
9	Head settle time in milliseconds
10	Motor start-up time in 1/8 second increments

Occasionally, you must change the contents of this table to perform certain BIOS operations, especially if you format 360K floppy disks on an IBM Personal Computer AT or compatible. (For additional information, refer to Chapter 15.)

C

Keyboard Interpretation Tables

This appendix contains two tables that will be useful when you interface to the keyboard, either through BIOS or directly through the hardware port.

BIOS Keyboard Codes

Table C.1 shows the scan code/ASCII value combinations that are returned through the BIOS keyboard services. The keyboard controller does not return the scan codes directly. Instead, BIOS translates (into the codes shown in this table) the codes it gives to the keyboard controller.

Table C.1. *BIOS keyboard codes.*

Scan Code		ASCII Value		
Decimal	Hex	Decimal	Hex	Keystroke
0	00	0	00	Break
1	01	27	1B	Esc
2	02	49	31	1
		33	21	!
3	03	50	32	2
		64	40	@
		0	00	Ctrl-@
4	04	51	33	3
		35	23	#
5	05	52	34	4
		36	24	$
6	06	53	35	5
		37	25	%
7	07	54	36	6
		94	5E	^
		30	1E	Ctrl-^
8	08	55	37	7
		38	26	&
9	09	56	38	8
		42	2A	* (shift-8)
10	0A	57	39	9
		40	28	(
11	0B	48	30	0
		41	29	)
12	0C	45	2D	–
		95	5F	_
		31	1F	Ctrl-_
13	0D	61	3D	=
		43	2B	+
14	0E	8	08	backspace
		127	7F	Ctrl-backspace

Scan Code		ASCII Value		
Decimal	Hex	Decimal	Hex	Keystroke
15	0F	9	09	tab
		0	00	back tab
16	10	113	71	q
		81	51	Q
		0	00	Alt-Q
		17	11	Ctrl-Q
17	11	119	77	w
		87	57	W
		0	00	Alt-W
		23	17	Ctrl-W
18	12	101	65	e
		69	45	E
		0	00	Alt-E
		5	05	Ctrl-E
19	13	114	72	r
		82	52	R
		0	00	Alt-R
		18	12	Ctrl-R
20	14	116	74	t
		84	54	T
		0	00	Alt-T
		20	14	Ctrl-T
21	15	121	79	y
		89	59	Y
		0	00	Alt-Y
		25	19	Ctrl-Y
22	16	117	75	u
		85	55	U
		0	00	Alt-U
		21	15	Ctrl-U
23	17	105	69	i
		73	49	I
		0	00	Alt-I
		9	09	Ctrl-I
24	18	111	6F	o
		79	4F	O

***Table C.1.** continues*

Table C.1. continued

| Scan Code | | ASCII Value | | |
Decimal	Hex	Decimal	Hex	Keystroke
		0	00	Alt-O
		15	0F	Ctrl-O
25	19	112	70	p
		80	50	P
		0	00	Alt-P
		16	10	Ctrl-P
26	1A	91	5B	[
		123	7B	{
		27	1B	Ctrl-[
27	1B	93	5D	]
		125	7D	}
		29	1D	Ctrl-]
28	1C	13	0D	Return
30	1E	97	61	a
		65	41	A
		0	00	Alt-A
		1	01	Ctrl-A
31	1F	115	73	s
		83	53	S
		0	00	Alt-S
		19	13	Ctrl-S
32	20	100	64	d
		68	44	D
		0	00	Alt-D
		4	04	Ctrl-D
33	21	102	66	f
		70	46	F
		0	00	Alt-F
		6	06	Ctrl-F
34	22	103	67	g
		71	47	G
		0	00	Alt-G
		7	47	Ctrl-G
35	23	104	68	h
		72	48	H
		0	00	Alt-H
		8	08	Ctrl-H

| Scan Code | | ASCII Value | | |
Decimal	Hex	Decimal	Hex	Keystroke
36	24	106	6A	j
		74	4A	J
		0	00	Alt-J
		10	0A	Ctrl-J
37	25	107	6B	k
		75	4B	K
		0	00	Alt-K
		11	0B	Ctrl-K
38	26	108	6C	l
		76	4C	L
		0	00	Alt-L
		12	0C	Ctrl-L
39	27	59	3B	;
		58	3A	:
40	28	39	27	'
		34	22	"
41	29	96	60	` (accent grave)
		126	7E	
43	2B	92	5C	\
		124	7C	|
		28	1C	Ctrl-\
44	2C	122	7A	z
		90	5A	Z
		0	00	Alt-Z
		26	1A	Ctrl-Z
45	2D	120	78	x
		88	58	X
		0	00	Alt-X
		24	18	Ctrl-X
46	2E	99	63	c
		67	43	C
		0	00	Alt-C
		3	03	Ctrl-C
47	2F	118	76	v
		86	56	V
		0	00	Alt-V
		22	16	Ctrl-V

Table C.1. *continues*

Table C.1. continued

Scan Code		ASCII Value		
Decimal	Hex	Decimal	Hex	Keystroke
48	30	98	62	b
		66	42	B
		0	00	Alt-B
		2	02	Ctrl-B
49	31	110	6E	n
		78	4E	N
		0	00	Alt-N
		14	0E	Ctrl-N
50	32	109	6D	m
		77	4D	M
	0	00	Alt-M	
	13	0D	Ctrl-M	
51	33	44	2C	,
		60	3C	<
52	34	46	2E	.
		62	3E	>
53	35	47	2F	/
		63	3F	?
55	37	42	2A	* (next to keypad)
		0	00	Alt-Pause
56	38	0	00	Alt-Break
57	39	32	20	space
58	3A	0	00	Caps Lock
59	3B	0	00	F1
60	3C	0	00	F2
61	3D	0	00	F3
62	3E	0	00	F4
63	3F	0	00	F5
64	40	0	00	F6
65	41	0	00	F7
66	42	0	00	F8

| Scan Code | | ASCII Value | | |
Decimal	Hex	Decimal	Hex	Keystroke
67	43	0	00	F9
68	44	0	00	F10
69	45	0	00	Num Lock
70	46	0	00	Scroll Lock
71	47	0	00	Home
		55	37	7 (keypad)
72	48	0	00	up-arrow
		56	38	8 (keypad)
73	49	0	00	PgUp
		57	39	9 (keypad)
74	4A	45	2D	− (next to keypad)
75	4B	0	00	left-arrow
		52	34	4 (keypad)
76	4C	0	00	center key on keypad
		53	35	5 (keypad)
77	4D	0	00	right-arrow
		54	36	6 (keypad)
78	4E	43	2B	+ (next to keypad)
79	4F	0	00	End
		49	31	1 (keypad)
80	50	0	00	down-arrow
		50	32	2 (keypad)
81	51	0	00	PgDn
		51	33	3 (keypad)
82	52	0	00	Ins
		48	30	0 (keypad)
83	53	0	00	Del
		46	2E	. (keypad)
84	54	0	00	shift-F1
85	55	0	00	shift-F2
86	56	0	00	shift-F3

***Table C.1.** continues*

Table C.1. *continued*

| Scan Code | | ASCII Value | | |
Decimal	Hex	Decimal	Hex	Keystroke
87	57	0	00	shift-F4
88	58	0	00	shift-F5
89	59	0	00	shift-F6
90	5A	0	00	shift-F7
91	5B	0	00	shift-F8
92	5C	0	00	shift-F9
93	5D	0	00	shift-F10
94	5E	0	00	Ctrl-F1
95	5F	0	00	Ctrl-F2
96	60	0	00	Ctrl-F3
97	61	0	00	Ctrl-F4
98	62	0	00	Ctrl-F5
99	63	0	00	Ctrl-F6
100	64	0	00	Ctrl-F7
101	65	0	00	Ctrl-F8
102	66	0	00	Ctrl-F9
103	67	0	00	Ctrl-F10
104	68	0	00	Alt-F1
105	69	0	00	Alt-F2
106	6A	0	00	Alt-F3
107	6B	0	00	Alt-F4
108	6C	0	00	Alt-F5
109	6D	0	00	Alt-F6
110	6E	0	00	Alt-F7
111	6F	0	00	Alt-F8
112	70	0	00	Alt-F9

Scan Code		ASCII Value		
Decimal	Hex	Decimal	Hex	Keystroke
113	71	0	00	Alt-F10
114	72	0	00	Ctrl-PrtSc
115	73	0	00	Ctrl-left arrow
116	74	0	00	Ctrl-right arrow
117	75	0	00	Ctrl-End
118	76	0	00	Ctrl-PgDn
119	77	0	00	Ctrl-Home
120	78	0	00	Alt-1 (keyboard)
121	79	0	00	Alt-2 (keyboard)
122	7A	0	00	Alt-3 (keyboard)
123	7B	0	00	Alt-4 (keyboard)
124	7C	0	00	Alt-5 (keyboard)
125	7D	0	00	Alt-6 (keyboard)
126	7E	0	00	Alt-7 (keyboard)
127	7F	0	00	Alt-8 (keyboard)
128	80	0	00	Alt-9 (keyboard)
129	81	0	00	Alt-0 (keyboard)
130	82	0	00	Alt − (keyboard)
131	83	0	00	Alt-= (keyboard)
132	84	0	00	Ctrl-PgUp

Keyboard Controller Codes

Table C.2 shows the key codes returned when you access the keyboard controller through hardware port 60h. Notice that this table is a good deal shorter than table C.1. The keyboard controller does no translation on the Shift, Ctrl, and Alt keys. Each key is given a specific position value, which BIOS translates into the appropriate scan code/ASCII value combination.

Table C.2. *Keyboard controller codes*

Key Code		
Decimal	Hex	Key
1	01	Esc
2	02	1
3	03	2
4	04	3
5	05	4
6	06	5
7	07	6
8	08	7
9	09	8
10	0A	9
11	0B	0
12	0C	—
13	0D	=
14	0E	backspace
15	0F	tab
16	10	q
17	11	w
18	12	e
19	13	r
20	14	t
21	15	y
22	16	u
23	17	i
24	18	o
25	19	p
26	1A	[

Key Code		
Decimal	Hex	Key
27	1B	]
28	1C	Enter
29	1D	Ctrl
29/69	ID/45	Pause
30	1E	a
31	1F	s
32	20	d
33	21	f
34	22	g
35	23	h
36	24	j
37	25	k
38	26	l
39	27	;
40	28	'
41	29	` (accent grave)
42	2A	left shift
42/52	2A/34	PrtSc (enhanced keyboard)
42/71	2A/47	Home (middle, enhanced keyboard)
42/72	2A/48	up-arrow (middle, enhanced keyboard)
42/73	2A/49	PgUp (middle, enhanced keyboard)
42/75	2A/4B	left-arrow (middle, enhanced keyboard)
42/77	2A/4D	right-arrow (middle, enhanced keyboard)
42/79	2A/4F	End (middle, enhanced keyboard)
42/80	2A/50	down-arrow (middle, enhanced keyboard)

Table C.2. continues

Table C.2. *continued*

	Key Code	
Decimal	*Hex*	*Key*
42/81	2A/51	PgDn (middle, enhanced keyboard)
42/82	2A/52	Insert (middle, enhanced keyboard)
42/83	2A/53	Del (middle, enhanced keyboard)
43	2B	\
44	2C	z
45	2D	x
46	2E	c
47	2F	v
48	30	b
49	31	n
50	32	m
51	33	,
52	34	.
53	35	/
54	36	right shift
55	37	* (next to keypad)
56	38	Alt
57	39	space
58	3A	Caps Lock
59	3B	F1
60	3C	F2
61	3D	F3
62	3E	F4
63	3F	F5
64	40	F6
65	41	F7
66	42	F8

Decimal	Key Code Hex	Key
67	43	F9
68	44	F10
69	45	Num Lock
70	46	Scroll Lock
71	47	Home (keypad)
72	48	up-arrow (keypad)
73	49	PgUp (keypad)
74	4A	− (next to keypad)
75	4B	left-arrow (keypad)
76	4C	5 (keypad)
77	4D	right-arrow (keypad)
78	4E	+ (next to keypad)
79	4F	End (keypad)
80	50	down-arrow (keypad)
81	51	PgDn (keypad)
82	52	Ins (keypad)
83	53	Del (keypad)
84	54	[currently unused]
85	55	[currently unused]
86	56	[currently unused]
87	57	F11
88	58	F12

Some keys, especially on the enhanced 101-key keyboard, return double values. These values are shown with a slash between the two numbers and are placed in the order designated by the first number of the pair.

Each key is designated by the unshifted value shown on the keycap.

Glossary

Align type. An assembly language directive specifying how the start of the segment is to be aligned in memory. The align type is specified on the same line as the segment name. See also *BYTE*, *PAGE*, *PARA*, and *WORD*.

ALU. Arithmetic/Logic Unit, the portion of the CPU that performs arithmetic functions on data. The ALU controls the settings of the bits in the flags register.

ASCII. American Standard Code for Information Interchange.

ASCIIZ. An ASCII string that is terminated with a nul character (value of 0). ASCIIZ is used extensively in DOS interrupt services.

Assembler. The software program that translates (assembles) assembly language mnemonics into machine language for direct execution by the computer.

Assembly language. The pseudo-English language, called *source code*, that is written and hopefully readable by humans. Assembly language is not directly executable by a computer.

Assembly. The process of code conversion performed by an assembler. Assembly language source code is translated into machine language through this process.

AT. A segment combine type used generally to prepare a template to be used for accessing fixed location data. In the format *AT XXXX* (where *XXXX* is a memory address), *AT* signifies that addresses and offsets are to be calculated relative to the specified memory address. See also *Combine type*, *COMMON*, *MEMORY*, *PUBLIC*, and *STACK*.

Auxiliary carry flag. The bit in the flag register that indicates whether the previous decimal operation resulted in a carry out of or borrow into the four low-order bits of the byte.

AX. A general-purpose data register.

Base register. A register containing an address that is used as a base in indirect addressing methods. The base register is usually the BP or BX register.

BCD. Binary Coded Decimal.

Binary. A numbering system based on only two digits. The only valid digits in a binary system are 0 and 1. See also *Bit*.

Bit. Binary digit, the smallest unit of storage on a computer. Each bit can have a value of 0 or 1, indicating the absence or presence of an electrical signal. See also *Binary*.

BP. The base pointer register.

BX. A general-purpose data register.

Byte. A basic unit of data storage and manipulation. A byte is equivalent to 8 bits and can contain a value ranging from 0 through 255.

BYTE. A segment align type that directs the assembler to place the segment at the next available byte after completing the preceding segment. See also *Align type*, *PAGE*, *PARA*, and *WORD*.

CALL. An assembly language instruction telling the assembler to perform the subroutine.

Carry flag. The bit in the flag register that indicates whether the previous operation resulted in a carry out of or borrow into the high-order bit of the resulting byte or word.

CGA. Color Graphics Adapter.

Class type. An assembler directive indicating how individual segments are to be grouped when linked. Segments having the same class type are loaded contiguously in memory before another class type is begun. The class type is specified on the same line as the segment name and is enclosed by single quotation marks.

Combine type. An optional assembler directive that defines how segments with the same name will be combined.

COMMON. A segment combine type. It causes individual segments of the same name and of the COMMON combine type to begin at a common memory address. All COMMON segments with the same name begin at the same point, with the resulting segment equal in length to the longest individual segment. All addresses and offsets in the resulting segment are relative to a single segment register. See also *AT*, *Combine type*, *MEMORY*, *PUBLIC*, and *STACK*.

Control Word. A 16-bit register used in the NPX/FPU to govern how the chip works.

CPU. The microprocessor (central processing unit) responsible for operations within the computer. These operations generally include system timing, logical processing, and logical operations.

CS. The code segment register.

CX. A general-purpose data register, usually used for counting functions.

DASD. Direct access storage device. The term was coined by IBM and is used extensively in their documentation.

DI. The destination index register.

Direction flag. The bit in the flag register that indicates whether string operations should increment (DF clear) or decrement (DF set) the index registers.

Displacement. An offset from a specified base point.

DMA. Direct memory access; a method of data transfer involving direct access of the RAM buffer area through specialized circuitry. DMA frees the CPU for other operations and results in a more efficient use of computer resources.

DOS. Disk Operating System.

DS. The data segment register.

DTA. A memory area (disk transfer area) used with FCB file operations for the transfer of information to and from the floppy disk. See also Chapter 13, service 21/1A.

DX. A general-purpose data register.

EGA. Enhanced Graphics Adapter.

ENDP. An assembler directive indicating the end of a procedure. See also *PROC*.

EQU. An assembly language directive (equate). See also *Equate*.

Equate. The full-word form of the assembly language instruction EQU. Equate assigns a value to a mnemonic label that is later substituted for other occurrences of the label during program assembly. See also *EQU*.

ES. The extra segment register.

Exception. An NPX/FPU term relating to a flag set in the status word register if an operation renders an exceptional result (outside normal bounds).

FAR. A procedure that pushes the full return address (effectively the contents of CS:IP) on the stack. FAR is assumed to be in a code segment different from the current segment.

FCB. File Control Block.

Flag. An indicator used to control or signal other software or hardware functions.

FPU. An acronym for *Floating Point Unit*. This is the equivalent of an 80387 NPX built into the 80486 microprocessor.

FS. An additional "extra" segment register for the 80286 and 80386. Identical in use to the ES register.

Function. A self-contained coding segment designed to do a specific task. A function is sometimes referred to as a procedure or subroutine.

GDT. Global Descriptor Table. Used in protected mode programming of the 80286, 80386, or 80486 to detail segment register contents and other descriptors for the entire operation of the CPU.

Graphics. A video presentation consisting mostly of pictures and figures instead of letters and numbers. See also *Text*.

Group. A collection of segments that fit within a 64K segment of RAM. At link time, LINK.EXE uses segment group classifications to determine how segments are combined.

GS. An additional "extra" segment register for the 80286 and 80386. Identical in use to the ES register.

Hexadecimal. A numbering system based on 16 elements. Digits are numbered 0 through F, as follows: 0, 1, 2, 3, 4, 5, 6, 7, 8, 9, A, B, C, D, E, F.

HGA. Hercules Graphics Adapter.

IDT. Interrupt Descriptor Table. Used in protected mode programming of the 80286, 80386, or 80486 to replace the interrupt vectors normally located in low memory on the 8086/8088.

Index register. A register assumed to contain an address for use in indirect addressing modes. Usually, the index register consists of the SI (source index) or DI (destination index) registers.

Instruction Set. The group of mnemonic directions used to control a processor.

Interrupt flag. The bit in the flag register that indicates whether the CPU should handle maskable interrupts. If this flag is set, interrupts are handled. If it is clear, interrupts are ignored.

IP. The instruction pointer register.

LDT. Local Descriptor Table. Used in protected mode programming of the 80286, 80386, or 80486 to detail segment register contents and other descriptors for a local task.

LIB.EXE. The library management software distributed by Microsoft and IBM with their assemblers.

Library. A collection of object code modules saved in a single file. The assembler searches this file during the linking process to resolve external references in the main programs.

Linking. The process of resolving external references and address references in object code, resulting in machine language instructions that are directly executable by the computer.

Machine language. The series of binary digits that a microprocessor executes to perform individual tasks. People seldom (if ever) program in machine language. Instead, they program in assembly language, and an assembler translates their instructions into machine language.

MASM. Macro Assembler, sold and supported by Microsoft.

MCB. Memory Control Block.

MCGA. Multi-Color Graphics Array.

MDA. Monochrome Display Adapter.

Memory map. An organized method of depicting the use of an area of computer memory.

MEMORY. A segment combine type that results in all segments with the same name being joined into one segment when linked. All addresses and offsets in the resulting segment relate to a single segment register. See also *AT*, *Combine type*, *COMMON*, *PUBLIC*, and *STACK*.

MMU. An acronym for *Memory Management Unit*, a specialized section of the 80486.

Monochrome. A single color.

MSW. Machine Status Word.

NaN. An acronym for *Not a Number*. This is a term used in conjunction with NPX/FPU chips. It represents a floating point value that does not represent a numeric or infinite quantity value. It is typically generated as the result of a serious error and can contain error information that can indicate the source of the error.

NEAR. An assembly language directive that indicates the type of procedure you are creating. Issued on the same line as the PROC directive, NEAR controls how you call and return from the procedure.

NPX. Numeric Processor Extension. This is the 8087, 80287, or 80387 numeric coprocessor.

Object code. A "halfway step" between source code and executable machine language. Object code consists mostly of machine language but is not directly executable by the computer. It must first be linked in order to resolve external references and address references.

Offset. A distance from a given paragraph boundary in memory. The offset is usually given as a number of bytes.

OptASM. Optimizing Assembler, sold and supported by SLR, Inc.

Overflow flag. The bit in the flag register that indicates whether the signed result of the preceding operation can be represented in the result byte or word.

PAGE. A segment align type that directs the assembler, after it completes the preceding segment, to place the segment at the next available hexadecimal address ending in 00. See also *Align type, BYTE, PARA,* and *WORD.*

PARA. A segment align type that directs the assembler, after it completes the preceding segment, to place the segment at the next available hexadecimal address ending in 0. See also *Align type, BYTE, PAGE,* and *WORD.*

Parity flag. The bit in the flag register that indicates whether the low-order 8 bits of the result contain an even number (PF set) or odd number (PF clear) of bits equal to 1.

PROC. An assembly language directive indicating the start of a procedure. See also *ENDP.*

Procedure. A self-contained coding segment designed to do a specific task, sometimes referred to as a subroutine.

Protected Mode. An alternative operating mode of the 80286, 80386, and 80486 chips. Protected mode causes a different use of the segment registers and memory than real mode.

Pseudo-Op. A type of operation code that is not a direction to the micro-processor but a command for the assembler or linker to follow when producing the executable file.

PSP. Program Segment Prefix.

PUBLIC. A segment combine type that results in all segments with the same name being joined into one segment when linked. All addresses and offsets in the resulting segment relate to a single segment register. See also *AT*, *Combine type*, *COMMON*, *MEMORY*, and *STACK*.

RAM. Random-Access Memory.

Real Mode. The native operating mode of the 8086/8088. Also available as the default operating mode on later Intel CPUs.

Register. The data-holding areas, usually 16 bits in length, used by the processor in performing operations.

ROM. Read-Only Memory.

RPL. Requested Privilege Level.

Run-time system. A system manager that oversees proper operation of the language during program execution.

Segment. A particular area of memory, 64K in size.

Segment offset. The value to be added to the result of 16 times the segment value, thereby producing an absolute memory address.

Segment register. Any of the CPU registers designed to contain a segment address. They include the CS, DS, ES, and SS registers.

SI. The source index register.

Sign flag. The bit in the flag register that is set equal to the high-order bit of the result of the last operation.

Significand. This is the portion of a floating point number that contains the most significant nonzero bits of the number.

Source code. The assembly language instructions, written by humans, that an assembler translates into object code.

SP. The stack pointer register.

SS. The stack segment register.

Stack. An area of memory set aside for the temporary storage of values in a computing environment. The stack operates in a LIFO fashion. In an 8088-based environment, only whole words (16 bits) can be pushed on and popped from the stack.

STACK. A segment combine type resulting in all segments with this combine type being joined to form one segment when linked. All addresses and offsets in the resulting segment are relative to the stack segment register. The SP register is initialized to the ending address of the segment. This combine type normally is used to define the stack area for a program. See also *AT*, *Combine type*, *COMMON*, *MEMORY*, and *PUBLIC*.

Status Word. A 16-bit register used in the NPX/FPU to indicate the status or result of certain operations.

Subroutine. A self-contained coding segment designed to do a specific task, sometimes referred to as a procedure.

TASM. Turbo Assembler, sold and supported by Borland International.

Text. A video presentation scheme consisting mostly of letters and numbers. See also *Graphics*.

TLB. Translation Lookaside Buffer, the 80486 on-chip cache for page table entires.

Trap flag. The bit in the flag register that indicates a single-step instruction execution mode. If the trap flag is set, a single-step interrupt occurs. The flag then is cleared after the assembler executes the next instruction.

VGA. Video Graphics Array, a type of display adapter.

Virtual Mode. An alternative operating mode of the 80386 and 80486 chips under which a protected-mode task can appear to be running in a virtual real-mode 8086 environment.

WAIT. An assembly language instruction (wait).

Word. In general usage, two consecutive bytes (16 bits) of data.

WORD. A segment align type that directs the assembler, after it completes the preceding segment, to place the segment at the next available even address. If the preceding segment ends on an odd address, WORD effectively is equivalent to BYTE. See also *Align type*, *BYTE*, *PAGE*, and *PARA*.

Zero flag. The bit in the flag register that indicates whether the result of the preceding operation is zero. If the result is zero, the flag is set. If the result is not zero, the flag is clear.

INDEX

B

C

D

E

H

I

J

K

L

M

N

S

W

X

More Computer Knowledge from Que

DOS Programmer's Reference, 2nd Edition
by Terry Dettmann

Updated for DOS Version 4! This combination of reference and tutorial discusses DOS functions, BIOS functions, and using DOS with other programming languages—including C, BASIC, and assembly language. Must reading for experienced applications programmers!

Order #1006
$27.95 USA
0-88022-458-4, 850 pp.

Using Turbo Pascal
by Michael Yester

An excellent introduction to Turbo Pascal 5.5! This combination of tutorial and reference teaches you the fundamentals of the Pascal language and protocol, plus disciplined programming techniques.

Order #883
$21.95 USA
0-88022-396-0, 724 pp.

Power Graphics Programming
by Michael Abrash

This unique text is a compilation of articles by programming authority Michael Abrash, originally published in *Programmer's Journal*. Packed with programming techniques to help users optimize their use of graphics!

Order #1039
$24.95 USA
0-88022-500-9, 325 pp.

SQL Programmer's Guide
by Umang Gupta and William Gietz

Pre-eminent SQL authorities Gupta and Gietz present the definitive book for SQL programming. Covers SQL fundamentals, including queries, virtual tables, indexes, variables, database utilities, and function calls.

Order #881
$29.95 USA
0-88022-390-1, 302 pp.

ORDER YOUR PROGRAM DISK TODAY!

Why get frustrated? Save yourself hours of tedious, error-prone typing by ordering the companion disk to **Using Assembly Language, 2nd Edition**. This valuable disk contains the source code for every listing in the book.

Simply make a copy of this page, enclose payment information, and send to:

Discovery Computing Inc.
P.O. Box 88
South Jordan, UT 84065

Orders are normally processed within 48 hours of receipt.

Item	Disk Size	Format	Copies	Price Each	Amount
UAL2E Code Disk	5.25"	360K	_____	14.95	_____
UAL2E Code Disk	3.5"	720K	_____	19.95	_____

Utah residents, add 6.25% sales tax: _____

Subtotal: _____

If COD, add shipping & handling charge of $5.00: _____

Total: _____

Payment method:
Check: _____   Money Order: _____   COD: _____

Please make checks or money orders payable to Discovery Computing Inc. Credit card orders are not accepted. This offer is made by Discovery Computing Inc., not by Que Corporation. For assistance contact Discovery Computing Inc. at 801-254-3636 (voice), 801-254-3933 (FAX), or on CompuServe (72561,2207).

Free Catalog!

Mail us this registration form today, and we'll send you a free catalog featuring Que's complete line of best-selling books.

Name of Book _____

Name _____

Title _____

Phone (____) _____

Company _____

Address _____

City _____

State _____ ZIP _____

Please check the appropriate answers:

1. Where did you buy your Que book?
   - [ ] Bookstore (name: _____)
   - [ ] Computer store (name: _____)
   - [ ] Catalog (name: _____)
   - [ ] Direct from Que
   - [ ] Other: _____

2. How many computer books do you buy a year?
   - [ ] 1 or less
   - [ ] 2-5
   - [ ] 6-10
   - [ ] More than 10

3. How many Que books do you own?
   - [ ] 1
   - [ ] 2-5
   - [ ] 6-10
   - [ ] More than 10

4. How long have you been using this software?
   - [ ] Less than 6 months
   - [ ] 6 months to 1 year
   - [ ] 1-3 years
   - [ ] More than 3 years

5. What influenced your purchase of this Que book?
   - [ ] Personal recommendation
   - [ ] Advertisement
   - [ ] In-store display
   - [ ] Price
   - [ ] Que catalog
   - [ ] Que mailing
   - [ ] Que's reputation
   - [ ] Other: _____

6. How would you rate the overall content of the book?
   - [ ] Very good
   - [ ] Good
   - [ ] Satisfactory
   - [ ] Poor

7. What do you like *best* about this Que book?
   _____
   _____

8. What do you like *least* about this Que book?
   _____
   _____

9. Did you buy this book with your personal funds?
   - [ ] Yes   [ ] No

10. Please feel free to list any other comments you may have about this Que book.
    _____
    _____
    _____

— **QUe** —

Order Your Que Books Today!

Name _____

Title _____

Company _____

City _____

State _____ ZIP _____

Phone No. (____) _____

Method of Payment:

Check [ ] (Please enclose in envelope.)

Charge My: VISA [ ]   MasterCard [ ]
American Express [ ]

Charge # _____

Expiration Date _____

Order No.	Title	Qty.	Price	Total

You can **FAX** your order to **1-317-573-2583**. Or call **1-800-428-5331, ext. ORDR** to order direct.
Please add $2.50 per title for shipping and handling.

Subtotal	
Shipping & Handling	
Total	

— **QUe** —

BUSINESS REPLY MAIL
First Class Permit No. 9918   Indianapolis, IN

Postage will be paid by addressee

11711 N. College
Carmel, IN 46032

NO POSTAGE
NECESSARY
IF MAILED
IN THE
UNITED STATES

BUSINESS REPLY MAIL
First Class Permit No. 9918   Indianapolis, IN

Postage will be paid by addressee

11711 N. College
Carmel, IN 46032